P9-CKY-104

COOK'S ILLUSTRATED

2015

$35.00

Published by
America's Test Kitchen
17 Station Street
Brookline, MA 02445

ISBN: 978-1-940352-39-8
ISSN: 1933-639X

BC = Back Cover

COOK'S ILLUSTRATED INDEX 2015

A

B

C

D

E

F

J

K

L

M

N

O

P

T

U

V

W

Y

Z

NUMBER 132

JANUARY & FEBRUARY 2015

COOK'S ILLUSTRATED

Slow-Roasted Chicken
Crisp Skin, Juicy Meat

Tuscan Beef Stew
Rich Red Wine Flavor

French-Style Pork Chops
A Sauce That Breaks the Rules

Best Carving Board
Is Simpler Better?

Foolproof New York Cheesecake
Mahogany Top, Velvety Texture

Stir-Fried Noodles
Flavor-Packed Japanese Version

Secrets of Great Pan Sauce

Homemade Vegetable Broth

Mexican Drunken Beans

Best Roasted Mushrooms

CooksIllustrated.com

$6.95 U.S. & CANADA

CONTENTS

January & February 2015

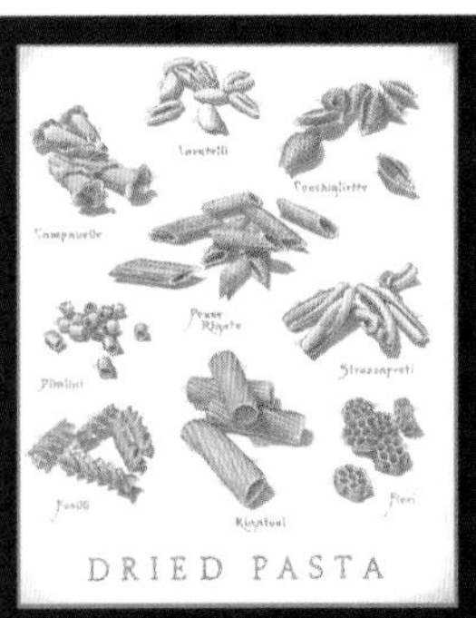

DRIED PASTA The shape of dried pasta determines what type of dish it will be used in. FUSILLI's corkscrew shape offers many crevices to hide pesto, ricotta, or crushed tomatoes. The more relaxed twists of STROZZAPRETI, which means "priest stranglers" in Italian, also offer nooks and crannies for sauces. Fluted CAMPANELLE catches toppings like fresh herbs, olive oil, or grated Parmesan in its ruffles. Cylindrical ridged varieties like RIGATONI and PENNE RIGATE match well with hearty ragus. Concave CONCHIGLIETTE provides a cradle for rich cheese sauces in its shell-like shape and is often baked *al forno*. CAVATELLI's pursed sides create a cavity for fruity olive oil. Tiny tubular DITALINI is a classic ingredient in *pasta e fagioli*. FIORI, which is similar to rotelle, is a striking base for warm dishes or cold salads.

COVER *(Tangerines)*: Robert Papp; BACK COVER *(Dried Pasta)*: John Burgoyne

America's Test Kitchen is a very real 2,500-square-foot kitchen located just outside Boston. It is the home of *Cook's Illustrated* and *Cook's Country* magazines and the workday destination of more than three dozen test cooks, editors, and cookware specialists. Our mission is to test recipes until we understand how and why they work and arrive at the best version. We also test kitchen equipment and supermarket ingredients in search of products that offer the best value and performance. You can watch us work by tuning in to *America's Test Kitchen* (AmericasTestKitchen.com) and *Cook's Country from America's Test Kitchen* (CooksCountry.com) on public television.

PRINTED IN THE USA

AN ISLAND TO ONESELF

In 1952, a New Zealander named Tom Neale hitched a ride to a small Pacific atoll, Suwarrow, that had been abandoned since World War II. He was well provisioned, with two cats, kerosene, bully (corned) beef, fishing gear, knives, various canned foods, baking staples, a basic medicine chest, and a few well-chosen books. When he got to Suwarrow, he found a badly damaged boat (he fixed it up using rope that he unraveled and made into caulk), water storage tanks, a few broken-down huts, wild chickens and pigs, and a protected atoll that held an infinite store of easy-to-spear fish. His diet consisted of seafood, chicken, eggs, pawpaw, coconut, and breadfruit. He constructed a native oven and a grill, learned to cook fish wrapped in leaves overnight, and just missed being attacked by a bull shark that was after the large fish on the end of his fishing line. He had to kill the wild pigs after they devastated his garden; this involved luring them in with food at night while sitting in a tree with spear at the ready. After he spent six months reconstructing a pier, a hurricane washed it away in hours. He returned to civilization after experiencing debilitating back pain from arthritis. He returned to Suwarrow in 1960 and stayed another four years. His final and longest stay began in 1967 and ended a decade later due to ill health.

A friend of mine, a landscape architect, now lives in Vermont but grew up in Connecticut. Just a couple of miles into the woods from where he lived, there was a hermit who had built his own shelter and furniture, made his own clothes, started his own orchard, and preserved his own food. And until about 10 years ago, there was a trapper who lived alone in a remote area of southern Vermont and made do on his own, selling pelts for a subsistence living. And even today, as I hike up in the woods, far away from any settlement, there are fallen-down barns and farmhouses, cellar holes, and plenty of stone walls and sheep fencing, evidence that many families lived far off the grid, up in the mountains, a good hike from the valley below.

Christopher Kimball

In this new century, however, we are social animals. We have social media. We are afraid of being lonely.

Hence this paean to loneliness. To being in the woods and not quite knowing what lies over the next ridge. To riding a tractor in August, looking up, and seeing red-tailed hawks soaring on thermals. To waking up in the middle of the night, alone, in an old farmhouse, with the sound of pipes banging. To the disquiet of the unfamiliar. To what you don't know and never will. To the phone not ringing. To the end of email. To standing in the falling snow in late afternoon, listening to the distant baying of a beagle chasing a rabbit. To trying something for the first time. To being unsure of yourself. To getting lost. To trying and failing.

I've never met a Vermonter who hungered for my approval. The old-timers decide on their own how far apart to plant their potatoes, when to put in their garden, or whether it's a good day to cut hay. They know the best spot to hunt deer, whether it's going to be a harsh winter, and whether to take the shortcut during mud season. And they don't need any help figuring out when to pull maple syrup off the pans, which pie to choose at the firehouse dinner in July (the pink fluffy one), or whether to have a second cider doughnut at Sherman's during early morning coffee hour.

Being alone is not the same as being lonely. One can be alone in a well-stuffed armchair, book in hand, surrounded by Oliver Twist, the ghost of Prince Hamlet, George Smiley, Peter Pan, or the trolls of Mordor. We are well-met with memories of friends departed, the stillness of twilight, the crackle of birch on the fire, and the company of a black Lab or a glass of wine. But we are not truly lonely.

Some of us have a true fondness for being alone. I have been alone in barns during thunderstorms so powerful that harnesses rattled on their hooks. I have fished alone in pools beneath waterfalls in remote pine forests with only half-light dappled on the water. I have driven the panhandle of Texas alone at night, jackrabbits and headlights for company. I have sat in tree stands, alone, before sunrise, in biting cold, the light above the mountains developing slowly, turning from sepia to watercolor. And I have been alone in the half-light of subway platforms in New York, midnight having passed, waiting desperately for the rumble of the next train.

Loneliness is called a disease. But older generations understood that one is poor company without loneliness as a companion. Loneliness sharpens the wits, makes one discriminate in the choice of words, and increases the appetite for fellowship. It gives one pause before speaking, puts a spring in the step, quiets the inner voice, and gives one the balance needed to survive the ups and downs of life with equanimity.

To paraphrase Nietzsche, one should struggle to avoid being overwhelmed by the tribe. No price is too high to pay for the privilege of owning oneself.

FOR INQUIRIES, ORDERS, OR MORE INFORMATION

CooksIllustrated.com
At CooksIllustrated.com, you can order books and subscriptions, sign up for our free e-newsletter, or renew your magazine subscription. Join the website and gain access to 22 years of *Cook's Illustrated* recipes, equipment tests, and ingredient tastings, as well as companion videos for every recipe in this issue.

COOKBOOKS
We sell more than 50 cookbooks by the editors of *Cook's Illustrated*, including *The Cook's Illustrated Cookbook* and *The Science of Good Cooking*. To order, visit our bookstore at CooksIllustrated.com/bookstore.

***COOK'S ILLUSTRATED* MAGAZINE**
Cook's Illustrated magazine (ISSN 1068-2821), number 132, is published bimonthly by Boston Common Press Limited Partnership, 17 Station St., Brookline, MA 02445. Copyright 2014 Boston Common Press Limited Partnership. Periodicals postage paid at Boston, MA, and additional mailing offices, USPS #012487. Publications Mail Agreement No. 40020778. Return undeliverable Canadian addresses to P.O. Box 875, Station A, Windsor, ON N9A 6P2. POSTMASTER: Send address changes to *Cook's Illustrated*, P.O. Box 6018, Harlan, IA 51593-1518. For subscription and gift subscription orders, subscription inquiries, or change of address notices, visit AmericasTestKitchen.com/support, call 800-526-8442 in the U.S. or 515-248-7684 from outside the U.S., or write to us at *Cook's Illustrated*, P.O. 6018, Harlan, IA 51593-1518.

FOR LIST RENTAL INFORMATION Contact Specialists Marketing Services, Inc., 777 Terrace Ave., 4th Floor, Hasbrouck Heights, NJ 07604; phone: 201-865-5800.

EDITORIAL OFFICE 17 Station St., Brookline, MA 02445; 617-232-1000; fax: 617-232-1572. For subscription inquiries, visit AmericasTestKitchen.com/support or call 800-526-8442.

QUICK TIPS

⋟ COMPILED BY SHANNON FRIEDMANN HATCH ⋞

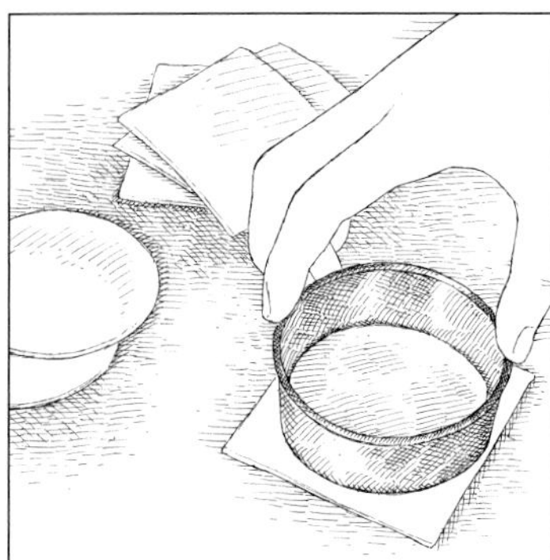

Shaping Up Square Cheese Slices

Melting square slices of cheese on round English muffins presents a problem: The edges of cheese that drape over the side can drip on the bottom of the oven and burn. To prevent this, Jackie Price of Cranston, R.I., uses a biscuit cutter (a canning jar lid also works) to cut out a circular shape from the cheese slice—it fits perfectly on the muffin.

Reheat Soft-Cooked Eggs

Nicole Perry of San Francisco, Calif., likes to make a large batch of soft-cooked eggs for the week and suggests this quick method for reheating them once they've been refrigerated.

Place the cold egg(s) in a bowl—or, if taking on the go, a food storage or deli container—and fill with hot water. Let sit for 3 minutes, drain, and serve.

Lid Gripper

When simmering a long-cooking sauce or stew partially covered, Kathleen Monaghan of Walnut Creek, Calif., found a way to give a slightly ajar lid more purchase: Nick a slit in a wine cork and insert it on the pot's rim. The prop creates enough space for the steam to escape, while ensuring that the lid stays in place.

Transporting Wine Glasses

When Shaun Breidbart of Pelham, N.Y., brings extra wine glasses to a party, he keeps them from breaking by fitting them into an empty wine-case box. Just as the cardboard dividers cushioned the bottles, they also create a buffer for the glasses.

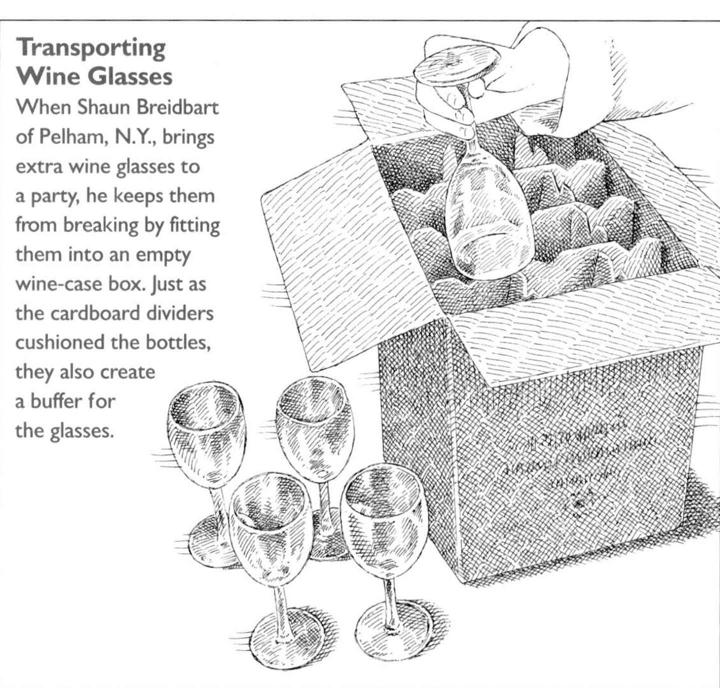

Alternative Spoon Rest

When making a recipe, like chili, that calls for an entire 14- or 28-ounce can of an ingredient such as tomatoes, Nancy Knop of Delaware, Ohio, uses the empty vessel as a spoon rest. The can's tall sides keep the spoon upright and steady, and when she's done cooking, she can recycle the can.

Stain-Free Beet Prep

Rather than stain her hands when peeling roasted beets, Susan Frank of Culver City, Calif., wears disposable plastic gloves that she simply throws away after she's done with the messy job.

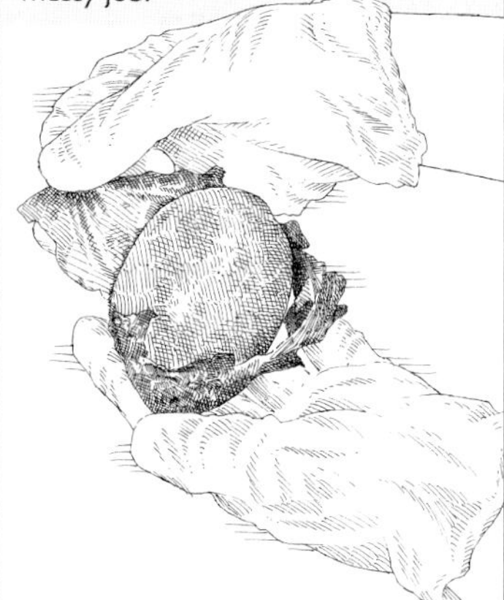

SEND US YOUR TIPS We will provide a complimentary one-year subscription for each tip we print. Send your tip, name, address, and daytime telephone number to Quick Tips, *Cook's Illustrated*, P.O. Box 470589, Brookline, MA 02447, or to QuickTips@AmericasTestKitchen.com.

An Efficient Way to Stuff Shells

To quickly stuff cooked pasta shells with cheese filling, Yvonne Pannucci of Pawleys Island, S.C., uses her ice cream scoop. Not only does the scoop portion the filling evenly, but its release lever helps deposit the filling neatly in the cooked pasta.

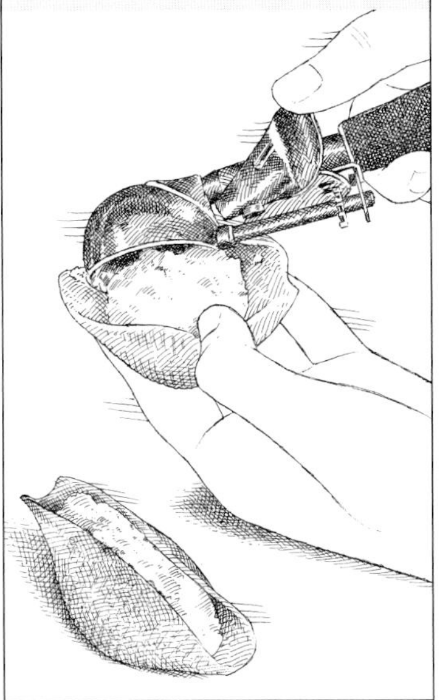

A Twist on Tying Bags

Heather Tuttle of Watertown, Mass., had always secured open bags of frozen vegetables with a twist tie or rubber band until she realized the answer was already in the bag—she simply cuts a strip of plastic from the top and then uses that strip to tie the bag closed.

Toaster Oven Baking Stone

Azim Mazagonwalla of Lincoln, R.I., likes the convenience of heating up slices of leftover pizza or panini in the toaster oven but wishes the results were as crisp as those heated on a baking stone. So he makes a mini stone for the toaster oven with unglazed quarry tiles (like those sold at home improvement stores) covered with parchment paper. For the crispest results, preheat the tiles for at least 15 minutes at 425 degrees before baking.

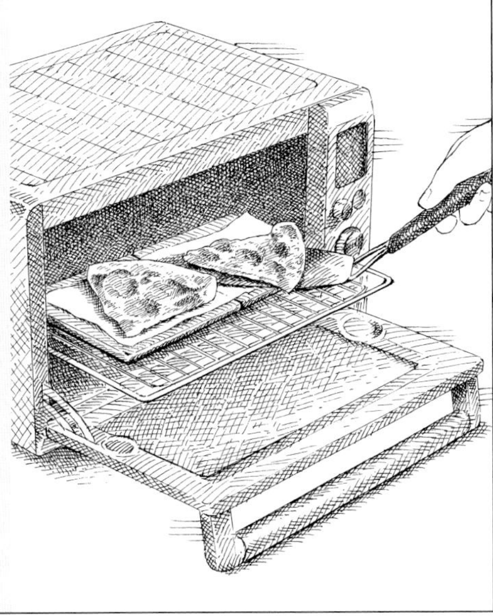

Proof That Yeast Works

When Rachel Shin of Medford, Mass., is about to bake bread or pizza, she uses this trick to make sure her yeast is fresh.

1. Add ½ teaspoon of yeast and ⅛ teaspoon of sugar to 2 tablespoons of warm (between 100 and 120 degrees) water. Stir to dissolve completely.

2. If the yeast is active, bubbles will start to form on the surface after 5 minutes; after 10 minutes, there will be a foamy layer. If only a few bubbles form on the surface after 10 minutes, the yeast is dead. (To use the tested yeast in a recipe, subtract ½ teaspoon of yeast and 2 tablespoons of water from the total amount in the recipe and add the tested yeast with the remaining water.)

A Stand-In for Counter Space

Kate Darnell of Salado, Texas, has limited counter space and doesn't have a place to rest a pot lid when she stirs a soup or stew. Her solution: placing the pot lid on a sturdy plate stand, which takes up less space and holds the lid (including larger slow cooker covers) upright and out of the way.

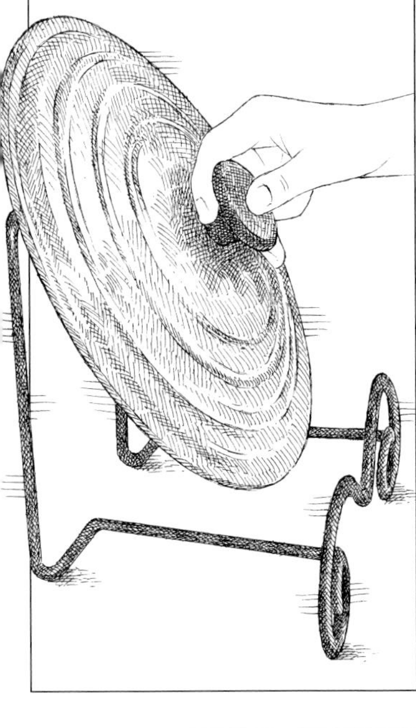

A Delicate Way to Test for Fish Doneness

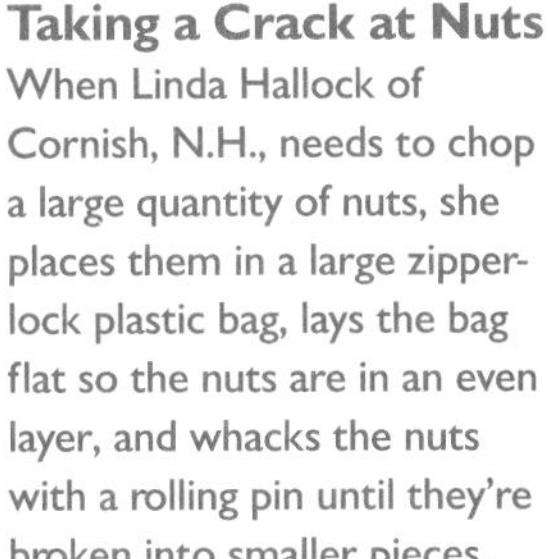

A quick way to tell if fish is cooked is to see if it flakes easily with a fork, but the pronged utensil can leave an unsightly gap in the fillet, ruining presentation. Wayne Drady of Little Compton, R.I., uses a gentler approach: a cake tester. Its thin point allows him to separate just a few flakes of fish to check for doneness without marring the fillet's appearance.

Taking a Crack at Nuts

When Linda Hallock of Cornish, N.H., needs to chop a large quantity of nuts, she places them in a large zipper-lock plastic bag, lays the bag flat so the nuts are in an even layer, and whacks the nuts with a rolling pin until they're broken into smaller pieces.

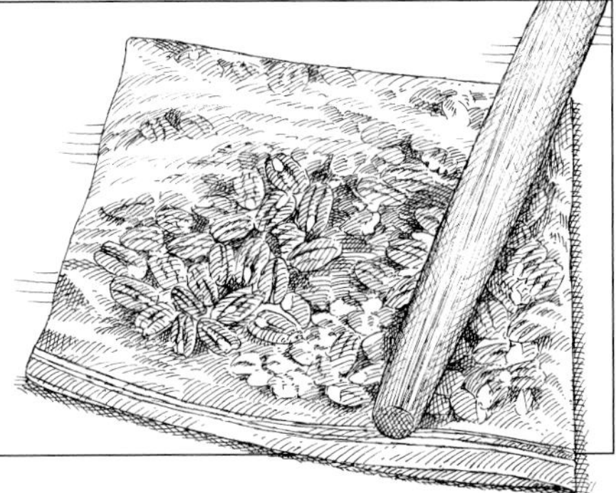

Introducing Tuscan Beef Stew

In this simple yet rich stew, just two ingredients—Chianti and black pepper—provide most of the complexity. But when you add them to the pot makes all the difference.

BY ANDREW JANJIGIAN

Peposo was supposedly created in the 15th century by Tuscan *fornaciai*, the furnace workers responsible for producing the more than 4 million terra-cotta tiles that line the dome of Florence's famous Basilica di Santa Maria del Fiore. As the story goes, the tilemakers would lay cheap cuts of beef into clay pots along with a head's worth of garlic cloves, a handful of peppercorns, and at least a liter of Chianti wine. The pots were said to be left uncovered near the kilns, where they would cook slowly while the tilemakers worked, until the meat was tender and the sauce reduced to a rich nap, perfect for serving over slabs of saltless Tuscan bread. True or not, it makes for a vivid story, just the sort of thing to get me into the kitchen, eager to experiment.

Shallots, carrot, and a few aromatics infuse the dish with flavor during the simmer; then we remove them for a stew that's about the sauce and meat.

Modern interpretations of peposo incorporate tomatoes or tomato paste (the now-ubiquitous fruit hadn't yet made its way to Italy at the time of the basilica's construction), along with other ingredients the tilemakers didn't have on hand: onions, carrots, celery, herbs, pancetta, and even things like frozen peas or butternut squash. I tested a fair number of these recipes, along with more purportedly traditional versions, and learned a few important things. I was drawn to the pared-down "classic" versions for their simplicity, but they were just a little too simple. With so few—and such basic—ingredients, these stews ended up tasting a little thin (or simply mouth-puckeringly tart, thanks to all that wine). On the other hand, recipes that took the dish too far from the basics were even more flawed. Some called for an excessive amount of tomatoes, which gave the dish an undesirable ragu-like consistency and masked the wine's flavor. Others were just overcomplicated. I wanted a version of peposo that hewed to its roots—tender, sumptuous beef in a rich yet simple sauce, centered on a complex wine and peppercorn flavor—but which also boasted balance and depth. To achieve that goal, I'd need to make use of at least a few additional ingredients beyond the basics, as well as some modern techniques. With that in mind, I got down to refining a recipe.

See When to Add What
Video available free for 4 months at CooksIllustrated.com/feb15

Building the Foundation

The tilemakers would have likely used shin meat, which makes an excellent choice for stewing: As part of a very active set of muscles, it's got plenty of tough collagen-containing connective tissue, which breaks down into gelatin during a long braise. This gelatin thickens the cooking liquid, giving it a silky, unctuous texture, and lubricates the fibers of the meat, keeping them moist (long-braised meat that lacks gelatin is typically dry as a bone). However, shin isn't always readily available, so I needed a substitute.

In our Chinese Braised Beef recipe (May/June 2014), we came up with a solid alternative to the shin: boneless short ribs, plus salt and powdered gelatin. Short ribs have less collagen than shin meat, but they are marbled with fat, which serves to keep the meat moist in a similar way. Salting them briefly helps them further retain moisture after long cooking (salt helps meat proteins retain water), and adding powdered gelatin gives the sauce a silky texture in lieu of the collagen.

I cut 4 pounds of short ribs into 2-inch chunks and placed them in a Dutch oven along with a head of garlic separated into cloves and lightly crushed, a few teaspoons of coarsely cracked peppercorns, and a bottle of Chianti. I covered the pot and placed it in the oven, set to a gentle 300 degrees, for about 2 hours.

The meat came out perfectly tender as I'd expected, but otherwise the dish was a bit unimpressive. The peppercorn flavor was lacking, while the wine had lost its aromatic qualities and came across as only acidic. Overall, the sauce just tasted flat. To shore up its underlying flavor, I seared half of the short ribs to give the sauce a bit more meaty complexity. (Searing all the meat would have required two batches, and I had some other easier tricks to turn to.) A tablespoon of tomato paste lent depth without calling attention to itself. Similarly, I added a teaspoon of anchovy paste, a common test kitchen practice that boosts meatiness without adding any noticeable fishiness. For a little sweetness that would help balance the wine's tartness, I added a few shallots and carrots. I left both in large pieces so that

Cheap Wine Is Fine

Early recipes for *peposo* relied on inexpensive Chianti, while modern versions call for a midpriced bottle (whether Chianti or a similar Tuscan wine such as Montepulciano or Brunello). We made batches using cheap ($5), midpriced ($12), and pricey ($20) Chianti, along with other varieties we often use in the kitchen: Cabernet Sauvignon, Pinot Noir, and Côtes du Rhône.

We were surprised that the stew made with the cheapest Chianti went over well with most tasters. While the midpriced wine was agreeable to everyone, there was no advantage to cooking with the expensive bottle. Highly oaked, tannic wines like Cabernet became harsh when cooked, but cheap bottles of fruitier Pinot and Côtes du Rhône made good stand-ins for the Chianti.

SCIENCE Maximizing the Flavors from Wine and Pepper

The flavor compounds in wine and pepper can be classified by their behavior during cooking. Stable compounds don't change, but volatile compounds evaporate, and unstable compounds break down. Over time, the result is a loss of flavor. Most recipes we found for this stew call for adding all the wine and pepper at once, at the start of a 2½-hour simmer. At the end of cooking, the flavors remaining were only those of the stable compounds. By adding some of the wine and pepper 15 minutes before finishing cooking, and the remainder of wine and pepper at the end, we were able to preserve more of the volatile and unstable compounds, capturing the most fleeting, bright, fresh flavors from both the wine and the pepper.

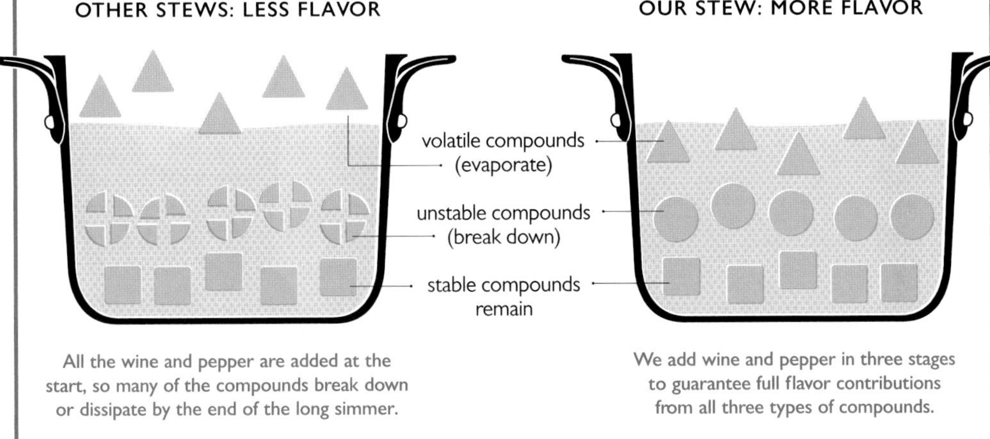

All the wine and pepper are added at the start, so many of the compounds break down or dissipate by the end of the long simmer.

We add wine and pepper in three stages to guarantee full flavor contributions from all three types of compounds.

they'd be easy to discard before finishing the sauce. Finally, bay leaves and fresh rosemary brought just the right herbal notes.

Thrice Is Nice

Now for the key players: wine and pepper. Every peposo recipe that I found called for adding all the wine right at the start. But this was clearly problematic: Its aromatic characters were lost; its color suffered, turning from a rich purply red to a muddy brown; and its acidity was concentrated. I tried using less wine (as little as 1 cup), along with water or stock to make up the difference, but that just made the wine flavor weaker.

A little research informed me that wine is made up of three types of flavor compounds. Only the stable type can sustain long cooking times; the other two (unstable and volatile) eventually either break down and become flavorless or evaporate. With that in mind, I wondered whether a two-stage approach might work better: 2 cups of wine to give the stable flavors time to infuse the meat, plus 1 cup of water (to ensure that the meat would be sufficiently submerged) at the start, and then a second hit of wine toward the end so some of the delicate volatile and unstable flavor components would still be in the pot when cooking finished. This did improve the flavor considerably, but the sauce ended up rather loose and thin. For a sauce with the proper consistency, I was better off adding a second portion of wine after straining the cooking liquid and then reducing the mixture for about 15 minutes. During this brief cooking time, most of the wine's flavor remained intact. To give the sauce a bit more body without boiling it down any further, I also added a few teaspoons of cornstarch. Saving a small amount of wine to add at the very end gave the finished sauce brightness.

At this point, there was little obvious pepper flavor to speak of, and without it, the dish wouldn't be worthy of its name. I tried simply adding more cracked pepper at the start, but the dish lacked the familiar floral pungency pepper is known for. However, adding pepper at the very end of cooking wasn't the answer either. While it brought that missing floral flavor to the dish, now the dish was lacking depth. I dug a little deeper into my science books and realized that, like wine, pepper possesses the same three types of flavor compounds. It seemed like the layered approach I had used with the wine would be appropriate with the pepper, too.

To confirm my hunch, I steeped peppercorns in water for 2½ hours to mimic the stew's cooking time. Sure enough, I found that though the infusion lacked the pungency contributed by volatile and unstable compounds, it still had a uniquely earthy layer of flavor due to its stable compounds (see "Black Pepper's Hidden Flavors," page 31, for more). So having some cracked peppercorns in the stew from the start made sense. I also began adding ground pepper along with the second addition of wine. Finally, a sprinkle of cracked peppercorns at serving ensured a heady aroma.

With tender, succulent meat; a rich, silky wine sauce; and a deep, peppery bite, there was nothing more this peposo needed, beyond a second bottle of Chianti to serve alongside and a hunk of crusty bread or a bowl of polenta to soak up the stew. I'd added a few modern twists and a couple of measured refinements to the recipe, but I'd like to think that, given the results, they were nothing the fornaciai of the basilica would object to.

TUSCAN-STYLE BEEF STEW

SERVES 6 TO 8

We prefer boneless short ribs in this recipe because they require very little trimming. If you cannot find them, substitute a 5-pound chuck roast. Trim the roast of large pieces of fat and sinew, and cut it into 2-inch pieces. If Chianti is unavailable, a medium-bodied wine such as Côtes du Rhône or Pinot Noir makes a nice substitute. Serve with polenta or crusty bread.

- 4 pounds boneless beef short ribs, trimmed and cut into 2-inch pieces
- Salt
- 1 tablespoon vegetable oil
- 1 (750-ml) bottle Chianti
- 1 cup water
- 4 shallots, peeled and halved lengthwise
- 2 carrots, peeled and halved lengthwise
- 1 garlic head, cloves separated, unpeeled, and crushed
- 4 sprigs fresh rosemary
- 2 bay leaves
- 1 tablespoon cracked black peppercorns, plus extra for serving
- 1 tablespoon unflavored gelatin
- 1 tablespoon tomato paste
- 1 teaspoon anchovy paste
- 2 teaspoons ground black pepper
- 2 teaspoons cornstarch

1. Toss beef and 1½ teaspoons salt together in bowl and let stand at room temperature for 30 minutes. Adjust oven rack to lower-middle position and heat oven to 300 degrees.

2. Heat oil in large Dutch oven over medium-high heat until just smoking. Add half of beef in single layer and cook until well browned on all sides, about 8 minutes total, reducing heat if fond begins to burn. Stir in 2 cups wine, water, shallots, carrots, garlic, rosemary, bay leaves, cracked peppercorns, gelatin, tomato paste, anchovy paste, and remaining beef. Bring to simmer and cover tightly with sheet of heavy-duty aluminum foil, then lid. Transfer to oven and cook until beef is tender, 2 to 2¼ hours, stirring halfway through cooking time.

3. Using slotted spoon, transfer beef to bowl; cover tightly with foil and set aside. Strain sauce through fine-mesh strainer into fat separator. Wipe out pot with paper towels. Let liquid settle for 5 minutes, then return defatted liquid to pot.

4. Add 1 cup wine and ground black pepper and bring mixture to boil over medium-high heat. Simmer briskly, stirring occasionally, until sauce is thickened to consistency of heavy cream, 12 to 15 minutes.

5. Combine remaining wine and cornstarch in small bowl. Reduce heat to medium-low, return beef to pot, and stir in cornstarch-wine mixture. Cover and simmer until just heated through, 5 to 8 minutes. Season with salt to taste. Serve, passing extra cracked peppercorns separately. (Stew can be made up to 3 days in advance.)

Perfect Slow-Roasted Chicken

The juiciest meat demands low heat; the crispiest skin, a hot sear. Could we achieve both?

⋟ BY DAN SOUZA ⋞

Cooking whole chicken slowly at low temperatures is a hugely popular restaurant technique these days. When done properly, slow roasting allows the meat to retain far more of the natural juices than high-temperature roasting does, delivering ultramoist results. That said, I've never eaten a slow-roasted whole chicken where the skin was as perfectly cooked as the meat. Typically, the skin is a bit flabby and padded with unrendered fat. For brown, supercrisp results, the skin demands high heat to render fat, drive off moisture, and speed the Maillard reaction. To address that lack, many recipes incorporate a stint under the broiler or a final bast of heat at 500 degrees, both of which are problematic. Cranking up the heat at the end of cooking improves the skin, but usually overcooks the meat just under it. And it's simply too difficult to get even rendering and browning on a whole chicken under the broiler.

Slow roasting chicken parts actually makes a lot more sense. With parts, I'd quickly sear and render the skin in a skillet before any meat below the surface was affected. And since in my house there's never enough roast chicken to go around, using parts would mean that I could easily cook enough chicken for eight people by searing in two batches.

I began by patting dry and seasoning four split breasts and four leg quarters before searing them on both sides in a superhot skillet slicked with a tablespoon of oil. I then transferred the parts to a wire rack set in a baking sheet and popped them into a 250-degree oven, placing the leg quarters at the back of the oven where the temperature is typically highest, hoping they'd finish cooking at the same time as the white meat, which needs less time in the oven.

After about 90 minutes of slow roasting, the chicken was ready to come out. At first blush, it seemed perfect: Both white and dark meat finished cooking at the same time. Moreover, every piece was evenly cooked throughout and topped with golden-brown skin. One bite, however, revealed that the skin had turned soft and yielding during its time in the low oven. I'd already rendered a fair amount of fat and driven off at least some moisture—I wondered if I could get away with a really fast stint under the broiler to render more fat and recrisp the skin. As a precaution against overcooking, I first rested the cooked chicken briefly before broiling. To my delight, it worked. This chicken had shatteringly crisp skin giving way to ultrajuicy, tender meat.

To make a pan sauce, I poured off the excess fat from the skillet and browned some shallots and garlic in butter, added a sprinkling of coriander, and deglazed with chicken broth. To achieve the rich body of a jus from a chicken roasted at a high temperature, I added a little powdered gelatin and finished with cornstarch. A last-minute addition of lemon juice and parsley and I had a pretty good pan sauce. But my tasters sought more intense chicken flavor.

My unusual but effective solution: Instead of patting the chicken dry before searing as we normally do, I left it wet to promote sticking. I also used only ¼ teaspoon of oil and added the chicken to the pan when the oil was only shimmering (versus smoking). More initial sticking (the chicken releases naturally after it starts to brown) meant more fond and, in the end, a better pan sauce. (See "Better Pan Sauce? Ignore the Rules," page 31.) Finally, I'd achieved the promised superiority of slow-roasted chicken: perfect meat and perfect skin.

Searing in a skillet before slow-roasting on a rack helps ensure crisp skin without compromising the juicy meat.

SLOW-ROASTED CHICKEN PARTS WITH SHALLOT-GARLIC PAN SAUCE

SERVES 8

To serve four people, halve the ingredient amounts.

- **5** pounds bone-in chicken pieces (4 split breasts and 4 leg quarters), trimmed
- Kosher salt and pepper
- **¼** teaspoon vegetable oil
- **1** tablespoon unflavored gelatin
- **2¼** cups chicken broth
- **2** tablespoons water
- **2** teaspoons cornstarch
- **4** tablespoons unsalted butter, cut into 4 pieces
- **4** shallots, sliced thin
- **6** garlic cloves, sliced thin
- **1** teaspoon ground coriander
- **1** tablespoon minced fresh parsley
- **1½** teaspoons lemon juice

1. Adjust 1 oven rack to lowest position and second rack 8 inches from broiler element. Heat oven to 250 degrees. Line baking sheet with aluminum foil and place wire rack on top. Sprinkle chicken pieces with 2 teaspoons salt and season with pepper (do not pat chicken dry).

2. Heat oil in 12-inch skillet over medium-high heat until shimmering. Place leg quarters skin side down in skillet; cook, turning once, until golden brown on both sides, 5 to 7 minutes total. Transfer to prepared sheet, arranging legs along 1 long side of sheet. Pour off fat from skillet. Place breasts skin side down in skillet; cook, turning once, until golden brown on both sides, 4 to 6 minutes total. Transfer to sheet with legs. Discard fat; do not clean skillet. Place sheet on lower rack, orienting so legs are at back of oven. Roast until breasts register 155 degrees and legs register 170 degrees, 1¼ hours to 1 hour 35 minutes. Let chicken rest on sheet for 10 minutes.

3. While chicken roasts, sprinkle gelatin over broth in bowl and let sit until gelatin softens, about 5 minutes. Whisk water and cornstarch together in small bowl; set aside.

4. Melt butter in now-empty skillet over medium-low heat. Add shallots and garlic; cook until golden brown and crispy, 6 to 9 minutes. Stir in coriander and cook for 30 seconds. Stir in gelatin mixture, scraping up browned bits. Bring to simmer over high heat and cook until reduced to 1½ cups, 5 to 7 minutes. Whisk cornstarch mixture to recombine. Whisk into sauce and simmer until thickened, about 1 minute. Off heat, stir in parsley and lemon juice; season with salt and pepper to taste. Cover to keep warm.

5. Heat broiler. Transfer sheet to upper rack and broil chicken until skin is well browned and crisp, 3 to 6 minutes. Serve, passing sauce separately.

Watch It Cook and Crisp
Video available free for 4 months at CooksIllustrated.com/feb15

Best Roasted Mushrooms

Could a single addition produce both deep roasted flavor and even seasoning?

� BY ADAM RIED ⋐

Even when I'm not in the mood for beef, I'll go to a steakhouse just for the side dishes: wedge salad, potatoes au gratin, and creamed spinach. But there's an exception: the mushroom sides, which are often uninspired. Awful? No. Dull? You bet. Still, rich, meaty-tasting mushrooms are an ideal side dish since they partner well with almost any protein. Outdoing the restaurants? It ought to be a cinch.

Right away I knew that sautéing was out since I didn't want to labor with multiple batches (crowding the pan would cause them to steam, not brown). That left roasting—the best way to develop flavorful browning without requiring my constant attention.

I wanted to avoid relatively bland white buttons, so I cut four full-flavored types—cremini, portobellos, oysters, and shiitakes—into chunks, tossed them in olive oil and salt, and roasted them both alone and in combination. Each batch emerged nicely browned, and a duo of cremini and shiitakes took top honors, the former providing pronounced earthiness and the latter a meaty, smoky taste.

But while I was testing oven temperatures—I settled on 450 degrees—a problem popped up. No matter how carefully I sprinkled on the salt, the mushrooms emerged unevenly seasoned: Some were oversalted (usually in the gills, the ribbed area underneath the mushroom cap), while others tasted flat. Plus, the shiitakes were cooking up somewhat dry.

I started brainstorming ways to make the shiitakes juicy: Use more oil, arrange them gill side down (to trap moisture), microwave them prior to roasting, add liquid to the pan, or cover them with foil. One by one, I ticked each test off my list, and one by one, each idea failed. I began to feel for the restaurants whose mushrooms I had once maligned.

It was then that a colleague offered an unconventional suggestion: brining. I was intrigued. While working on a recipe for stuffed mushrooms, we learned that the cap of any fungi is covered with a layer of hydrophobic (water-repellent) proteins that prevent water from seeping in. But could saltwater soak through the gills? I dissolved 3 tablespoons of salt in 2 quarts of water, dumped in the mushrooms, and left them to soak for 10 minutes. After blotting the mushrooms dry, I proceeded with oiling and roasting. Now they were too salty, but, encouragingly, they were *all* too salty: The brine had delivered consistent seasoning. I tinkered with the salt amount, finally reducing it to 5 teaspoons. After about an hour of roasting, this batch was darkly browned and evenly seasoned. And the shiitakes were as juicy as could be.

Why did brining work? Relatively dry shiitakes contain roughly 70 percent water (cremini, about 90 percent). The shiitakes sponged up the water from the brine (through the gills and any cut surfaces) via osmotic pressure, and because of this, they also retained moisture in the oven. The already succulent cremini didn't absorb enough water to noticeably alter their texture, yet—like the shiitakes—they held on to enough salt from the brine to be well seasoned.

Jazzing up the roasted mushrooms was as simple as glossing them with melted butter and mixing in a few fresh herbs and spices. Maybe I'd still hit up a steakhouse for the creamed spinach, but from now on I'd be enjoying mushrooms at home.

ROASTED MUSHROOMS WITH PARMESAN AND PINE NUTS

SERVES 4

Quarter large (more than 2 inches) mushrooms, halve medium (1 to 2 inches) ones, and leave small (under 1 inch) ones whole. For our free recipe for Roasted Mushrooms with Roasted Garlic and Smoked Paprika, go to CooksIllustrated.com/feb15.

- Salt and pepper
- 1½ pounds cremini mushrooms, trimmed and left whole if small, halved if medium, or quartered if large
- 1 pound shiitake mushrooms, stemmed, caps larger than 3 inches halved
- 2 tablespoons extra-virgin olive oil
- 2 tablespoons unsalted butter, melted
- 1 teaspoon lemon juice
- 1 ounce Parmesan cheese, grated (½ cup)
- 2 tablespoons pine nuts, toasted
- 2 tablespoons chopped fresh parsley

1. Adjust oven rack to lowest position and heat oven to 450 degrees. Dissolve 5 teaspoons salt in 2 quarts room-temperature water in large container. Add cremini mushrooms and shiitake mushrooms to brine, cover with plate or bowl to submerge, and let stand for 10 minutes.

2. Drain mushrooms in colander and pat dry with paper towels. Spread mushrooms evenly on rimmed baking sheet, drizzle with oil, and toss to coat. Roast until liquid from mushrooms has completely evaporated, 35 to 45 minutes.

3. Remove sheet from oven (be careful of escaping steam when opening oven) and, using thin metal spatula, carefully stir mushrooms. Return to oven and continue to roast until mushrooms are deeply browned, 5 to 10 minutes longer.

Believe it or not, briefly soaking mushrooms in a salt-water solution is the key to perfectly roasted results.

4. Combine melted butter and lemon juice in large bowl. Add mushrooms and toss to coat. Add Parmesan, pine nuts, and parsley and toss. Season with salt and pepper to taste; serve immediately.

ROASTED MUSHROOMS WITH HARISSA AND MINT

Substitute 1 tablespoon extra-virgin olive oil for butter and increase lemon juice to 2 teaspoons. Whisk 1 garlic clove, minced to paste; 2 teaspoons harissa; ¼ teaspoon ground cumin; and ¼ teaspoon salt into oil mixture in step 4. Omit Parmesan and pine nuts and substitute mint for parsley.

ROASTED MUSHROOMS WITH SESAME AND SCALLIONS

Substitute 2 teaspoons toasted sesame oil for butter and ½ teaspoon rice vinegar for lemon juice. Omit Parmesan and substitute 2 teaspoons toasted sesame seeds for nuts and 2 thinly sliced scallions for parsley.

Watch Adam Roast
Video available free for 4 months at CooksIllustrated.com/feb15

French-Style Pork Chops and Apples

Classic French versions call for lighting the sauce on fire. Does this technique really make a difference—or is it just kitchen theatrics?

BY LAN LAM

Dishes featuring the classic duo of pork and apples usually aren't anything special—think weeknight chops and applesauce. But *porc à la Normande* is a different story. A dish that has graced French tables for hundreds of years, it features an elegant presentation of pork, accompanied by sautéed apples cut into chunks, rings, or even *tournées* (oblong football shapes), while a sauce, complex with layers of apple flavor and a touch of richness, brings it all together.

When I tried a few versions, the potential and the pitfalls were clear. The pork was usually dry and the apples undercooked. Many of the sauces—the component that should really take this dish from everyday to exceptional—were too sweet and tasted flat. And every recipe required hours and an arsenal of pots. My challenge: deliver an elegant version with perfectly cooked pork and apples and a savory-rich sauce with complex apple flavor without requiring a lot of time or cookware.

Apples cut into rings look elegant but are functional, too—we use them as a bed to raise the chops off the skillet's bottom for even cooking.

Meat of the Recipe

The issue of dry pork starts with the selection of chops. I opted for center-cut bone-in rib chops since, unlike sirloin or blade chops, they contain just one muscle group (the loin), which makes them easier to cook evenly. Using 1-inch-thick chops would give me some leeway to help avoid overcooking, and salting the chops for an hour would help them retain their juices.

When the hour was up, I followed our protocol for cooking thick cuts: Sear on the stovetop, transfer to a wire rack set in a baking sheet, and finish in a 300-degree oven. These chops browned nicely and cooked up juicy and tender, so I moved on to the apples.

Cutting the apples into ½-inch-thick rings was clearly the way to go. Rings looked more elegant than chunks and would be easier to brown and cook through evenly (and less fussy to prepare) than tournées. I could have simply cooked the apples on the stovetop while the chops were in the oven, but I saw an opportunity for efficiency, as well as a flavor boost. Why not ditch the wire-rack-and-sheet-pan setup for the chops and instead use the apples to elevate the chops so they would cook evenly?

I browned some apple rings on one side, flipped them over, and added some chicken broth for even cooking and more flavor. Next, I placed my browned chops on top of the apples and moved the whole setup to the oven. The apples picked up fantastic meaty flavor while the chops, elevated off the skillet's bottom, cooked perfectly.

See How to Flambé
Video available free for 4 months at CooksIllustrated.com/feb15

Apples to Apple Sauce

The bulk of the sauce would be made from some form of apple-y liquid. I settled on apple cider. Apple juice lacks complexity because it's filtered, while hard ciders vary greatly and pack much less apple punch. All the recipes I'd tried also included Calvados, for good reason. This apple brandy from Normandy would provide an essential woodsy apple essence. For yet another hit of fruitiness, I chopped a couple of apples and added them to the pot with the liquids. They broke down as the sauce reduced and helped give it body as well as apple flavor.

Another thing about the traditional recipes: Many of them call for flambéing the sauce, igniting it after adding the Calvados. In the past we've touted the flavor flambéing adds to a dish, but I wondered if it was really necessary here since I'd be adding a number of flavorful ingredients. I decided to skip it. I sautéed some shallots; added a glug of Calvados, followed by cider, chicken broth, and the chopped apples; and brought the sauce to a simmer. Once it had reduced to a spoon-coating consistency, I stirred in some crème fraîche for richness.

This sauce was good, but I wanted great. Cooking two slices of chopped bacon and sautéing the shallots in the rendered fat boosted the savoriness. Nutmeg and thyme lent warmth and herbal depth. And instead of the crème fraîche, which gave the sauce a muddy appearance, I whisked in butter plus cider vinegar. This sauce had a great consistency when I quickly sampled it, but come serving time, after I'd prepared the chops and apples, I hit a snag: The butter had floated to the surface instead of staying emulsified.

I could have whisked for much longer to break the butter into droplets tiny enough to stay emulsified, or I could have whisked in the butter just before serving, but I came up with an easier solution. My inspiration came from my restaurant days of making chicken and beef stock. The chef had told us to gently simmer and avoid a hard boil. If a stock bubbles too vigorously, the fat will emulsify and make the stock cloudy. What he'd advised *against* then was exactly what I *needed* now: emulsification. I made another batch, this time adding the butter along with the cider and letting the sauce reduce at a vigorous simmer. *Voilà*, by serving time the sauce was still picture-perfect. However, it was a little boozy and lacked complexity.

Firing Up the Flavor

Maybe the flambé step was more important than I'd thought. Or could I get away with simply boiling the Calvados for several minutes to simulate the rapid evaporation caused by flambéing, instead of

STEP BY STEP | HOW—AND WHY—WE FLAMBÉ

We found that flambéing this sauce not only removes some alcohol but also makes a real difference in flavor, producing a more complex-tasting sauce through caramelization, the Maillard reaction, and changes in the shape of the flavor molecules, which leads to a changed flavor perception. Adding the alcohol in two stages keeps the size of the flames manageable and shortens the amount of time it burns.

ADD HALF OF BRANDY
Off heat, add ¼ cup Calvados and let warm through, about 5 seconds.

LIGHT SAUCE
Fully extend arm and wave flame over pan until Calvados ignites; shake pan gently to distribute flames.

LET BURN AND COVER
Let burn until flames subside on their own, 30 to 60 seconds. Cover for 15 seconds to ensure flame is extinguished.

REPEAT WITH REMAINING BRANDY
Add remaining ¼ cup Calvados and repeat flambéing (flames will subside after 1½ to 2 minutes).

actually lighting it on fire? I ran a side-by-side test: my working recipe with a flambéing step added, and a version for which I boiled the mixture after adding the Calvados. Tasters' votes were unanimous: Both were more complex than my previous versions, but the flambéed sauce was noticeably the most complex (See "How—and Why—We Flambé" for more details). Adding the Calvados in two stages, flambéing after each addition, kept the height of the flames and their burning time to a minimum.

Requiring just a couple of pots and an hour and a half start to finish, the whole recipe came together pretty easily. And thanks to its little bit of French-style flair, it had moved from ordinary to impressive.

For an Emulsified Sauce, Break the Rules

As the sauce in this recipe sits for 30 minutes while the chops and apples are prepared, butter that's simply whisked in after the sauce has been reduced (the standard procedure for most butter-enriched sauces) will separate out. To keep the butter emulsified longer, one option would have been to whisk more thoroughly to break the butter into even tinier droplets that would stay suspended for more than a few minutes. Or we could have whisked in the butter just before serving. Instead, we came up with an even easier approach, drawing inspiration from—and then breaking—a classic French rule for making stock.

French tomes dictate that you should never allow a stock to vigorously simmer: The bubbling action can break up the fat so that it disperses throughout the liquid, turning the stock cloudy. But since breaking up the fat was what we wanted to do for our sauce, we added the butter at the start of the long reduction time and then turned up the heat to keep the sauce at a vigorous simmer. The constant agitation during the 30 minutes breaks the butter into tiny droplets that stay so well emulsified that the sauce won't break for a full hour.

FRENCH-STYLE PORK CHOPS WITH APPLES AND CALVADOS

SERVES 4

We prefer natural pork, but if the pork is enhanced (injected with a salt solution), decrease the salt in step 1 to ½ teaspoon per chop. To ensure that they fit in the skillet, choose apples that are approximately 3 inches in diameter. Applejack or regular brandy can be used in place of the Calvados. Before flambéing, be sure to roll up long shirtsleeves, tie back long hair, and turn off the exhaust fan and any lit burners. Use a long match or wooden skewer to flambé the Calvados. The amount of vinegar to add in step 4 will vary depending on the sweetness of your cider.

- 4 (12- to 14-ounce) bone-in pork rib chops, 1 inch thick
- Kosher salt and pepper
- 4 Gala or Golden Delicious apples, peeled and cored
- 2 slices bacon, cut into ½-inch pieces
- 3 shallots, sliced
- Pinch ground nutmeg
- ½ cup Calvados
- 1¾ cups apple cider
- 1¼ cups chicken broth
- 4 sprigs fresh thyme, plus ¼ teaspoon minced
- 2 tablespoons unsalted butter
- 2 teaspoons vegetable oil
- ½–1 teaspoon apple cider vinegar

1. Evenly sprinkle each chop with ¾ teaspoon salt. Place chops on large plate, cover loosely with plastic wrap, and refrigerate for 1 hour.

2. While chops rest, cut 2 apples into ½-inch pieces. Cook bacon in medium saucepan over medium heat until crisp, 5 to 7 minutes. Add shallots, nutmeg, and ¼ teaspoon salt; cook, stirring frequently, until shallots are softened and beginning to brown, 3 to 4 minutes. Off heat, add ¼ cup Calvados and let warm through, about 5 seconds. Wave lit match over pan until Calvados ignites, then shake pan gently to distribute flames. When flames subside, 30 to 60 seconds, cover pan to ensure flame is extinguished, 15 seconds. Add remaining ¼ cup Calvados and repeat flambéing (flames will subside after 1½ to 2 minutes). (If you have trouble igniting second addition, return pan to medium heat, bring to bare simmer, and remove from heat and try again.) Once flames have extinguished, increase heat to medium-high; add cider, 1 cup broth, thyme sprigs, butter, and chopped apples; and bring to rapid simmer. Cook, stirring occasionally, until apples are very tender and mixture has reduced to 2⅓ cups, 25 to 35 minutes. Cover and set aside.

3. Adjust oven rack to middle position and heat oven to 300 degrees. Slice remaining 2 apples into ½-inch-thick rings. Pat chops dry with paper towels and evenly sprinkle each chop with pepper to taste. Heat oil in 12-inch skillet over medium heat until beginning to smoke. Increase heat to high and brown chops on both sides, 6 to 8 minutes total. Transfer chops to large plate and reduce heat to medium. Add apple rings and cook until lightly browned, 1 to 2 minutes. Add remaining ¼ cup broth and cook, scraping up any browned bits with rubber spatula, until liquid has evaporated, about 30 seconds. Remove pan from heat, flip apple rings, and place chops on top of apple rings. Place skillet in oven and cook until chops register 135 to 140 degrees, 11 to 15 minutes.

4. Transfer chops and apple rings to serving platter, tent loosely with foil, and let rest for 10 minutes. While chops rest, strain apple/brandy mixture through fine-mesh strainer set in large bowl, pressing on solids with ladle or rubber spatula to extract liquid; discard solids. (Make sure to use rubber spatula to scrape any apple solids on bottom of strainer into sauce.) Stir in minced thyme and season sauce with vinegar, salt, and pepper to taste. Transfer sauce to serving bowl. Serve chops and apple rings, passing sauce separately.

Slow-Cooked Whole Carrots

Who would ever slow-cook whole carrots for an hour? We would—if the results were superbly concentrated flavor and dense, meaty texture from end to end.

⋟ BY KEITH DRESSER ⋞

As a chef, I get particular enjoyment from dining out: It's my chance to keep up with the ever-changing culinary landscape by experiencing cutting-edge techniques and trendy ingredients. But at home I rarely have the desire to re-create restaurant food. (Who has the time to whip up a frothy bacon emulsion or labor over a batch of green apple taffy?) Still, every so often I come across a dish or approach that I absolutely have to try in my own kitchen. The most recent was a gorgeous platter of slow-cooked whole carrots. Fork-tender and without a hint of mushiness, they had a dense, almost meaty quality to them. And the carrot flavor was superconcentrated: sweet and pure, but still earthy. I pictured these carrots as an accompaniment to everything from a holiday beef tenderloin to a basic roast chicken.

A search for recipes that would produce similar results generated a lot of slow-roasted and braised carrots, but none came close to what I had been served. The roasted carrots boasted plenty of sweetness because of their significant browning, but this obscured their true flavor. On the other hand, braised carrots inevitably took on the flavor of whatever liquid they were cooked in—I wanted carrots that tasted like carrots, not like chicken broth or white wine. It was obvious that I would need to use another cooking method to spotlight the carrots in the best possible way.

The natural sugar from the carrots and a pat of butter added to the cooking water reduce to create a light glaze.

Saving Sweetness

I got my bearings by slowly simmering 12 whole peeled carrots (I chose similarly sized specimens so that they would cook as evenly as possible) in a full saucepan of salted water (about 6 cups) until they were tender. This test shed light on two issues. The first was inconsistent cooking: By the time the thick end of the carrot was tender, the thinner tapered end was mushy and waterlogged. The second was that the carrots had been robbed of their inherent sweetness. Simmering had drawn out the soluble sugar in the vegetable and, unfortunately, all of that flavorful sugar flowed down the drain when I poured off the cooking water.

Look: Perfect Carrots
Video available free for 4 months at CooksIllustrated.com/feb15

The latter problem would be solved by coming up with an approach that didn't call for discarding the sweet cooking water. Switching from a saucepan to a skillet (whose shallow sides would facilitate evaporation) and reducing the amount of water to just 3 cups were my first moves. I arranged the carrots in a single layer and simmered them uncovered until all the water evaporated and the carrots were fully tender when I pierced them with a paring knife, which took about 45 minutes. I also added a tablespoon of butter to the water at the beginning of simmering, which, in combination with the sugar released from the carrots, reduced to a light glaze that coated the carrots with a handsome sheen.

Unfortunately, even with this specialized method, the inconsistent doneness from the thick end of the carrot to the narrow end remained. I experimented with squirting some lemon juice into the water, hoping that its acid would firm up the pectin in the carrots and balance out the textural inconsistencies. The good news: It worked. The bad: In order for the lemon juice to have an effect, I needed to squeeze in so much of it that it buried the carrots' sweetness.

Pectin Power

Looking for a better solution, I was reminded of a phenomenon called "persistent firmness." Here's how it works: Precooking certain fruits or vegetables at a low temperature sparks an enzymatic reaction that helps the produce remain tender-firm during a second cooking phase at a higher temperature. If I could use persistent firmness to my advantage in this recipe, it would mean that the thin ends of the carrots wouldn't turn mushy while the thicker ends fully cooked through. (For more, see "Persistent Firmness—It's a Real Thing.")

To put the science to the test, I outfitted my skillet with a probe thermometer, brought 3 cups of salted water (along with the pat of butter) to a boil, removed the skillet from the heat, arranged the carrots in a single layer in the water, covered the skillet, and let the carrots stand for 20 minutes. During this time, the water temperature clocked in at 135 to 150 degrees, right in the ideal range for the enzymatic reaction to work its magic. After 20 minutes, I removed the lid and switched over to my newly developed cooking method, returning the carrots to the heat and simmering them until the water evaporated. These carrots were tender from end to end, yet they still boasted a firm, meaty texture.

The carrots were now just about perfect, but I did notice that the top sides of some of them were occasionally a little underdone. I suspected that because I was using a relatively small amount of water, the level was falling below the tops of the carrots before they had time to become tender. Using a lid wasn't the answer since covering the pan only slowed evaporation. Partially covering the skillet was a no-go since finding the sweet spot would take trial and error and might not be the same for every pot. Finally, rolling the carrots during cooking to promote even cooking was a pain in the neck and imperfect at best: Some of the carrots inevitably rolled back into their initial positions, thwarting my efforts.

That's when I thought of a trick I'd learned in restaurant kitchens: using a cartouche—a piece of parchment paper that sits directly on the food as it cooks, regulating the reduction of moisture in cooking. I topped my next batch of carrots with a cartouche and was happy to find that it solved the problem. The paper allowed the perfect rate of evaporation but also trapped more of the escaping steam and kept it concentrated on top of the carrots, ensuring perfectly tender, evenly cooked results.

I was happy to eat these carrots, with their firm, tender texture and pure carrot flavor, without any embellishment. But to make them real showstoppers, I dressed them up a bit. I settled on easy relishes that could be whipped up while the carrots cooked. These toppings, made with bold ingredients like sherry vinegar, olives, fresh herbs, and nuts, packed an acidic punch that complemented the carrots' sweet, earthy flavor. Garnishing with just a small amount of relish kept the focus on the carrots. I may not be a restaurant chef any more, but no one will know that from eating these carrots.

SCIENCE Persistent Firmness—It's a Real Thing

Precooking certain fruits or vegetables at a low temperature can help them retain a firm yet tender texture during a second cooking phase at a higher temperature. This phenomenon, called "persistent firmness," is the key to achieving evenly cooked whole carrots—especially those that are thick on one end and tapered on the other. To initiate persistent firmness, we found that our carrots need to be precooked in 120- to 160-degree water for 20 minutes. During this warm bath, an enzyme in the carrot called pectin methylesterase (PME) is activated. PME alters the pectin in the vegetable in such a way that it is able to bind with calcium ions that are also present in the cells. This, in turn, fortifies the pectin, creating a strong network that is more resistant to breaking down when the carrots finish cooking at a higher temperature. The upshot? Carrots that are perfectly tender—but not at all mushy—from end to end.

Making the Case for Paper

Going to the trouble of making a parchment paper lid with a small hole in the middle, or a cartouche, is worth it. It works better than a metal lid to keep steam concentrated on the top of the carrots, so they cook at the same rate as the underside of the vegetables. For more information, see "Why Use Parchment Instead of a Lid?" on page 30.

SLOW-COOKED WHOLE CARROTS

SERVES 4 TO 6

Use carrots that measure ¾ to 1¼ inches across at the thickest end. The carrots can be served plain, but we recommend topping them with one of our relishes (recipes follow). For our free recipes for Onion-Balsamic Relish with Mint and Red Pepper and Almond Relish, go to CooksIllustrated.com/feb15.

- 3 cups water
- 1 tablespoon unsalted butter
- ½ teaspoon salt
- 12 carrots (1½ to 1¾ pounds), peeled

1. Fold 12-inch square of parchment paper into quarters to create 6-inch square. Fold bottom right corner of square to top left corner to create triangle. Fold triangle again, right side over left, to create narrow triangle. Cut off ¼ inch of tip of triangle to create small hole. Cut base of triangle straight across where it measures 5 inches from hole. Open paper round.

2. Bring water, butter, and salt to simmer in 12-inch skillet over high heat. Remove pan from heat, add carrots in single layer, and place parchment round on top of carrots. Cover skillet and let stand for 20 minutes.

3. Remove lid from skillet, leaving parchment round in place, and bring to simmer over high heat. Reduce heat to medium-low and simmer until almost all water has evaporated and carrots are very tender, about 45 minutes. Discard parchment round, increase heat to medium-high, and continue to cook carrots, shaking pan frequently, until they are lightly glazed and no water remains in skillet, 2 to 4 minutes longer. Transfer carrots to platter and serve.

TECHNIQUE | MAKING A PARCHMENT LID (CARTOUCHE)

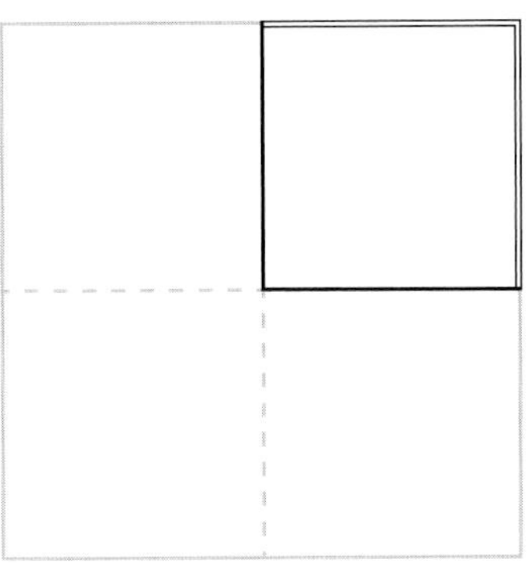

1. Fold 12-inch square of parchment into quarters to create 6-inch square.

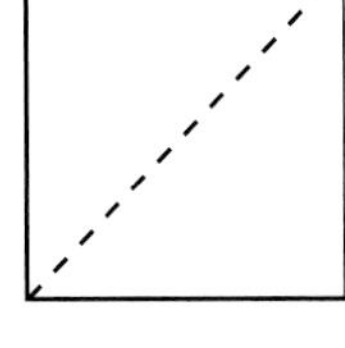

2. With openings at top and right sides, fold bottom right corner of square to top left corner.

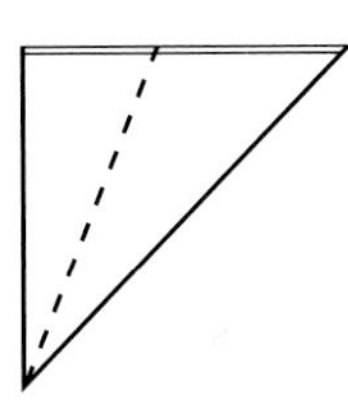

3. Fold triangle again, right side over left, to create narrow triangle.

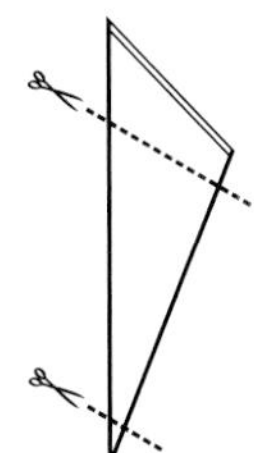

4. Cut off ¼ inch of tip to create hole. Cut base of triangle straight across where it measures 5 inches from hole.

GREEN OLIVE AND GOLDEN RAISIN RELISH

MAKES ABOUT 1 CUP

- ⅓ cup golden raisins
- 1 tablespoon water
- ⅔ cup pitted green olives, chopped
- 1 shallot, minced
- 2 tablespoons extra-virgin olive oil
- 1 tablespoon red wine vinegar
- ½ teaspoon ground fennel
- ¼ teaspoon salt

Microwave raisins and water in bowl until steaming, about 1 minute. Cover and let stand until raisins are plump, about 5 minutes. Add olives, shallot, oil, vinegar, fennel, and salt to plumped raisins and stir to combine.

PINE NUT RELISH

MAKES ABOUT ¾ CUP

Pine nuts burn easily, so be sure to shake the pan frequently while toasting them.

- ⅓ cup pine nuts, toasted
- 1 shallot, minced
- 1 tablespoon sherry vinegar
- 1 tablespoon minced fresh parsley
- 1 teaspoon honey
- ½ teaspoon minced fresh rosemary
- ¼ teaspoon smoked paprika
- ¼ teaspoon salt
- Pinch cayenne pepper

Combine all ingredients in bowl.

Japanese Stir-Fried Noodles with Beef

Springy noodles in a bold, complex sauce make *yakisoba* a standout among noodle stir-fries. The problem: replicating those qualities without the hard-to-find ingredients.

BY LAN LAM

Lo mein has long been my go-to noodle stir-fry to make at home because it's quick to prepare and contains meat and vegetables that add up to a satisfying one-dish meal. But when I want those qualities and also a bit more character, the Japanese equivalent called *yakisoba* comes to mind. This dish shares the same hearty combination of springy noodles, meat (often beef), and vegetables, but instead of the typical soy-garlic profile of Chinese American stir-fries, it boasts a bright, sweet-savory-tangy sauce. Its bold garnishes—namely, pickled ginger and a spice blend with sesame seeds and orange peel known as *shichimi togarashi*—make the dish even more distinctive. Then there's the noodles themselves. Like many Asian wheat noodles (including lo mein), yakisoba strands have a springy quality; they also have an ultraslick surface that takes up just a thin coating of sauce and makes the strands fun to slurp.

Wanting to add a homemade version to my repertoire, I paged through some cookbooks and found that recipes all followed a basic approach: Brown the vegetables and beef in a skillet and set them aside, boil up the noodles and then add them to the skillet, stir in the sauce and cook until it thickens, toss the sauced noodles with the beef and vegetables, and serve with the garnishes.

The bright, complex flavor of *yakisoba* is due as much to its sauce as it is to the classic garnishes: pickled ginger and a sesame-orange spice blend.

The problem: Springy, slippery yakisoba noodles and the distinctive spice blend were impossible to find outside an Asian market, as was the key ingredient to the sauce—a Japanese condiment modeled after British Worcestershire sauce that bears the same name.

I was certain I could fine-tune the cooking approach by using the foolproof techniques that the test kitchen has developed over the years for stir-fries. But could I make yakisoba taste the way it's meant to without all the hard-to-find ingredients? I set out to try.

See Every Step
Video available free for 4 months at CooksIllustrated.com/feb15

Beefing Up

Of the three beef cuts we tend to use in the test kitchen for stir-frying—blade steak, flap meat, or flank steak—I chose flank. It's a chewier cut, but its wide availability and easy preparation won me over. I sliced a 12-ounce portion into strips, cut each strip crosswise, and then seared the strips in two batches in a large nonstick skillet—a vessel that we've found makes better contact with flat Western burners than a round-bottomed wok does. The meat tasted great, and to soften its chew, I briefly soaked it in a solution of baking soda and water before searing. This treatment, we've discovered, raises the meat's pH, preventing its proteins from bonding excessively so that the meat is more tender and juicy.

As for the vegetables, thinly sliced carrots, shiitake mushrooms, cabbage, and onions are yakisoba standards; I had been adding these directly to the skillet, and my tasters and I were more or less happy with the results. The only changes I made were to swap conventional green cabbage for faster-cooking napa leaves, and grassy, more colorful scallions for the onion. The carrots and mushrooms also needed a bit more help softening. I browned them together and, once they'd developed color, added a splash of chicken broth to the pan, which generated a puff of steam that helped them turn tender.

Flavor Makers

Now for that complex sauce. While many recipes use sake or mirin as their base, the best always featured a generous amount of that Japanese Worcestershire sauce. The British original was a common substitute, but on its own this stand-in missed some of the fruity, savory notes of the Japanese kind; plus, it lacked body. Comparing the ingredient lists clarified their differences: Both contain vinegar and sweeteners, but instead of British Worcestershire's tamarind extract and anchovies, the Japanese sauce boasted tomato paste and pureed fruit, as well as dried sardines and yeast extract.

To doctor the British kind, I measured 2 tablespoons into a bowl and added ¼ cup of ketchup. That got me closer to the fruitiness of the Japanese sauce, but I didn't nail the sweet-tangy flavor until I whisked in rice vinegar and brown sugar. Meanwhile, ¼ cup of soy sauce took me partway to the savory flavor, and a few cloves of minced garlic helped, too. Dried sardines were out of the question, but a few finely minced anchovies added nice umami depth.

Noodling Around

It was time to figure out a suitably slick and snappy substitute for the yakisoba strands. As a longtime fan of the dish, I knew that chewy noodles like these are called "alkaline" noodles. With a little research I learned that's because they contain a pair of salts, sodium carbonate and potassium carbonate. These salts raise the pH of the dough, strengthening the network of protein strands, or gluten, that give the noodles structure so that they develop elasticity. (For more information, see "How Asian Noodles Get Their Spring.") The alkaline environment also imparts a golden tint to the noodles by turning compounds in the wheat, called flavones, yellow. Because lo mein has a similar texture (and color), I wasn't surprised to discover that these noodles also include the alkalizing salts. But before I settled on them as

SCIENCE How Asian Noodles Get Their Spring

Asian noodles come in countless varieties, but many, including *yakisoba*, ramen, and lo mein, are characterized by a satisfying chew. These springy noodles contain the same core ingredients as Italian pastas—wheat flour and water—along with two salts, sodium and potassium carbonates, that raise the pH of the dough. A little research confirmed that the alkaline environment increases the bonding between gluten strands, making the gluten network stronger and more elastic, for noodles that stretch and spring back. The effect of the alkalizing salts is clearly visible if you compare cooked Italian spaghetti strands with the alkaline noodles: The former swell more and have less give, while the latter stay firm and chewy.

HOLDING STRONG

Elastic alkaline noodles are so resilient that they can hold more than 4 ounces of weight before breaking. (Tender Italian spaghetti can hold only 1¾ ounces.)

my easier-to-find alternative to the yakisoba strands, I rounded up other widely available Asian noodles that also contained sodium and potassium carbonates. Besides fresh and dried lo mein, these included dried Chinese-style egg noodles, dried ramen, and even dried instant ramen. I boiled them all and then staged a taste test against proper yakisoba noodles.

Happily, all the alkaline noodles delivered respectable elasticity, but ultimately the lo mein strands (fresh as well as dried) were the closest match, as they were roughly the same width as yakisoba. But when I worked them into the stir-fry, they weren't slick like the yakisoba noodles I'd eaten in Japanese restaurants—and, frankly, neither were the actual yakisoba noodles I'd used in my earlier tests. In fact, the lo mein was rather sticky and soaked up so much of the sauce that the stir-fry was a bit dry. Adding ½ cup of chicken broth to the skillet along with the sauce helped hydrate the dish.

As for the stickiness, I looked back through my test recipes and discovered that a few called for rinsing the noodles under cool running water after boiling. Indeed, when I did the same, the lo mein's exterior became pleasantly slippery. Why? Rinsing with cold water removes the surface starches from the noodles. Less starch means that less sauce will cling, mitigating that sticky texture.

Back to the chile spice blend. The commercial togarashi that we sampled was both spicy and faintly sweet, so I mixed a spoonful of black pepper with a dash of cayenne and then incorporated sweetness with paprika. In lieu of dried orange peel, I stripped ¾ teaspoon of zest off the fruit and dried it in the microwave. Ground ginger and powdered garlic rounded out the sweet and savory notes, respectively.

This blend, along with a few slivers of pickled ginger, topped off a version of yakisoba that was as satisfying as any I'd eaten in a Japanese restaurant.

The Other Worcestershire

Yakisoba sauce (Japanese Worcestershire sauce) is a thicker, sweeter relative of the familiar British kind. To create a facsimile with similar flavor and body to the popular Bull-Dog brand's, we used widely available Lea & Perrins, doctoring it with ketchup, soy sauce, rice vinegar, and brown sugar.

JAPANESE-STYLE STIR-FRIED NOODLES WITH BEEF

SERVES 4 TO 6

This recipe calls for lo mein noodles, but use yakisoba noodles if you can find them and follow the same cooking directions. Garnish the noodles with pickled ginger (often found in the refrigerated section of the grocery store near tofu) and our Sesame-Orange Spice Blend (recipe follows) or, if you can find it, commercial *shichimi togarashi.*

- ⅛ teaspoon baking soda
- 12 ounces flank steak, trimmed, sliced lengthwise into 2- to 2½-inch strips, each strip sliced crosswise ¼ inch thick
- ¼ cup ketchup
- ¼ cup soy sauce
- 2 tablespoons Worcestershire sauce
- 1½ tablespoons packed brown sugar
- 3 garlic cloves, minced
- 3 anchovy fillets, rinsed, patted dry, and minced
- 1 teaspoon rice vinegar
- 1 pound fresh or 8 ounces dried lo mein noodles
- 1 tablespoon vegetable oil
- 6 ounces shiitake mushrooms, stemmed and sliced ¼ inch thick
- 1 carrot, peeled and sliced ⅛ inch thick on bias
- ¾ cup chicken broth
- 6 cups napa cabbage, sliced crosswise into ½-inch strips
- 7 scallions, cut on bias into 1-inch lengths
- Salt

1. Combine 1 tablespoon water and baking soda in medium bowl. Add beef and toss to coat. Let sit at room temperature for 5 minutes.

2. Whisk ketchup, soy sauce, Worcestershire, sugar, garlic, anchovies, and vinegar together in second bowl. Stir 2 tablespoons sauce into beef mixture and set aside remaining sauce.

3. Bring 4 quarts water to boil in large pot. Add noodles and cook, stirring often, until almost tender (center should still be firm with slightly opaque dot), 3 to 10 minutes (cooking times will vary depending on whether you are using fresh or dry noodles). Drain noodles and rinse under cold running water until water runs clear. Drain well and set aside.

4. Heat ½ teaspoon oil in 12-inch nonstick skillet over high heat until just smoking. Add mushrooms and carrot and cook, stirring occasionally, until vegetables are spotty brown, 2 to 3 minutes. Add ¼ cup broth and cook until all liquid has evaporated and vegetables are tender, about 30 seconds. Transfer vegetables to bowl.

5. Return skillet to high heat, add ½ teaspoon oil, and heat until beginning to smoke. Add cabbage and scallions and cook, without stirring, for 30 seconds. Cook, stirring occasionally, until cabbage and scallions are spotty brown and crisp-tender, 2 to 3 minutes. Transfer to bowl with mushrooms and carrot.

6. Return skillet to high heat, add 1 teaspoon oil, and heat until beginning to smoke. Add half of beef in single layer. Cook, without stirring, for 30 seconds. Cook, stirring occasionally, until beef is spotty brown, 1 to 2 minutes. Transfer to bowl with vegetables. Repeat with remaining beef and remaining 1 teaspoon oil.

7. Return skillet to high heat; add reserved sauce, remaining ½ cup broth, and noodles. Cook, scraping up any browned bits, until noodles are warmed through, about 1 minute. Transfer noodles to bowl with vegetables and beef and toss to combine. Season with salt to taste, and serve immediately.

SESAME-ORANGE SPICE BLEND

MAKES ¼ CUP

In addition to garnishing our stir-fry, this blend makes a great seasoning for eggs, rice, and fish. Store it in an airtight container for up to one week.

- ¾ teaspoon grated orange zest
- 2 teaspoons sesame seeds
- 1½ teaspoons paprika
- 1 teaspoon pepper
- ¼ teaspoon garlic powder
- ¼ teaspoon ground ginger
- ⅛ teaspoon cayenne pepper

Place orange zest in small bowl and microwave, stirring every 20 seconds, until zest is dry and no longer clumping together, 1 minute 30 seconds to 2 minutes 30 seconds. Stir in sesame seeds, paprika, pepper, garlic powder, ginger, and cayenne.

Drunken Beans

Cooking beans with beer and bacon can deliver results as full-flavored and satisfying as a rich stew—or it can lead to a pot of bitter, boozy beans.

BY ANDREW JANJIGIAN

Soupy beans, or *frijoles de la olla*, are a staple at most Mexican tables and for good reason. The humble preparation, which supposedly derives from the bean suppers that caballeros cooked over fires on the range, typically consists of beans, a bit of pork or lard, and just a few herbs and aromatics like onion, chiles, and maybe tomato. Once the flavors meld and the cooking liquid thickens slightly from the beans' starches, the dish is as satisfying as a rich stew. Add a side of rice and you've got a meal.

There are numerous iterations, but my favorite might be *frijoles borrachos*, or drunken beans, in which pinto beans are cooked with beer or tequila. The alcohol should be subtle, lending the pot brighter, more complex flavor than beans cooked in water alone. And yet, when I've made the dish at home, the alcohol tastes either overwhelmingly bitter, raw, and boozy or so faint that I can't tell it's there. I've also never gotten the consistency of the liquid quite right—that is, thickened just enough that it's brothy, not watery.

Our carefully orchestrated technique transforms humble dried beans into a rich, satisfying entrée.

I set my sights on a pot that featured creamy, intact beans and a cooking-liquid-turned-broth that wasn't awash in alcohol but that offered more depth than a batch of plain old pintos.

Humble Beginnings

My first step was to nail down the basics of Mexican pot beans. (I knew that canned beans were out here, since this recipe requires a full-flavored bean cooking liquid that only dried beans can impart.) Step one was to soak the dried beans overnight in salty water—an adjustment we make to the usual plain-water soak because we've learned that sodium weakens the pectin in the beans' skins and, thus, helps them soften more quickly. For the pork element, I chose bacon; plenty of recipes called for it, and its smoky depth would ratchet up the flavor of the dish. I browned a few sliced strips in a Dutch oven. Setting aside the meat, I left the rendered fat to sauté the aromatics: a chopped onion and a couple of poblano chiles, plus minced garlic. Once they had softened, I added the drained beans, a few cups of water, bay leaves, and salt and slid the vessel into a low (275-degree) oven, where the beans would simmer gently for the better part of an hour—no need to stir them or take the risk that they'd burst. (See "For Fewer Blowouts, Bake Your Beans," page 30.)

See Beans Get Tipsy
Video available free for 4 months at CooksIllustrated.com/feb15

Hop to It

I gave the beans an hour head start before adding the beer. Though some recipes call for incorporating it from the start of cooking, we've learned that cooking dried beans with acidic ingredients (and beer is definitely acidic) strengthens the pectin in the beans' skins and prevents them from fully softening. As for what type of beer to use, recipes were divided between dark and light Mexican lagers, but I reached for the former, figuring that a full-flavored pot of beans would surely require a full-flavored brew. I used 1 cup, splitting the difference between recipes that called for a full 12-ounce bottle and those that went with just a few ounces. I slid the pot back into the oven to meld the flavors and thicken the liquid. But the results I returned to half an hour later weren't what I was hoping for. Most noticeable was the beer's bitter flavor. The extra liquid had also thinned out the broth so that it lacked body.

I figured that reducing the amount of beer would thereby reduce the bitterness and the volume of liquid, too. But when I used just ½ cup, the "drunken" flavor was lost. Next, I tried cooking a full cup by itself before adding it to the pot when the beans were done cooking, hoping to increase its flavor and drive off some bitterness. Wrong again. The reduced beer tasted more bitter than ever, and some research explained why: The compounds responsible for the complex aroma and flavor of beer are highly volatile and dissipate quickly when boiled, while those that contribute bitterness are more stable and, in the absence of other flavors, become more pronounced. Given that, I tried adding the beer to the pot just before serving. This did help the beer retain a more complex flavor, but it also retained more of its raw-tasting alcohol.

A Cocktail of Flavor

I decided to switch gears and try tequila instead, since I'd seen it used in a number of recipes. I made more batches of beans, adding varying amounts of the liquor—from a few tablespoons all the way up to ½ cup. Further research told me that the flavor compounds in tequila are very stable and thus wouldn't be affected by a long simmer, so I added the tequila at the beginning of cooking to allow more time for some of the alcohol to evaporate.

In small amounts, the tequila's smoky-sweetness was very subtle, so I went with ½ cup, which added noticeable complexity. That said, my tasters and I all missed the beer's malty flavor, so I decided to use both types of alcohol. But this time I'd try a lighter (read: less bitter-tasting) lager. (For more information, see "Tasting Mexican Lagers" on page 28.)

Working up another batch, I poured in the tequila at the outset of cooking, but waited an hour

Perfect Beans—and Broth—Start Slow and Finish Strong

We like to cook beans in the oven because its heat is more even and gentle than that of the stovetop. If we're using the cooked beans in other recipes (see page 30 for complete instructions), we drain off the cooking liquid, but that liquid is a key component in dishes like our Drunken Beans. In these cases, we follow up the stint in the oven with a hard simmer on the stove. The higher, more direct heat jostles the beans, causing them to release starches that give the cooking liquid pleasant body.

START IN OVEN
Gentle cooking softens skins, saturates interiors.

FINISH ON STOVE
High heat causes starches to release into liquids.

You'd think that this vigorous simmer would also cause blowouts—exactly what we'd been avoiding by moving the initial cooking to the oven. But it didn't, because the beans fully cook in the oven—their flesh becomes saturated and their skins softened and flexible—and are therefore less vulnerable to blowing out. Just as you can simmer canned beans in a pot of soup with minimal blowouts, we found that our oven-cooked beans could be simmered without breaking down.

to add the beer, as I had in my first test. This time I got the booze flavor just right: faint bitterness and maltiness from the beer, with a deeper underpinning of flavor from the tequila. To underscore the pot's fresh and sweet flavors, I took a cue from other Mexican dishes and added a bundle of cilantro stems (I'd use the leaves from the bunch as a garnish) along with the bay leaves and a generous ¼ cup of tomato paste with the beer.

The only lingering issue: the too-thin broth. The low oven wasn't reducing the liquid enough, so when I pulled out the pot to add the beer, I simply moved it to the stove where it would simmer more rapidly. My only hesitation was that the beans might jostle and break down, but happily they held their shape, releasing just enough starch to turn the cooking liquid into a satisfying broth (see "Perfect Beans—and Broth—Start Slow and Finish Strong").

My drunken beans were still simple to prepare, but with two sources of alcohol; just the right depth from the bacon (I used the cooked pieces as a garnish), aromatics, and tomato paste; and a last touch of lime juice, chopped cilantro, and crumbled cheese, they were also incredibly satisfying.

SCIENCE Why Lots of Alcohol Doesn't Make Beans Boozy

Adding ½ cup of tequila and a cup of beer to our Drunken Beans lends the dish subtly bright, complex flavor—and doesn't make the final product as boozy as you might think. That's because we add the tequila before—rather than with—the other liquids and allow it to evaporate completely before adding first water and then beer. This allows all the tequila's alcohol to burn off while leaving its flavor compounds behind.

Here's why: When alcohol and water cook together, they form an azeotrope—a mixture of two different liquids that behaves as if it were a single compound. Because alcohol and water have a strong affinity for one another, it's not possible for alcohol molecules to evaporate without some water molecules present, and vice versa. This means that even though alcohol's boiling point is lower than water's, it will never fully boil off unless all the water does, too. The upshot: As long as there is water in the pot, there will also be alcohol.

We demonstrated how more alcohol ends up in a dish when it's cooked with other liquids by making two batches of our Drunken Beans. In one batch we incorporated the tequila together with the other liquids; in the other it was added on its own (as per our recipe). We then sent samples to an independent lab to measure the alcohol content of the final dishes. The batch in which the tequila had been added on its own contained 0.35 percent alcohol (from the beer, which we added partway through cooking to avoid having its acidity toughen the beans before they were sufficiently cooked), while the alcohol in the batch in which all the liquids were added simultaneously was 0.77 percent, more than double the amount.

BOOZE IN THE BACKGROUND
One cup of beer plus ½ cup of tequila may seem like a lot, but since we add the alcohol in stages, the beans taste complex, not boozy.

DRUNKEN BEANS

SERVES 6 AS A MAIN DISH

You'll get fewer blowouts if you soak the beans overnight, but if you are pressed for time, you can quick-brine your beans. In step 1, combine the salt, water, and beans in a large Dutch oven and bring to a boil over high heat. Remove the pot from the heat, cover, and let stand for 1 hour. Drain and rinse the beans and proceed with the recipe. Serve with rice.

- **Salt**
- **1 pound (2½ cups) dried pinto beans, picked over and rinsed**
- **30 sprigs fresh cilantro (1 bunch)**
- **4 slices bacon, cut into ¼-inch pieces**
- **1 onion, chopped fine**
- **2 poblano chiles, stemmed, seeded, and chopped fine**
- **3 garlic cloves, minced**
- **½ cup tequila**
- **2 bay leaves**
- **1 cup Mexican lager**
- **¼ cup tomato paste**
- **2 limes, quartered**
- **2 ounces Cotija cheese, crumbled (½ cup)**

1. Dissolve 3 tablespoons salt in 4 quarts cold water in large bowl or container. Add beans and soak at room temperature for at least 8 hours or up to 24 hours. Drain and rinse well.

2. Adjust oven rack to lower-middle position and heat oven to 275 degrees. Pick leaves from 20 cilantro sprigs (reserve stems), chop fine, and refrigerate until needed. Using kitchen twine, tie remaining 10 cilantro sprigs and reserved stems into bundle.

3. Cook bacon in Dutch oven over medium heat, stirring occasionally, until crisp, 5 to 8 minutes. Using slotted spoon, transfer bacon to paper towel–lined bowl and set aside. Add onion, poblanos, and garlic to fat in pot and cook, stirring frequently, until vegetables are softened, 6 to 7 minutes. Remove from heat. Add tequila and cook until evaporated, 3 to 4 minutes. Return to heat. Increase heat to high; stir in 3½ cups water, bay leaves, 1 teaspoon salt, beans, and cilantro bundle; and bring to boil. Cover, transfer to oven, and cook until beans are just soft, 45 to 60 minutes.

4. Remove pot from oven. Discard bay leaves and cilantro bundle. Stir in beer and tomato paste and bring to simmer over medium-low heat. Simmer vigorously, stirring frequently, until liquid is thick and beans are fully tender, about 30 minutes. Season with salt to taste. Serve, passing chopped cilantro, lime wedges, Cotija, and reserved bacon separately.

TO MAKE AHEAD: The finished beans can be refrigerated for up to 2 days. Before reheating, thin beans slightly with water.

Mexican Bouquet Garni

Cilantro leaves are a classic garnish for drunken beans, but since the herb's stems are also a source of aromatic flavor, we tied up 20 plucked stems and 10 more whole sprigs with twine and simmered them with the beans. Just as with a traditional bouquet garni, the spent bundle is easy to fish out of the pot before serving.

FLAVOR BUNDLE
Cilantro sprigs plus extra stems flavor the pot.

Making the Most of Lemons

Lemons are the key flavoring in countless recipes, but in the test kitchen, they are almost as indispensable as salt for seasoning and enhancing our cooking. BY LOUISE EMERICK

SCIENCE

What Makes a Lemon Lemony?

The juice and the zest of a lemon can be thought of as two different components, with each bringing a little something different to the table. Fresh juice gets its tart flavor primarily from citric acid and its distinctively lemony taste and scent from a mix of volatile aromatic compounds—chiefly limonene, pinene, and citral—contained in oil droplets in the juice sacs. The zest contains these compounds and many more (and likely in greater concentrations than in the juice), giving it a more intense and complex flavor and scent.

ZEST is packed with oil glands containing volatile aromatic compounds

JUICE gets its tart flavor from citric acid, while oils within the juice sacs provide aroma

PITH contains bitter phenolic compounds as well as pectin

When to Cook with Juice versus Zest

Juice and zest behave very differently when exposed to heat, primarily due to the way the volatile aroma compounds are bound up in each. The volatile compounds in juice are suspended in water, where they readily evaporate, so juice that's been heated loses its aroma and tastes flat (though it still contributes a tartness from citric acid, which isn't affected by heat). To retain its bright, fresh taste, we typically wait to add lemon juice toward the end of cooking or as a finishing touch, or we use it in uncooked applications like icings and glazes. When we use lemon juice in baked goods, while it can contribute tartness, its main purpose is to activate the leavening. Because the aromatic compounds in the zest are trapped in oil glands within the peel's cell walls, which make it harder for them to escape, zest retains a more complex lemony flavor when heated. For this reason, we tend to use zest in baked goods and other recipes that involve long exposure to heat.

SHOPPING

Choosing the Juiciest Lemons

Most lemons at the supermarket come in just two varieties. Lisbon lemons are often characterized by slightly smoother skin, a rounder shape, and a flatter stem end, while Eureka lemons are frequently distinguished by a more elliptical shape and knobs at both ends. No matter the variety, the most important trait to look for is fruit that gives under pressure, which indicates a thin skin and pith. We found that thin-skinned specimens yielded an average of 8 percent more of their weight in juice (or about 2½ teaspoons per medium lemon) than those that felt rock hard. Green skin is also not a problem. In our tests, as long as they were thin-skinned, lemons with a greenish cast had as much juice as their more uniformly yellow counterparts, and they did not taste more tart.

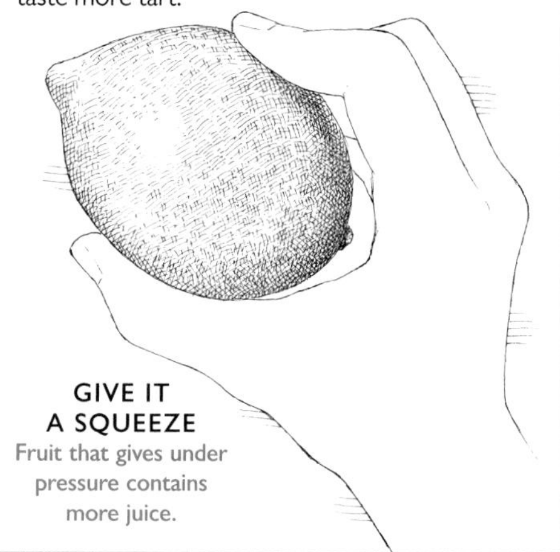

GIVE IT A SQUEEZE
Fruit that gives under pressure contains more juice.

BEST STORAGE OPTIONS

Like all citrus, lemons are nonclimacteric. On the down side, this means that they don't continue to ripen after harvest. On the plus side, it means that they retain their quality longer than other fruits. But to keep lemons as juicy as possible, store them chilled—and protect them from air.

Bag Whole Lemons
Unwrapped lemons will start to lose their moisture after about a week in the refrigerator. But we found that they'll stay in perfect condition for up to four weeks when sealed in a zipper-lock bag and chilled.

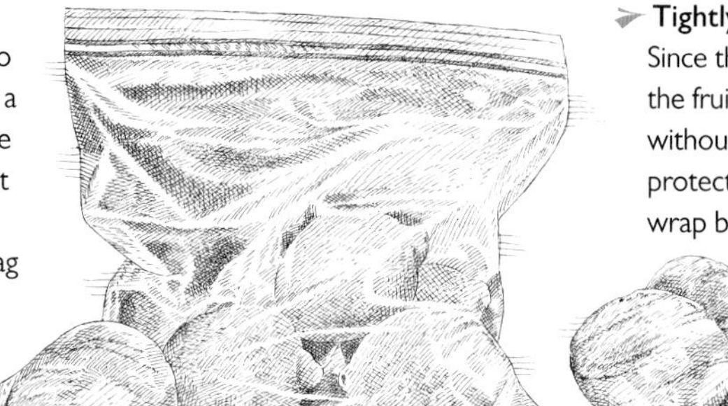

Tightly Wrap Zested Lemons
Since the oil in the zest protects the fruit from drying out, a lemon without its skin needs even more protection. Tightly wrap it in plastic wrap before refrigerating it.

Freeze Leftover Juice and Zest
In tests, we found that freezing leftover juice led to a deterioration in flavor, but it was still acceptable in recipes that call for only a small quantity, such as for a pan sauce. Freeze leftover zest in a zipper-lock bag for up to three weeks. Its color will fade, but it will still be fine for baking and cooking.

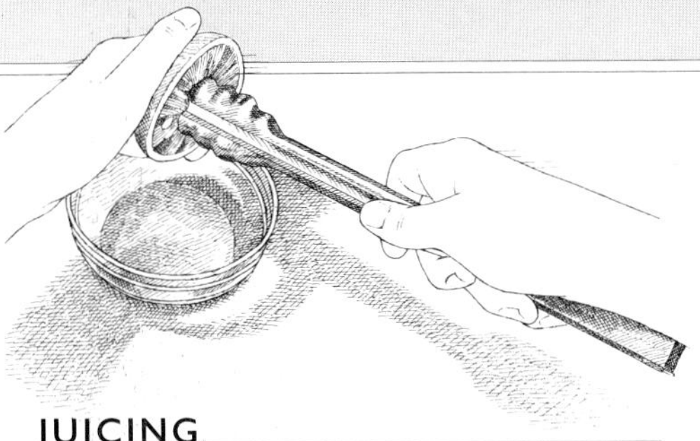

JUICING

- **Best Tools** Our preferred way to extract juice is to insert tongs, a reamer with a sharp tip, or even a fork into the lemon and twist over a bowl.
- **Avoid Cold Lemons** Room-temperature lemons are much more yielding and thus easier to squeeze than cold lemons. To quickly take the chill off a cold lemon, microwave it until it is warm to the touch.
- **Roll on a Hard Surface First** We found that rolling a lemon makes it easier to juice because it softens the membrane and tears the juice sacs.
- **Pantry Alternatives** In a pinch, ReaLemon 100% Lemon Juice from Concentrate is an acceptable substitute for fresh juice in most sweet and savory applications. Just don't try it in lemonade or other beverages; we found its flavor too flat to pass as fresh. Lemon extract is an acceptable, though less sour, substitute for 1 tablespoon of juice or less in baking recipes only (substitute ¼ teaspoon of extract per tablespoon of juice).

ZESTING

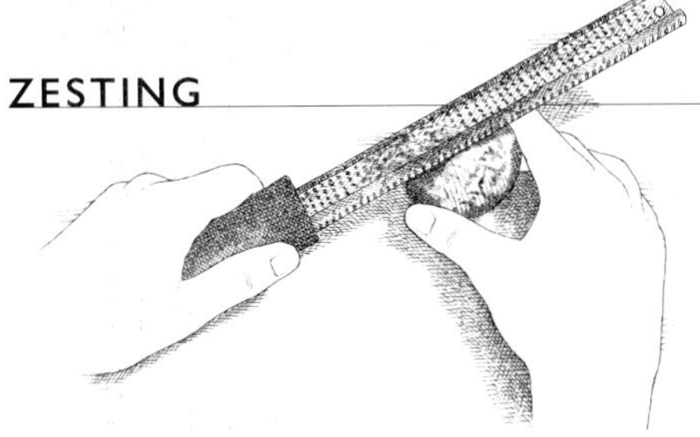

- **Best Tools** Use a rasp-style grater for fine zest and a vegetable peeler for strips of zest.
- **Don't Zest Too Soon** The volatile oils in the peel are strongest just after zesting; for maximum flavor, zest just before using.
- **Pack Lightly** To measure zest, pack it lightly into a measuring spoon.
- **Avoid the Pith** The oils in the zest are the key to its floral flavor; avoid the bitter white pith just beneath the zest by grating over the same area only once or twice.
- **Release the Oils** Grinding finely grated zest with the sugar included in a recipe will release more oils. To release oil in strips, crush or twist them.
- **Pantry Alternative** For a finishing touch or in baked goods where lemon is the main flavor, there is no substitute for fresh. But when lemon is only a background flavor, such as in blueberry muffins or a coffee cake, an equal amount of lemon extract is a fine stand-in. Because lemon extract is derived from oils in the peel, it shares the same flavor compounds as the fresh zest.

GREAT WAYS TO USE LEMONS

Protect Poached Fish
Put slices under fish when poaching to lift it off the pan's bottom to ensure even cooking or around fish when steaming to infuse it with a delicate flavor.

Prevent Sticky Pasta
Tap water is often slightly alkaline, which can weaken the protein network in pasta, allowing surface starches to absorb water and burst, leaving a sticky residue. Adding 2 teaspoons of lemon juice to 4 quarts of cooking water strengthens the pasta's protein mesh and helps keep starch granules intact.

Dress Mild Greens
Vinaigrette made with lemon is better suited for dressing milder greens, such as green leaf, Bibb, and Boston lettuces, than dressings made with sharper-tasting vinegar. Use a 3:1 ratio of oil to lemon juice.

Perk Up Soups and Stews
Add lemon juice to taste before serving to brighten chicken, fish, or vegetable soups and stews, or add a strip or two of zest at the start of cooking (discard before serving) for an infusion of floral lemon flavor.

Enhance Side Dishes
Seasoning rice, grains, and vegetables (even mashed potatoes) with juice and zest before serving brightens and enhances flavor. Use ¼ teaspoon of juice and 2 teaspoons of grated zest for four servings.

Grill and Squeeze Over Proteins
Grill halved lemons until charred and then squeeze over finished fish or poultry or add to a dressing. Grilling lemons caramelizes the sugars in the juice, creating more complex flavor. (You can also use lemons to cap the ends of skewers, so food at the ends won't overcook.)

Keep Pesto Green
It's common knowledge that lemon juice prevents cut vegetables from browning. But we found that the citric and ascorbic acids it contains can also keep basil pesto from oxidizing and losing its bright color: Add 2 teaspoons lemon juice for every cup of the packed herb.

Brighten Basting Oil
Add 1 teaspoon of grated zest, 1 tablespoon of juice, and 1 teaspoon of a minced herb such as rosemary to ½ cup of extra-virgin olive oil for a basting oil with a hint of citrus flavor.

Brighten Brown Butter Sauce
Lemon juice is a perfect complement to the nuttiness of brown butter. Add 1 tablespoon of juice for every 4 tablespoons of butter.

Substitute for Wine
To replace up to ½ cup of wine in soups and pan sauces, add ½ cup of chicken broth plus 1 teaspoon of lemon juice.

A Rest Makes Lemonade Better

- **Age Juice**
Letting lemon juice rest for up to 6 hours will allow the aromatic compounds in the fruit's oil to oxidize, making the lemon flavor more mellow and complex, a benefit most noticeable when juice is used in beverages. But don't let it sit too long—it will eventually lose potency and develop off-flavors.

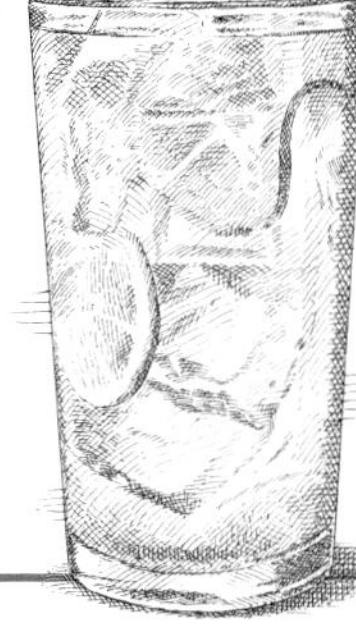

- **Steep Zest**
We've found that steeping zest in lemon juice for lemonade pulls out the zest's water-soluble flavor compounds, lending a deeper, more complex flavor (we discard the zest before serving). You can also use less sugar because compounds in the zest known as flavanones mask bitter flavors in the lemonade so it tastes sweeter.

Homemade Vegetable Broth

Our winning store-bought broth is OK in a pinch.
But we wanted a homemade version that beat it on flavor and was just as convenient.

BY ANDREA GEARY

Ask someone to make a list of extravagant foods and they're unlikely to mention vegetable broth. But consider how it's traditionally made: You take a lovely pile of produce, chop it up, and boil it for about an hour. Then you fish out all the food, throw it away, and keep the liquid. And after all that, what you have is not a meal but an ingredient.

It's no surprise that most cooks opt for store-bought vegetable broth (or even water). But even the best of the commercial stuff is not ideal (see our tasting on page 27), which is a shame, since a good broth can be the difference between a ho-hum vegetarian dish and a flavorful one that satisfies all diners, vegetarian or otherwise.

I wanted to make a broth that would boost my vegetarian meals the same way that chicken or beef stock boosts my meat-based cooking. But since vegetarian dishes can be more nuanced and subtle in their flavor, I would need a broth that wouldn't overpower the other ingredients or call too much attention to any one vegetable. If possible, I also wanted my recipe to generate minimal waste and be economical and simple to produce, so I could consider it a staple rather than a luxury.

Our stock concentrate, made from uncooked vegetables, produces just 1¾ cups of base, but that translates to 28 cups of prepared broth.

Taking Stock

Meat broths are a straightforward concept: Chicken broth tastes like chicken, and beef broth tastes like beef. But extending that logic to vegetable broth doesn't work because all vegetables taste different. To begin, I worked my way through several recipes using various vegetables and methods. I was drawn to one that was made almost entirely from scraps: carrot peels, celery leaves and ends, parsley stems, onion skins, and leek greens. But the earthy flavor of the carrot peels and celery ends dominated. A modern *sous-vide* broth made with 10 vegetables and herbs and cooked in a 185-degree water bath for 3 hours was flavorful, but the yield was only 1½ cups. I couldn't see myself going to that kind of trouble for such a small amount.

One recipe made with roasted vegetables required both the oven and the stove and took longer than 2 hours to make, and the caramelization of the vegetables made it too sweet. And my wild card, a raw puree whizzed in the blender like a vegetable smoothie and then strained through a fine-mesh sieve, was also a bust: Heavy on celery and watery tomatoes and cucumbers, the strained liquid had a murky orange-brown color and an unsuitably tangy flavor reminiscent of bad gazpacho. I considered changing the vegetables, but doing so would still result in what was basically vegetable juice. I was certainly getting an idea of what I *didn't* want.

I had almost given up when I happened upon a recipe in *The River Cottage Preserves Handbook* by Pam Corbin. For her souper mix, vegetables, herbs, and salt are ground in a food processor. Stir a spoonful of this paste into boiling water and there you have it: vegetable broth. These days, commercial options abound for vegetarian bouillon cubes and concentrates, but I had never seen a homemade version.

The potential was clear. Grinding vegetables was quick, with no cooking required. And unlike the failed smoothie concept, this base was undiluted and kept all the flavorful ingredients in the final product—those flavors would be extracted by the hot water to make an infusion. I appreciated that there was little waste, along with an unexpected advantage: more compact storage. Instead of ending up with several quarts of broth, I'd just have one container.

I loaded chopped leeks, fennel, carrots, celery root, sun-dried tomatoes, garlic, parsley, cilantro, and more than ¾ cup of salt into the food processor, as the recipe directed. The reasoning behind all that salt was persuasive: It would discourage spoilage so the base could be stored for weeks in the refrigerator. There was also a benefit Corbin didn't mention: The salt prevents the base from solidifying in the freezer, so it's easy to scoop out only what is required.

Compared to the previous versions, this broth was fresh-tasting. The leeks, carrots, and celery root gave it a balanced flavor, and the sun-dried tomatoes, rich in savory amino acids, contributed depth.

But there were problems. The vegetable flavor was weak, and the 7 ounces of herbs (a huge amount; consider supermarket bags of greens that weigh 6 ounces) dominated the broth and turned swampy during storage. The garlic didn't fare well either. Its flavor continued to develop and became too hot. With their sweet-sour undertone, the sun-dried tomatoes were too identifiable to be an anonymous umami booster. Although fennel added a pleasant licorice-like flavor, it wouldn't be welcome in every application. And, yes, ¾ cup of salt was too much. Still, I was intrigued by the possibilities.

From the Ground Up

A *mirepoix*, a mixture of two parts chopped onion to one part each of carrots and celery, is the classic base for many broths, so I started there. Corbin's recipe featured celery root and leeks, but I hoped that regular celery and onions would work just as well. I pureed 6 ounces of chopped onion, 3 ounces each of chopped carrots and celery stalks, and 2 ounces of salt, which was less than half the amount in the

Look: Here's How to Make It
Video available free for 4 months at CooksIllustrated.com/feb15

What's In? What's Out? Building a Balanced Broth

The key to our concentrate was finding a combination of vegetables that produced a broth that was unobtrusive but still had enough backbone to give a dish depth and complexity.

IN | OUT

CELERY ROOT, BUT NOT CELERY
Celery root contributes a mild yet complex celery flavor, while celery comes across as bitter and sour. Celery gets its bitter flavor from a compound called sedanolide. Celery root possesses it, too, but in lesser quantities.

LEEKS AND FREEZE-DRIED ONION, BUT NOT ONION
Onion made the stock sulfurous and sweet (and too watery). Low-moisture, low-sugar leeks are more neutral, while freeze-dried minced onions provide depth.

TOMATO PASTE, BUT NOT TOMATO
Fresh tomatoes were too mild and watery, while sun-dried tomatoes were too sweet-sour; tomato paste adds a savory depth without identifying itself.

previous batch. (I measured by weight for consistency since chopped vegetables pack unevenly.) Since cilantro has a more prominent flavor than parsley, I stuck with the latter and added only ½ ounce of it.

Celery root was in the recipe for a reason. The regular celery added bitterness and a slightly sour flavor. It turns out that celery root is not just milder than celery; it also has a more complex, creamy flavor. Both celery root and celery get their characteristic flavor from several phthalide compounds, but celery has more of one called sedanolide, which has a notably bitter flavor. Celery root was back in.

It was a similar story with the leek/onion swap. The higher moisture content of the onions made the base watery, so it solidified in the freezer. Worse, it was simultaneously sweeter and more sulfurous than the base made with leeks, which also possess the least sugar of all the alliums. So leeks went back in as well.

My broth was better now, but it still tasted a bit lightweight, so I went in search of an extra boost.

A Pungent Punch

The onions had been a failure, but their diluting effect did give me an idea. What if I took the opposite tack and concentrated my vegetables' flavor? That way, I could use more of them. I sliced leeks, carrots, and celery root and dried them for hours in a low oven. Then I ground them up in the food processor and added parsley and salt. Despite my starting with twice the amount of vegetables as in my previous batch, the vegetable flavor was weaker.

It turns out that water was not the only thing my vegetables lost in the oven; a lot of their volatile flavor compounds had evaporated, too. But this test was not a waste. It got me thinking about concentrated sources of flavor, which in turn led me to consider an option I've been quite snooty about in the past: those dried minced onions found in bottles in the spice aisle.

Dried minced onions aren't simply dehydrated; they're freeze-dried. Our science editor filled me in on the process: Frozen food is placed in a vacuum-sealed chamber. In this vacuum, the ice transitions into vapor and is pulled out of the food. Whereas the heat of a conventional oven pulls out flavor compounds along with the water, freeze-drying leaves many more of those compounds in place, just waiting to be reactivated by water.

I'll admit that I went overboard at first. When I swapped them for more than half the leeks, the broth tasted like onion soup. But a little experimentation led me to the sweet spot: 5 ounces of leeks augmented with 3 tablespoons of dried minced onions.

Savory Salvation

The distinct flavor of the sun-dried tomatoes in the first batch had been problematic, but I appreciated their umami quality, so I considered other options. Canned and fresh tomatoes took my base back to a slurry, so next I tried tomato paste. Just 1½ tablespoons contributed an appealing savoriness.

That hint of umami left me wanting more. I went to the pantry and pulled out savory non-meat powerhouses. Shiitake mushrooms were too earthy, and miso paste was too subtle in small amounts and too identifiable in larger. Kombu, a dried seaweed, worked well, but I settled on a less exotic option: soy sauce. Three tablespoons gave my broth the muscle it had lacked. To compensate for the added sodium, I cut the salt back to 2 tablespoons, which was still enough to prevent the mixture from freezing solid.

This broth had it all: easy preparation, minimal waste, convenient storage, and, best of all, fresh, balanced vegetable flavor that worked well in everything from soups and sauces to pastas and risotto. If I had to find a fault with this recipe, it would be that because it lasts about 6 months I don't get to make it very often. But I can live with that.

VEGETABLE BROTH BASE

MAKES ABOUT 1¾ CUPS BASE;
ENOUGH FOR 7 QUARTS BROTH

For the best balance of flavors, measure the prepped vegetables by weight. Kosher salt aids in grinding the vegetables. The broth base contains enough salt to keep it from freezing solid, making it easy to remove 1 tablespoon at a time. To make 1 cup of broth, stir 1 tablespoon of fresh or frozen broth base into 1 cup of boiling water. If particle-free broth is desired, let the broth steep for 5 minutes and then strain it through a fine-mesh strainer.

- 2 leeks, white and light green parts only, chopped and washed thoroughly (2½ cups or 5 ounces)
- 2 carrots, peeled and cut into ½-inch pieces (⅔ cup or 3 ounces)
- ½ small celery root, peeled and cut into ½-inch pieces (¾ cup or 3 ounces)
- ½ cup (½ ounce) parsley leaves and thin stems
- 3 tablespoons dried minced onions
- 2 tablespoons kosher salt
- 1½ tablespoons tomato paste
- 3 tablespoons soy sauce

Process leeks, carrots, celery root, parsley, minced onions, and salt in food processor, scraping down sides of bowl frequently, until paste is as fine as possible, 3 to 4 minutes. Add tomato paste and process for 1 minute, scraping down sides of bowl every 20 seconds. Add soy sauce and continue to process 1 minute longer. Transfer mixture to airtight container and tap firmly on counter to remove air bubbles. Press small piece of parchment paper flush against surface of mixture and cover. Freeze for up to 6 months.

A Broth Base You Can Freeze—and Never Thaw

Our recipe calls for 2 tablespoons of kosher salt (we use Diamond Crystal). That might seem like a lot, but once the base is diluted, it contains just 399 milligrams of sodium per 1-cup serving; commercial broth ranges from 240 to 1,050 milligrams per cup.

Furthermore, because salt depresses water's freezing point, the concentrate will never freeze solid. This means that you can keep it in the freezer for months and scoop out exactly the amount you need without ever having to thaw it.

SCOOP AND RECONSTITUTE
Mix 1 tablespoon of base with 1 cup of boiling water.

Really Good Savory Corn Muffins

We wanted a muffin full of cornmeal flavor. Could it also be moist and light-textured?

BY DAN SOUZA

A great sweet cornmeal muffin might be easy to come by, but a passable version of the savory type is the Bigfoot of the muffin world: We've all heard of its existence, but good luck finding physical evidence to support the claim. Most often, these muffins are unappealing, with insufficient cornmeal flavor and/or a dense, heavy crumb. Could I tip the scales in favor of the cornmeal?

I knew the reason for the flavor deficit: Recipes generally call for only 1 part cornmeal to 1 part wheat flour. Using more cornmeal would surely produce the distinctive flavor I wanted. But it would also affect texture: Wheat flour helps form an elastic network of gluten that provides structure and traps gas during baking. Cornmeal, on the other hand, can't form gluten. For an attractive rise, some wheat flour would be essential, but I wanted to use as little as possible to keep the cornmeal flavor at the fore.

I tested several proportions before settling on 2 cups cornmeal to 1 cup flour, along with milk, melted butter, baking powder and soda, salt, and eggs. These muffins boasted excellent flavor with enough gluten to push the batter above the rim of the muffin tin, but they were way too dry.

Muffins stay moist with the help of a few key ingredients; namely, water, fat, and sugar. Because a batter that's too runny won't form the proper shape during baking, I wanted to avoid, at least for the moment, increasing the milk I was already using or even adding water. Instead I tried sour cream, which has some water and a lot of fat. But the thick dairy wasn't enough to turn the tide: These muffins were still on the dry side. Next on the docket? Sugar.

Yes, sugar makes things sweet, but it also has a huge impact on the moisture level of baked goods. That's because sugar is hygroscopic, meaning that it attracts and traps moisture. It's not uncommon for a sweet muffin to call for more than 1 cup of sugar, an absolute nonstarter for my savory muffins. But a little sugar could provide some moisture retention without making the muffins sweet. I started small, maxing out at 3 tablespoons of sugar before the muffins began to taste too sweet.

But frustratingly, even with the help of sour cream and sugar, the crumb was still dry. In the past, we've improved moistness by adding a surplus of liquid to other types of batter and then letting it rest to thicken up prior to baking. The upshot is extra liquid in the mix without having to sacrifice the attractive dome achieved by a drier, stiffer batter. I tried it, increasing the milk and letting the batter rest for 20 minutes. No dice: The cornmeal-rich batter never fully absorbed the extra liquid and the muffins baked up flat.

Our recipe incorporates twice as much cornmeal as is typical, without compromising texture.

Then I had a thought: Could I add more moisture without thinning the batter by precooking the cornmeal with extra milk? I'd give it a try. I microwaved ½ cup of the cornmeal with 1¼ cups of milk (almost double the amount I'd used previously) until a thick, polenta-like porridge formed. I then whisked in the rest of the ingredients, divided the batter among the muffin tin cups, and placed the tin in the oven. Fifteen minutes later, I pulled out 12 idyllic muffins: golden brown, rich with buttery cornmeal flavor, and, most important, perfectly moist.

Why did this work? The starch granules in cornmeal absorb only a limited amount of moisture (less than 30 percent of their own weight) when mixed into a cold liquid. But when the liquid is heated, it weakens the starch granules so that they are able to soak up more fluid. Using this technique, I could add nearly twice the amount of liquid to my batter without turning it too thin to form a dome.

And just like that, I had my proof: Great savory cornmeal muffins really do exist.

How to Make Them
Video available free for 4 months at CooksIllustrated.com/feb15

SAVORY CORN MUFFINS

MAKES 12 MUFFINS

Don't use coarse-ground or white cornmeal.

- 2 cups (10 ounces) cornmeal
- 1 cup (5 ounces) all-purpose flour
- 1½ teaspoons baking powder
- 1 teaspoon baking soda
- 1¼ teaspoons salt
- 1¼ cups whole milk
- 1 cup sour cream
- 8 tablespoons unsalted butter, melted and cooled slightly
- 3 tablespoons sugar
- 2 large eggs, beaten

1. Adjust oven rack to upper-middle position and heat oven to 425 degrees. Grease 12-cup muffin tin. Whisk 1½ cups cornmeal, flour, baking powder, baking soda, and salt together in medium bowl.

2. Combine milk and remaining ½ cup cornmeal in large bowl. Microwave milk-cornmeal mixture for 1½ minutes. Whisk thoroughly and continue to microwave, whisking every 30 seconds, until thickened to batter-like consistency (whisk will leave channel in bottom of bowl that slowly fills in), 1 to 3 minutes longer. Whisk in sour cream, melted butter, and sugar until combined. Whisk in eggs until combined. Fold in flour mixture until thoroughly combined. Using portion scoop or large spoon, divide batter evenly among prepared muffin cups (about ½ cup batter per cup; batter will mound slightly above rim).

3. Bake until tops are golden brown and toothpick inserted in center comes out clean, 13 to 17 minutes, rotating muffin tin halfway through baking. Let muffins cool in muffin tin on wire rack for 5 minutes. Remove muffins from muffin tin and let cool 5 minutes longer. Serve warm.

SAVORY CORN MUFFINS WITH CHEDDAR AND SCALLIONS

Add ½ teaspoon pepper, ¼ teaspoon dry mustard, and pinch cayenne to dry ingredients in step 1. Whisk in 1½ cups shredded cheddar cheese and 5 thinly sliced scallions with eggs.

SAVORY CORN MUFFINS WITH ROSEMARY AND BLACK PEPPER

Whisk in 1 tablespoon minced fresh rosemary and 1½ teaspoons pepper with eggs.

Foolproof New York Cheesecake

Our recipe produced lush texture and a beautiful brown top—but not for everyone. To solve this mystery, we had to delve into the secrets of ovens.

BY ANDREA GEARY

The uniformly sleek, custardy consistency; smooth, flat top; and soft cream color of most cheesecakes is undeniably appealing. But I've always been partial to the textural and visual contrast of the New York kind. In particular, I like this version's characteristic dark brown surface and gentle downward slope from the edge to the center, which acts as a map of the interior's texture: Its slightly puffed-up perimeter gives way to a more luxurious, plush core that lingers on the palate—rich suede to other cheesecakes' slippery satin.

Somewhat surprisingly, both styles are made with the same basic components—a cream cheese–based filling atop a buttery graham cracker crumb crust. It's their baking methods that are different. While most cheesecakes are set in an insulating water bath and baked gently at a moderate temperature to ensure that all-over creaminess, the iconic recipe for the New York kind goes straight into a blazing-hot oven without the water bath, which causes the cake's rim to puff up and the top to brown. After a short time, the temperature is turned down very low, and it remains there until the filling is set.

Besides foolproofing the cake, we came up with a novel approach to making the crust that keeps it from getting soggy.

We used this gutsy baking technique in our 2002 recipe for New York–Style Cheesecake, which we made countless times to perfection in the test kitchen. But as the years passed, the recipe started to be problematic, with the cheesecakes sometimes turning out cracked and burned or oozy and undercooked. I was stumped as to why this might be happening. We were using the same recipe, the same ingredients, the same mixers, and the same pans. So why did this recipe sometimes fail? Eventually I realized that there was one variable that we could not control, either in readers' homes or in our lab-like test kitchen: ovens.

I'm not questioning the reliability of our test kitchen ovens; we are constantly testing and calibrating them, so we know they are accurate. But in the years since we developed that earlier recipe, almost every oven in the test kitchen has been replaced. All the other factors were constants, so the problem had to be related in some way to the ovens. To test my theory, I made the 2002 recipe in four different ovens, both older and newer models.

Sure enough, out of the four cheesecakes, only one turned out to have the requisite smooth brown top and velvety texture. Two of the others were grainy and had large cracks on top as well as burned edges. The fourth, baked to the very end of the given time range, had a promisingly sleek, nut-brown exterior, but it concealed a dishearteningly soupy center.

It was time for a new New York cheesecake recipe, one that would work in any oven. But we also agreed that when our existing recipe worked, it was fantastic—tangy, creamy, and rich. So I resolved to change the recipe as little as possible and to fix only what was broken: namely, the baking method.

Goodbye, High to Low

Here's how that original New York cheesecake recipe goes: Press a mixture of graham cracker crumbs, sugar, and melted butter into a 9-inch springform pan and bake it until it is dry and set. Fill it with a mixture of cream cheese, whole eggs and egg yolks, sugar, and some sour cream and lemon juice to underscore the cheese's tang. Place it on the lower-middle rack in the oven and bake it at 500 degrees for 10 minutes; then turn down the oven to 200 degrees for the remainder of the baking time, about 90 minutes.

Because this method had worked well in the past in the test kitchen, and because we know our ovens are perfectly accurate when they reach a given temperature, I suspected that the problem was neither the high temperature nor the low temperature, per se, but what was happening in the oven once the temperature was dialed down.

My next test involved no cheesecake, just thermometers. I set three of the four ovens I had used in my previous test to 500 degrees and placed a remote temperature probe in each one. After the ovens spent 10 minutes at 500 degrees, I turned the dials to 200 degrees, and I noted how long it took for the temperature of each oven to fall. The results were very revealing.

In one of the ovens, the temperature fell very slowly; in fact, it didn't even hit 200 degrees until well after the recommended baking time of 90 minutes. Not surprisingly, this was the oven that had produced a cracked, burned cheesecake in my previous test. Conversely, the temperature in the second oven fell to 200 degrees in just 40 minutes, explaining why its cheesecake had been underbaked. The only acceptable cheesecake had come from the oven that reached 200 degrees in a little over an hour.

With this test, I realized that oven temperatures that fell at just the right rate were the exception, not the rule. In fact, the results prompted me to contact an oven expert. She explained that energy efficiency is the modern consumer's priority when choosing an oven, and manufacturers have responded by improving insulation. The upshot is that newer ovens hold heat much more effectively than older ones. Our newer ovens are exceptionally well insulated, which explained the one model's very slow temperature decline—and why the cheesecake it produced was cracked and burnt.

See Our Foolproof Method
Video available free for 4 months at CooksIllustrated.com/feb15

Four Familiar Failures

A nut-brown surface, puffed-up rim, velvety interior, and buttery graham cracker crust are classic New York cheesecake traits. Unfortunately, so are these common pitfalls.

CRACKED
When exposed to high heat for too long, the cheesecake will overbake and develop unsightly fissures.

BURNT
Too much high heat can also cause the cheesecake to burn.

SPOTTY
Air bubbles that rise to the batter's surface during baking brown faster, giving the facade an undesirably mottled appearance.

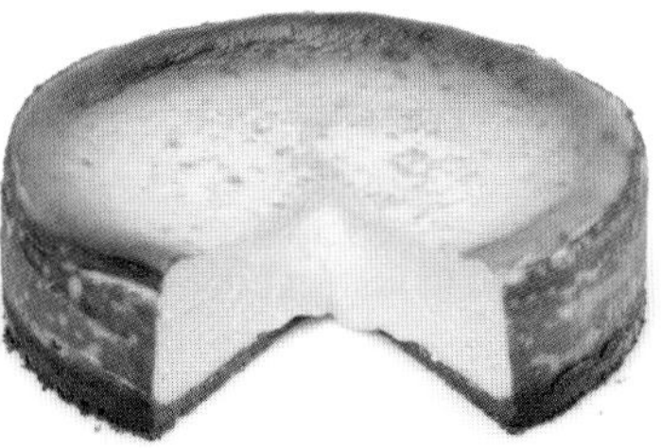

SOUPY
Even when the exterior is nicely set, the interior can be underdone and runny at the core.

No Middle Ground

Since I couldn't make the high-to-low method work consistently, my next idea was to compromise between the two extremes. I hoped that baking my cheesecake at a constant moderate 350 degrees might give me the best of both worlds—a browned top and the tiniest bit of lift for that velvety texture.

Instead, it gave me the worst of both: a cake that was pallid but also cracked and grainy after spending the entire baking time at a temperature that was too high.

Taking an even more conservative approach to address the overbaking problem, I baked my next cheesecake at a constant 200 degrees. Its surface was predictably pale and perfectly flat, but I hadn't anticipated the interior texture: consistently dense and satiny from edge to edge, as if it had been baked in an insulating water bath. In other words, I'd produced the ideal custard cheesecake—nice in its own way, but not at all what I was after.

Hello, Low to High

The high-temperature phase in the traditional New York technique was obviously vital to developing the proper browned exterior, but up to this point I had underestimated its importance in developing this cheesecake's characteristic suede-like texture. Here's how it works: That blast of heat causes the cheesecake to puff a good inch above the rim of the pan, much like a soufflé does, especially at the edges, where it is least protected. During that brief high-heat phase, the proteins in the eggs and the dairy just begin to form bonds that subtly interrupt the silky-smooth texture of the filling. The fall in temperature halts that protein bonding process, preventing the filling from turning coarse and curdled. What you're left with is that luxurious, velvety texture.

But what if I turned the traditional high-to-low technique on its head and went low to high instead? My rationale was this: As an oven's temperature increases, it's actively and almost constantly producing heat; when it cools down, it's passively—and unpredictably—releasing heat. Since the rate at which the temperature fell was out of my control, it made sense to eliminate that variable altogether. Instead, I'd bake the cheesecake at 200 degrees until it had set completely (at which point its internal temperature would register 165 degrees) and then crank the heat for the final minutes of cooking.

First I tried simply leaving the cake in the oven while it came up to 500 degrees. But that took a full 15 minutes and then another 10 minutes for the cheesecake to brown. With 25 minutes in a hot oven, this sample was unacceptably dry and grainy, not to mention overbaked at the edges and along the top. But I wasn't giving up on my low-to-high method just yet.

In my next test, I first removed the fully set cheesecake from the oven and then increased the heat. Once the oven reached 500 degrees, I placed the cheesecake back in the oven near the top, where it browned in just 10 minutes—so quickly that overcooking was not a problem.

This time, my low-to-high method produced a cake that was nicely browned (if a bit spotty) and had just the right textural contrast, and I was confident that it would work in any oven. But my innovative solution had also made a classic New York cheesecake problem—a soggy crust—even worse.

A Strong Foundation

A crumb crust is prone to turning soggy even in the best of circumstances because it is very porous; the abundance of surface area between the crumbs allows moisture to easily seep in and saturate the starch granules in the crackers. Here in particular, the crust didn't stand a chance at staying crisp because the cake is baked at such a low temperature that the bottom of the filling didn't set for—I checked—a good 2 hours.

But interestingly, some research revealed that many of the first American cheesecakes had pastry on the bottom, not graham crackers. That also brought to mind the moisture-resistant crust that I'd developed for our French Apple Tart (November/December 2014). Its compact, shortbread-like crumb has relatively little porosity—more like a sheet of rock versus the absorbent, packed-down "sand" of a crumb crust. I also used a lot of melted butter in this crust, which thoroughly coats the starches in the flour to make the dough even more resistant to soaking up water.

So I swapped out the crumbs, pressed the rich pastry into the base of the pan, and baked it before adding the filling. Indeed, this crust remained firm and dry even under the wet cheesecake batter. The problem (which, admittedly, I saw coming) was that my tasters missed that familiar graham cracker flavor.

But what about a hybrid crust? I combined a half recipe of my pastry dough with half the amount of crushed graham crackers I had used in the earlier crumb crust, pressed it into the pan, and baked it. The crumbs provided the classic flavor, and the dough bound them, creating a crust that was more cohesive and less vulnerable to moisture.

Problem Solving: A Crust That Won't Sog Out

A typical graham cracker crust turns soggy because the structure of the crushed-up crackers is loose and porous. As a result, moisture from the heavy, wet cream cheese filling seeps into the crevices and saturates the crumbs before the water has a chance to evaporate during baking.

The key to a more moisture-resistant crust was to "waterproof" the crumbs, which we did by working them into a pastry dough. Because the structure of pastry dough is much less porous than a crumb crust—picture a sheet of rock versus the absorbent "sand" of a crumb crust—water from the filling never soaks into it and simply evaporates in the oven. Furthermore, our pastry dough contains a high ratio of butter, which coats both the crumbs and the starch granules in the flour, making the dough even more resistant to soaking up water.

WATERPROOF CRUST

Smooth Sailing

That left me with just the spottily browned surface to fix, and I had a hunch as to the root of that problem. Beating together the filling ingredients causes tiny air bubbles to form in the batter; if they rise to the top of the batter, they brown more quickly than the surrounding surface, giving the cake an unattractively blistered appearance. The traditional high-to-low baking method doesn't give the bubbles a chance to rise because the initial blast of heat causes the top of the cheesecake to quickly swell and set smoothly, but switching to the reverse method meant that there was plenty of time for air bubbles to move up through the wet filling and settle at the surface.

The trick would be to remove as much air from the filling as possible before I baked the cheesecake. First, I passed the mixed filling through a fine-mesh strainer, which removed any large air pockets. I let the filled cheesecake sit for 10 minutes, which allowed any remaining bubbles to make their lazy way to the surface, and then I drew the tines of a fork gently across the surface of the cake to burst the bubbles that had appeared. The extra care paid off. When this cheesecake emerged from its high-temperature bake, it sported a smooth, brown top.

Despite the topsy-turvy baking method, this cheesecake had the same texture, flavor, and appearance as the one from our original recipe. But there was one important difference: I knew that this recipe would succeed no matter what oven it was baked in.

Baker Beware: Ovens Cool Down at Different Rates

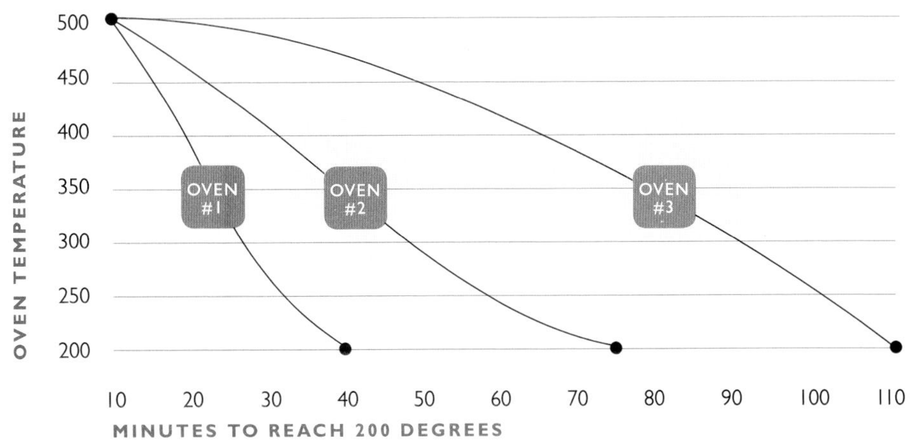

The textural and visual contrast that defines a New York cheesecake is typically produced by a high-to-low oven method: an initial blast of heat that puffs the sides and browns the top before the temperature is turned way down for the duration of baking to ensure just the right velvety interior. But baking cheesecakes in a variety of test kitchen ovens made us realize that this method works only in ovens that lose heat at a particular rate. If the oven is more thoroughly insulated and the temperature falls too slowly, the cheesecake will overcook; if the oven is less well insulated and the temperature falls too quickly, the beautifully browned exterior of the cheesecake is likely to hide a soupy, raw interior.

We confirmed this theory after monitoring the time it took three different ovens in the test kitchen to fall from 500 to 200 degrees. The results were all over the map. Even more compelling was that in the slowest oven, the temperature took almost 2 hours to reach 200 degrees—45 minutes longer than the recommended baking time for our previous recipe for New York–Style Cheesecake.

THE SOLUTION To eliminate the drop in oven temperature as a variable, we took the bold step of reversing the typical high-to-low method. We baked the cake in a 200-degree oven until it was completely set, removed it, and then cranked the heat to 500 degrees. Once the oven came up to temperature, we placed the cake on the upper rack, where in just 10 minutes the top browned and the edges puffed, creating that characteristic slope from edge to center.

FOOLPROOF NEW YORK CHEESECAKE

SERVES 12 TO 16

This cheesecake takes at least 12 hours to make (including chilling), so we recommend making it the day before serving. An accurate oven thermometer and instant-read thermometer are essential. To ensure proper baking, check that the oven thermometer is holding steady at 200 degrees and refrain from frequently taking the temperature of the cheesecake (unless it is within a few degrees of 165, allow 20 minutes between checking). Keep a close eye on the cheesecake in step 5 to prevent overbrowning.

Crust

- 6 whole graham crackers, broken into pieces
- ⅓ cup packed (2⅓ ounces) dark brown sugar
- ½ cup (2½ ounces) all-purpose flour
- ¼ teaspoon salt
- 7 tablespoons unsalted butter, melted

Filling

- 2½ pounds cream cheese, softened
- 1½ cups (10½ ounces) granulated sugar
- ⅛ teaspoon salt
- ⅓ cup sour cream
- 2 teaspoons lemon juice
- 2 teaspoons vanilla extract
- 6 large eggs plus 2 large egg yolks

1. FOR THE CRUST: Adjust oven racks to upper-middle and lower-middle positions and heat oven to 325 degrees. Process cracker pieces and sugar in food processor until finely ground, about 30 seconds. Add flour and salt and pulse to combine, 2 pulses. Add 6 tablespoons melted butter and pulse until crumbs are evenly moistened, about 10 pulses. Brush bottom of 9-inch springform pan with ½ tablespoon melted butter. Using your hands, press crumb mixture evenly into pan bottom. Using flat bottom of measuring cup or ramekin, firmly pack crust into pan. Bake on lower-middle rack until fragrant and beginning to brown around edges, about 13 minutes. Transfer to rimmed baking sheet and set aside to cool completely. Reduce oven temperature to 200 degrees.

2. FOR THE FILLING: Using stand mixer fitted with paddle, beat cream cheese, ¾ cup sugar, and salt at medium-low speed until combined, about 1 minute. Beat in remaining ¾ cup sugar until combined, about 1 minute. Scrape beater and bowl well; add sour cream, lemon juice, and vanilla and beat at low speed until combined, about 1 minute. Add egg yolks and beat at medium-low speed until thoroughly combined, about 1 minute. Scrape bowl and beater. Add whole eggs two at a time, beating until thoroughly combined, about 30 seconds after each addition. Pour filling through fine-mesh strainer set in large bowl, pressing against strainer with rubber spatula or back of ladle to help filling pass through strainer.

3. Brush sides of springform pan with remaining ½ tablespoon melted butter. Pour filling into crust and set aside for 10 minutes to allow air bubbles to rise to top. Gently draw tines of fork across surface of cake to pop air bubbles that have risen to surface.

4. When oven thermometer reads 200 degrees, bake cheesecake on lower rack until center registers 165 degrees, about 3 to 3½ hours. Remove cake from oven and increase oven temperature to 500 degrees.

5. When oven is at 500 degrees, bake cheesecake on upper rack until top is evenly browned, 4 to 12 minutes. Let cool for 5 minutes; run paring knife between cheesecake and side of springform pan. Let cheesecake cool until barely warm, 2½ to 3 hours. Wrap tightly in plastic wrap and refrigerate until cold and firmly set, at least 6 hours. (Leftovers can be refrigerated for up to 4 days.)

6. To unmold cheesecake, remove sides of pan. Slide thin metal spatula between crust and pan bottom to loosen, then slide cheesecake onto serving plate. Let cheesecake stand at room temperature for about 30 minutes. To slice, dip sharp knife in very hot water and wipe dry between cuts. Serve.

More than Just a Carving Board?

Clever features on new carving boards promise easier carving and serving. But does clever always mean useful?

BY KATE SHANNON

A carving board may seem like a luxury when you pull it out only a few times a year—but anyone who's tried carving a roast on a flat cutting board knows what a disaster that can be, with juices dribbling onto the counter from all sides. Carving boards are designed to avoid this mess, traditionally by relying on a trench around their perimeter that traps the liquid. Eight years ago we selected the J.K. Adams Maple Reversible Carving Board ($69.95) as our favorite. With a poultry-shaped indentation on one side and generous trenches on both, it's simple but effective. But when we noticed some new boards with features like pour spouts, clever liquid channeling designs, and innovative ways to anchor the meat, we decided an update was in order. We pitted our winner against nine boards (priced from $19.99 to $142.94) made from various materials (wood, bamboo, plastic, wood composite) and showcasing a range of features. After roasting turkeys and juicy 5-pound beef roasts for each board, we got to work carving.

We knew from our previous testing that we should consider only boards at least 18 inches long—enough space for a large turkey, with room to work. But bigger wasn't necessarily better. The three models that were nearly 2 feet long felt bulky and hogged counter space. This time around, we also learned that width is important, too. The turkey dwarfed the tiny cutting surface of one board that measured only 12¼ inches across. The ideal proportions turned out to be 20 by 14 or 15 inches.

As for height, boards around 1 inch tall had enough heft to sit securely on the counter but were still easy to lift. We liked that thinner boards could be stored easily, but they tended to slip on the counter. Taller boards added unwanted height and weight. The heaviest one tipped the scales at more than 17 pounds and was too cumbersome to carry.

In the Trenches

We expect a carving board to trap at least ½ cup of liquid, roughly the amount released by a midsize turkey as it rests. Traditionally, a trench about 1 inch from the board's perimeter is designed to handle the job. Because the fat released during carving gels as it cools, it will cause the juices to slow down, so boards with narrow, shallow trenches tended to clog and overflow. We were surprised that the two boards with the largest footprints had trenches that held just 2 ounces. At the other extreme, one of the trenches on our old winner held 10 ounces (the most of any board); its other trench held a respectable 5 ounces.

The lone model to stray from the standard trench had flared sides like those on a cafeteria tray. It kept juices off the counter, but the food sat in a puddle. The raised sides also made carving turkey difficult.

Going Overboard

Two models sported pour spouts to direct liquid from the trench off one corner of the board. We had hoped that they would make cleanup easy, but because the spouts were cut at such a shallow angle, juices diverted into the spouts during carving, causing liquid to dribble out.

Many models employed innovative features in the centers of the boards. Some were designed to trap and move liquid, like one board's three-pronged channel that directed juices to a well at the end of the board. It worked, but cutting over the channels, not to mention the huge divot, wasn't easy, especially when we required the full workspace for carving the turkey.

Small grids and pencil-shaped grooves carved into other boards were designed to not only trap liquid but also hold roasts firmly in place during carving. They worked moderately well, but they also hampered slicing. We were least impressed by the board with 172 tiny wooden pyramids in the center. Because our carving knife made contact with the pyramids at odd angles, our slices of beef and turkey were ragged at the bottom.

Bad by Design

A carving board is a simple concept, yet many of the boards we tested missed the mark.

SIZE MATTERS
The narrow Dexas board couldn't accommodate the turkey.

BLOCKED CHANNELS
Too-skinny trenches on the Totally Bamboo board led to overflowing juices.

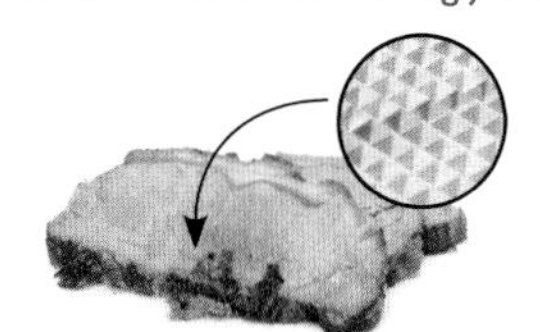

PYRAMID SCHEME
Tiny pyramids on the John McLeod board prevented clean cuts.

Wear and Tear

Finally, we considered upkeep and maneuverability. To test their resistance to knife marks, we made 50 slow, deliberate slices on each board. Of the eight solid wood and bamboo boards, seven showed a few light marks easily treated with mineral oil, but one was left with unsightly dark marks that we couldn't cover up. The wood fiber composite model easily scarred, but the marks were readily touched up with the oil. Meanwhile, the lone plastic board in the lineup was mostly scratch-resistant, showing only very faint marks.

In terms of cleanup, only the plastic board was truly dishwasher-compatible. (The wood composite board is labeled as dishwasher-safe but didn't fit in our dishwasher.) Of the wood and bamboo carving boards, bulkier, heavier models were a struggle to hand-wash. Some didn't fit comfortably in our sink, requiring testers to constantly lift and reposition them to rinse them. Midweight boards with simple designs (i.e., minimal crevices) were easiest to clean and won top marks.

In the end, we can't even recommend eight of the 10 boards we tested; they were either poorly sized, flimsy, or cumbersome, and their innovative attempts to collect liquid just got in our way. In fact, none could best our old favorite, the J.K. Adams Maple Reversible Carving Board. Its reversible design boasts a flat side suited to slicing roasts and an indented side with a poultry-shaped well to hold chicken and turkey snugly in place. Both sides allow for neat, even slicing without interference, and each sports a spacious trench that holds an ample ½ cup of liquid. It's also durable, handsome, and easy to clean and one of the least expensive boards in our lineup. This is one case where simpler really is better.

Why the J.K. Adams Won
Video available free for 4 months at CooksIllustrated.com/feb15

KEY

Good ★★★
Fair ★★
Poor ★

TESTING CARVING BOARDS

We tested 10 carving boards, listed below in order of preference. All were purchased online.

LIQUID CAPACITY
We poured ½ cup of water into the boards' trenches, approximating the amount of liquid released by a midsize turkey after a 30-minute rest. We also measured the trenches' overall capacity and evaluated the effectiveness of features designed to collect and move liquid.

CUTTING SURFACE
We carved 5-pound roast beefs, cooked rare for maximum juiciness, and 15-pound turkeys. Boards rated highest if they were roomy enough for large roasts and steady on the counter. We downgraded boards if features designed to hold meat in place interfered with our knives.

EASE OF USE
We rated each board on how easy and comfortable it was to lift, carry, carve on, and clean. We preferred boards that fit in our kitchen sink and didn't develop deep or unsightly knife marks.

	CRITERIA	TESTERS' COMMENTS
HIGHLY RECOMMENDED		
J.K. ADAMS Maple Reversible Carving Board **Model:** TBS-2014 **Price:** \$69.95 **Material:** Maple **Dimensions:** 20 by 14 by 1¼ in **Weight:** 5.75 lb **Source:** williams-sonoma.com 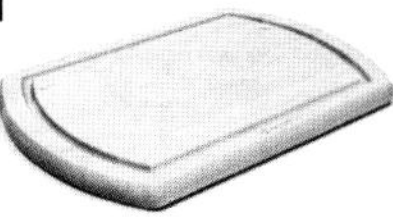	Liquid Capacity ★★★ Cutting Surface ★★★ Ease of Use ★★★	Our longtime favorite boasts trenches on both sides that easily accommodate ½ cup of liquid. One side provides uninterrupted cutting space, while the other features a poultry-shaped well that steadied turkeys during carving but didn't obstruct our knife. Midweight and moderately sized, it's easy to handle.
RECOMMENDED		
J.K. ADAMS Pour Spout Board **Model:** PSB-2014 **Price:** \$64.95 **Material:** Maple **Dimensions:** 20 by 14 by 1 in **Weight:** 5.75 lb **Source:** amazon.com 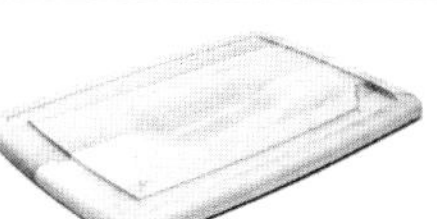	Liquid Capacity ★★ Cutting Surface ★★★ Ease of Use ★★★	This board is nearly identical to our winning board but with a few key differences. A new pour spout is cut at a shallow angle and nearly overflowed. It also downsized the large-capacity trench that our winner features, though it was still sufficient.
NOT RECOMMENDED		
JOHN BOOS & CO. Maple Countertop Board **Model:** KNEB23 **Price:** \$142.94 **Material:** Hard rock maple **Dimensions:** 23¾ by 17¼ by 1¼ in **Weight:** 13.45 lb	Liquid Capacity ★★★ Cutting Surface ★★ Ease of Use ★	One-inch lips on either end of this board gripped the counter's edge so it stayed in place. But the orientation was wrong; testers had to carve at the short end, wasting space at the other end. It was also cumbersome and the most expensive in our lineup.
IRONWOOD GOURMET Kansas City Carving Board, by Fox Run **Model:** 28103 **Price:** \$68.98 **Material:** Acacia wood **Dimensions:** 22 by 15 by 2¼ in **Weight:** 7.15 lb	Liquid Capacity ★★★ Cutting Surface ★ Ease of Use ★½	In addition to a trench, this board sports a three-pronged channel that directs liquid to a well on one end of the board. It worked, but the well's nearly 3-cup capacity is more than necessary and takes up valuable workspace. It scarred badly, and the padded feet, each nearly 1 inch tall, raised the board uncomfortably high.
JOHN BOOS & CO. Maple Cutting Board with Groove and Pour Spout **Model:** RAPA02 **Price:** \$113.95 **Material:** Hard rock maple **Dimensions:** 20 by 15 by 2¼ in **Weight:** 17.20 lb	Liquid Capacity ★★ Cutting Surface ★★★ Ease of Use ½	Twice as thick as our winning board, it stood a whopping 2¼ inches high. It was also brutally heavy and downright unsafe to carry when weighted with a heavy roast. A too-shallow pour spout almost overflowed before the rest of the trench had filled.
JOHN McLEOD Angus Carving Board **Model:** N/A **Price:** \$119.95 **Material:** Yellow birch **Dimensions:** 21 by 15 by 1 in **Weight:** 7.50 lb	Liquid Capacity ★★★ Cutting Surface ★ Ease of Use ★½	This board's tiny rows of pyramids interfered with our knife, resulting in slices that were jagged and torn at the bottom. They were also difficult to clean. The only positive: Liquid that accumulates around the pyramids is neatly channeled out to the trench.
PROTEAK Edge Grain Cutting Board with Hand Grip and Juice Canal **Model:** 108 **Price:** \$89.99 **Material:** Teak **Dimensions:** 24 by 18 by 1½ in **Weight:** 14.30 lb	Liquid Capacity ★ Cutting Surface ★★★ Ease of Use ★½	Made by the manufacturer of our favorite cutting board, it had the same elegant, durable construction. It also had the narrowest trench in our lineup, which meant that it overflowed almost instantly. It was also heavy and fit awkwardly in our sink.
TOTALLY BAMBOO Bamboo Carving Board with Gravy Well and Juice Groove **Model:** 30-CM09 **Price:** \$49.95 **Material:** Bamboo **Dimensions:** 23 by 16 by 1 in **Weight:** 7.70 lb	Liquid Capacity ★ Cutting Surface ★★★ Ease of Use ★	This carving board had ample cutting space, but its trench, which we found holds just over 2 ounces of water (less than half of what we expect from our carving boards), overflowed every time. It also slipped and spun on the counter.
DEXAS Chop & Serve Cutting Board & Serving Tray **Model:** 329-32-25 **Price:** \$19.99 **Material:** Plastic (polypropylene with TPE feet and handles) **Dimensions:** 20¼ by 12¼ by ¾ in **Weight:** 1.60 lb 	Liquid Capacity ★★ Cutting Surface ★ Ease of Use ★★	While this smaller, lightweight board kept up with bigger models when we carved roast beef, its narrow footprint was dwarfed by the turkey. Because it had raised sides instead of a trench, roasts sat in a puddle, turning crusts soggy. On the upside: It's dishwasher-safe and mostly scratch-resistant.
EPICUREAN Carving Board **Model:** N/A **Price:** \$79.99 **Material:** Wood fiber composite **Dimensions:** 20 by 15 by ½ in **Weight:** 3.80 lb 	Liquid Capacity ★★★ Cutting Surface ★ Ease of Use ★	This board's trench held plenty of liquid, but the trench had a yellow-green tinge and emitted an unpleasant odor when wet. It scratched easily, but mineral oil covered up most marks. Although marketed as dishwasher-safe, it couldn't fit in our machine.

More Vegetables, Better Broth?

We tasted a slew of products and discovered that, in most cases, the answer is no.

⋺ BY LISA McMANUS ⋲

If chicken broth is supposed to taste like chicken, and beef broth like beef, it stands to reason that vegetable broth should taste like vegetables. After all, this ingredient's core purpose is the same as that of any other broth: to augment the flavors of and add depth to dishes such as soups, stews, sauces, and risottos. Vegetable broth is also often called on as a meatless stand-in for the chicken or beef kind—and while it shouldn't taste like meat, it should provide a complex, balanced, unassuming backbone of flavor to a wide range of dishes.

The problem is that most commercial vegetable broths do neither of those things. When we tasted 10 products several years ago, we found that the vast majority were awful—sour, cloyingly sweet, or bitter. In fact, we could recommend only one product from that tasting, a broth from Swanson that was loaded with salt (940 milligrams per cup, about 40 percent of your daily allowance) and a slew of flavor-boosting additives.

Homemade Is Best
For a broth with complex vegetable taste and no off-flavors, try our recipe for Vegetable Broth Base (page 19).

Since then, however, dozens more vegetable broth products have popped up on supermarket shelves. Like commercial meat-based broths, these are sold not just in liquid form but also as powders, pastes, concentrates, and cubes. Would any of these new products be worthier of a place in our pantry?

Overwhelmed by the options, we scooped up 25 nationally available products that represented every style category. (We also held a separate tasting of low-sodium vegetable broths; go to CooksIllustrated.com/feb15.) Most were billed as vegetable broths, while four bore labels reading "no chicken" or "vegan chicken flavored," indicating that they are engineered to be meatless imitations of poultry-based products. We then narrowed the pack, eliminating broths that had more than 750 milligrams of sodium per serving and holding taste-offs within brands. In the end, we had 10 finalists, which we sampled warmed up straight from the package (when products needed to be reconstituted, we followed manufacturer directions), as well as in vegetable soup and Parmesan risotto. The last application, where the broth reduces considerably during cooking, would be a good measure of its flavor when concentrated.

Our hope that these products were any better than the last lot dimmed with our first sips of plain broth. Though the broths ranged dramatically in color and body, in the main they fell into two broad flavor categories: those that tasted "weirdly savory," with "super MSG impact," and those with actual vegetable flavor, albeit mostly unappealing. At best, these latter broths tasted bland (like "dishwater"); at worst, they ranged from overly bitter to horribly sweet (like "stewed socks and sugar") to downright sour (like "old tomatoes"). Once added to recipes, however, some broths redeemed themselves. Products that tasted like "umami bombs" sampled plain made both soup and risotto taste "savory" and "well seasoned," with "good depth." Others that tasted only "vaguely" of vegetables on their own moved into an effective supporting role, giving soup "nicely balanced" vegetable flavor.

When we examined their labels to see what went into these products, what was striking was that the product we liked most in recipes, a powder from Orrington Farms, contained only a smattering of vegetables. At the same time, many of the broths we either soundly disliked (Kitchen Basics) or had serious reservations about (Pacific and Rachael Ray) were traditional liquid broths with lots of vegetables positioned high on their ingredient lists. Could it actually be that more vegetables make bad commercial broth?

In the Mix

According to industry experts we spoke to, the answer is yes. Capturing appealing vegetable flavor in processed food turns out to be difficult. First, the bitter taste in certain fresh vegetables and herbs, such as celery and parsley, becomes more noticeable when these vegetables are concentrated during processing. Broths sold in liquid form can also oxidize, creating sour, musty off-flavors. In addition, nearly all the flavor of vegetables is due to volatile aroma molecules that are vulnerable to dissipating in liquid broths, leaving the flavor weak.

To offset bitter, sour notes and add flavor, some manufacturers load up their products with salt and/or sweeteners. Others increase sweetness by using vegetables that are naturally high in sugar. But as the bottom-ranked Kitchen Basics broth demonstrated, this strategy can backfire. With carrots, tomatoes, and red peppers in the mix, it had the highest amount of sugar (and the lowest amount of salt) in the lineup and tasted like "corn syrup."

Winning Formula

So what did our winner, Orrington Farms Vegan Chicken Flavored Broth Base & Seasoning, use to flavor its product if not lots of vegetables? For starters, maltodextrin, a common food additive used to add bulk as well as ensure even distribution of flavors. Next came salt and yeast extract, a foodstuff derived from the cells of fresh yeast. It has a deeply savory taste in its own right and is also full of glutamates and nucleotides, which bring an umami boost to other foods. (For more information, see "Commercial Broth's Secret Weapon: Yeast Extract.") While this product didn't add vegetable undertones, it did a good job of bringing savory depth to soup and risotto. We can also recommend a liquid stock from Swanson, which brought some savoriness and a little more vegetable flavor to recipes, and a paste from Better Than Bouillon, which, with the help of yeast extract, made food taste "robust" as well as "rich and meaty without tasting like beef."

Each of these products is undeniably convenient to use. But considering that our new homemade vegetable concentrate is quick, inexpensive, makes enough concentrate for 7 quarts of broth, and—most important of all—boasts complex, well-rounded vegetable flavor, we'll keep the commercial stuff on hand only for emergencies.

Commercial Broth's Secret Weapon: Yeast Extract

Our three recommended broths were notable for using yeast extract. This substance is made by extracting the proteins and amino acids from fresh yeast and is considered a foodstuff rather than an additive. It has a natural savory flavor as well as a substantial amount of glutamates and nucleotides, which give an umami boost to other foods. Though some noticed that it made broths taste "glutamate flavored," most thought that our winner from Orrington Farms added "great savory depth" to recipes.

Yeast extract can also act as a flavor potentiator of salt, allowing for as much as a 50 percent boost in salty taste without any increase in salt. But as we found in our tasting, this effect can backfire if a manufacturer isn't careful to balance flavor. Though it had the same amount of salt as our winner, yeast extract likely caused the Knorr broth to taste like a "salt bomb" in comparison.

SIMILARLY SAVORY
Yeast extract is the main ingredient in Marmite, which the British spread on toast.

TASTING VEGETARIAN BROTH

We tasted 10 top-selling national vegetable and nonmeat broth products (compiled from data from IRi, a Chicago market research firm) as warm broth, as well as in vegetable soup and Parmesan risotto, rating the broths on flavor, saltiness, off-flavors, and overall appeal. Nutritional data for a 1-cup serving is taken from product labels. Results of the soup and risotto tastings were averaged and products appear in order of preference. We ruled out 15 products in a preliminary round of tasting; for more information, go to CooksIllustrated.com/feb15.

RECOMMENDED

ORRINGTON FARMS Vegan Chicken Flavored Broth Base & Seasoning

Price: $3.50 for 6 oz ($0.02 per fl oz)
Style: Powder (2 tsp per cup of water, makes 28 cups)
Sodium: 750 mg **Sugar:** 0 g
Ingredients: Maltodextrin, salt (includes sea salt), yeast extract, dehydrated onion, spice [includes white pepper, celery seed, turmeric (spice & color), rosemary], dehydrated carrot, dehydrated garlic, dextrose, natural flavor, parsley, spice extract
Comments: With barely any vegetables, this powder didn't suffer from some of the off-flavors that plagued more vegetable-heavy products. In risotto, numerous tasters commented on its saltiness, but it also made the dish "very flavorful." In soup, it lent "great savory depth." Another bonus: It's cheap and easy to store.

SWANSON Certified Organic Vegetable Broth

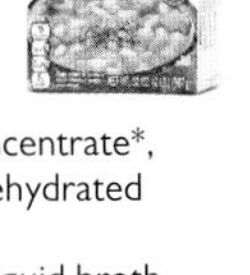

Price: $3.69 for 32 oz ($0.12 per fl oz)
Style: Liquid
Sodium: 530 mg **Sugar:** 2 g
Ingredients: Vegetable broth* (prepared from water and concentrated juices of carrot*, onion*, celeriac*). Contains less than 2% of: sea salt, natural flavoring*, vegetables* (carrots*, onions*, celery*), pear juice concentrate*, cane juice*, yeast extract*, (wheat*), canola oil*, dehydrated carrots*, dehydrated onions*, potato flour*, black pepper*. *Certified organic
Comments: Pear and cane juices and three forms of carrot made this liquid broth notably sweet, particularly when reduced in risotto. While some found that it contributed "nice vegetal flavor" to soup, in the main it was "neutral" and "inoffensive."

BETTER THAN BOUILLON Vegetable Base, Reduced Sodium

Price: $5.69 for 8 oz ($0.02 per fl oz)
Style: Paste (1 tsp per cup of water, makes 38 cups)
Sodium: 500 mg **Sugar:** 0 g
Ingredients: Vegetables and vegetable juice concentrate (carrots, celery, onion, tomato), yeast extract, salt, organic cane sugar, maltodextrin (from corn), canola oil, malted barley extract (gluten), onion powder, dried potato, garlic powder, natural flavor
Comments: Tasters described soup and risotto made with this reconstituted paste as "earthy," "mushroomy," and "carroty." While some tasters found it too salty (the "reduced sodium" label refers to its sodium content in relation to its regular vegetable base), most thought it provided a savory base that let "other flavors come through."

RECOMMENDED WITH RESERVATIONS

IMAGINE Organic Vegetarian No-Chicken Broth

Price: $3.79 for 32 oz ($0.12 per fl oz)
Style: Liquid
Sodium: 520 mg **Sugar:** less than 1 g
Ingredients: Filtered water, organic onions, organic celery, organic carrots, sea salt, organic spices, organic expeller pressed canola oil and/or organic safflower oil and/or organic sunflower oil*, organic garlic. *Adds a trivial amount of fat
Comments: Some tasters picked up on the onions and carrots in this liquid broth, finding it sweet, while others noted slightly "sour" or "bitter" aftertastes. Most agreed with the taster who called it "nothing offensive; nothing stellar."

SEITENBACHER Vegetarian Vegetable Broth and Seasoning

Price: $6.99 for 5 oz ($0.02 per fl oz)
Style: Powder (1 tsp per cup of water, makes 40 cups)
Sodium: 420 mg **Sugar:** 0 g
Ingredients: Nutritional yeast extract (yeast, salt), carrots, onions, turmeric root, parsley, leek, nutmeg, garlic, lovage, celery, pepper, balm, dill, paprika, rosemary, mustard
Comments: With yeast extract as its first ingredient, this powder gave soup a "funky packaged soup taste," but some found it "nicely neutral" when reduced in risotto.

RECOMMENDED WITH RESERVATIONS CONTINUED

PACIFIC FOODS Organic Vegetable Broth

Price: $3.99 for 32 oz ($0.12 per fl oz)
Style: Liquid
Sodium: 540 mg **Sugar:** 2 g
Ingredients: Water, carrots, onion, celery, tomatoes, leeks, sea salt, mushrooms, garlic, savory leaf, ground bay leaf (organic)
Comments: This broth made risotto taste "too carroty"; in soup it was mainly "boring," though a few found that it contributed a "very vegetal taste."

RACHAEL RAY Stock-in-a-Box All-Natural Veggie Stock

Price: $2.99 for 32 oz ($0.09 per fl oz)
Style: Liquid
Sodium: 480 mg **Sugar:** 0 g
Ingredients: Vegetable stock (from carrot, celery, onion), natural flavors, sea salt, cornstarch, bay leaf, marjoram, and thyme
Comments: While a few deemed this broth "savory" and "complex" in recipes, the majority felt that its "roasted vegetable flavor" was out of place. "It feels heavy and tastes oniony," one taster said. Others picked up on "bitter celery notes."

KNORR Homestyle Stock—Vegetable

Price: $3.99 for 4.66 oz ($0.04 per fl oz)
Style: Paste (1 tub per 3½ cups of water; 4-tub package makes 14 cups)
Sodium: 750 mg **Sugar:** less than 1 g
Ingredients: Water, salt, palm oil, carrots, tomato paste, sugar, leeks, autolyzed yeast extract, red bell peppers, parsley, maltodextrin (corn, potato), celery, xanthan gum, natural flavor, onion juice concentrate, spices, locust bean gum, caramel color, mustard oil, coconut oil, sulfur dioxide (used to protect quality)
Comments: Like the Orrington Farms powder, this paste was loaded with salt and yeast extract that gave it "depth" in recipes—but it lacked the winner's balance. It's "a salt bomb," tasters said, comparing it to "Lipton Cup-a-Soup." Each tub makes 3½ cups of broth, an amount that doesn't match most recipes.

KITCHEN ACCOMPLICE Veggie Broth Concentrate, Reduced Sodium

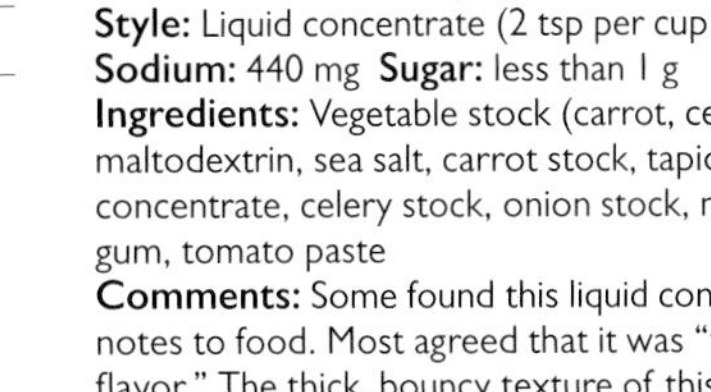

Price: $8.75 for 12 oz ($0.04 per fl oz)
Style: Liquid concentrate (2 tsp per cup of water, makes 28 cups)
Sodium: 440 mg **Sugar:** less than 1 g
Ingredients: Vegetable stock (carrot, celery, and onion stocks), maltodextrin, sea salt, carrot stock, tapioca starch, cabbage juice concentrate, celery stock, onion stock, natural flavors, mushroom stock, xanthan gum, tomato paste
Comments: Some found this liquid concentrate "pretty decent" for adding "herbal" notes to food. Most agreed that it was "too sweet"; others picked up a "canned soup flavor." The thick, bouncy texture of this concentrate made it difficult to squeeze a small amount into a measuring spoon.

NOT RECOMMENDED

KITCHEN BASICS Unsalted Vegetable Stock

Price: $3.49 for 32 oz ($0.11 per fl oz)
Style: Liquid
Sodium: 240 mg **Sugar:** 3 g
Ingredients: Vegetable stocks (onion, celery, carrot, mushroom, red pepper), tomato paste
Comments: With no added salt (some salt occurs naturally in vegetables) and the most sugar, this liquid broth made soup taste like "cheap marinara sauce." In risotto, it was "awful" with "weird onion flavor" and too much carrot. It also had an "unpleasant, bitter finish." (Note: The company slightly reformulated its broth just after our tasting—making it even sweeter, adding herbs, and lowering the sodium. We tried it and still do not recommend this broth.)

INGREDIENT NOTES

BY ANDREA GEARY, ANDREW JANJIGIAN & LAN LAM

Tasting Mexican Lagers

While developing our recipe for Drunken Beans (page 15), we decided to give Mexican lagers a closer look. We sampled the four best-selling imported Mexican lagers plain (after all, we'd likely be investing in a six-pack) and in our Drunken Beans.

All four lagers were developed at Mexican breweries and continue to be brewed there, but big-name marketing and distribution companies based in Europe now own them all. They're also often classified as American Adjunct Lagers. Technically, any ingredient beyond those used in traditional German brewing—water, yeast, barley, hops—is considered an unessential, or adjunct, ingredient. While adjunct grains like corn or rice can be used to enhance the beer's flavor, body, and aroma, they can also be used to cut costs. All four lagers in our lineup use corn.

The best beers of the group had a crisp, clean, lingering bitterness, while the lowest-ranking one had decent fizz but little flavor, "like a bland champagne." In Drunken Beans the playing field leveled off a bit; they all performed acceptably well (though some tasters found the lowest-ranking brew "raw" and "boozy").

Finally, we compared our front-runner with our go-to lager in the test kitchen, Budweiser (also an adjunct lager, made with rice). There was a clear difference. Tasted plain, Budweiser was deemed "fruitier" and "sweeter," yet still "weak" in both flavor and body compared with our imported favorite. In the beans, Bud contributed a one-note sweetness that was underwhelming compared with our favorite import. Deemed "off-dry but not sweet," with "mild bitterness on the finish," Tecate, our winner, offers nice complexity and balance. We'll grab a six-pack when a southwestern- or Mexican-inspired recipe calls for beer, or simply for serving at our next taco night. For complete tasting results, go to CooksIllustrated.com/feb15. –Kate Shannon

RECOMMENDED

TECATE
Price: $7.69 for six 12-oz bottles ($1.28 per bottle)
Comments: A "crisp, clean, lingering bitterness" set this beer apart, especially in our plain tasting. A few members of our panel detected subtle "citrusy" notes that made it especially refreshing. It's also the cheapest product in our lineup.

CORONA Extra
Price: $9.69 for six 12-oz bottles ($1.62 per bottle)
Comments: We liked the "fizzy" carbonation and "light," "smooth" flavor of this cookout classic.

MODELO Especial
Price: $9.69 for six 12-oz bottles ($1.62 per bottle)
Comments: This beer started slightly "sharp" and "bitter" but subsided quickly and had "very little aftertaste."

RECOMMENDED WITH RESERVATIONS

DOS EQUIS Lager Especial
Price: $9 for six 12-oz bottles ($1.50 per bottle)
Comments: Tasters found this beer "thin" and "flat" in flavor when tasted plain. In Drunken Beans, some found it "boozy" and "raw."

KEEPING IT FRESH
Following the lead of shrink-wrapped English cukes, we wrap American cukes in plastic to keep them crisp.

Storing Cucumbers Under Wraps

The common American cucumber has a thick, tough skin and is also coated in a food-safe wax to preserve its freshness, but we wondered recently if wrapping these cucumbers in plastic—as thin-skinned, so-called seedless English cucumbers are packaged to preserve freshness—could help them last even longer.

We stored American cucumbers in three different ways—loose, in a zipper-lock bag, and wrapped tightly in plastic wrap—and put them all in the refrigerator crisper bin. The cukes stored loose gave up the ghost first: They started to soften and desiccate after five days. The bagged ones began to rot within a week. The cucumbers wrapped in plastic wrap lasted a full 10 days before they started to soften.

Why the difference? The zipper-lock bag and the plastic wrap both helped slow moisture loss due to evaporation. But because the cucumbers in the bag could still "breathe," water that evaporated from their skins condensed inside the bag, providing a great atmosphere for microorganisms that cause rot. The plastic wrap formed an airtight second skin, keeping moisture from leaving the fruit and nearly preventing moisture loss from occurring.

We found that this storage method also worked well with related produce like zucchini and summer squash. It will also help slow deterioration of cut cucumbers and squash, but generally once they're cut, they won't last nearly as long since the cut end is very prone to rotting. –A.J.

Don't Buy Garlic That Smells Like Garlic

At the grocery store, we often give produce a sniff to size it up for freshness and flavor. Garlic is one product where a strong fragrance is a sign of questionable quality rather than potency: The main compound responsible for garlic's aroma, allicin, is formed only after cells have been damaged during cutting or crushing. This means that a head of garlic that smells at all of garlic has likely been manhandled during transport or storage.

To demonstrate this, we put a few heads of garlic in a plastic bag and whacked at them with a rolling pin (forcefully enough to mean business, but not so much that it left visible damage). After a day in storage, they were pungent, while heads that we didn't mistreat had no aroma at all. After a few more days, we peeled both sets, and the manhandled garlic was soft and beginning to rot in multiple places, while the carefully handled garlic was firm and unblemished.

The takeaway? Appearances can be deceiving, but the nose knows: Even if a head of garlic feels firm and looks good, if it smells like garlic, leave it in the bin. –A.J.

Make the Leap to Aleppo

ALEPPO PEPPER
Add flakes for an earthy, slightly sweet flavor and gentle heat.

We've long reached for ordinary red pepper flakes when we want to add straightforward spiciness to a dish. But a more nuanced red flake, Aleppo pepper, is becoming increasingly available. Made from dried, crushed Aleppo peppers (a name that comes from the northern Syrian city), these brick-red flakes are so widely used in Syria and nearby regions that they're often placed on the table along with salt and pepper.

When we added Aleppo pepper flakes to rice pilaf, tasters noted a complex, almost raisin-like sweetness and a slow-to-build heat with rich, roasty notes. We also found that Aleppo's heat, tanginess, and salt (salt is sometimes added during processing) work well when it's sprinkled on pizza and eggs. When we substituted Aleppo for regular red pepper flakes in a spice rub for steak, tasters said that it added a more complex and earthy flavor, with a sweet, gentle heat that let the other flavors come through more. We also compared Aleppo and ordinary flakes when added to a simple pasta dish with garlic and oil and liked the Aleppo for the tart, smoky, rich yet bright flavor that it added compared with the straightforward regular flakes. In our testing we found that Aleppo flakes distributed more evenly because they are ground more finely than regular flakes. Also, because of Aleppo's added salt, you should season lightly with salt and adjust as needed after adding Aleppo. You can find Aleppo pepper flakes at Middle Eastern markets and online sources like Penzeys Spices. –A.G.

Using Whipped Cream Cheese in Recipes

Many of us are as likely to have tubs of whipped cream cheese in our refrigerators as the more traditional blocks. To find out if the two are interchangeable, we used both types (measured by weight) in our Foolproof New York Cheesecake (page 23) and in cream cheese frosting.

Though some tasters found the frosting made with whipped cream cheese slightly less tangy than the one made with block cream cheese, all found it acceptable. In fact, it had a lighter, smoother texture that many preferred. The cheesecake was another story. While both cakes looked the part, the one made with whipped cream cheese had an unacceptably granular and slightly wet consistency in comparison with the dense, creamy texture of the one made with block cream cheese.

TAKES THE CAKE
Block cream cheese makes luxuriously creamy, dense cheesecake.

GOT WHIPPED
The whipped product produced grainy, wet results.

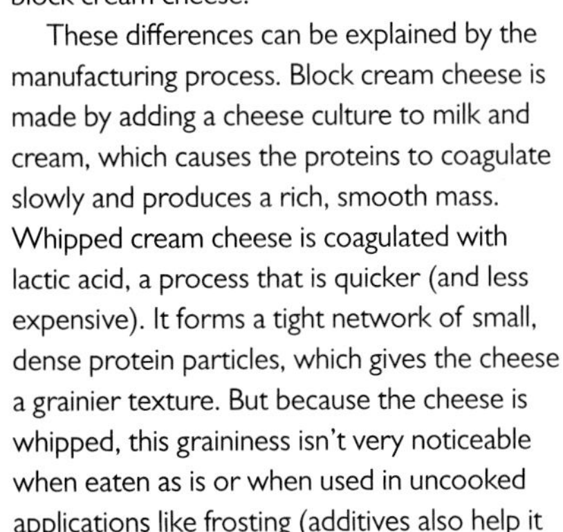

These differences can be explained by the manufacturing process. Block cream cheese is made by adding a cheese culture to milk and cream, which causes the proteins to coagulate slowly and produces a rich, smooth mass. Whipped cream cheese is coagulated with lactic acid, a process that is quicker (and less expensive). It forms a tight network of small, dense protein particles, which gives the cheese a grainier texture. But because the cheese is whipped, this graininess isn't very noticeable when eaten as is or when used in uncooked applications like frosting (additives also help it maintain that lighter, spreadable consistency). But when baked, the tight networks will tighten up even more and expel water. Hence, a cheesecake that is grainy and watery. And finally, a test using our pH meter confirmed why the whipped cheese tasted less tangy than the block style: The whipped product has a higher pH, an indicator that it contains less lactic acid, a result of being coagulated much more quickly.

Our bottom line: In recipes for which cream cheese is cooked, we recommend sticking with the traditional block. In cases where it is not heated, the whipped product is acceptable provided you substitute by weight. –A.G.

DIY RECIPE New-tella

We're huge fans of Nutella chocolate-hazelnut spread, but as with almost anything, homemade is even better than store-bought. Without the additives and palm oil, homemade spread doesn't have a plasticky texture or muted flavor—instead, it's more similar to natural peanut butter, and it packs a deeply nutty, chocolaty punch. Spread it on toast, croissants, or banana bread; use it in our recipe for Crêpes with Bananas and Nutella (May/June 2011); swirl it into ice cream; or put a good slathering inside your next s'more. Hazelnut oil is the best choice here, but walnut oil also works well; in a pinch you can get away with vegetable oil—you'll still get a product that is superior to the store-bought versions. We've found that blanching raw hazelnuts is the easiest way to remove their skins. –Mari Levine

CHOCOLATE HAZELNUT SPREAD

MAKES 1½ CUPS

- **2 cups hazelnuts**
- **6 tablespoons baking soda**
- **1 cup (4 ounces) confectioners' sugar**
- **⅓ cup (1 ounce) unsweetened cocoa powder**
- **2 tablespoons hazelnut oil**
- **1 teaspoon vanilla extract**
- **⅛ teaspoon salt**

1. Fill large bowl halfway with ice and water. Bring 4 cups water to boil. Add hazelnuts and baking soda and boil for 3 minutes. Transfer nuts to ice bath with slotted spoon, drain, and slip skins off with dish towel.

2. Adjust oven rack to middle position and heat oven to 375 degrees. Place hazelnuts in single layer on rimmed baking sheet and roast until fragrant and golden brown, 12 to 15 minutes, rotating sheet halfway through roasting.

3. Process hazelnuts in food processor until oil is released and smooth, loose paste forms, about 5 minutes, scraping down sides of bowl often.

4. Add sugar, cocoa, oil, vanilla, and salt and process until fully incorporated and mixture begins to loosen slightly and becomes glossy, about 2 minutes, scraping down sides of bowl as needed.

5. Transfer spread to jar with tight-fitting lid. Chocolate hazelnut spread can be stored at room temperature or refrigerated for up to 1 month.

1. After blanching, transfer hazelnuts to ice bath using slotted spoon.

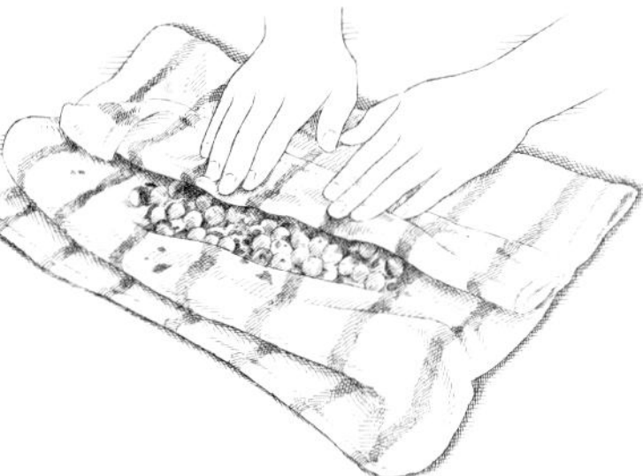

2. Drain nuts, then rub with dish towel to remove skins.

Storing Leftover Coconut Milk

We've found that leftover coconut milk will last up to a week in the fridge with no depreciation in quality, but we wondered if we could freeze it to make it last even longer. We purchased our favorite brands (Chaokoh and Ka-Me), transferred the milk to airtight containers, and stored them in the freezer until frozen solid.

Once defrosted, both brands of coconut milk broke (the milk proteins and fat separated from the liquid), much like what happens when you freeze buttermilk. So when used as is in Thai chicken curry and Thai chicken soup, the results weren't acceptable; the agglomerations of protein speckled both dishes, and they both lacked the rich viscosity that control samples made with unbroken (whether refrigerated or fresh from the can) coconut milk displayed. But we found a simple fix: Blend the defrosted coconut milk with an immersion blender for about 30 seconds to re-emulsify; then use it as directed in recipes. When we did this, the recipes were as good as those made with just-opened cans. Coconut milk will keep in the freezer for up to one month. –L.L.

KITCHEN NOTES

BY KEITH DRESSER, JARED HUGHES, ANDREW JANJIGIAN & DAN SOUZA

WHAT IS IT?

This copper mold is used to prepare a French confection known as *canelé de Bordeaux* (or *cannelé bordelais*), which dates back about 300 years. The molds, which range from 1¼ to 2 inches tall, are said to be key for producing a dark caramelized crust, the perfect contrast to the vanilla- and rum-spiked custardy interior of these little cakes.

CANELÉ MOLD
These fluted copper molds produce pastries worth the trouble but not the price.

We followed the lead of a few respected recipes, seasoning a half-dozen of the largest-size copper molds, lightly coating them with a beeswax and oil mixture known as white oil (which purportedly encourages caramelization while preventing sticking), and freezing them before filling them with batter and baking them. The results were impressive. Still, these days silicone canelé molds can be purchased online, and we found that they made respectable canelés (though the exterior was less impressive) and they didn't require the seasoning and white oil steps. Plus, they cost a fraction of the price (you can buy a sheet for 18 small canelé for $13, the same price as one copper mold). If we find bargain copper molds, we'll snatch them up, but until then we'll settle for silicone. C'est la vie.

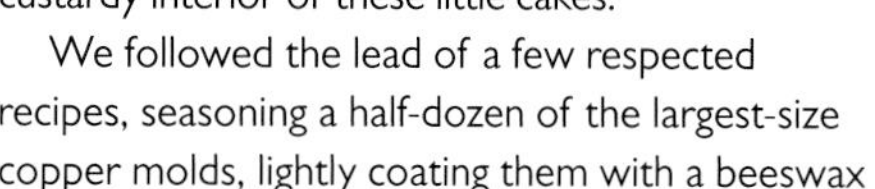

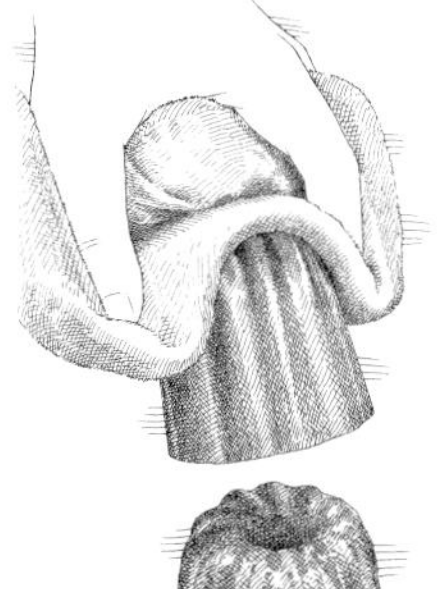

–Shannon Friedmann Hatch and Lan Lam

Why Use Parchment Instead of a Lid?

In our recipe for Slow-Cooked Whole Carrots (page 11), we found that using a cartouche—a round of parchment paper placed directly on top of food during cooking—was key for cooking the carrots efficiently and evenly. Why not just use a partially covered pan? The cartouche was able to trap steam directly on top of the carrots while still allowing it to escape around the edges of the paper, leaving the carrots perfectly cooked through and with just the light coating of glaze that we wanted. We found that although a partially covered pan traps some steam, the cooking isn't as even, fast, or consistent.

Here's why: A metal lid absorbs heat energy more readily than parchment does, so the steam in a lid-covered pot loses much of its energy to the lid and condenses. There is actually less steam cooking the food in a lid-covered pot, and the cooking and evaporation are slowed. Also, because condensation is uneven across the bottom of the lid, some areas are cooler than others, leading to uneven cooking. –K.D.

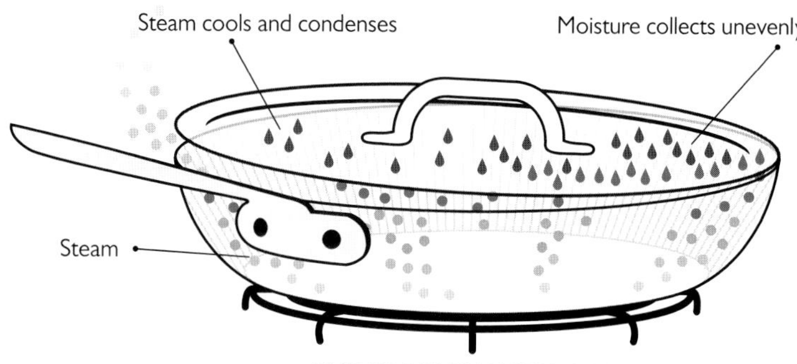

THE PROBLEM WITH A LID
A metal lid absorbs heat much more readily than parchment does, which leads to much slower cooking and evaporation.

TECHNIQUE | REHEATING SOFT POLENTA

Soft polenta is a perfect match for our Tuscan-Style Beef Stew (page 5). If you have leftovers, reheating the stew is easy enough, but what about the polenta? Not so easy. Soft polenta gels and turns firm in the refrigerator, and simply reheating it won't return its soft, scoopable texture. Cutting the leftovers into squares and frying them is always an option, but we wondered if we could find a way to make the polenta creamy again.

First we tried blending the polenta, cut into small cubes, with hot milk in a blender, but the violent action released a lot of starch, making the mixture gluey. Using the paddle attachment in a stand mixer released far less starch, but it left lumps. Here's the best approach. We pushed the cubes through a potato ricer, added a small amount of liquid, and reheated the mixture over a low flame or in the microwave (time will vary depending on volume, but typically it will take no longer than 5 minutes). The polenta won't return to its original smoothness, but it will come close. –A.J.

1. Cut polenta into 2-inch cubes, then push through fine plate of potato ricer.

2. Stir in ¼ to ½ cup milk, water, or broth per 1 cup polenta to reach desired consistency.

3. Reheat polenta over low flame or in microwave, stirring periodically, until warmed through.

For Fewer Blowouts, Bake Your Beans

We've cooked a lot of dried beans on the stovetop, but even if we take all the extra measures, some blowouts or broken beans and uneven cooking are inevitable. When developing our Drunken Beans (page 15), we found that cooking them in the oven significantly improves the odds of turning out a perfect batch.

On the stovetop, stirring the pot helps even out the cooking, but it isn't perfect; plus, some beans break. Jostling during simmering can also lead to broken beans. In the oven, it's easy to maintain essentially a subsimmer, and the heat is even so stirring isn't necessary. Furthermore, the beans' flesh absorbs liquid faster than the skin, and because the heat is higher on the stovetop, the beans' flesh swells before the skin has become sufficiently flexible, making the beans more likely to burst.

Our oven technique for cooking beans for use in other recipes (the liquid is discarded) works well with any variety, but it is especially good for thin-skinned beans like pinto, kidney, cannellini, black, flageolet, and navy. Here's our method: Pick through and rinse beans. For every pound of beans, dissolve 3 tablespoons of salt in 4 quarts of water in a large container. Add the beans and let soak for at least 8 hours or up to 24 hours. (To quick-soak: Start with boiling water instead of cold and let the beans soak at room temperature for 1 hour.) Adjust the oven rack to the lower-middle position and heat the oven to 275 degrees. Drain and rinse the beans and transfer them to a Dutch oven along with 4 quarts of water and 1 teaspoon of salt. Bring to a boil over high heat, cover, and transfer to the oven until the beans are tender, 40 to 60 minutes. –A.J.

Home Remedies for Grease Stains

FUN, BUT FAILED

Unsurprisingly, remedies like Cheez Whiz and cornmeal only made stains worse.

A CLEAN LIFT

Shampoo and dish soap were impressive stain removers.

Search the Internet and you'll find all sorts of home remedies for grease stain removal. We tested no less than 16 methods on white cotton T-shirts that we stained with ¼ teaspoon of peanut oil and let sit for 5 minutes before treating. A number of the treatments are reputed to work as absorbents: Put them on the stain, let them sit for at least 30 minutes or up to 1 hour so that they can pull out the oil, and then brush them off and wash the clothing. None of the suggested absorbents we tried—cornstarch, cornmeal, baking powder, baking soda, talcum powder, or salt—worked very well. While they pulled some oil out of the fabric, they also caused stains to spread.

Even though they were long shots, we also gave some unusual treatments a fair shake: hair spray, WD-40, Coca-Cola, aloe vera, and even Cheez Whiz. These all claim to work for different reasons (Cheez Whiz allegedly contains oil-fighting enzymes, while the soda's carbon dioxide and phosphoric acid are its purported keys to success). Sadly, none were successful, plus several also created stains of their own. Detergents and similar products were most promising. Lestoil, a concentrated cleaner that claims to remove clothing stains such as grease and tar, was a disappointment, while white bar soap (we used Dial) was only somewhat effective, likely because it was harder to work into the fabric. But shampoo (we used a type marketed for greasy hair) and liquid dish soap both worked effectively, on the fresh stains and on those that had sat overnight before treating.

For the best results, rub a clear liquid soap/shampoo into the fabric vigorously on both sides (a toothbrush works well) and let it sit for 15 minutes or up to 1 hour before rinsing thoroughly with cool water and air drying. Depending on how deeply set the stain is, you may need to repeat the process. –J.H.

Black Pepper's Hidden Flavors

We know that pepper's floral aroma comes from fleeting volatile compounds—during a long cooking time, they will dissipate. Yet most classic recipes for *peposo* (page 5) call for adding large amounts of peppercorns to the beef at the start of the long simmer. We wondered if they were really making any worthwhile flavor contribution.

To find out, we simmered 4 teaspoons of whole peppercorns in 4 cups of water for 2½ hours and then strained off the peppercorns. Tasters described the resulting infusion as "earthy," "meaty," and "tea-like." Further testing confirmed that cracked peppercorns will contribute the same stable flavor compounds to the stew during the long simmer but will release them more efficiently. For that reason (and because ground pepper in such high quantities created an unappealing muddy, gritty texture), we settled on using cracked over whole.

The takeaway? While pepper's most recognizable flavors will dissipate during a long cooking time, don't skip early additions of pepper when a recipe calls for it. It will infuse the dish with a noticeable depth. –A.J.

PEPPERCORN TEA?

During a long simmer, peppercorns will infuse a liquid with an earthy, tea-like flavor.

SCIENCE

Better Pan Sauce? Ignore the Rules

A pan sauce takes advantage of the flavorful browned bits, or fond, left in a pan after searing food. There are rules we follow when making such a sauce, but we decided to see what would happen if we broke all those rules.

EXPERIMENT

We browned four bone-in, skin-on chicken breasts following our usual protocol: patting the chicken dry, heating 1 tablespoon of vegetable oil over medium-high until smoking, and then searing the chicken, starting skin side down, until both sides were deeply browned. We repeated the test three more times, skipping the step of patting the chicken dry for one, reducing the oil to ¼ teaspoon for the second, and adding the chicken to the pan when the oil was only shimmering for the third. We also tested a batch for which we made all three of these changes at once.

RESULTS

While each change resulted in a bit more sticking and greater fond development, the batch in which we made all three changes at once delivered the best results. It took this batch 1 to 2 minutes longer on each side to reach the same level of browning as the batch cooked the standard way, but the fond it produced covered about 25 percent more of the skillet's surface.

EXPLANATION

When bonds form between sulfur-containing amino acids in the food's protein and the iron atoms in the pan, the food sticks. So the more bonds that form, the more fond that is left in the pan. The bonds will be limited if there's a significant barrier of oil, and they will break when exposed to high heat. Both of these factors detracted from fond development in our first batch. In contrast, using less oil encourages bonding. It is also encouraged in a cooler pan because it allows the bonds to remain intact longer. Placing wet skin in the pan caused the pan's temperature to drop because water removes heat from the pan during evaporation. Adding the chicken when the oil is shimmering also means a cooler pan and more sticking. Combining these three factors made the biggest difference.

LESS FOND

Lots of oil and high heat limit sticking and, thus, fond development.

MORE FOND

Less oil, wet skin, and lower heat encourage fond development.

TAKEAWAY

For a really chicken-y pan sauce, don't pat skin-on chicken dry, use ¼ teaspoon oil in a 12-inch skillet, and add the chicken when the oil starts to shimmer. Note: This method is best for skin-on poultry; without a protective layer like the chicken's skin, steaks, chops, and skinless chicken will develop too much of an overcooked band. –D.S.

SCIENCE OF COOKING: Pan Sauce Breakdown

To make the perfect pan sauce for chicken, you have to break all the rules. Free for 4 months at CooksIllustrated.com/feb15

EQUIPMENT CORNER

⋟ BY HANNAH CROWLEY & KATE SHANNON ⋞

HIGHLY RECOMMENDED

BREVILLE Tea Maker
Model: BTM800XL
Price: $249.99
Source: amazon.com

Tea Machines

Tea machines are designed to automate tea making by adding a removable brew basket to an electric kettle. Some also include extra features like a programmable timer, adjustable temperature settings, a keep-warm function, and automatic steeping. We brewed a variety of loose leaves in three models (priced from $86.44 to a staggering $249.99) and found that the Cuisinart ($99.00) and Breville ($249.99) made excellent cups, thanks to their fully perforated baskets that allow for thorough infusion. However, only the Breville was fully customizable. Users could program any temperature between 120 and 212 degrees and steep times from 0 to 10 minutes. Plus, whereas the other pots required the user to manually insert and remove the brew basket, the Breville did so automatically: The basket lowered and lifted itself based on an internal timer and thermometer. It's a worthy splurge for tea aficionados, while the Cuisinart makes a good Best Buy. –K.S.

Apple Corers

We used six new apple corers (priced from $8.99 to $23.90) as well as our old favorite from OXO ($8.99) to core bushels of apples. Sharp, serrated barrel edges pierced effortlessly into the apples, while the smooth, angled edge of the lone outlier struggled to break the skin. Barrels that measured ¾ to 1 inch wide removed cores without taking off too much flesh, while narrower models left behind bits of seed and stem. Releasing the extracted core depended on the length of the collar—the ring of metal that grips the extracted core—and, on some models, innovative features that promised to eject the core. Only the hinged barrel on the Cuisipro Apple Corer ($9.95) worked well with the press of a lever. That feature, plus its sharp teeth, wide barrel, and offset handle, made the Cuisipro our new favorite. –K.S.

HIGHLY RECOMMENDED

CUISIPRO Apple Corer
Model: 74-7150
Price: $9.95
Source: amazon.com

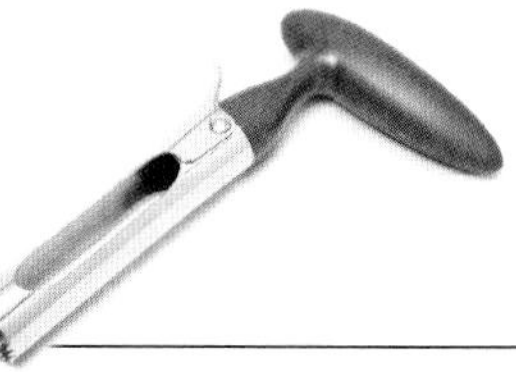

HIGHLY RECOMMENDED

STAYBOWLIZER
Model: 0013
Price: $24.95
Source: amazon.com

Bowl Stabilizer

The Staybowlizer ($24.95) solves the problem of mixing bowls that spin or rock on the counter by attaching the bowl to the work surface. This double-sided silicone gadget accommodates bowls from 6 to 21 inches in diameter. When it's oriented for small bowls, applying gentle pressure to a bowl's rim forms an impressive suction seal; flip it over and the cradle keeps larger bowls in place. The Staybowlizer kept bowls of all sizes fastened to a variety of counter surfaces, leaving our hands free to whisk oil into vinaigrette, beat eggs, and mix cookie dough. It also allowed us to set bowls at an angle (ideal for whisking) and functioned well in a double boiler. But the real test was when we beat egg whites with a hand mixer: The vessel rocked gently but never loosened. Best of all, it's dishwasher-safe. –K.S.

RECOMMENDED

BROILKING Professional Stainless Warming Tray
Model: NWT-1S, **Price:** $126.06
Source: amazon.com

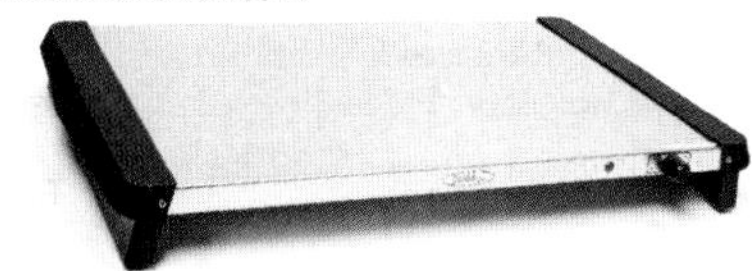

Warming Trays

Warming trays are portable flat surfaces that are designed to keep food piping hot as it sits out. They plug into the wall like electric griddles and, after preheating for about 10 minutes, can be topped with fully cooked food, either directly on the tray or in a serving vessel.

We loaded four models ($38.15 to $126.06) with a saucepan of tomato soup, a ceramic dish of spinach-artichoke dip, a glass casserole of macaroni and cheese, and small quiches set directly on the trays, tracking their temperature over 4 hours to see if they remained above the food safety threshold of 140 degrees. We also noted how easy they were to handle and clean.

The Toastess ($70.99), a complete failure, allowed foods to cool to a lukewarm 128 degrees after just 1 hour. We became wary of the Waring when its metal sheet popped in and out during use and its heating element burned light marks onto the steel surface after just a few uses. But the Oster ($38.15) and BroilKing ($126.06) are both worth considering. The former's lone heat setting kept food hot in all but the deepest pots—and its low price earned it our Best Buy recommendation—while the BroilKing offered a range of heat settings, the highest of which did a better job in our final head-to-head test: keeping a Dutch oven full of chili piping hot for 4 hours. –H.C.

For complete testing results, go to CooksIllustrated.com/feb15.

U.S. POSTAL SERVICE STATEMENT OF OWNERSHIP, MANAGEMENT AND CIRCULATION

1. Publication Title: Cook's Illustrated; 2. Publication No. 1068-2821; 3. Filing Date: 9/16/14; 4. Issue Frequency: Jan/Feb, Mar/Apr, May/Jun, Jul/Aug, Sep/Oct, Nov/Dec; 5. No. of Issues Published Annually: 6; 6. Annual Subscription Price: $41.70; 7. Complete Mailing Address of Known Office of Publication: 17 Station Street, Brookline, MA 02445; 8. Complete Mailing Address of Headquarters or General Business Office of Publisher: 17 Station Street, Brookline, MA 02445; 9. Full Names and Complete Mailing Address of Publisher, Editor and Managing Editor: Publisher: Christopher Kimball, 17 Station Street, Brookline, MA 02445; Editor: Jack Bishop, 17 Station Street, Brookline, MA 02445; Managing Editor: Rebecca Hays, 17 Station Street, Brookline, MA 02445; 10. Owner: Boston Common Press Limited Partnership, Christopher Kimball, 17 Station Street, Brookline, MA 02445; 11. Known Bondholders, Mortgagees, and Other Securities: None; 12. Tax Status: Has Not Changed During Preceding 12 Months; 13. Publication Title: Cook's Illustrated; 14. Issue Date for Circulation Data Below: September/October 2014; 15a. Total Number of Copies: 1,078,991 (Sep/Oct 2014: 1,088,124); b. Paid Circulation: (1) Mailed Outside-County Paid Subscriptions Stated on PS Form 3541: 848,431 (Sep/Oct 2014: 876,596); (2) Mailed In-County Paid Subscriptions Stated on PS Form 3541: 0 (Sep/Oct 2014: 0); (3) Paid Distribution Outside the Mail Including Sales Through Dealers and Carriers, Street Vendors, Counter Sales, and Other Paid Distribution Outside the USPS: 56,578 (Sep/Oct 2014: 46,436); (4) Paid Distribution by Other Classes of Mail Through the USPS: 0 (Sep/Oct 2014: 0); c. Total Paid Distribution: 905,010 (Sep/Oct 2014: 923,032); d. Free or Nominal Rate Distribution: (1) Free or Nominal Rate Outside-County Copies Included on PS Form 3541: 4,859 (Sep/Oct 2014: 4,592); (2) Free or Nominal Rate In-County Copies Included on Form PS 3541: 0 (Sep/Oct 2014: 0); (3) Free or Nominal Rate Copies Mailed at Other Classes Through the USPS: 0 (Sep/Oct 2014: 0); (4) Free or Nominal Rate Distribution Outside the Mail: 515 (Sep/Oct 2014: 515); e. Total Free or Nominal Rate Distribution: 5,374 (Sep/Oct 2014: 5,107); f. Total Distribution: 910,383 (Sep/Oct 2014: 928,139); g. Copies Not Distributed: 168,608 (Sep/Oct 2014: 159,985); h. Total: 1,078,991 (Sep/Oct 2014: 1,088,124); i. Percent Paid: 99.41% (Sep/Oct 2014: 99.45%).

INDEX

January & February 2015

RECIPE VIDEOS

Want to see how to make any of the recipes in this issue? There's a video for that.

MORE VIDEOS

Science of Cooking: Pan Sauce Breakdown

Testing Carving Boards

Recipes, reviews, and videos available free for 4 months at
CooksIllustrated.com/feb15

FOLLOW US ON SOCIAL MEDIA

facebook.com/CooksIllustrated
twitter.com/TestKitchen
pinterest.com/TestKitchen
google.com/+AmericasTestKitchen
instagram.com/TestKitchen
youtube.com/AmericasTestKitchen

Slow-Cooked Whole Carrots, 11

Savory Corn Muffins, 20

French-Style Pork Chops with Apples, 9

Foolproof New York Cheesecake, 23

Drunken Beans, 15

Roasted Mushrooms, 7

Vegetable Broth Base, 19

Slow-Roasted Chicken Parts, 6

Tuscan-Style Beef Stew, 5

Japanese Stir-Fried Noodles with Beef, 13

PHOTOGRAPHY: CARL TREMBLAY; STYLING: MARIE PIRAINO

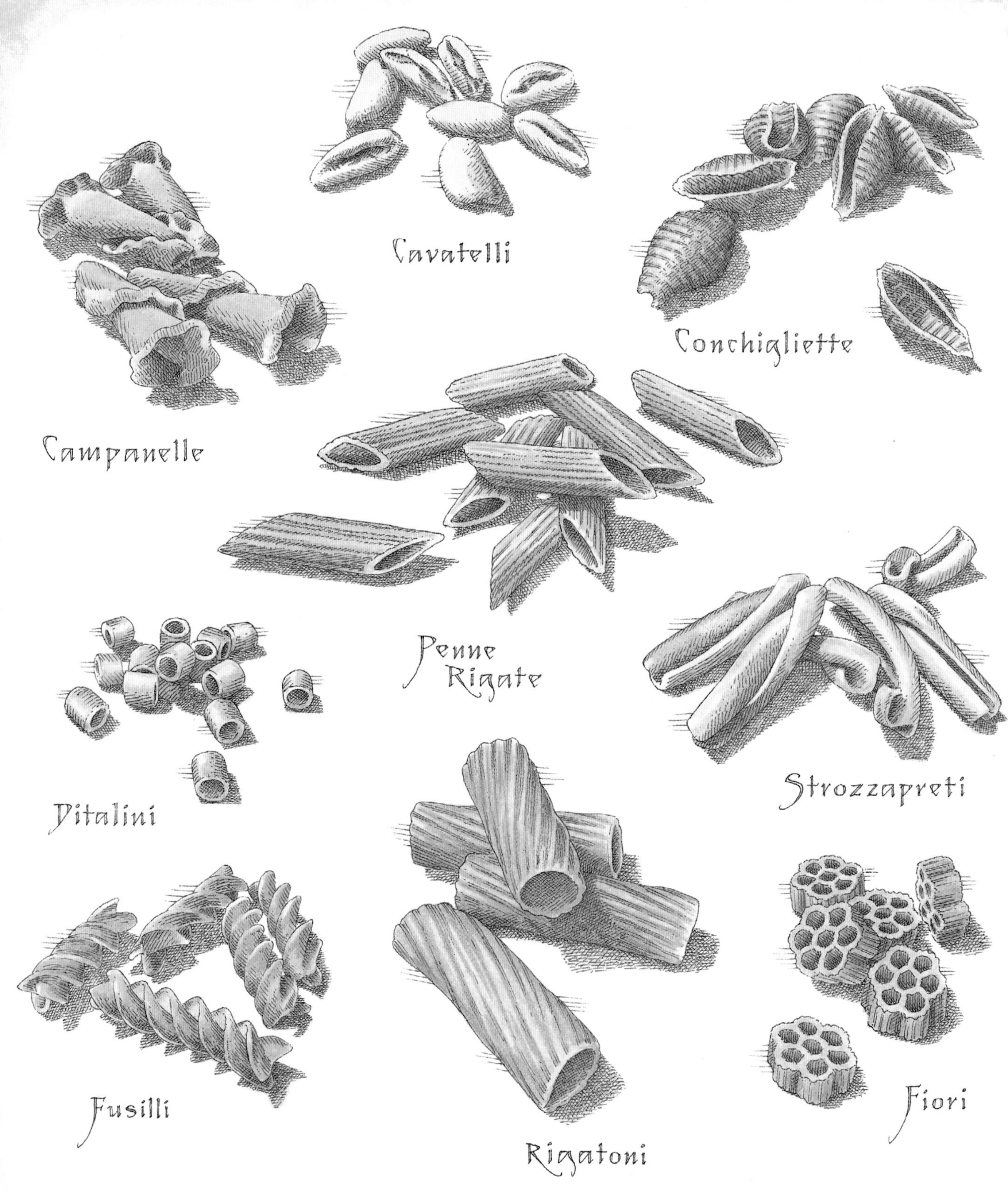
Cavatelli
Conchigliette
Campanelle
Penne Rigate
Strozzapreti
Ditalini
Fusilli
Rigatoni
Fiori

DRIED PASTA

NUMBER 133

MARCH & APRIL 2015

COOK'S ILLUSTRATED

Real Sicilian Pizza
Best Thick-Crust Pizza Ever

Coq au Riesling
Classic Chicken Dish Updated

Cuban Braised Beef
Hearty but Tender

Quick Sauces for Chicken

Secrets of Salting
When Should You Add It?

Best Dijon Mustard
Youth and Fat Are Key

Raspberry Charlotte
Showstopper Simplified

Mu Shu Pork at Home
Root Vegetable Gratin
Testing Stain Removers
Pasta with Peas and Prosciutto

CooksIllustrated.com
$6.95 U.S. & CANADA

CONTENTS

March & April 2015

SHEEP'S-MILK CHEESES Higher in fat and protein than cow's or goat's milk, sheep's milk makes cheese that is creamy, nutty, and subtly sweet. RICOTTA SALATA can be aggressively salty on its own but brings a clean, briny note to dishes. Sheep's milk is traditional in FETA, although contemporary makers often sub in goat's or cow's milk. BERKSWELL takes its saucer-like shape from the colander in which it matures; its rust-colored rind envelops a firm, crumbly cheese reminiscent of toasted nuts. A basket-weave exterior distinguishes MANCHEGO—its interior is dry and crumbles like cheddar but tastes milky with a muted sharpness. Ivory OSSAU-IRATY is supple and rich, herbal and earthy. PECORINO PEPATO is punctuated by peppercorns, which add heat, aroma, and crunch. Cave-aged ROQUEFORT is robust and complex—buttery, spicy, herbal, and acidic.

COVER (*Endive*): Robert Papp; BACK COVER (*Sheep's-Milk Cheeses*): John Burgoyne

America's Test Kitchen is a very real 2,500-square-foot kitchen located just outside Boston. It is the home of *Cook's Illustrated* and *Cook's Country* magazines and the workday destination of more than three dozen test cooks, editors, and cookware specialists. Our mission is to test recipes until we understand how and why they work and arrive at the best version. We also test kitchen equipment and supermarket ingredients in search of products that offer the best value and performance. You can watch us work by tuning in to *America's Test Kitchen* (AmericasTestKitchen.com) and *Cook's Country from America's Test Kitchen* (CooksCountry.com) on public television.

PRINTED IN THE USA

ELEMENTARY, MY DEAR WATSON!

Footsteps in fog on London streets. Mrs. Hudson. Tobacco stuffed in a stocking. Oatmeal and kippers for breakfast. Holmes alternately praising Watson for his loyalty and fellowship and then staging, on two separate occasions, his own death. (In an oddly cruel follow-up, he surprises Watson with his deception from beneath a three-penny stage disguise.) *The Spider Woman. The Woman in Green. The Scarlet Claw.* Watson filling in for Holmes at the flat with near-fatal results. Lestrade shouting "Coincidence!" when the audience knows a sinister plot is afoot. And the purely Victorian means of death: a giant spider; a dagger spring-loaded into a dictionary; the Hoxton Horror, who breaks a man's back for no apparent reason since a nonfatal robbery would have sufficed.

Basil Rathbone and Nigel Bruce are a peculiar on-screen pairing. Their relationship is equal parts domination and fellowship, humor and ego, and their cinematic friendship developed apart from the original Arthur Conan Doyle stories. Since the pairing is one of my favorite things, a cheerful pick-me-up on a winter's night, it started me thinking. My other favorite things are equally odd—neither packages tied up with string nor raindrops on roses. (Apologies—my 16-year-old daughter just sang the part of a nun in *The Sound of Music.*) My list is darker.

I loved the moment when my second child, Caroline, came in dead last in the 1-mile run at her school's Field Day. She remained steadfast and cheerful. Or when my son, Charlie, sang terribly off-key in the musical version of *Tom Sawyer* but brought the house down by singing louder and more animatedly than everyone else. Or when Charlie disappeared in a London hotel during an afternoon nap. After 20 minutes of heart-stopping panic (including reviewing the security tapes of the front entrance), I discovered him sleeping in the room next door where he had sleepwalked from his sister's room. Life has never been sweeter.

Christopher Kimball

Death has its own appeal. A bucks fills the scope, the trigger is pulled, and he drops to the snow. The chase of dog after rabbit. A neighbor who cheerfully orchestrated her own "going-away party" and then her own ending after receiving a terminal diagnosis. And my first and most lasting vision of death from early childhood—a black-suited farmer stretched out in an open coffin on a sunny day at our small Methodist church at the edge of a cornfield.

All these favorite things contain an element of suffering. This seems odd, I suppose, but Buddhists embrace the potential of suffering. They teach that pain is not to be avoided; it is part of life, the flip side of happiness. As they say, "Inhale pain, exhale joy." For some, it turns us inward. For others, it is the connection to the rest of the human experience; it opens us up to the world.

Joyful moments are created when we see ourselves connected to others. And this, if I may, is the appeal of Holmes and Watson. Holmes sees himself above the crowd—he even manipulates his best friend to gain advantage over an adversary. But the audience knows that Holmes could not exist without Watson, without his essential kindness, his good fellowship and loyalty. Holmes solves the crime but is unable to unravel the mystery of his own existence.

Holmes is parsimonious with his affection for Watson. Once in a while he says, "Good old Watson," but he is more often cruel than kind. In *The Spider Woman*, Holmes fakes his own death. He comes back to life in the guise of a quarrelsome postman who, for no apparent reason, baits Watson to violence by questioning Holmes's own reputation. He says, "He was no great detective from what I heard. Just one of them easy chair Johnnies. Would sit on his tail and let everybody else do the dirty work." He adds, ". . . it's my opinion that Mr. Sherlock Holmes was nothing more but an old herring gut," at which point Watson punches him in the face. Once he reveals his true identity, Watson is stunned and asks, "How could you play such a trick on me?" Incredibly, Holmes responds by blaming Watson, "You brought it on yourself, old man, throwing open my records to the public, tipping off every criminal in the country. The sheer addle-headedness, you've surpassed yourself." Watson replies, "I'll never forgive you for this, Holmes, not until my dying day." Of course, forgiveness is indeed at hand, usually by the next scene.

The most poignant moment in all the Rathbone/Bruce series is during *Pursuit to Algiers.* While on a boat to Algiers, Watson reads a telegram that confirms the crash of a plane that supposedly carried Holmes. (Yet another cruel Holmes deception.) Watson looks down and says, "No. It can't be true. Holmes. Holmes gone." Then he steps out on deck and stands by the rail, his back dark and to the camera. This scene lasts 20 seconds with little movement.

That image, a grieving Watson, his back to the camera, peering down into the depths is what gives life to the character of Sherlock Holmes. If nobody cared about Holmes the man, the audience wouldn't care about Holmes the detective. And, for the most part, Holmes was a vain, arrogant Victorian and an ofttimes heartless companion who humiliated his best friend.

The suffering of one makes the other more human.

Or as the Buddhists would say, in suffering, and in the suffering of others, we discover our own humanity.

And, as Sherlock would say, "Elementary, my dear Watson."

FOR INQUIRIES, ORDERS, OR MORE INFORMATION

CooksIllustrated.com
At CooksIllustrated.com, you can order books and subscriptions, sign up for our free e-newsletter, or renew your magazine subscription. Join the website and gain access to 22 years of *Cook's Illustrated* recipes, equipment tests, and ingredient tastings, as well as companion videos for every recipe in this issue.

COOKBOOKS
We sell more than 50 cookbooks by the editors of *Cook's Illustrated*, including *The Cook's Illustrated Cookbook* and *The Science of Good Cooking*. To order, visit our bookstore at CooksIllustrated.com/bookstore.

COOK'S ILLUSTRATED MAGAZINE
Cook's Illustrated magazine (ISSN 1068-2821), number 133, is published bimonthly by Boston Common Press Limited Partnership, 17 Station St., Brookline, MA 02445. Copyright 2015 Boston Common Press Limited Partnership. Periodicals postage paid at Boston, MA, and additional mailing offices, USPS #012487. Publications Mail Agreement No. 40020778. Return undeliverable Canadian addresses to P.O. Box 875, Station A, Windsor, ON N9A 6P2. POSTMASTER: Send address changes to *Cook's Illustrated*, P.O. Box 6018, Harlan, IA 51593-1518. For subscription and gift subscription orders, subscription inquiries, or change of address notices, visit AmericasTestKitchen.com/support, call 800-526-8442 in the U.S. or 515-248-7684 from outside the U.S., or write to us at *Cook's Illustrated*, P.O. 6018, Harlan, IA 51593-1518.

FOR LIST RENTAL INFORMATION Contact Specialists Marketing Services, Inc., 777 Terrace Ave., 4th Floor, Hasbrouck Heights, NJ 07604; phone: 201-865-5800.

EDITORIAL OFFICE 17 Station St., Brookline, MA 02445; 617-232-1000; fax: 617-232-1572. For subscription inquiries, visit AmericasTestKitchen.com/support or call 800-526-8442.

QUICK TIPS

⋟ COMPILED BY SHANNON FRIEDMANN HATCH ⋞

Utensil Storage Takes a Turn

Filling her countertop utensil holder with frequently used tools helps Lucia Alfaro of Turlock, Calif., keep what she needs at hand, but it's so jam-packed that it's hard to access everything it contains. She now stores the holder on a lazy Susan so that she can rotate the container until she finds exactly what she needs.

Finding a Perfect Match

To speedily locate the matching lids to her plastic storage containers, Isabella Jacob of Piermont, N.Y., uses a permanent marker to label each container and its lid with the same letter of the alphabet. Now, finding a matching set is literally as easy as ABC.

Space-Saving Pasta Rack

Kate Donovan of New York, N.Y., often makes fresh pasta but doesn't have room for a drying rack in her small kitchen. Instead, she drapes the sheets of pasta over clean plastic coat hangers hung on her cabinets' handles.

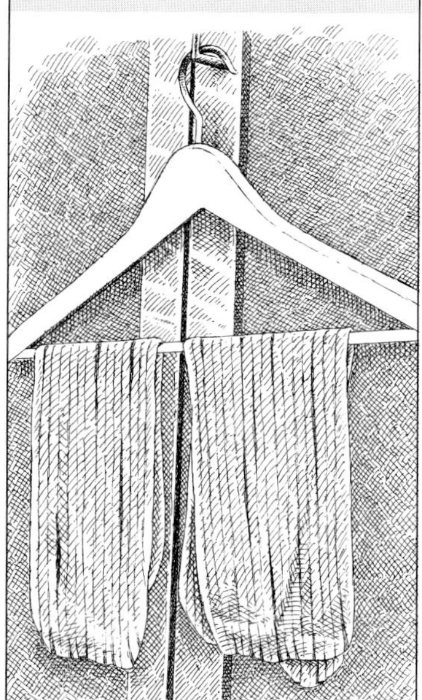

Truly Instant Oatmeal

Joann Sherman of Cold Spring, N.Y., didn't always have time in the morning to prepare a hot breakfast—until she started freezing prepared oatmeal, complete with all the toppings. Here's how:

1. Portion prepared oatmeal into lightly greased muffin tins and top with desired toppings, pressing them in slightly to adhere.

2. Place tin in freezer. When oatmeal is frozen, remove and store portions in zipper-lock freezer bag. To serve, place portion(s) in bowl and microwave until warm, 1 to 2 minutes.

Erasing Coffee Cup Stains

To remove dingy tea and coffee stains left inside mugs, Quinton Carlson of Lake Oswego, Ore., scrubs the stains with a mixture of 1 tablespoon of baking soda and 1½ teaspoons of water. This alkaline solution removes dark acidic stains like brewed tea and coffee more effectively than soap and water.

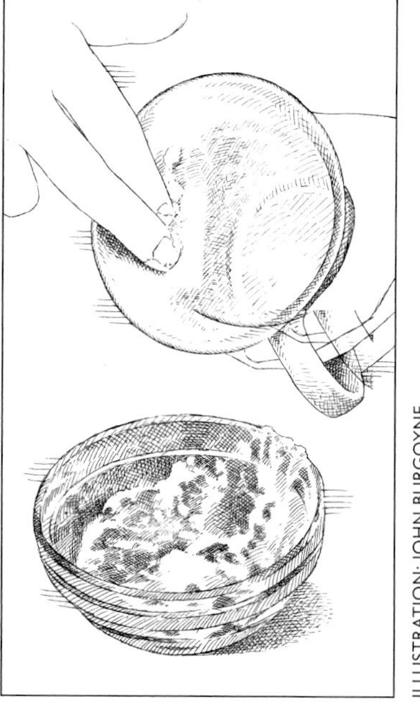

ILLUSTRATION: JOHN BURGOYNE

SEND US YOUR TIPS We will provide a complimentary one-year subscription for each tip we print. Send your tip, name, address, and daytime telephone number to Quick Tips, *Cook's Illustrated*, P.O. Box 470589, Brookline, MA 02447, or to QuickTips@AmericasTestKitchen.com.

Easier Sliced Bread

It can be difficult to saw through the tough exterior of a crusty loaf of bread. To make the task easier, Jessica Nare of San Diego, Calif., turns the bread on its side, where the crust is not only thinner but also slightly softer and thus easier to cut through.

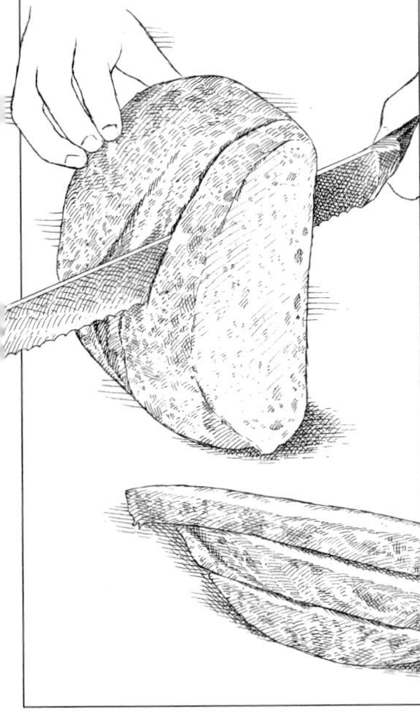

Ice Water, Hold the Ice

When a recipe calls for ice water, Peter Spinner of Middletown, Conn., has a nifty trick: He puts the ice and water in a fat separator. When he pours the water, the ice stays in the pitcher while the cold water pours from the spout.

A More Efficient Way to Dry Bags

Terry Buckman of Papillion, Neb., likes to wash and reuse her gallon-size food storage bags, but they slouch on the drying rack and take a long time to dry. Her solution: Place the bag over a cheese grater set on a towel. The washed bag remains upright, allowing droplets of water to more quickly drip away.

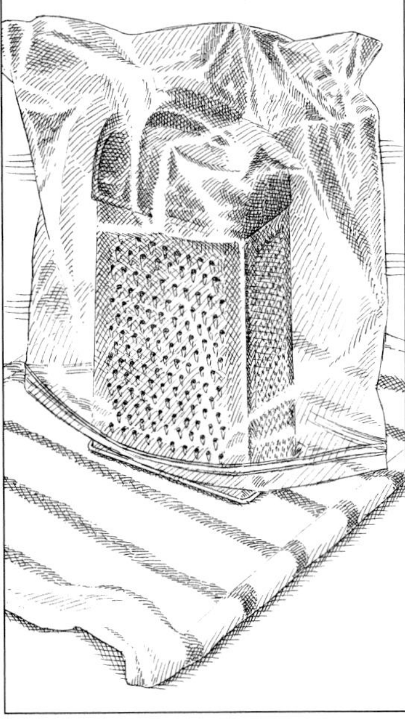

Cake Plate Stand-In

Often finding himself in need of an additional platter for serving desserts, J. Matthew Mitchell of San Bruno, Calif., borrows the removable turntable from his microwave. Its perfectly flat surface and large diameter easily accommodate most cakes, pies, and tarts.

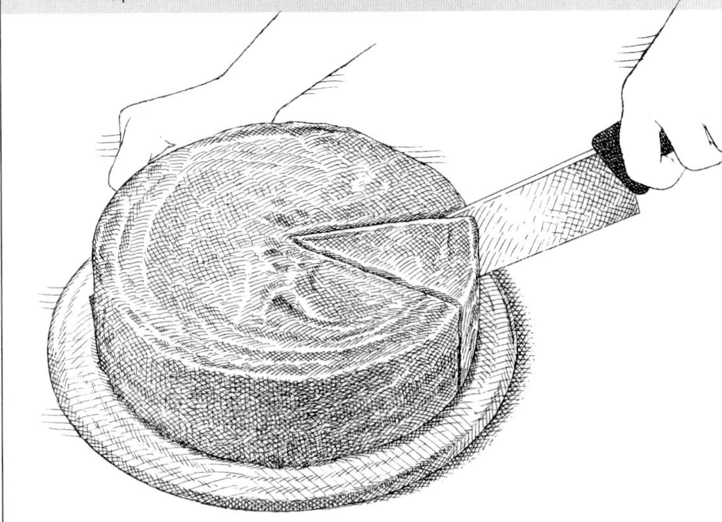

A Cap That Makes the Cut

When Mike D'Angelo of New York, N.Y., misplaced his cookie cutter, he quickly improvised with the cap of his nonstick cooking spray. Its thin edges easily cut through the dough (it works for biscuits and homemade ravioli, too). It's smaller than a drinking glass—the usual stand-in—and has a finer edge.

Smart (Phone) Grocery List

Beth Johnson of Leicester, Mass., uses this smart trick to keep track of what she needs to pick up at the store: She snaps a picture on her phone of items as soon as they run out and adds them to an album titled "groceries." She can scroll through the photos at the store and then delete any items she purchases.

Toting Totes

Susy Sedano of Los Angeles, Calif., offers this tip to keep reusable grocery bags organized: Roll them up and stick them in a wine-bottle tote.

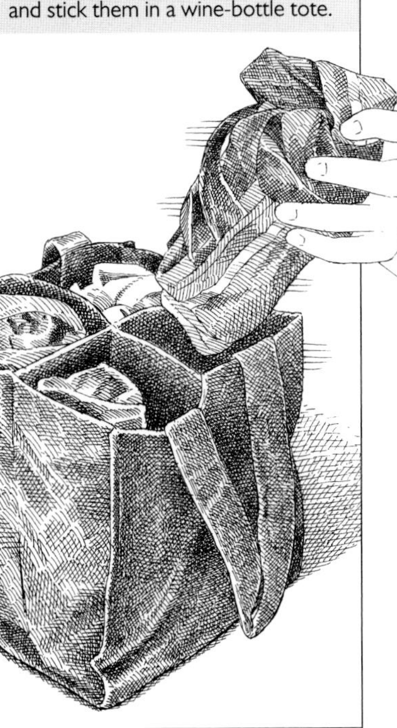

Introducing Coq au Riesling

Julia Child made the French classic red wine–based coq au vin a popular dish, but we were drawn to the rich and refined white wine version.

⋟ BY ANDREW JANJIGIAN ⋞

For most American cooks, coq au vin means chicken stewed in red wine with bacon, mushrooms, and onions, the version first popularized on Julia Child's television show *The French Chef*. The dish has humble origins: It was originally a way to use roosters or stewing hens, since cooking older birds for a long time in acidic wine theoretically helped tenderize their tough, sinewy meat and lend it flavor. In turn, the wine, enriched by gelatin from the chicken, transformed into a rich, velvety sauce. Served with a mound of mashed potatoes or buttered noodles and a bottle of wine for drinking alongside, it is still a perfect dish for a cold winter evening.

But here's something I'd wager most home cooks don't realize: In France, coq au vin is often made with white wine. One of the most common renditions hails from Alsace and features the local white, Riesling. When I rounded up a handful of recipes, I wasn't surprised to discover that they could be just as much of a production to make as the red wine braise. In traditional approaches, you cut a whole chicken into pieces and marinate it overnight. The next day you cook lardons, or pieces of fatty pork, in a Dutch oven, set them aside to sear the chicken, and then set aside the chicken and sauté a *mirepoix* of carrots, celery, and onions with flour and herbs. Then wine and broth go into the pot and the chicken is added back in and simmered until tender. The cooking liquid, now thickened to a rich nap, is strained so that it's velvety smooth. The main difference: The red version is usually garnished with sautéed mushrooms and pearl onions, while the white typically skips the onions and is finished with cream or crème fraîche.

I was sold on coq au Riesling's promise of a richer, more subtle and elegant dish. I was also determined that my version would be far less of a project than the original.

Straining the cooking liquid once the chicken is done and stirring in ¼ cup of crème fraîche before serving creates a silky, rich sauce.

Look: Skin Tricks
Video available free for 4 months at CooksIllustrated.com/apr15

Out with the Old—and New

I quickly discovered that many of the old practices were not necessary. Marinating the chicken in wine for a long time might have helped in the days of old stringy birds, but with modern chickens, it was not only unnecessary but ill-advised. The acidity of the wine tended to literally cook the exterior of the meat, denaturing the proteins in the same way that heat would and thereby making them less able to hold on to moisture. What's more, we have found that the flavor of wine in a marinade barely penetrates the meat. I came to a similar conclusion about the long cooking times in traditional recipes. While probably essential for tough meat, with today's birds it robbed the chicken of both flavor and moisture.

Next I moved on to testing more modern, streamlined recipes. Many eschewed the whole-bird approach in favor of using prepackaged parts. While this was simpler, it also made ensuring even cooking difficult, since the parts in a package may come from different chickens of varying sizes. Other recipes went so far as to opt for boneless skinless thighs or cut-up boneless skinless breast meat. That certainly sped things along, but the lack of skin and bones and the very rapid cooking time produced drier meat and a sauce lacking flavor and body. I wanted a manageable, pared-down approach, but not at such expense. Cutting up a whole chicken was mandatory. (For detailed instructions on butchering chicken, see our video at CooksIllustrated.com/apr15.) I would just have to figure out how to speed up things elsewhere.

Saving Skin

I began prepping a new batch, and as soon as I'd finished breaking down the chicken, I realized another advantage to a whole bird beyond ensuring even-size pieces: I had the back and wings to put to use. By browning them in the pot along with the parts and leaving them there during the simmering time, I found that I could give the sauce a good boost of meaty flavor. It was enough of an improvement that I realized the store-bought chicken broth I'd been adding along with the wine wasn't even necessary, so I swapped in a few cups of water instead. For a little more complexity, I increased the amount of mirepoix and herbs.

Since I wasn't marinating the chicken and was cooking the meat for only about 30 minutes, most of my effort and time went into what happened before I even added the liquids and cooked the chicken: namely, browning the bacon and setting it aside, browning the chicken parts and setting them aside, and finally sautéing the mirepoix. Searing the chicken pieces had to be done in at least two batches to avoid crowding, and each batch took about 10 minutes. Plus, all the moving in and out of the pot made for a lot of dirty dishes. To simplify, I tried browning only half the chicken, but the sauce came out a little flat—much of its flavor, it turned out, came from the fond produced during searing.

Throughout these early tests, I noticed that most tasters, myself included, were removing the skin before eating the chicken, since it had turned unappealingly wet and flabby from the 30-minute simmer. If the skin was going to be discarded anyway,

Picking the Right White

Shopping for Riesling can be tricky. For this recipe, don't worry about the wine's origin, but do make sure to get a drier style of Riesling rather than a sugary one. Since this information isn't always clearly indicated on labels, here are a few tips:

- Austrian Rieslings are usually a safe bet; most are dry.
- On bottles of German Riesling, look for the word "trocken," which means dry.
- On the back label of some Rieslings, you'll find a sliding scale indicating where the wine falls on the dry-sweet spectrum. Make sure it falls on the drier half.
- Look for Riesling that is 11 percent alcohol by volume or above. The higher the alcohol level, the drier the wine.
- Alternately, we found that Sauvignon Blanc or Chablis will work. Avoid oaky Chardonnays, which can turn bitter when reduced.

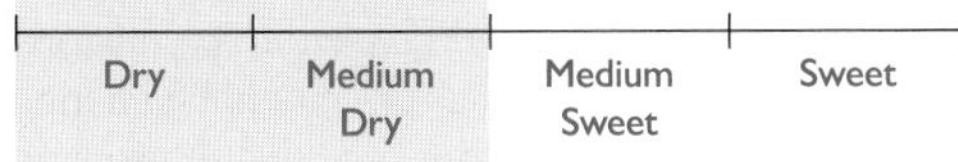

WHEN SELECTING RIESLING, KEEP LEFT

why not separate it from the meat and sear it by itself? This would not only save diners the trouble of removing it themselves but, more important, allow me to sear all the skin in a single batch. When the simmering time was up, the skin could be easily strained off with the other flavor additions.

Next time around, after cooking the bacon and setting it aside, I added the skin to the pot along with the back and wings. When the skin was well browned and the pot had developed a decent fond, I returned the bacon to the pot, added the mirepoix, and carried on as usual. The results were as good as when I'd seared the skin-on pieces, but the whole process took a fraction of the time. I was able to shave off more time (and end up with one less dirty dish) by cooking the bacon alone in the pot until its fat began to render and then leaving it there to brown along with the skin, back, and wings.

A Refined Finish

Now I just needed to refine the sauce. It was time to focus on the Riesling. Most recipes call for almost a full bottle, but when I added that much, most tasters found the sauce too sour and the acidity overpowered the chicken. When I cut back the wine to 2½ cups, the sauce was much more balanced. As for the quality and the variety of the wine, we found that—as is usually the case when cooking with wine—there's no sense spending a lot, but that if you wouldn't want to drink the wine, you wouldn't want to use it for cooking either. Bottles in the $7-to-$10 range did the trick. A dry Riesling was best here—or a comparable French wine like Sauvignon Blanc or Chablis (see "Picking the Right White").

As for finishing with either cream or crème fraîche, tasters preferred the tartness of the latter. Plus, unlike cream, the thicker dairy didn't loosen up the sauce too much. After straining the sauce and reducing it for a few minutes, I stirred in the crème fraîche. For the garnish, mushrooms are typically sautéed in butter in a separate skillet until brown, but I saw one last chance to simplify. It was just as effective to cook them in a few tablespoons of reserved chicken fat in the Dutch oven before returning the strained sauce to the pot. With that, I had my own take on coq au Riesling that was as streamlined to prepare as it was elegant.

COQ AU RIESLING

SERVES 4 TO 6

A dry Riesling is the best wine for this recipe, but a Sauvignon Blanc or Chablis will also work. Avoid a heavily oaked wine such as Chardonnay. Serve the stew with egg noodles or mashed potatoes.

- 1 (4- to 5-pound) whole chicken, cut into 8 pieces (4 breast pieces, 2 drumsticks, 2 thighs), wings and back reserved
- Salt and pepper
- 2 slices bacon, chopped
- 3 shallots, chopped
- 2 carrots, peeled and chopped coarse
- 2 celery ribs, chopped coarse
- 4 garlic cloves, lightly crushed and peeled
- 3 tablespoons all-purpose flour
- 2½ cups dry Riesling
- 1 cup water
- 2 bay leaves
- 6 sprigs fresh parsley, plus 2 teaspoons minced
- 6 sprigs fresh thyme
- 1 pound white mushrooms, trimmed and halved if small or quartered if large
- ¼ cup crème fraîche

1. Remove skin from chicken breast pieces, drumsticks, and thighs and set aside. Sprinkle both sides of chicken pieces with 1¼ teaspoons salt and ½ teaspoon pepper; set aside. Cook bacon in large Dutch oven over medium-low heat, stirring occasionally, until beginning to render, 2 to 4 minutes. Add chicken skin, back, and wings to pot; increase heat to medium; and cook, stirring frequently, until bacon is browned, skin is rendered, and chicken back and wings are browned on all sides, 10 to 12 minutes. Remove pot from heat and carefully transfer 2 tablespoons fat to small bowl and set aside.

2. Return pot to medium heat. Add shallots, carrots, celery, and garlic and cook, stirring occasionally, until vegetables are softened, 4 to 6 minutes. Add flour and cook, stirring constantly, until no dry flour remains, about 30 seconds. Slowly add wine, scraping up any browned bits. Increase heat to high and simmer until mixture is slightly thickened, about 2 minutes. Stir in water, bay leaves, parsley sprigs, and thyme and bring to simmer. Place chicken pieces in even layer in pot, reduce heat to low, cover, and cook until breasts register 160 degrees and thighs and legs register 175 degrees, 25 to 30 minutes, stirring halfway through cooking. Transfer chicken pieces to plate as they come up to temperature.

3. Discard back and wings. Strain cooking liquid through fine-mesh strainer set over large bowl, pressing on solids to extract as much liquid as possible; discard solids. Let cooking liquid settle for 10 minutes. Using wide shallow spoon, skim fat from surface and discard.

4. While liquid settles, return pot to medium heat and add reserved fat, mushrooms, and ¼ teaspoon salt; cook, stirring occasionally, until lightly browned, 8 to 10 minutes.

5. Return liquid to pot and bring to boil. Simmer briskly, stirring occasionally, until sauce is thickened to consistency of heavy cream, 4 to 6 minutes. Reduce heat to medium-low and stir in crème fraîche and minced parsley. Return chicken to pot along with any accumulated juices, cover, and cook until just heated through, 5 to 8 minutes. Season with salt and pepper to taste, and serve.

Chicken Skin: Turning a Liability into an Asset

The flabby chicken skin produced by braising is always unappealing. But the crisp, well-browned skin on a great roast chicken can be the best part of the dish. That's because when skin is sautéed or roasted, its unsaturated fats oxidize, producing deeply flavorful compounds. At the same time, once the skin reaches temperatures over 300 degrees, amino acids, the building blocks of the skin's proteins, react with some of its carbohydrates to set off the Maillard reaction, which produces browning and hundreds of additional complex flavor compounds.

To capitalize on these assets and avoid flabby texture, we treat the skin like a stand-alone ingredient, removing it from the cut-up chicken and then browning it in the pot along with the bacon and chicken wings and back. Leaving the skin in the pot throughout the simmer and only straining it out at the end of cooking ensures that all its flavors dissolve into the sauce.

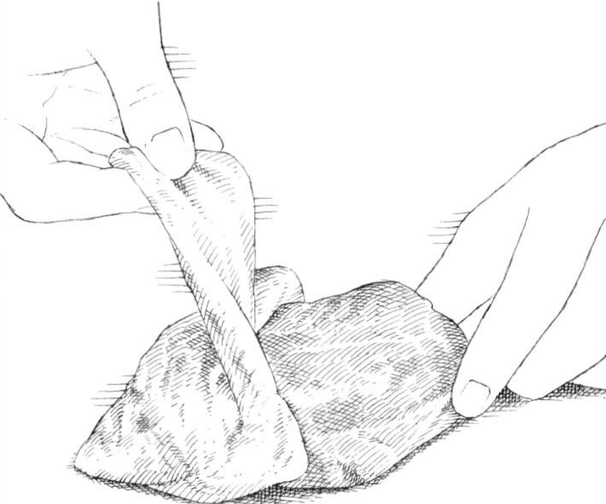

DON'T DITCH THE SKIN

We brown the skin along with the back and wings to extract flavor and then simmer it in the sauce before discarding it.

The Best Sicilian Pizza

Dense, doughy slabs of thick-crust pizza are all too familiar—and forgettable. We wanted to give the real-deal Sicilian pie its due.

BY ANDREW JANJIGIAN

As pizza goes, the category commonly known as "Sicilian" gets a bad rap. At most American pizzerias, food courts, and cafeterias, these thick, rectangular slabs baked in sheet pans are often just larger masses of the same dough that's used for round thin-crust pies—a halfhearted concession to customers who prefer a thick crust to a thin one. Usually, that crust is bready and dense, lacks textural contrast between the interior crumb and the bottom, and offers little in the way of interesting flavor. A tomato sauce that might be flavorful enough on thin-crust pizza is lackluster on the thicker dough, and the cheese (often just mozzarella) is one-dimensional.

The few worthy exceptions I've had came from Sicilian shops in New York City, where the pies featured a tight, even, cake-like crumb that was pale yellow and almost creamy. The underside of the crust was delicately crisp. Spread over the top was a layer of tomato sauce that was concentrated and complex and, following that, a blanket of cheese—a dusting of Parmesan underneath mozzarella and sometimes provolone. The combined effect was terrific, and exactly what I wanted for my own version.

For a bold, concentrated sauce that stands up to a thick crust, we slow-cook tomatoes with aromatics and spices.

A Crumby Start

Most Sicilian pizza recipes that I found called for a combination of white and semolina flours. The latter, a variety made from durum wheat, is the same type used to make many Italian pastas, couscous, and many Sicilian breads and is the source of a Sicilian pizza crumb's creamy yellow color (for more information, see page 28). The question was how much of each type would produce the cake-like crumb I wanted, so I started with a ratio test. In a stand mixer, I combined all-purpose flour with increasing amounts of semolina (from 20 to 100 percent semolina), plus yeast, salt, a touch of sugar, a couple of tablespoons of olive oil for richness and tenderness, and 2 cups of ice water; the water's cold temperature would keep the dough from overheating during kneading. I mixed each batch for about 6 minutes, by which time the dough was smooth, and then I kneaded it for another minute by hand. I let it ferment for a few hours at room temperature to allow flavor to develop and the dough to rise. I then stretched it and placed it into a rimmed baking sheet coated with both nonstick spray and extra-virgin olive oil (the spray would prevent sticking on the sides of the pan, while the oil would "fry" the crust during baking). Because Sicilian-style pies should rise tall, I let the dough proof for another hour to double in thickness, topped it with (for now) a simple cooked tomato sauce and a mixture of grated mozzarella and Parmesan cheeses, and baked it in a 450-degree oven for 20 minutes or so, until the underside was golden and the cheese brown and bubbly.

The clear takeaway from that first test: More semolina made the crust more cake-like—but only up to a point. Once I got above about 50 percent, the crumb became dense and the exterior tough. Some further semolina research helped explain why. This flour is very high in protein (about 16 percent by weight compared with 11 percent for all-purpose flour), but unlike other high-protein flours, it doesn't form gluten that is strong enough to hold air and allow the dough to expand and produce a chewy texture. As a result, doughs made with semolina were more cakey—that is, finer, with fewer bubbles and less chew—but too much semolina made the crust dense and tough. So I settled on using slightly less than a 1:1 ratio of semolina to all-purpose flour, which gave me a relatively cakey crumb and crisp exterior. Increasing the amount of oil in the dough to 3 tablespoons also increased tenderness.

To create an even finer crumb with yet-smaller bubbles, I chilled the dough as it rested, a process we call cold fermentation. When dough ferments at room temperature, its sugars, alcohol, and acids rapidly convert to carbon dioxide, which causes bubbles in the dough to expand. At colder temperatures, less carbon dioxide forms, and bubbles in the dough stay small.

The cold rest certainly got me closer to that tight crumb, but I'd have to figure out another way to make it even finer. At least the 24-hour rest in the fridge had boosted the flavor of the crust, since a longer fermentation produces a more complex-tasting array of flavor compounds. The day-long rest also gave it make-ahead convenience.

Pressing On

The reason the crumb wasn't as tight and fine as I'd hoped, I eventually realized, was that the dough was puffing up unevenly during the second rise. I wondered if I could skip the second proof, but one test confirmed that the answer was no: The single-proofed dough baked up dense and heavy, reminding me that the second proof was needed to restore texture-lightening gases that were pressed out during shaping.

But what if I compromised by tempering the rise? My thought—which was admittedly radical—was to roll instead of stretch the dough, since a rolling pin would surely make it evenly flat. I removed the dough from the fridge, lightly floured its surface to prevent sticking, pressed the dough into a rough rectangle, rolled it to fit the rimmed baking sheet, and baked it as I had before. When I cut a slice, I was pleased to see that the crumb was tighter and more even, though still not quite as fine as I wanted.

Thinking about other fine-textured breads, I had another idea, this one inspired by Pullman-style sandwich breads. These loaves are proofed and baked in metal pans with tight-fitting lids that limit the expansion of the dough and, thus, help produce a fine-textured crumb. I couldn't bake my pizza in an enclosed pan, but I could limit its expansion as it proofed by compressing the dough.

After fitting the next batch of dough into the baking sheet, I covered it with plastic wrap and then placed a second baking sheet over it as it proofed. After an hour, the dough had visibly risen, but its surface was perfectly flat. Topped and baked, it was exactly as I wanted: tender, fine, and even.

Top It Off

All that remained was to perfect the toppings, starting with the sauce. For concentrated flavor and body that would stand up to the thicker crust, I slowly cooked tomatoes and a touch of sugar with bold seasonings: sautéed garlic, dried oregano, minced anchovies (for savory, not fishy, depth), tomato paste, and a dash of hot pepper flakes. Tangy and savory-sweet, this sauce was the perfect match for the combination of rich, gooey mozzarella and salty, sharp Parmesan.

With a fine, tender, rich-tasting crust, bold sauce, and creamy-salty cheese, this pizza was nothing like the dense dough bricks at most pizzerias. In fact, I'd wager that it's a Sicilian pie that can't be topped.

THICK-CRUST SICILIAN-STYLE PIZZA

SERVES 6 TO 8

This recipe requires refrigerating the dough for 24 to 48 hours before shaping it. King Arthur all-purpose flour and Bob's Red Mill semolina flour work best in this recipe. It is important to use ice water in the dough to prevent overheating during mixing. Anchovies give the sauce depth without a discernible fishy taste; if you decide not to use them, add an additional ¼ teaspoon of salt. For tips on applying additional toppings, see page 30.

Dough

- 2¼ cups (11¼ ounces) all-purpose flour
- 2 cups (12 ounces) semolina flour
- 1 teaspoon sugar
- 1 teaspoon instant or rapid-rise yeast
- 1⅔ cups (13⅓ ounces) ice water
- 3 tablespoons extra-virgin olive oil
- 2¼ teaspoons salt

Sauce

- 1 (28-ounce) can whole peeled tomatoes, drained
- 2 teaspoons sugar
- ¼ teaspoon salt
- ¼ cup extra-virgin olive oil
- 3 garlic cloves, minced
- 1 tablespoon tomato paste
- 3 anchovy fillets, rinsed, patted dry, and minced
- 1 teaspoon dried oregano
- ¼ teaspoon red pepper flakes

Pizza

- ¼ cup extra-virgin olive oil
- 2 ounces Parmesan cheese, grated (1 cup)
- 12 ounces whole-milk mozzarella, shredded (3 cups)

1. **FOR THE DOUGH:** Using stand mixer fitted with dough hook, mix all-purpose flour, semolina flour, sugar, and yeast on low speed until combined, about 10 seconds. With machine running, slowly add water and oil until dough forms and no dry flour remains, 1 to 2 minutes. Cover with plastic wrap and let dough stand for 10 minutes.

2. Add salt to dough and mix on medium speed until dough forms satiny, sticky ball that clears sides of bowl, 6 to 8 minutes. Remove dough from bowl and knead briefly on lightly floured counter until smooth, about 1 minute. Shape dough into tight ball and place in large, lightly oiled bowl. Cover tightly with plastic wrap and refrigerate for at least 24 hours or up to 48 hours.

3. **FOR THE SAUCE:** Process tomatoes, sugar, and salt in food processor until smooth, about 30 seconds. Heat oil and garlic in medium saucepan over medium-low heat, stirring occasionally, until garlic is fragrant and just beginning to brown, about 2 minutes. Add tomato paste, anchovies, oregano, and pepper flakes and cook until fragrant, about 30 seconds. Add tomato mixture and cook, stirring occasionally, until sauce measures 2 cups, 25 to 30 minutes. Transfer to bowl, let cool, and refrigerate until needed.

4. **FOR THE PIZZA:** One hour before baking pizza, place baking stone on upper-middle rack and heat oven to 500 degrees. Spray rimmed baking sheet (including rim) with vegetable oil spray, then coat bottom of pan with oil. Remove dough from refrigerator and transfer to lightly floured counter. Lightly flour top of dough and gently press into 12 by 9-inch rectangle. Using rolling pin, roll dough into 18 by 13-inch rectangle. Transfer dough to prepared baking sheet, fitting dough into corners. Spray top of dough with vegetable oil spray and lay sheet of plastic wrap over dough. Place second baking sheet on dough and let stand for 1 hour.

5. Remove top baking sheet and plastic wrap. Gently stretch and lift dough to fill pan. Using back of spoon or ladle, spread sauce in even layer over surface of dough, leaving ½-inch border. Sprinkle Parmesan evenly over entire surface of dough to edges followed by mozzarella.

6. Place pizza on stone; reduce oven temperature to 450 degrees and bake until bottom crust is evenly browned and cheese is bubbly and browned, 20 to 25 minutes, rotating pizza halfway through baking. Remove pan from oven and let cool on wire rack for 5 minutes. Run knife around rim of pan to loosen pizza. Transfer pizza to cutting board, cut into squares, and serve.

Keys to the Ideal Thick Crust

Unlike the moderately fine, chewy crumb that defines good thin-crust pizza, the Sicilian kind should boast air bubbles that are smaller and more evenly dispersed, with a texture that's rich and tender. Here's how we deliver the ideal.

USE TWO TYPES OF FLOUR

A combination of semolina and all-purpose flours produces a crust with creamy flavor and color and cakey (rather than chewy) texture. (For more information about semolina flour, see page 28.)

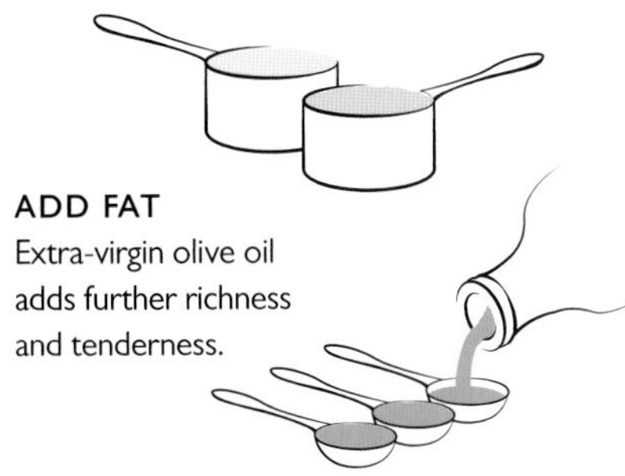

ADD FAT

Extra-virgin olive oil adds further richness and tenderness.

FERMENT IN THE FRIDGE

Refrigerating the dough as it proofs limits the formation of carbon dioxide, and, in turn, large gas bubbles. It also allows more complex flavors to develop.

ROLL, DON'T STRETCH

Flattening the dough with a rolling pin presses out some of the air so that the bubbles are fine and even.

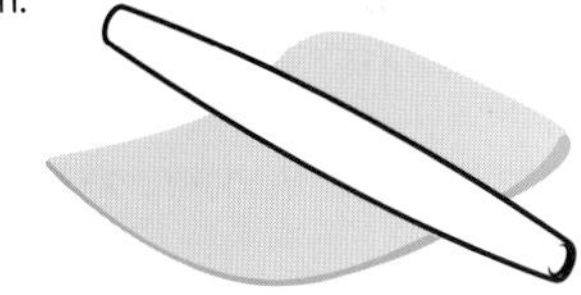

APPLY PRESSURE

Weighing down the dough with a baking sheet for its final proof allows it to rise a bit but prevents large air bubbles from forming and keeps the crumb uniform.

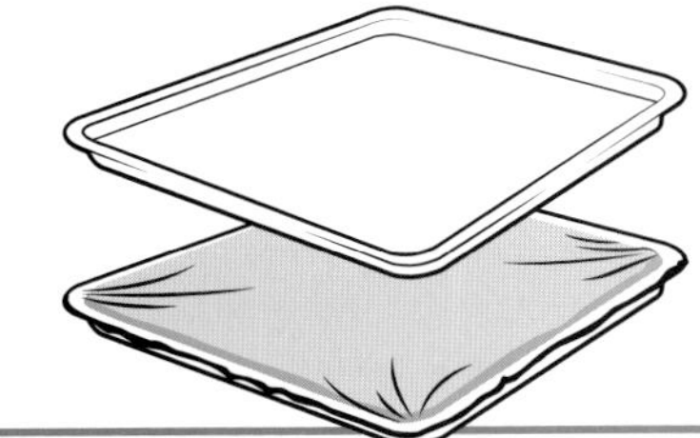

Andrew Shows You How
Video available free for 4 months at CooksIllustrated.com/apr15

A New Way to Cook Fish

Braising is not just for tough roasts. It can also give you supple, perfectly cooked fish—with a vegetable side and a silky sauce, to boot.

⋺ BY LAN LAM ⋲

Braising is a great way to cook large pork and beef roasts, but you rarely see recipes for braised fish. Why is that? Sure, braising is ideal for making tough cuts of meat succulent—cooking them slowly over long periods with a little bit of liquid will turn them meltingly tender. But at its core, braising is simply a gentle, moist-heat cooking method, which actually makes it ideally suited to producing moist, supple fish. And unlike poaching—a more familiar moist-heat approach to cooking fish—the cooking liquid isn't thrown out but instead is used as the basis for a sauce. Add a vegetable to the pot and you've got an entrée, sauce, and side that just needs rice or some good bread.

Of the braised fish recipes I did find, some called for doing all the cooking in the oven, others on the stove. The vegetables, fish, and liquid all varied quite a bit, and Dutch ovens, skillets, and sauté pans, with and without lids, were all used (a lid is a must on the stovetop to trap the steam, but not required in the oven). Yet no matter the approach, they all had problems. Timing was the biggest issue: Either the vegetables were perfectly done while the fish was overcooked and dry, or the vegetables were underdone and the fish was just right. The sauces were generally thin and bland. Despite braised fish's potential, no recipe could deliver. As someone who is always up for a good challenge, I set out to get it right.

As the fish and leeks cook, they release juices that dilute the wine in the pan. By the end of cooking, you have an entrée, vegetable, and sauce.

Breaking Down a Braise

I started with the fish. After a few initial rounds, I eliminated thin, flaky fillets like flounder and sole; they fell apart far too easily when I transferred them from cooking vessel to plate. Lean tuna steaks were also a no-go because they dried out, and the strong flavors of oily fish like salmon and mackerel overwhelmed the sauce. Halibut was my favorite. Its dense flesh is easy to manipulate in the pan and it has a clean, sweet flavor that would pair well with a simple sauce and most any vegetable. (The recipe also worked with similar firm-fleshed white fish such as sea bass or striped bass.)

For the cookware, I skipped the Dutch oven and sauté pan in favor of a 12-inch skillet. My halibut fillets needed gentle handling to stay in one piece, and the low sides of a skillet would allow me to easily slide spatulas under the fish. And while long-cooking meat braises benefit from the steady, even heat of the oven, my fish would cook through so quickly that keeping it on the stovetop was the much more logical choice.

I decided to follow the lead of most meat braises and quickly sear my fish to give it some color and a deeper flavor. I heated some oil in the skillet, seasoned the fillets with salt and pepper, and seared each side for a couple of minutes until browned. I then removed the fish from the pan and added leeks, a vegetable that would hold its shape but be quick-cooking enough to be done at the same time as the fish. The leeks' mild allium flavor would also complement the halibut nicely.

I sliced the leeks and then wilted them in a little oil before resting the fillets neatly on top. The bed of leeks lifted the fish off the pan's bottom, allowing for more even cooking while also infusing the fillets with flavor. I added just enough white wine and water to bring the liquid halfway up the sides of the fish (white wine was a natural choice, and cutting it with water would mellow its sharpness). I covered the fillets and waited until they were cooked through, which took about 20 minutes.

While the result wasn't bad, the sauce was too thin, bland, and lean-tasting, and the fish, though perfectly moist at the center, was a bit dry and overcooked on the exterior. The reason for the diluted sauce was pretty clear: I'd underestimated how much liquid the fish and leeks would release as they cooked. As for the fish's slightly dry exterior, I had the searing step to blame. While a pork or beef roast might be more forgiving, lean fish didn't have that wiggle room for doneness.

For the next test, I placed the leeks in the skillet along with a dollop of Dijon mustard and let them wilt before adding just enough wine to cover the vegetables. I then placed the fillets (not seared this time) on top and proceeded. I had hoped that the liquid released by the fish and vegetables would temper the wine's flavor and produce just the right amount of sauce. I was headed in the right direction, but the wine came across as a bit harsh and, not too surprisingly, the sauce's consistency was still too thin. And while the fish had improved from the previous batch—it wasn't dried out on both sides—it was slightly overcooked on just the underside this time.

Butter Makes It Better

I saw a way to fix the lean flavor and thin texture of the sauce in one fell swoop. In a traditional meat braise, the sauce thickens and becomes silky because tough cuts of meat possess a lot of collagen, which transforms into gelatin over the duration of the braise. This gelatin gives the cooking liquid body. Halibut, of course, doesn't have much collagen, so I needed another source of thickening power. Taking a cue from traditional pan sauces, I turned to butter. While a couple of tablespoons will thicken and enrich a pan sauce, I was working with a lot more liquid here. Six tablespoons delivered the flavor and texture I was after.

As for the unevenly cooked fish, I'd been expecting the foolproof, moist-throughout results that poaching delivers, but I realized I'd run into a problem unique to braising. With poaching, the fish is fully submerged in liquid, but in the case of braising, I was dealing with multiple cooking mediums. Here the simmering liquid was cooking the submerged portion more quickly than the upper portion, which was cooking through in the steam. (For more information, see "Secrets to Perfect Braised Fish.") I needed to give the upper portion a jump start, so I cooked the fillets, skinned side up, in the skillet for 3 or 4 minutes on one side, just until opaque but not browned (and rather than add more fat to the pan, I simply used the butter I needed for thickening the sauce for this step). I set them aside while I wilted the leeks and added the wine. Then I returned the fish to the pan, this time cooked side up, before proceeding as before. After transferring the cooked fish and vegetables to a platter, I simmered the sauce for a couple of minutes to reduce it to just the right consistency. This time I nailed it. The fish was perfectly cooked throughout and the sauce was silky, with just the right subtle flavor to complement the leeks and halibut. All my braised fish dinner needed was a little fresh parsley and a squeeze of lemon juice for freshness before it was ready for the table.

After coming up with a couple of variations, one featuring carrots (shaved lengthwise into thin ribbons with a vegetable peeler for quick cooking) and coriander and another with slivers of fennel and chopped fresh tarragon, one thing was pretty clear to me: With such a simple recipe and great flavorful options at the ready, I was going to be braising a lot more fish.

Secrets to Perfect Braised Fish

While braising fish offers a lot of appeal, it does have a downside: Because the fish is partially submerged in a small amount of cooking liquid, you are essentially half steaming, half simmering it. In tests comparing steaming halibut to completely submerging it in water and simmering it, we found that steaming took 57 percent longer. Why? For the fish to cook, molecules have to transfer their energy to the food through direct contact. Not only does simmering water generate only a small amount of steam, but many of those steam molecules condense on the lid rather than hitting, and transferring their energy to, the fish. Thus, far more molecules come in contact with the food in the simmering water than they do in the steam, making simmered food cook faster.

So it's no surprise that in our early tests for braised fish fillets, by the time the steamed portion had cooked through, the simmered portion had overcooked.

To address this discrepancy, we parcook one side of the fillets by sautéing them briefly, and then we arrange them atop a bed of wine and vegetables, raw side down, for the braise. This gives the upper portion that cooks through more slowly by steam a jump start. The result: perfectly moist, evenly cooked fillets.

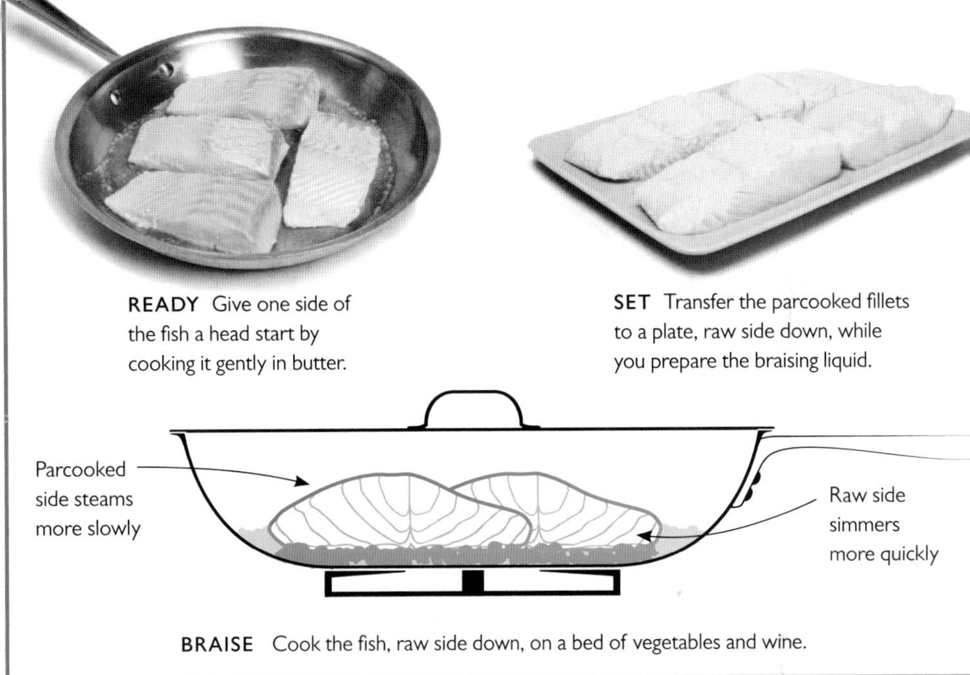

READY Give one side of the fish a head start by cooking it gently in butter.

SET Transfer the parcooked fillets to a plate, raw side down, while you prepare the braising liquid.

BRAISE Cook the fish, raw side down, on a bed of vegetables and wine.

BRAISED HALIBUT WITH LEEKS AND MUSTARD

SERVES 4

We prefer to prepare this recipe with halibut, but a similar firm-fleshed white fish such as striped bass or sea bass that is between ¾ and 1 inch thick can be substituted. To ensure that your fish cooks evenly, purchase fillets that are similarly shaped and uniformly thick. For our free recipes for Braised Halibut with Leeks and Mustard for Two, Braised Halibut with Carrots and Coriander for Two, and Braised Halibut with Fennel and Tarragon for Two, go to CooksIllustrated.com/apr15.

- 4 (6- to 8-ounce) skinless halibut fillets, ¾ to 1 inch thick
- Salt and pepper
- 6 tablespoons unsalted butter
- 1 pound leeks, white and light green parts only, halved lengthwise, sliced thin, and washed thoroughly
- 1 teaspoon Dijon mustard
- ¾ cup dry white wine
- 1 teaspoon lemon juice, plus lemon wedges for serving
- 1 tablespoon minced fresh parsley

1. Sprinkle fish with ½ teaspoon salt. Melt butter in 12-inch skillet over low heat. Place fish in skillet, skinned side up, increase heat to medium, and cook, shaking pan occasionally, until butter begins to brown (fish should not brown), 3 to 4 minutes. Using spatula, carefully transfer fish to large plate, raw side down.

2. Add leeks, mustard, and ½ teaspoon salt to skillet and cook, stirring frequently, until leeks begin to soften, 2 to 4 minutes. Add wine and bring to gentle simmer. Place fish, raw side down, on top of leeks. Cover skillet and cook, adjusting heat to maintain gentle simmer, until fish registers 135 to 140 degrees, 10 to 14 minutes. Remove skillet from heat and, using 2 spatulas, transfer fish and leeks to serving platter or individual plates. Tent loosely with aluminum foil.

3. Return skillet to high heat and simmer briskly until sauce is thickened, 2 to 3 minutes. Remove pan from heat, stir in lemon juice, and season with salt and pepper to taste. Spoon sauce over fish and sprinkle with parsley. Serve immediately with lemon wedges.

BRAISED HALIBUT WITH CARROTS AND CORIANDER

Substitute 1 pound carrots, peeled and shaved with vegetable peeler lengthwise into ribbons, and 4 shallots, halved and sliced thin, for leeks. Substitute ½ teaspoon ground coriander seed for Dijon mustard. Increase lemon juice to 1½ teaspoons and substitute cilantro for parsley.

BRAISED HALIBUT WITH FENNEL AND TARRAGON

Substitute 2 (10-ounce) fennel bulbs, stalks discarded, bulbs halved, cored, and sliced thin, and 4 shallots, halved and sliced thin, for leeks. Omit Dijon mustard and substitute tarragon for parsley.

See the Braise
Video available free for 4 months at CooksIllustrated.com/apr15

Root Vegetable Gratin

Root vegetables add complex flavor to the all-potato classic, but how do you get the different types to cook evenly? A glass of wine helps.

BY LAN LAM

It's hard to beat the earthy flavor, lush creaminess, and golden-brown crust of classic potato gratin, but it's also hard to eat an entire helping of a dish that rich. A good alternative, I've often thought, would be a gratin that trades some of the starchy spuds for the cleaner, more dynamic flavors of other root vegetables and the usual glut of rich dairy and cheese for a lighter, brighter sauce.

Apparently, plenty of other cooks have had the same idea, because recipes for root vegetable gratin abound. But when I tried a few, not one nailed the even cooking, cohesive structure, and crisp crust that define any good potato casserole. Instead, the recipes delivered myriad failures: slices that slid apart, sauces that were either sticky or soupy, and vegetable flavor that was often dull. Surely I could make a root vegetable gratin that offered as much flavor and textural appeal as the all-potato kind, but without its heft.

Light and crispy panko bread crumbs, plus Parmesan cheese and butter, make for a savory and crunchy topping.

Down to the Roots

The recipes I liked best from the early trials were those that paired earthy yet somewhat neutral-tasting potatoes with vegetables boasting more pronounced flavors, such as rutabagas, carrots, parsnips, turnips, beets, and celery root. I was also partial to the gratins made with layers of similarly sized, thin-sliced vegetables (rather than cubed, mashed, or grated ones) because I found that the uniform layers produced the neatest servings. So I eliminated slender carrots and parsnips; their small coins didn't layer as well with the larger potato rounds.

From there I knocked out a few basic cooking tests that I hoped would further narrow my vegetable choices. In greased baking dishes, I layered 2 pounds of thinly sliced Yukon Gold potatoes—a test kitchen favorite for their buttery flavor and moderate amount of starch, which I hoped would keep the gratin layers intact but not sticky—with combinations of turnips, beets, rutabaga, and celery root. In each dish, I made sure to sandwich these other root vegetables between layers of potatoes, both to break up the starchier spuds and to ensure that each bite would contain a variety of flavors. Then I poured in a placeholder cooking liquid (a combination of water and some heavy cream that I hoped would not be too rich) until the top layer was barely submerged. I covered the baking dishes with aluminum foil to trap the heat, hoping that would help the vegetables cook evenly from top to bottom, and baked the casserole in a moderately hot oven until the denser root vegetables were mostly cooked through. Then I removed the foil and put the dish back in the oven to allow most of the liquid to evaporate. (I'd get to the casserole's golden crust later.)

Not surprisingly, the beets stained the other vegetables pink; meanwhile, the turnips shed a considerable amount of liquid and turned mushy. So I crossed both off my list. But the flavor of the rutabagas and celery root complemented the potatoes nicely, the former adding pungent sweetness, the latter some savory complexity.

Look: Layers of Flavor
Video available free for 4 months at CooksIllustrated.com/apr15

Keep It Together

Of course, the problem with pairing potatoes and denser rutabaga and celery root is that the spuds cook faster. That was certainly the case with my gratin—particularly the bottom layer of potatoes, which saw the most heat and were so soft that they were breaking apart. In addition, because the rutabaga and celery root contain less starch than the potatoes, they weren't sticky enough to hold the gratin layers together when I cut a slice.

I recalled that in the past we added a pinch of baking soda to potatoes as they boiled for a recipe in which we deliberately wanted to turn them mushy; the alkali raised their pH, which caused the pectin holding their cell walls together to become more soluble and break down rapidly, allowing the potatoes' starches to leach out. So it stood to reason that if I wanted to keep potatoes more firm, I should try adding acid to the cooking liquid, which would lower the pH, making the pectin less soluble and thus slower to break down. As a side benefit, I also hoped that acid would brighten the flavor of the gratin.

I didn't want the harsh acidity of vinegar or the distinct fruitiness of lemon juice, but white wine had potential to add acidity with subtler flavor, so I prepared another gratin, replacing a generous ⅔ cup of the water with wine. As I'd hoped, the bottom layer of potatoes now held their shape nicely. And though I'd wondered if the wine would make the denser rutabaga and celery root too firm, I needn't have worried. Because they have less starch than potatoes, the firming effect of the acid was less noticeable on their texture.

As for keeping the slices bound together, I sprinkled a couple of teaspoons of flour between the layers to make up for the lack of starch in the other root vegetables. Where the flour mixed with moisture from the vegetables, a "glue" did form that kept the slices together, but the effect was patchy; the spots with more flour (and thus more glue) held together nicely, while other parts continued to slide apart. I evened out the distribution by making a slurry of flour and a splash of water (plus some salt for seasoning) and whisking that with the cooking liquid so that it evenly coated the vegetables. I also

PHOTOGRAPHY: CARL TREMBLAY

RECIPE TESTING | FOUR THAT FAILED

In our quest for the best gratin, we tried recipes featuring a range of vegetable preparations: shredded, sliced, cubed, and mashed. But not one lived up to our idea of what a good gratin should be—either because the vegetables were unevenly cooked, the sauce was sticky or soupy, or the flavor was dull and heavy.

stirred in a spoonful of Dijon mustard to kick up the flavor a notch. Finally, to ensure that the slices got a good hold on one another, I pressed down on the gratin with a spatula before baking and let the hot casserole rest for a full 25 minutes when it came out of the oven, which allowed the sauce to thicken and provide more grip.

Top It Off

With wine and mustard, the gratin tasted bright and clean but still needed a savory boost. Adding aromatics seemed like an obvious answer, so I scattered chopped onion, minced garlic, and fresh minced thyme—classic au gratin flavors—between the layers of vegetables. At least, I tried to scatter them, but the tiny pieces of garlic and thyme were clingy and difficult to evenly disperse, leaving some bites overwhelmingly garlicky and others bland. I was much better off tossing the garlic and thyme (plus some black pepper) with the chopped onion, which was easier to distribute evenly between the layers of vegetables.

The other savory component in most potato gratins is that golden crust. Thus far, I'd held off on adding cheese between the layers so that the flavors of the vegetables could dominate, but a cheese crust seemed like a subtler way to get at that rich savory flavor; I also hoped it would crisp up nicely. My first attempt was to sprinkle the casserole with a handful of grated Parmesan when I removed the foil cover and then put the dish back in the oven to bake until the cheese turned golden brown. That it did, but the results weren't nearly as crisp as I'd hoped, so for the next batch I reached for the ingredient we turn to when we want an ultracrisp crust: panko bread crumbs. When mixed with the Parmesan and a few tablespoons of melted butter, the bread crumbs formed a topping that was crisp, attractively brown, and rich and savory enough to contrast with the earthy, sweet flavors of the potatoes, celery root, and rutabaga.

Finally, my gratin had just enough richness to harken back to the classic version. And if my tasters were any indication, the gratin was also so light and flavorful that my dinner guests not only would have room for more but wouldn't be able to resist a second helping.

ROOT VEGETABLE GRATIN

SERVES 6 TO 8

Uniformly thin slices are necessary for a cohesive gratin. We recommend a mandoline for quick and even slicing, but a sharp chef's knife will also work. Because the vegetables in the gratin are tightly packed into the casserole dish, it will still be plenty hot after a 25-minute rest.

- **1 tablespoon plus 1½ cups water**
- **1½ teaspoons Dijon mustard**
- **2 teaspoons all-purpose flour**
- **Salt and pepper**
- **⅔ cup dry white wine**
- **½ cup heavy cream**
- **½ onion, chopped fine**
- **1¼ teaspoons minced fresh thyme**
- **1 garlic clove, minced**
- **2 pounds large Yukon Gold potatoes, peeled and sliced lengthwise ⅛ inch thick**
- **1 large celery root (1 pound), peeled, quartered, and sliced ⅛ inch thick**
- **1 pound rutabaga, peeled, quartered, and sliced ⅛ inch thick**
- **¾ cup panko bread crumbs**
- **1½ ounces Parmesan cheese, grated (¾ cup)**
- **4 tablespoons unsalted butter, melted and cooled**

1. Adjust oven rack to middle position and heat oven to 375 degrees. Grease 13 by 9-inch baking dish. Whisk 1 tablespoon water, mustard, flour, and 1½ teaspoons salt in medium bowl until smooth. Add wine, cream, and remaining 1½ cups water; whisk to combine. Combine onion, thyme, garlic, and ¼ teaspoon pepper in second bowl.

2. Layer half of potatoes in prepared dish, arranging so they form even thickness. Sprinkle half of onion mixture evenly over potatoes. Arrange celery root and rutabaga slices in even layer over onions. Sprinkle remaining onion mixture over celery root and rutabaga. Layer remaining potatoes over onions. Slowly pour water mixture over vegetables. Using rubber spatula, gently press down on vegetables to create even, compact layer. Cover tightly with aluminum foil and bake for 50 minutes. Remove foil and continue to bake until knife inserted into center of gratin meets no resistance, 20 to 25 minutes longer.

3. While gratin bakes, combine panko, Parmesan, and butter in bowl and season with salt and pepper to taste. Remove gratin from oven and sprinkle evenly with panko mixture. Continue to bake until panko is golden brown, 15 to 20 minutes longer. Remove gratin from oven and let stand for 25 minutes. Serve.

SCIENCE

Firming Up Potatoes with Wine

The wine in our root vegetable gratin brightens the flavor of this typically starchy-tasting dish, but more important, it also prevents the potatoes from breaking down and turning mushy while the denser celery root and rutabaga cook. Here's how it works: Potato cells have an abundance of starch granules; when these granules swell with water during cooking, they press against the cell walls, eventually causing them to burst and release starch. But when potatoes cook in water with wine, the wine lowers the pH, which strengthens the pectin in and around the cell walls, helping them resist bursting. The upshot is a pliable, not mushy, potato.

Of course, the acid also strengthens the pectin in the celery root and rutabaga, but since they contain less starch than potatoes, the acid's effect on them is less noticeable.

To demonstrate acid's effect on potatoes, we simmered two batches of ⅛-inch-thick potato slices, one in plain water and the other in 1½ cups of water acidulated with ⅔ cup of white wine. After just 10 minutes of simmering, the potatoes cooked in plain water fell apart, while those cooked in acidulated water remained whole and firm but pliable.

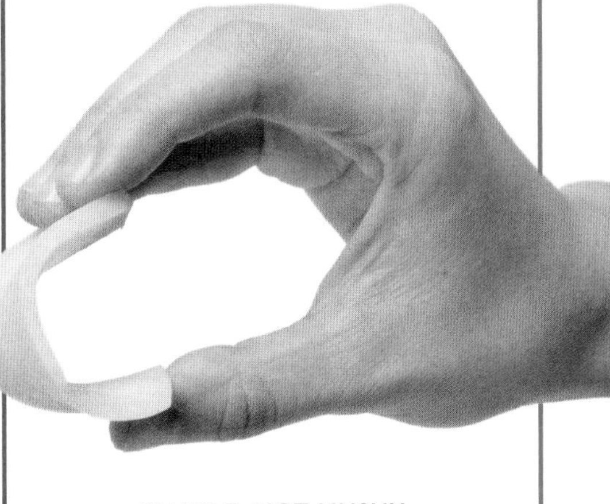

PLIABLE, NOT MUSHY

Cooking potatoes in water with wine strengthens their cell walls, so they resist bursting as they cook.

Cuban Braised Shredded Beef

Tender yet hearty strands make *ropa vieja* stand out from other Latin braised beef dishes. But to get the texture just right, we had to start with an unusual cut.

⇚ BY DAN SOUZA ⇛

I've always loved old recipes that carry with them well-worn, colorful—if generally unfounded—histories. One of my favorites is *ropa vieja* (literally "old clothes"), a comforting Cuban dish of braised and shredded beef, sliced peppers and onions, chopped green olives (in some versions), and a brothy sauce based on the meat's cooking liquid, wine, tomatoes, and warm spices. As the story goes, a peasant who couldn't afford meat to feed his family added some old clothes to the stew pot. By the powers of hope and love alone, the clothes magically turned into beef.

The ropa vieja at my favorite Cuban restaurant features tender and toothsome beef napped in sauce that's rich and meaty but bright and faintly sweet from the tomatoes—the perfect seasoning for rice and beans. But when I've followed recipes for the dish in my own kitchen, it's as if I've made that same clothes-for-meat substitution, minus the magic. The beef—flank steak is the traditional cut—has been either dry or much too chewy, or both. Most of the sauces have lacked meaty depth; instead, they've either tasted so much like canned tomatoes that they could be mistaken for pasta sauce or have been overly acidic from a too-heavy pour of wine. I'd hoped the Cuban restaurant would share its recipe with me, but when they declined my request, I knew I was on my own.

We skip chewy flank steak, the traditional choice for this dish, in favor of more tender (but still hearty) brisket.

Making the Cut

Looking for a replacement for flank steak seemed like a logical place to begin testing. In the test kitchen, we treat this beefy, relatively chewy cut like a proper steak, searing it on both sides until the center reaches medium-rare and then slicing it thin against the grain to make its texture as tender as possible.

I prepared a basic recipe for ropa vieja in which I compared flank steak to our preferred braising cuts, chuck roast and short ribs, both of which offer beefy flavor and turn tender when braised. Step one was to gently simmer the meat (seasoned simply with salt and pepper) in a few cups of water with strips of onion and bell pepper, plus a couple of bay leaves, for about 2½ hours; at that point, the meat was fork-tender and the broth had taken on beefy flavor and body. From there, I shredded the meat into relatively thick and coarse 2-inch strips—a preparation that makes ropa vieja stand apart from other more finely shredded beef dishes. Lastly, I sautéed a *sofrito* (the Latin flavor base of onions, bell peppers, and garlic) in a skillet with a little cumin and oregano; deglazed the pan with white wine, a small can of tomato sauce, and some of the homemade beef broth; added the shredded meat; and quickly tossed the mixture to coat.

Is It Magic? Watch and See
Video available free for 4 months at CooksIllustrated.com/apr15

The sauces made with all three cuts tasted decently beefy, if washed out; I'd build up those flavors later. But none of the meat produced the broad, tender-chewy shreds I was after—and the tough, chewy flank steak was the worst offender. I made another batch and increased the braising time, but when it finally turned tender, the meat was very dry.

Meanwhile, the chuck and the short ribs failed for the opposite reason: They were tender to a fault, collapsing into fine, silky shreds that would have been ideal for a taco filling but didn't fit the tender-yet-meaty profile that defines ropa vieja.

That's when I thought of brisket. It's a workhorse muscle that must be cooked slowly to turn tender, which is why it's typically barbecued or braised. I had high hopes that its ample fat and collagen would boost the meat's perceived juiciness, and its relatively thick muscle fibers would shred coarsely for satisfying chew. (For more information, see "For Perfect Shreds, Pick the Right Cut—and Cut It Right.")

Brisket is typically sold in two pieces: the leaner, more widely available flat cut, and the fattier, harder-to-find point cut. I opted for a 2-pound piece of the former, trimmed down its fat cap, and sliced it against the grain into 2-inch-wide strips—a bit of quick knife work that would not only help the meat cook faster but also produce a pile of perfectly sized pieces when it came time to shred the cooked meat. Then I put the strips into the pot with water and aromatics, making a change to the cooking method: I'd braise the meat, covered, in a low oven, where it would simmer more gently and evenly.

Two hours later, I was pleased to see that my departure from tradition had paid off. The brisket was shreddable, tender, and juicy, with a pleasant hint of chew.

Method Man

While I was bucking tradition, I realized that I could pare down the two cooking vessels to just a Dutch oven. Doing so also meant that I could beef up the flavor of the sauce by first sautéing the peppers and onions until they developed a rich fond in the pan and then building the sauce on that flavor base. (I'd remove them before sautéing the aromatics or adding the liquid to prevent them from turning mushy and then return them to the pot at the end of cooking.)

My other plan for adding depth to the sauce was to switch out the water for chicken broth (a quick test revealed that commercial beef broth produced an unpleasant sourness). But while this latest sauce definitely had more savory depth and character, it

FOR PERFECT SHREDS, PICK THE RIGHT CUT—AND CUT IT RIGHT

Our favorite cuts of beef for braising, chuck roast and short ribs, are tender and full of collagen that keeps the meat juicy during cooking, but their muscle fibers are relatively thin. This isn't a problem in most recipes, where ultratender meat is the goal, but in *ropa vieja*, where we want more substantial shreds of beef, we turned to a cut with thicker fibers: brisket.

Before cooking, we cut the brisket against the grain into 2-inch-wide strips. This shortens the muscle fibers, making the meat easier to shred with the grain (we use two forks to make quick work of the job) after cooking. It also helps the meat cook faster.

didn't quite match the ultrameaty flavor of the ropa vieja at my local Cuban place.

I thought the restaurant might have doctored the dish with Sazón, a popular Latin seasoning mixture of monosodium glutamate (MSG), salt, and spices. Rather than track down this ingredient, I added a couple of minced anchovies to the pot with the aromatics, knowing that their naturally high glutamate content would mimic the savory effect of straight MSG. But some element of beefiness was still missing. That's when I realized I'd overlooked the simplest path to richer, meatier flavor: searing the beef.

Traditionally, this dish gets all its browned depth from caramelizing vegetables for the sofrito, but there was no reason I couldn't also sear the beef to develop ultrasavory browning before adding the vegetables and proceeding. One test was all it took to convince me: This was by far my beefiest, most robustly flavored ropa vieja. A handful of chopped green olives added along with the finished peppers and onions—plus a splash of white vinegar just before serving—made the flavors pop even more.

With hearty-but-tender shreds of meat, a beefed-up sauce, sweetness from the peppers and onions, and briny punch from the olives and vinegar—not to mention a modern streamlined approach—my ropa vieja was just as good as the real thing from down the street, no magical thinking required.

Beefing Up the Sofrito

Most versions of *ropa vieja* get their depth from a combination of a *sofrito*, the Latin flavor foundation created when you sauté aromatic vegetables until a rich fond forms on the bottom of the pot, and a salty seasoning mix called Sazón. We skipped the mix and instead made an ultrasavory fond by first searing the brisket pieces—an untraditional step—and then sautéing the peppers and onions on top of the beef fond to create even more flavorful browned bits that give the pot a meaty boost.

A SHORTCUT NOT TAKEN
Latin cooks boost meaty flavor with Sazón, but we use other methods.

CUBAN BRAISED SHREDDED BEEF (ROPA VIEJA)
SERVES 6 TO 8

Look for a brisket that is 1½ to 2½ inches thick. Serve with steamed white rice and beans. Another good accompaniment is Fried Sweet Plantains.

- 1 (2-pound) beef brisket, fat trimmed to ¼ inch
- Salt and pepper
- 5 tablespoons vegetable oil
- 2 onions, halved and sliced thin
- 2 red bell peppers, stemmed, seeded, and sliced into ¼-inch-wide strips
- 2 anchovy fillets, rinsed, patted dry, and minced
- 4 garlic cloves, minced
- 2 teaspoons ground cumin
- 1½ teaspoons dried oregano
- ½ cup dry white wine
- 2 cups chicken broth
- 1 (8-ounce) can tomato sauce
- 2 bay leaves
- ¾ cup pitted green olives, chopped coarse
- ¾ teaspoon white wine vinegar, plus extra for seasoning

1. Adjust oven rack to middle position and heat oven to 300 degrees. Cut brisket against grain into 2-inch-wide strips. Cut any strips longer than 5 inches in half crosswise. Season beef on all sides with salt and pepper. Heat 4 tablespoons oil in Dutch oven over medium-high heat until just smoking. Brown beef on all sides, 7 to 10 minutes; transfer to large plate and set aside. Add onions and bell peppers and cook until softened and pan bottom develops fond, 10 to 15 minutes. Transfer vegetables to bowl and set aside. Add remaining 1 tablespoon oil to now-empty pot, then add anchovies, garlic, cumin, and oregano and cook until fragrant, about 30 seconds. Stir in wine, scraping up any browned bits, and cook until mostly evaporated, about 1 minute. Stir in broth, tomato sauce, and bay leaves. Return beef and any accumulated juices to pot and bring to simmer over high heat. Transfer to oven and cook, covered, until beef is just tender, 2 to 2¼ hours, flipping meat halfway through cooking.

2. Transfer beef to cutting board; when cool enough to handle, shred into ¼-inch-thick pieces. Meanwhile, add olives and reserved vegetables to pot and bring to boil over medium-high heat; simmer until thickened and measures 4 cups, 5 to 7 minutes. Stir in beef. Add vinegar. Season with salt, pepper, and extra vinegar to taste; serve.

A Sweet and Savory Side

In Cuban restaurants, *ropa vieja* is often accompanied by *plátanos maduros*, or fried sweet plantains. This savory-sweet side dish features thick, soft slices of very ripe plantains that are fried in oil to create a caramel-like browned crust encasing a soft, sweet interior; a sprinkling of salt balances the sweetness. We deep-fry our plantains and stir the slices occasionally so that they brown evenly.

FRIED SWEET PLANTAINS (PLÁTANOS MADUROS)
SERVES 6 TO 8 AS A SIDE DISH

Make sure to use plantains that are very ripe and black.

- 3 cups vegetable oil
- 5 very ripe black plantains (8½ ounces each), peeled and sliced on bias into ½-inch pieces
- Kosher salt

Heat oil in medium saucepan over medium-high heat until it registers 350 degrees. Carefully add one-third of plantains and cook until dark brown on both sides, 3 to 5 minutes, stirring occasionally with a wire skimmer or slotted spoon. Using wire skimmer or slotted spoon, transfer plantains to wire rack set in rimmed baking sheet. (Do not place plantains on paper towel or they will stick.) Season liberally with salt. Repeat with remaining plantains in two more batches. Serve immediately.

Bringing Home Mu Shu Pork

Making the thin, stretchy pancakes that are the hallmark of this Chinese restaurant classic requires two unusual techniques—but the result is the easiest-ever dough to work with.

⋟ BY ANDREA GEARY ⋞

I'm happy to eat just about any pork stir-fry at a Chinese restaurant, but *mu shu* pork has always been my favorite, thanks to the dish's most unique element: the Mandarin pancakes. Elastic but tender and paper-thin, these wheat rounds are the ideal utensil for wrapping up the stir-fried mix of soy- and ginger-flavored pork, delicately crisp-tender shredded vegetables, and scrambled eggs. A smear of salty-sweet hoisin sauce on the pancakes gives the stir-fry a bit more purchase and bolsters its flavor.

As often as I order mu shu pork in restaurants, though, I've always hesitated to make it at home because I figured that the pancakes might be troublesome. But my skepticism turned to curiosity when I consulted a few recipes: The pancakes contained just three ingredients—water, flour, and sesame oil—and came together in less than an hour (including a half-hour of hands-off time for the dough to rest). I could definitely manage that and looked forward to unlocking the secrets of the pancakes' intriguing texture.

To give the filling pleasantly chewy texture and savory depth, we include dried shiitake mushrooms as well as their umami-rich soaking liquid.

A Balanced Meal

The stir-fry would be a simple affair, and I stuck pretty closely to the lead of most recipes I found. I cut a pork tenderloin (its supple texture is ideal in stir-fries) into thin strips and tossed them with soy sauce, dry sherry (a widely available substitute for more traditional Chinese rice wine), and fresh ginger. I also used the same liquids (thickened with a touch of cornstarch) to whisk up a sauce. While the meat marinated, I scrambled a couple of eggs in a large, oiled nonstick skillet until they were just shy of cooked through (they'd finish cooking when I added them back to the skillet with the sauce) and then set them aside while I stir-fried the pork, spreading the strips in a flat layer so that they would brown nicely. Beyond that, it was simply a matter of stir-frying the vegetables, adding the sauce, and then returning the proteins to the pan to warm through.

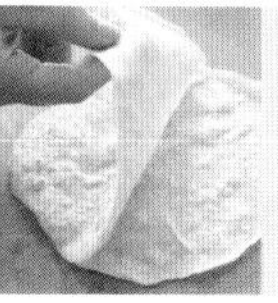

See How Easy It Is
Video available free for 4 months at CooksIllustrated.com/apr15

For the vegetables, authentic recipes called for just wood ear mushrooms and dried lily buds—and while my tasters and I enjoyed their pleasantly resilient chew, we found the mixture rather Spartan. (I later learned that mu shu pork is traditionally just one part of a banquet meal in which other dishes contribute the vegetable quota.) Both ingredients were also hard to come by, so I replaced them with dried shiitakes (rehydrated in hot water) and canned bamboo shoots. I also worked in shredded green cabbage and thin-sliced scallion whites.

The meat was moist and the vegetables crisp-tender, but the soy-sherry mixture lacked depth—and I wasn't convinced that a smear of hoisin on the pancakes would do enough to perk it up. So I made a few adjustments: In addition to seasoning the sauce with sugar and white pepper (which offers cleaner, more delicate heat than black pepper), I reserved and stirred in the umami-rich shiitake soaking liquid. Finally, I got the scallion whites good and brown in the pan to tease out more flavor. Those fixes produced a stir-fry that was good enough to eat on its own—but I still had the most important element to tend to.

Wrap It Up

The traditional method for making Mandarin pancakes is to combine flour with boiling water, knead the dough, and let it rest for about 30 minutes—not an inconvenience since I could prep the stir-fry ingredients. The next step is to shape small disks, sandwich pairs of those disks together with sesame oil, and roll out the sandwiched disks really thin. Finally, when the double pancakes are cooked on each side in a hot, dry skillet, something sort of magical happens: Water in the dough turns into steam, which makes the two layers of dough easy to pull apart into paper-thin pancakes.

Even though I had doubts about the dough at first—it felt dry initially, then tackier, and finally smooth after it rested—my results were flawless. But I had questions: For one, must the water be boiling hot or could it be cool? And was there more to sandwiching the dough than just the efficiency of rolling and cooking two pancakes at once?

I had a preliminary answer to my first query when I made a new batch of dough with cool water—and found it unmanageably sticky. Kneading and then resting the dough helps give the starches time to absorb the water. And from the Play-Doh-like smoothness of the hot-water dough, I could tell that the water had been soaked up. But the tackiness of this batch suggested that the cool water wasn't being readily absorbed. I did some digging and discovered that starch soaks up hot water faster than it does cool water. Hot water also produces dough that's easier to roll out because it makes the network of proteins that give the dough structure, known as gluten, looser and thus less prone to snapping back. (For more, see "What Hot Water Does to Dough.")

As for sandwiching the pancakes, I tried rolling

No Substitutions

Don't be tempted to substitute tortillas or other wrappers for homemade Mandarin pancakes; there is no replacement for their thin, delicate, stretchy texture. Plus, the pancakes can be made well in advance and refrigerated or frozen.

out individual rounds instead of double ones. The first problem: By the time they were appropriately thin, the wrappers were too delicate to pull off the counter. What's more, when I cooked each pancake on both sides, the dough dried out and lost a bit of the supple stretch it has when one side doesn't directly touch the heat.

Satisfied that I understood the mechanics of Mandarin pancakes, I prepared one last batch for a make-ahead test. Both the refrigerated and frozen pancakes revived nicely in the microwave, which meant that I could count on mu shu pork when I needed to throw together a quick weeknight stir-fry.

MU SHU PORK

SERVES 4

We strongly recommend weighing the flour for the pancakes. For an accurate measurement of boiling water, bring a full kettle to a boil and then measure ¾ cup. For tips on slicing cabbage, see page 31.

Pancakes

- 1½ cups (7½ ounces) all-purpose flour
- ¾ cup boiling water
- 2 teaspoons toasted sesame oil
- ½ teaspoon vegetable oil

Stir-Fry

- 1 ounce dried shiitake mushrooms, rinsed
- ¼ cup soy sauce
- 2 tablespoons dry sherry
- 1 teaspoon sugar
- 1 teaspoon grated fresh ginger
- ¼ teaspoon white pepper
- 1 (12-ounce) pork tenderloin, trimmed, halved horizontally, and sliced thin against grain
- 2 teaspoons cornstarch
- 2 tablespoons plus 2 teaspoons vegetable oil
- 2 eggs, beaten
- 6 scallions, white and green parts separated and sliced thin on bias
- 1 (8-ounce) can bamboo shoots, rinsed and sliced into matchsticks
- 3 cups thinly sliced green cabbage
- ¼ cup hoisin sauce

1. FOR THE PANCAKES: Using wooden spoon, mix flour and boiling water in bowl to form rough dough. When cool, transfer dough to lightly floured surface and knead until it forms ball that is tacky but no longer sticky, about 4 minutes (dough will not be perfectly smooth). Cover loosely with plastic wrap and let rest for 30 minutes.

2. Roll dough into 12-inch-long log on lightly floured surface and cut into 12 equal pieces. Turn each piece cut side up and pat into rough 3-inch disk. Brush 1 side of 6 disks with sesame oil; top each oiled side with unoiled disk and press lightly to form 6 pairs. Roll disks into 7-inch rounds, lightly flouring work surface as needed.

3. Heat vegetable oil in 12-inch nonstick skillet over medium heat until shimmering. Using paper towels, carefully wipe out oil. Place pancake in skillet and cook without moving it until air pockets begin to form between layers and underside is dry, 40 to 60 seconds. Flip pancake and cook until few light brown spots appear on second side, 40 to 60 seconds. Transfer to plate and, when cool enough to handle, peel apart into 2 pancakes. Stack pancakes moist side up and cover loosely with plastic. Repeat with remaining pancakes. Cover pancakes tightly and keep warm. Wipe out skillet with paper towel. (Pancakes can be wrapped tightly in plastic wrap, then aluminum foil, and refrigerated for up to 3 days or frozen for up to 2 months. Thaw wrapped pancakes at room temperature. Unwrap and place on plate. Invert second plate over pancakes and microwave until warm and soft, 60 to 90 seconds.)

4. FOR THE STIR-FRY: Microwave 1 cup water and mushrooms in covered bowl until steaming, about 1 minute. Let sit until softened, about 5 minutes. Drain mushrooms through fine-mesh strainer and reserve ⅓ cup liquid. Discard mushroom stems and slice caps thin.

5. Combine 2 tablespoons soy sauce, 1 tablespoon sherry, sugar, ginger, and pepper in large bowl. Add pork and toss to combine. Whisk together reserved mushroom liquid, remaining 2 tablespoons soy sauce, remaining 1 tablespoon sherry, and cornstarch; set aside.

6. Heat 2 teaspoons oil in now-empty skillet over medium-high heat until shimmering. Add eggs and scramble quickly until set but not dry, about 15 seconds. Transfer to bowl and break eggs into ¼- to ½-inch pieces with fork. Return now-empty skillet to medium-high heat and heat 1 tablespoon oil until shimmering. Add scallion whites and cook, stirring frequently, until well browned, 1 to 1½ minutes. Add pork mixture. Spread into even layer and cook without moving it until well browned on 1 side, 1 to 2 minutes. Stir and continue to cook, stirring frequently, until all pork is opaque, 1 to 2 minutes longer. Transfer to bowl with eggs.

7. Return now-empty skillet to medium-high heat and heat remaining 1 tablespoon oil until shimmering. Whisk mushroom liquid mixture to recombine. Add mushrooms and bamboo shoots to skillet and cook, stirring frequently, until heated through, about 1 minute. Add cabbage, all but 2 tablespoons scallion greens, and mushroom liquid mixture and cook, stirring constantly, until liquid has evaporated and cabbage is wilted but retains some crunch, 2 to 3 minutes. Add pork and eggs and stir to combine. Transfer to platter and top with scallion greens.

8. Spread about ½ teaspoon hoisin in center of each warm pancake. Spoon stir-fry over hoisin and serve.

SCIENCE What Hot Water Does to Dough

Most lean Western doughs, such as for pizza and rustic breads, are made with cold water primarily because the yeast they contain would die if exposed to hot water. But unyeasted Mandarin pancake dough calls for hot water, which eliminates two problems that plague most cold-water doughs: stickiness and springback.

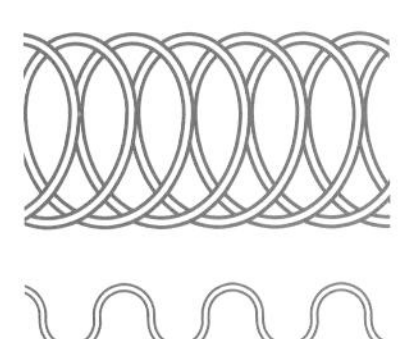

NOT SO WOUND UP
Hot water straightens the tightly coiled gluten proteins, making the dough easier to roll out.

Hot water makes the dough less sticky because it separates the tightly packed starch molecules faster than cold water does, allowing the starch to absorb the free water that would otherwise make the dough tacky.

Hot water also makes the dough easy to roll out because it straightens some of the coiled sections of gluten (the network of proteins that give dough structure). As a result, the dough is less elastic and less prone to snapping back. At the same time, the straightened proteins can move closer together and form tighter bonds, creating a stronger gluten network that allows the dough to be rolled out paper-thin without tearing and makes the pancakes stretchy.

PANCAKES MADE TWO BY TWO

Cooking two rounds together produces pancakes twice as fast.

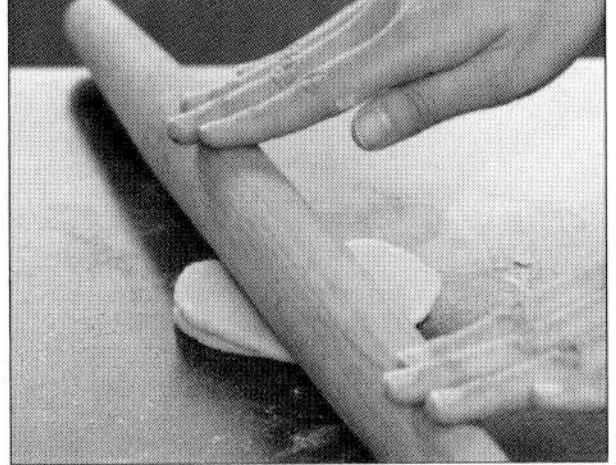

SANDWICH
Brush 6 disks with sesame oil. Top with unoiled disks. Press pairs together, then roll into thin rounds.

COOK
Heat each round until air pockets form between layers and underside is dry. Flip and cook second side.

PULL APART
When pancakes are cool enough to handle, peel apart into 2 pieces.

The Gooey Secrets of Melting Cheese

After making countless grilled cheese sandwiches, cheeseburgers, casseroles, and pizzas, we've learned a few tricks about how to melt cheese perfectly. BY ELIZABETH BOMZE

Whether it's oozing from a grilled cheese or a quesadilla, stretching from a slice of pizza, or making a pasta casserole rich and gooey, melted cheese has universal appeal. Plus, melted cheese has an ultrasavory umami quality that makes its flavor as addictive as its texture.

But achieving that perfect stretch or creaminess is harder than it looks—and too often the result is a greasy, stringy, clumpy mess. By understanding the way a cheese melts and how to manipulate it, you can produce perfect results every time.

HOW CHEESE MELTS—OR DOESN'T

All cheeses can be categorized into two groups based on how they are coagulated: with acid (such as vinegar or lemon juice) or with an enzyme known as rennet (which can be animal- or plant-derived).

Acid-coagulated cheeses (such as feta, ricotta, and fresh goat cheese) resist melting because the acid dissolves the calcium ions between the casein proteins and alters their electrical charge, both of which cause the proteins to link up tightly and clump. Heat then makes the proteins bond together even more tightly, which squeezes out the water and causes the cheese to dry out and stiffen.

Rennet-coagulated cheeses (such as cheddar, Monterey Jack, and mozzarella) melt in two stages: First, their fat globules change from solid to liquid, which makes the cheese more supple. Then, as the temperature continues to rise, the tightly bonded casein proteins loosen their grip on one another and the cheese flows like a thick liquid.

THREE TYPES OF MELTERS

GREAT MELTERS

Younger, moister cheeses contribute relatively mild flavor but melt beautifully on pizza and burgers and in grilled cheese, macaroni and cheese, lasagna, and enchiladas.

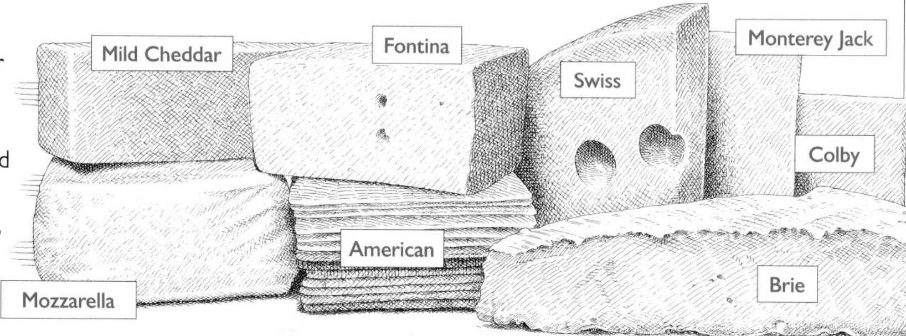

POOR MELTERS

Aged cheeses lend strong flavor to pasta casseroles, gratins, omelets, sandwiches, and sauces but must be paired with younger, moister cheeses or stabilizers like starch or fat to make them melt without "breaking."

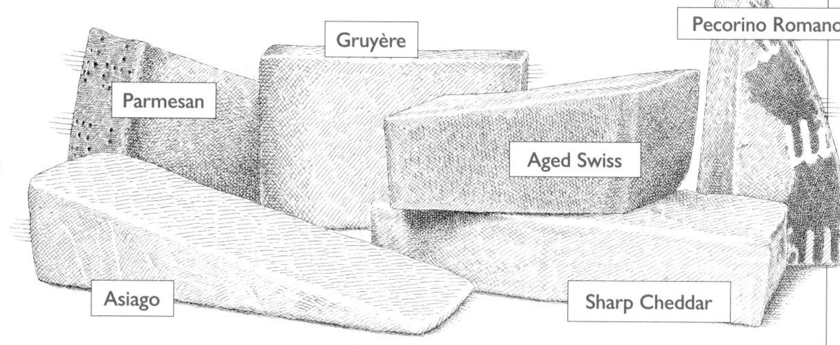

NONMELTERS

We use these acid-coagulated cheeses, which resist melting, as last-minute additions to pastas, salads, and crostini.

CHEESE STORAGE

The key to keeping cheese fresh for as long as possible is controlling moisture loss. If moisture evaporates too quickly, the cheese dries out; if it's trapped on the surface, it encourages mold. To find the best storage methods, we wrapped cheddar and Brie in a variety of materials and refrigerated them for one month, monitoring them for mold and dryness. We came away with the following recommendations.

In the Fridge: Allow Some Air

➢ Formaticum Cheese Paper and Bags

($9 for 15 sheets or bags): This wax-coated material lined with porous plastic kept cheeses mold-free for three weeks and can be reused.

➢ Parchment and Aluminum Foil

Wrapping cheese tightly in parchment (or waxed) paper and then loosely with aluminum foil mimics the two-ply construction of specialty cheese wraps; the paper wicks away moisture, while the foil traps just enough to keep the cheese from drying out.

In the Freezer: Airtight Only

Conventional wisdom holds that cheese should never be frozen—but we found that almost any variety can be frozen for up to two months with no decline in quality. The trick is to wrap the cheese tightly in plastic wrap and then seal it in a zipper-lock bag (vacuum sealing is also a good option). Thaw it overnight in the fridge or for a few hours on the counter.

How to Make Flavorful Cheeses Melt Well

We like to cook with aged cheeses because they offer stronger flavor, but they often melt poorly. This is because cheese loses moisture as it ages, so its proteins become more concentrated and cling together more tightly than those in younger cheeses. Heating makes the proteins loosen their grip on one another only slightly so they flow (i.e., melt) less readily and are more prone to recombining, leaving behind a gritty texture and pools of fat. To get the best flavor and texture, we turn to the following tricks.

Add a Moist Cheese

When we're making grilled cheese, baked pasta casseroles like macaroni and cheese, and fondue, we supplement flavorful aged cheeses like sharp cheddar and Gruyère with moister varieties like Monterey Jack, fontina, and even Brie, which helps the mixture melt smoothly. For pasta casseroles, a 50/50 ratio of aged-to-moist cheeses works well; for grilled cheese, increase the amount of aged cheese to between 75 and 80 percent.

Grate Fine

Smaller, finer shreds of hard cheeses like Parmesan will disperse more evenly throughout the dish than coarser shreds will and, thus, help stave off clumping. For thinner shreds, use a rasp-style grater or the fine holes of a box grater.

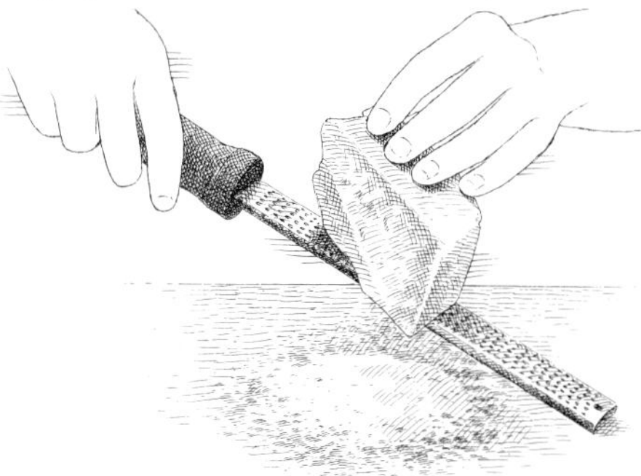

Add Dairy

Adding a couple of tablespoons of cream to a sauce made with aged cheese, as we do in our recipe for Spaghetti with Pecorino Romano and Black Pepper, can help keep it smooth. The cream contains molecules called lipoproteins that allow it to act as an emulsifier, keeping the fat and proteins together.

Add Starch

We toss shredded cheese for fondue with cornstarch (2 tablespoons for every pound of shredded cheese) and purposely cook pasta in a reduced amount of water to make a starch-concentrated liquid base for our spaghetti carbonara cheese sauce. The starch granules release threads of amylose, which bind to the cheese's casein proteins and prevent them from squeezing out fat and recombining into gritty curds.

For our free recipes for Grown-Up Grilled Cheese with Gruyère and Chives, Classic Macaroni and Cheese, Spaghetti alla Carbonara, and Spaghetti with Pecorino Romano and Black Pepper, go to **CooksIllustrated.com**; for our free recipe for Cheese Fondue from our sibling publication, *Cook's Country*, go to **CooksCountry.com/fondue**.

A Shred of Advice

Semifirm cheeses like cheddar, Monterey Jack, and mozzarella often smear, break apart, and clog the holes when shredding. Here's our three-part fix:

1. Freeze cheese for 30 minutes before grating to keep it firm while grating.
2. Use the large holes of a grater to prevent clumping.
3. Coat the face of the grater with nonstick cooking spray to prevent sticking.

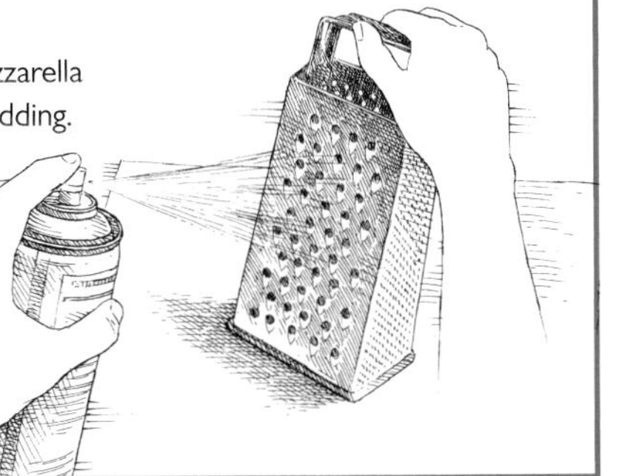

What Makes Mozzarella So Stretchy?

When melted, mozzarella has a distinctive, taffy-like elasticity that few other cheeses can match. This quality is due to its pH during processing: Mozzarella is less acidic than cheeses like cheddar or Monterey Jack, which allows it to retain more calcium—the "glue" that holds proteins in cheese together. More calcium means a more stable protein structure that's less prone to breaking apart when heated. What's more, when milk curds are stretched and pulled to make mozzarella, this stability allows its proteins to line up in a straight, uniform fashion (if you look closely, you can see a fine ribbed pattern in the cheese). When enough heat is applied, the strands loosen and flow in the same direction. Because cheeses like cheddar and Monterey Jack are more acidic during processing, they have less calcium. Their proteins are thus held together more loosely, and when heated, they flow in all directions, resulting in an amorphous mass.

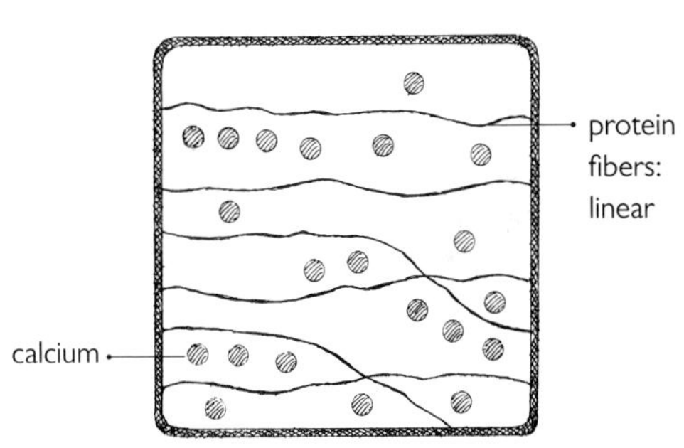

MOZZARELLA

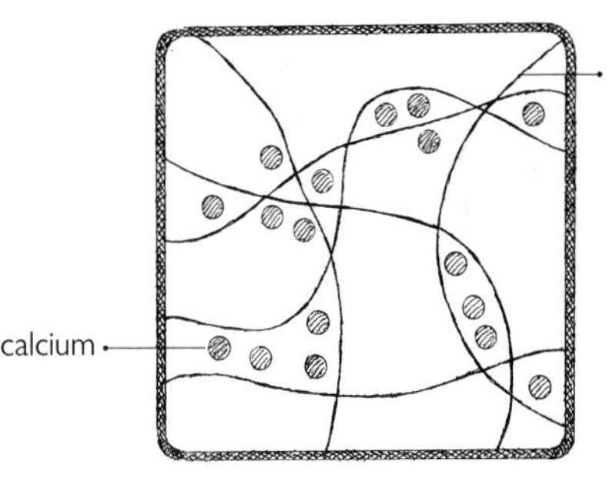

CHEDDAR

Don't Substitute Fresh for Block

While mozzarella in general stretches better than other cheeses, block mozzarella stretches much better than the fresh kind—so substituting one for the other is not a good idea. Why the difference? Again, the acidity during processing plays a critical role, as the pH of block mozzarella makes it ideal for stretching. It's basic enough that it doesn't lose calcium, so its proteins can flow and stretch. Meanwhile, fresh mozzarella is even less acidic, so its protein structure is even more stable and tight and less able to stretch; it's also processed at higher temperatures, which further stabilizes its structure. Another boon for block-style mozzarella: It bubbles and browns better than the fresh kind because it contains as much as 15 percent less moisture.

Pasta with Prosciutto and Peas

An ingredient from Switzerland—not Italy—takes this classic to a new level.

⋟ BY DAN SOUZA ⋞

The best Italian cooks source ingredients at their peak and then do only what is necessary to highlight them. One dish that exemplifies this ethos is *paglia e fieno* (straw and hay): ribbons of handmade egg and spinach pastas adorned with rich, nutty prosciutto and fresh sweet peas, bound with cream and bolstered with Parmesan. In Italy, during the height of pea season, cooks have easy access to all these ingredients and can follow the recipe to the letter. Bringing the dish to the American kitchen would mean breaking a few rules.

I started by doing a little ingredient sourcing of my own. The test kitchen has found that a good substitute for fresh pasta is dried egg pasta in a long ribbon shape like tagliatelle. While I'd be giving up the dramatic visual of green and pale yellow strands, I was willing to choose convenience over appearance for a weeknight recipe. As for fresh peas, even in early spring it can be difficult to catch them before they deteriorate from sweet to starchy. Luckily, frozen petite peas are consistently sweet; they would be my go-to choice. Since I'd be taking some shortcuts with the pasta and peas, I wanted to make the most of the star ingredients, imported prosciutto di Parma and Parmigiano-Reggiano, or Parmesan. Fortunately, both are easy to track down in the United States.

Recipes for paglia e fieno are remarkably similar: Boil the pasta until al dente. Meanwhile, soften a minced shallot in butter, add heavy cream, and then simmer prosciutto, minced or cut into strips, in the cream. Finally, combine the drained pasta with the sauce, add the Parmesan and peas, and ladle in some starchy pasta cooking water to bring it all together.

This method was dead simple, but whenever I cooked the prosciutto for more than a few seconds, its flavor changed dramatically. Why? The answer has to do with what we experience on our tongue versus in our nose. Our tastebuds register five tastes: salty, bitter, sour, sweet, and umami. Prosciutto is salty, a bit sweet, slightly sour, and rich in umami. The salt, sugars, acids, and glutamate responsible for these tastes are stable, so they stay put during cooking.

Then there's aroma, experienced through our noses. Aroma deeply affects how we perceive food, but aroma compounds are highly volatile and

Watch How It's Done
Video available free for 4 months at CooksIllustrated.com/apr15

We add strips of uncooked prosciutto at the end to preserve its delicate taste and silky texture.

therefore quickly escape during cooking. The aroma compounds that sensory panels have related to prosciutto include hazelnuts, almonds, strawberry, melon, cheese, and mushrooms, among others.

Now that I was armed with this information, the right approach seemed crystal clear. I'd simmer some minced prosciutto in cream to provide meaty depth and then finish with raw strips to retain the ham's impressive aromatic complexity. I gave it a shot, and, sure enough, I'd assembled the best of both worlds: a background salty/umami flavor of cooked prosciutto combined with the unique fruity, nutty fragrance of raw. Another benefit: This approach preserved the trademark silky texture of the raw ham.

This was all well and good, but I couldn't shake the feeling that I'd left my job unfinished by not examining the cheese. Was Parmesan the best choice?

Recent research has shown that there is much aromatic crossover between prosciutto and Parmesan, which explains why the pairing is so powerful and complementary. Digging deeper, I compared the most prevalent aroma compounds in prosciutto, Parmesan, and a number of other aged cheeses. It turned out that aged Gruyère—a cheese that is especially meaty- and fruity-tasting—contains two important compounds present in prosciutto but not in Parmesan: methanethiol, which aroma experts describe as meaty, fishy, and cheesy, and ethyl 2-methylbutyrate, which provides fruity apple- and strawberry-like scents.

Could incorporating some Gruyère in my recipe boost the flavor of the prosciutto? To put the science to the test, I mixed up batches of pasta with different ratios of the Parmesan and Gruyère. I was amazed when tasters agreed that 50 percent Parmesan and 50 percent aged Gruyère made the prosciutto taste, well, more like prosciutto. I had bucked Italian tradition with the help of aroma science, making the dish better than ever. After grinding in a bit of pepper for depth, I had nothing left to do—besides eat, that is.

TAGLIATELLE WITH PROSCIUTTO AND PEAS

SERVES 4 TO 6

We prefer imported prosciutto di Parma sliced 1/16 inch thick or domestically made prepackaged Volpi Traditional Prosciutto. Look for a hard Gruyère that is aged for at least 10 months. Pappardelle can be substituted for the tagliatelle. For our free recipe for Tagliatelle with Prosciutto and Peas for Two, go to CooksIllustrated.com/apr15.

- 6 ounces thinly sliced prosciutto
- 1 tablespoon unsalted butter
- 1 shallot, minced
- Salt and pepper
- 1 cup heavy cream
- 1 pound tagliatelle
- 1 1/2 cups frozen petite peas, thawed
- 1 ounce Parmesan cheese, grated (1/2 cup)
- 1 ounce Gruyère cheese, grated (1/2 cup)

1. Slice 5 ounces prosciutto crosswise into 1/4-inch-wide strips; set aside. Mince remaining 1 ounce prosciutto. Melt butter in 10-inch skillet over medium-low heat. Add shallot and 1/4 teaspoon salt and cook until softened, about 2 minutes. Stir in cream and minced prosciutto and bring to simmer. Cook, stirring occasionally, until cream mixture measures 1 cup, 5 to 7 minutes. Remove pan from heat and cover to keep warm.

2. Meanwhile, bring 4 quarts water to boil in large pot. Add pasta and 1 tablespoon salt and cook, stirring often, until al dente. Reserve 2 cups cooking water, then drain pasta and return it to pot.

3. Add 1 cup reserved cooking water, cream mixture, prosciutto strips, peas, Parmesan, Gruyère, and 1 teaspoon pepper to pasta. Gently toss until pasta is well coated. Transfer pasta to serving bowl and serve immediately, adjusting consistency with remaining reserved cooking water as needed.

Updated Cabbage Side Dishes

Brussels sprouts got an image makeover. Shouldn't cabbage get one, too?

⋟ BY SANDRA WU ⋞

Poor cabbage. Alternately viewed as a pauper's vegetable or a dieter's frenemy, cabbage can become overbearing, limp, and smelly when cooked. But this humble vegetable has loads of potential—if it is treated properly. I wanted to restore cabbage's reputation by highlighting its mild sweetness and maintaining a crisp-tender texture, all the while avoiding objectionable flavors and odors.

The trouble begins with cabbage's pungent-tasting sulfur compounds called isothiocyanates. Cooking can temper their taste, but it's possible to go overboard: The longer cabbage is cooked, the more odoriferous compounds—including hydrogen sulfide (typical of rotten eggs) and ammonia—are produced.

To avoid such aromas and flavors, then, it would be necessary to cook the vegetable as rapidly as possible. I also knew another tip: Immerse the cut cabbage in water to draw out the pungent sulfur compounds. Putting both tricks to work, I soaked sliced cabbage for various amounts of time, drained it, and then quickly sautéed it and compared it with unsoaked samples. Great news: A mere 3-minute soak, along with swift cooking, produced a noticeable reduction in unwanted flavors.

But all was not perfect: Cooked uncovered over medium-high heat, the cabbage lightly caramelized in some areas, adding nuttiness, but only some slices emerged tender while others were downright crunchy. Conversely, when I cooked the cabbage covered over lower heat, it emerged uniformly tender and sweet, yet slightly soggy and missing the depth provided by browning.

What if I used a hybrid method—starting with the lid on to create steam (generated by the moisture clinging to the cabbage after soaking) and then uncovering the pan to evaporate liquid and encourage browning? Sure enough, this cabbage was crisp-tender, with plenty of sweetness and nuttiness.

To turn the cabbage into a bona fide side dish, I added sautéed onions for depth, plus fresh parsley and lemon juice for vibrancy. For variations, I employed the same straightforward method and mixed in bold ingredients along with different herbs, spices, and acids to sway the dish toward a particular profile.

Look: Cabbage Is a Star
Video available free for 4 months at CooksIllustrated.com/apr15

Our 3-minute trick transforms the flavor of cabbage.

SAUTÉED CABBAGE WITH PARSLEY AND LEMON

SERVES 4 TO 6

For tips on slicing cabbage, see page 31. For our free recipe for Sautéed Cabbage with Miso and Scallions, go to CooksIllustrated.com/apr15.

- 1 small head green cabbage (1¼ pounds), cored and sliced thin
- 2 tablespoons vegetable oil
- 1 onion, halved and sliced thin
- Salt and pepper
- ¼ cup chopped fresh parsley
- 1½ teaspoons lemon juice

1. Place cabbage in large bowl and cover with cold water; let stand for 3 minutes. Drain well and set aside. Meanwhile, heat 1 tablespoon oil in 12-inch nonstick skillet over medium-high heat until shimmering. Add onion and ¼ teaspoon salt and cook, stirring occasionally, until softened and lightly browned, 6 to 7 minutes. Transfer onion to bowl.

2. Return now-empty skillet to medium-high heat, add remaining 1 tablespoon oil and heat until shimmering. Add cabbage and sprinkle with ½ teaspoon salt and ¼ teaspoon pepper. Cover and cook, without stirring, until cabbage is wilted and lightly browned on bottom, about 3 minutes.

3. Stir and continue to cook, uncovered, until cabbage is crisp-tender and lightly browned in places, about 4 minutes longer, stirring once halfway through cooking. Remove skillet from heat. Stir in onion, parsley, and lemon juice. Season with salt and pepper to taste, transfer to serving bowl, and serve.

SAUTÉED CABBAGE WITH BACON AND CARAWAY SEEDS

Substitute red cabbage for green. Whisk 1 tablespoon cider vinegar and 2 teaspoons packed brown sugar together in medium bowl. Omit oil. Cook 4 slices chopped bacon in skillet over medium-high heat until crisp, 5 to 7 minutes. Transfer bacon to paper towel–lined plate and pour off all but 1 tablespoon fat into bowl (reserve fat). Substitute red onion for onion and cook in fat in skillet until almost tender, 5 to 6 minutes. Add 1 teaspoon caraway seeds and cook for 1 minute. Transfer to bowl with vinegar mixture. Cook cabbage in 1 tablespoon reserved fat. Stir bacon into cabbage with onion mixture before serving.

SAUTÉED CABBAGE WITH CHILE AND PEANUTS

Substitute red onion for onion. Cook 1 thinly sliced jalapeño, seeds reserved (optional), with onion in step 1. Once onion is crisp-tender, about 4 minutes, add 2 garlic cloves, minced to paste, and continue to cook until fragrant, about 30 seconds. Substitute 4 teaspoons fish sauce and 2 teaspoons packed brown sugar for salt and pepper in step 2. Substitute ½ cup chopped fresh cilantro for parsley and 1 tablespoon lime juice for lemon juice. Add reserved jalapeño seeds, if desired. Sprinkle cabbage with 2 tablespoons chopped dry-roasted peanuts before serving.

SAUTÉED CABBAGE WITH FENNEL AND GARLIC

Substitute savoy cabbage for green. Substitute extra-virgin olive oil for vegetable oil and 1 fennel bulb, fronds minced, stalks discarded, bulb halved, cored, and sliced thin, for onion. Cook fennel bulb until softened, 8 to 10 minutes, then add 2 garlic cloves, minced to paste, and ¼ teaspoon red pepper flakes and continue to cook until fragrant, about 30 seconds. Omit pepper. Substitute fennel fronds for parsley and increase lemon juice to 2 teaspoons. Drizzle cabbage with 1 tablespoon extra-virgin olive oil and sprinkle with 2 tablespoons grated Parmesan before serving.

Quick Sauces for Sautéed Chicken

We wanted sauces that would be ready at the same time as the chicken.

BY KEITH DRESSER

Pan sauces based on the fond left behind after sautéing bone-in chicken are great. But when sautéing chicken cutlets made from boneless, skinless breasts, the process is so quick that it creates very little fond from which to build a sauce. I wanted sauce options that would offer bold flavors and interesting textures without depending on fond. I also wanted to be able to make them before the chicken hit the pan.

With this in mind, I tried a handful of speedy recipes, including vinaigrettes, mayonnaises, raw salsa-like toppings, and purees like pesto and romesco. The oil in the vinaigrette and mayonnaise added plenty of flavor and fatty richness, but these smooth sauces fell short in the texture department. Conversely, the bright-tasting salsas added pleasant crunch but were too lean. But tasters roundly praised the romesco-style sauce, a thick, coarse Spanish concoction of roasted red peppers, toasted hazelnuts, bread, sherry vinegar, olive oil, smoked paprika, and garlic that I whizzed in a food processor.

This sauce worked well to enliven the mild-tasting breast meat for a number of reasons: The roasted red peppers and paprika provided a sweet smokiness, the sherry vinegar gave it an acidic punch, and the underpinning of nuts and bread lent texture and body, as well as brought all the other ingredients together. Most romesco-style recipes call for first toasting the nuts and cubed bread in oil to enhance their flavor and add even more richness, and I followed suit. I also found that a teaspoon of honey added with the remaining ingredients helped bring all the flavors into focus.

I then cast about for other combinations I could use to build similar sauces, restricting myself to ingredients that needed no cooking. After some experimenting, I came up with two more sauces, each based on bread and nuts (or seeds) along with a tangy ingredient and extra-virgin olive oil. The first featured fresh and sun-dried tomatoes, balsamic vinegar (which was sweet enough that I skipped the honey in this variation), and pine nuts. In the second, I paired tomatillos and jarred jalapeños with pepitas. I then went on to flavor the pairings with bold herbs or spices.

Each of these sauces came together in about 5 minutes. Besides offering robust flavor and a little bit of contrasting texture, they had one more advantage over pan sauces: I could prepare them in advance.

See the Sauces
Video available free for 4 months at CooksIllustrated.com/apr15

For our free recipes for Sautéed Chicken Cutlets and Sautéed Chicken Cutlets for Two, go to CooksIllustrated.com/apr15.

QUICK ROASTED RED PEPPER SAUCE

MAKES ABOUT 1 CUP

You will need at least a 12-ounce jar of roasted red peppers for this recipe. For our free recipe for Quick Olive-Orange Sauce, go to CooksIllustrated.com/apr15.

- ½ slice hearty white sandwich bread, cut into ½-inch pieces
- ¼ cup hazelnuts, toasted and skinned
- 2 tablespoons extra-virgin olive oil
- 2 garlic cloves, sliced thin
- 1 cup jarred roasted red peppers, rinsed and patted dry
- 1½ tablespoons sherry vinegar
- 1 teaspoon honey
- ½ teaspoon smoked paprika
- ½ teaspoon salt
- Pinch cayenne pepper

Heat bread, hazelnuts, and 1 tablespoon oil in 12-inch skillet over medium heat; cook, stirring constantly, until bread and hazelnuts are lightly toasted, 2½ to 3 minutes. Add garlic and cook, stirring constantly, until fragrant, about 30 seconds. Transfer bread mixture to food processor and pulse until coarsely chopped, about 5 pulses. Add red peppers, vinegar, honey, paprika, salt, cayenne, and remaining 1 tablespoon oil to processor. Pulse until finely chopped, 5 to 8 pulses. Transfer to bowl and let stand, at least 10 minutes. (Sauce can be prepared up to 2 days in advance and refrigerated in airtight container.)

QUICK SUN-DRIED TOMATO SAUCE

MAKES ABOUT 1 CUP

For the best taste and texture, make sure to rinse all the dried herbs off the sun-dried tomatoes.

- ½ slice hearty white sandwich bread, cut into ½-inch pieces
- ¼ cup pine nuts
- 2 tablespoons extra-virgin olive oil
- 2 garlic cloves, sliced thin
- 1 small tomato, cored and cut into ½-inch pieces
- ½ cup oil-packed sun-dried tomatoes, rinsed
- 2 tablespoons coarsely chopped fresh basil
- 2 tablespoons balsamic vinegar
- ½ teaspoon salt

Heat bread, pine nuts, and 1 tablespoon oil in 12-inch skillet over medium heat; cook, stirring constantly, until bread and pine nuts are lightly toasted, 2½ to 3 minutes. Add garlic and cook, stirring constantly, until fragrant, about 30 seconds. Transfer bread mixture to food processor and pulse until coarsely chopped, about 5 pulses. Add tomato, sun-dried tomatoes, basil, vinegar, salt, and remaining 1 tablespoon oil to processor. Pulse until finely chopped, 5 to 8 pulses. Transfer to bowl and let stand, at least 10 minutes. (Sauce can be prepared up to 2 days in advance and refrigerated in airtight container.)

QUICK TOMATILLO SAUCE

MAKES ABOUT 1 CUP

You will need at least a 15-ounce can of tomatillos for this recipe.

- ½ slice hearty white sandwich bread, cut into ½-inch pieces
- ¼ cup pepitas
- 2 tablespoons extra-virgin olive oil
- 2 garlic cloves, sliced thin
- 1 cup canned tomatillos, rinsed
- 2 tablespoons jarred sliced jalapeños plus 2 teaspoons brine
- 2 tablespoons fresh cilantro leaves
- 1 teaspoon honey
- ½ teaspoon salt

Heat bread, pepitas, and 1 tablespoon oil in 12-inch skillet over medium heat; cook, stirring constantly, until pepitas and bread are lightly toasted, 2½ to 3 minutes. Add garlic and cook, stirring constantly, until fragrant, about 30 seconds. Transfer bread mixture to food processor and pulse until coarsely chopped, about 5 pulses. Add tomatillos, jalapeños and brine, cilantro, honey, salt, and remaining 1 tablespoon oil to processor. Pulse until finely chopped, 5 to 8 pulses. Transfer to bowl and let stand, at least 10 minutes. (Sauce can be prepared up to 2 days in advance and refrigerated in airtight container.)

Modern Raspberry Charlotte

Cake surrounding creamy fruit mousse promises the best of old-world elegance. But it doesn't matter how gorgeous it looks if the filling is rubbery and the cake is tough.

⋟ BY ANDREA GEARY ⋞

When I first read about charlotte russe, a classic and stately 19th-century French dessert composed of a creamy fruit filling encased in cake (usually in the form of sponge cake piped into lady fingers), I thought it might be just the thing to infuse my repertoire of homey desserts with a bit of old-world elegance. But after I made some, I understood why so few cooks today make it. First, there were a lot of steps: I had to make the sponge cake, let it cool, and line the mold with it. Next I had to make a Bavarian cream for the filling—a multistep procedure involving a fruit puree, crème anglaise (a stovetop custard sauce), gelatin, and whipped cream. Then there's still filling, chilling, and unmolding.

After all that, the fillings were downright bouncy, having been shored up with enough gelatin to ensure that the dessert would survive unmolding and slicing. Plus, they didn't have much fruit flavor. Additionally, the sponge cake came off as lean, even a bit chewy, and in some cases it had structural issues, with filling seeping between the gaps.

Spreading a raspberry jam mixture over the cake before pouring in the fruit filling and then topping it off with a jam swirl brings maximum fruit flavor.

I knew that this dessert had a lot of showstopper potential, but I didn't want to sacrifice texture for presentation. To bring back charlotte russe, I'd have to make the filling and the cake tender enough to be pleasant to eat but sturdy enough for the dessert to hold its shape. I also wanted bright fruit flavor that stood up to the cream and cake. I wouldn't mind putting in some effort, but in order to be worth it, my charlotte was going to have to be a stunner.

Expunge the Sponge

Charlottes are made in various fruit flavors—citrus, berries, stone fruit—but I settled on raspberries because they would lend visual appeal and a nice sweet-tart flavor. A charlotte mold, a specialized tinned steel pan with tall, flared sides, is traditional, but I was happy to follow the lead of more modern recipes, which called for a springform pan. Using a mixture of sweetened raspberry puree, gelatin, and whipped cream as a temporary filling, I turned my focus to the cake.

I made my first charlotte with the simplest option, store-bought ladyfingers, but they turned soggy and fell apart. I then tried making my own, combining whipped egg whites and sugar with flour and a bit of salt and vanilla for a traditional sponge cake batter, which I then piped into ladyfingers, baked, and cooled. These were more structurally sound, though if the edges were not perfectly straight, the filling seeped between the gaps. They were also fussy to make, a bit chewy, and prone to drying out around the edges. I wondered if I could address all these issues at once by baking the batter in a baking sheet and then cutting it to fit the bottom and sides of my springform. Alas, while this cake was certainly easier to make, its texture hadn't improved. I realized that the key to the sponge cake's structural integrity was also the reason for its troublingly resilient texture. Without the tenderizing influence of fat, the whipped egg whites had formed a sturdy protein network—excellent for keeping the sides of the charlotte in place, but not for producing the tender cake my tasters and I preferred. Taking inspiration from trifle and tiramisù, I tried soaking the cakes with liqueur and flavored syrups, but they stuck to the pan.

Following a different tack, I mixed up my favorite tender, rich butter cake and gave that a go, but it was not to be. Though this cake usually bakes up soft and moist, it was firm, dry, and crumbly in this application. Why? All its butter stiffened up in the fridge, ruining its texture.

Then I had a brainstorm. I knew I needed a cake that contained egg whites for structure, but some fat for tenderness. What has those qualities? Chiffon cake. It uses an egg white foam for strength, but it also contains some egg yolks and fat for tenderness. And since the fat is vegetable oil, which doesn't solidify at cool temperatures, the cake would stay soft even when refrigerated.

Chiffon cake is usually baked in a tube pan, which has tall sides that support its delicate structure, but such recipes take a long time to bake and cool, plus they make more cake than I'd need. Fortunately, a

The Many Forms of Flawed Charlottes

While the components of tender sponge cake and creamy fruit filling were a constant in all the charlotte recipes we tried, how the two came together varied. In the end, all the traditional recipes that we tried looked quite different, yet they all had serious flaws.

DOESN'T BEAR FRUIT
Lacks fruit flavor.

ROLL ON BY
Requires ultrafussy jelly roll cake.

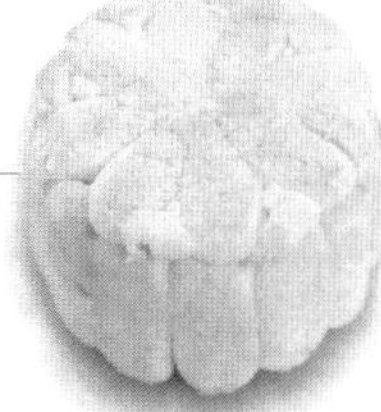

LEAK-PRONE
Filling seeps out.

RECIPE SHORTHAND Making Raspberry Charlotte

MAKE CURD
Prepare and strain raspberry curd. Set aside and stir occasionally.

PREPARE JAM MIXTURE
While curd cools, prepare jam and gelatin mixture and set aside.

BAKE CAKES
Bake cakes and let them cool completely.

PREPARE BASE AND SIDES
Spread cakes with jam, cut square cake into strips, and assemble in pan.

ADD FILLING
Whip cream and fold into curd; then pour filling into cake-lined pan.

SWIRL AND GARNISH
Drizzle remaining jam mixture over cake and swirl. Garnish with berries.

couple of years ago when I was developing a trifle recipe, I devised a modified chiffon cake that, with help from a little extra flour, had sufficient structure to be baked in a baking sheet. For my charlotte, I simply cut that recipe in half and baked 1 cup of batter in an 8-inch round cake pan and the rest in an 8-inch square pan. These shallow cakes took about 10 minutes to bake, and they cooled quickly.

I placed the cooled round cake in the bottom of my 9-inch springform pan, which left a ½-inch space between the cake and the sides of the pan. I then cut the square cake into four equal strips and tucked them, standing each on a narrow edge, between the round cake and the pan's sides. I had a bit of difficulty squeezing them in until I realized that I could simply loosen the clasp of the ring, put the cake strips in place, and then close the ring to cinch everything together snugly. A perfect fit.

However, I noticed an issue when I removed the ring. The bottom of the square cake—which was now facing outward as the sides—had browned, taking away from the assembled cake's elegant aesthetic. Putting the cake pans on a baking sheet insulated them as they baked and prevented browning on the bottom. Browning around the edges highlighted the seams, so I also trimmed the cake before assembly.

Giving the Bavarian the Boot

Making a Bavarian cream, the traditional filling for charlotte russe, is not for the fainthearted. First you make a crème anglaise, a cooked custard sauce. You add softened gelatin to that, let it cool to just the right degree, and then fold in whipped cream and either a fruit puree (that's more steps) or fruit-flavored liqueur.

Beyond the hassle of all these steps, the biggest problem is that crème anglaise is fairly fluid, and the fruit puree only loosens it further. So a Bavarian requires quite a lot of gelatin to firm up to a sliceable consistency—which in turn makes it bouncy. Perhaps I could come up with not only a simpler filling but one that also had more body to begin with so that I could get away with using less gelatin.

My placeholder filling was a reasonable and simple start, but without eggs, it lacked richness and depth. Why not make a fruit curd instead? Most people are familiar with lemon curd, an intensely flavored pudding made with lemon juice, sugar, butter, and egg yolks. But a curd can be made with almost any fruit, even raspberries, and it has a thicker, more set consistency that would allow me to use less gelatin. Plus, this was a great step toward streamlining; the curd would be doing the job of both the custard and the fruit puree in the Bavarian.

I whisked three egg yolks with 2 teaspoons of cornstarch in a bowl (the cornstarch would prevent the egg yolks from curdling when cooked) and set it aside. Then I cooked 1 pound of thawed frozen raspberries (they were just going to be mashed anyway, so this was a good place to economize) with ⅔ cup of sugar, 2 tablespoons of butter, and a pinch of salt in a saucepan over medium heat until the raspberries broke down. I stirred a bit of the raspberry mixture into the egg yolks to temper them and added the egg yolk mixture to the saucepan, cooking it until it was simmering and thickened. I strained the mixture into a bowl that held 1¼ teaspoons of unflavored gelatin (less than half what the traditional Bavarian filling required) that I had softened in water. After passing everything through a sieve to remove the raspberry seeds, I stirred my curd until the gelatin dissolved and set it aside to cool.

All that remained was to fold heavy cream that I had whipped to soft peaks into the gelatin-curd mixture. I poured the filling into my charlotte shell, smoothed the top, and placed it in the refrigerator to set.

This was a huge improvement. The springform ring came away easily from the base (though it was tricky to transfer the charlotte from the pan base to the platter). The cake and filling were tender, the dessert was sliceable but not overly gelled, and it had loads of raspberry flavor. Still, the overall visual effect was a bit austere.

Final Dressings

Some classic charlotte recipes call for garnishing the finished dessert with yet more whipped cream, but that struck me as too much of a good thing. Plus, the cream would only mute the fruit's flavor. Instead I thought of a way I could dress up my charlotte and bump up the raspberry flavor even more.

But first, a strategic improvement: For my next charlotte, I skipped the base of the springform pan altogether and put the ring directly on my serving platter. Why move the dessert if I didn't have to? Next, I mixed ½ cup of warm seedless raspberry jam with ½ teaspoon of gelatin that I had softened in lemon juice for extra brightness. I spread some of this jam onto the cakes before assembling the charlotte, and I swirled the remainder into the top of the filling. As a crowning touch, I arranged some fresh raspberries on the top of the charlotte before placing it in the fridge.

This charlotte met all my requirements. Its impressive appearance made it suitable for the most sophisticated of dessert tables, and its bright raspberry flavor, tender cake, and soft yet sliceable filling was sure to meet the demands of any 21st-century cook.

Bye-Bye Bounce

Traditionally, charlotte russe's filling is a Bavarian cream, in which a custard sauce known as crème anglaise gets combined with gelatin, whipped cream, and a fruit puree. The problem is that crème anglaise is so fluid that the filling requires a lot of gelatin to make it sliceable—which in turn creates an unappealing bouncy consistency. The solution? Instead of the usual crème anglaise as the main component of the filling, we turned to a fruit curd. The curd naturally has a more set—but not bouncy—consistency, so we were able to use less gelatin to get the necessary texture.

UH-OH: JELL-O
Most fillings are overloaded with gelatin, giving them an unappealing bouncy texture.

RASPBERRY CHARLOTTE

SERVES 12 TO 16

It is fine to use frozen raspberries in the filling. Thaw frozen berries completely before using and use any collected juices, too. It is important to measure the berries for the filling by weight. If you wish to garnish the top of the charlotte with berries, arrange 1 to 1½ cups fresh berries (depending on size) around the edge of the assembled charlotte before refrigerating. For clean, neat slices, dip your knife in hot water and wipe it dry before each slice.

Filling

- 1¼ teaspoons unflavored gelatin
- 2 tablespoons water
- 3 large egg yolks (reserve whites for cake)
- 2 teaspoons cornstarch
- 1 pound (3¼ cups) fresh or thawed frozen raspberries
- ⅔ cup (4⅔ ounces) sugar
- 2 tablespoons unsalted butter
- Pinch salt
- 1¾ cups heavy cream

Jam Mixture

- ½ teaspoon unflavored gelatin
- 1 tablespoon lemon juice
- ½ cup seedless raspberry jam

Cake

- ⅔ cup (2⅔ ounces) cake flour
- 6 tablespoons (2⅔ ounces) sugar
- ¾ teaspoon baking powder
- ⅛ teaspoon salt
- ¼ cup vegetable oil
- 1 large egg plus 3 large egg whites (reserved from filling)
- 2 tablespoons water
- 1 teaspoon vanilla extract
- ¼ teaspoon cream of tartar

1. FOR THE FILLING: Sprinkle gelatin over water in large bowl and set aside. Whisk egg yolks and cornstarch together in medium bowl until combined. Combine raspberries, sugar, butter, and salt in medium saucepan. Mash lightly with whisk and stir until no dry sugar remains. Cook over medium heat, whisking frequently, until mixture is simmering and raspberries are almost completely broken down, 4 to 6 minutes.

2. Remove raspberry mixture from heat and, whisking constantly, slowly add ½ cup raspberry mixture to yolk mixture to temper. Whisking constantly, return tempered yolk mixture to mixture in saucepan. Return saucepan to medium heat and cook, whisking constantly, until mixture thickens and bubbles, about 1 minute. Pour through fine-mesh strainer set over gelatin mixture and press on solids with back of ladle or rubber spatula until only seeds remain. Discard seeds and stir raspberry mixture until gelatin is dissolved. Set aside, stirring occasionally, until curd is slightly thickened and reaches room temperature, at least 30 minutes or up to 1 hour 15 minutes.

3. FOR THE JAM MIXTURE: Sprinkle gelatin over lemon juice in small bowl and let sit until gelatin softens, about 5 minutes. Heat jam in microwave, whisking occasionally, until hot and fluid, 30 to 60 seconds. Add softened gelatin to jam and whisk until dissolved. Set aside.

4. FOR THE CAKE: Adjust oven rack to upper-middle position and heat oven to 350 degrees. Lightly grease 8-inch round cake pan and 8-inch square baking pan, line with parchment paper, and lightly grease parchment. Whisk flour, sugar, baking powder, and salt together in medium bowl. Whisk oil, whole egg, water, and vanilla into flour mixture until smooth batter forms.

5. Using stand mixer fitted with whisk, whip egg whites and cream of tartar on medium-low speed until foamy, about 1 minute. Increase speed to medium-high and whip until soft peaks form, 2 to 3 minutes. Transfer one-third of egg whites to batter; whisk gently until mixture is lightened. Using rubber spatula, gently fold remaining egg whites into batter.

6. Pour 1 cup batter into round pan and spread evenly. Pour remaining batter into square pan and spread evenly. Place pans on rimmed baking sheet and bake until cakes spring back when pressed lightly in center and surface is no longer sticky, 8 to 11 minutes (round cake, which is shallower, will be done before square cake). Cakes should not brown.

7. Let cakes cool in pans on wire rack for 5 minutes. Invert round cake onto wire rack. Carefully remove parchment, then reinvert onto second wire rack. Repeat with square cake. Let cool completely, at least 15 minutes.

8. Place round cake in center of serving platter. Spread with 2 tablespoons jam mixture. Place ring from 9-inch springform pan around cake, leaving equal space on all sides. Leave clasp of ring slightly loose. Using sharp chef's knife, trim ⅛ inch off all edges of square cake. Spread square cake with 2 tablespoons jam mixture. Cut cake in half. Cut each half lengthwise into two pieces to make four equal-size long strips. Place cake strips vertically around round cake, jam side in, taking care to nestle ends together neatly. Fasten clasp of springform ring.

9. Using stand mixer fitted with whisk, whip cream on medium-low speed until foamy, about 1 minute. Increase speed to high and whip until soft peaks form, 1 to 2 minutes. Transfer one-third of whipped cream to curd; whisk gently until mixture is lightened. Using rubber spatula, gently fold in remaining cream until mixture is homogenous.

10. Pour filling into cake ring and spread evenly to edge. (Surface of filling will be above edge of cake.) Drizzle remaining jam mixture over surface of filling. Using knife, swirl jam through surface of filling, making marbled pattern. Refrigerate for at least 5 hours or up to 24 hours.

11. To unmold, run thin knife around edge of ring (just ½ inch down). Release ring and lift to remove. Let stand at room temperature for 20 minutes before slicing and serving.

Piece(s) of Cake

Surrounding a charlotte's creamy filling with sponge cake ladyfingers, as is often depicted in classic representations of this old-world dessert, certainly seems elegant. But in reality, the ladyfingers don't work that well—the filling seeps between the gaps, plus they taste lean and their texture is chewy. In our recipe, we swap the sponge for a more tender and rich chiffon cake. We bake part of it in a round cake pan and the rest in a square pan. The round cake serves as the base, while we cut the square cake into strips that fit snugly around its perimeter.

A SQUARE FOR THE SIDES
An 8-inch square cake is cut into four strips and used to line the sides of the pan.

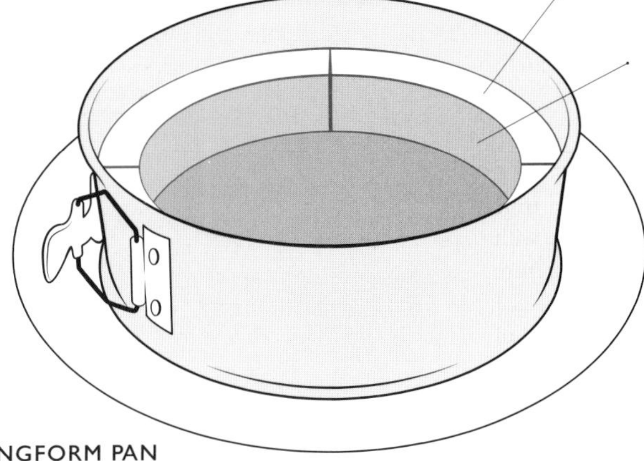

JAM ON THE INSIDE
A mixture of jam, gelatin, and lemon juice is spread onto the cakes before assembly.

SPRINGFORM PAN
The charlotte is constructed inside the ring of the springform pan, right on the serving platter.

A ROUND BASE
A thin 8-inch round cake serves as the bottom of our charlotte.

Watch a Charlotte Take Shape
Video available free for 4 months at CooksIllustrated.com/apr15

Spotting the Toughest Stain Remover

Stain removers abound, all guaranteeing spotless results on the first try. The reality? When it comes to getting out stubborn food stains, almost none of them work.

BY LISA McMANUS

Bacon sizzles and spits and your favorite shirt gets a grease spot. Frosting a cake, you find chocolate smeared on a sleeve. Food stains are all too commonplace in the kitchen, so we bought seven top-selling laundry stain removers and prepared to make a scientific mess with the goal of finding a reliable weapon against permanent stains. Label after label on the bottles vowed to "get stains out the first time!" and even offered "guaranteed" results. We wondered if we'd come away with a record number of winners. There was only one way to find out. Sets of white cotton T-shirts and yards of blue cotton fabric designed for button-down shirts (selected since natural fibers are more prone to stain than synthetics) would be our canvas. In the past, we found that many common laundry stain fighters had no trouble with coffee, red wine, and beet juice, so we focused on tougher stains. To each T-shirt and piece of blue fabric, we applied measured samples of six foods that make stubborn stains: melted dark chocolate, hot bacon fat, yellow mustard, black tea, a puree of chipotle chiles in adobo sauce, and pureed blueberries. (For more information, see "The Toughest Stain Sources We Could Find" at CooksIllustrated.com/apr15.) We would pit each stain remover against this array while noting its ease of use.

Promises, Promises

Most stain removers are applied in a similar way: Put the product on the spot, rub it in, wait briefly (each gives a specific wait time), and then launder. Two bottles featured built-in scrubbers to help the cleaner penetrate. Only one product worked completely differently: It's a powder that you dissolve in water to presoak the whole garment before laundering.

We wanted to see if we could get away with minimal effort. After applying the stains (and waiting 15 minutes to let them soak in), we applied our stain removers and soaked or waited the shortest time frame each product recommended. We did only light rubbing with our hands (or scrubby caps when included) and then washed in color-safe cold rather than warm or hot water (all the product directions make vague suggestions like "wash according to care label instructions in the warmest water recommended"). When labels suggested it, we added an extra capful of the product to the wash (throughout testing, we laundered using a measured amount of ordinary laundry detergent). As a control, we also laundered a stained T-shirt and piece of fabric with detergent alone, without treating the stains.

So much for guarantees—while a few products successfully removed the bacon grease, most of the stains were still clearly visible. One consolation: The untreated control shirt and fabric looked worse than any that we had treated—that is, except for the lowest-performing product in this test, which blended the six stains into one giant brownish blot and turned the white shirt a sickly yellow. Clearly, the least-effort approach wasn't enough. But two products stood out, lightening all the stains and completely erasing the tea and blueberries (one product also removed bacon grease) while leaving fabrics bright.

In the next round, we ran two tests at once: For the first, we reapplied stain removers to the old stains from the first round. For the second, we applied fresh stains to a new section of the same shirts and fabric pieces from the first test and took a more aggressive approach: After waiting 15 minutes, we applied the removers, but this time we scrubbed harder, waited (or soaked) for the maximum recommended time, and laundered in hot water.

Small changes made a big difference: While three of the products still failed across the board, the other four showed progress, erasing various stains. But one product, which had performed in the top two in the first round, pulled farther ahead of the pack. This time it removed all the previous stains and virtually all the newly applied ones.

But treating fresh stains isn't always realistic; sometimes you don't notice a spot until laundry day. So for our final round, we stained the pieces of fabric and shirts and waited a full 72 hours before treating them, scrubbing vigorously, and washing in hot water. Once again, the front-runner from previous tests outperformed the others, leaving the shirt and blue fabric looking bright and free of all but one stain. Only the adobo sauce left a faint orange mark on the shirt; however, even that virtually disappeared with one more round of soaking and washing.

So what about this product makes it work so much better than the others?

> **Out, Damned Spot**
>
> Our winner did a near-perfect job getting out all types of food stains, even stubborn adobo sauce.
>
> 
>
> BEFORE
>
> 
>
> AFTER

Stain Science

Our winner, a powdered product, was the only remover in our lineup to use sodium percarbonate, a combination of sodium carbonate and hydrogen peroxide. Activated when dissolved in water, the sodium percarbonate releases oxygen, which bubbles up and helps lift the stain from the fabric, while the hydrogen peroxide, a color-safe bleaching agent, decolorizes the stains. These ingredients are most effective on stains from natural substances, e.g., food-based stains. It also contains surfactants, which disrupt the surface tension of stain molecules, providing an entry for water and cleaning agents.

The rest of the products we tested attack stains using enzymes plus surfactants. Enzymes work by breaking down the stains' big, water-insoluble molecules into smaller, soluble components and disrupting the stain's bonds to the fabric. But each type of enzyme targets only a very specific type of stain, so manufacturers usually include a scattershot assortment of enzymes to make them more all-purpose. (For more information, see "Stain-Fighting Enzymes and Foods They Target" at CooksIllustrated.com/apr15.)

This explains why enzymes were less effective than sodium percarbonate when tackling a broad spectrum of stains. For that reason, we can enthusiastically recommend only OxiClean Versatile Stain Remover. It takes a little more time and effort to use than the other products, which call for just a few sprays and some rubbing and waiting before laundering. But however convenient a product may be, the real goal is spot-free clothing. Next time we stain our clothes in the kitchen, we'll reach for a bucket and the OxiClean Versatile Stain Remover.

See Stains Disappear—or Not
Video available free for 4 months at CooksIllustrated.com/apr15

KEY

Good ★★★
Fair ★★
Poor ★

TESTING LAUNDRY STAIN REMOVERS

We tested seven top-selling national laundry stain removers, chosen from data compiled by Chicago-based market research firm IRi. We stained plain white cotton T-shirts and blue cotton shirt fabric with 1 teaspoon each of melted bittersweet chocolate, warm bacon grease, yellow mustard, pureed blueberries, black tea, and pureed chipotle chiles in adobo sauce. We applied stain removers and washed the clothing in separate wash loads with two large towels, using a measured amount of identical laundry detergent (one without special stain-fighting ingredients or claims). Results from the tests were averaged and products appear below in order of preference. Prices were paid in Boston-area supermarkets. For complete testing results, go to CooksIllustrated.com/apr15.

CLEANING AGENTS
Ingredients in the product designed to remove stains were obtained from product websites and labels; not a complete listing of contents.

PERFORMANCE
We conducted three rounds of stain treatment in three different areas on white T-shirts and blue cotton shirt fabric. Products that removed stains under all conditions rated highest. We broke performance into three categories.

➢ **Fresh Stains**
We treated fresh stains after 15 minutes in two rounds. We first used minimal effort, laundering in cold water after the minimum recommended wait time; when products instructed to "rub in" the product, we scrubbed lightly with our hands or with scrubby bottle tops, if included. We then repeated this test but vigorously scrubbed the stains and waited the maximum recommended time before laundering in hot water.

➢ **Laundered Stains**
We re-treated any stains remaining after the first test using maximum scrubbing effort to remove the stains and laundering in hot water.

➢ **Old Stains**
We left stains to dry for 72 hours before treating using maximum scrubbing efforts to remove the stains and laundering in hot water.

EASE OF USE
Products received higher marks if they were simple and comfortable to use, were not messy to apply, and offered clear directions.

	CRITERIA	TESTERS' COMMENTS
HIGHLY RECOMMENDED		
OXICLEAN Versatile Stain Remover **Price:** $8.59 for 3-lb tub **Method:** Dissolve powder in water, soak garment for 1 to 6 hours, launder **Cleaning Agents:** Sodium percarbonate (oxygen-based bleach), surfactants  	Fresh Stains ★★½ Laundered Stains ★★★ Old Stains ★★½ Ease of Use ★★½	Though it required more time to dissolve this powder in water and presoak stained clothes for hours, the stellar results made it worthwhile. Only a ghost of adobo sauce remained on the shirt when we left stains untouched for 72 hours before treating, but even that virtually disappeared with another treatment.
RECOMMENDED WITH RESERVATIONS		
TIDE Ultra Stain Release **Price:** $5.85 for 25-oz bottle **Method:** Pour on, scrub with cap, launder **Cleaning Agents:** Surfactants, four enzymes, fabric brightener  	Fresh Stains ★★ Laundered Stains ★★ Old Stains ★ Ease of Use ★★★	The nubbly Zap! Cap, designed to rub the product onto the garment, was easy to use and did help this stain remover penetrate. It did a better job at removing more stains than most of the rest of the lineup and left fabrics looking brighter. That said, it wasn't effective on chocolate or mustard, and on stains that sat for 72 hours before treating, it left all but the grease stain clearly visible on our T-shirt.
NOT RECOMMENDED		
RESOLVE Spray & Wash Laundry Stain Remover **Price:** $3.79 for 22-oz spray **Method:** Spray, wait 5 minutes maximum, rub into stain, launder **Cleaning Agents:** Surfactant, solvent, one enzyme  	Fresh Stains ★½ Laundered Stains ★½ Old Stains ★ Ease of Use ★★½	This poorly focused spray is hard to keep off surrounding surfaces, and it instructs the user never to leave it on fabric for longer than 5 minutes or risk permanent damage (the label even warns that it could damage plastic and paint). It did remove bacon grease, but too many other spots were still clearly visible.
ZOUT Laundry Stain Remover **Price:** $4.45 for 22-oz spray **Method:** Spray, rub in, wait 1 to 5 minutes, launder **Cleaning Agents:** Surfactant, three enzymes  	Fresh Stains ★ Laundered Stains ★½ Old Stains ★ Ease of Use ★★★	Spraying on this "action foam" felt satisfying because it bubbled up, making it look like it was working right away. But the results were a huge letdown: The only stain it removed was grease (though it faded chocolate stains significantly, an especially tough stain for other products).
SHOUT Trigger Triple-Acting Formula **Price:** $3.59 for 22-oz spray **Method:** Spray, rub in, wait 1 to 5 minutes, launder **Cleaning Agents:** Surfactant, one enzyme  	Fresh Stains ★ Laundered Stains ★ Old Stains ★ Ease of Use ★★★	This spray was especially easy to pump, with good coverage where we wanted it. But the good news stopped there. While it lightened most stains, it removed only fresh grease stains.
CLOROX 2 Stain Remover & Color Booster Liquid **Price:** $7.19 for 33-oz bottle **Method:** Pour on, rub in gently, wait 5 to 10 minutes, launder (suggests adding capful to wash) **Cleaning Agents:** Hydrogen peroxide, surfactant, fabric brightener  	Fresh Stains ★ Laundered Stains ★ Old Stains ★ Ease of Use ★★	The only stain this product completely removed was grease; it especially failed on bright orange chipotles in adobo sauce. Leftover stains lightened up slightly when treated a second time but were still clearly present. It was also hard to control how much product poured out of the wide opening onto the stain.
RESOLVE Max Power Gel with Scrubnubs **Price:** $3.49 for 6.7-oz bottle **Method:** Squeeze onto stains, scrub with top of bottle, wait 1 to 5 minutes, wash **Cleaning Agents:** Surfactant, solvent, three enzymes  	Fresh Stains ½ Laundered Stains ★ Old Stains ★ Ease of Use ★	This "power gel" made stains worse, creating one giant blot. And it was a pain to use: The scrubnubs, which surround a hole that dispenses the gel, scooped up food residue and redeposited it on the clothes as we scrubbed. (We tried to rinse food out of the hole, but this was difficult.)

A Dijon That Passes Muster

What traits guarantee a Dijon mustard that packs a wallop of clean heat and balanced acidity? Youth and, surprisingly, a little fat.

BY KATE SHANNON

When Grey Poupon first posed its famous question to American television audiences 34 years ago, the company's sophisticated French-style mustard (which is actually made in the United States) wouldn't necessarily have been a pantry staple in most households. But over the years our taste for (and sales of) this spicy, smooth condiment has grown—to the tune of more than $45 million worth of mustard sold by Grey Poupon in this country each year.

In the test kitchen, we understand the appeal. Good Dijon mustard is creamy, with more body than conventional yellow mustard, and packs a wallop of clean, nose-tingling heat. We slather it on sandwiches, squirt it on hot dogs and sausages, and add it to everything from salad dressings and dips to pan sauces and glazes for roasted meats, fish, and vegetables.

When we last tasted Dijon mustards in 2008, Grey Poupon was our favorite for its "bold" yet "balanced" heat, but lately we've wondered if any other producers could top it. To find out, we purchased 10 Dijons made in the smooth style developed in France in the 1300s (we ignored coarse- and whole-grain products), tasting them plain and, to see how they paired with savory food, on boiled hot dogs.

As expected, clean flavor, intense heat, and creamy body were exactly the qualities we liked in a Dijon. Those that were "sweet," "too mild," or seasoned with ingredients beyond the standard formula simply didn't meet our expectations for what Dijon should be.

We prepared for our plain tasting by squirting each of the 10 mustards into numbered plastic cups.

Read the Label

The three best indicators of a strong, spicy Dijon are right on the label.

1. Fat content:
Even a small amount indicates more mustard seeds—and stronger flavor.

2. Sell-by date:
Fresher mustards are spicier, so buy jars as far from their dates as possible.

3. Preservative:
Sulfur dioxide is more effective than tartaric acid at staving off oxidation and, thus, preserving heat.

Some Like It Hot

The sources of those unexpected flavors became obvious when we scanned the package ingredient lists. All the bottom-ranking mustards contained "spices" or other seasonings, the product from Inglehoffer being the worst offender. Loaded with garlic, celery seed, paprika, sweeteners (including high fructose corn syrup), and thickeners, it actually "ruined a hot dog" for some tasters. Our favorite mustards stuck closer to the minimalist traditional French recipe: just mustard seeds, water, vinegar, salt (we preferred those with at least 100 milligrams per serving), and a few preservatives.

And what gave a mustard a good dose—or not—of heat? The answer wasn't quite as obvious as how high on the ingredient list mustard seeds appeared. It turns out that the acidity of the condiment, which comes from vinegar and sometimes from wine as well, can also affect its spiciness. That's because too much acidity can kill heat-producing compounds in the mustard seed called isothiocyanates. Sure enough, when we had an independent lab measure the pH of each sample, the values tracked with our heat assessments: Tasters found the Dijons with lower pHs (and thus greater acidity) to be the least spicy—even "a bit bland" on a hot dog—whereas mustards with relatively high pHs earned praise for "full, intense mustard flavor."

Another surprising indicator of a mustard's heat: fat content. While the majority of these Dijons contained no fat, our favorites had a tiny amount—just 0.5 grams per serving. It turns out that mustard seeds are the only ingredient in most Dijons that contains fat. Therefore the Dijons listing fat were likely to contain more mustard seeds than other products, which helped to explain their more potent heat.

Finally, we knew from a previous Dijon tasting that mustard's pungent isothiocyanate compounds are highly volatile and will fade with time or exposure to air. In fact, oxidation can even occur slowly inside new, unopened containers of mustard. All the Dijons we tasted contain preservatives that can help inhibit oxidation, but it turns out that the type of preservative used can influence heat. While our top three mustards included some form of sulfite or sulfur dioxide, most of the others relied on tartaric acid. Sulfur dioxide renders oxygen inactive, which makes it a very effective stabilizer, but tartaric acid merely removes traces of iron that promote oxidation, so it's less effective.

All these other factors being equal, the best way to ensure that your mustard will pack some heat is to buy the freshest possible product. The problem is that manufacturers don't make determining the age of a product easy. For one thing, a mustard's shelf life can range from six months to two years, depending on the manufacturer, and is not printed on the label—making it hard to know whether a mustard that's, say, five months away from a sell by date is still very fresh or getting close to the end of its time. (We determined the age of the mustards in our tasting by calling the manufacturers to find out their shelf life.) What's more, some brands print a cryptic manufacturing code that corresponds to a production date rather than an actual sell-by date. Even with this ambiguity, our advice is to, when possible, buy a mustard that does list a sell-by date, and make sure that date is as far away as possible.

Cuts the Mustard

Bringing together all the traits we were looking for was our favorite mustard, Trois Petits Cochons Moutarde de Dijon ($6.99 for a 7-ounce jar). Its pH was the highest of all the mustards in the lineup (3.80 versus 3.49 in the loser), and it contained a small amount of fat; in fact, it was the only mustard we tasted to list mustard seeds as the first ingredient. (Incidentally, it's also the only widely available supermarket Dijon produced in France.) It wowed tasters with the "sharp, nasal-clearing," "long, slow burn" that we associate with good Dijon.

TASTING DIJON MUSTARD

Twenty-one *Cook's Illustrated* staff members sampled 10 supermarket Dijon mustards plain and on boiled hot dogs, rating them on spiciness, texture, and overall appeal. Products were selected using data on top-selling national brands of mustard compiled by Chicago-based marketing research firm IRi. Products are listed below in order of preference. Sodium and fat are based on label information.

RECOMMENDED

TROIS PETITS COCHONS Moutarde de Dijon

Price: $6.99 for a 7-oz jar ($1.00 per oz)
Ingredients: Mustard seeds, vinegar, water, sea salt (may contain naturally occurring sulfites)
Fat: 0.5 g
Sodium: 115 mg per teaspoon
Comments: Thanks to a high ratio of mustard seeds (it's the only product we tasted to list them as the first ingredient), this pricey Dijon impressed tasters with "nasal-clearing" heat that "kicks in gradually" and "builds." It was balanced, too, delivering just enough salt and "tangy," "bright" flavor to even out its spiciness.

MAILLE Dijon Originale

Price: $4.49 for a 7.5-oz jar ($0.60 per oz)
Ingredients: Water, mustard seeds, vinegar, salt, citric acid, sulphur dioxide (preservative)
Fat: 0.5 g
Sodium: 125 mg per teaspoon
Comments: A good choice for those who prefer a more moderate heat level, this "well-rounded" Dijon was "fairly spicy but not too sharp" and boasted "bright flavor typical of Dijon."

ROLAND Extra Strong Dijon Mustard

Price: $5.16 for 10.1-oz jar ($0.51 per oz)
Ingredients: Water, mustard seeds, vinegar, salt, citric acid, sodium metabisulfate (as a preservative)
Fat: 0.5 g
Sodium: 125 mg per teaspoon
Comments: With "big, nasal-clearing heat" that reminded tasters of "wasabi" and "horseradish," this mustard was rated the hottest in our lineup. That made it an especially appealing condiment on hot dogs, where it "cut through the saltiness" of the meat.

FRENCH'S Dijon Mustard

Price: $2.99 for 12-oz jar ($0.25 per oz)
Ingredients: Distilled vinegar, water, #1 grade mustard seed, salt, chardonnay wine, citric acid, tartaric acid, spices and turmeric
Fat: 0 g
Sodium: 130 mg per teaspoon
Comments: This mustard was fairly spicy, but some tasters lamented that its heat "doesn't linger" as long as other products'. What they did pick up on was tanginess, noting its "kick from acid."

KOOPS' Dijon Mustard

Price: $4.98 for 12-oz jar ($0.42 per oz)
Ingredients: Water, mustard seed, vinegar, salt, white wine, citric acid, turmeric, tartaric acid, spices
Fat: 0 g
Sodium: 120 mg per teaspoon
Comments: Heat-seekers wanted more zip, depth, and bite from this "mellow" Dijon. But despite that, tasters found it "bright" and "pleasant" enough to recommend it. In sum: "It would do a grilled frank justice."

DID YOU KNOW?

All products reviewed by America's Test Kitchen, home of *Cook's Illustrated* and *Cook's Country* magazines, are independently chosen, researched, and reviewed by our editors. We buy products for testing at retail locations and do not accept unsolicited samples for testing. We do not accept or receive payment or consideration from product manufacturers or retailers. Manufacturers and retailers are not told in advance of publication which products we have recommended. We list suggested sources for recommended products as a convenience to our readers but do not endorse specific retailers.

RECOMMENDED CONTINUED

GREY POUPON Dijon Mustard

Price: $3.29 for 8-oz jar ($0.41 per oz)
Ingredients: Water, vinegar, mustard seed, salt, white wine, fruit pectin, citric acid, and tartaric acid, sugar, spice
Fat: 0 g
Sodium: 120 mg per teaspoon
Comments: The "familiar" flavor of our former winner combined "sharp vinegar tang" with a "creamy" texture, which one taster deemed "mustard heaven." But the consensus among most tasters was that this Dijon "could use more heat."

RECOMMENDED WITH RESERVATIONS

EMERIL'S Dijon Mustard

Price: $2.25 for 12-oz jar ($0.19 per jar)
Ingredients: Distilled vinegar, water, mustard seed, salt, white wine, citric acid, tartaric acid, spices, oleoresin turmeric
Fat: 0 g
Sodium: 135 mg per teaspoon
Comments: With "more vinegar than heat" and spices, this Dijon reminded tasters of "yellow mustard." Some also noticed a "slightly sweet" and "perfumey" flavor. As one taster summed up: "It's not a bad mustard, but it's not Dijon."

WOEBER'S Supreme Dijon Mustard

Price: $6.00 for 10-oz jar ($0.60 per oz)
Ingredients: Distilled vinegar, water, #1 mustard seed, salt, white wine, citric acid, tartaric acid, and spices
Fat: 0 g
Sodium: 120 mg per teaspoon
Comments: Heavy on the vinegar and wine flavors and light on the spiciness, this Dijon was "tart" and "tangy"—a "middle-of-the-road" mustard, tasters said. But its bright flavor was overwhelmed by the hot dog, and it had a "slightly bitter" aftertaste.

SILVER SPRING Dijon Mustard

Price: $4.83 for 9.5-oz jar ($0.51 per oz)
Ingredients: Vinegar, water, mustard seed, salt, white wine, citric acid, tartaric acid, turmeric, spices
Fat: 0 g
Sodium: 45 mg per teaspoon
Comments: Most tasters found this mustard "mellow." On its own, it offered only a "mild" burn; on a hot dog, it tasted "a little weak." Some even detected off-flavors in the form of a "weirdly fruity," "slightly sweet aftertaste," and even distracting hints of "garlic" and "clove."

NOT RECOMMENDED

INGLEHOFFER Traditional Dijon Mustard (also sold as Beaver Mild Dijon Mustard)

Price: $3.75 for 9-oz jar ($0.42 per oz)
Ingredients: Water, white distilled vinegar, mustard seed, white wine, salt, garlic, soybean oil, sugar, high fructose corn syrup, eggs, modified corn starch, xanthan gum, spices, natural flavors, citric acid, celery seed, turmeric, annatto, calcium disodium EDTA (retains product freshness), paprika
Fat: 0 g
Sodium: 60 mg per teaspoon
Comments: Loaded with spices, sweeteners, stabilizers, and acid—and lacking salt—this was anything but traditional Dijon. Tasters likened its flavor to a "dried spice packet" and complained that it "ruined" the hot dog.

INGREDIENT NOTES

BY JARED HUGHES, ANDREW JANJIGIAN & LAN LAM

Tasting Salted versus Unsalted Chicken Stock

Our favorite chicken broth is Swanson Chicken Stock, which we appreciate for its "rich," "meaty" flavor. This broth stood out because it's made with a relatively high percentage of meat-based protein compared with similar products and a moderate amount of sodium for the broth world—510 milligrams per 1-cup serving. Still, since many people monitor their sodium intake, we wondered how the "unsalted" version of this product would measure up.

Swanson Unsalted Chicken Stock has 130 milligrams of sodium, which is just under the United States Department of Agriculture's 140-milligram ceiling for "low-sodium" products. (In fact, "unsalted" means only that no salt was added during processing, so some unsalted broths can contain much more sodium per serving.) When we compared ingredient lists, we found that the company didn't simply omit the sodium in the unsalted version but reformulated it from the ground up. While both products begin their ingredient lists with "chicken stock," the regular broth adds salt next, followed by vegetables and an herb. In the unsalted version, the vegetables disappear, replaced by more chicken-centric ingredients, including dehydrated chicken and chicken fat. Despite these differences, both contain 4 grams of protein per cup, identically low levels of sugars, and trace amounts of fat per 1-cup serving.

To compare how each tasted, we sampled the broths side-by-side plain, in vegetable soup, and in a simple Parmesan risotto, rating them on flavor, saltiness, off-flavors, if any, and overall appeal. We weren't that surprised to find that our tasters preferred the regular chicken broth in all three tastings, but the unsalted broth fared surprisingly well. In fact, its scores were high enough to make it a recommended alternative. When we need to restrict sodium, we won't hesitate to reach for Swanson Unsalted Chicken Stock. –Lisa McManus

HIGHLY RECOMMENDED

SWANSON Chicken Stock
Sodium: 510 mg per cup
Protein: 4 g per cup
Ingredients: Chicken stock, salt, carrots, cabbage, onions, celery, celery leaves, parsley
Comments: "Bolder, more robust" as well as more "savory" and "chicken-y" than the unsalted version of this stock, "it brings out more flavor from the start."

RECOMMENDED

SWANSON Unsalted Chicken Stock
Sodium: 130 mg per cup
Protein: 4 g per cup
Ingredients: Chicken stock, dehydrated chicken, natural flavoring, chicken fat
Comments: "Subtle" and "light," "mild" and "clean-tasting," and "with mellow, distinct chicken flavor," this unsalted version of our winning chicken broth pleased most tasters.

CLOSE, BUT NOT THE SAME
Though they both have purple tops, turnips (below) are smaller and white, while rutabagas (left) are bigger, denser, and yellow in color.

Exploring Roots: Rutabagas and Turnips

Because of the purple coloring around their tops, rutabagas (used in our Root Vegetable Gratin, page 11) are often mistaken for purple-top turnips. The two are indeed related, but they have very different flavors and textures and need to be handled differently in recipes.

When we tried both in soups and stews, the rutabaga brought a mellow sweetness in comparison with turnips' mild pepperiness. Because rutabagas are much denser than turnips, we found that you should either add them earlier in the cooking process or cut them about 25 percent smaller (e.g., if the recipe specifies turnips cut into 1-inch cubes, cut the rutabagas into ¾-inch cubes).

Both can also be used raw in salads: Turnips will add a sharp peppery flavor and a firm but juicy texture, while raw rutabaga will be sweeter, with a crisp texture. Smaller turnips are fine sliced thin, but we prefer to cut larger, firmer rutabagas into thin matchsticks or to coarsely grate them. –L.L.

Why Is That Flour Yellow?

If you've ever seen cellophane bags of semolina flour at the supermarket, its yellow color and coarse texture might have led you to think that it was cornmeal. However, this flour is made from wheat. Specifically, it's the coarsely ground endosperm of durum wheat, the same variety used to make most dried Italian pasta and Moroccan couscous. Semolina's deep yellow color comes from high concentrations of carotenoids (the same compounds responsible for the brilliant colors of carrots, mangos, and apricots). We use semolina flour in our Thick-Crust Sicilian-Style Pizza (page 7) to give the dough a slightly sweet, rich flavor; a finer, more cake-like crumb; and an appealing buttery color. You can find durum semolina flour in many supermarkets near the flour or specialty grains (Bob's Red Mill durum semolina flour has a coarse texture that we like in our pizza dough) and in Italian and Indian markets. –A.J.

Low-Sodium Salt in Baking

We have previously found that LoSalt salt substitute, which replaces some of table salt's sodium chloride with potassium chloride (a salty-tasting compound), was acceptable in savory applications, but we wondered how it would fare in baked goods. To find out, we tested it in three recipes that called for varying concentrations of salt: yellow layer cake, blueberry muffins, and pie dough.

In the layer cake, all found the LoSalt version acceptable; in fact, half of tasters couldn't even detect a difference. In blueberry muffins, most tasters could identify the LoSalt batch, but still considered it to be fine. When it came to the pie crust, which contained the highest concentration of salt of the three recipes tested, all of our tasters were able to pick out the sample with LoSalt, but once we filled the crust, the difference wasn't noticeable.

A FINE SUB
LoSalt salt substitute works fine in baking.

To see if we could avoid a special purchase, we also tried simply adding less salt to these recipes by adding amounts of table salt equivalent to the amount of sodium chloride in the LoSalt. However, tasters unanimously agreed that flavor suffered when less table salt was used.

The bottom line? LoSalt will produce acceptable results in a wide range of baking applications; we don't recommend simply cutting back on the amount of table salt. Just be aware when using LoSalt that the higher proportion of salt the recipe calls for, the more likely you are to notice a difference. –J.H.

Cheater Couverture Chocolate

Couverture chocolate is manufactured specifically for dipping cookies and truffles and coating molds. It's ideal for the job because it produces a thinner layer of chocolate that's shinier and snappier than regular chocolate when set. It can also be costly—up to $20 per pound. But we found a cheaper way to get the same professional-looking results: Melt regular chocolate (we used our favorite dark chocolate, Ghirardelli 60 Percent Cacao Bittersweet Chocolate Premium Baking Bar) with a small amount of high-quality white chocolate (such as E. Guittard or Ghirardelli). Here's why the combination worked: When chocolate melts, the cocoa butter becomes liquid; all its other components are insoluble and are suspended in the liquid. Because white chocolate contains cocoa butter but no cocoa solids, it created a more fluid product that was easier to work with and allowed for a thinner coating. Also, the more cocoa butter there is, the more rigid (snappy) and glossy the final coating will be. Avoid white chocolate chips and any bars that contain partially hydrogenated palm oil, palm kernel oil, soybean oil, or cottonseed oil, as these are added in lieu of some or all of the cocoa butter and thus won't work as well.

SHINY, SNAPPY COATING
No expensive couverture chocolate needed.

Here's our cheater method: Finely chop or grate 4 ounces of chocolate and ¼ ounce of white chocolate. Microwave 3 ounces of the chocolate at 50 percent power until it is mostly melted, stirring frequently. Then add the remaining 1 ounce of chocolate and the white chocolate and stir it until melted, returning it to the microwave for no more than 5 seconds at a time to complete the melting. –L.L.

A SIMPLE FORMULA
Four ounces of dark chocolate melted with ¼ ounce of white chocolate makes a great dipping chocolate.

DIY RECIPE **Preserved Lemons**

Lemons that have been preserved in salt have a bright citrus flavor, balanced by brininess and sourness, that can add depth and nuance to all sorts of dishes, perhaps most famously to Moroccan tagines. Typically the rinds, which become soft in texture and mellow in flavor, are sliced thin or minced before being added to a dish, but the pulp can also be used. You can buy preserved lemons at specialty markets, but they're expensive. For a fraction of the price, you can make them yourself. You'll find all sorts of uses for them; we recommend adding them to pan sauces, combining them with a garlicky yogurt sauce for serving with grilled meats or fish, or incorporating them into vinaigrettes. You can also flavor the lemons by adding a cinnamon stick, bay leaf, coriander seeds, or other spices to the jar while they preserve.

We use Meyer lemons, which are a hybrid of a lemon and an orange, because they are a bit sweeter and more floral-tasting than common supermarket lemons. Look for them from August through March at higher-end supermarkets and gourmet shops. –Suzannah McFerran

PRESERVED LEMONS

MAKES 4 PRESERVED LEMONS

Don't substitute table salt for the kosher salt. We prefer to prepare this recipe with Meyer lemons, but regular lemons can be substituted. If using regular lemons, choose smaller fruit with thin skin (thin-skinned lemons will yield to gentle pressure). Also note that because regular lemons have thicker peels, they may take two to four weeks longer to soften.

- **12 Meyer lemons (4 whole, scrubbed and dried, 8 juiced to yield 1½ cups), plus extra juice if needed**
- **½ cup Diamond Crystal kosher salt**

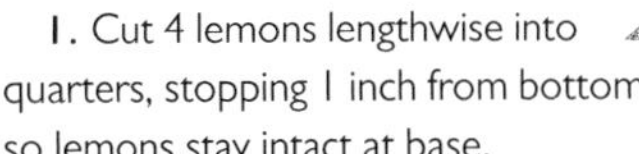

1. Quarter lemons, leaving base intact.

2. Pour salt into lemon cavity.

3. Submerge in lemon juice.

1. Cut 4 lemons lengthwise into quarters, stopping 1 inch from bottom so lemons stay intact at base.

2. Working with 1 lemon at a time, hold lemon over medium bowl and pour 2 tablespoons salt into cavity of lemon. Gently rub cut surfaces of lemon together, then place in clean 1-quart jar. Repeat with remaining lemons and salt. Add any accumulated salt and juice in bowl to jar.

3. Pour 1½ cups lemon juice into jar and press gently to submerge lemons. (Add more lemon juice to jar, if needed, to cover lemons completely.) Cover jar tightly with lid and shake. Refrigerate lemons, shaking jar once per day for first 4 days to redistribute salt and juice. Let lemons cure in refrigerator until glossy and softened, 6 to 8 weeks. Preserved lemons can be refrigerated for up to 6 months.

4. To use, cut off desired amount of preserved lemon. Using knife, remove pulp and white pith from rind. Slice, chop, or mince rind and pulp as desired.

KITCHEN NOTES

BY ANDREA GEARY, ANDREW JANJIGIAN, LISA McMANUS & DAN SOUZA

WHAT IS IT?

MOULI SALAD MAKER
Although it successfully grated carrots and cheese, it failed to impress when we tried it with a number of other vegetables and fruits.

A midcentury ad for this salad tool promised that it would "save fingers, time, food, and flavor." A precursor to the food processor (which didn't hit home kitchens until the 1970s), the Salad Maker claimed to make easy work of slicing, chopping, and shredding. It came with five interchangeable disks, three of which were for shredding at various sizes. Much like an oversize rotary grater, it was designed with a chamber above the cutting disk that held the food while a hand clamp kept the food in place and helped press it through the disk.

Assembly was simple: The foldaway legs popped into place, blades snapped on with a click, and the removable hand crank easily slid into its slot. But food had to be chopped into odd pieces to fit inside the shallow crescent-shaped chamber, and pressing on the clamp's handle took a lot of muscle to be effective. When we tried slicing, chopping, and shredding cabbage, potato, apple, and cucumber using various disks, the results were uneven, mangled, or even crushed slices and shreds. Carrot, however, grated acceptably well. We also discovered that the superfine disk was ideal for turning out grated Parmesan.

While the Salad Maker might be fine for grating or slicing very firm, nonwatery foods, anything softer is too difficult, if not impossible, to get through the blades cleanly. We'll stick with the food processor in our modern kitchens.
–Shannon Friedmann Hatch

Topping Tips for Sicilian Pizza

Our Thick-Crust Sicilian-Style Pizza (page 7) gets a topping of mozzarella and Parmesan cheeses, but if you want to embellish a bit, here are a few guidelines for how to handle different types of toppings.

HEARTY VEGETABLES

Aim for a maximum of 12 ounces spread out in a single layer. Vegetables such as onions, peppers, and mushrooms should be thinly sliced and lightly sautéed (or microwaved for a minute or two along with a little olive oil) until wilted before using.

DELICATE VEGETABLES AND HERBS

Leafy greens and herbs like spinach and basil are best placed beneath the cheese to protect them or added raw to the fully cooked pizza.

MEATS

Raw proteins (no more than 8 ounces per pizza) should be precooked and then drained to remove excess fat. We like to poach meats like sausage (broken up into ½-inch chunks) or ground beef for 4 to 5 minutes in a wide skillet along with ¼ cup of water, which helps render the fat while keeping the meat moist. Cured meats such as pepperoni or salami can be placed directly on top of the cheese in a single layer. –A.J.

COOKING CLASS

Cold Fermentation and Flavor in Yeasted Breads

In yeasted dough recipes like our Thick-Crust Sicilian-Style Pizza (page 7), fermentation is a key step that occurs after the dough has been mixed and kneaded. In this stage, the yeast consumes sugars in the dough, producing not only carbon dioxide, which is critical to give the dough the proper rise, but also numerous flavor and aroma molecules. The typical bread recipe calls for fermenting the dough on the counter. But we often let the dough ferment in the refrigerator—usually for at least 24 to 48 hours and sometimes up to 72 hours—because we've found that we get more flavorful results.

Here's why: Yeast left out at room temperature consumes sugars and leavens the batter rapidly. But then it's spent; it stops producing not just gas but also compounds that give bread flavor. At cool temperatures, yeast produces carbon dioxide more slowly, so refrigerating the batter allows yeast to leaven at a slow and steady pace, providing more time for a more complex-tasting combination of flavor compounds to develop. The net result? A more flavorful dough.

To demonstrate how temperature affects the rate of carbon dioxide production in dough, we prepared a yeasted batter (its more fluid consistency would be easier to use with our testing equipment) and split it into two batches. We placed each in a simple device we fashioned from a test tube and a semipermeable balloon to capture gas. We left one out at room temperature and placed the other in the refrigerator and then monitored the gas production of each at various intervals. –A.J.

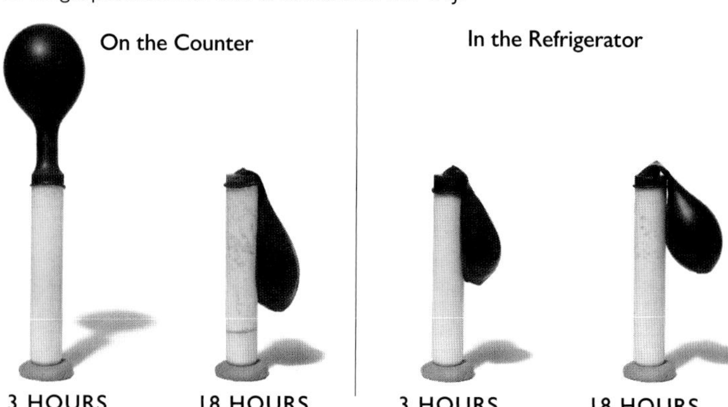

The yeast in the room-temperature batter produced enough gas to fill the balloon within 3 hours but then was spent, while the refrigerated batter continued to generate just enough gas to keep the balloon partially filled even after 18 hours.

Converting Muffins into Loaves

Over the years, a number of readers have asked us if they could bake a muffin recipe as a quick bread. We wanted to figure out if a simple formula could convert a variety of muffin recipes to loaf recipes.

Because muffins are small, they are generally baked at relatively high temperatures so they develop browning before their interiors overcook. In general, muffins bake for 15 to 20 minutes. Loaves, on the other hand, have a much greater volume-to-surface-area ratio and require longer baking at a lower temperature. We tested several fruit and nut muffin recipes, as well as a plain one, baking each in 8½ by 4½-inch pans at a range of oven temperatures and times.

Our findings? To convert a muffin recipe to make a loaf, set the oven rack in the middle position, decrease the oven temperature by 50 degrees, and bake until a toothpick inserted in the center of the loaf matches the visual cue (either "with few moist crumbs attached" or "clean"), 60 to 70 minutes. Recipes with sugary toppings like streusel should be tented with foil during the last 20 to 25 minutes to prevent them from getting too dark. –D.S.

THE EASY WAY TO SLICE CABBAGE

We make quick work of slicing a large quantity of cabbage for recipes like our cabbage side dishes (page 19) by breaking it into smaller pieces for easier handling. –A.G.

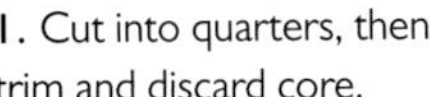

1. Cut into quarters, then trim and discard core.

2. Separate leaves into small, flat stacks.

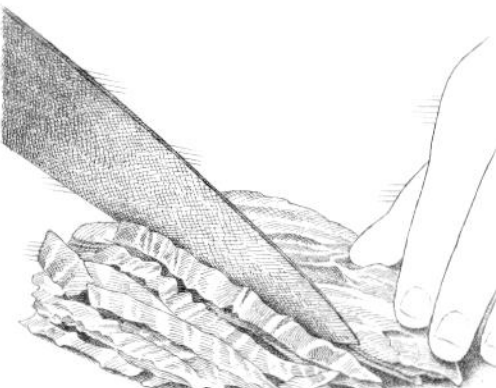

3. Cut each stack of leaves into thin slices.

Tips for Better Stain-Fighting

Many of the stain removers in our testing (page 24) gave only minimal instructions for how to get the best results. We found that if we followed these tips, we increased the effectiveness of all the products, including our winner.

➢ **Act fast.** Attacking a stain when it's fresh gives you the best likelihood of getting it out.

➢ **Use some elbow grease.** Don't just dab or spritz on a stain remover and expect results. We recommend applying the stain remover as directed and then using a toothbrush to work it into the fibers (be careful with delicate fabrics).

➢ **Launder in hot water if possible.** Hot water helps dissolve grease and soften chocolate, and it provides a more favorable climate for enzymes to do their work. We found that all the stains faded significantly more when we followed the stain treatment with a hot-water wash rather than using cold water (the only exception would be blood stains, which fade best in cold water).

➢ **Be patient.** When we applied the stain remover and waited the maximum recommended time before washing, nearly all the products performed better.

➢ **Examine before drying.** If stains remain, re-treat them right away. Dryer heat helps stains become permanent, and we found that older stains often continued to fade with further treatment. –L.M.

Swapping Noodles? Mind the Sauce

Most supermarket pasta is made with just wheat and water. But many stores also stock dried Italian pasta made with eggs. In our recipe for Tagliatelle with Prosciutto and Peas (page 18), we found that swapping one for the other has implications on how much pasta cooking water you need to add to the sauce: When cooked, regular dried pasta absorbs a lot less water than dried egg pasta. This is because regular pasta is most often extruded through Teflon dies that create a smooth, glossy surface that makes it less permeable to water, while Italian-brand egg pastas are extruded through bronze dies that create a rougher, more permeable surface. So if you use regular dried pasta in a recipe calling for egg pasta, add about 30 percent as much water as the recipe calls for, and increase from there to achieve the right sauce consistency. The opposite holds true: If you substitute egg pasta in a recipe calling for regular dried pasta, reserve twice as much pasta cooking water and be prepared to add it generously to achieve the proper sauce consistency. –D.S.

ADD MORE WATER

When using Italian dried egg pasta (such as Bionaturae or De Cecco), add extra pasta cooking water to your sauce.

SCIENCE When to Add Salt

Most recipes (and culinary schools) advise seasoning food with salt early in the cooking process, not just at the end. We decided to investigate this conventional wisdom to see if the timing of seasoning makes a notable difference.

EXPERIMENT

We roasted carrots and prepared beef stew in two ways: For one batch we seasoned the dishes at the very beginning of cooking and, in the case of the beef stew, also when we added the onions. For the other batch we withheld all the measured salt in the recipes and added it at the end.

RESULTS

The roasted carrot samples were drastically different from one another. Those seasoned before roasting, with 1½ teaspoons of salt, were properly seasoned and flavorful throughout. Meanwhile, the carrots seasoned with the same amount after roasting were seasoned only on their exteriors and also tasted far too salty.

When it came to the beef stew, when we salted the meat before cooking (with 1½ teaspoons of salt) and seasoned the onions (with ½ teaspoon of salt) when they went into the pot as directed, the stew and particularly the meat itself were more evenly and deeply seasoned than those in the sample salted only at the finish. Furthermore, as with the carrots, the stew's gravy tasted far too salty when the salt was added at the end.

EXPLANATION

We know that salt penetrates food slowly when cold. (In a previous experiment, we found that it took 24 hours for salt to diffuse into the center of a refrigerated raw turkey.) While the process is faster during cooking—for example, our science editor noted that the rate of diffusion of salt into meat will double with every 10-degree increase up to the boiling point—it's still not instantaneous. Furthermore, salt penetrates vegetables even more slowly than it does meat (this is because the salt must cross two rigid walls surrounding every plant cell, while the cells in meat contain only one thin wall). Adding salt at the beginning of cooking gives it time to migrate into the pieces of food, seasoning them throughout. Meanwhile, if you add salt only at the end, it provides a more concentrated, superficial coating that immediately hits your tongue.

TAKEAWAY

For the most even seasoning and well-rounded flavor, we strongly encourage seasoning foods early in the cooking process as we direct in our recipes. However, if you forget, do not make up for it by simply stirring it all in at the end. Instead, start with a very small amount of salt—we used a mere 8 percent of the original amount of salt for the carrots after roasting (⅛ teaspoon versus 1½ teaspoons) and 31 percent for the beef stew (just over ½ teaspoon versus 2 teaspoons)—and then taste and season further as desired. On the flip side, if you are watching your salt intake, you could wait until the end of cooking to season your food, knowing that you'll be able to get away with a lesser amount. –D.S.

FORGET TO SALT? ADD LESS

SCIENCE OF COOKING: Salt Secrets

Are you telling me that it really matters whether I add salt at the beginning of cooking or just before serving? Yes, we are, and this video shows why. Free for 4 months at CooksIllustrated.com/apr15

EQUIPMENT CORNER

BY HANNAH CROWLEY, LAUREN SAVOIE & KATE SHANNON

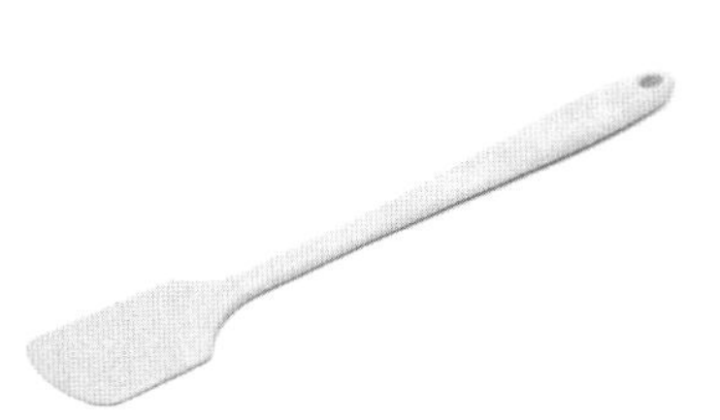

HIGHLY RECOMMENDED

GIR Skinny Spatula
Model: Skinny
Price: $12.95
Source: amazon.com

NOT RECOMMENDED

THERMOS
Stainless King Vacuum Insulated 16 oz. Food Jar with Folding Spoon
Model: SK3000BKTRI4
Price: $24.99

RECOMMENDED

SABITORU
Medium Grit Rust Eraser
Model: N/A
Price: $7.29
Source: amazon.com

RECOMMENDED WITH RESERVATIONS

ZOJIRUSHI
Home Bakery Virtuoso Breadmaker
Model: BB-PAC20
Price: $279.95

RECOMMENDED

MESSERMEISTER
Pro-Touch 4-Inch Grapefruit Knife
Model: 800-26
Price: $15.39
Source: amazon.com

Jar Spatulas

Jar spatulas, slim utensils designed to maneuver in tight spaces, supposedly get every last drop out of jars. We used nine models (priced from $5.18 to $12.95) to scrape out jars of marinara sauce, molasses, mayonnaise, honey, and Nutella. We also let each model sit in hot tomato sauce and ran each through the dishwasher 10 times to assess stain resistance and durability.

Most failed: Some handles were too short to keep our hands clear of sticky jars, while the heads on others were either flimsy or blunt and imprecise. The three best spatulas combined flexibility and firmness with a nimble tip for digging into corners. Of those, we preferred the GIR Skinny Spatula ($12.95), which emptied jars quickly and featured a uniformly flat surface that wiped clean with a single swipe. Alternatively, the slim head of the less-expensive OXO Good Grips Silicone Jar Spatula ($5.95) fit nicely in jars and can be pulled off the handle for cleaning. –K.S.

Thermal Food Jars

Thermal food jars are insulated vessels that promise to keep food hot or cold on the go. We wondered if any could keep their contents food-safe for several hours, since the U.S. Department of Agriculture discourages leaving food between 40 and 140 degrees for more than 2 hours. So we filled six models (priced from $19.95 to $41.99) with 200-degree tomato soup, 150-degree macaroni and cheese, and 38-degree tuna salad and monitored the foods' temperatures for 4 hours.

No jar kept the macaroni and cheese or tuna salad temperature-safe, and only three kept the soup safe. The best of those, the Thermos Stainless King Vacuum Insulated 16 oz. Food Jar with Folding Spoon ($24.99), is durable, leakproof, and cleans up in the dishwasher. –H.C.

Rust Erasers

Rust erasers, made from a rubber compound surrounded by an abrasive, are designed to rub away corrosion that can damage carbon-steel knives. You lubricate the eraser with water and rub it gently along the blade. We tested two (priced at $5.73 and $7.29) by letting new carbon-steel knives air dry and rust, scrubbing them, and repeating the process three times. We also compared the erasers with a medium-grit sandpaper sponge, metal polish, and kitchen cleansing powder.

All five products removed rust effectively, but they revealed black marks that indicated "pitting corrosion"—tiny holes where the corroded metal was removed. (An expert reassured us that the tiny pits won't weaken the strength of the blade as long as it doesn't rust further.) Ultimately, we preferred the dedicated erasers for their ease of use. The polish and the powder dirtied kitchen towels, while the sandpaper was less nimble to maneuver on the knife's sharp edges. Of the two erasers, the Sabitoru Medium Grit Rust Eraser ($7.29) proved exceptionally durable. –K.S.

Bread Machines

Bread machines take the work out of producing fresh loaves at home. Just add the ingredients, push a button, and come back a few hours later to the finished product. In each of the five models we tested (priced from $99 to $279.95), we baked white, whole-wheat, cinnamon-raisin, and gluten-free loaves using both our own recipes and those included with each machine.

A few machines produced loaves with a uniform crumb, but every bread was overbrowned and stiff on the sides, with a pallid, squishy top and punctured bottom where the mixing paddles remained during baking. The gluten-free loaves were failures—"squat," "mushy," and "doughy," testers reported. What's more, the nonstick coating on the Breville paddle rubbed off into the dough, creating inedible black spots. Some models suffered mechanical flaws, too: The Cuisinart shook noisily on its unsteady feet as it mixed, while the smaller of the two Zojirushi models started smoking when its mixing paddle sprayed flour on the heating element when we tried to make a full-sized loaf (it only fits its own scaled-down recipes).

Given those defects, we can't fully recommend any of the models. However, if you want the convenience of a bread machine despite the flaws in the loaves—and have the cash and counter space to spare—the microwave-size Zojirushi Home Bakery Virtuoso Breadmaker ($279.95) was the best of the bunch. Its dual mixing paddles (other machines had only one) produced a consistently uniform crumb in every loaf we made. Alternatively, the compact T-fal Balanced Living Breadmaker ($135) turned out passable loaves and cost less but is fussy to operate. –L.S.

Grapefruit Knives

A grapefruit knife, with a curved blade that's serrated on both sides, is designed to separate the sections from the peel and pith. Traditional models look like bent steak knives; we also found double-ended versions with a serrated blade on one end and a pair of close-set blades on the other that straddle and slice the membrane sections with fewer cuts. We tested five models (priced from $5.66 to $15.39): two traditional, two double-ended, and one that supposedly digs out fruit in one shovel-like motion.

The latter mangled the fruit, while the double-ended knives made work difficult because one blade always pressed against our palms. The dual blades also trapped pulp. Our favorite, the Messermeister Pro-Touch 4-Inch Grapefruit Knife ($15.39), is a traditional model with a gentle curve that was comfortable and didn't puncture the pulp. –L.S.

For complete testing results, go to CooksIllustrated.com/apr15.

INDEX

March & April 2015

FOLLOW US ON SOCIAL MEDIA

facebook.com/CooksIllustrated

twitter.com/TestKitchen

pinterest.com/TestKitchen

google.com/+AmericasTestKitchen

instagram.com/TestKitchen

Braised Halibut with Carrots and Coriander, 9

Root Vegetable Gratin, 11

Tagliatelle with Prosciutto and Peas, 18

Mu Shu Pork, 15

Raspberry Charlotte, 23

Sautéed Cabbage with Parsley and Lemon, 19

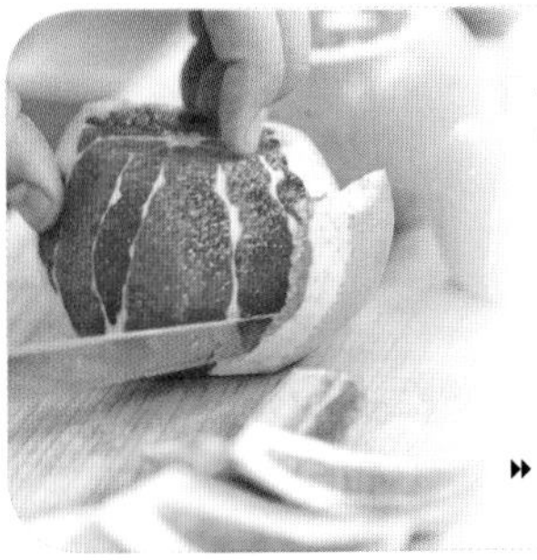

Thick-Crust Sicilian-Style Pizza, 7

Cuban Braised Shredded Beef (Ropa Vieja), 13

Coq au Riesling, 5

Quick Sauces for Chicken, 20

PHOTOGRAPHY: CARL TREMBLAY; STYLING: CATRINE KELTY, MARIE PIRAINO

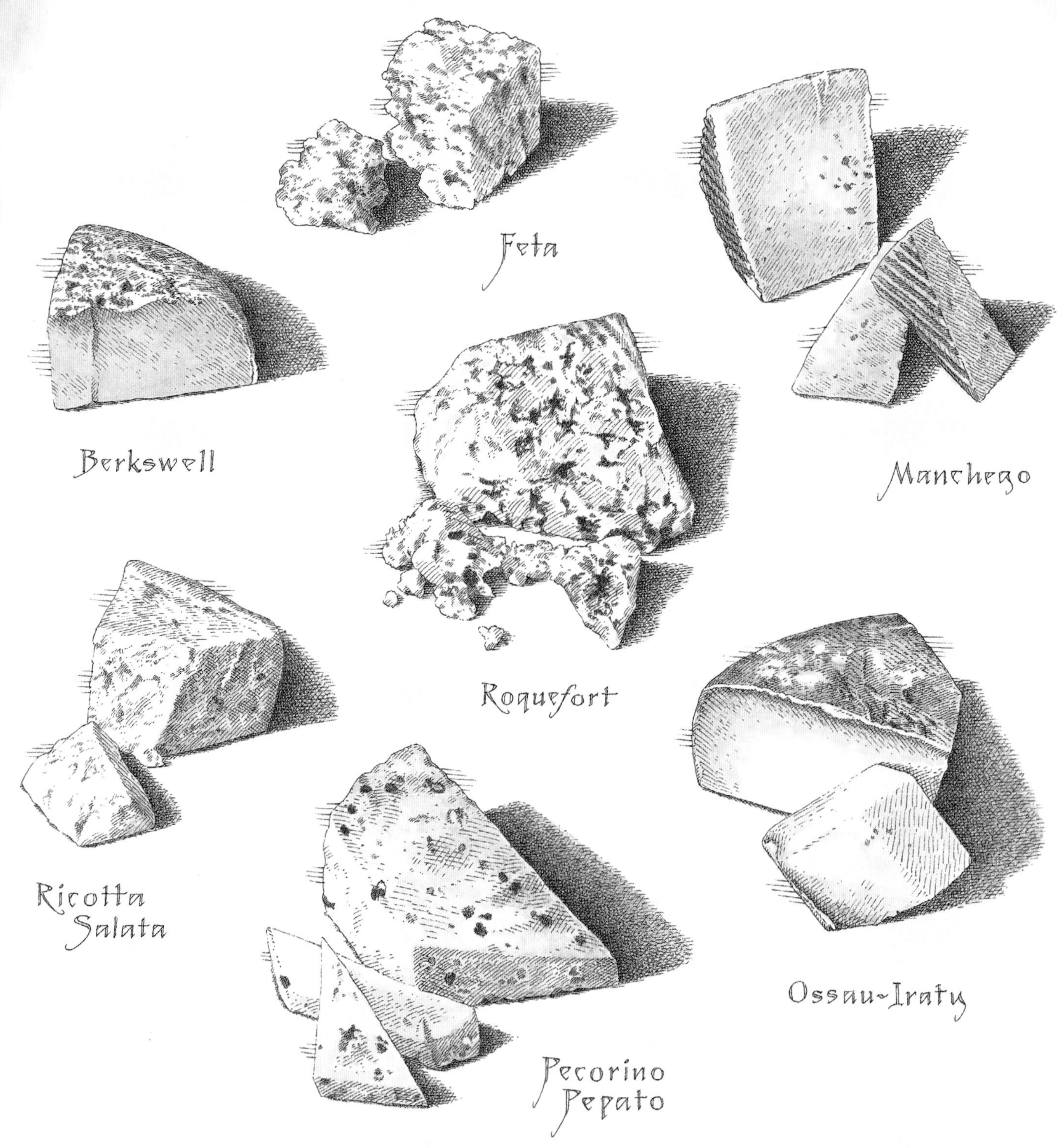

SHEEP'S-MILK CHEESES

NUMBER 134

MAY & JUNE 2015

COOK'S ILLUSTRATED

Grilled Pork Kebabs
How About Tenderloin?

Modern Pot-au-Feu
French Classic Simplified

Best Roasted Potatoes
Supercrisp and Tender

Vietnamese Chicken
Savory Caramel Sauce

Cast-Iron Skillets
Are Enameled Better?

N.Y. Bagels at Home
We Finally Did It

Strawberry-Rhubarb Pie Perfected

Best Supermarket Brie

Provençal Vegetable Soup

Semolina Gnocchi

How to Cook Farro

CooksIllustrated.com

$6.95 U.S. & CANADA

CONTENTS

May & June 2015

ASIAN PICKLES Gumball-size PICKLED PLUMS, or *umezuke*, ferment with salt and purple *shiso* leaves for a salty, sour taste. Their pickling liquid can be reused to make PICKLED GINGER, a sweet-spicy accompaniment. *Takuan*, or PICKLED DAIKON, dries in the sun before it is stuffed into a crock to develop a distinct musty taste. Crunchy, spicy LOTUS ROOTLETS in brine are chopped and tossed with shrimp, chiles, lime juice, fried shallots, and herbs in a popular Vietnamese salad. PICKLED SADAO FLOWER is a bitter complement to fatty fish or pork belly in many Southeast Asian dishes. Taiwanese PICKLED TREE SEEDS add umami richness to the food they garnish. Whole heads of Thai PICKLED GARLIC are brined in vinegar, salt, and sugar until their skins are soft enough to eat. Fiery PICKLED CHILES are served as a condiment at Thai tables so heat can be adjusted to taste. Spicy Vietnamese PICKLED GREEN MANGO is often served with grilled meats.

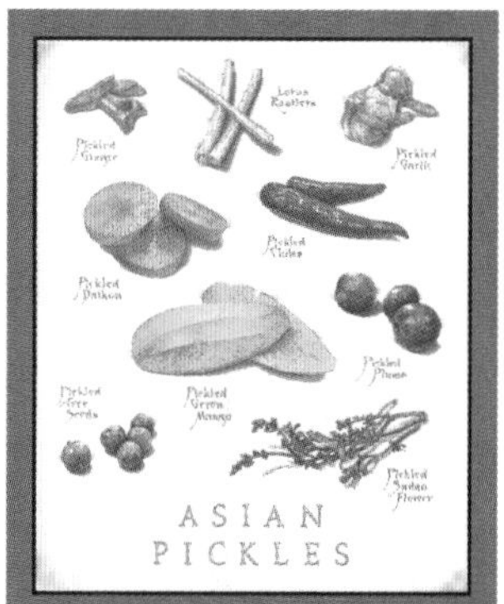

COVER *(Radishes)*: Robert Papp; **BACK COVER** *(Asian Pickles)*: John Burgoyne

America's Test Kitchen is a very real 2,500-square-foot kitchen located just outside Boston. It is the home of *Cook's Illustrated* and *Cook's Country* magazines and the workday destination of more than three dozen test cooks, editors, and cookware specialists. Our mission is to test recipes until we understand how and why they work and arrive at the best version. We also test kitchen equipment and supermarket ingredients in search of products that offer the best value and performance. You can watch us work by tuning in to *America's Test Kitchen* (AmericasTestKitchen.com) and *Cook's Country from America's Test Kitchen* (CooksCountry.com) on public television.

COOK'S ILLUSTRATED

Founder and Editor	Christopher Kimball
Editorial Director	Jack Bishop
Editorial Director, Magazines	John Willoughby
Executive Editor	Amanda Agee
Test Kitchen Director	Erin McMurrer
Managing Editor	Rebecca Hays
Executive Food Editor	Keith Dresser
Senior Editors	Hannah Crowley Andrea Geary Lisa McManus Dan Souza
Senior Editors, Features	Elizabeth Bomze Louise Emerick
Senior Copy Editor	Megan Ginsberg
Copy Editor	Krista Magnuson
Associate Editors	Andrew Janjigian Chris O'Connor
Test Cooks	Daniel Cellucci Lan Lam Annie Petito
Assistant Editors	Lauren Savoie Kate Shannon
Editorial Assistant	Rachel Shin
Assistant Test Cook	Matthew Fairman
Executive Assistant	Christine Gordon
Assistant Test Kitchen Director	Leah Rovner
Senior Kitchen Assistants	Michelle Blodget Alexxa Grattan
Kitchen Assistants	Maria Elena Delgado Ena Gudiel Jason Roman
Executive Producer	Melissa Baldino
Co-Executive Producer	Stephanie Stender
Associate Producer	Kaitlin Hammond
Contributing Editor	Dawn Yanagihara
Science Editor	Guy Crosby, PhD
Consulting Creative Director	Amy Klee
Managing Editor, Web	Christine Liu
Associate Editors, Web	Jill Fisher Roger Metcalf
Senior Video Editor	Nick Dakoulas
Product Manager, Cooking School	Anne Bartholomew
Senior Editor, Cooking School	Mari Levine
Design Director, Print	Greg Galvan
Photography Director	Julie Cote
Art Director	Susan Levin
Associate Art Director	Lindsey Timko
Art Director, Marketing	Jennifer Cox
Deputy Art Director, Marketing	Melanie Gryboski
Associate Art Director, Marketing	Janet Taylor
Designer, Marketing	Stephanie Cook
Staff Photographer	Daniel J. van Ackere
Associate Art Director, Photography	Steve Klise
VP, Print and Direct Marketing	David Mack
Circulation Director	Doug Wicinski
Circulation & Fulfillment Manager	Carrie Fethe
Partnership Marketing Manager	Pamela Putprush
Marketing Assistant	Marina Tomao
Chief Operating Officer	Rob Ristagno
VP, Digital Products	Fran Middleton
Production Director	Guy Rochford
Production & Imaging Specialists	Heather Dube Dennis Noble Lauren Robbins Jessica Voas
Director, Business Systems	Alice Carpenter
Project Manager	Britt Dresser
Director of Engingeering	Welling LaGrone
Senior Controller	Theresa Peterson
Customer Loyalty & Support Manager	Amy Bootier
Customer Loyalty & Support Reps	Rebecca Kowalski Andrew Straaberg Finfrock Juliet Tierney
VP, New Business Development	Michael Burton
Director, Marketing & Sales	Deborah Fagone
Client Services Manager	Kate Zebrowski
Sponsorship Sales Associate	Morgan Mannino
Director, Retail Book Program	Beth Ineson
Human Resources Director	Adele Shapiro
Publicity	Deborah Broide

PRINTED IN THE USA

THE NEXT TOWN OVER

I came back to town 10 years after my mother sold the family farm. Looking for a piece of land, I stopped by the Wayside Country Store and asked after Junior Bentley, the dairy farmer I had worked for as a kid. I was told that Junior could be in only one of three places, none of them farther afield than "the next town over." I finally found him haying by the Battenkill, and he directed me to an old dairy farm turned cornfield over on the west side.

Years later, it occurred to me that very few locals ever traveled farther than the next town over. Our village has limits: the edge of Mike Lourie's dairy farm as it butts up toward New York State and the town of Hebron. The steep run of mountains over to the east side, referred to as "The Oven." The Congregational church to the northwest, which has a good supper the first Saturday of every month. To the north, the high peaks of Merck Forest with its wild, rolling landscapes. And then the cornfields to the south, stretching out toward the flatlands of New York.

There are stories of neighbors who have ventured farther afield. Two years ago, Axel Blomberg went lake fishing in Maine and was shook up when a bear swam toward his canoe. Fifteen years ago a bar a few towns away hosted a Saturday a.m. lingerie show; some of the local carpenters and plumbers didn't get home until late afternoon. And, of course, locals do venture out in August and September for their once-a-year outing. They attend a country fair—the one up in Rutland, the Bondville Fair, or the famous Tunbridge World's Fair with the pig races and the giant pumpkin weigh-in—or they head to the drive-in in Hoosick Falls, setting up lawn chairs in the backs of pickups and eating double portions of the thick homemade French fries from the cement-block commissary. The only neighbors who really do travel are the horse people—they trailer their horses for gymkhana competitions. The rest of us might take in one rodeo every few years, perhaps heading up to Pond Hill Ranch in Castleton or driving over to Ballston Spa south of Saratoga, New York. (One or two neighbors have been known to take the bus down to Mohegan Sun to play blackjack, but that's hush-hush.)

Christopher Kimball

But for the most part, folks in our town don't travel much. They show up at exactly the same time every morning at Sherman's Country Store for coffee and doughnuts. (My neighbor Doug is there at 6:30 a.m. like clockwork.) Mike Lourie and his family are tending to their dairy herd 24/7, growing and storing silage, milking, and fixing equipment. There is always someone around at the fire department. Saturdays are busy at the historic town library. Jed is either baking sourdough (his Rupert Rising bread is world-class) or delivering it, and either Kelli or Dan (who both run Sherman's Store) is always at the counter with a quip and ready change. Improbably, our tiny town has two post offices and three churches—you can always run into neighbors there. During the summer, Skip Wilson's brood is always out and about running riding mowers and weedwacking until dark like some highly trained circus act. They do my lawn in 10 minutes flat.

So the question arises: What does one know about life if one hasn't seen Kevin Spacey on Broadway or ordered steak frites and a cheap bottle of Côtes du Rhône at a small café on Rue du Bac in Paris? Outsiders who drive through our town see a collection of old Vermont houses, almost all of them white clapboard, most neat and well cared for, but more than a few veterans of prior renovations, some thoughtful and some not. It just doesn't look special, unlike a tour of hill towns of Italy or a trip to the Dalmatian Coast. But when you spend time there, put down roots, you discover something unexpected.

What that is, exactly, I can't quite figure. I have walked through the Sahara Desert, I have visited the Hmong people in northern Vietnam, I have fished in Patagonia, and I have driven a Land Rover through the Mountains of the Moon in the Congo, but none of those adventures brought back wisdom. But a cup of coffee at Sherman's often leaves me happier and slightly more knowledgeable regarding the human condition.

Maybe small towns are unconnected to the march of history. I have yet to see a neighbor using any sort of portable electronic device other than a GPS hung around the neck of a hunting dog. Instead, I am invited to a viewing of the monster buck shot by Skip's wife last November, hanging skinned and headless in the small shed by his father's house. Or I stop by Axel's in late summer to get his report on that season's fishing—fewer than 100 brook trout is a bad year. Or I get a strong whiff of liquid manure spread by the honey truck on the cornfield out behind my house as I drink my morning coffee. Little things loom large—the gift of a slow cooker, a slice of well-made apple pie, a sunny day after a stretch of subzero weather, and a can of Labatt Blue after a long day haying or digging potatoes.

It's not idyllic. It's not romantic. People die unexpectedly, some by their own hand after a bad diagnosis, others due to accidents with chain saws or falling trees. Alcohol takes its toll as do hard times.

But life in our town isn't missing anything. It's not digital; it's personal. And in this day and age, that's saying something.

FOR INQUIRIES, ORDERS, OR MORE INFORMATION

CooksIllustrated.com
At CooksIllustrated.com, you can order books and subscriptions, sign up for our free e-newsletter, or renew your magazine subscription. Join the website and gain access to 22 years of *Cook's Illustrated* recipes, equipment tests, and ingredient tastings, as well as companion videos for every recipe in this issue.

COOKBOOKS
We sell more than 50 cookbooks by the editors of *Cook's Illustrated*, including *The Cook's Illustrated Cookbook* and *The Science of Good Cooking*. To order, visit our bookstore at CooksIllustrated.com/bookstore.

COOK'S ILLUSTRATED MAGAZINE
Cook's Illustrated magazine (ISSN 1068-2821), number 134, is published bimonthly by Boston Common Press Limited Partnership, 17 Station St., Brookline, MA 02445. Copyright 2015 Boston Common Press Limited Partnership. Periodicals postage paid at Boston, MA, and additional mailing offices, USPS #012487. Publications Mail Agreement No. 40020778. Return undeliverable Canadian addresses to P.O. Box 875, Station A, Windsor, ON N9A 6P2. POSTMASTER: Send address changes to *Cook's Illustrated*, P.O. Box 6018, Harlan, IA 51593-1518. For subscription and gift subscription orders, subscription inquiries, or change of address notices, visit AmericasTestKitchen.com/support, call 800-526-8442 in the U.S. or 515-248-7684 from outside the U.S., or write to us at *Cook's Illustrated*, P.O. 6018, Harlan, IA 51593-1518.

FOR LIST RENTAL INFORMATION Contact Specialists Marketing Services, Inc., 777 Terrace Ave., 4th Floor, Hasbrouck Heights, NJ 07604; phone: 201-865-5800.

EDITORIAL OFFICE 17 Station St., Brookline, MA 02445; 617-232-1000; fax: 617-232-1572. For subscription inquiries, visit AmericasTestKitchen.com/support or call 800-526-8442.

QUICK TIPS

⋛ COMPILED BY SHANNON FRIEDMANN HATCH ⋚

Disposable "Gloves" for Seeding Chiles

When Dan Siegel of Philadelphia, Pa., needs to seed chiles but doesn't have any latex gloves to protect against the burn of capsaicin, he covers his hands with a pair of plastic zipper-lock bags. Use sandwich bags if your hands are smaller, quart-size if they're larger.

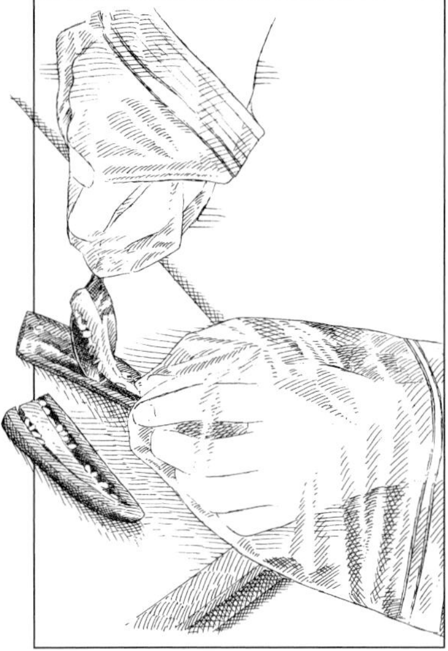

Stand-In Cookbook Stand

Barbara Brown of Elkins Park, Pa., has discovered an unconventional use for her large salad bowl: a cookbook stand. Unlike a flat countertop, it elevates the book at an angle for easy reference during cooking.

A More Efficient Way to Tenderize Kale

We've found that kneading and squeezing chopped raw kale tenderizes the hearty green, but since you can work only so much kale in your hands at one time, Joni McGary of Bloomington, Ind., came up with a more efficient approach: She places a few cups of leaves in a partially open zipper-lock bag and presses on them with a rolling pin for about 2½ minutes.

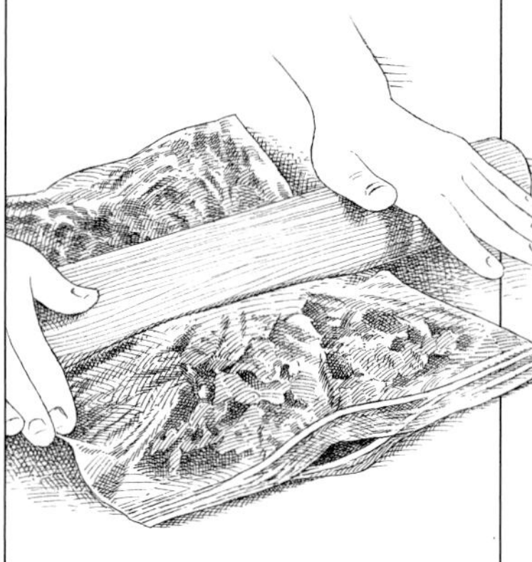

Cleaning Crevices

Cookware with tight crevices, like panini presses and grill pans, can be hard to clean. Karen Pizzuto-Sharp of Seattle, Wash., has found a solution in a compressed air duster. Designed to clean in between the keys on a keyboard, the can's fine blast of air also lifts off crumbs in narrow cooking spaces.

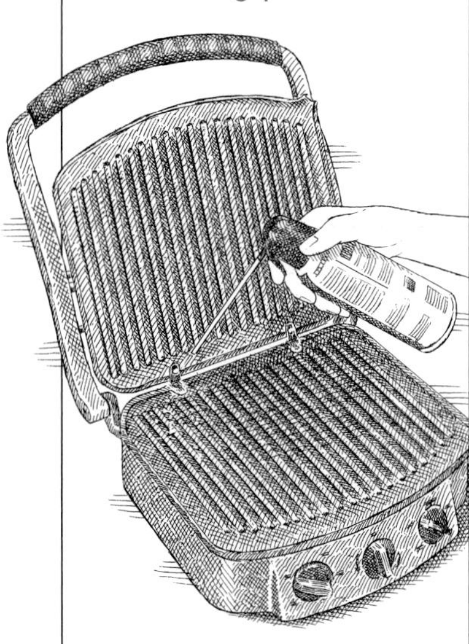

Confining Messy Cutting Jobs

When chopping juicy tomatoes or segmenting citrus fruits, Marjorie Thomsen of Cambridge, Mass., places her cutting board in a rimmed baking sheet. The shallow walls keep any runny juices contained while allowing easy access to the food.

Extra Holding "Platter"

When Susan Feller of West Tisbury, Mass., is batch-cooking meat in her cast-iron Dutch oven and needs a spot to hold the parcooked food while she sautés other ingredients, she uses the lid to the Dutch oven. The upturned lid makes a neat holding spot for items until they are ready to go back into the pot.

ILLUSTRATION: JOHN BURGOYNE

SEND US YOUR TIPS We will provide a complimentary one-year subscription for each tip we print. Send your tip, name, address, and daytime telephone number to Quick Tips, *Cook's Illustrated*, P.O. Box 470589, Brookline, MA 02447, or to QuickTips@AmericasTestKitchen.com.

Stringing Up Herbs to Dry

Wendy Bruck of Meadowbrook, Pa., often air-dries herbs by hanging them with kitchen twine but occasionally runs out of twine. As a backup, she uses unflavored dental floss, which is strong enough to hold the bundles and easy to cut on the built-in tab.

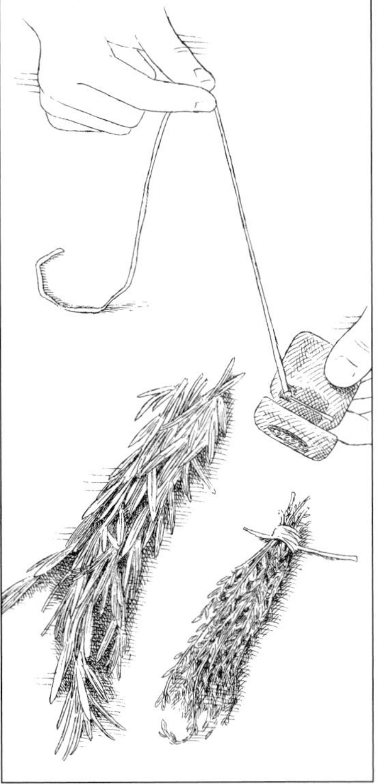

Pizza Cutter Cover

A sharp pizza wheel can be a dangerous hazard in a tool drawer, as many do not come with a guard to shield the blade. Drucie Andersen of McLean, Va., fashions a cover using a new sponge—just slice an opening in the side and insert the blade to store.

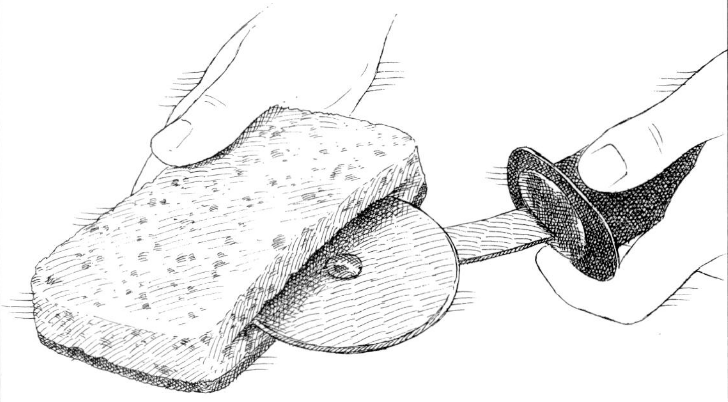

Alternative Sandwich Press

Karen Lacouture of Naples, Fla., doesn't own a panini press but gets by instead with her waffle iron. Like a panini press, the iron closes partially over the sandwich and compresses it while also imprinting appealing crosshatch marks.

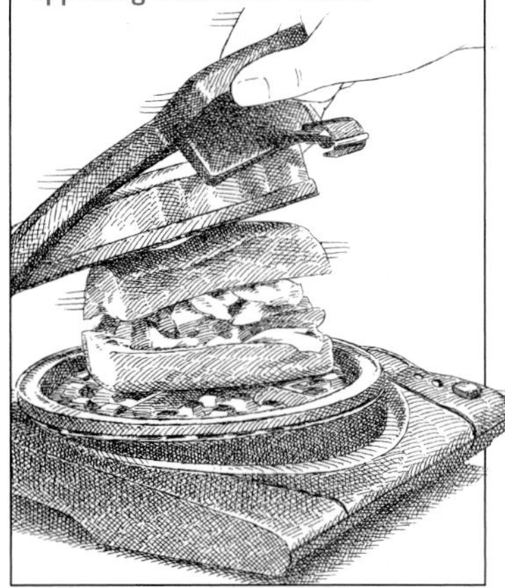

Streamlining Hard-Cooked Eggs

When making a large number of hard-cooked eggs at once, Kate Enroth of Milwaukie, Ore., skips the fussy step of fishing each one from the hot water with a slotted spoon. Instead, she cooks the eggs in her pasta pot with a strainer insert. When they're done, she can simply lift out the strainer and place it (with all the eggs inside) into a large bowl of ice-cold water.

Another Way to Keep Brown Sugar Soft

To prevent brown sugar from turning rock hard, Pam Danely of Raleigh, N.C., drops a large marshmallow into the package. Its moisture prevents the sugar from drying out.

A Better Way to Store Mushrooms

To keep loose mushrooms fresh for as long as possible, Theresa Hrach of Sewickley, Pa., places them in an empty strawberry container. Its vents allow spoilage-hastening ethylene gas to disperse.

Mess-Free Chocolate Chopping

Chopping baking chocolate usually leaves bits of the bar strewn all over the work surface, so Sheelagh El-Harbi of Skibbereen, Co. Cork, Ireland, came up with a neater solution: In lieu of chopping, she whacks the unwrapped bar against the edge of the counter to break it up into pieces while the wrapper keeps the pieces contained. (The uneven pieces will work fine in any recipe that calls for melted chocolate, such as brownies or ganache.)

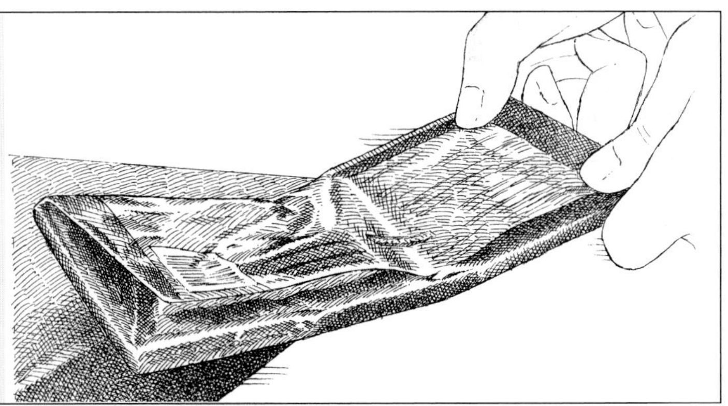

Simple Pot-au-Feu

The rich broth and tender meat and vegetables that define this French classic should be an easy way to feed a crowd. Why do so many recipes turn it into an ordeal?

⋟ BY DAN SOUZA ⋞

By many accounts, pot-au-feu—which translates literally to "pot on the fire"—has been France's most celebrated dish since the French Revolution, extolled for providing sustenance to rich, poor, and everyone in between. Typically, several cuts of meat (beef is most common) are simmered in a pot of water with potatoes and other root vegetables until tender, at which point the meat is carved and portioned into bowls with the vegetables and the clear, complex-tasting broth is ladled over the top. To give the dish kick, pungent condiments like mustard and the tiny French pickles known as cornichons are served alongside.

In search of a satisfying meal for spring, I decided it was time to try making the dish myself. But when I gathered recipes, I was met with surprise. I was expecting modest ingredient lists in keeping with pot-au-feu's reputation as a food of the people, but most were anything but. Instead of two or three meats, they called for practically an entire butcher's case: beef and veal shanks, oxtail, short ribs, veal breast, sausages, chicken livers—some even an entire bird. Even the more pared-down recipes specified cuts that most Americans can't easily find.

A robust parsley, mustard, and cornichon sauce goes directly on the meat before the savory broth is added, making this dish anything but bland.

Still, I wasn't ready to give up on the idea of a one-pot meal, especially one that seemed as tailor-made for a special occasion as for a family dinner. What could I do to make it more approachable?

Mixed Meats

My first step was putting aside the massive stockpot employed by most recipes in favor of a more manageable Dutch oven, which would still provide plenty of room for a recipe serving six to eight. Next, I looked to whittle down the meat on the shopping list. Since beef was common to all the recipes I found, I made the bold decision to limit myself to it—and to just one cut. I rounded up three good contenders: short ribs, brisket, and chuck-eye roast. Short ribs cooked relatively quickly (in just a couple of hours) and stayed juicy, but their steep price tag was a turnoff. Brisket, which is the foundation of a New England boiled dinner, performed reasonably well, but it was bested in both flavor and texture by chuck roast for its compact and uniform shape, deep flavor, and relative tenderness. Gently stewing a 4-pound roast (cut into two smaller roasts for faster cooking) for roughly 3½ hours in about 3 quarts of water until tender yielded plenty of juicy, sliceable meat, but the broth tasted a bit weak.

I'd already cut the amount of water back at the start when I swapped the stockpot for the Dutch oven. Why not cut it back further and turn what was basically a soup into a braise for even more concentrated, flavorful results? I gave it a try, covering the meat only halfway with water and flipping it partway through cooking. Sure enough, I ended up with a quart of deeply flavored broth. I also took this opportunity to move the cooking to a low oven so I wouldn't have to fiddle with the burner to keep the broth at a consistent gentle simmer.

Still, the broth was coming up short. Not meatiness, exactly, but something else. It occurred to me that in my haste to pare down the recipe, I'd overlooked a critical component: bones. Every single recipe I'd come across specified bone-in cuts, particularly beef shank. I knew from years of making stock that bones lend body to broth since their collagen breaks down into gelatin during cooking. But they also lend something else: marrow.

Marrow, the soft, flexible tissue found inside bones, is responsible for red blood cell production in animals. It is rich in amino acids, especially in glutamic acid, the primary compound responsible for the meaty taste called umami. It also contains a slew of volatile flavor compounds including, interestingly enough, diacetyl, a component of natural butter flavor. Marrow is present in bones from many parts of the cow, but the femur, where the shank is cut from, contains an especially high amount.

So where was I going to find a good source of marrow outside of buying beef shank? The good news was that marrow bones, often called soup bones, are not only readily available in most supermarkets but also inexpensive (for more information, see "Bone Up for Better Broth"). After running a few tests, I settled on using 1½ pounds of bones. Combined with the chuck, they gave me a broth with the beguiling mix of beefiness and butteriness that helps make traditional pot-au-feu a standout.

Clearing the Air

French cooks insist that a proper pot-au-feu broth be clear, not cloudy. To this end, most recipes called for skimming the foam, made up of proteins and fats, that rises to the top of the pot, lest it get suspended or emulsified into the broth during cooking. I tried omitting the skimming step and found that as long as the stock didn't boil (the physical action of boiling churns fat and particles into the broth and makes it cloudy), it didn't make a difference whether I skimmed—the proteins and fats settled to the bottom of the pot during cooking and were caught and discarded when I strained the liquid. (For more information, see "For a Clearer Stock, Simmer; Don't Boil," on page 31.)

Speaking of which, I was already passing the broth through a fine-mesh strainer, but classic recipes also call for straining the broth through layers of cheesecloth to further refine it. While I found that this step could get rid of more of the fine detritus, it didn't make enough of a difference to be worth the effort.

Nor did I see any need to fuss over bundling together a sachet of herbs and such in cheesecloth per tradition. Along the way I'd whittled down the list to what I thought was worth keeping. I'd ditched thyme and parsley stems and just kept it simple, using bay leaves and peppercorns along with a celery rib and a quartered onion, which were all easily removed during the straining step.

Making a Meal

The range of vegetables found in pot-au-feu varies as much as the meat. The classics include potatoes, carrots, leeks, parsnips, and turnips. In the name of simplicity, I narrowed it down to my tasters' top picks: potatoes and carrots. But I also tested some green vegetables to freshen up the pot, and I found that asparagus added brightness and appealing color. Because I had switched from stewing the meat to braising, I didn't have enough liquid in the pot to add the vegetables while the meat was in there. So I transferred the finished chuck to a serving platter and popped it back into the oven (which I had turned off) to keep warm; I then defatted and strained the broth and returned it to the pot. In went the vegetables for a quick simmer, and that was it.

I loved the meat sprinkled with sea salt and parsley, dabbed with Dijon mustard, and chased with a sour cornichon, as is traditional, but then I came up with something I liked even more: a simple sauce featuring those accompaniments plus chives, white wine vinegar, and pepper. This bright sauce needed some fat for balance, so I used the back of a spoon to harvest the soft marrow that was left in the center of the bones, minced it, and added it to the sauce. That beefy, buttery stuff elevated the sauce just as it had the broth. I not only dolloped it over the meat but also tossed a few tablespoons with the vegetables.

Here was a "pot on the fire" that was simple and as satisfying as any dish I could imagine.

ONE CUT IS PLENTY

Most pot-au-feu recipes call for a slew of different meats. To streamline, we settled on just one cut: chuck-eye roast, which delivers tender, beefy-tasting meat with a fraction of the effort or expense required by many classic renditions. This roast also needs very little prep.

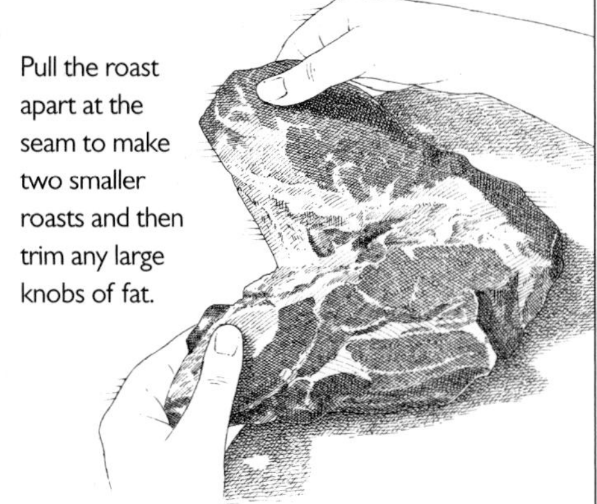
Pull the roast apart at the seam to make two smaller roasts and then trim any large knobs of fat.

SIMPLE POT-AU-FEU

SERVES 6 TO 8

Marrow bones (also called soup bones) can be found in the freezer section or the meat counter at most supermarkets. Use small red potatoes measuring 1 to 2 inches in diameter.

Meat

- **1 (3½- to 4-pound) boneless beef chuck-eye roast, pulled into two pieces at natural seam and trimmed**
- **Kosher salt**
- **1½ pounds marrow bones**
- **1 onion, quartered**
- **1 celery rib, sliced thin**
- **3 bay leaves**
- **1 teaspoon black peppercorns**

Parsley Sauce

- **⅔ cup minced fresh parsley**
- **¼ cup Dijon mustard**
- **¼ cup minced fresh chives**
- **3 tablespoons white wine vinegar**
- **10 cornichons, minced**
- **1½ teaspoons pepper**

Vegetables

- **1 pound small red potatoes, halved**
- **6 carrots, halved crosswise, thick halves quartered lengthwise, thin halves halved lengthwise**
- **1 pound asparagus, trimmed**
- **Kosher salt and pepper**

Flake sea salt

1. FOR THE MEAT: Adjust oven rack to lower-middle position and heat oven to 300 degrees. Season beef with 1 tablespoon salt. Using 3 pieces of kitchen twine per piece, tie each into loaf shape for even cooking. Place beef, bones, onion, celery, bay leaves, and peppercorns in Dutch oven. Add 4 cups cold water (water should come halfway up roasts). Bring to simmer over high heat. Partially cover pot and transfer to oven. Cook until beef is fully tender and sharp knife easily slips in and out of meat (meat will not be shreddable), 3¼ to 3¾ hours, flipping beef over halfway through cooking.

2. FOR THE PARSLEY SAUCE: While beef cooks, combine all ingredients in bowl. Cover and set aside.

3. Remove pot from oven and turn off oven. Transfer beef to large platter, cover tightly with aluminum foil, and return to oven to keep warm. Transfer bones to cutting board and use end of spoon to extract marrow. Mince marrow into paste and add 2 tablespoons to parsley sauce (reserve any remaining marrow for other applications). Using ladle or large spoon, skim fat from surface of broth and discard fat. Strain broth through fine-mesh strainer into large liquid measuring cup; add water to make 6 cups. Return broth to pot. (Meat can be returned to broth, cooled, and refrigerated for up to 2 days. Skim fat from cold broth, then gently reheat and proceed with recipe.)

4. FOR THE VEGETABLES: Add potatoes to broth and bring to simmer over high heat. Reduce heat to medium and simmer for 6 minutes. Add carrots and cook 10 minutes longer. Add asparagus and continue to cook until all vegetables are tender, 3 to 5 minutes longer.

5. Using slotted spoon, transfer vegetables to large bowl. Toss with 3 tablespoons parsley sauce and season with salt and pepper to taste. Season broth with salt to taste.

6. Transfer beef to cutting board, remove twine, and slice against grain ½ inch thick. Arrange servings of beef and vegetables in large, shallow bowls. Dollop beef with parsley sauce, drizzle with ⅓ cup broth, and sprinkle with flake sea salt. Serve, passing remaining parsley sauce and flake sea salt separately.

Bone Up for Better Broth

One thing our chuck-eye roast didn't deliver was the silky body and almost buttery flavor of a broth made from bone-in cuts. The solution was simple: Add marrow bones. The soft tissue found inside the bones is packed with the amino acids responsible for meaty, umami flavors. It also contains the volatile compound diacetyl, a component of natural butter flavor, and brings a subtle buttery taste to the broth. As an added bonus, at the end of cooking, we scrape the marrow from the bones and stir it into our sauce to give it a beefy, rich boost.

Look: It's Simple
Video available free for 4 months at CooksIllustrated.com/june15

The Best Way to Grill Pork Tenderloin

To make the most of this supertender—but very mild—cut, we turn it into kebabs.

BY ANDREA GEARY

When the National Pork Board began advertising its product as "The Other White Meat" in 1987, it spoke the truth. Pork tenderloin, in particular, has the same assets and liabilities as the ever-popular boneless, skinless chicken breast. On the plus side, it's economical, lean, and quick to prepare. The downside? It lacks flavor and has a tendency to dry out when cooked.

Brushing a pork tenderloin with a potent glaze and grilling it can mitigate one of the problems, to a degree: The intense heat creates some flavorful char on the outside of the meat—but only on the outside. This time around, I decided to embrace the reality of the situation: If the exterior was the best-tasting part, then I would increase the amount of exterior. That would mean cutting the meat into pieces, coating them in a glaze, and grilling them on skewers. More surface area would equal more glaze and more smoky char and, thus, more flavor. Problem solved.

Or so I thought. My first attempt didn't go well. I started by cutting two 12-ounce tenderloins into 1-inch chunks. Taking my inspiration from Chinese barbecued pork, I tossed the meat with a superquick, no-cook glaze: soy sauce, sugar (which would encourage charring), five-spice powder, and garlic powder. I threaded the chunks onto skewers and grilled the kebabs on a hot grill. After just 6 minutes, the pork had reached the target temperature of 140 degrees. But in that brief time, the thin glaze had dripped off, the pork had dried out, and the meat had stuck to the grill.

For my next attempt, I tossed the pork with salt and let it sit for 20 minutes while I heated the grill and mixed up the glaze. We've learned that salting raw meat changes the structure of its exterior proteins in a way that enables them to hold on to more moisture. I also swapped the watery soy sauce for thicker, sweeter hoisin, which meant that I could skip the sugar. After stirring in the garlic and five-spice powders, I coated the chunks with the viscous mixture. I threaded the pieces onto skewers, spritzed them with vegetable oil spray to reduce sticking, and arranged the kebabs on the hot grates.

This was an improvement: The meat didn't stick, and more of the glaze had clung to it. Still, the exterior didn't offer as much rich flavor as I had hoped.

Watch It Step by Step
Video available free for 4 months at CooksIllustrated.com/june15

I made two more changes. First, I added ½ teaspoon of cornstarch to the hoisin mixture. This would help the glaze cling better since the cornstarch would gelatinize (or soak up and trap excess liquid) in the heat of the grill. Second, thinking ahead, I set aside 1½ tablespoons of the glaze before tossing the pork in the rest of it. After I flipped the skewers on the grill, I brushed them with the reserved glaze.

Much better. Thanks to the cornstarch and the second glaze addition, each piece of moist, juicy pork boasted some crusty char and a sticky coating. To complete the Chinese barbecued pork vision, I garnished the skewers with a sprinkle of sliced scallions.

To adapt this approach to other flavor profiles, I devised a spicy-sweet variation combining Sriracha and brown sugar and an American barbecue version with ketchup, chili powder, and liquid smoke. Now the other white meat seems like a much more attractive option for a quick dinner.

Adding a bit of cornstarch to the glaze makes it just thick enough to cling.

GRILLED PORK KEBABS WITH HOISIN AND FIVE-SPICE

SERVES 4

You will need four 12-inch metal skewers. We prefer natural pork, but if your pork is enhanced (injected with a salt solution), do not salt it in step 1. For our free recipes for Grilled Pork Kebabs with Barbecue Glaze, Grilled Pork Kebabs with Barbecue Glaze for Two, Grilled Pork Kebabs with Hoisin and Five-Spice for Two, and Grilled Pork Kebabs with Sweet Sriracha Glaze for Two, go to CooksIllustrated.com/june15.

- 2 (12-ounce) pork tenderloins, trimmed and cut into 1-inch chunks
- 1 teaspoon kosher salt
- 1½ teaspoons five-spice powder
- ¾ teaspoon garlic powder
- ½ teaspoon cornstarch
- 4½ tablespoons hoisin sauce
- Vegetable oil spray
- 2 scallions, thinly sliced

1. Toss pork and salt together in large bowl and let sit for 20 minutes. Meanwhile, whisk five-spice powder, garlic powder, and cornstarch together in bowl. Add hoisin to five-spice mixture and stir to combine. Set aside 1½ tablespoons hoisin mixture.

2. Add remaining hoisin mixture to pork and toss to coat. Thread pork onto four 12-inch metal skewers, leaving ¼ inch between pieces. Spray both sides of meat generously with oil spray.

3A. FOR A CHARCOAL GRILL: Open bottom vent completely. Light large chimney starter filled with charcoal briquettes (6 quarts). When top coals are partially covered with ash, pour evenly over half of grill. Set cooking grate in place, cover, and open lid vent completely. Heat grill until hot, about 5 minutes.

3B. FOR A GAS GRILL: Turn all burners to high, cover, and heat grill until hot, about 15 minutes. Leave primary burner on high and turn off other burner(s).

4. Clean and oil cooking grate. Place skewers on hotter side of grill and grill until well charred, 3 to 4 minutes. Flip skewers, brush with reserved hoisin mixture, and continue to grill until second side is well charred and meat registers 140 degrees, 3 to 4 minutes longer. Transfer to serving platter, tent loosely with aluminum foil, and let rest for 5 minutes. Sprinkle with scallions and serve.

GRILLED PORK KEBABS WITH SWEET SRIRACHA GLAZE

Substitute 3 tablespoons packed brown sugar and 1½ tablespoons Sriracha sauce for five-spice powder, garlic powder, and hoisin sauce. Increase cornstarch to 1 teaspoon. Substitute ¼ cup minced fresh cilantro for scallions.

Ultimate Roasted Potatoes

For the crispest, most flavorful roasted potatoes, rethink the fat.

⋟ BY ANDREW JANJIGIAN ⋞

When I'm craving roast potatoes that are a step up from the norm, I dip into the stash of leftover bacon fat that I keep tucked away in my fridge. The meaty grease bolsters the dish with a flavor and richness that plain olive oil can't match.

Normally, I simply cut up whatever potatoes I have on hand, toss them with a few tablespoons of the grease, and roast them in a hot oven until tender. While the results are always good, I wanted to pull out all the stops and create an ultimate version: perfectly seasoned potatoes with supercrisp, golden-brown exteriors and moist interiors. It would also be fun, I decided, to experiment with duck fat instead of bacon fat. Once a rarity, this fat has become so popular during the past few years that it's now sold by the pint in many supermarkets.

I rounded up a bushel of Yukon Gold potatoes, which boast an ideal balance of starchiness and waxiness that would yield crisp-on-the-outside, moist-on-the-inside results. I peeled 3½ pounds of potatoes, cut them into chunks, and tossed them with 3 tablespoons of duck fat and some chopped fresh rosemary (its piney taste is a natural match for potatoes) before roasting them on a baking sheet in a 450-degree oven. Instead of painstakingly turning each individual piece, I used a scrape-and-toss approach, letting the potatoes brown on one side for 15 minutes and then using a sharp, thin spatula to shuffle them around. Repeating this twice during roasting ensured that any unbrowned sides got a shot at receiving direct heat from the bottom of the sheet. Finally, I sprinkled the chunks with kosher salt as they came out of the oven.

This first-round sample wasn't nearly as good as I'd hoped that it would be. For one, the potatoes were underseasoned, despite my generous hand with salt. They also lacked sufficient meaty flavor from the fat, and some of the rosemary had burned. What's more, the chunks shed moisture as they cooked, causing them to end up somewhat shriveled and parched on the interior. And their exteriors weren't sufficiently crisp.

I focused on the textural downfalls first. Covering the baking sheet with foil at the start of roasting trapped moisture, but once the foil was removed, the chunks were so wet that they took a long time to brown. By the time the outsides finally took on color, the insides were once again dried out.

I needed potatoes with a quick-browning, starchy exterior layer surrounding an interior that would stay moist during roasting. We faced the same conundrum when developing our Home Fries recipe (January/February 2012). The solution? Boil the potatoes for just 1 minute in water laced with baking soda. The soda rapidly degrades the pectin in the cells at the exterior of the potato, causing them to release a wet starch that rapidly browns. After draining the chunks, I further roughed up their exteriors by stirring them vigorously with 5 tablespoons of the duck fat—enough to boost meaty flavor without causing greasiness—and more salt. This left them coated in a thick paste that I hoped would transform in the oven into an ultracrisp shell.

A surprise ingredient helps produce a crisp, golden-brown outer layer that envelops a moist, fluffy interior.

To prevent the rosemary from burning, I mixed it with an extra tablespoon of fat and stirred this mixture into the potatoes toward the end of cooking. When this batch came out of the oven, I seasoned it with ground black pepper and a little more salt. These were some seriously good spuds: richly flavored with spot-on seasoning, golden brown and crisp on the outside, and moist and fluffy on the inside.

Lastly, I experimented with other types of animal fat. Unsurprisingly, chicken fat and lard produced outstanding results. Bacon fat worked better when cut with olive oil so that its salty and smoky flavors didn't take over. With a little know-how (and a little fat), I'd produced crispy roasted potatoes that taste just as good as they sound.

Saving Fat for Cooking

Saving the leftover fat from bacon, roasts, or poultry is easy to do. Pour the warm fat through a fine-mesh strainer into a Mason jar and discard any solids. (Alternatively, let the fat cool and harden and then scoop it into the jar, leaving any solids behind.) Put the lid on the jar, label it, and refrigerate it for up to one month or freeze it for up to six months, adding more fat as desired.

DUCK FAT–ROASTED POTATOES

SERVES 6

Duck fat is available in the meat department in many supermarkets. Alternatively, substitute chicken fat, lard, or a mixture of 3 tablespoons of bacon fat and 3 tablespoons of extra-virgin olive oil.

- **3½ pounds Yukon Gold potatoes, peeled and cut into 1½-inch pieces**
- **Kosher salt and pepper**
- **½ teaspoon baking soda**
- **6 tablespoons duck fat**
- **1 tablespoon chopped fresh rosemary**

1. Adjust oven rack to top position, place rimmed baking sheet on rack, and heat oven to 475 degrees.

2. Bring 10 cups water to boil in Dutch oven over high heat. Add potatoes, ⅓ cup salt, and baking soda. Return to boil and cook for 1 minute. Drain potatoes. Return potatoes to pot and place over low heat. Cook, shaking pot occasionally, until surface moisture has evaporated, about 2 minutes. Remove from heat. Add 5 tablespoons fat and 1 teaspoon salt; mix with rubber spatula until potatoes are coated with thick paste, about 30 seconds.

3. Remove sheet from oven, transfer potatoes to sheet, and spread into even layer. Roast for 15 minutes.

4. Remove sheet from oven. Using thin, sharp, metal spatula, turn potatoes. Roast until golden brown, 12 to 15 minutes. While potatoes roast, combine rosemary and remaining 1 tablespoon fat in bowl.

5. Remove sheet from oven. Spoon rosemary-fat mixture over potatoes and turn again. Continue to roast until potatoes are well browned and rosemary is fragrant, 3 to 5 minutes. Season with salt and pepper to taste. Serve immediately.

See How Ducky They Are
Video available free for 4 months at CooksIllustrated.com/june15

Introducing Semolina Gnocchi

These Roman-style dumplings are rich, creamy, and satisfying. The only problem? Getting them out of the pan.

BY DAVID PAZMIÑO

Gnocchi to me has always meant pillowy, thimble-size dumplings shaped from a dough of riced potato, flour, and egg, and so that's what I was expecting when I ordered so-called Roman gnocchi at a recent dinner out. But instead of the familiar little boiled pouches, these gnocchi turned out to be plump 2-inch rounds that arrived at the table shingled in a baking dish. One bite and I was sold: Made from semolina flour, egg, and cheese, with a creamy, slightly dense texture more like that of polenta than potato dumplings, they were pure comfort food. And though I ate them plain, I could easily see their potential as a light dinner when served with a sauce. I would definitely be making these at home the first chance I got.

When I gathered recipes, I found that all followed the same basic approach. Each began with semolina, a deep yellow flour made from durum wheat that has a richer flavor and coarser texture than regular wheat flour. The semolina is whisked into a heated liquid (usually milk) and stirred over the heat until it comes together to make a pourable batter or dough (much like the process for making polenta). Eggs, butter, and cheese are then stirred in to enrich the mixture and help it set up. At that point, most recipes call for spreading the dough out on a flat surface into a thick slab and letting it cool until stiff enough to cut into rounds with a biscuit cutter. The disks are then shingled (which helps keep them moist), topped with additional butter and cheese, and reheated in a baking dish.

These polenta-like gnocchi are fashioned from a dough made of semolina flour, butter, egg, and cheese. In our version, baking powder provides lift.

When I took these recipes into the kitchen, I found that the process was indeed straightforward, but the results presented a host of issues. The cooked mixture often took an awfully long time to cool and firm up to a stiff enough consistency to allow for stamping out the dumplings, and even then it was problematic, with a wet consistency that made cleanly cutting out circles and transferring them to a baking dish difficult at best. I also didn't like that much of the semolina mixture was wasted in the cutting-out process. And because the dough was fairly soft, the dumplings tended to fuse together in the heat of the oven, which made it impossible to lift them out individually for neat, attractive portions. And finally, there was the flavor—or lack thereof. Most versions tasted bland or starchy. I wanted a recipe that gave me individual dumplings with enough flavor to stand alone with a salad or be served with a simple sauce.

Watch the Shaping Process
Video available free for 4 months at CooksIllustrated.com/june15

Flour Power

Finding the proper ratio of milk to semolina flour seemed like the most promising way to address the consistency problems. Recipes that called for significantly more liquid than flour took too long to cook, barely set up once cooled, and formed a unified and barely distinguishable mass once baked. Those that relied on a ratio on the lower end of that spectrum resulted in gnocchi that took much less time to cook to the desired thick consistency and set up much more firmly. Unfortunately, they also tasted floury and had a pasty texture because the semolina wasn't able to fully hydrate. Several tests later, I found the happy medium: 2½ cups liquid to 1 cup semolina gave me a dough with the right consistency but without that raw-flour flavor.

Now that I had the texture right, I was ready to further improve the flavor. First, the liquid. I tested versions using all water, all milk, a 50/50 combination of the two, and all chicken broth. All milk contributed the best flavor.

Next I addressed the butter, egg, and cheese, which are added to the dough after it comes off the heat. Three tablespoons of butter (plus one more to grease the pan) lent adequate flavor and richness without tipping my gnocchi over into greasy territory.

But figuring out the eggs wasn't as easy. Recipes were all over the map: Some called for whole eggs, others only yolks, while yet others relied on a combination of whole eggs plus yolks. Still others specified yolks plus whipped egg whites. After testing all the options, I found that simplest was best: One lightly beaten whole egg provided sufficient binding power and lightness as well as some richness.

As for the cheese, softer varieties like mozzarella and fontina, which have more moisture than harder aged cheeses, resulted in gnocchi that were too tender and that were inclined to fuse together during baking. I eventually settled on firmer Gruyère since it added flavor without having any negative effect on texture. A bit of grated Parmesan sprinkled over the gnocchi before baking provided another savory hit and gave the dumplings a nicely browned top. My final flavor tweak was to incorporate some minced rosemary and some nutmeg to add complexity and woodsy notes and a hint of warm spice.

Now the flavor was spot on and the texture was really close, but the dumplings were a little denser than I would have liked. Adding more egg would only loosen the mixture and put me back where I started. The answer? Stirring in ½ teaspoon of baking powder when I added the cheese. As it does in many doughs and batters, baking powder gave the dumplings lift.

STEP BY STEP | MAKING SEMOLINA GNOCCHI

By making a very stiff dough and then refrigerating the shaped dumplings before shingling them in the pan, we ensure that they don't fuse together in the oven.

START DOUGH Slowly whisk semolina into warm milk mixture.

FINISH DOUGH Cook over low heat until stiff dough forms. Add butter, egg, cheese, rosemary, and baking powder.

SHAPE GNOCCHI Use moistened ¼ cup measure to portion gnocchi, inverting onto tray.

CHILL Refrigerate gnocchi, uncovered, for 30 minutes.

ARRANGE IN PAN Shingle gnocchi in greased 8-inch square dish, then sprinkle with Parmesan and bake.

Chill Out

Up to this point, I had been cooling the dough by spreading it out in a baking dish and leaving it in the refrigerator for about an hour. But now that I had a very thick dough right off the stove, I didn't really need to let it cool; the dumplings would hold their shape even if warm. Was there a more efficient way to shape them?

One recipe I had seen skipped cutting out rounds and called instead for forming the still-warm dough into oblong torpedo-like shapes. I gave it a try, and while this method avoided waste, it was more labor-intensive than I wanted. There had to be an easier approach. Perhaps I could simply use a ¼-cup dry measuring cup, dipped in water between scoops to avoid sticking, to portion out each dumpling. When I tried this, I ended up with perfectly shaped disks. But there was one issue remaining: Though certainly better than in those early tests, my dumplings still fused together in the oven more than I would have liked.

To ensure easy-to-portion individual dumplings, I found that I could simply let the shaped dumplings cool for 30 minutes in the refrigerator before baking them in a 400-degree oven for 35 to 40 minutes. As our science editor explained, this allowed the swollen starches in the semolina flour to rebond on the exterior and form a "skin" through a process called retrogradation. This meant that, once baked, the dumplings were easy to separate and serve (I let the hot gnocchi sit for 15 minutes before serving so they had time to set up a bit). While a 30-minute stint in the fridge was the minimum, I discovered that the longer the dumplings sat in there—up to 24 hours—the better, so they turned out to be a great make-ahead dish.

These dumplings were just the savory, simple comfort food I was after, but they also lent themselves to some flavorful variations. A combination featuring prosciutto and chives and another with sun-dried tomatoes and basil nicely complemented semolina's nutty, buttery flavor. Whether I went with my simple version or a variation, my semolina gnocchi were as easy to prepare as they were satisfying to eat.

SEMOLINA GNOCCHI (GNOCCHI ALLA ROMANA)

SERVES 4 TO 6

Serve as a side dish or as a light entrée topped with Quick Tomato Sauce (recipe follows) or Broccoli Rabe, Sun-Dried Tomato, and Pine Nut Topping or Sautéed Cherry Tomato and Fresh Mozzarella Topping (go to CooksIllustrated.com/gnocchitoppings). For our free recipe for Semolina Gnocchi with Browned Butter, go to CooksIllustrated.com/june15.

- 2½ cups whole milk
- ¾ teaspoon salt
- Pinch ground nutmeg
- 1 cup (6 ounces) fine semolina flour
- 4 tablespoons unsalted butter
- 1 large egg, lightly beaten
- 1½ ounces Gruyère cheese, shredded (⅓ cup)
- 1 teaspoon minced fresh rosemary
- ½ teaspoon baking powder
- 2 tablespoons grated Parmesan cheese

1. Adjust oven rack to middle position and heat oven to 400 degrees. Heat milk, salt, and nutmeg in medium saucepan over medium-low heat until bubbles form around edges of saucepan. Whisking constantly, slowly add semolina to milk mixture. Reduce heat to low and cook, stirring often with rubber spatula, until mixture forms stiff mass that pulls away from sides when stirring, 3 to 5 minutes. Remove from heat and let cool for 5 minutes.

2. Stir 3 tablespoons butter and egg into semolina mixture until incorporated. (Mixture will appear separated at first but will become smooth and bit shiny.) Stir in Gruyère, rosemary, and baking powder until incorporated.

3. Fill small bowl with water. Moisten ¼-cup dry measuring cup with water and scoop even portion of semolina mixture. Invert gnocchi onto tray or large plate. Repeat, moistening measuring cup between scoops to prevent sticking. Place tray of gnocchi, uncovered, in refrigerator for 30 minutes. (Gnocchi can be refrigerated, covered, for up to 24 hours.)

4. Rub interior of 8-inch square baking dish with remaining 1 tablespoon butter. Shingle gnocchi in pan, creating 3 rows of 4 gnocchi each. Sprinkle gnocchi with Parmesan. Bake until tops of gnocchi are golden brown, 35 to 40 minutes. Let cool for 15 minutes before serving.

SEMOLINA GNOCCHI WITH PROSCIUTTO AND CHIVES

Stir 1½ ounces finely chopped thinly sliced prosciutto into semolina mixture with Gruyère. Substitute 1 tablespoon minced fresh chives for rosemary.

SEMOLINA GNOCCHI WITH SUN-DRIED TOMATOES AND BASIL

Stir ⅓ cup rinsed and patted dry oil-packed sun-dried tomatoes into semolina mixture with Gruyère. Substitute 1 tablespoon minced fresh basil for rosemary.

QUICK TOMATO SAUCE

MAKES ABOUT 3 CUPS

Our favorite crushed tomatoes are Tuttorosso Crushed Tomatoes in Thick Puree with Basil.

- 2 tablespoons unsalted butter
- ¼ cup grated onion
- 1 teaspoon minced fresh oregano or ¼ teaspoon dried
- Salt and pepper
- 2 garlic cloves, minced
- 1 (28-ounce) can crushed tomatoes
- ¼ teaspoon sugar
- 2 tablespoons chopped fresh basil
- 1 tablespoon extra-virgin olive oil

Melt butter in medium saucepan over medium heat. Add onion, oregano, and ½ teaspoon salt and cook, stirring occasionally, until onion is softened and lightly browned, 5 to 7 minutes. Stir in garlic and cook until fragrant, about 30 seconds. Stir in tomatoes and sugar, bring to simmer, and cook until slightly thickened, about 10 minutes. Off heat, stir in basil and oil and season with salt and pepper to taste.

Vietnamese Caramel Chicken

The savory caramel sauce in this braised chicken dish is far more complex than its short ingredient list suggests. The trick, though, is knowing just how long to cook the sugar.

⋙ BY ANNIE PETITO ⋘

In an American kitchen, caramel sauce is the sweet treat that we like to pour over ice cream and other desserts. In Vietnam, it's a different thing entirely. There, *nuoc mau*, or "colored water," as it's known, is commonly prepared in large batches and added to a variety of savory dishes. To make the caramel, the sugar is cooked long enough that the results are a little sweet and also bitter. Stirring in a good amount of fish sauce adds an essential savory, salty flavor, while ginger, pepper, or chile lend heat. In the best versions, the result is a potent yet perfectly balanced sauce that lends a rich brown color to everything from meat to catfish to tofu. Steamed rice and a vegetable to soak up the extra sauce are the typical accompaniments.

There are certainly more exotic options, but I've always been drawn to the chicken-based version. When I tried a few recipes, though, none of the results lived up to the promise. The chicken, which is braised in the sauce, was usually leathery, and the sauce was either gloppy or so thin that it slid off the meat. When it came to flavor, most of the recipes fell into one of two camps: either too sweet or too salty and pungent. I wanted an authentic but approachable recipe that produced tender, juicy chicken bathed in just the right amount of a sauce that balanced bitter, sweet, salty, and spicy.

Halved chicken thighs provide good surface area to soak up the sauce and keep the cooking time long enough to allow its flavors to penetrate.

Finding the (Bitter)Sweet Spot

I started with the sauce. Modern recipes were convenient—they called for building the entire dish in a skillet—but trying to evenly caramelize sugar over the large surface of a skillet proved difficult. So instead I followed the lead of traditional Vietnamese recipes and pulled out a deep, small saucepan for the caramel. Once it was prepared, I'd move the sauce to a skillet to braise the chicken.

Traditional recipes call for cooking the caramel until it's almost black, but I decided to start more cautiously. I brought 7 tablespoons of sugar and 3 tablespoons of water to a boil in my saucepan over moderately high heat until it started to turn golden. (The water was helpful in dissolving the sugar so it spread evenly over the bottom of the pan.) As the sugar began to take on color more rapidly, I turned down the heat and swirled the pan occasionally to ensure that the caramel cooked evenly. The color progressed from light amber to auburn. When a reddish-brown hue was just starting to develop, I turned off the heat and carefully added another ¾ cup of hot water to stop the cooking (adding hot water rather than cold ensured that the mixture didn't harden). After the caramel sputtered and bubbled for a few seconds, I moved on to adding the fish sauce.

The hallmark of nuoc mau is its careful balance of bittersweet and salty, so determining the correct ratio of fish sauce to caramel was key. Recipes called for anywhere from a 1:1 to a 1:2 ratio of fish sauce to caramel. After a lot of tinkering, I was surprised to find that something closer to a 1:4 ratio of fish sauce to caramel was best. Just ¼ cup of fish sauce produced the right savory, salty punch without tasting fishy. But something was off. The caramel's flavor was more purely sweet—closer to a dessert sauce—than the bittersweet flavor I was after.

I started up another couple of batches of caramel, following the same process but cooking the caramels progressively longer. For one batch, I watched as it turned reddish-brown as before, but when a few wisps of smoke wafted up from the pan, I quickly pulled it off the heat and added the water. For the other batch, I went against all my instincts and left it on the heat, even after I saw the wisps of smoke. Soon, the bubbles took on an orange hue. I swirled the pan and saw that the color beneath was like molasses or black coffee. I immediately turned off the heat and poured in the water. I added the ¼ cup of fish sauce to both batches and sampled them side by side. Hands down, the darker batch was superior to anything I'd tried yet. It was still slightly sweet, but it also had a notable bitterness that added complexity and brought the whole sauce into remarkable balance. (For more information, see "Taking Some Sweet Out of Caramel.") For a final touch, I stirred in a couple of tablespoons of freshly grated ginger for warmth and brightness.

Wondering how easily I could hit the target again, I repeated the cooking process multiple times. I found that it really wasn't hard or scary. The key was to use an instant-read thermometer—I learned that the desired dark-molasses color corresponded to temperatures between 390 and 400 degrees—in addition to visual cues.

Getting to the Meat of It

It was time for the chicken. The traditional approach would have been to whack a whole bird across the bones into bite-size bone-in chunks. I ruled this out from the start for being too much work. I tried using bone-in thighs, but tasters found the bones annoying. So I followed the lead of many modern recipes, which call for boneless, skinless chicken thighs cut into small pieces. While small bits of meat provided a lot of great surface area for the sauce to cling to, the flavor was only skin deep—the chicken had cooked through too quickly to absorb much flavor. I found that I achieved a happy medium by cutting boneless, skinless thighs in half.

See Exactly How It's Done
Video available free for 4 months at CooksIllustrated.com/june15

SCIENCE Taking Some Sweet Out of Caramel

Most of us think of caramel as a sweet sauce. But if cooked long enough, caramel will become less sweet and more complex. Here's what happens: When table sugar is heated, a cascade of chemical reactions occurs that transforms some—and eventually all—of its single type of molecule into literally hundreds of different compounds that bring new flavors, aromas, and colors. At first these compounds are mild and buttery in flavor, and the caramel still tastes very sweet. With continued cooking, even more sugar molecules break down, and the caramel begins to taste markedly less sweet; meanwhile bitter, potent-tasting molecules also begin to form (along with those that bring a darker color). We found that cooking sugar to between 390 and 400 degrees produced a caramel with subtle sweetness and an appealingly bitter edge. Any additional cooking, though, made the caramel taste acrid and burnt.

SIMPLY SWEET
Only some sucrose molecules have broken down. Color is amber, and flavor is mild and still very sweet.

BITTERSWEET
More sucrose has broken down. Color is molasses-like, and flavor is less sweet and more complex.

TESTING Rice Cookers

Cooking rice using the traditional method is not all that hard, so to be worth purchasing, a rice cooker had better be both convenient and foolproof. We purchased five models, priced from $19.99 to $170.45, in which we cooked white and brown rice, as well as sushi rice.

When we made the smallest possible batches of white and sushi rice (1 to 2 cups uncooked), all the machines performed well. Making brown rice and maximum-capacity batches of white rice revealed greater differences; rice made in the losing models was either inconsistent or blown out.

The cookers' various features were really what set them apart. While the automatic keep-warm function was standard across all models (we confirmed that each of the cookers held the rice at a food-safe temperature for the entirety of their keep-warm cycles), a few included extra features that weren't worth paying for. We liked the rice from the simpler—and affordable—Aroma machine at least as much as that made in the other models, and we were happy with its few perks: separate settings for white and brown rice (brown rice settings generally include a soaking period to soften the rice before cooking), a digital timer and audio alert, a delayed-start function, clear water line indications, and a removable lid insert that made cleanup a breeze. For complete testing results, go to CooksIllustrated.com/june15. –Kate Shannon

HIGHLY RECOMMENDED
AROMA 8-Cup Digital Rice Cooker and Food Steamer
Price: $29.92
Model: ARC-914SBD

Next question: How long should I cook the chicken? In some recipes the meat was just cooked through, while others called for cooking it so long that it was nearly falling apart. I liked the latter approach since it meant more time for sauce absorption, but tasters found the resulting chicken dry. Luckily, I had a solution. In the past, we've found that treating meat with baking soda can help. The soda raises the meat's pH, which causes enzymes called calpains to become more active and cut the meat's muscle fibers. As the fibers break down, the meat's texture softens and its looser consistency retains water better. The net result: juicier, more tender meat.

I dissolved 1 tablespoon of baking soda in 1¼ cups of cold water and let the chicken soak for 15 minutes before rinsing it and adding it to the sauce in a 12-inch skillet. (This size worked best since the chicken could sit in a single layer in the sauce.) Even when simmered for more than 30 minutes, to 205 degrees, the chicken was still juicy—plus, it was pull-apart tender and fully infused with the flavor of the sauce.

I was really close, but the sauce wasn't clinging to the chicken like I'd hoped. It certainly started out thick enough, but as the chicken cooked, it released its juices, thinning out the sauce. Cooking it down to the desired consistency made it too salty and left too little for serving. Whisking in 2 teaspoons of cornstarch gave my sauce just enough body. In addition to the ginger, a few tasters asked for a little more spice. Chiles, whether dried or fresh, overpowered the ginger, but ½ teaspoon of ground black pepper added depth and just the right amount of gentle heat.

For the last detail, I steamed some broccoli to provide a pleasant textural and visual contrast to the chicken. I poured a small amount of sauce over both the chicken and broccoli and saved the rest to serve alongside. Finally, this was the complex, addictive dish that I'd been imagining.

VIETNAMESE-STYLE CARAMEL CHICKEN WITH BROCCOLI

SERVES 4 TO 6

The saltiness of fish sauce can vary; we recommend Tiparos. When taking the temperature of the caramel in step 2, tilt the pan and move the thermometer back and forth to equalize hot and cool spots; also make sure to have hot water at the ready. This dish is intensely seasoned, so serve it with plenty of steamed white rice.

- 1 tablespoon baking soda
- 2 pounds boneless, skinless chicken thighs, trimmed and halved crosswise
- 7 tablespoons sugar
- ¼ cup fish sauce
- 2 tablespoons grated fresh ginger
- 1 pound broccoli, florets cut into 1-inch pieces, stalks peeled and sliced ¼ inch thick
- 2 teaspoons cornstarch
- ½ teaspoon pepper
- ½ cup chopped fresh cilantro leaves and stems

1. Combine baking soda and 1¼ cups cold water in large bowl. Add chicken and toss to coat. Let stand at room temperature for 15 minutes. Rinse chicken in cold water and drain well.

2. Meanwhile, combine sugar and 3 tablespoons water in small saucepan. Bring to boil over medium-high heat and cook, without stirring, until mixture begins to turn golden, 4 to 6 minutes. Reduce heat to medium-low and continue to cook, gently swirling saucepan, until sugar turns color of molasses and registers between 390 and 400 degrees, 4 to 6 minutes longer. (Caramel will produce some smoke during last 1 to 2 minutes of cooking.) Immediately remove saucepan from heat and carefully pour in ¾ cup hot water (mixture will bubble and steam vigorously). When bubbling has subsided, return saucepan to medium heat and stir to dissolve caramel.

3. Transfer caramel to 12-inch skillet and stir in fish sauce and ginger. Add chicken and bring to simmer over medium-high heat. Reduce heat to medium-low, cover, and simmer until chicken is fork-tender and registers 205 degrees, 30 to 40 minutes, flipping chicken halfway through simmering. Transfer chicken to serving dish and cover to keep warm.

4. Bring 1 inch water to boil in Dutch oven. Lower insert or steamer basket with broccoli into pot so it rests above water; cover and simmer until broccoli is just tender, 4½ to 5 minutes. Transfer broccoli to serving dish with chicken.

5. While broccoli cooks, bring sauce to boil over medium-high heat and cook until reduced to 1¼ cups, 3 to 5 minutes. Whisk cornstarch and 1 tablespoon water together in small bowl, then whisk into sauce; simmer until slightly thickened, about 1 minute. Stir in pepper. Pour ¼ cup sauce over chicken and broccoli. Sprinkle with cilantro and serve, passing remaining sauce separately.

Sautéed Swiss Chard

We transform this twofer of tender leaves and hearty stems into a satisfying side dish.

BY SANDRA WU

In the Mediterranean, where Swiss chard originated (it doesn't hail from Switzerland despite what its name suggests), the vegetable is hugely popular. It's no wonder: With its earthy, mineral-y undertones and a slightly more substantial texture than spinach, the quick-cooking green has a lot to offer. We're fond of chard in the test kitchen, too, incorporating it into everything from soups and pasta dishes to braises. But this time around, I wanted to feature the green on its own as a side dish.

I knew that I wouldn't be discarding the sizable center stems of the chard, since they become tender-crisp with cooking and can add volume and texture to a dish. I also knew that I wanted to sauté the vegetable since this method would offer stems with a bit of bite plus supple leaves in just minutes. The challenge would be getting both elements to cook evenly.

Because the thickness of the chard stems varies from leaf to leaf, it was imperative that they be cut to the same size for consistent cooking. To achieve not only uniformity but also an elegant look, I sliced the stems ¼ inch thick on the bias.

Since the leaves cook much more quickly than the stems, I gave the stems a head start. Sautéing them (along with a sprinkle of salt) in olive oil over medium heat worked, but boosting the temperature to medium-high encouraged the development of flavorful caramelization while also reducing the cooking time by a few minutes. Once the slices were nearly crisp-tender, I added in as many of the leaves that would fit comfortably in the pan. After they wilted slightly, I packed in the remaining leaves, added a little more salt, and cooked it all for about 3 more minutes, until all the leaves were tender but still had some texture.

To give this simple dish some interest, I toasted a couple of thinly sliced garlic cloves in the oil just prior to adding the stems and finished the chard with freshly squeezed lemon juice. Finally, I devised a couple of variations. In a nod to Mediterranean cooking, I created a version featuring pine nuts and currants. Another incorporated caramelized shallots, meaty pancetta, and sweet-tart balsamic vinegar.

With these interesting variations and an easy technique, Swiss chard is no longer going to be relegated to merely supporting roles in my kitchen.

Chard Comes Alive
Video available free for 4 months at CooksIllustrated.com/june15

Slicing the stems thin and on the bias helps them cook quickly.

SAUTÉED SWISS CHARD WITH GARLIC

SERVES 4

This recipe will work with any color of Swiss chard. For our free recipes for Sautéed Swiss Chard with Sesame Sauce and Sautéed Swiss Chard with Ginger, go to CooksIllustrated.com/june15.

- 2 tablespoons extra-virgin olive oil
- 3 garlic cloves, sliced thin
- 1½ pounds Swiss chard, stems sliced ¼ inch thick on bias (3 cups), leaves sliced into ½-inch-wide strips (10 cups)
- Kosher salt and pepper
- 2 teaspoons lemon juice

Heat oil in 12-inch nonstick skillet over medium-high heat until just shimmering. Add garlic and cook, stirring constantly, until lightly browned, 30 to 60 seconds. Add chard stems and ¼ teaspoon salt and cook, stirring occasionally, until spotty brown and crisp-tender, 5 to 6 minutes. Add two-thirds of chard leaves and cook, tossing with tongs, until just starting to wilt, 30 to 60 seconds. Add remaining chard leaves and ¼ teaspoon salt and continue to cook, stirring frequently, until leaves are tender, about 3 minutes longer. Remove pan from heat, stir in lemon juice, and season with salt and pepper to taste. Serve immediately.

SAUTÉED SWISS CHARD WITH CURRANTS AND PINE NUTS

Decrease amount of garlic to 1 minced clove and add ¼ teaspoon ground cumin to skillet with garlic. Substitute sherry vinegar for lemon juice and stir 3 tablespoons dried currants and 3 tablespoons toasted pine nuts into chard with vinegar.

SAUTÉED SWISS CHARD WITH PANCETTA AND CARAMELIZED SHALLOTS

Omit extra-virgin olive oil. Heat 1 tablespoon vegetable oil in 12-inch nonstick skillet over medium heat until shimmering. Add 3 thinly sliced shallots and cook, stirring frequently, until well browned and softened, 10 to 12 minutes. Transfer shallots to bowl and use paper towels to wipe out skillet. Heat 1 tablespoon vegetable oil and 2 ounces pancetta, cut into ¼-inch pieces, in now-empty skillet over medium-high heat. Cook, stirring occasionally, until rendered and crisp, 6 to 8 minutes. Using slotted spoon, transfer pancetta to paper towel–lined plate. Pour off all but 2 tablespoons fat from skillet and return to medium-high heat. Proceed with recipe, adding ¼ teaspoon kosher salt and ⅛ teaspoon red pepper flakes to skillet with chard stems. Omit garlic, pepper, and any additional salt. Substitute 1 tablespoon balsamic vinegar for lemon juice and stir pancetta and shallots into chard with vinegar off heat.

TECHNIQUE | REMOVING STEMS

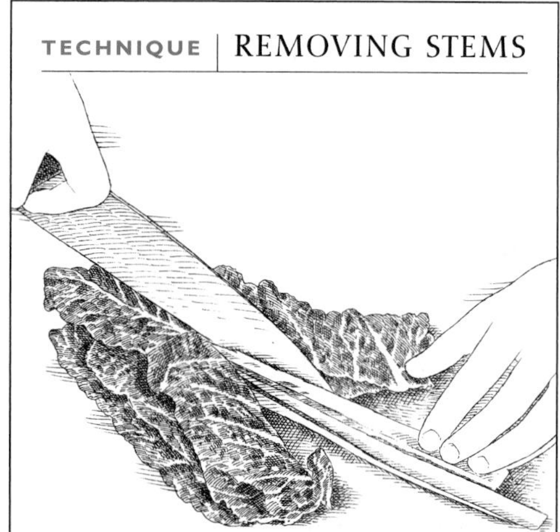

Stack two to three leaves, aligning their central stems. Slice along each side of the stem. Repeat with remaining leaves.

New York Bagels for All

It doesn't get any better than the crackly-crisp shell, tender chew, and subtle malty flavor of a New York bagel. So what do you do if you don't live in New York?

BY ANDREW JANJIGIAN

The average bagel is nothing special and not hard to come by: a uniformly soft, swollen, tasteless ring that's mass-produced and sold at supermarkets, convenience stores, coffee shops, and bagel chains nationwide. It requires a run through the toaster to crisp up the crust and develop any flavor, and it typically functions as a vehicle for condiments like butter and cream cheese, deli cold cuts, or pizza toppings.

But a proper New York bagel—that's in a class by itself. In New York City, where great bagels abound, these rings have a fine, uniform crumb and a substantial chew. (*New York Times* columnist Mimi Sheraton once said that a good bagel should "give your facial muscles a workout.") Their exterior is glossy and lightly browned with a thin, crackly-crisp shell, and their flavor is complex: wheaty, with both a faint sourness and a malty sweetness. Unfortunately, bagels like these are all but impossible to find outside the New York City area. That's not because the city's water makes bagels better, as many devotees claim (see "Is It Something in the Water?"); it's because good bagel shops use specialized ingredients, equipment, and techniques that help the dough develop a crisp exterior, satisfying chew, and complex flavor.

Before baking, bagels are boiled, which helps them spring up and also develops a crisp, shiny crust.

Replacing those ingredients, tools, and techniques with home baker–friendly alternatives was precisely the challenge I faced. And I wouldn't be satisfied unless the results rivaled the real deal in New York.

A Protein Boost

Generally speaking, making bagel dough is a lot like making a typical bread dough: You mix flour, water, yeast, and salt in a stand mixer until it forms a mass; you shape the dough (in this case, into rings); and you let it proof so that gases can form that leaven and flavor the dough.

However, bagel dough differs from most other bread doughs in three significant ways, each of which helps produce a bagel's fine, even crumb and chew. First, the dough contains less water—usually between 50 and 55 percent, versus about 60 to 70 percent in loaf breads. Minimizing the water reduces the extensibility of the dough's gluten network (that is, the network of proteins that give baked goods their elasticity) and thus yields a very stiff dough that bakes up chewy. Second, while most bread doughs proof twice—once after mixing and again after shaping—bagel dough is shaped into rings immediately after mixing and is proofed only once to prevent its yeast from developing too much gas, which would make the bagel's crumb airy. Third, bagels are often proofed in the refrigerator for the better part of 24 hours, a process known as cold fermentation. Not only does the colder temperature further minimize the yeast's gas production, but it also encourages the yeast to produce a more intricate mix of flavor compounds.

I confirmed that the hydration of the dough directly affects a bagel's chew when I tried a handful of existing bagel recipes. An outlier dough with about 60 percent water produced soft, fluffy bagels, while those that stuck closer to 55 percent hydration yielded chewier results. The only downside to working with the drier, stiffer dough was that it strained the mixer. So I moved the operation to the food processor, the sharp blades of which easily handled the dense, stiff mass. I also made two other tweaks: I used ice water to keep the dough as cool as possible during mixing, and I let the shaped bagels ferment at room temperature for an hour before chilling to give the yeast a chance to jump-start the fermentation process a bit.

The other ingredient that clearly influenced the bagels' texture was the flour, as the chewiest results came from doughs made with high-gluten flour. This product, a staple in bread bakeries and available only via mail order, contains a high proportion (14 to 15 percent) of the gluten-forming proteins, glutenin and gliadin, that make up the strong elastic networks in chewy New York bagels and pizza. Bread flour was surely the best supermarket alternative, since it's the highest-protein flour that's widely available, but the bread-flour bagels I made were still a distant second to the high-gluten-flour batch.

Fortunately, there was another, more widely available product I could add to strengthen the dough. Vital wheat gluten, a powdered form of wheat gluten, is often used by professional bakers to create a stronger network and thus a chewier product. Adding about 1½ teaspoons per cup of bread flour brought the texture of these bagels closer to that of the high-gluten-flour bagels—but still not as close as I wanted.

Adding even more vital wheat gluten was not the solution—I found that it made the bagels tough. So I pursued the other avenue for strengthening the dough: the shaping technique.

Do the Twist

Traditionally, bagels are shaped by stretching each round into a log, which purposely puts a lot of stress on the dough to tighten the gluten network, and then wrapping it around your palm

Behind the Bagel Process
Video available free for 4 months at CooksIllustrated.com/june15

and pressing both ends together to seal. To stress the dough even further, I flattened out the ball with a rolling pin and then rolled it up like a carpet before stretching it out, which strengthened the dough and pressed out any large air bubbles. I'd also seen some bagels with a subtle spiral pattern in the dough, and testing proved that it wasn't merely cosmetic: When I twirled the ends of the dough in opposite directions before sealing them, that twist further tightened up the gluten network and gave the bagels true New York–caliber chew.

STEP BY STEP | SHAPING BAGELS LIKE A PRO

Thoroughly working the dough during shaping helps a New York bagel develop its characteristic chew.

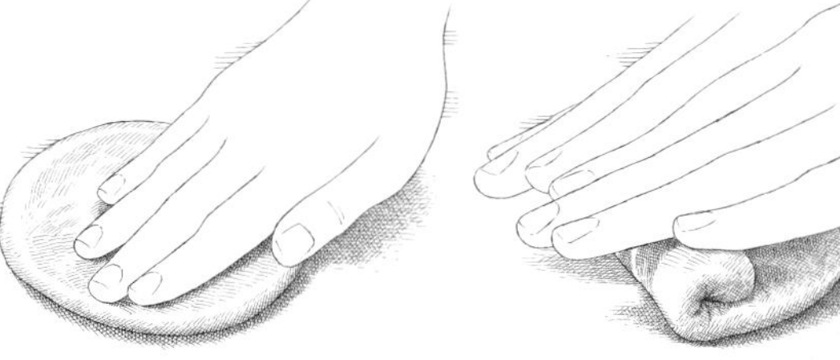

1. Pat and roll dough ball (lightly coated with flour) with rolling pin into 5-inch round.

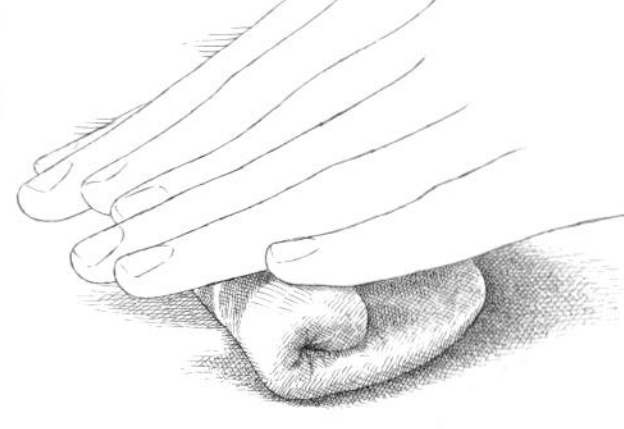

2. Roll into tight cylinder, starting with far side of dough.

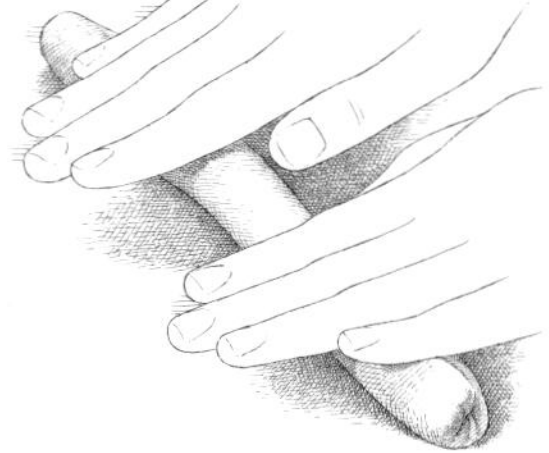

3. Roll and stretch dough into 8- to 9-inch-long rope, starting at center of cylinder (don't taper ends).

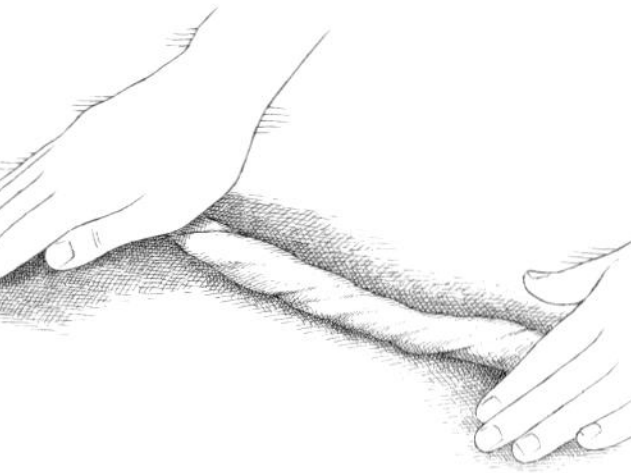

4. Twist rope to form tight spiral by rolling ends of dough under hands in opposite directions.

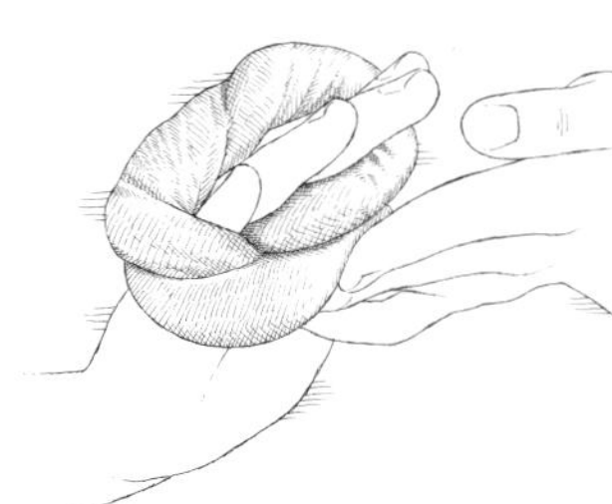

5. Wrap rope around fingers, overlapping ends by 2 inches, to create ring. Pinch ends together.

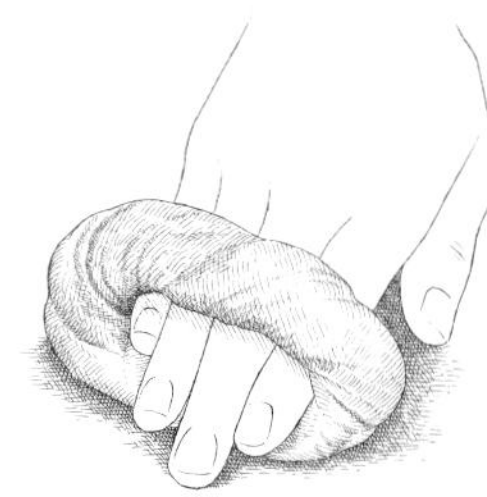

6. Press and roll seam (positioned under your palm) using circular motion on counter to fully seal.

Rack 'em Up

In New York bakeries, bagels undergo a two-step boil-and-bake process: They are dropped into malt syrup–infused boiling water for about 20 seconds and then placed on water-soaked wood boards lined with burlap and sprinkled with cornmeal (to prevent sticking) that sit directly on the hot oven floor. Once the bagels have started to brown, they're flipped directly onto the oven floor to finish browning.

Boiling bagels "wakes up" their yeast (sluggish from being kept cold) so that they spring up during baking. It also hydrates and cooks the starches on the bagel's exterior to create the glossy, crisp crust. And finally, it lends the dough that subtle malt sweetness. Bagel boards are mostly about crust development. They protect the exterior from burning during the first half of baking and give off steam that performs three functions: It keeps the dough's exterior moist and pliable so that it can expand, it further cooks the surface starches, and it efficiently transfers heat so that the bagels crisp.

To mimic the professional setup, I placed a wire rack (coated with vegetable oil spray) in a rimmed baking sheet and slid a baking stone into the oven to act as the "hearth." As for a source of steam, I've had success placing a pan of water on the bottom of the oven when baking other breads—but here I figured that I didn't need the extra vessel, since the rimmed baking sheet could hold enough water.

My ersatz setup got me almost all the way there: The ½ cup of boiling water I poured into the baking sheet provided plenty of steam. But once I transferred the bagels to the hot stone and removed the pan of water from the oven, they started to burn and turn leathery. I kept the next batch on the rack for the duration of baking, but not surprisingly, the bagels were too pale. Lowering the oven temperature helped even out the browning, but after baking longer, the bagels' crust was thick and tough, not thin and crisp.

Out of ideas for the baking method, I thought back to the malt-infused boiling water. Browning is influenced by pH—acidic foods don't darken as readily as alkaline ones do—so I removed the slightly acidic malt syrup from the water and instead added a tablespoon of alkaline baking soda (an addition I'd seen in some recipes), plus a little sugar. That just about did it, as these bagels baked up with a nice, glossy tan and a lightly crisp exterior. Not surprisingly, they lacked that distinct malt flavor, but the fix was easy: I added the syrup to the dough instead.

Complexly flavored with a delicate crisp crust and substantial chew, these plain bagels rivaled some of the best I've had in New York. As for toppings, poppy and sesame seeds, as well as my own "everything" mix, were easily applied. I simply poured the toppings into a small bowl and pressed the just-boiled bagels in face first so that the seasonings stuck securely to their surfaces. Meanwhile, making a cinnamon-raisin variation was as simple as kneading a handful of the fruit into the mixed dough and incorporating a mixture of cinnamon and sugar during shaping.

There I had it: New York bagels without New York—or its water.

Is It Something in the Water?

It's often said that what makes New York bagels distinctively crisp, chewy, and flavorful is something available only in that city: the local water. Curious if that claim is true or merely an urban legend, we set up taste tests pitting bagels made with water that we brought back from Brooklyn against those made with our local Brookline water. The results: The vast majority of tasters found the two batches virtually identical.

For due diligence, we then sent samples of water from both sources to an independent lab to test for factors that might affect the dough's gluten and, thus, its texture: mineral content, pH, titratable acidity, and chlorine level. The only significant difference between the two samples was in their respective pHs: The Brooklyn water was mildly acidic (5.48 pH), while Brookline water was slightly basic (7.34 pH). But when we measured the pH of the two doughs after they'd fermented, the differences were negligible.

That's good news for bagel enthusiasts outside New York, since it means that all anyone really needs to make a good bagel is a good recipe.

Storage towers like these supply New York City with its water.

NEW YORK BAGELS

MAKES 8 BAGELS

This recipe requires refrigerating the shaped bagels for 16 to 24 hours before baking them. This recipe works best with King Arthur bread flour, although other bread flours will work. Vital wheat gluten and malt syrup are available in most supermarkets in the baking and syrup aisles, respectively. If you cannot find malt syrup, substitute 4 teaspoons of molasses. The bagels are best eaten within a day of baking; fully cooled bagels can be transferred to heavy-duty zipper-lock bags and frozen for up to one month. For our free recipe for New York Cinnamon-Raisin Bagels, go to CooksIllustrated.com/june15.

- 1¼ cups ice water (10 ounces)
- 2 tablespoons malt syrup
- 2⅔ cups (14⅔ ounces) bread flour
- 4 teaspoons vital wheat gluten
- 2 teaspoons instant or rapid-rise yeast
- 2 teaspoons salt
- ¼ cup (1¼ ounces) cornmeal
- ¼ cup (1¾ ounces) sugar
- 1 tablespoon baking soda

1. Stir ice water and malt syrup together in 2-cup liquid measuring cup until malt syrup has fully dissolved. Process flour, wheat gluten, and yeast in food processor until combined, about 2 seconds. With processor running, slowly add ice water mixture; process until dough is just combined and no dry flour remains, about 20 seconds. Let dough stand for 10 minutes.

2. Add salt to dough and process, stopping processor and redistributing dough as needed, until dough forms shaggy mass that clears sides of workbowl (dough may not form one single mass), 45 to 90 seconds. Transfer dough to unfloured counter and knead until smooth, about 1 minute. Divide dough into 8 equal pieces (3½ ounces each) and cover loosely with plastic wrap.

3. Working with 1 piece of dough at a time and keeping remaining pieces covered, form dough pieces into smooth, taut rounds. (To round, set piece of dough on unfloured counter. Loosely cup your hand around dough and, without applying pressure to dough, move your hand in small circular motions. Tackiness of dough against counter and circular motion should work dough into smooth, even ball, but if dough sticks to your hands, lightly dust your fingers with flour.) Let dough balls rest on counter, covered, for 15 minutes.

4. Sprinkle rimmed baking sheet with cornmeal. Working with 1 dough ball at a time and keeping remaining pieces covered, coat dough balls lightly with flour and then, using your hands and rolling pin, pat and roll dough balls into 5-inch rounds. Starting with edge of dough farthest from you, roll into tight cylinder. Starting at center of cylinder and working toward ends, gently and evenly roll and stretch dough into 8- to 9-inch-long rope. Do not taper ends. Rolling ends of dough under your hands in opposite directions, twist rope to form tight spiral. Without unrolling spiral, wrap rope around your fingers, overlapping ends of dough by about 2 inches under your palm, to create ring shape. Pinch ends of dough gently together. With overlap under your palm, press and roll seam using circular motion on counter to fully seal. Transfer rings to prepared sheet and cover loosely with plastic, leaving at least 1 inch between bagels. Let bagels stand at room temperature for 1 hour. Cover sheet tightly with plastic and refrigerate for 16 to 24 hours.

5. One hour before baking, adjust oven rack to upper-middle position, place baking stone on rack, and heat oven to 450 degrees.

6. Bring 4 quarts water, sugar, and baking soda to boil in large Dutch oven. Set wire rack in rimmed baking sheet and spray rack with vegetable oil spray.

7. Transfer 4 bagels to boiling water and cook for 20 seconds. Using wire skimmer or slotted spoon, flip bagels over and cook 20 seconds longer. Using wire skimmer or slotted spoon, transfer bagels to prepared wire rack, with cornmeal side facing down. Repeat with remaining 4 bagels.

8. Place sheet with bagels on preheated baking stone and pour ½ cup boiling water into bottom of sheet. Bake until tops of bagels are beginning to brown, 10 to 12 minutes. Using metal spatula, flip bagels and continue to bake until golden brown, 10 to 12 minutes longer. Remove sheet from oven and let bagels cool on wire rack for at least 15 minutes. Serve warm or at room temperature.

TECHNIQUE

HOW TO ADD TOPPINGS

Place ½ cup poppy seeds, sesame seeds, caraway seeds, dehydrated onion flakes, dehydrated garlic flakes, or coarse/pretzel salt in small bowl. Press tops of just-boiled bagels (side without cornmeal) gently into topping and return to wire rack, topping side up.

For Everything Topping, combine 2 tablespoons poppy seeds, 2 tablespoons sesame seeds, 1 tablespoon onion flakes, 2 teaspoons garlic flakes, 2 teaspoons caraway seeds, and ½ teaspoon coarse or pretzel salt.

Secrets to a Glossy Crust, Great Flavor, and Big Chew

Here's how we created the hallmarks of a New York bagel without the ingredients and equipment (or tap water) used by the local pros.

HIGH-PROTEIN DOUGH
Lots of gluten is key to achieving that jaw-working chew, so we used relatively high-protein bread flour supplemented with vital wheat gluten, a powdered form of the protein that is sold in most supermarkets.

COLD FERMENTATION
Proofing the dough overnight in the fridge allows it to develop an especially complex mix of flavor compounds.

ROUGH HANDLING
We roll, stretch, and twist the dough to shape it into rings—actions that help tighten the gluten network and thus yield a bagel with substantial chew.

A BETTER BOIL
Adding baking soda and sugar to the water in the boiling step helps encourage consistent browning.

STEAM TREATMENT
Baking the bagels on a rack set in a rimmed baking sheet (set on a baking stone) and adding a small amount of boiling water creates steam that leads to a crisp, delicate crust.

Our New York–style bagels, made here in Brookline.

Shellfish Without Fear

It's not just about shrimp. Other shellfish also require little prep, cook quickly, and can fit any occasion. Our tips will inspire you to buy and cook them with the same confidence.

BY LOUISE EMERICK

MUSSELS

Common Misconception:
Mussels often harbor unsafe bacteria; plus, it's hard to tell if the ones you are buying are fresh.

Reality: The vast majority of mussels for sale today are farmed, and they're widely regarded as one of the cleanest, safest shellfish you can eat. But their small mass means they deteriorate rapidly when dead, so they must be live when you cook them—which is actually very easy to determine (see below).

IMPORTANT TIPS

➢ **To determine freshness, use your nose.** Live mussels will smell pleasantly briny. Those that have died will smell sour or sulfurous and should be discarded. Also discard any with cracked or open shells that won't close when lightly tapped.

➢ **To store, keep in a wet, breathable environment.** Mussels can come in contact with ice, but you don't want them sitting in water. Place them in a colander set in a bowl, surround them with ice in the colander and cover with wet paper towels (wet newspaper is even better as it retains moisture longer). They will keep in the fridge for up to three days.

➢ **Cleaning is easy.** Farmed mussels are virtually free of sand and grit and need only a quick rinse under the tap. If any have a fibrous beard sticking out of their shells, just grasp it with a clean dish towel and pull firmly to remove.

➢ **Unopened cooked mussels needn't be discarded.** Try microwaving any unopened mussel briefly (30 seconds or so) to see if the muscle that keeps the shell closed will relax with more heat. If the shell still won't open, then throw out the mussel.

➢ **Don't crowd the pot.** Tightly packing mussels in a pot to steam them will overcook those at the bottom. For this reason, when cooking several pounds, we prefer to cook them spread out in a large roasting pan, covered, in the oven.

OVEN-STEAMED MUSSELS

SERVES 4

- **1 tablespoon extra-virgin olive oil**
- **3 garlic cloves, minced**
- **Pinch red pepper flakes**
- **1 cup dry white wine**
- **3 sprigs fresh thyme**
- **2 bay leaves**
- **4 pounds mussels, scrubbed and debearded**
- **¼ teaspoon salt**
- **2 tablespoons unsalted butter, cut into 4 pieces**
- **2 tablespoons minced fresh parsley**

1. Adjust oven rack to lowest position and heat oven to 500 degrees. Heat oil, garlic, and pepper flakes in large roasting pan over medium heat; cook, stirring constantly, until fragrant, about 30 seconds. Add wine, thyme sprigs, and bay leaves and bring to boil. Cook until wine is slightly reduced, about 1 minute. Add mussels and salt. Cover pan tightly with aluminum foil and transfer to oven. Cook until most mussels have opened (a few may remain closed), 15 to 18 minutes.

2. Remove pan from oven. Push mussels to sides of pan. Add butter to center and whisk until melted. Discard thyme sprigs and bay leaves, sprinkle parsley over mussels, and toss to combine. Serve immediately.

Mussels keep best if surrounded with ice, as long as melted ice can drain off.

CLAMS

Common Misconception:
As with mussels, clams can be unsafe, and it's hard to tell if what you're buying is fresh.

Reality: Most hard-shell clams sold today are farmed and very clean and safe to eat. It's also equally easy to distinguish fresh clams from those that have expired (see below).

IMPORTANT TIPS

These tips apply to hard-shell clams, which are the easiest to find nationally (soft-shell clams like steamers are sold primarily in the Northeast and are also more perishable).

➢ **Fresh, live clams should smell clean.** Discard any that have a bad odor as well as those that have cracked shells or won't close when lightly tapped.

➢ **Fresh water will kill clams, so avoid contact with ice when storing.** Place them in a bowl, cover with wet paper towels or newspaper, and set in another bowl filled with ice. They will keep in the fridge for up to one week.

➢ **Cleaning is easy.** Because farmed hard-shell clams are typically held on flats submerged in saltwater for several days after being dug up, they usually expel any grit that they have ingested prior to making it to market. You need only to scrub their shells before cooking.

➢ **Unopened cooked clams needn't be discarded.** As with mussels, unopened clams may just need more cooking. Microwave them briefly to see if their shells open; discard clams if they don't.

➢ **Easiest to steam on the stovetop.** Unlike mussels, clams can cook evenly on the stovetop. This is because per pound there are fewer clams than mussels, so even if you are cooking 4 pounds of them, there aren't that many in the pot to deal with. This allows for easy stirring and more even cooking.

Four pounds of clams will cook evenly on the stovetop.

CLAMS STEAMED IN WHITE WINE

SERVES 4

How fast the clams cook depends on the pot and clam size; to prevent overcooking, start checking for doneness after 4 minutes.

- **1½ cups dry white wine**
- **3 shallots, chopped fine**
- **4 garlic cloves, minced**
- **1 bay leaf**
- **4 pounds littleneck clams, scrubbed**
- **3 tablespoons unsalted butter**
- **2 tablespoons minced fresh parsley**
- **Lemon wedges**

Bring wine, shallots, garlic, and bay leaf to simmer in Dutch oven over medium heat; continue to simmer to blend flavors, 3 minutes. Increase heat to high. Add clams, cover, and cook, stirring twice, until clams open, 4 to 8 minutes. Using slotted spoon, remove clams from liquid and transfer to large serving bowl. Once all clams have been removed from pot, whisk butter into liquid to make emulsified sauce. Pour sauce over clams, sprinkle with parsley, and serve immediately with lemon wedges.

SEA SCALLOPS

Common Concern:

Many sea scallops seem to have an unpleasant chemical taste.

Reality: This is true for "wet" scallops, which have been treated with a solution of water and sodium tripolyphosphate to preserve them. Untreated, or "dry," scallops have more flavor and a creamy texture and also brown better. That said, we've found it easy to eliminate the chemical taste of wet scallops (see below).

IMPORTANT TIPS

➢ **Pink scallops taste sweeter.** Female scallops will turn pink when spawning. We found that they have a sweeter, richer taste than white scallops.

➢ **Store scallops as you would fish fillets or steaks.** Keep scallops in the refrigerator in a bag or sealed container on a bed of ice. Dry scallops can be kept for up to 5 days; wet scallops for up to one week.

➢ **Don't worry if scallops smell mildly fishy.** Scallops release gas as soon as they have been shucked, which you may smell when you first open the bag or container. The smell should dissipate after a few minutes. (However, if it doesn't, the scallops are past their prime.)

➢ **Check if scallops are wet or dry.** Treated scallops typically look more uniformly white than those that haven't been treated, but to find out for sure, microwave one scallop on a paper towel–lined plate for 15 seconds. A wet scallop will leave a sizable ring of moisture on the towel (the scallop can then be cooked as is).

➢ **Soak wet scallops to improve their taste.** Combine 1 quart of cold water, ¼ cup of lemon juice, and 2 tablespoons of salt and soak scallops in mixture for 30 minutes.

➢ **Remove tough muscle.** Most scallops have a crescent-shaped muscle attached to their sides that cooks up tough. Use your fingers to peel it off before cooking.

➢ **Use a thermometer to check doneness.** Many scallop recipes simply use visual clues for gauging doneness. The most foolproof method is to cook them until their centers reach 115 degrees. Off heat, carryover cooking will increase their temperature to the ideal 125 to 130 degrees.

PAN-SEARED SCALLOPS

SERVES 4

You can substitute Orange-Lime Vinaigrette, Ginger-Butter Sauce, or Caper-Mustard Sauce (for the free recipes, go to CooksIllustrated.com/panseAredscallops) for the lemon wedges.

- **1½ pounds dry sea scallops, 10 to 20 per pound, tendons removed**
- **Salt and pepper**
- **2 tablespoons vegetable oil**
- **2 tablespoons unsalted butter**
- **Lemon wedges**

1. Place scallops on rimmed baking sheet lined with clean dish towel. Place second clean dish towel on top of scallops and press gently on towel to blot liquid. Let scallops sit at room temperature for 10 minutes while towels absorb moisture.

2. Sprinkle scallops on both sides with salt and pepper. Heat 1 tablespoon oil in 12-inch nonstick skillet over high heat until just smoking. Add half of scallops in single layer, flat side down, and cook, without moving them, until well browned, 1½ to 2 minutes.

3. Add 1 tablespoon butter to skillet. Using tongs, flip scallops; continue to cook, using large spoon to baste scallops with melted butter (tilt skillet so butter runs to 1 side) until sides of scallops are firm and centers are opaque and register 115 degrees, 30 to 90 seconds longer (remove smaller scallops as they finish cooking). Transfer scallops to large plate and tent loosely with aluminum foil. Wipe out skillet with paper towels and repeat with remaining oil, scallops, and butter. Serve immediately with lemon wedges.

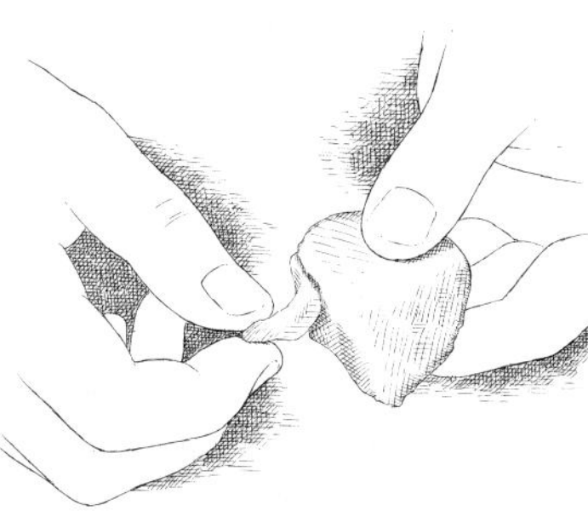

Use your fingers to peel away the crescent-shaped muscle before cooking.

LOBSTERS

Common Concern:

Lobsters are difficult to work with because they move around a lot.

Reality: While a lively lobster can be challenging to handle, its movement is a good thing as it indicates good health and the best texture and flavor once the lobster is cooked. And luckily, we've found a very simple method to keep a lobster still when you're trying to get it in the pot (see below).

Freezing lobsters briefly puts them in a coma-like state that makes them easier to handle.

IMPORTANT TIPS

➢ **Hard-shell versus soft-shell.** Most of the year the lobsters you find are hard-shell, but due to their molting cycle, the lobsters available during the late summer into early fall are generally soft-shell. Consider buying extra when lobsters are soft-shell, since they haven't fully grown into their shells and yield less by weight—about 17 percent compared with the 25 percent yield from a hard-shell.

➢ **Avoid contact with ice when storing.** Keep lobsters in the refrigerator in the breathable seafood bag many fishmongers sell them in or in an open container, covered with wet paper towels or newspaper. Hard-shell lobsters are best eaten within 24 hours. Weaker soft-shell lobsters are more perishable; eat them as quickly as possible after purchase.

➢ **Freeze lobsters briefly before cooking to minimize their movements.** A short 30-minute stint in the freezer will sedate lobsters and help keep them still when you put them in the pot.

➢ **Steam lobsters that you plan to serve whole at the table.** They're less waterlogged and messy than boiled lobsters.

➢ **Boil lobsters that you're shelling ahead of time.** Use salted water for well-seasoned meat. Shell them over the sink, since water trapped in the shells will make a mess.

➢ **Use a thermometer to check doneness.** Most recipes simply give you a cooking time based on weight, but the only way to know for sure that the lobster is cooked just right is to go by temperature. We cook most fin fish to between 130 and 140 degrees, but we cook lobster to 175 degrees. Its muscle fibers are longer and require more heat to shrink to the length that delivers a tender, pleasantly resilient texture.

STEAMED WHOLE LOBSTERS

SERVES 4

- **4 (1¼-pound) hard-shell lobsters**
- **8 tablespoons butter, melted (optional)**
- **Lemon wedges**

Bring about 1 inch water to boil over high heat in large pot set up with wire rack. Add lobsters, cover, and return to boil. Reduce heat to medium-high; steam until tails register 175 degrees, 13 to 14 minutes. Serve with melted butter, if using, and lemon wedges.

Cook the lobsters until their tails register 175 degrees.

For the best way to extract lobster meat, go to **CooksIllustrated.com/lobstermeat.**

Provençal Vegetable Soup

Minestrone's French cousin is bright and fresh—and hearty, thanks to a key pantry staple.

⋟ BY KEITH DRESSER ⋞

Just about every Western cuisine lays claim to a vegetable soup, but my favorite is the version native to the south of France called *soupe au pistou.* The French equivalent of minestrone, this broth is chock-full of vegetables, beans, and herbs—a celebration of the fresh produce that returns to the markets in early summer. Virtually any vegetables can and do go into the pot, but aromatics like carrots, celery, and leeks are typical, along with zucchini and the thin French green beans called haricots verts. Pasta often makes an appearance, along with a white bean known as *coco de Mollans.* The only component that's an absolute constant is the pesto-like condiment for which the soup is named; stirring a spoonful into each bowl lends the broth a jolt of fresh basil and garlic, along with salty Parmesan.

But when I've made the soup with the supermarket produce that is my main option most of the year, what should be a flavorful, satisfying soup often lacks character and body. I also find that when I don't have time to soak and simmer dried white beans (cannellini or navy are a typical substitute for hard-to-find coco de Mollans) and instead shortcut with canned ones, the soup suffers. But what if there was a way to have both—that is, a hearty, full-flavored soupe au pistou that I could throw together anytime?

Most classic versions use water for the soup base, but for more flavor I would make a vegetable broth. Ordinarily, that's a labor-intensive process, but our homemade Vegetable Broth Base (January/February 2015) takes minutes to make—just a handful of vegetables and pantry seasonings buzzed to a paste in the food processor and stirred into boiling water, 1 tablespoon per cup. I made 3 cups of broth and added an equal amount of water, which would produce a base that was flavorful but delicate enough to let other ingredients come forward.

I wanted the mixture of vegetables to be abundant but not cluttered. I softened a leek with celery and carrot, added minced garlic, poured in the broth and water, and brought it all to a simmer. I added 8 ounces of haricots verts that I had cut into short lengths. When they were bright green but still crisp, I added a can of drained cannellini beans and some chopped zucchini and tomato, which added fresh flavor and color and a touch of fruity brightness.

A dollop of pistou enlivens this simple vegetable soup.

Within minutes, the soup's flavors seemed balanced and on target and the vegetables were tender. But there was the thin broth to address. Adding pasta to the soup helped: Not only did it make the soup heartier, but the pieces sloughed off starch as they boiled, giving the broth more body—though not enough.

But there was an ingredient already at my disposal that I hadn't yet employed: the starchy liquid from the canned cannellini beans. As we've discovered, this viscous, seasoned "broth" can be invaluable in dishes that call for canned beans, lending a body and flavor similar to that which you get from cooking dried beans and using their liquid. Adding it to the pot with the beans made all the difference in my recipe, producing a soup that was still brothy but also had some body.

As for the namesake pistou, this mixture is even simpler to make, and brighter-tasting, than Italian pesto because it lacks toasted nuts. Pureeing a generous handful of fresh basil with Parmesan, a clove of garlic, and plenty of extra-virgin olive oil yielded a bold, grass-green sauce that was sharp and rich—the perfect accompaniment for the fresh, clean soup.

And with that, I had soupe au pistou that was both fast and flavorful, not to mention satisfying enough to stand on its own.

Keith Shows You How
Video available free for 4 months at CooksIllustrated.com/june15

PROVENÇAL VEGETABLE SOUP (SOUPE AU PISTOU)

SERVES 6

We prefer broth prepared from our Vegetable Broth Base (recipe available free at CooksIllustrated.com/june15), but store-bought vegetable broth can be used.

Pistou

- ¾ cup fresh basil leaves
- 1 ounce Parmesan cheese, grated (½ cup)
- ⅓ cup extra-virgin olive oil
- 1 garlic clove, minced

Soup

- 1 tablespoon extra-virgin olive oil
- 1 leek, white and light green parts only, halved lengthwise, sliced ½ inch thick, and washed thoroughly
- 1 celery rib, cut into ½-inch pieces
- 1 carrot, peeled and sliced ¼ inch thick
- Salt and pepper
- 2 garlic cloves, minced
- 3 cups vegetable broth
- 3 cups water
- ½ cup orecchiette or other short pasta
- 8 ounces haricots verts or green beans, trimmed and cut into ½-inch lengths
- 1 (15-ounce) can cannellini or navy beans
- 1 small zucchini, halved lengthwise, seeded, and cut into ¼-inch pieces
- 1 large tomato, cored, seeded, and cut into ¼-inch pieces

1. FOR THE PISTOU: Process all ingredients in food processor until smooth, scraping down sides of bowl as needed, about 15 seconds. (Pistou can be refrigerated for up to 4 hours.)

2. FOR THE SOUP: Heat oil in large Dutch oven over medium heat until shimmering. Add leek, celery, carrot, and ½ teaspoon salt and cook until vegetables are softened, 8 to 10 minutes. Stir in garlic and cook until fragrant, about 30 seconds. Stir in broth and water and bring to simmer.

3. Stir in pasta and simmer until slightly softened, about 5 minutes. Stir in haricots verts and simmer until bright green but still crunchy, 3 to 5 minutes. Stir in cannellini beans and their liquid, zucchini, and tomato and simmer until pasta and vegetables are tender, about 3 minutes. Season with salt and pepper to taste. Serve, topping individual portions with generous tablespoon pistou.

Strawberry-Rhubarb Pie

Because strawberries and rhubarb both contain loads of moisture, avoiding a mushy, soupy pie requires a clear strategy.

BY ANDREA GEARY

It's hard to pin down exactly when American cooks began adding strawberries to rhubarb pie. One early source of the practice is the 1936 edition of the *Settlement Cook Book*, wherein Mrs. Simon Kander suggests adding an equal amount of strawberries to the rhubarb filling "for variety." Suffice it to say, the two have been paired together for so long that we think of them as a great match. Except that they're not. The trouble lies not in their differences—fruit and vegetable, sweet and sour—but in an important similarity: Both are loaded with water (92 and 95 percent water by weight, respectively). When the two are enclosed in pastry and baked, that water heats up and causes both to soften dramatically, albeit differently: Rhubarb often blows out completely, releasing all that moisture into the filling and collapsing into mush, while strawberries remain intact but become unappealingly bloated.

By controlling the water shed by the rhubarb and berries, we produce a pie filling that doesn't ooze out when you cut a slice.

To shore up the exuded liquid, most recipes call for some sort of starchy thickening agent (usually flour, cornstarch, or tapioca), but adding enough to thicken a pie this juicy turns the bright, flavorful liquid into a dull, starchy goo. Some recipes also preemptively remove some of the water by precooking the rhubarb, but that only guarantees that the stalks will blow out before they make it into the pie.

My task: bring together delicately sweet strawberries and bracingly tart rhubarb in a bright-tasting filling that gels softly and contains plenty of intact fruit and vegetable pieces.

A Sweet Start

Rhubarb frequently blows out because its rigid walls can't accommodate the expansion that occurs when heat converts its abundant moisture to steam—a fact that I confirmed early on in my testing when I tried to precook the rhubarb, both on the stove and in the oven. I knew I had to remove water (at least 1 cup was my goal), but applying heat was out of the question, so I tried the most obvious no-heat method I could think of: macerating the stalks in sugar. Sugar is hygroscopic—that is, it has an affinity for water molecules and draws moisture out of plant cells via osmosis, which leaves the flesh compact but intact.

I tossed 1½ pounds of the trimmed rhubarb stalks (chopped into small pieces to maximize their surface area and, I hoped, speed up their moisture loss) with a generous 1¼ cups sugar and let the mixture sit. And sit. In fact, 90 minutes passed before the full cup of liquid I wanted had been drawn out. Obviously, that was far too long to wait, but I decided to see how the drained rhubarb would function in the finished dessert, so I threw together a basic pie.

I combined the sugared and drained rhubarb pieces with 1 pound of cut-up strawberries and 3 tablespoons of instant tapioca, as we've previously had good luck using it to thicken fruit pies. I poured the strawberry-rhubarb filling mixture into a pie plate lined with our Foolproof Pie Dough—this pastry contains vodka, which makes it moist and pliable enough to roll out easily but doesn't encourage gluten development the way water does, and thus doesn't toughen the crust. (There's no trace of alcohol flavor in the finished pie.) Then I placed a second pastry round on top of the filling, neatly crimped the edges, cut several vents to allow steam to escape, and finally, brushed the top crust with egg wash and sprinkled it with a teaspoon of sugar before baking it in a hot oven to ensure that the crust browned nicely.

The macerating step was definitely worth the effort; the sugar drew moisture out of the stalks without rupturing their cell walls or causing them to collapse and turn mushy the way heat does—in essence, macerating was a gentler form of dehydration. However, going forward I'd need to find a way to dramatically expedite the process. There was another issue as well: As I might have expected, discarding the sugary rhubarb liquid robbed the filling of sweetness and left the pie unpalatably tart.

It occurred to me that the microwave might help speed up the macerating process since its heat would provide more energy to drive the process of osmosis, thus helping the sugar dissolve faster and thus pull moisture from the cells more quickly. Encouragingly, when I microwaved the sugared rhubarb pieces for a couple of minutes, some of the sugar dissolved, but the rhubarb got only slightly warm and was therefore not in danger of blowing out and collapsing. When I found that after just 30 minutes of resting the microwaved rhubarb had exuded even more juice—a full 10 ounces—than it had in 90 minutes at room temperature, I knew the microwave method was a keeper.

Simmer Down

As for that flavorful rhubarb syrup, I simmered it in a saucepan to reduce it and concentrate its flavor. While the flavor of this concentrated syrup was good, adding even some of it back to the filling made it loose, not softly gelled. Plus, the excess moisture caused the strawberries to bloat. Increasing the amount of tapioca in the mix thickened the liquid, but predictably it also dulled its flavor.

See How It's Done
Video available free for 4 months at CooksIllustrated.com/june15

What? Run It Under Water?

It sounded crazy when my colleague (who got the trick from his mother) suggested I do it, but here's why sticking a pie under the tap before baking makes sense: It thoroughly moistens the dough so it can hold on to more sugar, which gets transformed into a candy-like layer in the oven. Ultimately, I opted for a safer (albeit less dramatic) method for the same result: I brushed the pastry thoroughly with water. Even this approach produced a crust that was able to grip a full 3 tablespoons of sugar.

That's when I realized I might be able to take care of both the runny rhubarb syrup and the bloated berry problem at the same time if I just cooked down the strawberries in the rhubarb syrup. I hoped the berries would give the syrup more body and an extra boost of fruity flavor, while also giving up some of their own moisture; essentially, I'd be making a sort of strawberry-rhubarb jam. I simmered the syrup with the strawberries until it had reduced and the berries were starting to break down. (I mashed up any solid pieces with a fork until the mixture was soft and pulpy, but not completely smooth.) Finally, I combined the berry mixture with the microwaved rhubarb, poured the filling into the pastry shell, and slide another pie into the oven.

I was finally getting somewhere. Now the filling comprised tender yet intact chunks of rhubarb that were lightly coated with a glossy, perfectly thickened, jammy gel that was neither too stiff nor too runny. My tasters' only comment: Now that they were being cooked down and mashed, the strawberries didn't offer much of their own presence in the pie filling. Fortunately, the fix turned out to be as simple as macerating a portion (1 cup) of the cut-up berries with the microwaved rhubarb so that the final filling contained intact rhubarb and strawberry pieces glossed with the soft, jammy, gelled liquid.

A Sweet Finish

The filling tasted bright and pleasantly tart, so I thought that an extra burst of sugar on the top crust would be a subtle way to add contrasting sweetness, not to mention a hint of crystalline crunch against the soft filling. But when I sprinkled any more than a couple of teaspoons of sugar onto the pastry before baking, most of the granules didn't stick; they either sat loose on the crust's surface and fell off when I sliced the pie or slid into the crevices at the crust's edge.

When I mentioned the sugar sticking problem to a colleague, he suggested a trick he'd learned from his mother that, quite frankly, sounded insane: Instead of brushing on an egg wash, or even lightly moistening the crust with water or milk as most pie recipes suggest, she actually runs her pies under a faucet. Flooding the surface of the pastry with water, she claims, makes it tackier so that it can grip more sugar.

I was at once intrigued and skeptical. Wouldn't running the pie under the faucet potentially sog out the crust, not to mention tear it from the water pressure? Still, it was such a novel idea that I had to try it—and, admittedly, I was startled by the impressive results. For one thing, the wetter pastry held a whopping 3 tablespoons of sugar, dramatically increasing the amount I'd started with. Even better, that heavy coat of sugar worked its hygroscopic magic once again: The ample amount of water allowed the sugar granules to dissolve and then dry into a glassy candy-like shell. The effect: visual appeal, delicate crunch, and just the right amount of sweetness to balance the tart filling. My only change was to brush on the water; as much as I liked the novelty of drenching the crust, I didn't want to risk that the pressure of water direct from the faucet might tear the pastry.

With chunks of strawberries and rhubarb clearly visible in the perfectly gelled filling, and all of it encased in a sweet, crunchy crust, I had finally come up with a way to make the classically flawed pairing a perfect match.

The Runniest of All Pies

Most fruit pies are runny by nature, but the strawberry-rhubarb kind is the worst. That's because the abundance of liquid in rhubarb floods the pie during baking, and the berries soak up some of the juices and bloat. We devised specific treatments for each component, resulting in a filling that gels softly and tastes bright. We also fixed rhubarb's mushy texture.

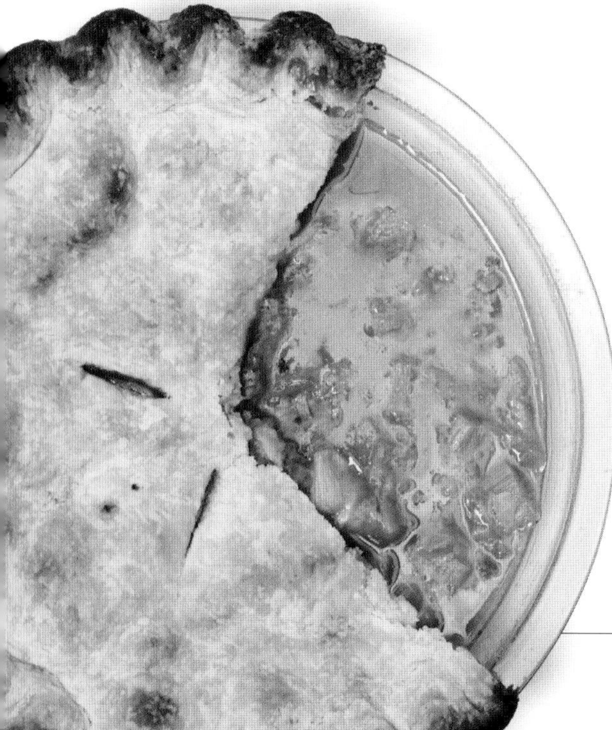

PROBLEMS

MUSHY RHUBARB
Rhubarb in pie fillings tends to "blow out" because its rigid structure can't accommodate the expansion that occurs when the heat of the oven converts the stalk's abundant moisture to steam. The result: pieces that have exploded rather than remained tender and intact.

BLOATED BERRIES
Strawberries also soften during baking but remain intact because their structure is more flexible and better able to withstand expansion. In fact, strawberries in pie filling not only contain their own juices during baking but also soak up moisture thrown off by the rhubarb, which makes them unappealingly bloated.

SOLUTIONS

MICROWAVE
To rid the rhubarb of some water without cooking it too much, we toss the cut-up pieces with sugar (which helps draw out moisture) and briefly microwave them.

MACERATE; THEN DRAIN
Resting the sugared rhubarb and some of the berries for 30 minutes draws out even more moisture that can then be drained off.

REDUCE
We further minimize the juices but retain their flavor by reducing the shed liquid with the rest of the berries until the mixture turns jammy.

STRAWBERRY-RHUBARB PIE

SERVES 8

This dough is unusually moist and requires a full ¼ cup of flour when rolling it out to prevent it from sticking. Rhubarb varies in the amount of trimming required. Buy 2 pounds to ensure that you end up with 7 cups of rhubarb pieces. For tips on crimping the dough, see "Crimping with Style" on page 31. If desired, serve the pie with whipped cream or ice cream.

Crust

- 2½ cups (12½ ounces) all-purpose flour
- 2 tablespoons sugar, plus 3 tablespoons for sprinkling
- 1 teaspoon salt
- 12 tablespoons unsalted butter, cut into ¼-inch slices and chilled
- ½ cup vegetable shortening, cut into 4 pieces and chilled
- ¼ cup vodka, chilled
- ¼ cup cold water, plus extra for brushing

Filling

- 2 pounds rhubarb, trimmed and cut into ½-inch pieces (7 cups)
- 1¼ cups (8¾ ounces) sugar
- 1 pound strawberries, hulled, halved if less than 1 inch, quartered if more than 1 inch (3 to 4 cups)
- 3 tablespoons instant tapioca

1. FOR THE CRUST: Process 1½ cups flour, 2 tablespoons sugar, and salt in food processor until combined, about 5 seconds. Scatter butter and shortening over top and process until incorporated and mixture begins to form uneven clumps with no remaining floury bits, about 15 seconds.

2. Scrape down sides of bowl and redistribute dough evenly around processor blade. Sprinkle remaining 1 cup flour over dough and pulse until mixture has broken up into pieces and is evenly distributed around bowl, 4 to 6 pulses.

3. Transfer mixture to large bowl. Sprinkle vodka and cold water over mixture. Using rubber spatula, stir and press dough until it sticks together.

4. Divide dough in half. Turn each half onto sheet of plastic wrap and form into 4-inch disk. Wrap disks tightly in plastic and refrigerate for 1 hour. Let chilled dough sit on counter to soften slightly, about 10 minutes, before rolling. (Wrapped dough can be refrigerated for up to 2 days or frozen for up to 1 month. If frozen, let dough thaw completely on counter before rolling.)

5. FOR THE FILLING: While dough chills, combine rhubarb and sugar in bowl and microwave for 1½ minutes. Stir and continue to microwave until sugar is mostly dissolved, about 1 minute longer. Stir in 1 cup strawberries and set aside for 30 minutes, stirring once halfway through.

6. Drain rhubarb mixture through fine-mesh strainer set over large saucepan. Return drained rhubarb mixture to bowl and set aside. Add remaining strawberries to rhubarb liquid and cook over medium-high heat until strawberries are very soft and mixture is reduced to 1½ cups, about 10 to 15 minutes. Mash berries with fork (mixture does not have to be smooth). Add strawberry mixture and tapioca to drained rhubarb mixture and stir to combine. Set aside.

7. Roll 1 disk of dough into 12-inch circle on well-floured counter. Loosely roll dough around rolling pin and gently unroll onto 9-inch pie plate, letting excess dough hang over edge. Ease dough into plate by gently lifting edge of dough with your hand while pressing into plate bottom with your other hand. Wrap dough-lined plate loosely in plastic and refrigerate until dough is firm, about 30 minutes.

8. Roll other disk of dough into 12-inch circle on well-floured counter, then transfer to parchment paper–lined baking sheet; cover with plastic and refrigerate for 30 minutes. Adjust rack to middle position and heat oven to 425 degrees.

9. Transfer filling to chilled dough-lined plate and spread into even layer. Loosely roll remaining dough round around rolling pin and gently unroll it onto filling. Trim overhang to ½ inch beyond lip of plate. Pinch edges of top and bottom crusts firmly together. Tuck overhang under itself; folded edge should be flush with edge of plate. Crimp dough evenly around edge of plate using your fingers or butter knife. Brush surface thoroughly with extra water and sprinkle with 3 tablespoons sugar. Cut eight 2-inch slits in top crust.

10. Place pie on parchment-lined rimmed baking sheet and bake until crust is set and begins to brown, about 25 minutes. Rotate pie and reduce oven temperature to 375 degrees; continue to bake until crust is deep golden brown and filling is bubbling, 30 to 40 minutes longer. If edges of pie begin to get too brown before pie is done, cover loosely with aluminum foil. Let cool on wire rack for 2½ hours before serving.

TECHNIQUE | VENTING GUIDES

Cutting vents in a pie's top crust allows steam to escape—important for juicy fruit pies like strawberry-rhubarb. By cutting eight evenly spaced slits in a spoke-like pattern, we also create slicing guidelines that help produce even portions.

Testing Ice Cream Scoops

Our favorite ice cream scoop from Rösle ($26.95) produces tidy, smooth spheres, but its narrow handle has always felt small for users with larger hands. Plus, it's pricey. So we compared six models ($11 to $18.44) with the Rösle by scooping ice cream and sorbet.

Both slightly curved and round bowls made neat scoops, but the formers' shallower shape helped ice cream release more easily. As for the grip, testers rejected models with spring-loaded handles, whose wide spans made them uncomfortable to squeeze while scooping. They preferred simple rounded handles that measured 3 to 4 inches around their widest point.

The best scoops, from Zeroll and OXO, offered wide, comfortable handles and shallow oval bowls. But the Zeroll handle had an extra perk: It contains a heat-conductive fluid that warms on contact with your hand; when that heat travels to the bowl, the warm metal slightly melts the ice cream so that it's particularly easy to scoop. For complete testing results, go to CooksIllustrated.com/june15. –Kate Shannon

HIGHLY RECOMMENDED

ZEROLL Original Ice Cream Scoop
Model: 1010
Price: $18.44
Comments: This gently curved bowl scoops perfect orbs that release easily. Its comfy handle contains a special fluid that warms up on contact with your hand; when that heat travels to the bowl, it slightly melts the ice cream so that it's easier to scoop.

RECOMMENDED WITH RESERVATIONS

TOVOLO Tilt Up Ice Cream Scoop
Model: N/A
Price: $11
Comments: The thin-edged bowl plowed through and released ice cream, but its large shape scooped balls that were too big for a cone. The "feet" sticking out the back of the bowl kept the scoop from dripping on the counter when we set it down, but they snagged on the rim of the container and left their own puddles.

NOT RECOMMENDED

NORPRO EZ-Scoop 2-Tablespoon Stainless Steel Scoop
Model: 703
Price: $13.33
Comments: A portion scoop that doubles for ice cream, this bowl releases ice cream when its spring-loaded handles are squeezed—but the handles' span was uncomfortable. Thin strips of ice cream became stuck under the wiper, jamming the mechanism so it wouldn't release cleanly.

How to Cook Farro

We were sold on this nutty grain even before we realized how fast and easy it is to cook.

BY ANDREA GEARY

I've always been a fan of the hearty texture and nutty taste of whole grains—not to mention their versatility. Because each grain has a protective layer of bran, these starches stay fresh and separate (rather than sticking together in starchy clumps) for days after they've been cooked. I can boil up a batch of wheat berries or brown basmati on the weekend and toss it into salads, soups, and side dishes all week long.

Farro is a perfect example. This ancient form of wheat boasts a mildly earthy flavor that is similar to that of wheat berries, but the grains are smaller and the skin surrounding each capsule is a little more delicate, which makes farro a bit more tender. Until recently, it was rarely seen outside Italy, so when whole farro began showing up at local supermarkets, I was eager to develop a basic cooking method so I could start incorporating it into a variety of dishes.

I found a bewildering array of contradictory advice on how to cook farro. Some claimed that an overnight soak before cooking was essential, presumably to help the grains hydrate so that they'd cook faster. Others said 25 minutes would do the job, and still others skipped the soak altogether. As for actually cooking the farro, simmering the grains in a large pot of salted water was a common method, but the suggested times varied wildly—from as little as 20 minutes to as long as an hour.

It turned out that boiling the grains in a couple of quarts of salted water for about 20 minutes and then draining them yielded nicely firm but tender results. (For more information, see "Farro: The Fast-Cooking Whole Grain" on page 29.) Soaking the farro before simmering was detrimental, as the grains ruptured after even a brief simmer and cooked up mushy. My final cooking test was to try toasting the farro (with and without oil or butter) before incorporating water, as we often do for quinoa, rice, and pasta. In the end, the flavor gain was so minimal that it would surely be obscured by any mix-ins that I would use to dress up the grains.

With the farro perfected, I devised two summery sides. For the first, I tossed the grain with cherry tomatoes, asparagus, and sugar snap peas; dressed the salad with a lemon and dill vinaigrette; and topped it with feta. For the second, I put together a simple warm side dish with onion, fresh herbs, and lemon.

Look: Quick and Easy
Video available free for 4 months at CooksIllustrated.com/june15

SIMPLE FARRO

MAKES 2½ CUPS

We prefer the flavor and texture of whole-grain farro. Pearled farro can be used, but cooking times vary, so start checking for doneness after 10 minutes. Do not use quick-cooking farro in this recipe. Warm farro can be tossed with butter or olive oil and salt and pepper for a simple yet hearty side dish. It can also be added to soups or, when cooled, added to salads.

- 1½ cups whole farro, rinsed
- 1 tablespoon salt

Bring 2 quarts water to boil in large saucepan. Add farro and salt. Return to boil, reduce heat, and simmer until grains are tender with slight chew, 15 to 20 minutes. Drain well. (Farro can be refrigerated for up to 5 days.)

FARRO SALAD WITH ASPARAGUS, SUGAR SNAP PEAS, AND TOMATOES

SERVES 6

For our free recipe for Farro Salad with Butternut Squash and Radicchio, go to CooksIllustrated.com/june15.

- 6 ounces asparagus, trimmed and cut into 1-inch lengths
- 6 ounces sugar snap peas, strings removed, cut into 1-inch lengths
- Salt and pepper
- 3 tablespoons extra-virgin olive oil
- 2 tablespoons lemon juice
- 2 tablespoons minced shallot
- 1 teaspoon Dijon mustard
- 1 recipe Simple Farro, room temperature
- 6 ounces cherry tomatoes, halved
- 3 tablespoons chopped fresh dill
- 2 ounces feta cheese, crumbled (½ cup)

1. Bring 2 quarts water to boil in large saucepan. Add asparagus, snap peas, and 1 tablespoon salt. Cook until vegetables are crisp-tender, 2 to 3 minutes. Using slotted spoon, transfer vegetables to rimmed baking sheet and let cool for 15 minutes.

2. Whisk oil, lemon juice, shallot, mustard, ¼ teaspoon salt, and ¼ teaspoon pepper together in large bowl. Add cooled vegetables, farro, tomatoes, dill, and ¼ cup feta to dressing and toss to combine.

After just 20 minutes of cooking, farro is ready to be incorporated into salads, pilafs, and more.

Season with salt and pepper to taste and transfer to serving bowl. Sprinkle salad with remaining ¼ cup feta and serve.

WARM FARRO WITH LEMON AND HERBS

SERVES 6

For our free recipe for Warm Farro with Cranberries, Pecans, and Herbs, go to CooksIllustrated.com/june15.

- 3 tablespoons unsalted butter
- 1 onion, chopped
- Salt and pepper
- 1 garlic clove, minced
- 1 recipe Simple Farro
- ¼ cup chopped fresh parsley
- ¼ cup chopped fresh mint
- 2 teaspoons lemon juice

Melt butter in 12-inch skillet over medium heat. Add onion and ¼ teaspoon salt and cook, stirring frequently, until onion is softened but not browned, 6 to 8 minutes. Add garlic and cook until fragrant, about 1 minute. Add farro and cook until warmed through, 3 to 5 minutes. Remove from heat and stir in parsley, mint, and lemon juice. Season with salt and pepper to taste, and serve.

A Better Cast-Iron Skillet?

Cheap and tough, a cast-iron skillet is a kitchen workhorse, but the upkeep makes some cooks balk. Could enameled cast-iron pans, which need no special care, top the classic?

BY LISA McMANUS

Few pieces of kitchen gear improve after years of heavy use. In fact, I can think of only one: the cast-iron pan. As you cook in it, a cast-iron pan gradually takes on a natural, slick patina that releases food easily. Well-seasoned cast iron can rival, and certainly outlast, a nonstick pan. Cast-iron pans are virtually indestructible and easily restored if mistreated. Their special talent is heat retention, making them ideal for browning, searing, and shallow frying. Our longtime favorite has been the Lodge Classic Cast Iron Skillet ($33.31) for its low price, generous size, sturdiness, smooth factory preseasoning, and ability to get ripping hot.

Whether traditional or enameled, a cast-iron pan should be slick enough to easily release scrambled eggs, unlike the top pan above.

Fortunately, cast iron is having a renaissance. Manufacturers have launched new versions of traditional cast-iron pans with innovative design tweaks to their handles and overall shapes in an attempt to rival the bare-bones pans like the Lodge Classic. Perhaps more notably, there's been a boom in the number of enameled cast-iron skillets. These pans cloak the rough surface inside and out with the same kind of porcelain coating found on Dutch ovens. Enameling promises a cast-iron pan with advantages: The glossy coating prevents the metal from rusting or reacting with acidic foods, both of which are concerns with traditional cast iron. It also lets you thoroughly scrub dirty pans with soap—generally taboo with traditional pans since soap will remove the patina. (The patina can be restored; see "What's the Deal with Seasoning?") While a handful of expensive enameled skillets have been around for years, new models are now appearing at lower prices. We had to wonder: Should we be trading out our traditional pan for an enameled one?

We bought 10 cast-iron skillets, six enameled and four traditional, each about 12 inches in diameter. Prices ranged from $21.99 to a whopping $179.95. We included our old favorite, from Lodge, in the lineup, along with our former Best Buy, from Camp Chef ($21.99). Comparing the new pans with our old winners, we set about scrambling eggs, searing steaks, making a tomato-caper pan sauce (to check if its acidity reacted with the pan surface), skillet-roasting thick fish fillets that went from stove to oven, baking cornbread, and shallow-frying breaded chicken cutlets. At the end of testing, we scrambled more eggs to see whether the pans' surfaces had evolved. To simulate years of kitchen use, we plunged hot pans into ice water, banged a metal spoon on their rims, cut in them with a chef's knife, and scraped them with a metal spatula.

No Lightweights

For this story, we skipped over "lightweight" cast-iron skillets. We tried this category in a previous testing and found that they lacked the outstanding heat retention of traditional heavy cast-iron pans. (For more information, see CooksIllustrated.com/lightcastiron.)

Sticking Points

All the traditional pans arrived preseasoned from the factory. Traditional pans from T-fal and Calphalon offered potential design improvements over the Lodge: the T-fal a longer, more ergonomic handle and the Calphalon a rounded shape with an unusual cupped helper handle. Both were generally pleasing to use, but with their pebbly finishes, they took longer than the Lodge to establish seasoning, and by the end of testing, neither matched the Lodge's shiny surface. The T-fal pan also required an hour of preseasoning in the oven with oil before the first use, even though it was sold as "preseasoned." Despite this dual preseasoning, the acidic pan sauce picked up a slightly funky, metallic taste. The Camp Chef looked less refined in general compared with the Lodge and was not as thoroughly preseasoned. Thus, it took longer to develop a good, slick surface, but it's still a sturdy performer at a great price. Still, in test after test, we preferred the solid, effortless performance of the Lodge Classic skillet. It held its spot as the gold standard in the traditional category.

That left enameled pans. The pricey Le Creuset skillet ($179.95) was glassy smooth inside, while the rest were matte. Despite their enamel coatings, some cooking surfaces were nearly as rough as sandpaper, tearing lint from towels as we wiped them. But surprisingly, the finish didn't always relate directly to how much the food stuck—the top pan was quite smooth, but its closest competitor was rough. In recipes that required plenty of fat, such as steaks or fried chicken cutlets, the enameled pans all released foods well and delivered good browning. But with foods that often stick—fish, eggs, and cornbread—the differences between the enameled and traditional pans finally emerged. While in the main the enameled pans performed reasonably well, they tended to grab on to the food a little more. All the traditional skillets instantly turned out crisp-crusted cornbread loaves when we flipped them, but four of six enameled models held on to the cornbread and tore out a chunk of bottom crust. Our lowest-ranked enameled pan, by Tramontina, pulled off a 4 by 6-inch chunk; it also broke up fish fillets when we tried to flip them. Most telling, traditional pans became slicker each time we used them, but enamel coatings remained the same, and a few even released slightly less well by the end of testing.

See How We Tested Them
Video available free for 4 months at CooksIllustrated.com/june15

Heating Things Up

Next we looked more generally at how the pans handled and functioned. One of cast iron's selling points is that it holds heat well, producing excellent browning. But, for the same reason, it's slow to heat up and can have hot spots. You must preheat thoroughly to give the heat time to spread. We found that the enamel coatings didn't dramatically affect how quickly the pans heated or cooled down. Rather, the pan's ability to retain heat, whether traditional or enameled, is related mainly to the thickness and overall mass of the cast iron. The pans in our lineup ranged in thickness from 4.1 to 5.6 millimeters. Pans on the thicker end of the range proved problematic. Two of the thickest pans, both enameled (plus another pan that was thinner but had an unusually large cooking surface), were more sluggish to heat, hung on to hot spots for longer, and finally became too hot, making it a challenge to brown food evenly.

Another note about heating: While traditional cast iron has no upper temperature limits, this is not true of enamel because high temperatures can cause the coating to develop numerous small cracks (called "crazing"). This restriction makes them less versatile; one pan's maximum was just 400 degrees. However, there was one exception. Our favorite enameled pan fell in line with the traditional pans; with no recommended upper limit by the manufacturer, it's even broiler-safe. It also proved itself above the rest on the abuse front. After all the scraping and banging and cutting, it was the only enameled pan to emerge perfectly unmarked.

Enameled or not, weight, handle length, and breadth made a big difference in how easy the pans were to use. Our pans ranged from 6½ pounds to nearly 9 pounds. Longer handles gave better leverage, though shorter ones worked if the pan had a good helper handle. The worst helper was a mere ¾-inch tab on the Staub pan; the best were big enough to feel secure, even through potholders. As for shape, low, flaring, curved sides are usually ideal in a skillet to encourage evaporation and help food brown. But a thoroughly preheated cast-iron skillet radiates heat so intensely that browning was easy even in pans with higher, straighter sides, as long as they had a broad enough cooking surface. Our top pans were at least 10 inches across the cooking surface, which provided enough room for even the biggest steaks to brown without crowding and steaming.

Which Cast Iron Is Right for You?

Buy a **TRADITIONAL** cast-iron pan if:

- **You're never going to baby your cookware.** You want to use it at any temperature, under the broiler or on the grill, with metal utensils, and bang it around with no fear of damage.
- **You don't want to spend a lot.** Our favorite 12-inch traditional skillet will cost around $30 and last a lifetime.
- **You don't mind simple maintenance.** Wash, dry thoroughly, and lightly oil to prevent rust.
- **You are OK with using little to no soap** (hot water and a scrub brush suffice).
- **You don't plan to make long-simmered acidic sauces like marinara in it.**
- **You won't leave it soaking.**

Buy an **ENAMELED** cast-iron pan if:

- **You never want to think about seasoning the pan.** Enamel doesn't need it.
- **You don't mind spending more.** Our recommended 12-inch skillets range from $50 to $180.
- **You're prepared to protect the glass-like enamel.** You won't use it under the broiler (unless you're prepared to buy our durable, and expensive, winner); you'll avoid metal utensils and banging or scraping the pan; and you'll stack with care.
- **You dislike the idea of not using soap.**
- **You plan to use it for long-simmered acidic sauces.**
- **You don't mind that the enamel will not become more nonstick.** An enameled pan will never become as nonstick as a well-seasoned traditional pan.

Weighing the Options

In the final analysis, neither enameled nor traditional cast iron was "best." Both offer great heat retention and superior browning, but beyond that it's a matter of comparing pros and cons and determining what's best for your own needs. If you find seasoning traditional cast iron intimidating, paying more up front for an enameled pan is probably worth it. But keep in mind, while a good enameled pan may be more "nonstick" than a traditional stainless-steel pan, it isn't ever going to match a well-seasoned traditional cast-iron pan (in fairness, enameled pans aren't marketed as nonstick). On the flip side, if you don't want to pamper your pan to prevent chipping and scratching and are OK with maintaining the seasoning, traditional cast iron is for you. What's more, if you want to use metal utensils and high heat, if you want a pan that over time will release food more easily, and if you want to save some money, choose traditional cast iron. (For more, see "Which Cast Iron Is Right for You?")

Our favorite among the traditional pans is still the Lodge Classic Cast Iron Skillet. At $33.31, it's a real bargain. Our enameled winner is the Le Creuset Signature 11¾" Iron Handle Skillet ($179.95), a new version of a pan we tested in 2007, now with a bigger helper handle and broader cooking surface. It browned foods beautifully, performed admirably on the sticking tests, and cleaned up easily. While it's expensive, the value is evident in its toughness; it took abuse with nary a scratch. For a more economical option, we were impressed by the consistently solid performance of the Mario Batali by Dansk 12" Open Sauté Pan ($59.95), our Best Buy enameled pan.

What's the Deal with Seasoning?

Cast-iron skillets used to be sold uncoated, and you had to season them from scratch. But all that is in the past: Cast-iron skillets are now sold factory preseasoned. The manufacturer sprays on a proprietary, food-safe oil and bakes it onto the pan. (However, if the seasoning becomes damaged or if you own an old-fashioned uncoated pan, the surface can oxidize, causing rust to form.) As soon as you start cooking in the pan, heat makes fats in the pan polymerize, meaning that the fat's molecules link together and bond to the rough iron surface, forming a natural hard, protective coating. This coating not only keeps the pan from rusting or reacting with acidic food but also helps food release more easily. Every time you cook in your cast-iron pan, you're improving this natural polymerized coating, which is called the pan's "seasoning."

EVERYDAY UPKEEP: To maintain and improve your pan's seasoning, don't scrub with abrasives, use harsh soap, or leave it soaking. Instead, clean the pan by rinsing it with hot water and a scrub brush. (It's OK to use a few drops of dish soap if you need to.) You can also mix kosher salt with oil to make a DIY scrubber that can remove stuck-on food without scraping off your pan's seasoning.

Once the pan is clean, wipe it all over with paper towels and then put it on the stove on medium-low heat until all moisture disappears. Add a few drops of vegetable oil and, using paper towels, rub the oil into the interior of the skillet, creating an even, thin coat that, by the time you're done wiping, should feel almost dry to the touch.

OVERHAUL: If you think your skillet needs just a touch-up, heat the pan and repeatedly wipe it with a thin coat of oil until the surface looks dark black and slightly glossy but isn't sticky or greasy to the touch. However, if you do damage the seasoning, and your pan looks dry and patchy, it's not the end of the world. To reestablish the seasoning, follow one of our methods found at CooksIllustrated.com/castiron.

CAST-IRON SKILLETS

We tested ten 12-inch cast-iron skillets. Pans were purchased online and appear in order of preference. Oven-safe temperature ratings are from manufacturers.

KEY
Good ★★★
Fair ★★
Poor ★

BROWNING
We seared steaks and made an acidic sauce, looking for good crust and flavor without off-notes. We rated browning with skillet-roasted fish fillets, shallow-fried breaded chicken cutlets, and cornbread.

STICKING
We cooked thick fish fillets and baked cornbread; we scrambled eggs as first and last tests to evaluate changes in the pans' surfaces.

EASE OF USE
We considered features that helped make the pans easy to use and clean.

DURABILITY
We heated pans to 400 degrees and then plunged them into ice water, made five cuts inside with a chef's knife, scraped with a metal spatula 10 times, and whacked a metal spoon five times on the rims and sides of pans.

TRADITIONAL CAST IRON

HIGHLY RECOMMENDED

LODGE Classic Cast Iron Skillet, 12"
Model: L10SK3
Price: $33.31
Weight: 7 lb, 10⅛ oz
Cooking Surface: 10 in
Ovensafe to: At least 1,000°

Browning ★★★
Sticking ★★★
Ease of Use ★★★
Durability ★★★

Our old winner arrived with the slickest preseasoned interior, and it only got better. It browned foods deeply, and its thorough seasoning ensured that our acidic pan sauce picked up no off-flavors. Though its handle is short, the pan has a helper handle that made lifting easy. It survived abuse testing without a scratch.

CALPHALON 12-in. Pre-Seasoned Cast Iron Skillet
Model: 1873975
Price: $34.95
Weight: 6 lb, 12 oz
Cooking Surface: 10¼ in
Ovensafe to: "Well above broiler level"

Browning ★★★
Sticking ★★½
Ease of Use ★★★
Durability ★★★

Even browning made this pan stand out; we also liked the unusual helper handle and curved sides, which added to its cooking area. However, its pebbly surface stuck to food a bit more than our smoother top-rated pan and took a little more effort to scrub clean.

RECOMMENDED

CAMP CHEF 12" Seasoned Cast Iron Skillet
Model: SK12
Price: $21.99
Weight: 7 lb, ¾ oz
Cooking Surface: 9¾ in
Ovensafe to: 600°

Browning ★★★
Sticking ★★
Ease of Use ★★½
Durability ★★★

This inexpensive choice browned steak, chicken, and cornbread beautifully and made a pan sauce with no off-flavors. Nevertheless, its preseasoning seemed thin, looking patchy after washing; fish and eggs stuck at first, but the pan acquired good seasoning in time and endured abuse well.

RECOMMENDED WITH RESERVATIONS

T-FAL Pre-Seasoned Cast Iron Skillet, 12"
Model: E8340763
Price: $34.97
Weight: 8 lb, 8¾ oz
Cooking Surface: 10 in
Ovensafe to: 600°

Browning ★★
Sticking ★★
Ease of Use ★★
Durability ★★½

This pan is supposedly preseasoned, but instructions had us season it again in the oven. Its nonstick quality improved slowly, leaving us scrubbing eggs. When we flipped steaks, the pan seemed to lose heat, leading to uneven browning. It turned the pan sauce faintly metallic, and spatula scrapes left scratches. We did love the long, rounded handle.

ENAMELED CAST IRON

HIGHLY RECOMMENDED

LE CREUSET Signature 11¾" Iron Handle Skillet
Model: LS2024-30
Price: $179.95
Weight: 6 lb, 8⅝ oz
Cooking Surface: 10 in
Ovensafe to: No maximum set by company

Browning ★★★
Sticking ★★½
Ease of Use ★★★
Durability ★★★

With flaring sides, an oversize helper handle, wide pour spouts, a satiny interior, and balanced weight, this expensive but beautifully made pan is a pleasure to cook in. Our only quibbles: A small piece of cornbread stuck, and scrambled eggs stuck a little (but scrubbed out easily). After abuse testing, the pan still looked nearly new.

RECOMMENDED

MARIO BATALI by Dansk 12" Open Sauté Pan
Model: 826782 (cobalt color)
Price: $59.95
Weight: 8 lb, 10½ oz
Cooking Surface: 10¼ in
Ovensafe to: 475°

BEST BUY

Browning ★★★
Sticking ★★★
Ease of Use ★★½
Durability ★★

This pan felt well-balanced, and its ample size and great heat capacity rendered deep browning on every food we cooked. Its surface resisted sticking, releasing cornbread perfectly. It's a bit less durable than others: Half-inch areas of enamel chipped off both of the handles' tips, and the pan bottom looked blotchy.

LODGE Enamel Coated Cast Iron Skillet, 11"
Model: EC11S43
Price: $48.90
Weight: 6 lb, 13⅜ oz
Cooking Surface: 9¼ in
Ovensafe to: 400°

Browning ★★★
Sticking ★★½
Ease of Use ★★½
Durability ★★

The long handle on this small pan made it comfortable to lift, and its curved sides were easy to swipe with a spatula. It released cornbread perfectly but performed slightly less well with fish and eggs. Foods browned evenly. But two big steaks barely fit and steamed rather than seared. Good for small households.

RECOMMENDED WITH RESERVATIONS

RACHAEL RAY Cast Iron 12-inch Open Skillet with Helper Handle
Model: 59161
Price: $79.95
Weight: 7 lb, 14⅝ oz
Cooking Surface: 11 in
Ovensafe to: 500°

Browning ★★½
Sticking ★★½
Ease of Use ★★
Durability ★★

This pan is roomy but sluggish to heat up and then prone to run too hot. Once we'd adjusted, the pan behaved well, with good browning; however, fish and cornbread stuck and took some scrubbing. Knife scratches remained.

STAUB Cast Iron 12" Fry Pan
Model: 1223025
Price: $174.99
Weight: 6 lb, 6⅜ oz
Cooking Surface: 10 in
Ovensafe to: 500°

Browning ★★
Sticking ★★
Ease of Use ★★½
Durability ★★

We liked its low, flared sides, but this pan felt clunky and browned fish and steak unevenly. The cooking surface was prone to sticking. It was slower to heat and tended to run hot. The exterior scratched easily, and the bottom blackened in spots.

TRAMONTINA Gourmet Enameled Cast Iron 12 in Skillet with Lid
Model: 80131/058DS
Price: $69.60
Weight: 7 lb, 8⅝ oz
Cooking Surface: 9¾ in
Ovensafe to: 450°

Browning ★★½
Sticking ★★
Ease of Use ★½
Durability ★★½

While it browned steaks fairly well, delicate foods stuck to this pan and broke the biggest chunk off cornbread. Thick, heavy, and deep, with a narrow cooking surface, it felt awkward, heated sluggishly, and was prone to run hot. The uncoated rim required seasoning to prevent rust.

The Best Supermarket Brie

Think French pedigree and words like "triple crème" indicate the best examples of this cheese plate favorite? So did we—until we learned that good Brie is a matter of culture.

BY KATE SHANNON

A few decades ago, Brie was the pinnacle of sophistication on American cheese plates. Its longtime French reputation as the "cheese of kings," coupled with its lush, buttery, not-too-pungent profile and velvety edible rind, made it at once fashionable and approachable. But Brie sold in America has changed over the years. The original name-protected versions have been banned by the U.S. Food and Drug Administration (FDA) for using raw milk, and these days most products found in supermarkets are produced domestically. You're also increasingly likely to find specimens that are bland, rubbery, and encased in rinds as stiff as cardboard. And yet, if there was a creamy, satiny, richly flavorful Brie available in the average grocery store, we wanted to know about it. So we gathered 10 nationally available brands that ranged broadly in price (from $5.92 to $19.98 per pound), purposely selecting cheeses that spanned a variety of traits that we thought might affect flavor and texture—in particular, fat content (we included standard-fat, double, and triple crème cheeses), nationality (American or French), and format (some are sold as small wheels, others as wedges cut from larger wheels). We sampled the Bries plain at room temperature (the ideal serving temperature) and also baked into phyllo cups with dollops of red currant jelly to see how the cheeses behaved when heated.

Process of Elimination

We could tell just by handling the cheeses that their textures varied considerably: Wheels and wedges alike ranged from soft and pliable to almost rigid. When we tasted the cheeses, we found that their flavors varied just as much—some were "boring," with "almost no flavor," while others tasted "mushroomy" and "nutty-rich." Heating the cheeses only underscored these differences: Fuller flavors intensified and creamier textures became even plusher, while bland cheeses tasted the same and barely melted at all. When we tallied the scores, we were pleased to find that we could recommend without reservation four out of the 10 cheeses—in particular, a standout wedge that embodied everything we want in Brie: a lush, buttery, full-flavored interior encased in a pillowy rind.

But surprisingly, factors like origin, price, and format had no bearing on our preferences. Though our favorite was a wedge from France, our runner-up was an 8-ounce wheel made in California. And a bargain wedge from Michigan outranked French Bries costing two or three times as much.

We also assumed that Bries labeled triple and double crème would taste richer and creamier than standard-fat cheeses—but that wasn't always the case. Though cream is generally added to the milk when making both double and triple crèmes, the amount can vary substantially within each category. (Triple crèmes contain upwards of 75 percent butterfat while double crèmes range from 60 to 75 percent.)

Culture Shock

It wasn't until we dug deeper into the Brie-making process that we uncovered the key factor explaining what gave a cheese the lush texture and earthy flavor we liked best: the culturing process. Cultures in the milk and on the exterior of the Brie react with the milk proteins as the cheese ages—a process called proteolysis—and cause the proteins to break down. This results in a rind forming on the wheel and its interior softening and developing flavor from the outside in, a process known as surface-ripening.

According to Dean Sommer and Mark Johnson at the University of Wisconsin-Madison's Center for Dairy Research, the nature of that ripening—and the flavor and texture of Brie—largely depends on the type of cultures a cheesemaker uses. French *appellation d'origine contrôlée* (AOC) Bries are made exclusively with raw milk, which can contain enough natural bacteria to culture the cheese. But Bries made with pasteurized milk need added cultures. These fall into two main strains, mesophilic or thermophilic. Mesophilic cultures are more reactive with milk proteins and lead to so-called traditional Brie that more closely mimics the AOC raw-milk cheese with fuller flavor, gooier texture, and a thinner, spottier rind. Thermophilic cultures are less reactive and create milder, firmer cheese with a thicker, more uniform rind. Such cheeses are

Real Brie? Not in the States

Most Americans have never tasted authentic French Brie, which is a regional product made according to strict criteria governed by the *appellation d'origine contrôlée* (AOC). That's because AOC Brie is made with raw milk and is aged for only a few weeks, and the FDA bans raw-milk cheeses unless they've been aged at least 60 days.

Supermarket Brie: Two Styles

Both the United States and France produce facsimiles of AOC Brie in two distinct styles, each of which results from the type of cultures used. You won't see these named on the label, but visual clues can help you determine what style you're buying. We prefer "traditional" Brie: even when chilled at the supermarket, it has a gooey core that bulges at the cut sides (wheels will give slightly when pressed) and a soft, spotty rind. "Stabilized" Brie is typically stiffer, with a thicker white rind.

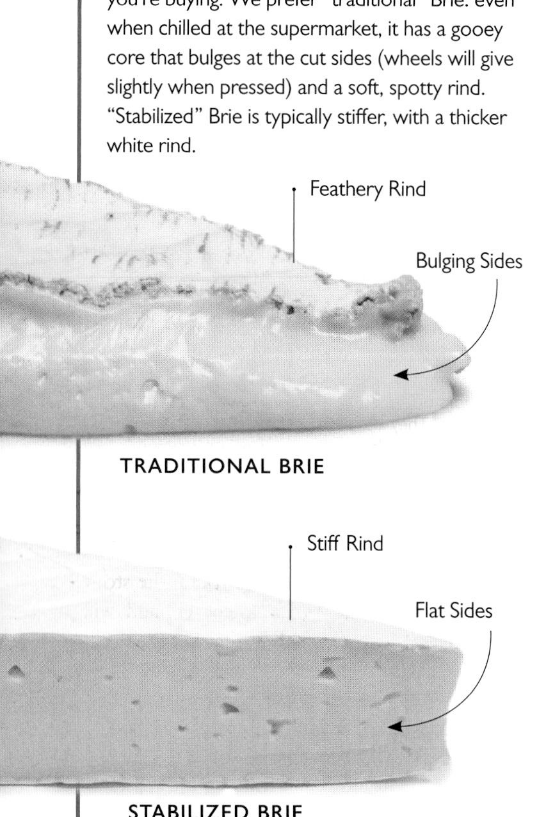

Eat the Rind!

A soft, pillowy rind isn't just a visual clue that a Brie likely has an appealingly gooey interior. It's great to eat, too, lending pleasant mushroomy flavor to the milder, more buttery-tasting core.

TASTING SUPERMARKET BRIE

Twenty-one *Cook's Illustrated* staff members tasted 10 nationally available Brie-style cheeses served plain at room temperature (the ideal serving temperature) and then baked with red currant jelly in phyllo cups, rating each sample on flavor, texture, and overall appeal. We obtained information about the age, butterfat, and style of cheese (either traditional or stabilized, dependent on the type of cultures used) from manufacturers. Products are listed in order of preference.

HIGHLY RECOMMENDED

FROMAGER D'AFFINOIS

Made in: France
Format and Price: Wedges, $17.99 per lb
Style and Age: Not disclosed, 14 days
Butterfat Classification: Double crème
Comments: The runaway favorite in both tastings, this Brie boasts "nutty richness," "ultracreamy" body, and a pillowy rind—all characteristics associated with traditional versions (though the manufacturer wouldn't confirm the culturing process). As one taster put it, eating this cheese was "sheer pleasure."

RECOMMENDED

MARIN Triple Crème Brie

Made in: USA
Format and Price: 8-oz wheels, $9.99 each ($19.98 per lb)
Style and Age: Traditional, 10 to 14 days
Butterfat Classification: Triple crème
Comments: The lone triple crème, this traditional Brie was "complex without being too pungent," "tangy," and "pleasantly earthy," but moderately so, with a "slight funk" that tasters found pleasant. Even more appealing was its "silky," "unctuous" texture that "almost melts in your mouth."

FROMAGE DE MEAUX

Made in: France
Format and Price: Wedges, $17.99 per lb
Style and Age: Traditional, 4 to 8 weeks
Butterfat Classification: Standard fat
Comments: This traditional Brie was aged up to twice as long as our other top scorers and offered "mushroomy" depth. Its texture was "beautifully runny," "creamy," and "so velvety." But don't mistake this for Brie de Meaux, one of just two name-protected Bries that are made in the Seine-et-Marne region of France according to strict laws.

RENY PICOT Brie

Made in: USA
Format and Price: 7-oz wedges, $2.59 each ($5.92 per lb)
Style and Age: Stabilized, 15 to 20 days
Butterfat Classification: Double crème
Comments: Tasters praised this Brie's "hint of ooze" and "good balance" of "tang" and "buttery flavor." But what made it really stand out was its bargain price—one-third the cost of other recommended products.

RECOMMENDED WITH RESERVATIONS

ALOUETTE Double Crème Brie

Made in: USA
Format and Price: 8-oz wheels, $6.49 each ($12.98 per lb)
Style and Age: Stabilized, not disclosed
Butterfat Classification: Double crème
Comments: Though this stabilized Brie, with a "thick, dry rind," was "pleasant" enough, the general consensus was that it was "unremarkable," "bland," and "boring." As one taster said, "This could almost be American cheese."

RECOMMENDED WITH RESERVATIONS CONTINUED

BRIE D'ISIGNY

Made in: France
Format and Price: Wedges, $11.99 per lb
Style and Age: Not disclosed, up to 4 weeks
Butterfat Classification: Double crème
Comments: Some tasters loved the texture of this "plush," "silky-smooth" Brie—traits that made us think it was a traditional version (the manufacturer wouldn't confirm the style), but most found its flavor "sharp" and "almost sour."

PRÉSIDENT Brie

Made in: USA
Format and Price: 8-oz wheels, $7.69 each ($15.38 per lb)
Style and Age: Not disclosed, 6 to 11 days
Butterfat Classification: Double crème
Comments: Tasters weren't offended by this well-known Brie, but they weren't impressed either. Most offered complaints about its "stiff," "plasticky" texture; "chalky rind"; and flavor that was "nothing special" (features that made us assume it was a stabilized Brie). In other words, "it's kind of boring" and "generic."

JOAN OF ARC Double Crème Brie

Made in: USA
Format and Price: Wedges, $13.99 per lb
Style and Age: Not disclosed, 7 to 10 days
Butterfat Classification: Double crème
Comments: "Mild" and "unremarkable," this Brie (which we assumed was stabilized) "verged on bland." As a result of its "bouncy" texture, the cheese remained "in firm little cubes" when we baked it in phyllo cups; tasters found this texture off-putting.

NOT RECOMMENDED

ILE DE FRANCE Brie

Made in: France
Format and Price: Wedges, $12.99 per lb
Style and Age: Stabilized, 7 to 10 days
Butterfat classification: Double crème
Comments: With "almost no flavor" and a texture that was firm to the point of being "rubbery," this "boring" Brie reminded tasters of "Velveeta" or "American cheese with a rind." "What's the point?" one taster asked.

BRIE DE NANGIS

Made in: France
Format and Price: Wedges, $17.99 per lb
Style and Age: Traditional, 4 to 8 weeks
Butterfat Classification: Standard fat
Comments: The "funky," "barnyardy" flavors of this Brie are often prized in France, but most of our tasters found them too strong. They also objected to the cheese's "sticky," "gluey" consistency, which was especially evident when it was baked in phyllo cups.

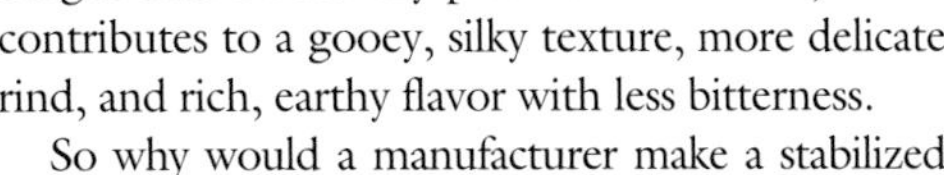

referred to as "stabilized" in the industry.

Since labels don't indicate whether a Brie is traditional or stabilized, we asked each manufacturer directly—and among those that answered, we saw a pattern. Most of our top-ranking cheeses were traditional, which correlated with our tasters' preferences for Brie with creamier body and somewhat fuller flavor, while stabilized cheeses dominated the middle and bottom of the pack. What's more, the makers of our top two Bries add *Geotrichum*, a yeast-like fungus that is naturally present in raw milk, which contributes to a gooey, silky texture, more delicate rind, and rich, earthy flavor with less bitterness.

So why would a manufacturer make a stabilized Brie? For one thing, there's a market demand for blander cheese both here and in France (where stabilized Brie is often fed to schoolchildren). Another more compelling reason is quality control: As long as a wheel of traditional Brie is left uncut, it will continue to soften and develop flavor, so makers must rely on supermarket staff to handle and rotate the stock appropriately. Stabilized Brie, on the other hand, will remain consistently firm and mild as it sits at the store.

The makers of our winner, a wedge called Fromager d'Affinois, wouldn't confirm that their cheese is made with mesophilic cultures but its silky body, buttery-rich flavor, and downy-soft rind are the qualities that we associate with traditional Brie. It's a double crème that we'll happily seek out for our cheese plates.

INGREDIENT NOTES

⋑ BY ANDREA GEARY, LAN LAM, ANNIE PETITO & DAN SOUZA ⋐

Tasting Smoked Salmon

We love bagels with smoked salmon (not to be confused with lox or gravlax, which are cured but not smoked), so we gathered up five top-selling, widely available products. We chose those labeled either smoked salmon or nova lox, both of which these days refer to salmon that has been salt-cured to remove moisture and add flavor and then rinsed and smoked at a low temperature (aka cold-smoked).

Whether tasted plain or on our New York Bagels (page 15), fish that had a good balance of smoke and fresh salmon flavor rated highest. Tasters were less enthusiastic about samples that were bland or came on too strong, with "fishy" or "campfire" flavors. Variety didn't matter; most of the samples were farm-raised Atlantic salmon, and the one wild sockeye salmon landed in the middle of the rankings. Neither did the type of wood used for smoking matter, nor the fat content of the fish. More important were the flavorings added during curing. When we asked manufacturers directly, we learned that only two products—including our favorite—relied on salt alone and didn't use spices or a sweetener. Thickness and texture also played a large part in our preferences. Tasters found thinner slices more tender than thicker slabs. We also gave a thumbs-down to products that were "mushy" or "mealy."

In the end we could fully recommend two of the five. Our favorite, Spence & Co. Traditional Scottish Style Smoked Salmon, was the only product we tasted that follows the Scottish tradition of trimming off the pellicle, the smokier, drier, browned surface. While costly for the manufacturer, this created a uniformly "buttery" texture and more subtle smoky flavor. Each thin slice was intact, flavorful, and tender. For complete tasting results, go to CooksIllustrated.com/june15. –Kate Shannon

HIGHLY RECOMMENDED

SPENCE & CO. Traditional Scottish Style Smoked Salmon
Price: $10.99 for 4 oz ($2.75 per oz)
Comments: Our winner balanced "clean" salmon taste and "rich smoke flavor." Its name refers to the Scottish technique of removing the pellicle, the layer that forms during salting and smoking, which leaves only the tender and delicately flavored meat below. Slices were "silky," "delicate," and "lush." Thin sheets layered between slices allowed for neat, easy separation.

RECOMMENDED

DUCKTRAP Kendall Brook Cold-Smoked Salmon
Price: $9.99 for 4 oz ($2.50 per oz)
Comments: Evaporated cane juice added a "slight sweetness" to this fish, which had "pleasant smoke" flavor and mild saltiness. Tasters liked the "thin, almost translucent" slices and silky texture. Although there are no plastic sheets separating slices, the thin pieces of salmon could be pulled apart fairly easily.

NOT RECOMMENDED

LASCCO Smoked Atlantic Nova Salmon
Price: $4.99 for 3 oz ($1.66 per oz)
Comments: Straight out of the package, these slices seemed oddly uniform and were by far the thickest of the samples; the rectangular pieces stood out from the rest of the lineup. This was also the only product to add coloring and preservatives. Slices separated fairly easily and kept their shape, but they were unpleasantly thick, "chewy," and "bland."

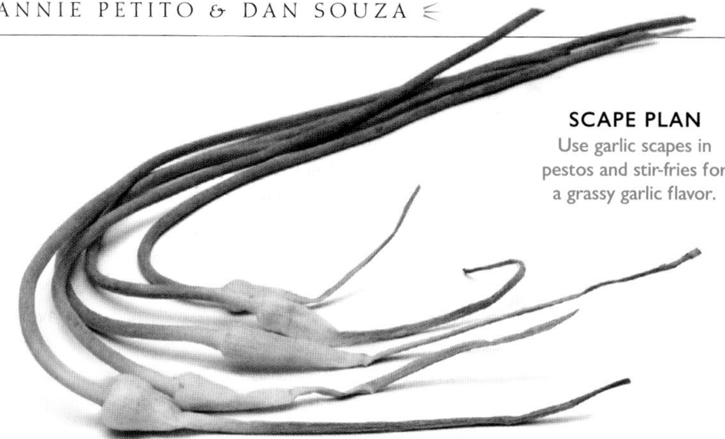

SCAPE PLAN
Use garlic scapes in pestos and stir-fries for a grassy garlic flavor.

Scoping Out Garlic Scapes

These slim, serpentine flower stems grow from the tops of hardneck garlic. Farmers have long known that removing them encourages the plant to direct its energy toward growing a plump underground bulb, but only recently has this agricultural byproduct begun to find its way to farmers' markets and community-supported agriculture boxes, usually in late spring.

Our tasters found that raw garlic scapes have an assertive garlic flavor that's less fiery and more grassy than that of raw cloves. Because garlic scapes have a tough and fibrous texture, we found that they worked best minced or pureed for raw applications. Pureed with olive oil, Parmesan cheese, and pine nuts, they produced a simple yet potent pesto.

When the scapes were cooked, tasters noted that the garlic flavor became more muted and sweet—more like roasted garlic than raw—and the texture was impressively dense and meaty. For the simplest preparation, we tossed the scapes with oil, salt, and pepper and cooked them on the grill over medium-high heat until they were softened and lightly charred, about 15 minutes. We also found that they worked very well when substituted for the green beans in a spicy stir-fry, as their mellow garlic flavor complemented the heat.

Garlic scapes are very hardy; we found that they can be refrigerated in a zipper-lock bag, left slightly open, for up to three weeks. The stem ends and the flower pods can be quite fibrous even when cooked, so we recommend trimming them before use. –A.G.

The Best Way to Rinse Rice

To ensure light, fluffy white rice, we always remove surface starch by rinsing the raw grains in a fine-mesh strainer under cold running water before cooking. But we've gotten letters from readers (and feedback from coworkers) noting that it can be hard to recognize when the water has become clear. This is because the water is aerated by its passage through the rice, which can give it a cloudy appearance; plus, typically we're rinsing in the sink and the rinse water goes quickly down the drain. Wondering if there might be a better approach, we pitted this method against another popular method—swishing the grains in a bowl of water, pouring off the cloudy water, and repeating the process until the water is clear. In the end, we still found the strainer method to be superior. Both approaches require the same amount of water, but our strainer method produced notably fluffier, more separate grains. This was because there was inevitably some starch left behind in the bowl with the rice when draining off the cloudy water. To make our method more foolproof, we recommend capturing some of the rinse water in a bowl to check whether it is starchy. Keep reserving and checking, a small amount at a time, until it is clear. –A.G.

DIY Decaf Tea? Don't Bother

Most decaf teas are generic blends that lack complexity, so many tea lovers try to decaffeinate high-quality tea at home. The most common method is to steep the leaves for a few minutes, discard the infusion, and then steep it again to produce a supposedly caffeine-free cup of tea. When we tried this method using loose-leaf white, green, oolong, and black teas and sent the teas to an independent lab for analysis, we learned that, in the main, the second infusions did not contain significantly less caffeine than the first, and in fact the green and oolong samples contained more. The exception was the black tea; this second infusion contained about 40 percent less caffeine than the first. Generally speaking, it was the third infusion of each tea that showed more impact on the caffeine content. White, green, and black all showed a marked drop from their original caffeine content (the oolong, however, actually contained a little more, likely attributed to the fact that these leaves are tightly rolled and it took the first infusion to start to open them up), but tasters found the tea at this point to be noticeably weaker in flavor and body.

The takeaway? Given how much the flavor suffers and the effort (and waste) required to notably decrease the caffeine, we don't think it's worth it. –D.S.

Farro: The Fast-Cooking Whole Grain

Usually, when a grain is sold as "semi-pearled" or "pearled"—that is, when its bran layer has been lightly abraded or almost completely rubbed away—it will cook faster than "whole" grains that have an intact bran layer. But farro is an exception. We found that whole farro often cooks faster and more consistently than the processed varieties. That's because the whole grain's heavier seed coat is rigid, so once water gets inside the grain, steam pressure builds up and causes it to rupture at the ends. Thus, water flows in a bit faster and speeds up cooking time. As for why processed grains don't cook consistently, pearling is not a standardized process; manufacturers remove as much of the grain's bran layer—and label it—as they wish. –A.G.

White Pepper: It's Not Just About Color

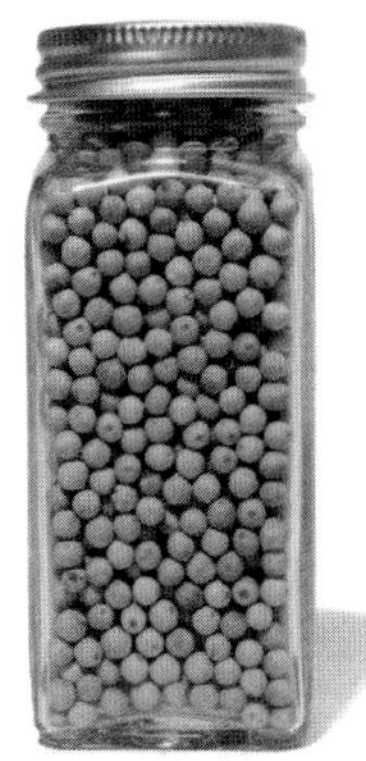

LESS HEAT, MORE COMPLEXITY
White pepper has a different flavor profile than black. Only substitute black pepper if the amount called for is small.

Some recipes call for white pepper when uniformly light-colored results are desired. But if looks aren't a consideration, does it matter if you substitute black pepper when a recipe specifies white? If it calls for a large enough amount—yes. We made two pots of hot-and-sour soup (which traditionally calls for white pepper), using 1 teaspoon of black pepper in one batch and 1 teaspoon of white pepper in the other. Tasters noted that the soup with black pepper was more aromatic and had more spicy heat but preferred the soup with white pepper for its floral, earthy flavor and greater complexity. However, when we tried the swap in a stir-fry that called for a lesser amount of white pepper, tasters had a hard time distinguishing them.

The difference in flavor between white and black pepper relates to how they are processed. To make black pepper, unripe berries from pepper plants are gathered and dried until the skins are blackened, which gives it its characteristic aroma and sharp bite. White peppercorns are fully ripened berries that have been soaked in water to ferment, and their outer skin is removed before drying. Although stripping the skin away removes much of the volatile oils and aroma compounds (most notably piperine, which is responsible for pepper's pungent heat), allowing the berries to ripen longer lets them develop more complex flavor, while fermenting adds another layer of flavor.

So if you have a recipe that relies on a fair amount of white pepper for flavor, we don't recommend swapping in the black type. –A.P.

DIY Sriracha

Sriracha is a Thai hot sauce known by its followers as rooster sauce (just look at a bottle from the popular Huy Fong Foods). Salty, sweet, sour, and hot but not searing, it's the perfect condiment for everything from rice and stir-fries to eggs and macaroni and cheese. The ingredient list is simple—chiles, sugar, salt, garlic, and distilled vinegar—and we kept the recipe simple, too. After blending the ingredients and simmering the mixture to reduce it to the right ketchup-y thickness, we blend it once more for smoothness. Refrigerating the sauce for at least one day before using it is key; the flavors deepen with age. If you want it spicier, add up to 1 tablespoon of the chile seeds. –Diane Unger

SRIRACHA

MAKES ABOUT 2 CUPS

- 1½ pounds red jalapeño chiles, stemmed and seeds reserved
- 12 garlic cloves, peeled
- 1 cup water
- ¾ cup distilled white vinegar
- 1 cup sugar
- 3 tablespoons salt

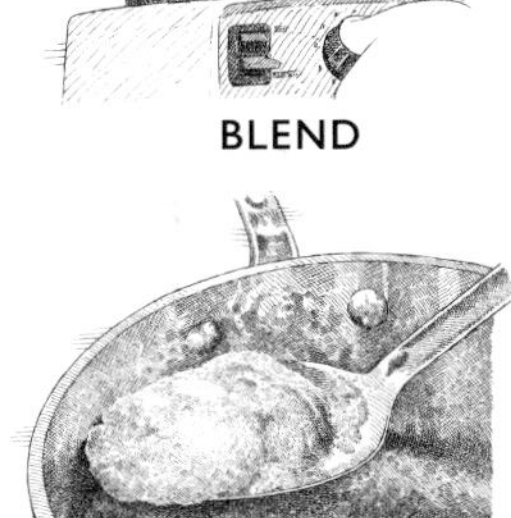

BLEND

SIMMER

1. In blender, process jalapeños; up to 1 tablespoon reserved jalapeño seeds, if desired; garlic; water; and vinegar until smooth, about 2 minutes. Transfer mixture to large saucepan and whisk in sugar and salt.

2. Bring to boil over high heat, then reduce heat to medium-low and simmer, stirring occasionally and skimming any surface foam, until mixture is thickened and reduced to 2 cups, about 25 minutes. Remove pan from heat and let cool for 5 minutes.

3. Return mixture to blender and process on low speed until smooth, about 20 seconds. Transfer to large liquid measuring cup and let cool completely. Pour cooled mixture into jar or plastic squeeze bottle with tight-fitting lid and refrigerate for at least 1 day before using. Sriracha can be refrigerated for up to 3 months.

Storing Half an Onion

To find the best way to store half a leftover onion, we gave the most popular recommendations a try, keeping samples in the refrigerator for two weeks before evaluating the results. The first sample, which was stored in water, turned brown (as did the water) and swelled noticeably. Swapping the water for oil, as some sources suggest, was also a failure; the onion became unmanageably greasy. However, those that were stored cut side down—either wrapped tightly in plastic wrap, in a zipper-lock bag, or in an airtight container—showed much more promise. The cut side dried out a little, so we cut a thin layer from the cut surface of all three samples before comparing each one, raw and cooked in a rice pilaf, to samples prepared using a freshly cut whole onion. Tasters found that when eaten raw, the older onion tasted metallic, sour, and harsh compared with the fresh onion. However, in the rice pilaf, no one could distinguish between the fresh and stored onion.

KEEP IT AIRTIGHT
Stored properly, a leftover halved onion works fine if cooked but not raw.

Bottom line? Store leftover halved onions wrapped tightly in plastic wrap or in a zipper-lock bag or airtight container in the fridge for up to two weeks. Be sure to use the stored onions only in cooked applications. –L.L.

KITCHEN NOTES

⋟ BY ANDREA GEARY, ANDREW JANJIGIAN & DAN SOUZA ⋞

WHAT IS IT?

BUTTER CHURN
This 4-quart hand-cranked butter churn by Standard Churn Company made 1½ pounds of butter.

Before butter was a supermarket staple, people made it at home using a number of methods to agitate the cream until the fat separated out and could be stored for cooking and baking. This hand-cranked butter churn, circa 1940, was geared toward rural cooks who had access to fresh dairy but not to prepackaged butter or even electricity.

We've made butter in the test kitchen before by whipping room-temperature heavy cream in a stand mixer for 2 to 5 minutes until the fat separated out, so we wondered how long this hand-cranked tool would take to deliver comparable results—and how tired our arms would be. We poured 1½ quarts of cream into the 4-quart vessel (there's a helpful "Fill to here" line embossed on one side) and started to turn the crank. Surprisingly, within 1 minute the cream had increased by half in volume. By 5 minutes it was very thick and increasingly hard to churn, and chunks of butter began to appear on the bottom of the jar. We stopped just shy of 7 minutes when the buttermilk had separated from the butter, which was a solid, yellow mass. After draining, washing, and shaping it, we had 1½ pounds of butter. It's not as easy or as fast as churning butter in our stand mixer, but this tool was effective, and we enjoyed the hands-on process. –Shannon Friedmann Hatch

Dough Whisks: Not Just for Dough

We've previously recommended the Danish dough whisk for mixing bread doughs, particularly those that are stiff, because it makes short work of combining flour with liquids. Unlike a wooden spoon, which doesn't agitate well, or a standard balloon whisk, which quickly gets gummed up with dough, the dough whisk's double loop of rigid wire provides good agitation while moving easily through the dough mixture.

Since then, we've come to realize that the dough whisk is more versatile than its name reveals. It works equally well for mixing muffin, cake, pancake, and crêpe batters, whether stiff or loose. It also easily handles polenta, grits, oatmeal, and other porridges cooking in a saucepan or pot, as well as folds whipped egg whites into a soufflé base. In all these situations, not only does the dough whisk stir the mixture efficiently and eliminate lumps, but the flat profile of the parallel wire loops makes it great for digging into corners of the pot in a way that a rounded whisk can't. –A.J.

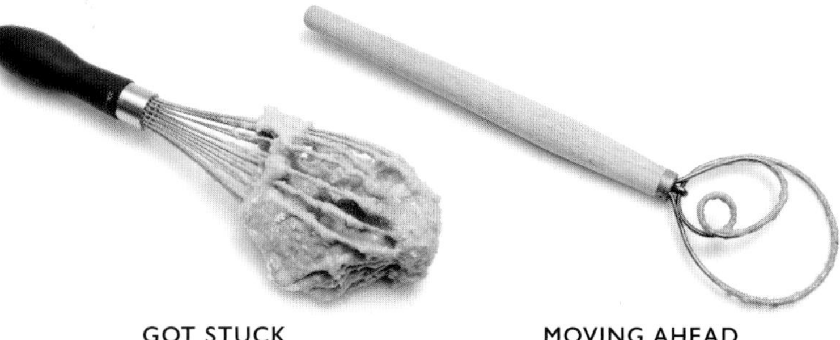

GOT STUCK **MOVING AHEAD**

Toasting in the Microwave

We've always toasted small amounts of nuts in a skillet on the stovetop (for larger amounts of nuts, we turn to the oven and spread them out in a single layer on a rimmed baking sheet), but this method requires a watchful eye and near-constant stirring to avoid burning. But there's another option: toasting nuts in the microwave. The cooking is more even in the microwave, so less stirring is required. Plus, there will be less carryover cooking in a microwave-safe vessel than in a highly conductive metal skillet, so you don't have to worry about quickly transferring the nuts to a cool bowl or plate.

We found that this microwave approach works well not only with nuts but also with other ingredients that need a quick toasting before use, such as bread crumbs, seeds (like pepitas, sesame, or sunflower), shredded coconut, and whole spices like coriander or cumin seeds. Whole spices need only a couple of minutes, while most other ingredients need about 5 minutes (your timing may vary depending on your microwave, of course).

Here's the method: Place the ingredient in a shallow microwave-safe bowl or pie plate in a thin, even layer. Cook on full power, stopping to check the color and stir every minute at first. As the food starts to take on color, microwave it in 30-second increments to avoid burning. –A.J.

NEW-WAVE APPROACH
To toast nuts or other ingredients in the microwave, spread them over a glass pie plate in a thin, even layer.

COOKING CLASS Macerating versus Salting

Many recipes, including our Strawberry-Rhubarb Pie (page 21), call for macerating fruit before incorporating it into a dish. Like salting watery produce such as cabbage, eggplant, or zucchini, tossing fruit with sugar and leaving it to sit draws out moisture that might otherwise lead to soupy fillings with bloated (or blown-out) produce. Like salt, sugar pulls water out of cells through osmosis: It creates a higher concentration of dissolved molecules at the surface of the fruit, which in turn causes water from inside the fruit's cell walls to be drawn out, since water has a tendency to move from a more dilute solution to a more concentrated one. But sugar and salt differ in their efficiency at the task. This is because the speed at which water is drawn out depends on the number of ions or molecules present. Sugar remains one molecule when dissolved, while salt molecules divide into two ions. So in any given solution, fewer sugar ions will be at work by volume than salt ions. But because we toss the produce with a comparatively high concentration of sugar when macerating, it still gets the job done in a reasonable amount of time. –A.G.

TECHNIQUE | CRIMPING WITH STYLE

Adding extra moisture in the form of vodka to our Foolproof Pie Dough, which we use in our Strawberry-Rhubarb Pie (page 21), makes it supple and easy to roll out, but some readers have reported that this softer dough doesn't hold an edge that's as defined as they would like. If your decorative edges are prone to drooping, try swapping the usual fluted crimp for a rope crimp, which sits squarely on the edge of the pie plate for optimum support. –A.G.

1. After pressing top and bottom crusts together and tucking the edge underneath, use the dull side of a butter knife held at a 45-degree angle to press into the dough at ½-inch intervals.
2. Work your way around the pie, pressing firmly enough to seal the layers of pastry together but not all the way down to the edge of the pie plate.

Why Animal Fats Taste So Good

In our recipe for Duck Fat–Roasted Potatoes (page 7), roasting our spuds in animal fat instead of olive oil gives them much richer flavor. But why does animal fat taste so much better? It has to do with the fatty acids that give any fat its particular flavor profile. In refined oils such as pure olive oil, many of the volatile fatty acids and aroma compounds have been stripped away to make a neutral-tasting oil that will work in a variety of applications. Meanwhile, unrefined oils like extra-virgin olive oil have plenty of flavor, but because some of their volatile fatty acids and aroma compounds evaporate when exposed to heat, they lose most of it after a few minutes of cooking. But when the fatty acids in an unrefined animal fat are exposed to heat, they oxidize to form new flavor compounds that actually improve flavor and make it taste more complex.

Animal fats can deepen the flavor of lots of foods beyond our potatoes. Try bacon fat instead of butter on the bread for a grilled cheese sandwich, or use it to sauté greens like kale or collards. Substitute the animal fat of your choice for the oil in fried eggs or roasted Brussels sprouts. Chicken fat is a great substitute for the butter in rice pilaf. See "Saving Fat for Cooking" on page 7 for tips on how to reserve these fats. –A.J.

COOKING CLASS
For a Clearer Stock, Simmer; Don't Boil

Nearly every recipe for the classic French dish pot-au-feu (page 5) calls for simmering rather than boiling once the meat has been added to the pot. Yes, this means you'll be cooking the meat for upwards of 3 hours, but there's a good reason for cooking low and slow here. Just as when you're making stock for soups or stews, boiling will cause soluble proteins and rendered fat to emulsify into the cooking liquid. By simmering, you avoid emulsifying the fat and thus keep the stock clearer, and we found that the scum created simply settled to the bottom of the pot. –D.S.

UNDER A CLOUD
Boiling produces a cloudy broth because the agitation emulsifies rendered fat and soluble proteins.

SCIENCE OF COOKING: Fresh versus Dried Herbs
Trying to substitute dried herbs for fresh? Stop and watch this video.
Free for 4 months at CooksIllustrated.com/june15

SCIENCE Substituting Dried Herbs for Fresh

In spring and early summer, before your freshly planted herbs are ready for use, it can be tempting to swap in dried herbs when a recipe calls for fresh. After all, they are more convenient and a lot cheaper than buying bunches of fresh herbs from the supermarket. We decided to look into the matter more thoroughly to find out when exactly this swap would be acceptable.

EXPERIMENT

We purchased fresh and dried versions of basil, chives, dill, oregano, parsley, rosemary, sage (in coarsely crumbled and rubbed forms), tarragon, and thyme. Then we cooked our way through 24 recipes (including marinades, sauces, and braises), making each with fresh and dried herbs and comparing differences in flavor.

RESULTS

In all but one application, tasters preferred fresh herbs to dry. Chili was the exception; in this dish, dried oregano was the favorite. A common criticism of dried herbs was that they had lost many of the subtleties and nuances of fresh herbs, tasting "dusty" and "stale." Meanwhile, fresh herbs tasted "clean" and "bright." Still, there were a few instances in which some dried herbs, though not preferred, were a passable substitute. In addition to oregano, dried rosemary, sage, and thyme fared reasonably well in recipes involving fairly long cooking times (more than 20 minutes) and a good amount of liquid.

EXPLANATION

The principal flavor compounds in herbs can be divided into four categories: hydrocarbons, aldehydes, ketones, and phenols. Some of these compounds are stable, which means they don't change at high temperatures and thus are able to maintain their flavor even through the drying process and cooking. Other compounds are volatile, meaning they are fragile and therefore are easily lost under those same conditions. The flavor compounds found in delicate herbs—basil, chives, dill, parsley, tarragon—tend to be more volatile, hence the fresh form always performs better than the dried. In contrast, the dominant flavor compounds in the herbs that work acceptably well when dried—rosemary, oregano, sage, and thyme—are nonvolatile and better survive drying and cooking. Dried herbs are best used in recipes with ample liquid because moisture will hydrate their cells, which makes them porous and able to release more of their aroma compounds. But even in circumstances ideal for dried herbs, they will always have a slightly dusty, stale flavor because the drying process leads to oxidation.

TAKEAWAY

When a recipe calls for delicate herbs, it's best to stick with fresh (as well as in all recipes that use herbs raw or to finish a dish). However, if a recipe calls for hardier herbs such as rosemary, oregano, sage, or thyme, their dried form can be an acceptable substitute. Just keep in mind that ounce for ounce, dried herbs are more potent than fresh. Our testing—in which we used only newly purchased jars of herbs—indicated that using 1 part dried herb to 3 parts fresh came closest to producing flavors of equal strength. –D.S.

	Includes	When to Substitute	Fresh : Dried Herb Substitution Ratio
Delicate herbs	Basil, chives, dill, parsley, tarragon	Never	N/A
Hardier herbs	Oregano, rosemary, crumbled or rubbed sage, thyme	In recipes with ample liquid and at least 20 minutes of cooking time	3:1

EQUIPMENT CORNER

⋺ BY HANNAH CROWLEY, LAUREN SAVOIE & KATE SHANNON ⋹

RECOMMENDED	HIGHLY RECOMMENDED	RECOMMENDED WITH RESERVATIONS	HIGHLY RECOMMENDED	RECOMMENDED WITH RESERVATIONS
IDEVICES **Kitchen Thermometer** **Model:** IKT0002 **Price:** $78	**BNTO by Cuppow** **Model:** N/A **Price:** $8.99	**PITMASTER IQ120** **Model:** IQ120 **Price:** $199.95	**WÜSTHOF** **Classic 3.5-Inch Fully Serrated Paring Knife** **Model:** 7/9/0663 **Price:** $39.95	**WHITE MOUNTAIN** **Wooden Bucket 6-Quart Electric Ice Cream Maker** **Model:** PBWMIME612 **Price:** $269.50

Remote Thermometers

Remote thermometers allow you to monitor, from a distance, the temperature of food as it cooks. We used six new models—four pager-style models and two that use Bluetooth and connect to your smartphone—(priced from $28.91 to $78) on the grill, on the stovetop, and in the oven to take the temperature of pulled pork, steak, and salmon fillets.

Most models were accurate to within 1 degree of our laboratory-quality calibrated thermometer, and while no model met its advertised distance (each company noted that ranges will vary depending on building materials and interference), a few receivers stayed in touch with their bases up to 250 feet away. The biggest divide came down to user-friendliness, as pager models were uniformly fussy to use. They were harder to set up, adjust, and reconnect. The Bluetooth devices, such as our favorite, from iDevices ($78), were more intuitive, worked with multiple smartphones, connected quickly, and delivered accurate temperature readouts. (Note: In our tests, this model's distance range was a modest 100 feet.) –L.S.

Mason Jar Adapters

From Brooklyn to Boise, Mason jars are being reused these days as everything from travel food-storage containers to drinking cups. We tested one product that promised to turn a jar into a two-part to-go container. The BNTO from Cuppow ($8.99), a 6-ounce plastic tub that drops into a widemouthed jar but stays aloft thanks to a wide rim, turned jars into two-part containers, perfect for housing snack duos like hummus and carrot sticks. The reCAP ($7), a screw-on, flip-top plastic drinking lid, transforms jars into drinking cups and was comfortable to sip from. Both products were virtually drip-proof, are dishwasher-safe, and resisted staining. Neither can be used for hot items, however; the uninsulated glass jars will burn your hand. –K.S.

Pitmaster IQ

Producing tender barbecued meat requires many hours of steady, gentle heat. We typically employ tricks like setting vents to regulate airflow, arranging the charcoal to burn gradually, and adding charcoal at intervals, but we were intrigued by the Pitmaster IQ120 ($199.95), a digitally controlled fan with temperature sensors that attaches to the grill to control airflow and regulate the temperature automatically.

We compared barbecuing with and without the Pitmaster on duplicate models of our favorite inexpensive charcoal grill, the Weber One-Touch Gold 22.5-Inch Charcoal Grill, preparing side-by-side batches of hot-smoked salmon, barbecued spareribs, and barbecued beef brisket. Though we were impressed by the food produced using the Pitmaster—salmon was more moist, brisket was juicier, and ribs were smokier and more tender—setting up and using the device was fussy and required a lot of trial and error to gauge the ideal amount of fuel and the target temperature for each recipe. Unless you're a barbecue aficionado with the patience to fiddle, it's not worth the high price. –H.C.

Serrated Paring Knives

Our favorite paring knife, from Wüsthof ($39.95), and our Best Buy, from Victorinox ($6.95), are nimble and durable enough to handle most small-knife tasks, but we were curious about their serrated equivalents, which are said to be handy for extra-delicate items like tomatoes and citrus segments. We purchased both, plus three other serrated paring knives ($5.95 to $39.95), and used them to segment citrus and slice cherry tomatoes. Two knives utterly failed. Their thick, dull blades struggled to slice through orange peels and required multiple passes to get through tomatoes. But three other knives impressed us with razor-sharp serrations on thin blades that allowed testers to race through tasks neatly and safely. Our new serrated winner, the Wüsthof Classic 3.5-Inch Fully Serrated Paring Knife ($39.95) won us over with its pleasant heft and superior slicing ability, but the Best Buy Victorinox Serrated Paring Knife ($5.95) offers a near-equal blade on a sturdy, lightweight frame, all for a bargain price. –K.S.

Large Ice Cream Makers

Large ice cream makers can produce a gallon or more in a single batch, handy for big gatherings. We purchased five models ($33.99 to $269.50) that make 4 or 6 quarts and tested them by churning vanilla ice cream and raspberry sorbet.

The ice creams ranged from moderately icy to appealingly smooth, but every batch of sorbet was grainy. Meanwhile, operating these machines might be a fun project or a messy chore, depending on how much space and time you have. They cool the base the old-fashioned way—you pour ice and rock salt around a metal canister that holds the base, which is set in a large bucket and spun through the salted ice. We had to replace the melted ice at least once during churning, the tall canisters didn't always fit in our freezers, many machines were loud, and one leaked.

The best ice cream came from the White Mountain Wooden Bucket 6-Quart Electric Ice Cream Maker ($269.50), but this machine is extremely loud and bulky. If you prefer a small, quiet, indoor machine, you're better off with our favorite small model, the Whynter SNÖ Professional Ice Cream Maker ($209.99), which churns continuous 2-quart batches that are hard enough to be eaten right away. –K.S.

For complete testing results, go to CooksIllustrated.com/june15.

INDEX

May & June 2015

FOLLOW US ON SOCIAL MEDIA

facebook.com/CooksIllustrated
twitter.com/TestKitchen
pinterest.com/TestKitchen
google.com/+AmericasTestKitchen
instagram.com/TestKitchen
youtube.com/AmericasTestKitchen

RECIPE VIDEOS

Want to see how to make any of the recipes in this issue? There's a video for that.

MORE VIDEOS

Recipes, reviews, and videos available free for 4 months at
CooksIllustrated.com/june15

New York Bagels, 15

Provençal Vegetable Soup, 18

Duck Fat–Roasted Potatoes, 7

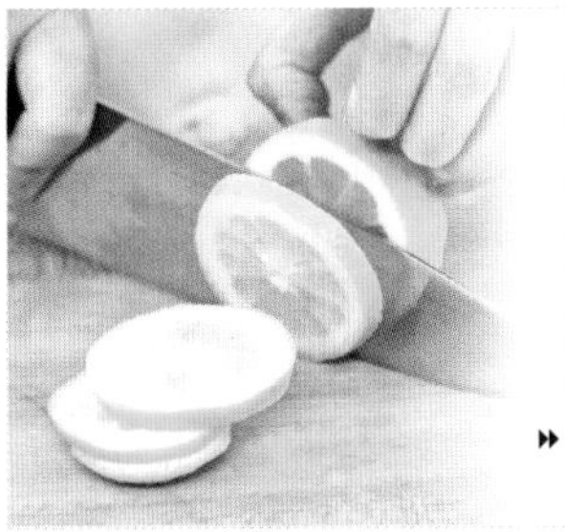

Vietnamese-Style Caramel Chicken, 11

Grilled Pork Kebabs, 6

Farro Salad with Asparagus and Tomatoes, 22

Simple Pot-au-Feu, 5

Strawberry-Rhubarb Pie, 21

Semolina Gnocchi, 9

Sautéed Swiss Chard, 12

PHOTOGRAPHY: CARL TREMBLAY; STYLING: MARIE PIRAINO

ASIAN PICKLES

NUMBER 135 JULY & AUGUST 2015

COOK'S ILLUSTRATED

Best Burger Ever
Learn the Secrets

Peri Peri Chicken
BBQ Chicken with a Kick

Fluffy Whole-Wheat Pancakes
Forget Everything You've Heard

The Ultimate Char-Grilled Steak

Balsamic Vinegars
The Truth Behind the Labels

Roasted Tomatoes
Concentrate the Flavor

Better Fried Rice
The Secret? Change the Rice

Testing Knife Sharpeners
Modern Succotash
Italian Sausage with Grapes

CooksIllustrated.com
$6.95 U.S. & CANADA

CONTENTS

July & August 2015

CLASSIC TAPAS In Spanish bars, tiny plates of food known as tapas are enjoyed as drinking snacks. Smooth, buttery MARCONA ALMONDS are a tad softer and sweeter than the more common California variety. They often accompany MANCHEGO, a salty, semifirm sheep's-milk cheese, and the tangy-sweet quince paste called MEMBRILLO. ACEITUNAS (olives) flavored with garlic, herbs, or spices offer a briny counterpoint to the richer choices on a tapas spread. Wrinkly, bright green PIMIENTOS DEL PADRÓN (peppers) are flash-fried until blistered. Frittata-like TORTILLA ESPAÑOLA features potato slices suspended in tender but set eggs. PATATAS BRAVAS, chunks of potatoes fried in oil, are topped with *alioli* or spicy tomato sauce. PAN CON TOMATE is simply slices of crusty bread drizzled with olive oil, rubbed with a fresh tomato half, and sprinkled with coarse salt. To make SALT COD FRITTERS, dried fish is soaked, drained, mixed into a batter, and deep-fried. Silky, paper-thin slices of JAMÓN (ham) deliver intensely nutty, salty flavor.

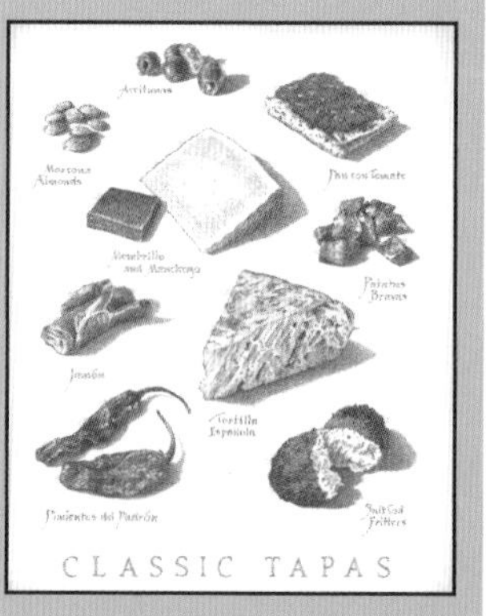

COVER *(Cherries)*: Robert Papp; **BACK COVER** *(Classic Tapas)*: John Burgoyne

America's Test Kitchen is a very real 2,500-square-foot kitchen located just outside Boston. It is the home of *Cook's Illustrated* and *Cook's Country* magazines and the workday destination of more than three dozen test cooks, editors, and cookware specialists. Our mission is to test recipes until we understand how and why they work and arrive at the best version. We also test kitchen equipment and supermarket ingredients in search of products that offer the best value and performance. You can watch us work by tuning in to *America's Test Kitchen* (AmericasTestKitchen.com) and *Cook's Country from America's Test Kitchen* (CooksCountry.com) on public television.

COOK'S ILLUSTRATED

PRINTED IN THE USA

THE DON'T LIST

The world is full of bucket lists—all sorts of wonderful things to do before shucking off the mortal coil. And one has all sorts of other "to do" lists as well: Ten things to do in Rome. Five books to read on vacation. Twenty classic movies in black and white.

All of this presupposes that life is about inclusion, not exclusion. That a sufficient number of items checked off the list ensures the good life because life is a function of what one has done, not what one has not done. I beg to differ.

One really bad decision—say, deep-frying a frozen turkey—can become your last act of free will. (I know since a friend of mine's uncle actually died from the aforesaid culinary challenge.) Or how about scuba diving off Mexico with no prior experience? (Yes, I have intimate knowledge of this life-ending activity as well.) Or lesser mistakes, such as driving a 1948 Farmall down a steep incline with a full load of hay on the back? You get the idea.

Life is about not making the huge mistakes while assembling an inventory of smaller steps in the right direction. Smart moves accumulate over time to your advantage. One major misstep and it may take a lifetime to work back to the beginning.

So here is my list of things to avoid at all costs.

1) Don't Shoot the Dog: When rabbit hunting, it is really bad form to shoot the dog instead of the rabbit. Tom, the president of The Old Rabbit Hunter's Association, had his beagle sprayed with buckshot by an overenthusiastic amateur hunter. The gentleman's shotgun was summarily wrapped around a large oak. Put another way, hold your fire unless you are darn sure you can see what you are shooting at.

2) Don't Cure the Symptom: On many occasions, I am awoken in the middle of the night by a smoke alarm. I grab a stepladder, rip the unit off the ceiling, remove the battery, and go back to bed. Always address the big problem, not the symptom.

3) Don't Listen to the Words: I once spent two weeks trying to negotiate a business deal with an investment group in the Far East on behalf of a friend of mine in magazine publishing. Every night, we would fax over a revised business plan. Every morning we were told, through an interpreter, that everything was fine, that the deal was almost done. What they were really saying was, "We would rather give our money to Charles Ponzi than invest one additional dollar in your enterprise." We finally got the message, about a week before we had to shut the doors. Read between the lines, not the lines themselves.

Christopher Kimball

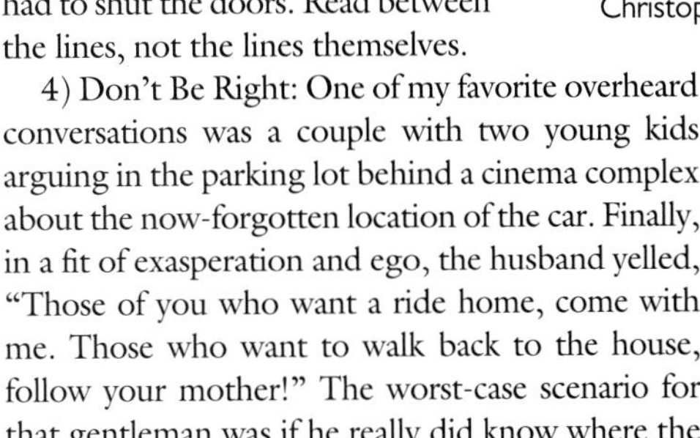

4) Don't Be Right: One of my favorite overheard conversations was a couple with two young kids arguing in the parking lot behind a cinema complex about the now-forgotten location of the car. Finally, in a fit of exasperation and ego, the husband yelled, "Those of you who want a ride home, come with me. Those who want to walk back to the house, follow your mother!" The worst-case scenario for that gentleman was if he really did know where the car was. As I said, it almost never pays to be right.

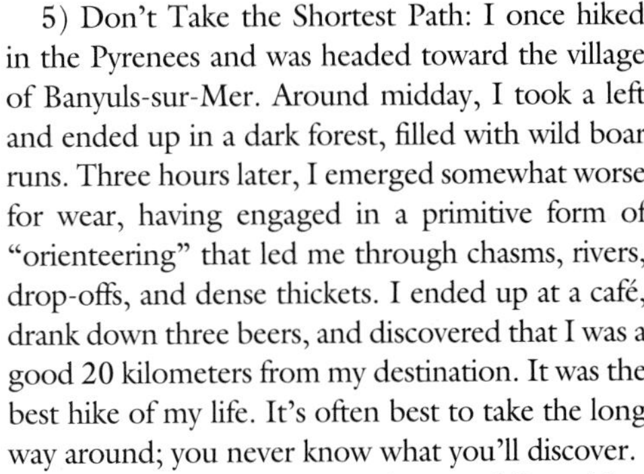

5) Don't Take the Shortest Path: I once hiked in the Pyrenees and was headed toward the village of Banyuls-sur-Mer. Around midday, I took a left and ended up in a dark forest, filled with wild boar runs. Three hours later, I emerged somewhat worse for wear, having engaged in a primitive form of "orienteering" that led me through chasms, rivers, drop-offs, and dense thickets. I ended up at a café, drank down three beers, and discovered that I was a good 20 kilometers from my destination. It was the best hike of my life. It's often best to take the long way around; you never know what you'll discover.

6) Don't Roll the Dice: Luck is not delivered free of charge; it is earned. A famous chef on the West Coast once sold her establishment for a few million dollars and then invested every penny of it with Bernie Madoff. She lost every penny. Today, she is back at work and, one hopes, happy in her second career, but I bet she thinks a lot about what might have been. Just get over it! You're not lucky. You've never been lucky. So don't test your luck.

7) Don't Have the Last Word: The word one regrets is almost always the last word. That's the one you can never take back. Like the time I argued with the highway patrolman who had pulled me over for using a radar detector. After an escalating back and forth, I ended the conversation by yelling, "Well, even if I had one, you'd never find it!" He immediately called for backup, threw me up against the car, and found the detector hidden under the driver's seat in about 20 seconds. It cost me $300 and half a day in court. The judge joked, "That sure is an expensive radar detector!"

8) Don't Follow Conventional Wisdom: When I launched *Cook's Illustrated*, I was betting on a food magazine that had no color photos and no advertising and had a painting on the front instead of a seductive plate of food. Simply put, convention is what worked in the past; it doesn't predict the future. Never take it seriously.

9) Don't Trust Your Instincts: If I had trusted my instincts, I would now be the oldest member of a commune outside Brattleboro, Vermont, playing Grateful Dead covers at the August 4-H fair. One's instincts almost always push one to do the fun or easy thing, almost never to choose the hard path. Maybe a better mantra would be, "Do the opposite of what you feel like doing right this minute." That will serve you better.

10) Don't Ignore Old People: Once a month I walk over to a friend's house for cocktail hour. He is a widower. He is 80 years old. And I rarely enjoy myself more. My generation's mantra was "Never trust anyone over 30." Experience forces me to reconsider that proposition. Above a certain age, you don't care whom you offend, you've exhausted your anxieties, you're good at conversation, and you have accumulated sufficient life experience to be a useful companion. If you want solid career or personal advice, talk to an "old person." They don't call us "grown-ups" for nothing.

FOR INQUIRIES, ORDERS, OR MORE INFORMATION

CooksIllustrated.com
At CooksIllustrated.com, you can order books and subscriptions, sign up for our free e-newsletter, or renew your magazine subscription. Join the website and gain access to 22 years of *Cook's Illustrated* recipes, equipment tests, and ingredient tastings, as well as companion videos for every recipe in this issue.

COOKBOOKS
We sell more than 50 cookbooks by the editors of *Cook's Illustrated*, including *The Cook's Illustrated Cookbook* and *The Science of Good Cooking*. To order, visit our bookstore at CooksIllustrated.com/bookstore.

COOK'S ILLUSTRATED MAGAZINE
Cook's Illustrated magazine (ISSN 1068-2821), number 135, is published bimonthly by Boston Common Press Limited Partnership, 17 Station St., Brookline, MA 02445. Copyright 2015 Boston Common Press Limited Partnership. Periodicals postage paid at Boston, MA, and additional mailing offices, USPS #012487. Publications Mail Agreement No. 40020778. Return undeliverable Canadian addresses to P.O. Box 875, Station A, Windsor, ON N9A 6P2. POSTMASTER: Send address changes to *Cook's Illustrated*, P.O. Box 6018, Harlan, IA 51593-1518. For subscription and gift subscription orders, subscription inquiries, or change of address notices, visit AmericasTestKitchen.com/support, call 800-526-8442 in the U.S. or 515-248-7684 from outside the U.S., or write to us at *Cook's Illustrated*, P.O. 6018, Harlan, IA 51593-1518.

FOR LIST RENTAL INFORMATION Contact Specialists Marketing Services, Inc., 777 Terrace Ave., 4th Floor, Hasbrouck Heights, NJ 07604; phone: 201-865-5800.
EDITORIAL OFFICE 17 Station St., Brookline, MA 02445; 617-232-1000; fax: 617-232-1572. For subscription inquiries, visit AmericasTestKitchen.com/support or call 800-526-8442.

QUICK TIPS

COMPILED BY SHANNON FRIEDMANN HATCH

Whipped Cream in Seconds

Rather than haul out her stand mixer to whip cream, Julie Lacouture of Los Angeles, Calif., uses her immersion blender.

1. Fill the tall canister that comes with the blender (a wide-mouth quart-size Mason jar also works well) with enough cream to submerge the head of the blender, keeping in mind that the cream will roughly double in volume.

2. With the motor running, move the head up and down through the cream to pull in air. The cream should whip in about 20 seconds.

Stacking Pots with Lids

Sheila Shapiro of West Tisbury, Mass., doesn't have much room to store her lidded pots but has found an easy way to maximize her cabinet space. By upturning the lids on her pots, she can stack them on top of one another. This works especially well for enameled cookware (like a Dutch oven), because it prevents the lid from getting scratched.

Spritzing Meat with Flavor

Joe Hild of Tampa, Fla., spritzes the food he smokes with apple juice to achieve extra flavor. Instead of filling a spray bottle with the juice, he inserts the tube from the sprayer directly into a juice box. That way, he uses just as much as he needs and doesn't need to store an entire bottle of leftover juice.

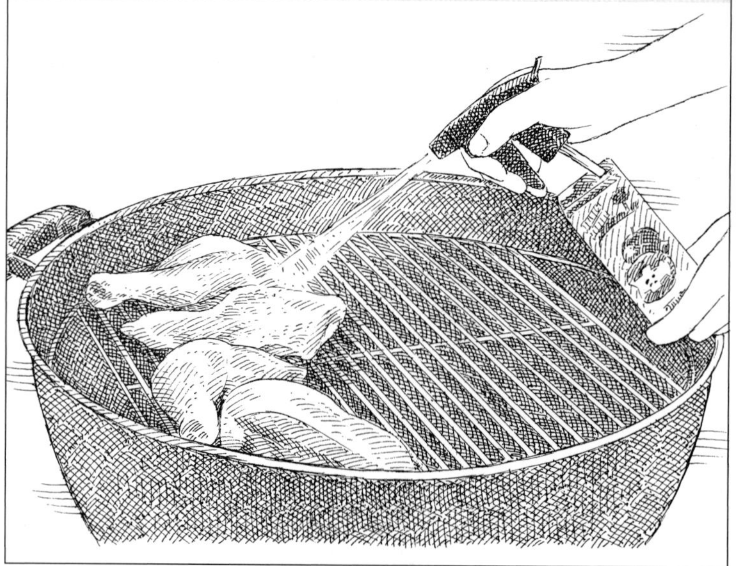

Fashioning Lids for Outdoor Drinks

Kelly Kaineg of Boise, Idaho, has devised a clever idea to keep bugs out of drinks when entertaining outdoors: Invert a cupcake liner on top and poke a straw through it for easy sipping. A bonus: She keeps track of each guest's glass by writing his or her name on each liner.

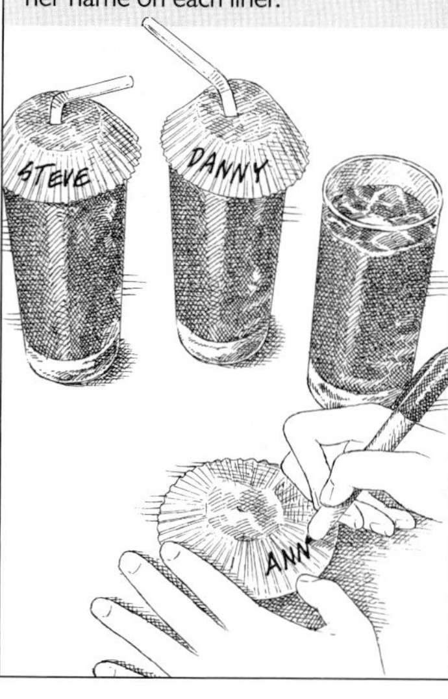

Scaling Fish with a Cookie Cutter

Occasionally when she buys whole fish, Darlene Brunswick of Springfield, Mass., finds that some scales are still intact. To remove them, she grabs her scalloped cookie cutter. The curved edges easily remove the scales when she drags the cutter against them along the length of the fish.

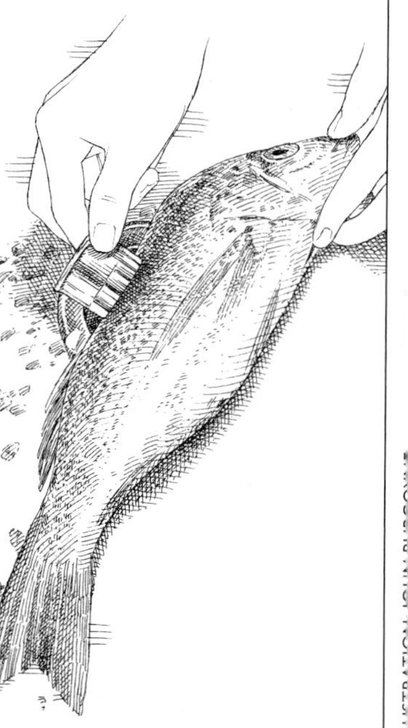

SEND US YOUR TIPS We will provide a complimentary one-year subscription for each tip we print. Send your tip, name, address, and daytime telephone number to Quick Tips, *Cook's Illustrated*, P.O. Box 470589, Brookline, MA 02447, or to QuickTips@AmericasTestKitchen.com.

Basting Brush Holder

Sarah Farma of San Carlos, Calif., often uses her silicone brush to baste food on the grill with a sauce, but the dirty brush has nowhere to rest. Now, she puts the basting sauce in a tall, heavy-bottomed drinking glass and rests the brush inside. The vessel supports the brush's long handle and prevents drips.

Alternative Cookware Rack

With little storage space in the kitchen, Rhonda Grace of Chicago, Ill., came up with a different place to keep her pots and pans: on an over-the-door coat rack that she hangs from her pantry door. The loop handles on her cookware easily hang from the rack's hooks.

Aerating One Glass of Wine

Recalling that we had good results aerating a bottle of wine in a blender, Diane Kiino of Kalamazoo, Mich., turned to her electric milk frother when she needed to aerate just one glass. Buzzing the wine with the tiny whisk for just a few seconds improved its flavor.

Flatware Pie Weights

When Sara Strong of Monroe, Conn., blind-bakes multiple pie crusts and doesn't have enough pie weights, she fills the shell with heavy stainless steel flatware (spoons fit best). Just as conventional weights do, the utensils prevent the pastry from puffing up during baking.

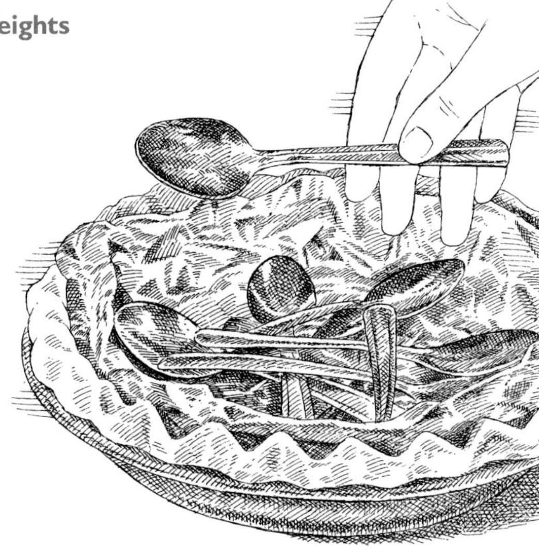

Muffin-Cup Ice Cubes

Susan Siegel of Boynton Beach, Fla., often makes a big bowl of punch when she entertains but finds that conventional-size ice cubes melt long before the party is over. Instead, she makes larger, longer-lasting cubes by freezing water in the cups of a muffin tin.

Stamping Out Pineapple Rings

Lisa Gillian of Sugar Grove, Ill., doesn't own a pineapple corer but likes to make rings from the fruit for serving.

1. After slicing off the skin, slice the fruit into disks.

2. Stamp out the core with a small biscuit cutter.

Introducing Peri Peri Chicken

The key to making this spicy African dish is to treat it like classic barbecued chicken—but give it kick.

� BY ANDREW JANJIGIAN ⋞

The spicy grilled dish known as *peri peri* chicken has old African roots and a meandering history, but the basic idea is this: Chicken is marinated overnight in a paste of garlic, herbs, spices, lemon juice, and *peri peri* chiles—fiery local peppers whose name means "pepper pepper" in Swahili. The next day the chicken is grilled over a hot fire until the meat is tender and the skin is crisp and charred. The result is a dish packed with complex, spicy flavor.

While doing some initial research, I found that published recipes for this dish vary greatly, but given its backstory, I wasn't all that surprised. Portuguese travelers brought the peri peri pepper from South America to East Africa, where it met up with the ancient tradition of cooking chicken over a live fire. When the sailors picked up and moved on to the next conquest, they took the pepper and the cooking method with them. With each landing, the dish assumed some of the flavors and character of its adopted homes, including India and the former Portuguese colony of Macao, located near Hong Kong.

In addition to salt, chiles, and aromatics, we use five-spice powder, tomato paste, and peanuts to give our spice paste complexity and balance.

The first time I ever had peri peri chicken was at a Chicago restaurant called Fat Rice that features the melting-pot cuisine of Macao. The meat was tender, the skin was perfectly crisped, and, most notably, the dish hit me with undeniable heat, yes, but also layers of complexity and richness. This chicken set the bar for my own adaptation.

Traditional versions described in African cookbooks used merely chiles, lemon juice, and a few herbs like oregano and ground bay leaves for seasoning. Macanese versions incorporated five-spice powder, which lent the dish a more Asian flavor. Recipes that had few ingredients yielded chicken with little more than grill flavor; more successful were those that used a lot of chiles and a generous amount of spice paste to ensure that the seasonings weren't overpowered by the smoke and char of grilling. But none of them really hit the mark for the spicy yet complex taste I was after. Since peri peri peppers (fresh or dried) are hard to come by in the States, I'd need to find a good substitute. I also wanted to iron out the cooking method for my version; most recipes simply said "grill over a hot fire."

Watch: Very Peri Peri
Video available free for 4 months at CooksIllustrated.com/aug15

Turning Up the Heat

Because peri peri chicken is really a type of barbecued chicken with a different flavor profile, I decided to use the test kitchen's foolproof approach to that dish: We spread charcoal evenly over half the grill, providing a hotter area where char is developed, while leaving the other half of the grill free of coals, creating a place to finish the cooking gently over indirect heat. We also put an aluminum pan filled with water on the grill to absorb heat and eliminate hot spots. This method calls for chicken parts for two reasons: They provide more surface area for charring and sauce (or in my case, spice paste), and they allow for more-even cooking since the more delicate breast pieces can be placed farther from the fire. Finally, we salt the chicken overnight. While salt might not have been a major component in the peri peri chicken recipes I'd tried (they called for ½ to 2 teaspoons at most), I'd use quite a bit more—2 tablespoons, in fact, based on our barbecued chicken recipe. During marinating, the salt not only penetrates the meat and seasons it throughout but also alters the proteins in the chicken so that the meat more tenaciously holds on to water during cooking—one more guarantee that it would come off the grill tender and juicy.

With the cooking method settled, I could focus on flavor. My spice paste started with a few ingredients whizzed together in the food processor: garlic, shallots, lemon zest and juice, bay leaves, paprika, and black pepper. I also added a generous amount of five-spice powder for complexity. Olive oil would help extract the fat-soluble components in the spices, while sugar would enhance all the flavors.

Now for the peri peri peppers. I was able to track down peri peri hot sauce, so I at least had a sense of the pepper's character: hot, but also fruity and complex. For the best available substitute, I settled on dried arbol chiles. But I quickly learned that tasters' tolerance for spiciness, and to some degree the spiciness of the chiles themselves, varied. If I added a little cayenne for baseline heat, I could use a range of arbols (from four to 10) and still get plenty of fruity chile flavor. I also sorted out an easy way to adjust the heat midstream. I began with a judicious amount of arbols and then tasted the paste before applying it to the chicken, adding more arbols until it was just past the point of being as hot as I wanted the finished chicken to be. The heat of the grill took the edge off, leaving the spiciness at just the right level (see "Taste the Paste").

A Nutty Way to Finish

I was close, but my recipe still lacked the richness and complexity of the version I'd had at Fat Rice. Stumped as to what to do next, I called the chef. Although he wouldn't reveal all his secrets, he did generously describe his technique, which he learned from a chef in Macao. He told me that once the chicken was cooked, he applied a sauce made from coconut milk, tomato paste, and finely chopped

CORE TECHNIQUE | GRILLING WITH WATER

Whether you're cooking this recipe or barbecued chicken, it's key to cook the meat through gently for tender, juicy results. To do this, in addition to setting up the grill with a cooler side that is left free of coals, we also put an aluminum pan or pie plates filled with water on the grill. Both the pan (or plates) and the water absorb heat, lowering the heat overall and eliminating hot spots.

GAS

1. Fill 2 disposable aluminum pie plates with 1 ½ cups water each.
2. Place pie plates on 1 burner, opposite primary burner, and set cooking grate in place.
3. Light burners as directed and proceed with recipe.

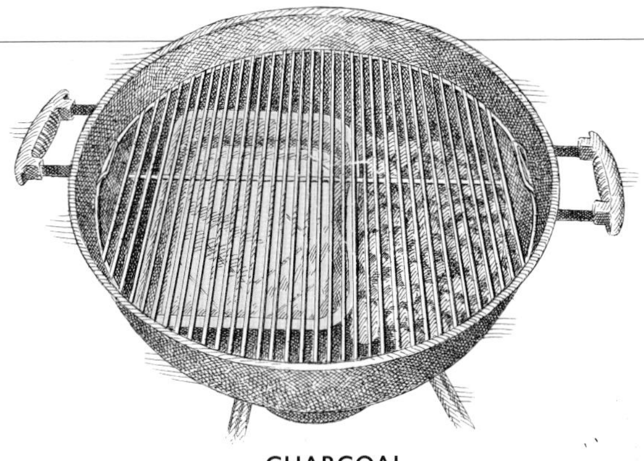

CHARCOAL

1. Fill 13 by 9-inch disposable aluminum pan with 3 cups water.
2. Place pan on 1 side of charcoal grate.
3. Once coals are lit, pour them next to pan, put cooking grate in place, and proceed with recipe.

peanuts and then returned the chicken to the grill to char it further.

I didn't want to complicate my recipe by adding a sauce, but I was game to try incorporating these ingredients into my spice paste. Coconut milk left the exterior of the grilled chicken pasty, but tomato paste and the chopped peanuts gave my dish the balancing richness and hint of sweetness it had been missing. This was a grilled chicken recipe I'd be turning to time and again; it's as delicious as it is easy to make.

PERI PERI GRILLED CHICKEN

SERVES 6 TO 8

This recipe requires refrigerating the spice paste–coated chicken for at least 6 hours or up to 24 hours prior to cooking. When browning the chicken, move it away from the direct heat if any flare-ups occur. Serve the chicken with white rice.

- **4–10** arbol chiles, stemmed
- **3** tablespoons extra-virgin olive oil
- **2** tablespoons salt
- **8** garlic cloves, peeled
- **2** tablespoons tomato paste
- **1** shallot, chopped
- **1** tablespoon sugar
- **1** tablespoon paprika
- **1** tablespoon five-spice powder
- **2** teaspoons grated lemon zest plus ¼ cup juice (2 lemons)
- **1** teaspoon pepper
- **½** teaspoon cayenne pepper
- **3** bay leaves, crushed
- **6** pounds bone-in chicken pieces (breasts, thighs, and/or drumsticks), trimmed
- **½** cup dry-roasted peanuts, chopped fine
- **1** (13 by 9-inch) disposable aluminum pan (if using charcoal) or 2 (9-inch) disposable aluminum pie plates (if using gas)
- Lemon wedges

1. Process 4 arbols, oil, salt, garlic, tomato paste, shallot, sugar, paprika, five-spice powder, lemon zest and juice, pepper, cayenne, and bay leaves in blender until smooth, 10 to 20 seconds. Taste paste and add up to 6 additional arbols, depending on desired level of heat (spice paste should be slightly hotter than desired heat level of cooked chicken), and process until smooth. Using metal skewer, poke skin side of each chicken piece 8 to 10 times. Place chicken pieces, peanuts, and spice paste in large bowl or container and toss until chicken is evenly coated. Cover and refrigerate for at least 6 hours or up to 24 hours.

2A. FOR A CHARCOAL GRILL: Open bottom vent halfway and place disposable pan filled with 3 cups water on 1 side of grill. Light large chimney starter filled with charcoal briquettes (6 quarts). When top coals are partially covered with ash, pour evenly over other half of grill (opposite disposable pan). Set cooking grate in place, cover, and open lid vent halfway. Heat grill until hot, about 5 minutes.

2B. FOR A GAS GRILL: Place 2 disposable pie plates, each filled with 1½ cups water, directly on 1 burner of gas grill (opposite primary burner). Turn all burners to high, cover, and heat grill until hot, about 15 minutes. Turn primary burner to medium-high and turn off other burner(s). (Adjust primary burner as needed to maintain grill temperature between 325 and 350 degrees.)

3. Clean and oil cooking grate. Place chicken, skin side down, on hotter side of grill and cook until browned and blistered in spots, 2 to 5 minutes. Flip chicken and cook until second side is browned, 4 to 6 minutes. Move chicken to cooler side of grill and arrange, skin side up, with legs and thighs closest to fire and breasts farthest away. Cover (positioning lid vent over chicken if using charcoal) and cook until breasts register 160 degrees and legs and thighs register 175 degrees, 50 to 60 minutes.

4. Transfer chicken to serving platter, tent with aluminum foil, and let rest for 10 minutes before serving, passing lemon wedges separately.

Picking the Right Stand-In for the Peri Peri Peppers

Traditionally, dried African *peri peri* peppers, which are about 10 times hotter than serrano chiles, give this dish its spicy heat, but they are hard to find in the States. Because they have a fruity, complex flavor in addition to heat, we found that no one chile could replace them. Instead, we landed on a combination of cayenne, for a baseline level of heat, and dried arbol chiles, which are spicy but, more important, have the right fruity note that mimics the peri peri chiles' flavor.

PERI PERI PEPPERS

ARBOLS PLUS CAYENNE

Taste the Paste

In test after test, we found that pastes that tasted exactly as spicy as we wanted before cooking had a more tempered flavor in the final dish. After some research, we learned that when exposed to high heat, capsaicin, the primary chemical compound responsible for the chile's heat, actually breaks down. After an hour on the grill, about 30 percent of the capsaicin will have broken down. To counteract this effect, your paste should taste just a bit spicier than you want prior to cooking. We call for using a relatively wide range of arbol peppers not only because tolerance for spiciness varies but also because the intensity of individual dried chiles can differ greatly. We suggest starting with four. Then, after mixing together the paste, give it a try and add up to six more chiles as necessary.

Really Good Whole-Wheat Pancakes

Forget everything you've heard. The more whole-wheat flour you use, the more tender (and foolproof) the pancakes will be. Just be sure your flour is fresh.

BY ANDREA GEARY

I've always liked the nutty flavor and slightly rustic texture of whole-wheat flour, so I'm glad to see it being added to everything from muffins to pizza crusts. But where, I wondered, were all the pancake recipes? A pancake would be a perfect place to swap whole-wheat flour for white flour because its robust flavor would be an ideal foil for the caramel-y sweetness of maple syrup—and the health benefits of eating whole grains don't hurt either.

Pancake recipes that feature a portion of whole-wheat flour do exist, of course, but those that call for 100 percent whole-wheat flour are surprisingly rare. Most cut the whole-wheat flour with an equal amount of white flour, while others call for grains like oats or buckwheat. Many recipes also call for fruit juice, fruit, vanilla, or cinnamon.

I wanted something different: a no-frills, all whole-wheat pancake that was simple to prepare and as light, tender, and fluffy as a pancake made with white flour.

Whole-wheat baked goods aren't always dense and leaden. In fact, these whole-wheat pancakes are as light as their white-flour counterpart.

A Bitter Disappointment

I was puzzled by most cooks' reluctance to use all whole-wheat flour in a pancake recipe. Maybe its nutty flavor was too strong for some; that would explain all the flavor additions. And I've experienced enough brick-like loaves of whole-wheat bread to suspect that it might also have something to do with concerns about the structure: 100 percent whole-wheat flour is notorious for producing squat, dense, tough baked goods.

Erring on the side of caution, I made one of the straightforward half wheat–half white recipes I had found. Except for the whole-wheat flour, this recipe was just like most other pancake recipes: I whisked the two flours with baking powder, baking soda, salt, and sugar in one bowl, and I whisked buttermilk (which I chose over milk since its tangy flavor would better complement the whole wheat), eggs, and vegetable oil in another. Then I folded the two mixtures together very carefully since the recipe, like most, cautioned that overmixing would lead to dense, tough pancakes.

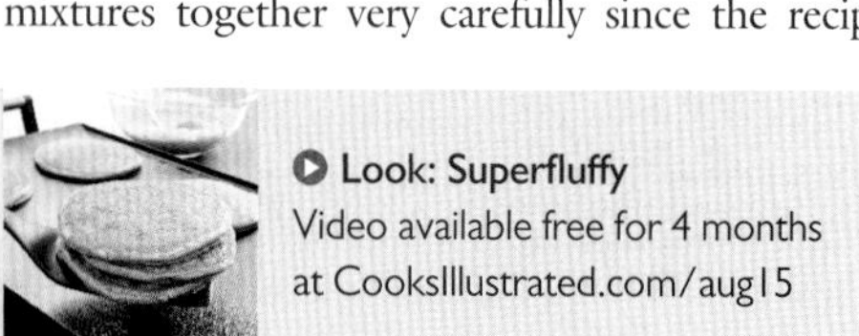

Look: Superfluffy
Video available free for 4 months at CooksIllustrated.com/aug15

Despite my concerns, there were no structural issues: These pancakes were as tender and fluffy as any white-flour pancakes I had ever made. But the taste was another story. Even using only 50 percent whole-wheat flour, the pancakes had a bitter flavor that overpowered the nuttiness. It wasn't terrible, but it didn't bode well for my 100 percent whole-wheat goal.

Before making any rash decisions, I did some research and learned that what we think of as "whole-wheat flavor" is actually two different flavors. That toasty, slightly tannic flavor comes from phenolic acid in the bran. This flavor is constant over time. The second is a bitter flavor that comes from the small amount of fat in the flour—specifically, the oxidation of that fat. This bitterness will build over time as the fat is exposed to air during storage (storing the flour in the freezer will slow oxidation).

No wonder I'd been put off by the results of that first test. I had used an open bag of flour I'd been keeping in my cupboard. For my next batch of pancakes, I made sure to use a fresh bag of flour (just opened and well within its expiration date). The results tasted much better. These pancakes were nutty and sweet.

Their surprisingly soft, light texture convinced me to try increasing the whole wheat, so I made the recipe again, this time using 75 percent whole-wheat flour and 25 percent white. As I had hoped, these pancakes had a bit more earthy, nutty whole-wheat flavor, but the real surprise was that they were even lighter and more tender than the previous batch. This pointed me to a really interesting discovery: Using all whole-wheat flour doesn't make pancakes tougher or denser. In fact, it makes them more foolproof. To understand why, it's helpful to understand a little about gluten.

The Gluten Factor

Both white and whole-wheat flour contain proteins that bond together in the presence of moisture to form an elastic network called gluten. Stirring or kneading a batter or dough builds and strengthens that gluten network. That's a good thing when you're making yeasted bread because it is this network that captures the gases given off by the yeast, enabling a loaf to swell and maintain its shape during its lengthy rise and baking time. The gluten network is also what gives the final baked bread its satisfyingly resilient chew.

But for quick breads such as pancakes, gluten is a liability. The foamy, delicate batter is leavened by fast-acting chemical leaveners (baking powder and baking soda), which create tiny air bubbles throughout the batter, and the viscosity of the batter is enough to hold the bubbles in place in the brief time between mixing and setting. A strong gluten network will actually restrict the air bubbles' expansion in a delicate pancake batter and thus hinder rise. Also, the resilient texture of gluten isn't desirable in a pancake, hence the dire warnings about overmixing.

But I realized that logic applies only to pancakes made with *white* flour. Whole-wheat flour behaves differently for two reasons. First, unlike white flour, whole-wheat flour contains the bran and germ, and these do not contribute gluten-forming proteins, so a cup of whole-wheat flour contains fewer gluten-forming proteins than does a cup of white flour.

Second, those bits of bran are quite sharp, and they slice across any gluten strands that do form, shortening them and weakening the network.

So whole-wheat flour is bad for gluten development. That makes it bad for yeasted loaves but ideal for pancakes. When I mixed the mostly whole-wheat pancake batter, the bran was weakening the gluten structure. Using whole-wheat flour meant that I could be much less cautious about my mixing technique and still produce perfectly tender, fluffy pancakes.

So what was stopping me from making a 100 percent whole-wheat version? Nothing. In my next batch, I used all whole-wheat flour and ended up with exactly what I'd been wanting. These pancakes had nutty, earthy flavor and they were as tall and tender as any white-flour pancake I'd ever had.

100 PERCENT WHOLE-WHEAT PANCAKES

MAKES 15 PANCAKES

An electric griddle set at 350 degrees can be used in place of a skillet. If substituting buttermilk powder and water for fresh buttermilk, use only 2 cups of water to prevent the pancakes from being too wet. To ensure the best flavor, use either recently purchased whole-wheat flour or flour that has been stored in the freezer for less than 12 months. Serve with maple syrup and butter.

- 2 cups (11 ounces) whole-wheat flour
- 2 tablespoons sugar
- 1½ teaspoons baking powder
- ½ teaspoon baking soda
- ¾ teaspoon salt
- 2¼ cups buttermilk
- 5 tablespoons plus 2 teaspoons vegetable oil
- 2 large eggs

1. Adjust oven rack to middle position and heat oven to 200 degrees. Spray wire rack set in rimmed baking sheet with vegetable oil spray; place in oven.
2. Whisk flour, sugar, baking powder, baking soda, and salt together in medium bowl. Whisk buttermilk, 5 tablespoons oil, and eggs together in second medium bowl. Make well in center of flour mixture and pour in buttermilk mixture; whisk until smooth. (Mixture will be thick; do not add more buttermilk.)
3. Heat 1 teaspoon oil in 12-inch nonstick skillet over medium heat until shimmering. Using paper towels, carefully wipe out oil, leaving thin film on bottom and sides of pan. Using ¼-cup dry measuring cup or 2-ounce ladle, portion batter into pan in 3 places. Gently spread each portion into 4½-inch round. Cook until edges are set, first side is golden brown, and bubbles on surface are just beginning to break, 2 to 3 minutes. Using thin, wide spatula, flip pancakes and continue to cook until second side is golden brown, 1 to 2 minutes longer. Serve pancakes immediately or transfer to wire rack in oven. Repeat with remaining batter, using remaining 1 teaspoon oil as necessary.

For the Sweetest Wheat, Use Fresh Flour . . . or Grind Your Own

After testing this recipe in a range of blenders, we found that a machine with a 450-watt motor and ice-crushing capability is essential.

The little bits of bran and germ in whole-wheat flour are a nutritional boon, but they're also a storage liability because they contain fats that are vulnerable to oxidation. If unchecked, this oxidation can give the flour a bitter taste. For the best flavor, we recommend starting with a freshly opened bag or one that you've stored in the freezer (where whole-wheat flour keeps well for up to a year). Or you can take it to the next level and grind your own grain. Sound hard-core? We thought so, too, until we tried it. The method is simple: Pulverize wheat berries (which are simply dried wheat kernels and widely available in the bulk section of supermarkets), sugar, and salt in a blender and then add liquid (we use buttermilk); keep blending and then add the rest of the pancake ingredients to create a batter that you can pour directly from the blender jar into the skillet. The whole process barely takes 5 minutes, and the result is the sweetest, nuttiest-tasting whole-wheat pancake you've ever experienced.

WHEAT BERRY PANCAKES

MAKES 12 PANCAKES

This recipe is for mixing only. For cooking directions refer to steps 1 and 3 of 100 Percent Whole-Wheat Pancakes and be sure to have extra vegetable oil on hand for the skillet. For efficient blending of the buttermilk and wheat berry mixture, it's important for the blender to create and maintain a vortex, which looks like a whirlpool. Watch the batter as it is mixing; if the vortex closes (or does not form), changing the blender speed or adding more buttermilk will bring it back. Because pulverizing the wheat berries creates some stress on a blender's motor, we recommend using a machine with at least a 450-watt motor and ice-crushing capability. If you are using a high-end blender like a Vitamix or Blendtec, the blending times will be shorter.

- 1½ cups wheat berries
- 2 tablespoons sugar
- ¾ teaspoon salt
- 1½ cups buttermilk
- 5 tablespoons vegetable oil
- 2 large eggs
- 1½ teaspoons baking powder
- ½ teaspoon baking soda

Process wheat berries, sugar, and salt in blender on high speed until as fine as possible, about 3 minutes. Transfer mixture to bowl. Add 1 cup buttermilk to blender and pour wheat berry mixture on top. Blend on high speed, adding additional buttermilk and changing speed as necessary to maintain vortex, until mixture is thick and has only small lumps, about 3 minutes. Add oil, eggs, and any remaining buttermilk and continue to blend until fully incorporated, about 30 seconds longer. With blender running, add baking powder and baking soda, and blend until incorporated, about 15 seconds.

SCIENCE Go Ahead: Beat the Heck out of This Batter

Recipes for white-flour pancakes always warn against overmixing. That's because it will create a strong, restrictive gluten network, and that makes for tough, dense cakes. But we discovered that the same rule doesn't apply to pancakes made with whole-wheat flour for two reasons. The first is that cup for cup, whole-wheat flour has fewer gluten-forming proteins than white flour. Second, whole-wheat flour contains bran, which is sharp and will cut through gluten strands that do form. When the gluten strands are shorter, the gluten network is weakened and the pancakes become even more tender.

WHITE-FLOUR PANCAKES

25 stirs

100 stirs

WHOLE-WHEAT-FLOUR PANCAKES

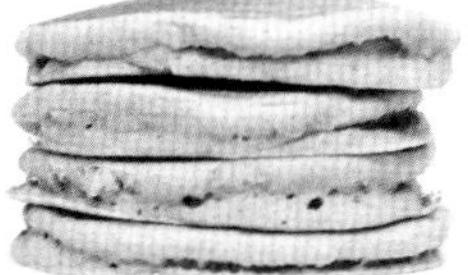

25 stirs

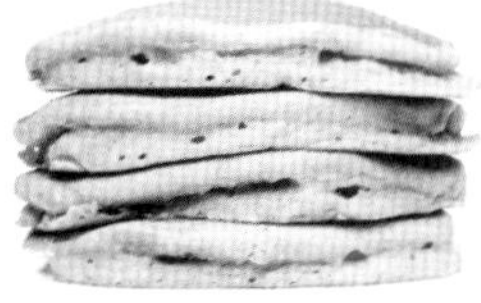

100 stirs

Ultimate Char-Grilled Steak

The secret to delivering a charcoal-grilled steak with a killer crust and perfectly cooked meat from edge to edge? Keep the coals in the chimney.

BY DAN SOUZA

While it's hard to beat the smoky char of a grilled thick-cut steak, I have to admit that since I started using the test kitchen method for pan-searing steaks, the indoor version more often approaches perfection. Our pan-searing technique calls for first baking a thick steak in a low oven and then searing it in a smoking-hot preheated skillet. The initial baking not only evenly cooks the meat but also dries and warms the steak's surface, resulting in lightning-fast searing—just a minute or so per side. The result of this approach is the platonic ideal of a steak: a crisp, well-browned crust and medium-rare meat from edge to edge. The time is so fast that, unlike with most methods, only a sliver of meat below the crust overcooks and loses its rosy hue.

But with grilling, though I've worked out some pretty hot grill setups over the years, even with my best efforts it takes so long to evenly brown the steak that I overcook a fair amount of meat below the surface. This summer I decided to hold grilled steak to a higher standard: perfectly cooked meat, a well-browned and crisp crust, and great charcoal-grilled flavor.

A charcoal chimney starter delivers intense heat for maximum char. And it happens so quickly that there's little overcooked meat beneath the surface.

Searing Question

To reach perfection, I suspected that I'd need to think outside the box—or as it turned out, the grill. In my research I came across a novel technique for cooking over a live fire that relied on a charcoal chimney starter to not just light the coals but actually do the cooking. To produce an amazing sear, celebrity chef and food science guru Alton Brown mimics the intensity of a steakhouse-caliber broiler by placing a porterhouse steak on the grill grate and then putting a lit chimney of coals right over it. I found other sources that took a similar approach but flipped the setup, placing the chimney on the grill's charcoal grate and then arranging the steak, set on the cooking grate, on top.

Dan Fans the Flames
Video available free for 4 months at CooksIllustrated.com/aug15

I gave both methods a try (I settled on strip over rib-eye steaks since the former don't have as much internal fat and would thus cause fewer flare-ups) and, variations aside, one thing was for certain: Searing over a chimney was faster than any traditional grill setup I'd ever used, browning one side of the steak in about 2 minutes. Why is it so fast? For much the same reason that a chimney is so effective at lighting a pile of coals: access to oxygen. In a chimney, the coals rest on a grate surrounded by big slits that let in lots of air, the sides of the chimney are perforated for additional airflow, and there is no bottleneck—both the top and bottom of the chimney have wide openings. Together, these features allow a huge supply of oxygen to access the coals, which makes them burn hot. Plus, the cylindrical shape is ideal for focusing intense radiant heat toward the open ends.

But there was a downside to the chimney-based recipes. They all cooked the steaks start to finish over high heat, which inevitably led to an overcooked interior. To address this, I decided I would cook the interior of my steaks using our low-temperature oven method for pan-seared steaks and then move outside to sear them and give them that charcoal-grilled flavor.

After cooking a few steaks in a 275-degree oven for 30 minutes until they reached 105 degrees, I tried searing them both under and on top of a chimney. I quickly developed a preference for the latter. While putting the steak under the chimney avoided any chance of flare-ups because the fat dripped away from the heat source, ashes fell on the steak as it cooked and monitoring the browning required picking up the blazing-hot chimney. Putting the steak on top avoided both of these problems.

That said, the technique still had its issues. Placing a grill grate, which measures more than 20 inches in diameter, on top of a glowing-hot 6-quart chimney starter that was a mere 7½ inches in diameter was precarious to say the least. In addition, the grate itself posed a problem: The hot bars of the grill grate seared the parts of the steak touching it faster than the radiant heat from the coals could brown the rest of the steak's surface. The result was blackened grill marks over an unappealing background of gray meat—not exactly the thorough edge-to-edge browning I was after. And finally, flare-ups were a problem, even with strip steaks. The intense heat of the chimney quickly rendered and torched the fat cap. Cutting off the fat cap was a simple way to extinguish the flare-up issue, but I didn't have a simple solution for the grill grate. Or maybe it *was* that simple. What would happen if I just ditched the grate entirely?

Chimney Champ

A chimney starter is central to this recipe. Our favorite model from Weber ($14.99) boasts sturdy construction, a generous 6-quart capacity, a heat-resistant handle plus a second handle for pouring control, and plenty of ventilation holes, virtually guaranteeing that the coals ignite quickly.

WEBER RAPIDFIRE CHIMNEY STARTER

Grilling Steak over a Chimney Starter?

Most of us have used a chimney starter only for lighting coals and getting them good and hot before we pour them into the grill. But the coals are actually at their hottest in the chimney—not in the grill, where airflow is far more restricted. So why not leave the coals in the chimney and cook over that? Sure enough, this setup produced a deeply browned sear in just 1 minute per side. Here's how it works.

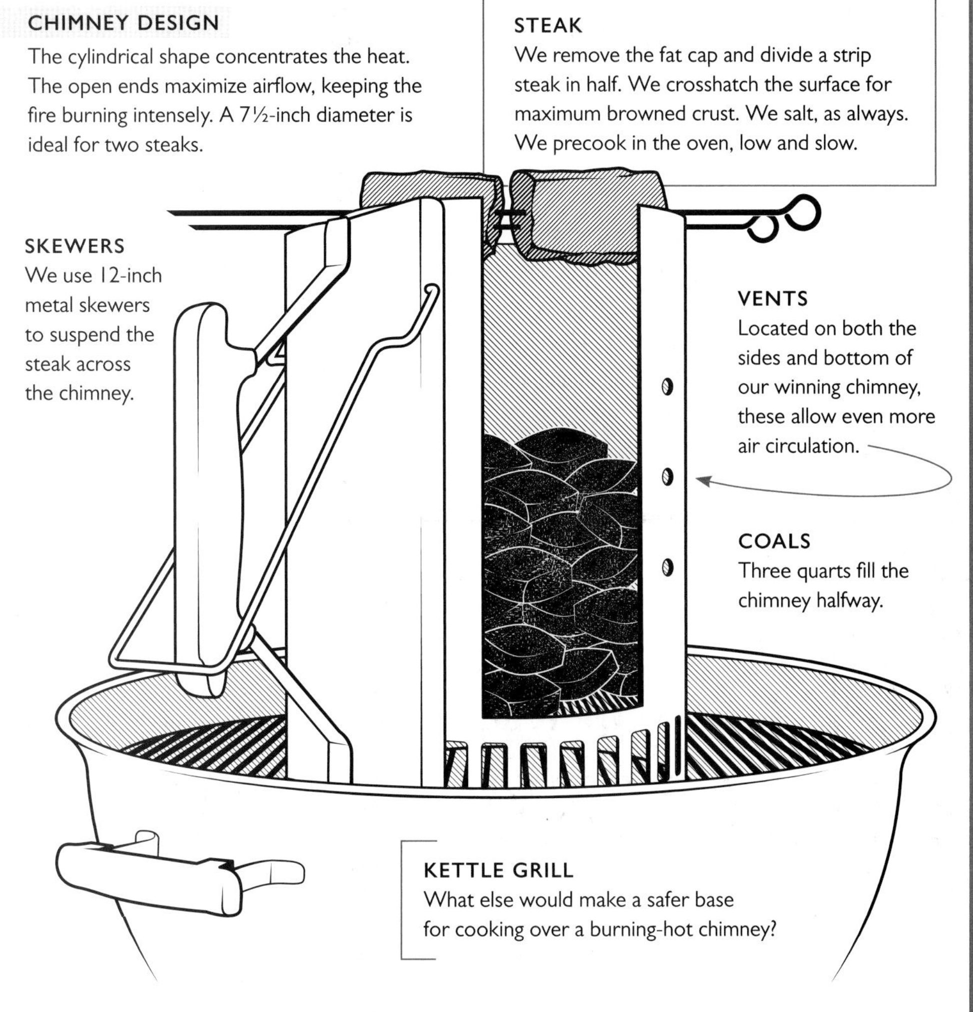

Better than Grate

There are many examples of cooking over a live fire without a grate—think of a pig suspended on a spit or even marshmallows toasted on sticks. But even with these precedents in mind, it felt a little odd as I ran two metal skewers, parallel to each other, lengthwise through the center of a 1¾-inch-thick strip steak. (One steak would easily serve two, so I figured that once I had my method down I could double the recipe.) After cooking my skewered steak through indoors, I moved outside and lit a chimney starter filled halfway with charcoal. As soon as the coals were ready, I set the skewered steak on top with the protruding ends of the skewers resting directly on the rim. I was finally onto something. In about 2 minutes the entire surface of the steak facing the coals turned a rich mahogany color and the edges charred beautifully. The gray band of overcooked meat was pretty small and the flavor was good. I just needed to make a few tweaks to reach perfection.

I had noticed that the steak charred best at the edges, which made sense because the edges have more exposed surface area and are thinner, making it easier for water to evaporate, a key factor for browning to occur. With that in mind, I sliced the steak in half crosswise before skewering to create two more edges and thus more browning. This worked well, with the added benefit of making serving a breeze—I simply slid the cooked steaks off the skewers and had two 8-ounce portions. Scoring the surface of the steaks in a crosshatch pattern before cooking provided additional edges to brown and char.

Many tasters complained that the interiors of the steaks were bland, so I salted the meat and let it sit for an hour before putting it in the oven. This made a big flavor difference, but I saw a chance for improvement. I salted some more steaks and immediately popped them into a superlow 200-degree oven to cook for about an hour and a half (I cooked them to 120 degrees since carryover cooking would be minimal). My bet paid off. The steaks were well seasoned and cooked internally to perfection because of the even-gentler cooking. And because the exterior had more time to dehydrate, these steaks browned and charred in just 60 seconds per side.

All that was left was to double the recipe to make four 8-ounce steaks on two sets of skewers. Since I was working with two strip steaks, each cut in half crosswise, I paired up the narrower ends from the two steaks on one set of skewers and the wider ends on another to ensure even cooking. I could only sear one pair at a time given the chimney's diameter, but it happened so fast that this didn't pose a problem.

With that, I had grilled steaks that lived up to the highest standards.

ULTIMATE CHARCOAL-GRILLED STEAKS
SERVES 4

Rib-eye steaks of a similar thickness can be substituted for strip steaks, although they may produce more flare-ups. You will need a charcoal chimney starter with a 7½-inch diameter and four 12-inch metal skewers for this recipe. If your chimney starter has a smaller diameter, skewer each steak individually and cook in four batches. It is important to remove the fat caps on the steaks to limit flare-ups during grilling.

2 (1-pound) boneless strip steaks, 1¾ inches thick, fat caps removed
Kosher salt and pepper

1. Adjust oven rack to middle position and heat oven to 200 degrees. Cut each steak in half crosswise to create four 8-ounce steaks. Cut 1⁄16-inch-deep slits on both sides of steaks, spaced ¼ inch apart, in crosshatch pattern. Sprinkle both sides of each steak with ½ teaspoon salt (2 teaspoons total). Lay steak halves with tapered ends flat on counter and pass two 12-inch metal skewers, spaced 1½ inches apart, horizontally through steaks, making sure to keep ¼-inch space between steak halves. Repeat skewering with remaining steak halves.

2. Place skewered steaks on wire rack set in rimmed baking sheet, transfer to oven, and cook until centers of steaks register 120 degrees, flipping steaks over halfway through cooking and removing them as they come to temperature, 1½ hours to 1 hour 50 minutes. Tent skewered steaks (still on rack) with aluminum foil.

3. Light large chimney starter filled halfway with charcoal briquettes (3 quarts). When top coals are completely covered in ash, uncover steaks (reserving foil) and pat dry with paper towels. Using tongs, place 1 set of steaks directly over chimney so skewers rest on rim of chimney (meat will be suspended over coals). Cook until both sides are well browned and charred, about 1 minute per side. Using tongs, return first set of steaks to wire rack in sheet, season with pepper, and tent with reserved foil. Repeat with second set of skewered steaks. Remove skewers from steaks and serve.

A New Approach to Fried Rice

We figured out a single substitution that both eliminates the need for leftover rice and makes the dish less greasy.

BY ANDREA GEARY

Traditional fried rice recipes vary widely in terms of ingredients, but there's one component that's common to all of them: leftover (as in cold and stale) white rice. Take it from someone who's tried to rush the process: moist, freshly cooked white rice doesn't hold up to frying. It quickly absorbs oil, leaving you with a mushy, greasy mass. In addition, recently cooked white rice naturally clumps; it needs to stale a bit (a process known as retrogradation) to firm up so that the grains will stay separate when stir-fried. The problem for me is that I almost never have leftover white rice in the fridge—so I rarely make fried rice. However, since brown rice takes longer to cook, I sometimes make big batches of it so I will have leftovers. Curious one evening to see how brown rice would fare in lieu of traditional white rice, I took a chance and improvised a simple fried-rice supper.

To balance brown rice's nutty flavor, we use more ginger, garlic, and soy sauce than you would find in a version made with white rice.

I noticed a promising difference as soon as I began cooking: Because each grain is encased in bran, these grains stayed much more separate than white rice. And that meant I could use a lot less oil—less than half the amount, in fact—than I would have used to stir-fry white rice. In the finished dish, the brown rice added an appealingly robust nuttiness that blank-slate white rice can't match; I'd just need to bump up the other flavors to balance it out. I also found that it was a bit too chewy and dry, so I wanted to tone that down. And lastly, while I often have leftover brown rice in my fridge, I know many people are put off by its long cooking time—it can take about 45 minutes on the stovetop or over an hour in the oven—so they simply don't make it very often. But I had an idea about how to address that.

It's Cool to Be Warm

One reason it takes so long to cook brown rice is that the bran hinders the hydration of the rice. Another reason is that most cooks make brown rice using the absorption method—that is, they cook it over low heat in just enough water to allow for hydration and a bit of evaporation, no stirring permitted.

This ultragentle method is the best way to cook delicate white rice because boiling the grains over high heat in a lot of water would cause them to tumble around, break up, and become mushy and sticky. That's because white rice is mostly unprotected starch. But we've found that since the starch in brown rice is enclosed and protected by the bran, it can actually be cooked like pasta, with plenty of water and plenty of heat. Preparing it this way whittled the cooking time down to 25 minutes. So much for brown rice's time-consuming reputation.

But here's the possibility that really interested me: If brown rice's bran coating had prevented clumping enough to allow me to cook the rice using the pasta method and to fry it in very little oil, might the bran also allow me to skip the chilling step that traditional white-rice recipes require? In fact, I had to wonder if refrigerating the brown rice was the cause of the too-chewy and dry texture that I'd found objectionable in that first test.

To find out, I boiled and drained a pot of brown rice and then immediately moved ahead with the recipe. To keep the focus on the rice's texture, I kept things simple. I heated some oil in a nonstick skillet, scrambled a couple of eggs until they were just cooked, and added the warm, just-cooked rice to the pan. Then I mixed the eggs into the rice (breaking the curds into smaller pieces), seasoned it with salt, and stirred in some chopped scallions.

The difference between this sample and that initial batch I'd made with my leftover brown rice was significant. This freshly cooked rice was pliable and moist. It still had a bit more texture than was ideal, but ditching the chilling was definitely a step in the right direction. I wondered if I might not even notice the extra chew once I'd incorporated the add-ins, so I moved on.

Balancing Act

I needed to incorporate some heartier flavors and textures to balance the brown rice, so I decided to model my recipe on a more elaborate Chinese restaurant version, which augments the rice and egg with Chinese barbecued pork, shrimp, and vegetables to make the dish into a main course.

Once I started stir-frying, things would move quickly, so I got all my ingredients together while the rice boiled. For a quick version of Chinese barbecued pork, I cut some boneless country-style pork ribs across the grain into bite-size slices and tossed them in hoisin sauce, honey, and five-spice powder. I chopped some scallions and shrimp, beat some eggs, grated some ginger, and minced some garlic, and I was ready to go.

For even cooking and because the skillet would be quite full by the end, I cooked the components in batches: first the shrimp and eggs and then the pork. I kept these off to the side in a bowl while I browned the scallion whites in sesame oil along with a good amount of garlic and ginger. I then added half the warm rice, which left me plenty of space in the skillet to break up the clumps of aromatics. Because I'd learned in my early experiments that fried brown rice would need a bit more seasoning than white, I added some soy sauce even though it's not traditional in

See Why Brown Is Better
Video available free for 4 months at CooksIllustrated.com/aug15

fried rice. Then I added the remainder of the rice, the cooked proteins, and some frozen peas for color and sweetness. I finished it all off by stirring in the scallion greens.

The new flavors worked really well with the brown rice, but the firm texture of the bran still stood out too much. I wanted grains that were a bit smoother and plumper.

The Long and the Short of It

I use all kinds of white rice: long-grain for pilaf, medium-grain for paella, and short-grain for risotto, so why was I limiting myself to long-grain brown rice for this recipe? With their rounder, plumper shapes, shorter-grain rices, I realized, were a much better option than long-grain rice for this recipe. Medium-grain brown rice was a bit hard to find, but I bought some short-grain and boiled up a batch. Though it was fully cooked after 25 minutes like the long-grain brown rice, I found that it actually benefitted from a little extra cooking. While long-grain rice is prone to blowing out and turning mushy if overcooked, giving the short-grain rice an extra 10 minutes made it just a bit softer.

So how did short-grain brown rice work in the fried rice? Beautifully. The smooth, rounded grains had a pleasantly resilient texture that melded well with the other components. Now that I know I can make fried rice with brown rice, less oil, and less forethought, I'll be making it a lot more often.

Benefits of the Bran

Unlike refined grains of white rice, brown rice grains are still surrounded by the bran. We found that this is a big advantage when it comes to making fried rice.

No Need for Leftovers
Fresh white rice naturally clumps, so it has to be refrigerated overnight to stale and harden before stir-frying. Brown rice's bran helps prevent clumping, so it can be used immediately after cooking.

Quick Cooking Method
The bran protects the starch within each grain, so brown rice can be cooked aggressively, and thus quickly, like pasta.

Less Oil Required
Because the bran helps brown rice grains stay separate, you need to use only about half the oil a recipe calling for white rice would require.

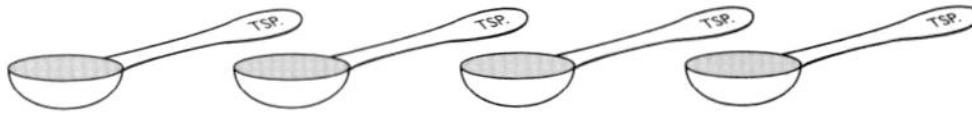

FRIED BROWN RICE WITH PORK AND SHRIMP

SERVES 6

Freshly boiling the short-grain rice gives it the proper texture for this dish. Do not use leftover rice, and do not use a rice cooker. The stir-fry portion of this recipe moves quickly, so be sure to have all your ingredients in place before starting. This recipe works best in a nonstick skillet with a slick surface. Serve with a simple steamed vegetable, if desired.

- 2 cups short-grain brown rice
- Salt
- 10 ounces boneless country-style pork ribs, trimmed
- 1 tablespoon hoisin sauce
- 2 teaspoons honey
- ⅛ teaspoon five-spice powder
- Small pinch cayenne pepper
- 4 teaspoons vegetable oil
- 8 ounces large shrimp (26 to 30 per pound), peeled, deveined, tails removed, and cut into ½-inch pieces
- 3 eggs, lightly beaten
- 1 tablespoon toasted sesame oil
- 6 scallions, white and green parts separated and sliced thin on bias
- 2 garlic cloves, minced
- 1½ teaspoons grated fresh ginger
- 2 tablespoons soy sauce
- 1 cup frozen peas

1. Bring 3 quarts water to boil in large pot. Add rice and 2 teaspoons salt. Cook, stirring occasionally, until rice is tender, about 35 minutes. Drain well and return to pot. Cover and set aside.

2. While rice cooks, cut pork into 1-inch pieces and slice each piece against grain ¼ inch thick. Combine pork with hoisin, honey, five-spice powder, cayenne, and ½ teaspoon salt and toss to coat. Set aside.

3. Heat 1 teaspoon vegetable oil in 12-inch nonstick skillet over medium-high heat until shimmering. Add shrimp in even layer and cook without moving them until bottoms are browned, about 90 seconds. Stir and continue to cook until just cooked through, about 90 seconds longer. Push shrimp to 1 side of skillet. Add 1 teaspoon vegetable oil to cleared side of skillet. Add eggs to clearing and sprinkle with ¼ teaspoon salt. Using rubber spatula, stir eggs gently until set but still wet, about 30 seconds. Stir eggs into shrimp and continue to cook, breaking up large pieces of egg, until eggs are fully cooked, about 30 seconds longer. Transfer shrimp-egg mixture to clean bowl.

4. Heat remaining 2 teaspoons vegetable oil in now-empty skillet over medium-high heat until shimmering. Add pork in even layer. Cook pork without moving it until well browned on underside, 2 to 3 minutes. Flip pork and cook without moving it until cooked through and caramelized on second side, 2 to 3 minutes. Transfer to bowl with shrimp-egg mixture.

Brown Rice in Less Time

Because the bran is removed from each grain during processing, white rice is mostly unprotected starch. Agitation and jostling during cooking will cause that starch to release and make the rice gummy—which is why it's best cooked using the gentle absorption method (i.e., simmering the rice in a set amount of liquid). But grains of brown rice still possess their bran, which means they can handle more aggressive cooking. With that in mind, we opt to cook brown rice like pasta, boiling it in plenty of water. The advantage? It cuts down the cooking time, and here's why.

First, boiling water gets hotter than the water in the absorption method—212 degrees versus around 204 degrees—so cooking is faster. Second, the more water in the pot, the more energy there is to be transferred to the rice. We were able to cut the usual 45 minutes (on the stove) to 60 minutes (in the oven) needed for the absorption method down to 35 minutes.

5. Heat sesame oil in now-empty skillet over medium-high heat until shimmering. Add scallion whites and cook, stirring frequently, until well browned, about 1 minute. Add garlic and ginger and cook, stirring frequently, until fragrant and beginning to brown, 30 to 60 seconds. Add soy sauce and half of rice and stir until all ingredients are fully incorporated, making sure to break up clumps of ginger and garlic. Reduce heat to medium-low and add remaining rice, pork mixture, and peas. Stir until all ingredients are evenly incorporated and heated through, 2 to 4 minutes. Remove from heat and stir in scallion greens. Transfer to warmed platter and serve.

Sausage with Grapes and Vinegar

This humble Italian supper celebrates the natural pairing of sweet and savory. But to make it great, we had to test every possible way to cook sausage.

⋟ BY ANNIE PETITO ⋞

I've always enjoyed the pairing of rich, salty pork and bright, sweet fruit—think pork chops and applesauce or prosciutto draped around cantaloupe. So naturally I'm intrigued by the Italian combination of pork sausage links with grapes and balsamic vinegar, a humble dish that originated in Umbria as a quick meal for vineyard laborers. Rich, juicy, and well browned, the sausages are a great match for the tangy-sweet vinegar-based sauce with grapes that soften and caramelize in the pan. Take into account that this dish can be on the table in less than 30 minutes and it's no wonder it became an Italian classic.

But like most preparations based on just a couple of simple components, the fewer the ingredients, the more important the technique. I tried recipes that failed at every turn, starting with grapes that were barely cooked and bouncy and vinegar that tasted harsh instead of in balance with the meat's richness.

But the real problem was the sausage itself. Some recipes weren't explicit about how to cook the links—and as I discovered, you can't just throw them into a skillet and hope for the best. But even the recipes that did specify a method came up short: Cooked over high—and even somewhat over medium—heat, the sausages tended to burn in spots before they had cooked all the way through, or their casings split, allowing their flavorful juices to leak into the pan and leaving their interiors dry and mealy. Cooking them over a low flame solved those problems but introduced new ones—namely, that their exteriors wrinkled and toughened, and their color was pallid at best.

In fact, these outcomes were all too familiar to me from other times I've tried to produce sausage that's both well-browned on the outside and juicy on the inside. If I could finally figure out the best way to cook the sausage, I'd have this dish, not to mention a host of others, at my disposal.

Watch the Stovetop Action
Video available free for 4 months at CooksIllustrated.com/aug15

A thinly sliced onion and dry white wine balance the grapes' sweetness and add body to the quick pan sauce.

Dry Run

Those early tests proved that the sausages needed at least medium heat to develop color—and I hoped that with some adjustments to the searing method, I could prevent them from burning or splitting.

My first idea was to keep the links moving as they cooked so that no one spot would get too dark. I heated a little oil in the pan and added 1½ pounds of sweet Italian sausages, the kind most recipes called for, and proceeded to turn them constantly as they cooked so that their heat exposure was as even as possible. But while such careful monitoring did help prevent burning, the casings split and the meat dried out nonetheless. Plus, that method was way too fussy.

It turns out that sausages split when the links' natural casings, which are composed largely of collagen, lose moisture and thus become more rigid. At the same time, the moisture in the sausage turns to steam, causing the meat to expand and strain the casing so much that it eventually bursts.

Some recipes I found called for pricking the sausages with a fork before cooking them, which supposedly prevents the buildup of pressure that causes the casings to split. And it did. The downside was that the nicks gave the precious juices too many escape routes and yielded results that were only marginally moister than the sausages that had split.

As a last resort, I skipped the pricking and tried roasting the sausages on a baking sheet in a 400-degree oven—an attempt at developing good browning without the direct heat of searing. But it was another dead end, as the sausages lacked the deep browning I'd achieved with the stove's more direct heat.

The Missing Link

Until now, I'd been avoiding moist-heat cooking methods because steaming or boiling the links would surely sacrifice flavorful browning. But I also knew that including some liquid would ensure that the meat cooked relatively gently and keep the casings hydrated and pliable. A combination of dry and moist heat seemed worth a shot.

I spent the next several tests fiddling with hybrid cooking methods: poaching or steaming followed by searing, or the reverse. The trouble with poaching or steaming first was that I had to use two vessels to cook the sausages, one with water and one without. Plus, introducing moisture from the get-go washed out the flavor of the links, so they never tasted as savory as they should have.

I had much better luck when I browned the links first. Borrowing the classic Chinese method for cooking potstickers, I cooked the sausages over medium heat, turning them once so that they browned on two sides, and then added ¼ cup of water to the pan. It was just enough to generate some steam but not so much that the water submerged the sausages and washed away their flavor. I immediately covered the pan so that the links could steam gently; after about 10 minutes, they hit their target temperature of 160 to 165 degrees (for more information about sausage doneness, see "Don't Judge a Link by Its Color"). I let the links rest for about 5 minutes and then took a taste: Well-browned outside and juicy within, they were ideal—and even better, this quick one-pan method would work for just about any stovetop sausage preparation.

SCIENCE Don't Judge a Link by Its Color

When we were perfecting our method for cooking sausage, we kept running into a weird phenomenon: Sometimes sausages that were fully cooked to 160 degrees looked pink inside. Deep, hammy pink. Naturally, nobody wanted to touch those links, but we later learned that persistent pinkness can be due to a variety of factors unrelated to the meat's doneness: the seasonings, the age of the pork when it's processed, and how it was stored. But according to Joseph Sebranek and Melvin Hunt, professors and meat experts at Iowa State University and Kansas State University, respectively, the most significant factor affecting the pigment is the pork's pH: The higher the pH, the more stable its pink pigment will be, even when the meat is fully cooked.

We confirmed this effect by adding increasing amounts of alkaline baking soda to ground pork to raise its pH and then cooking all the samples via *sous vide* to exactly 160 degrees. Sure enough, the samples with the highest pH were noticeably pinker, proving that the color of the pork is not a good indication of its doneness. Instead, we'll trust our instant-read thermometers.

COLOR OF SAUSAGE WHEN COOKED TO 160°

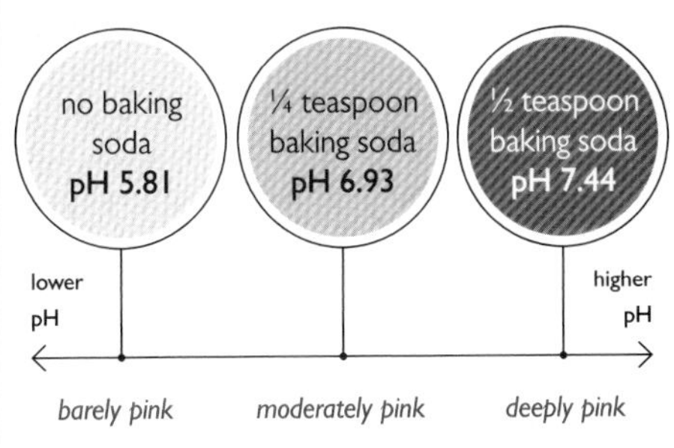

Grape Expectations

With my sausage method settled, all I had left to do was plug the grapes and a quick pan sauce into the equation. I wanted the fruit to break down a little, so I halved 1 pound of red grapes (their darker pigment would look nicer with the inky balsamic vinegar than paler green grapes would) lengthwise and added them to the skillet with the browned links just before adding the water. Once the sausages were cooked through, I removed them from the pan but continued to cook the grapes, raising the heat to cook off excess moisture so that they would soften and caramelize but still retain their shape. Off heat, I stirred a couple of tablespoons of vinegar into the pan and promptly spooned the glazy sauce over the sausages.

The grapes were nicely cooked, but the sauce was a tad greasy, sweet, and one-dimensional. Removing some fat from the skillet before adding the grapes solved the first problem, while adding a thinly sliced onion along with the grapes lent the dish some savory-sweet backbone. Then, to loosen up the vinegar sauce's syrupy consistency and balance its sweetness, I deglazed the pan with ¼ cup of dry white wine (lighter and brighter than red) and added a tablespoon of chopped fresh oregano during the last minute of cooking. That way, the sauce would work as a dip for crusty bread or spooned over a heartier accompaniment like polenta. Sprinkling chopped mint over the finished dish added a touch of color and freshness.

ITALIAN SAUSAGE WITH GRAPES AND BALSAMIC VINEGAR

SERVES 4 TO 6

Our favorite supermarket balsamic vinegar is Bertolli Balsamic Vinegar of Modena (for more tasting information, see page 27). Serve this dish with crusty bread and salad or over polenta for a heartier meal. For our free recipe for Italian Sausage with Grapes and Balsamic Vinegar for Two, go to CooksIllustrated.com/aug15.

- 1 tablespoon vegetable oil
- 1½ pounds sweet Italian sausage
- 1 pound seedless red grapes, halved lengthwise (3 cups)
- 1 onion, halved and sliced thin
- ¼ cup water
- ¼ teaspoon pepper
- ⅛ teaspoon salt
- ¼ cup dry white wine
- 1 tablespoon chopped fresh oregano
- 2 teaspoons balsamic vinegar
- 2 tablespoons chopped fresh mint

1. Heat oil in 12-inch skillet over medium heat until shimmering. Arrange sausages in pan and cook, turning once, until browned on 2 sides, about 5 minutes. Tilt skillet and carefully remove excess fat with paper towel. Distribute grapes and onion over and around sausages. Add water and immediately cover. Cook, turning sausages once, until they register between 160 and 165 degrees and onions and grapes have softened, about 10 minutes.

2. Transfer sausages to paper towel–lined plate and tent with aluminum foil. Return skillet to medium-high heat and stir pepper and salt into grape-onion mixture. Spread grape-onion mixture in even layer in skillet and cook without stirring until browned, 3 to 5 minutes. Stir and continue to cook, stirring frequently, until mixture is well browned and grapes are soft but still retain their shape, 3 to 5 minutes longer. Reduce heat to medium, stir in wine and oregano, and cook, scraping up any browned bits, until wine is reduced by half, 30 to 60 seconds. Remove pan from heat and stir in vinegar.

3. Arrange sausages on serving platter and spoon grape-onion mixture over top. Sprinkle with mint and serve.

Wrong Ways to Cook Sausage

We cooked sausage every way we could think of before we landed on the ideal method.

TEST 1
POACH
Problems: Cooking in water produced sausages that were moist—but pale and washed out.

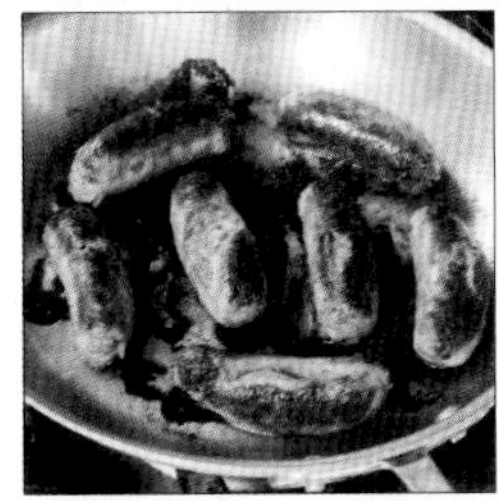

TEST 2
SAUTÉ OVER HIGH HEAT
Problems: Searing caused the casings to split and leak juices and the meat to dry out.

TEST 3
SAUTÉ OVER LOW HEAT
Problems: Prolonged exposure to low heat caused the casings to shrivel and toughen.

TEST 4
ROAST
Problems: The oven's gentler heat kept the links juicy but resulted in pale color and bland flavor.

TEST 5
POACH AND SEAR
Problems: Introducing moist heat first required two vessels and washed out the sausages' flavor.

The Right Way to Cook Sausage

SAUTÉ AND THEN STEAM
Moderate heat develops flavorful browning without burning. Then, adding a little water to the pan and covering it gently steams the sausages so they cook up juicy.

Cherry Clafouti

This baked French custard studded with fresh fruit would be a simple and satisfying dessert—if we could nail its finicky texture and prevent the cherries from turning soggy.

⋟ BY DAN SOUZA ⋞

When I have a surplus of summer fruit and not much time to make dessert, I usually throw together a crisp or cobbler—easy, satisfying, and crowd-pleasing. But I've often admired France's answer to those simple desserts: clafouti, a rustic yet graceful baked custard that is studded with fresh fruit such as apricots, plums, or—most classic and my favorite—cherries. To make it, you mix up a batter without any chemical leaveners (similar to that used for crêpes) using flour, sugar, eggs, milk and/or heavy cream, and a touch of vanilla or almond extract; pour it into a buttered baking dish; scatter the cherries (usually unpitted) on top; and bake it for the better part of half an hour. When finished, the custard should be rich and tender but resilient enough to be neatly sliced and the fruit plump enough to disrupt the custard with bright, sweet-tart flavor.

Baking our clafouti in a metal skillet, rather than a glass baking dish, helps it develop flavorful browning on the bottom and makes it easier to slice.

But simple as clafouti is, the texture of the custard is tricky to get right: It can easily end up either pasty and bready or loose and creamy like crème brûlée. It can turn out too thin to sink a fork into or so tall that it overwhelms the cherries. As for the fruit, whole cherries never integrate well in the custard and often burst, leaking juices into the custard that render it soggy and (thanks to the acid in the fruit juice) curdled in isolated patches. Plus, I've always found the inclusion of pits curious; spitting them out when snacking is one thing, but doing so at the dinner table seems indecorous. I hoped that with a little work, I could come up with a recipe that consistently turned out a rich, tender custard punctuated with bright cherry flavor.

Custard's Last Stand

Whether a custard bakes up bready, creamy, or somewhere in between depends largely on the ratio of dairy and flour to eggs. Why? Well, the proteins in whole eggs provide structure; adding fat (from heavy cream, milk, or egg yolks alone) and starch (from flour) dilutes that structure as each buffers the proteins and keeps them from linking up too tightly. The more the protein network is diluted, the looser the custard will be.

For the tender but set texture I wanted, I analyzed the quantities of these core components in a dozen published clafouti recipes and compared the textures they produced. Not surprisingly, the flour-heavy recipes (which called for as much as 1 cup) were the ones that baked up tough and bready, while richer batters (which called for up to 2¼ cups heavy cream) produced custards that were too tender and creamy to slice.

It took several more rounds of tinkering before I hit on the ideal: four whole eggs, 1 cup of heavy cream plus ⅔ cup of whole milk (a combination that lent the batter more than double the amount of fat that an equal amount of half-and-half would have but considerably less than heavy cream alone) and a modest ½ cup of flour. Baked at 350 degrees for about 20 minutes, this custard could be sliced into neat wedges but still yielded to the pressure of a fork.

But as nice as its texture was, this custard was a tad dull, and my tasters and I agreed that some browning on the top and bottom would go a long way toward creating more complex flavor. So I started cranking up the oven temperature. By the time I got to 425 degrees, the very top edge was browning nicely, but the underside remained pale—which made me wonder if the glass baking dish I was using wasn't transferring heat quickly enough to the bottom of the custard.

A 12-inch metal skillet would surely conduct heat faster, I thought. And I was right—the browning improved in the pan. But what really helped was preheating the skillet on the oven's lower rack (close to the heat source), removing it from the oven and adding a pat of butter, and then pouring the batter over the top. The butter browned quickly, adding rich flavor to the custard's underside, and the blast of heat souffléed the edges for a dramatic appearance and nicely browned crust. A bonus: It was much easier to cut and serve neat slices from the skillet, with its flared sides, than from the straight-sided baking dish.

Secret Source of Cherry Flavor: Pits

Cherry clafouti is traditionally made with unpitted cherries because, surprisingly, the stones lend the dessert a fragrant spice flavor—but they also make it tricky to slice and eat. The solution? Use pitted cherries and toss them with a little cinnamon. If that sounds like an odd solution, it's not; both cherry pits and cinnamon contain a compound called linalool that lends the dessert a similarly warm, floral complexity.

Cherry Picking

Most classic clafouti recipes call for whole, unpitted cherries because, they claim, the pits add stronger cherry flavor; not pitting the cherries also saves prep time. But I wondered if the pits made a real flavor difference in clafouti. Even if they did, they made it difficult to slice (and eat) the dessert.

A side-by-side tasting of custards baked with pitted and unpitted cherries proved that the flavor difference was real—my tasters noted a pleasantly warm, cinnamon-like flavor in the unpitted batch. And as it turned out, they were onto something: Cherry pits and cinnamon share a fragrant, floral compound called linalool.

This got me thinking: Why not simply add a touch of cinnamon to pitted cherries? Removing the pits would, of course, add time to the recipe, but the results were well worth the effort. Not only did the cinnamon-dusted pitted cherries taste virtually identical to the unpitted ones, but doing away with the fruits' stones meant that I could halve the cherries, which would prevent them from bursting during baking.

But simply tossing halved cherries into the clafouti didn't prevent them from shedding juice that created those damp, curdled pockets. To fix that, I'd need to drive off some of their moisture before incorporating them into the custard. I tried both microwaving the halved cherries and roasting them (cut side up) on a foil-lined rimmed baking sheet for about 15 minutes. I found that the latter did a better job of driving off moisture; roasting also nicely concentrated the fruits' flavor. As they cooled briefly, I splashed the cherries with fresh lemon juice for a jolt of bright flavor. Then to sop up any of their residual juices, I added a couple of teaspoons of flour to the cinnamon I was already tossing with the fruit. My final tweak, sprinkling granulated sugar over the baked custard, added just a hint of sweet crunch that contrasted nicely with the tender custard.

This clafouti—with its creamy but set interior, rich-tasting crisp crust, and bursts of concentrated cherry flavor—was an improvement on classic renditions but still simple enough to stand in for a casual cobbler.

Roast the Cherries First

Briefly roasting halved and pitted cherries for our clafouti adds a little time to traditional approaches that call for tossing whole raw cherries into the batter—but we think it's worth the effort. Instead of bursting and leaking juices into the custard, which leave it soggy and stained red, the fruit adds bright, sweet-tart flavor that complements the rich custard.

CHERRY CLAFOUTI

SERVES 6 TO 8

We prefer whole milk in this recipe, but 1 or 2 percent low-fat milk may be substituted. Do not substitute frozen cherries for the fresh cherries.

- 1½ pounds fresh sweet cherries, pitted and halved
- 1 teaspoon lemon juice
- 2 teaspoons all-purpose flour, plus ½ cup (2½ ounces)
- ⅛ teaspoon ground cinnamon
- 4 large eggs
- ⅔ cup (4⅔ ounces) plus 2 teaspoons sugar
- 2½ teaspoons vanilla extract
- ¼ teaspoon salt
- 1 cup heavy cream
- ⅔ cup whole milk
- 1 tablespoon unsalted butter

1. Adjust oven racks to lowest and upper-middle positions; place 12-inch skillet on lower rack and heat oven to 425 degrees. Line rimmed baking sheet with aluminum foil and place cherries, cut side up, on sheet. Roast cherries on upper rack until just tender and cut sides look dry, about 15 minutes. Transfer cherries to medium bowl, toss with lemon juice, and let cool for 5 minutes. Combine 2 teaspoons flour and cinnamon in small bowl; dust flour mixture evenly over cherries and toss to coat thoroughly.

2. Meanwhile, whisk eggs, ⅔ cup sugar, vanilla, and salt in large bowl until smooth and pale, about 1 minute. Whisk in remaining ½ cup flour until smooth. Whisk in cream and milk until incorporated.

3. Remove skillet (skillet handle will be hot) from oven and set on wire rack. Add butter and swirl to coat bottom and sides of skillet (butter will melt and brown quickly). Pour batter into skillet and arrange cherries evenly on top (some will sink). Transfer skillet to lower rack and bake until clafouti puffs and turns golden brown (edges will be dark brown) and center registers 195 degrees, 18 to 22 minutes, rotating skillet halfway through baking. Transfer skillet to wire rack and let cool for 25 minutes. Sprinkle clafouti evenly with remaining 2 teaspoons sugar. Slice into wedges and serve.

Batter Up: Getting the Ratio Right for Tender, Sliceable Clafouti

Custards can range from soft and creamy, like pastry cream, to more resilient and bready, like a crêpe. The textural difference largely depends on the ratio of three key ingredients: eggs, dairy, and flour. The proteins in the eggs provide the structure, linking together into a network as the custard heats, while both fat from the dairy and starch from the flour dilute that structure by interrupting the egg proteins and preventing them from knitting together too tightly.

So when we set out to achieve the tender-but-set texture of our Cherry Clafouti, we conducted more than a dozen tests, fiddling with the amounts of each component. Not surprisingly, too much flour made the custard too bready, whereas an excess of dairy yielded custard that was too loose. Ultimately, we settled on a relatively moderate amount of each: 1⅔ cups of dairy, four eggs, and ½ cup of flour, which yielded a clafouti that was soft but sliceable.

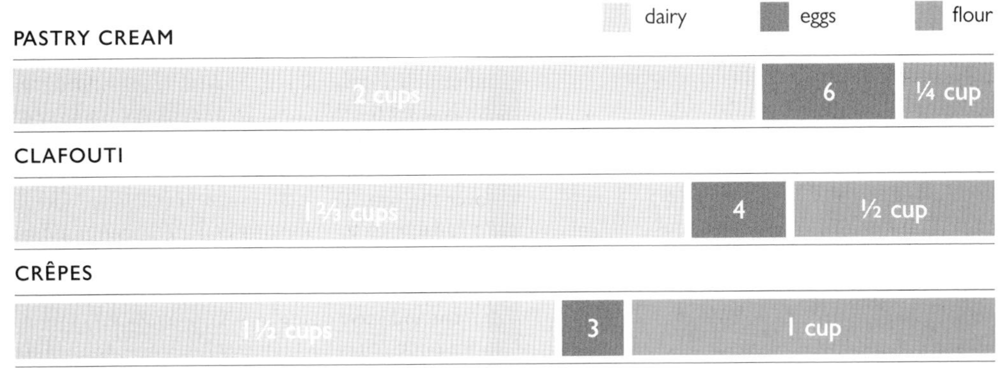

Look: Dan Cooks Clafouti
Video available free for 4 months at CooksIllustrated.com/aug15

Making the Burger Lover's Burger

Nothing is more satisfying than a juicy burger. After making hundreds over the years, we've sorted out the ingredients and techniques that produce the perfect patty.

BY ELIZABETH BOMZE

GRIND THE MEAT YOURSELF

Grinding your own meat leads to a burger that's far superior to those made from commercially ground beef because it allows you to control the cut and how finely you grind it. And you don't need special equipment to do it—just a food processor. The trick is to grind the meat fine enough to ensure tenderness but coarse enough that the patty will stay loose.

Use the Best Cut

Chuck is often used for commercial ground beef, but it contains lots of connective tissue that must be removed before grinding. Instead, we use sirloin steak tips (or "flap meat"), which are well marbled and require little trimming.

Trim and Cut

After removing any excess fat and gristle, cut the steak tips into ½-inch chunks, which will process evenly during grinding.

Add Butter for Juiciness

The fat in butter helps burgers cook up superjuicy, and the butter's protein encourages browning. To ensure that the butter pieces are consistent and evenly distributed, cut the butter into small cubes.

Freeze Beef and Butter

To firm up the meat and butter before grinding, freeze the pieces on a plate or rimmed baking sheet in a single layer for about 30 minutes. That way, the food processor cuts them cleanly instead of smashing them, which leads to pasty, dense results.

Work in Batches

Process the beef and butter in small batches, stopping to redistribute them around the bowl as necessary, to ensure a precise, even grind.

Inspect the Grind

After grinding, spread the mixture on a rimmed baking sheet and discard any long strands of gristle or large chunks of hard meat or fat.

FORM THE PATTIES

Seasoning and handling the meat carefully will result in flavorful, tender burgers.

Wait to Season

Salting ground beef before forming the patties thoroughly seasons the meat and keeps it juicy. But don't season the meat until you're ready to form the patties and don't add too much salt; over time, salt dissolves meat proteins, causing them to bind together, which makes for dense, tough patties. We found that ¾ teaspoon of kosher salt mixed into 1½ pounds of meat produces juicy burgers that are still tender. In addition, we sprinkle the formed patties with salt and pepper just before cooking.

Shape with a Light Touch

The more you handle ground meat, the more its proteins will link together and the tougher the burger will be. So we take care to handle the meat gently when forming burgers.

PORTION Divide ground beef into equal-size balls.

PACK Toss each ball between your hands until lightly packed.

PRESS Flatten into patties ¾ inch thick and 4½ inches in diameter.

For Well-Done Burgers, Add a Panade

If you prefer to cook burgers to well-done, a panade can help keep the meat moist and tender. This paste of starch and liquid (typically made from bread and milk) gets between the meat proteins so that they don't bind together tightly and forms a gel that lubricates the proteins so that they stay moist. In tests, we've found that burgers made with a panade retained twice as much liquid as burgers without one. **FORMULA:** For 1½ pounds of beef, combine 1 slice of hearty white sandwich bread, torn into pieces, with 2 tablespoons of milk. Let the mixture sit for about 5 minutes until the bread is soaked and then mash it to a paste with a fork; you'll have about ¼ cup. Gently mix the panade into the meat before forming the burgers.

If You Don't Grind Your Own Meat

When you don't have time to grind the meat yourself, follow these guidelines for buying the best possible commercial ground beef.

DO buy ground beef labeled 80 percent lean, ideally "ground chuck," which is well marbled and cooks up relatively tender, juicy, and flavorful (preground chuck contains little gristle).

DON'T buy packages labeled "ground round," a lean, tough cut that lacks beefy flavor, or "ground beef," which can contain cuts from any part of the cow and might be livery or tough.

DON'T buy ground beef that looks brown or that has leached juices into the package—signs that it may not be freshly ground and that it may have been previously frozen, respectively.

DON'T splurge on grass-fed ground beef. It costs about 50 percent more than grain-fed beef, and we've found that the leaner meat lacks the flavor and juiciness we expect in a burger.

DO consider cooking commercial ground beef to 160 degrees, per U.S. Department of Agriculture guidelines.

BURGER LOVERS' BURGERS
SERVES 4

When stirring the salt and pepper into the ground meat and shaping the patties, take care not to overwork the meat or the burgers will be dense. Sirloin steak tips are also sold as flap meat. If desired, toast the buns while the cooked burgers rest. Serve the burgers with your favorite toppings.

- **1½ pounds sirloin steak tips, trimmed and cut into ½-inch chunks**
- **4 tablespoons unsalted butter, cut into ¼-inch pieces**
- **Kosher salt and pepper**
- **1 (13 by 9-inch) disposable aluminum pan (if using charcoal)**
- **1 teaspoon vegetable oil (if using stovetop)**
- **4 hamburger buns**

1. **FREEZE MEAT** Place beef chunks and butter on large plate or rimmed baking sheet in single layer. Freeze until meat is very firm and starting to harden around edges but still pliable, about 35 minutes.
2. **GRIND MEAT** Place one-quarter of meat and one-quarter of butter pieces in food processor and pulse until finely ground into rice-grain-size pieces (about 1/32 inch), 15 to 20 pulses, stopping and redistributing meat around bowl as necessary to ensure beef is evenly ground. Transfer meat to baking sheet. Repeat grinding with remaining meat and butter in 3 batches. Spread mixture over sheet and inspect carefully, discarding any long strands of gristle or large chunks of hard meat, fat, or butter.
3. **FORM PATTIES** Sprinkle 1 teaspoon pepper and ¾ teaspoon salt over meat and gently toss with fork to combine. Divide meat into 4 balls. Toss each between your hands until uniformly but lightly packed. Gently flatten into patties ¾ inch thick and about 4½ inches in diameter.

GRILL METHOD

4. Using your thumb, make 1-inch-wide by ¼-inch-deep depression in center of each patty. Transfer patties to platter and freeze for 30 to 45 minutes.

5A. FOR A CHARCOAL GRILL: Using skewer, poke 12 holes in bottom of disposable pan. Open bottom vent completely and place disposable pan in center of grill. Light large chimney starter two-thirds filled with charcoal briquettes (4½ quarts). When top coals are partially covered with ash, pour into disposable pan. Set cooking grate in place, cover, and open lid vent completely. Heat grill until hot, about 5 minutes.

5B. FOR A GAS GRILL: Turn all burners to high, cover, and heat grill until hot, about 15 minutes. Leave all burners on high.

6. Clean and oil cooking grate. Season 1 side of patties liberally with salt and pepper. Using spatula, flip patties and season other side. Grill patties (directly over coals if using charcoal), without moving them, until browned and meat easily releases from grill, 4 to 7 minutes. Flip patties and continue to grill until browned on second side and meat registers 120 to 125 degrees for medium-rare or 130 to 135 degrees for medium, 4 to 7 minutes longer.

7. Transfer burgers to plate and let rest for 5 minutes. Transfer burgers to buns and serve with toppings.

STOVETOP METHOD

4. Season 1 side of patties liberally with salt and pepper. Using spatula, flip patties and season other side. Heat oil in 12-inch skillet over high heat until just smoking. Using spatula, transfer burgers to skillet and cook, without moving them, for 3 minutes. Using spatula, flip burgers and continue to cook until burgers register 120 to 125 degrees for medium-rare or 130 to 135 degrees for medium, 2 to 3 minutes longer.

5. Transfer burgers to plate and let rest for 5 minutes. Transfer burgers to buns and serve with toppings.

For Flat Burgers, Make an Impression

Making a slight dimple in the center of a raw patty can prevent it from bulging as it cooks, which happens when the meat's protein exceeds 140 degrees and shrinks, squeezing the edges of the patty like a belt. But only grilled burgers need to be dimpled. Why? Because while grilled burgers will be exposed to high heat all over even without direct contact with the cooking surface, only the portions of pan-seared burgers that make contact with the cooking surface will get very hot. Plus, pan-seared burgers cook more quickly, so the meat is less susceptible to shrinking.

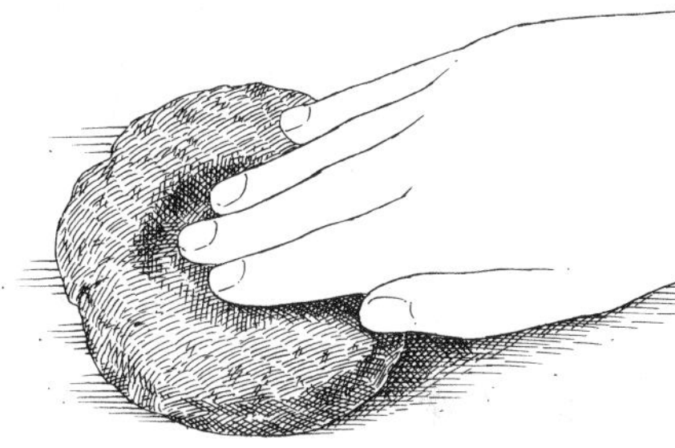

DIMPLE DOS AND DON'TS
Dimple burgers cooked on the grill, but don't bother dimpling burgers cooked in a skillet.

Chill Before You Grill

In addition to freezing the meat before grinding it, we briefly freeze the patties before grilling. Why? Freezing firms up the loosely packed meat so it holds together on the grill long enough for a thick crust to form, which also makes the burgers easier to flip.

Doneness Chart

To take the temperature of burgers without breaking them apart, leave them in the pan (or on the grill), slide the tip of the thermometer into the top edge, and push it toward the center, making sure to avoid hitting the pan (or grill grate) with the probe.

	DEGREES (before rest)
Medium-rare	120–125
Medium	130–135
Medium-well	140–145
Well-done	160+

TIP

Track Doneness with Toothpicks

When cooking for a crowd, it can be tricky to distinguish well-done burgers from medium-rare at a glance. Assign each level of doneness a particular number of toothpicks (e.g., one for rare, two for medium, three for well-done) and peg the proper marker(s) into the patties as they come off the heat.

Make It a Cheeseburger

Adding cheese at the right time and trapping heat around the burgers help the slices melt quickly and evenly.

Wait to Add Cheese

When the burgers are nearly done—about 2 minutes to go on the grill and 90 seconds on the stove—top them with sliced cheese (we like cheddar or American).

Add a Lid

Cover grilled burgers with an overturned disposable aluminum roasting pan and stovetop burgers with a lid.

How to Grill Whole Trout

Grilling whole trout is quick and easy; plus, its crisp, smoky skin is a perfect complement to its mild-tasting meat. The only problem? Getting it off the grill in one piece.

⋟ BY LAN LAM ⋞

I'm always surprised that more people don't grill whole fish. The grill infuses fish with smoky flavor, while the intense heat crisps the skin beautifully, lending contrast to the moist flesh beneath. And because the skin acts as a buffer during cooking, it helps ensure that the interior cooks through gently. The skin also keeps the delicate flesh contained, making a whole fish easier to handle than fillets.

So why don't more people grill them? One reason might be that the idea of cleaning and scaling whole fish sounds like a chore; plus, they need to be boned at the table or before serving. But there's an easy answer to those obstacles: Choose whole trout. Not only are whole trout almost always sold cleaned and scaled, but their backbones and pinbones are also removed. And they're small, weighing about 10 ounces each, so one fish can serve one person—no need to fuss with portioning.

There's just one problem with grilling whole trout: The skin is prone to sticking to the cooking grate (as it is with any fish), which can cause the flesh to come off in ragged pieces. As straightforward as this might sound, it's a problem I've never been able to fully solve. I decided it was time to really tackle this challenge head-on.

Applying a mixture of mayonnaise and honey (neither of which you can taste) to the fish helps it brown and release from the grill before it overcooks.

Attach and Release

When I researched recipes, I realized that there was a dearth of promising solutions. Most recipes called for wrapping the whole fish in things like foil, wet newspaper, or banana leaves or in something edible like bacon or prosciutto. Since all these approaches would prevent the skin from crisping—one of the key selling points to me of grilling whole fish in the first place—they were of no use. My best bet would be to just start grilling and see what inspiration came to me.

Before I fired up the grill, I prepped the trout, which didn't require much. I simply snipped off the fins with scissors since they would burn, seasoned the interior with salt and pepper (I'd come back to flavorings later), and brushed the exterior with oil.

When grilling fish in the past, I've noticed that sticking is more of an issue on gas grills than on charcoal grills, so I decided to start there, figuring that adapting to charcoal afterward wouldn't be a problem. I also settled on cooking over high heat. This might seem like the wrong tactic for delicate fish, but I knew that it could be beneficial in preventing sticking. This is because foods stick to the cooking grate (and pans, for that matter) when bonds form between sulfur-containing amino acids in the food's proteins and the iron atoms in the cooking grate. Fortunately, though, these bonds will eventually break when exposed to high enough heat for a long enough time. (For more information, see "Why Browned Food Doesn't Stick.")

A Clean Start

Properly cleaning your grate before cooking is critical since leftover gunk on your grate can impart off-flavors and encourage sticking. For the best results, preheat the grill (a hot grate is easier to clean) and use a good grill brush to scrub off debris. Our favorite is the Grill Wizard 18-Inch China Grill Brush ($31.50).

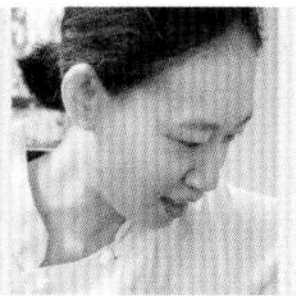

Look: Proper Flipping
Video available free for 4 months at CooksIllustrated.com/aug15

I proceeded to cook my fish, flipping them just once as soon as they'd browned (a clear sign that the grill had reached a temperature hot enough to release the fish). After 10 minutes, the fish were beautifully browned on both sides and released nicely. But there was a problem: The flesh had reached 150 degrees, about 20 degrees higher than the target for perfect doneness. I needed the skin to brown more quickly.

A Sweet Solution

I knew that for food to brown (a process known as the Maillard reaction), heat must first break down its proteins into amino acids and its carbohydrates into simpler sugars known as reducing sugars, freeing these molecules to recombine into hundreds of new compounds that bring darker color and more complex flavor. To speed up this reaction—and thus get my fish to brown faster so it would release more quickly—my first thought was to boost the amount of reducing sugars present. In past similar situations, we've used honey, which is basically a solution of the reducing sugars fructose and glucose. I figured that it wouldn't take much, just ⅛ teaspoon or so per fish. There was only one problem. Evenly coating the fish with a small amount of honey was a messy, difficult task. I tried whisking the honey into the oil I was already brushing on the fish, but because honey is water-based, the two wouldn't combine. After a conversation with our science editor, I had an unusual but effective answer: ditching the oil in favor of mayonnaise. Mayonnaise is an emulsion of oil droplets suspended in water, so when I stirred the honey into the mayo, the honey simply dissolved into the water portion, allowing it to evenly disperse. I found that ½ teaspoon of honey combined easily with 2 tablespoons of mayonnaise.

It was time to fire up the grill and try again. My fish browned beautifully on the first side after they'd been on the grill for just 3 minutes—2 minutes sooner than in my previous test. Using a pair of thin metal fish spatulas, I had no trouble flipping the fish over, and after another 3 minutes, they were ready. My tasters noted that the skin was perfect, with great grill flavor and not a hint of honey or mayo, and the fish itself was moist, tender, and perfectly cooked.

It was time to move on to charcoal. I understood now why sticking was less of a problem on charcoal: A charcoal grill can get hotter than a gas grill, in part because you can manipulate the heat output by varying charcoal setups and using the vents to make the charcoal burn hotter and faster. Still, I'd keep my mayo coating in play for added insurance. And to concentrate the heat of the coals for maximum heat output, I picked up a trick we've used before: corralling the coals in the center of the grill with the help of a disposable aluminum pan that I'd poked a few holes in to increase airflow. Using a chimney filled two-thirds of the way with charcoal delivered perfectly cooked fish in just minutes.

My recipe just lacked a little flavor boost. In addition to serving the fish with lemon wedges, I used lemon zest and marjoram, an herb that goes well with char-grilled flavor. For variations, I paired lime zest with coriander and orange zest with ground fennel.

This recipe is so quick, easy, and flavorful that it's sure to win many converts to grilling whole fish.

SCIENCE Why Browned Food Doesn't Stick

When cooking on the stovetop or grill, if you try to flip a piece of protein—whether fish, chicken, pork, or beef—too soon, the skin or the outer layer of meat will stick (or worse, with delicate fish, flake apart into shreds). But wait long enough and, as soon as the exterior browns, the protein releases from the pan. Why does this happen?

The food sticks because cysteine, an amino acid in the protein molecules, contains a sulfur atom that will bond at low temperatures with iron atoms that are present in the pan or the bars of a grill grate. High heat will break these bonds, but getting your pan or grill ripping hot isn't enough—as soon as you put the food down, the temperature of the cooking surface will drop, and the food will stick. You have to wait patiently for the temperature to climb back up and then cook the exterior of the food to a high enough temperature to break the bonds.

But how do you know when that point has been reached? Conveniently, there is a visual cue: browning. Food browns when a series of chemical reactions take place, which generally happens at around the same high temperature that is required to break the sulfur-iron bonds between the food and pan. *Voilà*, the food releases.

STUCK
At low temperatures, proteins bond to a pan or grill grate and stick.

RELEASED
At high temperatures, food browns and releases.

TECHNIQUE | HOW TO FLIP A WHOLE FISH

Given whole trout's long shape and delicate skin, you can't just push a spatula under it and flip it over like a burger. You need two spatulas and a little maneuvering.

1. Slide spatula scant 1 inch under backbone edge and lift edge up. Slide second spatula under, then remove first spatula, allowing fish to ease onto second spatula.

2. Place first spatula on top of fish so it's oriented in same direction as second spatula and flip fish over.

GRILLED WHOLE TROUT WITH MARJORAM AND LEMON

SERVES 4

We prefer marjoram in this recipe, but thyme or oregano can be substituted. Do not flip the fish over in one motion. Instead, use two thin metal spatulas to gently lift the fish from the grate and then slide it from the spatula back onto the grate. The heads can be removed before serving, if desired.

- 2 teaspoons minced fresh marjoram
- 1 teaspoon grated lemon zest, plus lemon wedges for serving
- Kosher salt and pepper
- 4 (10- to 12-ounce) whole trout, gutted, fins snipped off with scissors
- 2 tablespoons mayonnaise
- ½ teaspoon honey
- 1 (13 by 9-inch) disposable aluminum pan (if using charcoal)

1. Place marjoram, lemon zest, and 2 teaspoons salt on cutting board and chop until finely minced and well combined. Rinse each fish under cold running water and pat dry with paper towels inside and out. Open up each fish and sprinkle marjoram mixture evenly over flesh of fish. Season each fish with pepper. Close up fish and let stand for 10 minutes. Stir mayonnaise and honey together. Brush mayonnaise mixture evenly over entire exterior of each fish.

2A. FOR A CHARCOAL GRILL: Using kitchen shears, poke twelve ½-inch holes in bottom of disposable pan. Open bottom vent completely and place disposable pan in center of grill. Light large chimney starter two-thirds filled with charcoal briquettes (4 quarts). When top coals are partially covered with ash, pour into even layer in disposable pan. Set cooking grate over coals with bars parallel to long side of disposable pan, cover, and open lid vent completely. Heat grill until hot, about 5 minutes.

2B. FOR A GAS GRILL: Turn all burners to high, cover, and heat grill until hot, about 15 minutes. Leave all burners on high.

3. Clean and oil cooking grate. Grill fish (directly over coals if using charcoal and with lid closed if using gas) until skin is browned and beginning to blister, 2 to 4 minutes. Using thin metal spatula, lift bottom of thick backbone edge of fish from cooking grate just enough to slide second thin metal spatula under fish. Remove first spatula, then use it to support raw side of fish as you use second spatula to flip fish over. Grill until second side is browned, beginning to blister, and thickest part of fish registers 130 to 135 degrees, 2 to 4 minutes. Transfer fish to platter and let rest for 5 minutes. Serve with lemon wedges.

GRILLED WHOLE TROUT WITH LIME AND CORIANDER

Substitute 1 teaspoon ground coriander for marjoram, lime zest and wedges for lemon zest and wedges.

GRILLED WHOLE TROUT WITH ORANGE AND FENNEL

Substitute 1 teaspoon ground fennel for marjoram and orange zest for lemon zest.

Saving Succotash

Move over, limas. A new type of bean relieves this side dish of its suffering.

⋟ BY KEITH DRESSER ⋞

In 17th-century Plymouth, Massachusetts, Pilgrims and Native Americans frequently cooked up what was later referred to as "Plymouth succotash"—a stew of corn or hominy, dried beans, and bits of dried or fresh meat or fish. By the 19th century, succotash had evolved into the meatless side dish that we know today. But just because a dish boasts longevity doesn't mean that it's well liked. In fact, many folks crinkle their noses at the mention of succotash, since they have always known it as a dish of canned or frozen corn and lima beans swamped in a thick, dull cream sauce. This is a shame, since a quick, easy mix of crisp, sweet corn and creamy beans should be a summertime staple. I set out to modernize succotash by nixing the dull dairy and freshening up the lackluster vegetables.

The quality of the corn and beans would be crucial to success, so using fresh corn was a must. But fresh limas are hard to come by, so I tried alternatives—with no luck. Dried limas took hours to cook; frozen were inconsistent, as some cooked up creamy while others were grainy; and canned were unattractively washed out in flavor and color. But canned limas did boast a pleasant creamy texture that made me wonder if other canned beans might fare better.

After surveying the possibilities, I decided to try butter beans, which are closely related to limas. (Both beans are variants of the *Phaseolus lunatus* legume.) Sure enough, the larger butter beans offered mild flavor, decent looks, and the same appealing texture. After stripping the kernels from 4 ears of corn, I sautéed them in butter with the rinsed and drained beans. This warmed the beans through while retaining the crispness of the corn.

Purists say that true succotash contains only corn and beans. However, I found a lot of recipes that mixed in seasonal vegetables like eggplant, tomatoes, and squash. While the duo of beans and corn seemed too plain, a medley was too busy. Moderation was in order. An onion and two cloves of garlic provided a savory base; half a red bell pepper provided crispness and color; and final additions of minced parsley and lemon juice focused the freshness.

I was happy with the way the dish was shaping up but had one lingering concern: Without the traditional cream sauce to bind the ingredients, the dish resembled salsa instead of succotash. I tried "milking" the corn after removing the kernels by scraping the cob with the back of a knife, but there was never enough liquid to create a light coating for the vegetables. Mixing chicken broth with a little cornstarch did a better job of giving the dish some cohesion, but the chicken flavor was distracting. The cornstarch gave me an idea, though: I could add a splash of the starchy bean "broth" in the can—a sleeper ingredient we sometimes call on to lend body to bean soups and pasta dishes. Just 2 tablespoons delicately bound the ingredients and accentuated the bean taste without overpowering the other flavors.

With classic succotash flavors in place, I varied the recipe by swapping out the butter beans for a few alternative varieties—pink, pinto, and cannellini—as well as tweaking the vegetable and herb additions. The result is a handful of easy-to-prepare, fresh side dishes that should restore the status of succotash.

MODERN SUCCOTASH

SERVES 4 TO 6

Do not use frozen or canned corn in this dish.

- 1 (15-ounce) can butter beans, 2 tablespoons liquid reserved, rinsed
- 2 teaspoons lemon juice
- 3 tablespoons unsalted butter
- 1 small onion, chopped fine
- ½ red bell pepper, cut into ¼-inch pieces
- Salt and pepper
- 2 garlic cloves, minced
- Pinch cayenne pepper
- 4 ears corn, kernels cut from cobs (3 cups)
- 2 tablespoons minced fresh parsley

1. Stir reserved bean liquid and lemon juice together in small bowl; set aside. Melt butter in 12-inch nonstick skillet over medium-high heat. Add onion, bell pepper, and ½ teaspoon salt and cook, stirring frequently, until softened and beginning to brown, 4 to 5 minutes. Add garlic and cayenne and cook until fragrant, about 30 seconds.

2. Reduce heat to medium and add corn and beans. Cook, stirring occasionally, until corn and beans have cooked through, about 4 minutes. Add bean liquid mixture and cook, stirring constantly, for 1 minute. Remove skillet from heat, stir in parsley, and season with salt and pepper to taste. Serve.

MODERN SUCCOTASH WITH FENNEL AND SCALLIONS

Thinly slice white and green parts of 4 scallions on bias. Substitute cannellini beans for butter beans; 1 fennel bulb, cut into ¼-inch pieces, and scallion whites for onion and bell pepper; ¼ teaspoon ground fennel for cayenne; and scallion greens for parsley.

The secret to our fresh, light succotash comes in a can.

MODERN SUCCOTASH WITH LEEKS AND BLACK PEPPER

Substitute pink beans for butter beans; 1 leek, white and light green parts halved lengthwise, sliced thin, and washed, for onion and bell pepper; 1 teaspoon pepper for cayenne; and 3 tablespoons minced chives for parsley.

MODERN SUCCOTASH WITH POBLANO, BACON, AND CILANTRO

Substitute pinto beans for butter beans and lime juice for lemon juice. Cook 2 slices chopped bacon in 12-inch nonstick skillet over medium-high heat, stirring occasionally, until crisp, 5 to 7 minutes. Using slotted spoon, transfer bacon to paper towel–lined plate and set aside. Reduce butter to 2 tablespoons and add it to fat in skillet. Proceed with recipe, substituting poblano chile for bell pepper, ¼ teaspoon ground coriander for cayenne, and cilantro for parsley. Sprinkle with reserved bacon before serving.

Keith Saves Succotash
Video available free for 4 months at CooksIllustrated.com/aug15

The Best Way to Roast Tomatoes

Our method concentrates the flavor of peak-season and supermarket tomatoes alike.

BY LAN LAM

If you've never roasted tomatoes, you should. It's a largely hands-off technique that yields the ultimate condiment: bright, concentrated tomatoes that are soft but retain their shape. They can be used right away or frozen, and they perk up just about any dish—from sandwiches and crostini to pastas and salads.

And yet I rarely roast tomatoes because most recipes take hours, which is no fun on a hot day. Faster recipes yield pulpy, bland results—an unappealing phase between raw and roasted. I wanted bright-tasting, soft-but-intact tomatoes in less time.

I started with larger round tomatoes, which boast a higher ratio of the flavorful "jelly" to skin than do the denser plum variety, and a lower ratio of chewy skin than smaller cherry or grape tomatoes. And since the main goal of roasting tomatoes is to burn off much of their moisture, I sliced them into ¾-inch-thick rounds—a shape that maximized their surface area for efficient evaporation and allowed me to fit 3 pounds in a single layer on a foil-lined rimmed baking sheet.

I drizzled the slices with a couple of tablespoons of extra-virgin olive oil, sprinkled them with kosher salt and pepper, and slid them into a 300-degree oven, hoping the low temperature would dry them out gradually without burning. But gradual was an understatement. They took about 5 hours to collapse and shrivel sufficiently and made almost no progress during the first hour because in the low oven, the water inside them evaporated slowly.

What they needed was a blast of heat to get them hotter faster, so for the next batch I cranked the oven temperature to 425 degrees. Half an hour in, their edges were nicely dried out—good progress. Then to keep them from burning, I dropped the temperature back to 300 degrees, propped open the oven door so that the oven cooled quickly, and flipped them so they'd cook evenly. That brought the cooking time down to just under 4 hours, but I wanted to cut the time more.

Great Uses for Roasted Tomatoes

Savory-sweet roasted tomatoes can punch up countless dishes:

TOPPINGS Sandwiches, crostini, pizza, polenta, scrambled eggs

MIX-INS Frittata, quiche, pasta, deli salads, bread dough

DRESSING During roasting, the oil picks up concentrated flavor that makes it great for whisking into salad dressings; drizzling over meat, fish, vegetables, or pasta; or using as a dip for crusty bread.

See How They Change
Video available free for 4 months at CooksIllustrated.com/aug15

I'd seen a few recipes that called for not just coating but submerging the tomatoes in oil. When I thought about it, I realized that because oil is more efficient than air at transferring heat, the tomatoes would probably cook faster. Sure enough, when I roasted the next batch in 1 cup of oil, they cooked up nicely concentrated and caramelized in about 2 hours. The only problem: A full cup of oil filled the sheet pan to the rim, making it difficult to maneuver. Scaling back to ¾ cup made handling easier and prolonged the roasting time by only about a half-hour.

A quick tweak—scattering the tomatoes with garlic cloves and dried oregano before roasting—added just enough fragrance and flavor. In fact, the results were so good with farmers' market tomatoes that I tried my method with supermarket specimens and was thrilled when it rendered these blander fruits sweet-savory and concentrated.

ROASTED TOMATOES

MAKES 1½ CUPS

Avoid using tomatoes smaller than 3 inches in diameter, which have a smaller ratio of flavorful jelly to skin than larger tomatoes. To double the recipe, use two baking sheets, increase the baking time in step 2 to 40 minutes, and rotate and switch the sheets halfway through baking. In step 3, increase the roasting time to 1½ to 2½ hours. For our free recipe for Chunky Roasted Tomato Sauce, go to CooksIllustrated.com/aug15.

- 3 pounds large tomatoes, cored, bottom ⅛ inch trimmed, and sliced ¾ inch thick
- 2 garlic cloves, peeled and smashed
- ¼ teaspoon dried oregano
- Kosher salt and pepper
- ¾ cup extra-virgin olive oil

1. Adjust oven rack to middle position and heat oven to 425 degrees. Line rimmed baking sheet with aluminum foil. Arrange tomatoes in even layer on prepared sheet, with larger slices around edge and smaller slices in center. Place garlic cloves on tomatoes. Sprinkle with oregano and ¼ teaspoon salt and season with pepper to taste. Drizzle oil evenly over tomatoes.

For the best flavor and texture, roast large tomatoes.

2. Bake for 30 minutes, rotating sheet halfway through baking. Remove sheet from oven. Reduce oven temperature to 300 degrees and prop open door with wooden spoon to cool oven. Using thin spatula, flip tomatoes.

3. Return tomatoes to oven and continue to cook until spotty brown, skins are blistered, and tomatoes have collapsed to ¼ to ½ inch thick, 1 to 2 hours. Remove from oven and let cool completely, about 30 minutes. Discard garlic and transfer tomatoes and oil to airtight container. (Tomatoes can be refrigerated for up to 5 days or frozen for up to 2 months.)

ROASTED TOMATO RELISH

MAKES 1¼ CUPS

Use this relish to top bruschetta, chicken, or pork tenderloin or to dress up scrambled eggs or polenta.

- 1 cup Roasted Tomatoes, chopped coarse, plus 1 tablespoon reserved tomato oil
- 1 small shallot, minced
- ¼ cup chopped fresh cilantro
- ¾ teaspoon red wine vinegar
- ½ teaspoon capers, rinsed and minced
- Salt and pepper

Combine all ingredients in bowl and season with salt and pepper to taste.

Israeli Couscous Salads

These pasta pearls can revitalize a picnic salad—but first you have to cook them right.

⋟ BY ERIN McMURRER ⋞

When a recession hit Israel in the early 1950s, rice—a kitchen staple—became scarce. In response, prime minister David Ben-Gurion called on food manufacturers to develop a wheat-based alternative. The result was the dense, pasta-like spheres called *ptitim* or, outside Israel, Israeli couscous. Like tiny, granular North African couscous, the Israeli kind is made from semolina flour, but the latter boasts smooth, tapioca-size spheres and a pleasant chew. The little balls are produced in the same way that Italian pasta is made: by forcing dough through an extruding machine. But unlike most pasta, which is air-dried, Israeli couscous is traditionally dried over a flame, giving it toasty, rich flavor.

That flavor, plus its springy, toothsome texture, makes Israeli couscous a fresh choice for pasta salad, offering an alternative to customary shapes like fusilli or penne. The only real barrier is that the compact spheres are tricky to cook just right.

Whereas North African couscous is so minuscule that it can be hydrated with boiling water off heat, the Israeli kind needs to spend time on the stove. After reviewing package directions and paging through cookbooks, I noted two possible techniques. For the less common pasta method, the couscous is boiled and then drained. But when I tried this, it yielded spheres that overcooked and turned gummy on the exterior before the interior had a chance to become tender. The other option, the absorption method, seemed more promising, since it calls for slowly simmering the couscous in a measured amount of water that is entirely soaked up during cooking. Sure enough, this gentler approach produced more consistent results. After some tinkering, I determined that a 1:1¼ couscous-to-water ratio was ideal. To ensure perfectly even cooking, I stirred the pot occasionally during simmering and then let the couscous stand covered off heat for 3 minutes.

Before moving on, I briefly backtracked and tried toasting the couscous in fat before adding the water—a technique known as the pilaf method. This was well worth the effort, as the fat accentuated the unique nuttiness of the pearls. Oil was best since butter tended to solidify once the orbs cooled enough to be incorporated into a salad.

Although my tender-chewy Israeli couscous was good enough to eat warm as a simple side dish, I needed to quickly cool it down to use in salad. To do so, I spread it into a single layer on a baking sheet. (When left to cool in a bowl, it continued to steam and became mushy in spots.)

I mixed the cooled couscous with a basic vinaigrette, but it was far too mild. I bumped up the acid, eventually using equal parts acid and oil to dress the starchy orbs. Next came plenty of fragrant herbs, along with fresh vegetables and salty cheese. Whereas many pasta salads include large, chunky mix-ins, I chopped the ingredients small to ensure that each bite contained a balance of flavors and textures. With a sprinkling of crunchy toasted nuts on top, these salads were ready for backyard parties, potlucks, or even as a standalone for a simple meal.

Erin Makes It Clear
Video available free for 4 months at CooksIllustrated.com/aug15

SIMPLE ISRAELI COUSCOUS
MAKES ABOUT 4 CUPS

The warm couscous can be tossed with butter or extra-virgin olive oil and salt and pepper for a side dish or cooled and used in a salad. If you're making a salad, transfer the couscous to a rimmed baking sheet and let it cool completely, about 15 minutes. Our favorite brand of Israeli couscous is Roland (for more information, see page 28).

- 2 cups Israeli couscous
- 1 tablespoon extra-virgin olive oil
- 2½ cups water
- ½ teaspoon salt

Heat couscous and oil in medium saucepan over medium heat, stirring frequently, until about half of grains are golden brown, 5 to 6 minutes. Add water and salt; stir to combine. Increase heat to high and bring to boil. Reduce heat to medium-low, cover, and simmer, stirring occasionally, until water is absorbed, 9 to 12 minutes. Remove saucepan from heat and let stand, covered, for 3 minutes. Serve.

ISRAELI COUSCOUS WITH LEMON, MINT, PEAS, FETA, AND PICKLED SHALLOTS
SERVES 6

For efficiency, let the shallots pickle while you prepare the remaining ingredients. For our free recipes for Israeli Couscous with Tomatoes, Olives, and Ricotta Salata and Israeli Couscous with Radishes and Watercress, go to CooksIllustrated.com/aug15.

For rich flavor, toast the couscous before adding water.

- ⅓ cup red wine vinegar
- 2 tablespoons sugar
- Salt and pepper
- 2 shallots, sliced thin
- 3 tablespoons extra-virgin olive oil
- 3 tablespoons lemon juice
- 1 teaspoon Dijon mustard
- ⅛ teaspoon red pepper flakes
- 1 recipe Simple Israeli Couscous, cooled
- 4 ounces (4 cups) baby arugula, roughly chopped
- 1 cup fresh mint leaves, torn
- ½ cup frozen peas, thawed
- ½ cup shelled pistachios, toasted and chopped
- 3 ounces feta cheese, crumbled (¾ cup)

1. Bring vinegar, sugar, and pinch salt to simmer in small saucepan over medium-high heat, stirring occasionally, until sugar dissolves. Add shallots and stir to combine. Cover and let cool completely, about 30 minutes. Drain and discard liquid.

2. Whisk oil, lemon juice, mustard, pepper flakes, and ⅛ teaspoon salt together in large bowl. Add cooled couscous, arugula, mint, peas, 6 tablespoons pistachios, ½ cup feta, and shallots and toss to combine. Season with salt and pepper to taste and transfer to serving bowl. Let stand for 5 minutes. Sprinkle with remaining ¼ cup feta and remaining 2 tablespoons pistachios and serve.

Next-Generation Knife Sharpeners

What if you could buy a sharpener that not only repaired the new breed of ultrathin chef's knives but also honed the wider cutting edge of more traditional blades?

⪢ BY HANNAH CROWLEY ⪡

Japanese bladesmiths have long favored chef's-style knives with blades that are ultraslim—that is, sharpened to about 15 degrees on either side of the blade—and for good reason: In addition to being thin and lightweight, these blades have a supernarrow cutting edge, which helps make them razor-sharp. We've also come to favor a thinner edge. After years of testing dozens of knives, our repeat favorite is from Victorinox, a Swiss-made knife that is sharpened to 15 degrees on either side of the edge, allowing it to push and slide through food more easily than do more traditional European blades sharpened to at least 20 degrees.

To maintain that narrow edge, we use a tool specifically designed to sharpen a blade to 15 degrees. Our favorite models, both from Chef'sChoice, are a manual and an electric sharpener that each do a fine job of restoring an ultrakeen edge to an Asian-style knife. But in recent years the trend toward slimmer knives—and slimmer knife sharpeners—has spread west, as European manufacturers including Wüsthof, Henckels, Messermeister, and Mercer have launched their own 15-degree knives and sharpeners. (In fact, Wüsthof and Henckels have discontinued their 20-degree knives.) We were curious to see what these new sharpeners had to offer—and were especially eager to test the claim of one that it can even hone a 20-degree knife to 15 degrees.

As part of our testing process, we dulled and sharpened knives five times.

So we rounded up nine models (including our previous favorites), five manual and four electric, from both Western and Asian manufacturers and priced from roughly $20 to $200. To evaluate them, we bought nine of our favorite Victorinox chef's knives and assigned one to each sharpener; we then dulled the knives identically and sharpened them according to manufacturer instructions. To assess sharpness, we slashed sheets of copy paper and sliced delicate tomatoes, repeating the dulling, sharpening, and slicing process four more times with multiple testers (for more information, see "Testing Knife Sharpness" on page 31).

Material World

All knife sharpeners work similarly: The user repeatedly drags the blade against an abrasive surface at a set angle, which trims and reshapes the blade by removing microscopic amounts of metal that are blunted or too far out of alignment. (Honing a blade on a steel is for knives that are less dull, as it simply repositions metal that is only slightly out of alignment.) With electric sharpeners, the abrasives are on motorized wheels that spin against the blade; with manual sharpeners, they're either on nonmotorized wheels or the abrasive material itself is fashioned into a V-shaped chamber through which the user pulls the knife.

Despite sharing similar mechanisms, the sharpeners we tested produced dramatically varied results. There were differences in user-friendliness: Some came with unintuitive directions and designs or fussy cleaning requirements; others made jarring vibrations or piercing grinding noises. We docked points for all these flaws.

But what really divided the pack was how sharp—or not—the knives were after we sharpened them. Some models barely restored the knife's edge and others actually damaged it, rendering it uneven or jagged so that the knife struggled when it came in contact with the food. And then there were the best sharpeners, which put such a keen edge on the blade that it felt sharper than it did out of the box.

We first checked to see if electric and manual sharpeners performed comparably—and for routine sharpening, they did. (Repairing deep nicks was another story; more on that later.) It wasn't until we examined the inner workings of the sharpeners that we realized that two key factors were determining how effectively they sharpened.

First, the type of abrasive. The models we tested used three different kinds: carbides (a combination of metal and carbon), ceramic, and diamond. Our least favorite models featured carbides or ceramic, materials that proved problematic in part because they have what Mike Tarkanian at the Massachusetts Institute of Technology's Department of Materials Science and Engineering calls a "high coefficiency of friction." This means that they are relatively sticky and grab at the surface of the blade more than diamond does. As a result, sharpeners made of these materials rough up the surface of the blade, making it move through food less efficiently. In addition, ceramic and carbides are also softer than diamonds and degrade more quickly, shortening the life span of the sharpener; in fact, the ceramic wheels on the electric Shun sharpener sent up a puff of white dust every time we pulled the blade through its chamber.

Diamond, on the other hand, is the hardest

Bad to the Blade

To get a closer look at how well—and poorly—the sharpeners performed, we examined the sharpest and dullest knives under a high-powered laboratory microscope at the Massachusetts Institute of Technology's Department of Materials Science and Engineering.

SMOOTH AND SHARP
Chef'sChoice Trizor XV

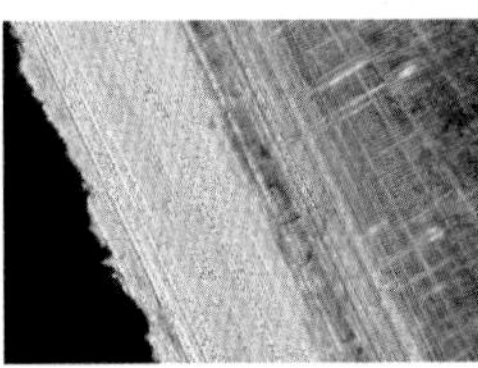

ALL CHEWED UP
Kuhn Rikon

Clean, precise cuts like these are particularly easy with a razor-sharp, 15-degree edge.

Manual or Electric? It's a Personal Choice

Our two favorite sharpeners from Chef'sChoice, one manual and one electric, are both fitted with strong, durable diamond abrasives that produce sharp, smooth edges. They're also dead easy to use. Which one you pick depends on your needs and your budget.

HANDY AND AFFORDABLE

Chef'sChoice Pronto Manual Diamond Hone Asian Knife Sharpener ($49.99)

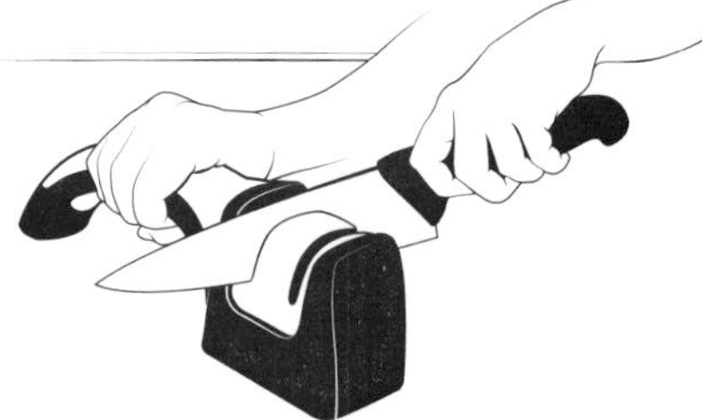

High Sides
Tall walls hold the knife steady so that the user can draw the blade through the chamber with even pressure.

Compact Design
The slim body easily stows in a drawer, making it more convenient for routine upkeep.

HIGH-POWERED, HIGH-PRICED

Chef'sChoice Trizor XV Knife Sharpener ($149.99)

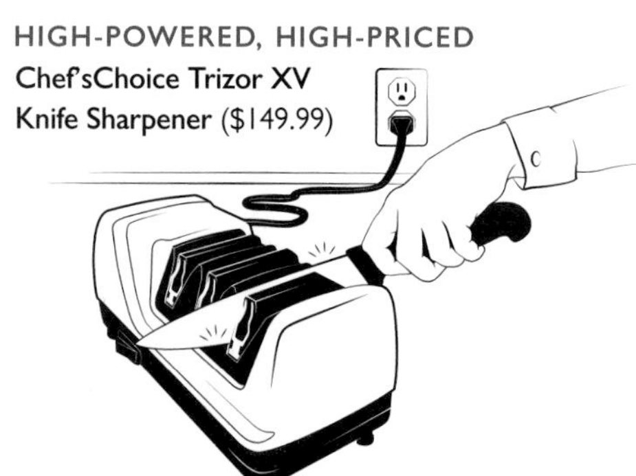

Supportive Chambers
Spring-loaded guides restrict the knife's movement so that the entire edge makes steady contact with the abrasive at a precise angle.

Angle Conversion Slot
The aggressive first slot can quickly repair extensive damage and narrow a 20-degree Western knife to a sharper 15-degree edge.

Angling for a Sharper Edge

The manufacturers advertise that the aggressive first slot on the Chef'sChoice Trizor XV can narrow the angle of a 20-degree Western blade to 15 degrees—a function that would make this pricey model worth considering even if you don't own a 15-degree knife.

We tested that claim by running a brand-new 20-degree chef's knife through the Trizor for 20 strokes on either side of the blade (per manufacturer's directions). We then compared its sharpness to a second new copy of that knife, as well as a new copy of our favorite 15-degree chef's knife from Victorinox, by having multiple testers slice through crates of produce. The results were convincing: Testers reported that the copy with the narrowed edge felt noticeably sharper than its sibling and almost as sharp as the 15-degree Victorinox.

DEGREES OF SHARPNESS

When manufacturers report that a knife has a 15- or 20-degree angle, they're referring to the angle of the bevel—the slim strip on either side of the blade that narrows to form the cutting edge. The more acute that angle, the sharper the blade will feel.

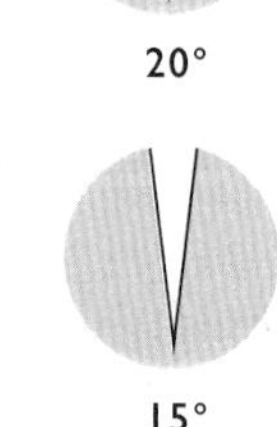

20°

15°

BEVEL

Lisa Explains It All
Video available free for 4 months at CooksIllustrated.com/aug15

material in the world, which makes it strong and durable for sharpening. Its coefficiency of friction is also relatively low, which allows it to glide smoothly over a knife blade as it sharpens and thus produce a smoother, sharper edge.

In Chambers

The second factor affecting sharpness was the design of the sharpening chamber. For the abrasive to put a consistently smooth edge on the entire blade, the blade must move through the chamber as steadily as possible; if there's any wiggle room, the blade can shift position slightly from stroke to stroke and emerge unevenly sharpened. The Wüsthof, Victorinox, and Kuhn Rikon sharpeners, for example, all had poor blade support, so testers naturally eased up on pressure when the blades were almost through their chambers, lest they push the blades off the sharpeners and onto the counter. As a result, the knives assigned to these sharpeners had noticeably duller tips that couldn't cut through paper and squashed tomatoes flat. Examining the blades under a high-powered microscope at MIT confirmed that they were utterly ragged from all that wobbling (see "Bad to the Blade").

The best designs came from Chef'sChoice. Both of its electric models feature spring-loaded guides in their chambers that supported the entire edge, allowing for smooth, consistent contact with the abrasive; on its manual model, the company built high sides that held the blade at a precise, secure angle so that testers could draw it through the chamber with even pressure.

Power Hungry?

With diamond abrasives, supportive chambers, and intuitive design, all three Chef'sChoice models (two electric and one manual) put razor-sharp edges on very dull knives and were easy to use. But whether you buy a manual or electric model depends on your needs and personal preferences. Manual sharpeners are smaller, lighter, cheaper—our repeat top-rated Chef'sChoice Pronto Manual Diamond Hone Asian Knife Sharpener costs about $50—and easier to store. They also don't need to be unpacked and plugged in for use, making them a more convenient option for routine upkeep.

But what even the best manual sharpener can't do is repair extensive damage to a blade. When we filed two identical notches into the ends of each knife and then ran them through their respective sharpeners, the winning manual Chef'sChoice hadn't made much progress after 300 strokes. But since the electric models put the abrasive in contact with the blade at a much higher speed, they quickly repaired the damage, giving them a distinct advantage over manual models. Our winning electric model, the Chef'sChoice Trizor XV ($149.99)—the only model to feature a dedicated slot for heavy damage—required only 76 strokes to make a severely damaged knife look and cut like a brand-new blade. Meanwhile, the runner-up electric model, the Chef'sChoice Diamond Sharpener for Asian Knives ($79.99) got the job done in about 220 strokes.

While the Trizor does have a hefty price tag, its heavy damage slot offers another compelling reason to buy it, even if you don't own a 15-degree knife: As advertised, it can indeed narrow the angle of a traditional Western blade, converting it from 20 degrees to 15 (see "Angling for a Sharper Edge"). With this ability, it may just be the last sharpener you'll ever need to buy.

KEY

Good ★★★
Fair ★★
Poor ★

TESTING KNIFE SHARPENERS

We tested nine knife sharpeners, four electric and five manual. Models are listed in order of preference. All were purchased online.

ROUTINE SHARPENING
We bought new copies of our winning chef's knife, the Victorinox 8" Swiss Army Fibrox, and assigned one to each sharpener. We dulled them identically and sharpened each according to manufacturer instructions. To rate their sharpness, we slashed sheets of paper and sliced tomatoes and then repeated the dulling, sharpening, and slicing process four more times with different testers. Those that made clean cuts without crumpling the paper or damaging the fruit rated highest.

NOTCH REMOVAL
We filed notches in both ends of each blade and ran them through their respective electric sharpeners (manual models could not remove notches), timing how long—and counting the number of strokes—it took to repair the damage.

DESIGN
Sharpeners that had clear, precise instructions, were intuitive to use, and cleaned up easily rated highest.

ELECTRIC

HIGHLY RECOMMENDED

	CRITERIA		TESTERS' COMMENTS
CHEF'SCHOICE Trizor XV Knife Sharpener **Model:** 15 **Price:** $149.99 **Abrasive:** Diamond 	Routine Sharpening Notch Removal Design	★★★ ★★★ ★★★	With diamond abrasives and a spring-loaded chamber that precisely and gently guided the blade, this sharpener "purred" with perfection, consistently producing edges that were sharper than on brand-new knives from edge to tip. "I'm cutting this paper into confetti," said one tester. It was the only sharpener to quickly remove nicks in the blade; in 10 minutes, a severely damaged knife looked and cut like a brand-new blade. A big perk: It can convert a 20-degree edge to a sharper 15 degrees.

RECOMMENDED

CHEF'SCHOICE Diamond Sharpener for Asian Knives (BEST BUY) **Model:** 316 **Price:** $79.99 **Abrasive:** Diamond 	Routine Sharpening Notch Removal Design	★★½ ★★ ★★★	Also fitted with diamond abrasives and a spring-loaded chamber that "cradled" the blade, our previous recommended electric 15-degree sharpener was quick and easy to use. It wasn't quite as effective at sharpening as its winning sibling—the blade dragged just a bit when cutting paper—but the result was comparable to the factory-sharpened edge. It removed nicks in the blade, though it took 30 minutes and a tiring 223 swipes.

NOT RECOMMENDED

KITCHEN IQ Angle Adjust Adjustable Electric Knife Sharpener **Model:** 50353 **Price:** $199.99 **Abrasive:** Diamond and ceramic	Routine Sharpening Notch Removal Design	★½ ★★★ ★★	This electric sharpener's adjustable knob sets the edge angle anywhere from 10 to 30 degrees per side for different types of knives. But its vibrating motor, which felt as if it was "kicking the knife around" was problematic. The tip ricocheted back and forth out of the slot, which dented it badly. With these flaws, we didn't care that it removed nicks in 96 strokes.
SHUN Electric Sharpener **Model:** AP0119 **Price:** $79.95 **Abrasive:** Ceramic 	Routine Sharpening Notch Removal Design	★½ ★★ ★★	Though this model put a reasonably sharp edge on the knife, it worked too aggressively: Not only did it remove an alarming 3 grams of metal from the blade after four rounds of sharpening (other models removed statistically insignificant amounts), but its ceramic wheels sprayed dust as it worked, making us question its durability. It left a zipper-like pattern on the blade and was the only model you have to clean each time after using. Removing nicks from the knife's edge took longer than 30 minutes.

MANUAL

RECOMMENDED

	CRITERIA		TESTERS' COMMENTS
CHEF'SCHOICE Pronto Manual Diamond Hone Asian Knife Sharpener **Model:** 463 **Price:** $49.99 **Abrasive:** Diamond	Routine Sharpening Notch Removal Design	★★½ N/A ★★★	Our previous favorite manual sharpener quickly and easily restores a razor-sharp edge to blades that have no serious damage. Its high guides ensured that the blade met the abrasive at a precise and secure angle so we could put even pressure along the entire edge. The handle was grippy and comfortable, "anchoring itself in your hand," and the tool can easily be stored in a drawer.

RECOMMENDED WITH RESERVATIONS

VICTORINOX SwissSharp **Model:** 49002 **Price:** $32.40 **Abrasive:** Carbide	Routine Sharpening Notch Removal Design	★★ N/A ★★	This sharpener put a decent edge on the knife, was quick to operate, and was compact enough to stow in a drawer. The blade teetered back and forth in the V-shaped chamber; when we looked at it microscopically, it showed a wavy, irregular edge.

NOT RECOMMENDED

MIYABI 2-Stage Diamond/Ceramic Handheld Knife Sharpener **Model:** 34536-007 **Price:** $49.99 **Abrasive:** Diamond, ceramic polishing slot	Routine Sharpening Notch Removal Design	★★ N/A ★	This sharpener secured the knife at a precise angle and produced an acceptably sharp edge. But its lightweight plastic body felt cheap and was scratched up after only a few uses, and its tall plastic case blocked the last ½ inch of the knife's heel from contacting the sharpening wheel, which would eventually create a misshapen edge. For the same price, the manual Chef'sChoice sharpener is a much better product.
WÜSTHOF Two Stage Hand-Held Sharpener **Model:** 2922 **Price:** $19.99 **Abrasive:** Carbide	Routine Sharpening Notch Removal Design	★½ N/A ★	This sharpener was sturdy to hold but didn't secure the knife because its ⅛ inch of extra space at the top of its chamber allowed the knife to teeter as it slid over the abrasives. That extra space forced testers to ease up on pressure as they pulled the knife through the chamber (lest they push too hard and have the knife clunk down on the counter as it slid out of the chamber), which made for an inconsistent edge.
KUHN RIKON Dual Knife Sharpener **Model:** 2949 (black) **Price:** $19.50 **Abrasive:** Ceramic 	Routine Sharpening Notch Removal Design	★ N/A ★	Because this model didn't support even pressure along the length of the blade, the knife never got very sharp; under a microscope, it looked jagged and rutted at the tip and heel. Instructions were unintuitive, and pronounced ridges on the handle dug into our hands.

Supermarket Balsamic, Unmasked

In recent years, Italy has created a new set of guidelines for mass-produced balsamic vinegar. We wanted to know if these new laws guarantee a better-quality product.

BY KATE SHANNON

The first thing to understand when you set out to buy balsamic vinegar at the grocery store is that it has little to do with the traditionally made, name-protected Italian artisanal product called *aceto balsamico tradizionale*. It's not even made for the same purpose. The traditional stuff is a small-batch, long-aged product that bears a *Denominazione di Origine Protetta* (DOP) seal indicating use of locally grown ingredients and adherence to strict guidelines. Costing as much as $250 for a tiny 3.4-ounce bottle, it's meant to be drizzled sparingly over steak or strawberries—or even sipped. Masking its flavors in vinaigrette or burning them off in a cooked application would be a tragic mistake.

That's where the supermarket stuff comes in. This inexpensive mass-produced product is designed for salad dressing or to make a sweet-tart reduction to drizzle over vegetables or grilled meats. While its flavor isn't anywhere near as complex as traditional balsamic, it can still have a pleasing fruity bite, which makes it a staple in most American kitchens.

Since we last tasted supermarket balsamic vinegar in 2007, a new certification process for this product has been put in place. Vinegars that are produced in either Reggio Emilia or Modena (the only two provinces where traditional balsamic can be made) and follow certain other guidelines can call themselves "balsamic vinegar of Modena" and bear an *Indicazione Geografica Protetta*, or IGP, seal on their labels. Curious if this certification process would raise the standards and give us a better supermarket option at the same affordable price, we rounded up nine widely available balsamic vinegars of Modena with an IGP seal (including our former winner), all sold for no more than $15 a bottle, and conducted a series of blind taste tests. We sampled them plain, whisked into vinaigrette, and reduced to make a quick glaze that we served over asparagus.

The In-Between Balsamic

For drizzling, midrange balsamics can be a great alternative to expensive traditional balsamics.

Inexpensive supermarket balsamic is best for everyday use, while costly traditional vinegar should be reserved for drizzling on berries, steaks, or a good cheese. But there's another category of balsamic vinegar, sold in specialty shops and some supermarkets, that falls between the two. Many of these vinegars hold themselves to a higher standard, including adding less wine vinegar and aging longer. We bought three bottles of these midrange balsamics (La Vecchia Dispensa Organic Condiment, San Giacomo Essenza Riserve Balsamic, and Oliviers & Co. Velluto Balsamic Condiment), priced between $4 and $10 per ounce, recommended by a local gourmet shop. We tried them plain, drizzled on berries, and in vinaigrette.

Straight out of the bottle we noticed that they had a syrupy consistency closer to that of traditional vinegar, and when we drizzled them over berries, tasters actually deemed their consistency, honeyed sweetness, and fruity complexity a surprisingly close approximation of 25-year-aged *tradizionale*, though the nuances of each vinegar varied a bit. But also like a traditional balsamic, these midrange vinegars were ill-suited to vinaigrette—the dressings made with them were all sticky and gloppy, more like a tart caramel sauce than a salad dressing. This is because like the traditional balsamics, these vinegars have more of what are known as polymeric pigments, which form gel-like droplets with oil, than supermarket vinegars. Our recommendation? For use as an everyday ingredient in dressings and cooking, opt for balsamic vinegar of Modena from the supermarket. But if you want a vinegar that can affordably do the job of the pricey traditional vinegar, these midprice balsamics are a great option. Because the flavor and consistency can vary from brand to brand, ask for recommendations at your local gourmet shop.

When it comes to making a vinaigrette, stick with supermarket balsamics; anything pricier will make a gloppy mess.

Label Laws

Straight from the bottles, the vinegars ranged from nearly as thick as traditional balsamic to as watery and thin as distilled white vinegar. The plain tasting revealed a similarly wide array of flavors. The best versions tasted of caramelized sugar or roasted fruit and had a smooth, pleasant tang; others had a fake, candy-like sweetness or, at the opposite end of the spectrum, tasted harshly acidic. We were puzzled. How could all these products qualify under the exact same standards?

We did a little investigating and discovered that the guidelines governing the use of the seal are pretty loose. IGP laws do outline a list of approved ingredients—namely, that the vinegar begin with the must (the skin, seeds, and juice) from select native Italian grape varietals. But they require that only 20 percent of the finished product consist of grape must (compared with the 100 percent required for traditional balsamic). So what makes up the remaining 80 percent? Regular wine vinegar made anywhere. Second, although some aging is mandatory, 60 days are all that's required—a far cry from traditional vinegar's 12-year minimum. And finally, while production must take place within Reggio Emilia or Modena and certain varieties of grapes are required, the grapes can be grown anywhere in the world.

But here's the kicker: Unlike batches of traditional balsamic vinegar, which are subjected to a final taste test so rigorous that roughly 20 percent of submissions fail it, nearly every vat of vinegar that follows the loose IGP rules for production becomes certified, explaining the wide range we'd observed in our tastings.

Ferreting Out a Winner

We now knew why vinegars bearing the IGP seal could taste so different. And yet we couldn't find a trend in our plain tasting results that connected our preferences to any particular manufacturing

Seal of Quality?

Just as high-end traditional vinegars bear the DOP (*Denominazione di Origine Protetta*) seal, some supermarket balsamics bear the name-protected IGP (*Indicazione Geografica Protetta*) seal. But don't be fooled. While this IGP designation seems like it's lending credibility, we learned that the rules are very loose.

TASTING SUPERMARKET BALSAMIC

Twenty-one *Cook's Illustrated* staff members sampled nine top-selling balsamic vinegars of Modena with *Indicazione Geografica Protetta*, or IGP, certification. We tasted our lineup plain, in vinaigrette, and as a glaze over asparagus to assess flavor, consistency, and overall appeal. Ingredients are based on label information. Results were averaged and products appear below in order of preference.

RECOMMENDED

BERTOLLI Balsamic Vinegar of Modena
Ingredients: Wine vinegar, concentrated grape must, cooked grape must, caramel color, antioxidant: sulphites
Price: $3.49 for 8.5 fl oz ($0.41 per fl oz)
Comments: Served plain, this balsamic vinegar tasted of dried fruit like figs, raisins, and prunes. Some of these nuances disappeared once it was reduced or whisked into vinaigrette, but it still tasted pleasantly sweet. While its texture was fairly thin, its flavor earned high marks in the dressing and the glaze.

MONARI FEDERZONI Balsamic Vinegar of Modena
Ingredients: Wine vinegar, concentrated grape must, caramel color, contains sulfites
Price: $2.50 for 16.9 fl oz ($0.15 per fl oz)
Comments: Tasters praised the consistency of this vinegar, which was viscous but not too thick to coat greens or asparagus. It had a bright acidity and "nice fruit flavor" that made for a sweet glaze and boasted hints of blueberries and wine when served plain.

COLAVITA Balsamic Vinegar of Modena
Ingredients: Wine vinegar, concentrated grape must, caramel color, contains sulfites
Price: $2.99 for 17 fl oz ($0.18 per fl oz)
Comments: Although some tasters noted harshness in this vinegar when sampling it plain, this was tempered to a "nice bite" in vinaigrette and glaze. In those applications, a fruity sweetness came to the forefront. As one taster said, "It's perfectly balanced."

ORTALLI Balsamic Vinegar of Modena
Ingredients: Wine vinegar, cooked grape must, caramel color, contains sulfites
Price: $6.69 for 16.9 fl oz ($0.40 per fl oz)
Comments: Tasters approved of the full and "balanced" flavors of this balsamic. Plain, it tasted of cooked fruit; in vinaigrette and glaze, it showcased flavors of plum, honey, and molasses. Although it was a little thin in body even when reduced, its rich flavor and pleasant acidity more than made up for it.

BELLINO Balsamic Vinegar of Modena
Ingredients: Wine vinegar, concentrated grape must, caramel color, contains sulfites
Price: $5.49 for 16.9 fl oz ($0.32 per fl oz)
Comments: This vinegar consistently scored in the middle of the lineup. Although it was both sweet and acidic, it lacked complexity and was deemed "not outstanding," even a bit "boring." It showed to its best advantage in the vinaigrette, where its sweet start and pleasantly bright finish made it a crowd-pleaser.

RECOMMENDED CONTINUED

LUCINI Aged Balsamic Vinegar of Modena
Ingredients: Contains sulfites from grapes
Price: $13.99 for 8.5 fl oz ($1.65 per fl oz)
Comments: The only aged product in our lineup, this vinegar was so viscous and thick when tasted plain that tasters compared it with port and dessert wine. Whisked in vinaigrette and reduced to a glaze, it became sticky and syrupy—appealing to some tasters, but overwhelming to others. Although the label does not list the ingredients, the company confirmed that it uses a mix of grape must and wine vinegar.

RECOMMENDED WITH RESERVATIONS

STAR Balsamic Vinegar of Modena
Ingredients: Wine vinegar, concentrated grape must, boiled grape must, caramel color, potassium metabisulfite as a preservative
Price: $2.99 for 8.5 fl oz ($0.35 per fl oz)
Comments: Though this vinegar earned some favorable reviews, we still have reservations. Namely: It was too sharp and "puckery" when tasted plain and maintained its harshness even when reduced to a glaze. What we did like: a consistency that was pleasantly thick in vinaigrette and became "syrupy" when reduced.

CENTO Balsamic Vinegar of Modena
Ingredients: Wine vinegar, concentrated grape must, caramel E 150d, antioxidant: (sulfites) E 224
Price: $3.49 for 16.9 fl oz ($0.21 per fl oz)
Comments: At our plain tasting, the berry notes of this vinegar drew comparisons to candy, juice, and even Kool-Aid. Similar comments came up during the vinaigrette tasting: "like jelly candy." It was also panned for being harsh and "astringent," with "an assertive and unpleasant bite, like alcohol." It mellowed to an acceptable level of fruitiness when reduced to a glaze. As for the consistency, it scored in the middle of the pack straight from the bottle and became "nice and thick" when reduced or whisked in vinaigrette.

DE NIGRIS Balsamic Vinegar of Modena, White Eagle
Ingredients: Wine vinegar, concentrated grape must, caramel, contains sulfites
Price: $5.49 for 16.9 fl oz ($0.32 per fl oz)
Comments: This sample consistently fell to the bottom of our rankings. Although it lent acidic brightness to vinaigrette and glaze, it had a one-note flavor that bordered on "tannic," and some tasters noticed a "harsh" aftertaste. It remained thin and mild-tasting even when reduced.

methods. Some products use more of the native grape must than others and/or cook the must in open vats as do traditional balsamic makers (cooking in vats allows for caramelization and, thus, more complex flavor development than what is produced by mechanical processing)—but neither of these variables was necessarily linked to the vinegars we preferred. Seven of the nine manufacturers confirmed that they age their balsamics for the minimum time. Of the two remaining, one cited the vague range of "60 days to two years," and the other, our former winner, qualified as what is known as *invecchiato*, meaning that it is aged for more than three years. Our front-runner ages for the minimum time.

But we still had the reduction and vinaigrette tastings to go, and interestingly, after these two tastings the playing field leveled off just a bit. Six of the products we tried were perfectly acceptable once incorporated into a vinaigrette or reduced and drizzled over asparagus. The additional ingredients in the dressing softened any sharp acidity, while reducing these vinegars added body to thinner products but didn't adversely affect the thickest. Our objections to the other three vinegars in the lineup only mellowed enough to recommend them with reservations. Though they'd do in a pinch, they retained the artificial sweetness or harshness tasters had objected to in the plain tasting.

While each of our top six balanced fruity sweetness with bright acidity, one came out on top. Bertolli Balsamic Vinegar of Modena has a "lush," "syrupy" texture in vinaigrette and an "almost drinkable" flavor with notes of apple, molasses, and dried fruit. Best of all, at only $3.49 for an 8.5-ounce bottle ($0.41 per fluid ounce), it's affordable enough to use every day.

INGREDIENT NOTES

BY ANDREA GEARY, ANDREW JANJIGIAN, LAN LAM, ANNIE PETITO, & DAN SOUZA

TASTING ISRAELI COUSCOUS

Israeli couscous, a round semolina pasta about the size of tapioca (distinct from the tiny, grain-like North African couscous), provides wheaty flavor and pleasantly chewy starch to soups, salads, and pilafs. We tasted five supermarket products, plain and in our recipe for Israeli Couscous with Lemon, Mint, Peas, Feta, and Pickled Shallots (page 22).

ISRAELI COUSCOUS

NORTH AFRICAN COUSCOUS

Cooked according to package directions, most passed muster, but one was a mushy mess. Its directions demanded almost twice the usual quantity of water and had us boiling it far longer than the others. We learned that better texture is also a result of the protein-carbohydrate ratio. The firmer, springier products had a higher ratio of protein to carbohydrates than the mushy product; proteins enhance texture by holding the carbohydrates together like an adhesive. When we tasted them again using our preferred pilaf cooking method, all the products got passing grades, although one stood out as especially "sweet" and "toasty." This couscous contained slightly more natural sugars, called fructans, which enhanced the Maillard reaction (when protein is heated, especially in combination with sugars, new flavor compounds are created) and provided a subtle flavor boost.

Regarding shape, our tasters preferred larger pearls, and the airtightness of the packaging may also have influenced our preferences: Our top two products are sold in jars, while our lowest-ranked couscous is sold loose in a cardboard box. While we recommend most of the products we tasted, we'll be buying our top-ranked one, Roland Israeli Couscous. For complete tasting results, go to CooksIllustrated.com/aug15. –Lisa McManus

RECOMMENDED

ROLAND Israeli Couscous
Price: $7.19 for 21.16 oz ($0.34 per oz)
Comments: Our favorite couscous had a "rich and nutty flavor." It was "chewy but tender," with "big round pieces," and was "a little starchier than others" but "firm and bouncy." In salad, it had "the great nutty flavor I expect from Israeli couscous," summed up one taster.

RECOMMENDED WITH RESERVATIONS

NEAR EAST Original Plain Pearled Couscous
Price: $3.49 for 6 oz ($0.58 per oz)
Comments: We recommend this product with the reservation that you should ignore the package directions, which call for too much water and time, leading to a mushy, pasty mess. Cooked in our pilaf style or salad, its scores crept up, but the pearls still "seemed smaller, pebblier" than others and "delicate," with "distinct granules." Some tasters noted that the taste was on the "mild," "bland" side.

Cooking with Kohlrabi

Kohlrabi, which can be either purple or green, is a member of the brassica family, which also includes broccoli, turnips, and cabbage. Its leaves are tender when young and can be added to salads for a peppery bite. More mature leaves and their fibrous stems can be cut into small pieces and cooked in the same manner as collards or kale and offer a similar minerally flavor. After removing the skin and the tough fibrous layer underneath it with a vegetable peeler, tasters found that the raw flesh had a crisp texture and peppery flavor similar to that of turnip but milder and with a sweetness like that of jícama or even apple. It's a good appetizer sliced thin and sprinkled with salt and lime or lemon juice and makes a nice addition to salads. It also shows up in all sorts of cooked applications, from stir-fries to sautés to soups. We've found, however, that overcooked, it becomes flavorless. This makes it best-suited for quick-cooking dishes like stir-fries; if you want to use it in soups and stews, wait and add it toward the end of cooking. –L.L.

TURNIP'S PEPPERY, SWEET COUSIN
To maintain kohlrabi's delicate flavor in applications like stir-fries and soups, cook it only briefly.

A Substitute for Shortening

Many pie dough recipes use both butter and vegetable shortening. While the butter contributes richness and flavor, the shortening helps ensure tenderness, since, unlike butter, it doesn't contain water. That helps minimize the production of gluten, which can make crusts tough. Shortening also has a higher melting point than butter, so it helps keep the dough from getting overly soft during rolling and shaping.

Because some cooks avoid shortening, we wondered whether clarified butter or ghee, a type of clarified butter popular in Indian cooking, might make a worthy substitute. Made by simmering butter until all the water has evaporated, ghee and clarified butter are water-free and also melt at higher temperatures than butter (though still at temperatures lower than shortening).

To test it out, we kept the regular butter and replaced the shortening with ghee in our Foolproof Pie Dough (which also contains vodka in place of some of the water to help prevent gluten formation) and in a more traditional pie dough recipe. We then compared them with the original recipes.

CLEAR ALTERNATIVE
Ghee, a type of clarified butter (which you can make or buy), can be subbed for shortening in pie dough.

Crusts in which we swapped ghee for shortening had a rich, buttery flavor that the shortening crusts lacked. In terms of texture, our Foolproof Pie Dough was as tender and flaky as the shortening version. The traditional pie dough made with ghee—while still tender and perfectly acceptable—puffed up, almost like a puff-pastry dough. This is because the recipe contained more water (from both butter and the use of water rather than vodka) than our Foolproof Pie Dough recipe. Also, because of ghee's lower melting range compared with shortening, the crust separated into layers earlier in the baking process and the crust puffed more. It also meant that both crusts made with ghee were slightly greasier than their shortening counterparts.

The takeaway? Substituting ghee or clarified butter for shortening in pie crusts will deliver a tender, flaky crust with a richer, more buttery flavor; be aware that it will be a bit greasier and in some cases the crust might puff up slightly. For instructions on making clarified butter and ghee, go to CooksIllustrated.com/aug15. You can also buy ghee at Indian and Middle Eastern markets, as well as in natural foods stores. –A.J.

Pitting Cherries Without a Pitter

For recipes like our Cherry Clafouti (page 15), a cherry pitter makes the pitting process quick and simple. But since not everyone owns this tool, we looked for alternatives. We tried setting the cherry on the mouth of an empty wine bottle and using a chopstick to push the pit through; fishing the pit out with a bent paper clip; and pushing the pit out by pressing the cherry on the end of an inverted funnel. In the end, we found that using a wine bottle with a straw worked best. The hollow end of a straw helped it grip the pit, and the narrow opening of the wine bottle (a beer bottle would work too) held the cherry in place while we pushed the pit through. The bottle caught the pits and juices, making cleanup easy. –L.L.

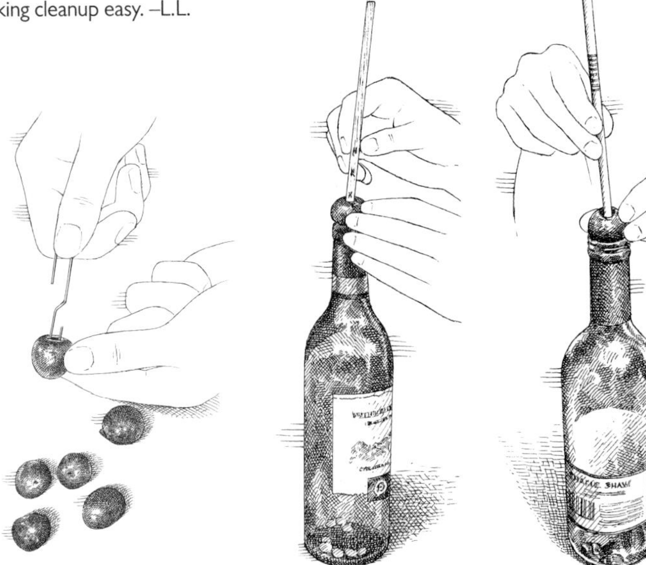

GOOD Bent paper clip | **BETTER** Chopstick plus wine bottle | **BEST** Straw plus wine bottle

Skip the Salt When Cooking Corn

Almost 15 years ago we found that cooking fresh corn in salted water made the skins of the kernels tougher than those of corn cooked in plain water. Back then we attributed the toughening effect to the presence of the calcium used in the salt's anticaking agent. Recently, however, we noticed that the skins turned tougher even when we seasoned the water with calcium-free kosher salt. When it comes to cooking corn on the cob or blanching corn kernels, we'll still refrain from adding salt to the cooking water, as we'd prefer to have tender skins and simply season after cooking. –D.S.

A Better Way to Seed Jalapeños

We often remove the seeds and ribs from jalapeño chiles to tone down their heat. In the past we've suggested running a melon baller or small spoon along the inside of a halved chile to accomplish this task. But sometimes stem removal isn't complete or easy; plus, jalapeño juice will occasionally spray up. Recently, we found a better method, which also allows you to cut around the core to yield flat, even planks (rather than a pair of curved sides), which makes subsequent chopping or mincing easier. This method will also work with other straight-sided chiles, such as serranos. –A.P.

With chile flat on cutting board, use chef's knife to cut down 1 side, using edge of chile's crown as guide for where to position knife. Place chile on cut side and repeat on remaining sides to create 4 planks. Discard stem and core, reserving seeds if specified in recipe.

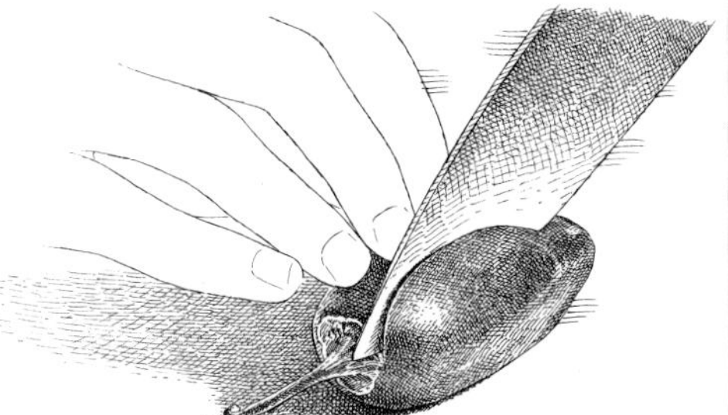

DIY Strawberry Refrigerator Jam

The beauty of refrigerator jams lies in their simplicity. They generally make a small batch, which means you don't need to invest in bushels of fruit and there's no need for canning equipment to sterilize the jars for long-term storage; you can keep the one or two jars of jam the recipe makes in the fridge and finish them off in a few weeks. Another bonus? A small batch of fruit will cook down quickly to the proper consistency, and the less you cook fruit, the more of its fresh taste is preserved. A shorter cooking time also preserves more of the naturally occurring pectin in the fruit, which is necessary for proper gelling. In addition to the fruit's pectin, lemon juice and sugar are key to ensuring that this jam sets up, since acidity and sugar help pectin form a strong gel without the need for adding commercial pectin. –Addy Parker

STRAWBERRY REFRIGERATOR JAM

MAKES ABOUT 2 CUPS

Crushing the berries jump-starts the release of pectin and decreases the cooking time, ensuring maximum fresh flavor.

- **1½ pounds strawberries, hulled and cut into ½-inch pieces (3 cups)**
- **1 cup sugar**
- **3 tablespoons lemon juice**

1. Place metal spoon in freezer to chill. Combine strawberries, sugar, and lemon juice in large saucepan. Bring to boil over medium-high heat, then reduce heat to medium. Mash fruit with potato masher until fruit is mostly broken down. Simmer vigorously until fruit mixture thickens and spatula leaves trail that does not fill in immediately, 15 to 25 minutes.

2. To test for proper thickness, remove saucepan from heat. Dip chilled spoon into jam and allow jam to run off spoon; jam should slowly fall off spoon in one thickened clump. If jam is runny, return to medium heat and simmer for 2 to 4 minutes before retesting. Transfer jam to jar and let cool completely. Cover with tight-fitting lid and refrigerate for up to 3 weeks.

SPOON TEST
Properly cooked jam should slowly slide off a chilled spoon in a clump. If the jam runs off quickly, keep cooking it.

Don't Skimp on Frozen Shrimp

Frozen shrimp are individually encased in icy shells that add weight, so if a recipe calls for 8 ounces of shrimp, should you defrost some extra to allow for the weight that will be lost when the ice melts? If so, how much?

Attempting to find a useful rule of thumb, we weighed out seven batches of frozen shrimp (testing across brands, sizes, and peeled versus unpeeled) and weighed them again after they were thawed and drained. We found that the thawed shrimp were 12 to 25 percent lighter and that a batch of smaller shrimp had proportionately more loss due to its greater surface area.

Our advice? When it comes to frozen shrimp, skip weighing them. Instead, note that in addition to being labeled small, medium, large, etc., shrimp are labeled with the range of pieces per pound, such as 26/30 for large shrimp. This number (which is clearly marked on the packaging) represents raw, unfrozen weight, so if your recipe calls for 8 ounces of large shrimp, simply count out 15 shrimp—half of the top of the range. That way you'll be sure to have enough post-thaw. –A.G.

KITCHEN NOTES

⋟ BY HANNAH CROWLEY, ANDREA GEARY, LAN LAM & DAN SOUZA ⋞

WHAT IS IT?

When food was first put into tin cans in the early and mid-1800s, home cooks opened them up with whatever tool they had on hand, such as a chisel or even a hammer. It wasn't until the 1850s that the first can-opening tool was invented, and in 1892 this "Never Slip" opener was patented. The tool features a curved blade with a sharp tip and a notched rest. To use it, you punch a hole in the can with the sharp tip, insert the blade, and pump up and down to cut around the can. The notched rest sits on the can's lip for a secure grip.

Punching the initial hole required some force, and it took more effort to work our way around large cans of tomatoes and beans than a modern-day opener would require, but it was manageable. But the opener proved to be too long for 6-ounce cans; the tip of the blade cut into the opposite side of the can. And in all cases, we could never cut all the way around the can; when we were about an inch from the starting point, there wasn't anything to anchor the lid when we tried to make the last couple of cuts. As for the safety factor, the opener felt a bit unstable to testers, as if it might slip—though it never actually did. While we appreciated the compact size of the Never Slip opener and it worked reasonably well, we're glad can openers have evolved. –L.L.

NEVER SLIP CAN OPENER
Despite its name, this tool didn't feel particularly secure even though it effectively opened 15- and 28-ounce cans.

Doubling Rice Pilaf? Don't Double the Water

We have a rice pilaf recipe (March/April 2000) that works without fail when made using 1½ cups of rice, but many readers have written us to ask why they end up with an inch of mushy rice on the bottom of the pot when they try to double it. The reason is that, despite what many cookbooks suggest, rice-to-water ratios can't simply be scaled up proportionally. After running a series of tests, we confirmed that rice absorbs water in a 1:1 ratio, no matter the volume. So in our original rice pilaf recipe, which calls for 1½ cups of rice and 2¼ cups of water, the rice absorbed 1½ cups of water. The remaining ¾ cup of water evaporated. But here's the catch: The amount of water that evaporates doesn't double when the amount of rice is doubled. In fact, we found that when cooking a double batch of rice using the same conditions—the same large pot and lid and on the same stove burner over low heat—as we'd used for a single batch, the same quantity of water evaporated: ¾ cup. Hence, simply doubling the recipe—increasing the amount of rice to 3 cups and the water to 4½ cups—leads to mushy rice because there is an excess of water in the pot. The bottom line: To double our rice pilaf recipe, use 3 cups of rice and only 3¾ cups of water. –D.S.

ERRATUM In our March/April 2015 issue, we incorrectly printed that if you forget to season with salt during the cooking process as directed in recipes, you should season at the end of cooking with 8 percent of the original amount of salt called for. That amount should be 25 percent, not 8 percent.

Going Two Rounds with Charcoal

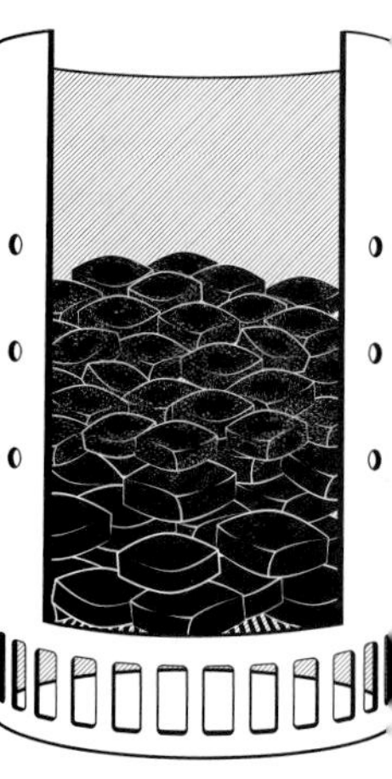

RECYCLE COALS
Save partially used coals and put them on top of fresh charcoal the next time you grill.

With quick-cooking grilling recipes, like our Ultimate Charcoal-Grilled Steaks (page 9), we often end up with a fair amount of coals that are only partially used by the end of cooking. In the name of frugality, we wondered, if we immediately extinguished the coals by cutting off the air supply (the best way to do this is to dump them into a small, metal lidded container such as a garbage can), could we then save them to reignite in a future round of grilling?

We discovered that the answer is yes, with one caveat. Trying to light a chimney starter filled entirely with used coals was a nonstarter—these smaller coals nestled tightly together, greatly restricting airflow and delaying or even preventing the coals from igniting. However, we found that it does work to replace up to half of the fresh coals called for in a recipe with used coals. Before you get started, make sure to place your previously used, cooled briquettes in the charcoal chimney and shake and rap it over the trash to dislodge ash, which would impede the coals from properly igniting. To maximize airflow, be sure to place the fresh coals in the chimney first and top them with the used coals. –D.S.

Turning Stainless Steel Nonstick

When cooking delicate foods like fried eggs, we usually turn to a nonstick skillet. But what if you don't have one? To find out if we could make a regular stainless-steel skillet more nonstick with the help of a vegetable oil spray like PAM, we sprayed the entire surface of a 10-inch skillet and heated it over medium heat (any hotter and the spray discolored) until shimmering before adding an egg, which we also sprayed on top. For comparison, we heated 1 tablespoon of vegetable oil (a generous amount for a 10-inch pan) in an identical stainless-steel skillet over medium heat until shimmering before adding an egg, which we drizzled with oil before flipping.

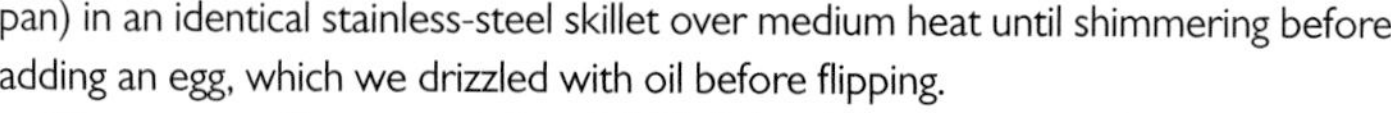

Vegetable oil sprays, which contain lecithin, can make a stainless-steel pan nearly nonstick.

The spray easily trumped the oil. Why? As oil heats up, it tends to form an uneven layer because the surface of the pan heats unevenly, causing the oil to pool in cooler areas and disappear in other areas. Vegetable oil sprays prevent sticking better because they contain more than just oil—they also include lecithin, an emulsifier that bonds the oil to the pan so it forms a thin, complete layer of oil between the pan and the food.

The takeaway? In lieu of a nonstick skillet, vegetable oil spray and a stainless-steel skillet can work nearly as well. Be sure to spray the entire surface of the pan, including the flared sides. (Foods like scrambled eggs won't work with this method. Because the food is moved around the pan during cooking, the layer of nonstick spray is lifted from the bottom of the pan.) –D.S.

Testing Knife Sharpness

Owning a knife sharpener (see page 25 for our winning model) makes tuning up your knife easy, but how do you know when it's time? The best way to tell if a knife is sharp is to put it to the paper test. Holding a sheet of paper (basic printer/copy paper is best) firmly at the top with one hand, draw the blade down through the paper, heel to tip, with the other hand. The knife should glide through the paper and require only minimal pushing. If it snags, try realigning the blade's edge using a honing, or sharpening, steel and then repeat the test. If the knife still doesn't cut the paper cleanly, use your sharpener. Repeat the paper test to make sure the knife is properly sharpened; if it catches on the paper, note where along the blade it happens. You can minimize the amount of metal removed by focusing on just this section of the blade to fine-tune the sharpening (just make sure you don't overdo it and end up making the blade uneven). –H.C.

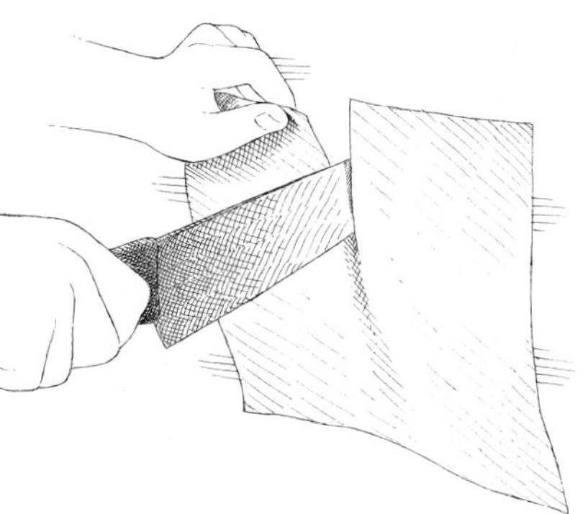

MAKING THE CUT
A properly sharpened knife will glide through paper with minimal pushing, no snagging.

Cracks in Your Pie Crust? Patch Without Scraps

To ensure a crisp, not soggy, crust, most of our tart and single-crust pie recipes start with a crust that is either partially or fully baked before being filled.

But occasionally cracks or holes form during this prebaking step, and these imperfections allow wet filling to leak through, making the crust soggy and difficult to serve. These holes can be patched with leftover dough, but what if you threw it away after fitting the dough, or you simply don't have any, as is always the case with press-in crusts? We devised a solution.

Simply stir together 4 tablespoons of all-purpose flour, 2 tablespoons of melted butter, and a pinch of sugar until it has the soft consistency of Play-Doh. Using your fingers, take a small amount of the mixture and press it gently into the hole or crack in the warm pie crust, smearing the edges to seal them to the baked crust. Bake the crust (without weights or foil) until the spackled area is firm and dry to the touch, 5 to 10 minutes. The spackled area won't have exactly the same flavor, texture, or appearance as the rest of the crust, but once the pie or tart is filled and baked, no one will know. –A.G.

Ensuring Complete Seasoning

In recipes that call for seasoning meat with a specified amount of salt, it can be tempting to sprinkle very close to the meat so that none of the salt is lost to the cutting board. Unfortunately, this leads to an uneven distribution of salt. Here's a better way:

Place the meat on a rimmed baking sheet and sprinkle with the specified amount of salt from up high (we've found that starting 12 inches above the food seasons it more evenly than from closer distances). Then simply pick up each piece of meat and roll it in any salt that has landed on the baking sheet. –D.S.

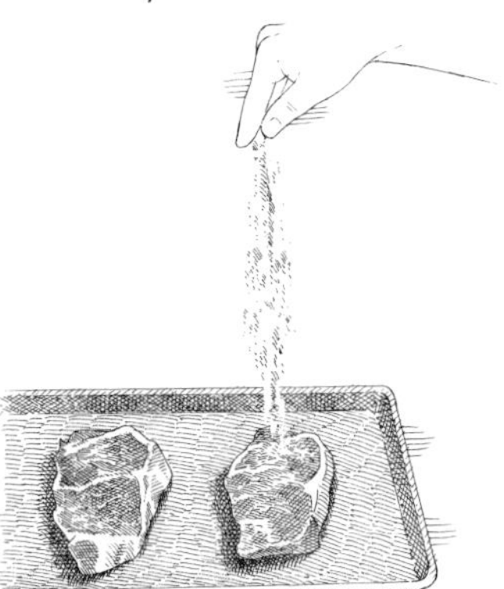

Season meat, set on baking sheet, from up high, then roll meat in seasoning on baking sheet.

EXPERIMENT With Whipped Cream, Temperature Matters

Conventional wisdom says to make sure your cream is cold before whipping it, but we wondered exactly how much temperature matters, so we decided to run a few tests.

EXPERIMENT

We whipped three batches, each consisting of 1 cup of whipping cream, to stiff peaks: one that came straight from the refrigerator and was 40 degrees; another that had sat out for 1 hour and reached 57 degrees; and a third that was at room temperature, 72 degrees. We recorded how long it took to whip the cream to its maximum volume without overwhipping and noted the final texture.

RESULTS

The refrigerated sample yielded 2¼ cups of smooth, stiff peaks after 1¼ minutes of whipping. The sample that sat out for an hour yielded 2 cups of slightly grainy stiff peaks after 1 minute and 50 seconds of whipping, and the room-temperature sample yielded 1¾ cups of grainy whipped cream but never reached stiff peaks, even after 2½ minutes of whipping.

72 DEGREES
Yield: 1¾ cups
Time: 2½ minutes

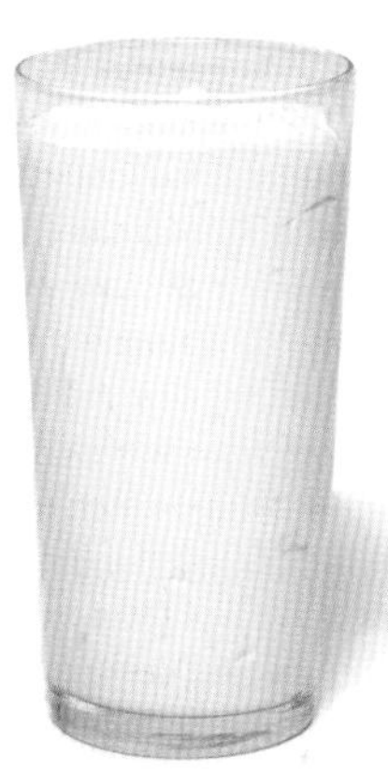

57 DEGREES
Yield: 2 cups
Time: 1 minute, 50 seconds

40 DEGREES
Yield: 2¼ cups
Time: 1¼ minutes

EXPLANATION

Whipping cream introduces air bubbles. When the cream is cold, these bubbles are held in place by a network of tiny globules of solid fat, which allow the cream to eventually expand into a light, airy mass. At warmer temperatures, that fat starts to soften and the globules collapse, so the cream can't whip up as fully, and it takes longer to reach its maximum (diminished) volume. This extended whipping time also gives the cream a grainy texture, as the fat forms small, irregular clumps rather than microscopic, smooth solid globules that surround the air bubbles.

TAKEAWAY

For maximum volume and the best texture, it's crucial to use cream straight from the refrigerator. Chilling the bowl and beaters can also help ensure that your cream stays cold through the whipping process. –L.L.

EQUIPMENT CORNER

⋟ BY LISA McMANUS, LAUREN SAVOIE & KATE SHANNON ⋜

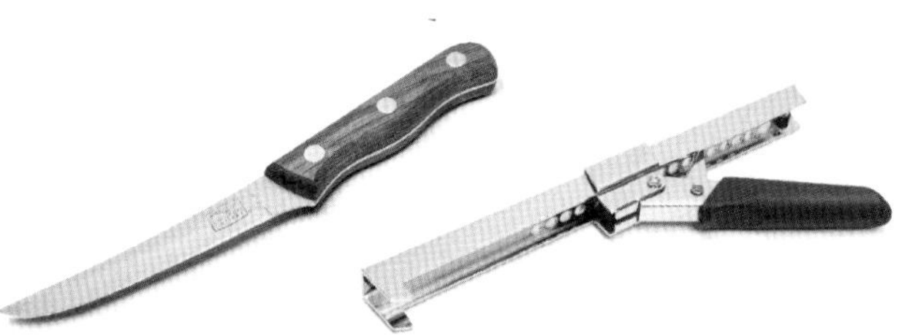

RECOMMENDED

CHICAGO CUTLERY
Walnut Tradition 4-Piece Steak Knife Set
Model: B144
Price: $17.95 for set of four knives

RECOMMENDED

AMCO
Swing-A-Way Jar Opener
Model: 711BK
Price: $10.09

NOT RECOMMENDED

GRILLBOT
Grill Cleaner
Model: GBU101
Price: $120.71

HIGHLY RECOMMENDED

RACHAEL RAY
ChillOut Thermal Tote
Model: 7-62570-03-99
Price: $17.99

RECOMMENDED

TODDY
Cold Brew System
Model: BXTCM
Price: $34.95

UPDATE Inexpensive Steak Knives

When our favorite steak knife set, the Victorinox Swiss Army 6-Piece Rosewood Steak Set, increased in price from $80 to $170, we wondered if we could find comparable knives that wouldn't slice into our savings. We rounded up four less expensive sets and tested them against our winning Victorinox set ($28.46 per knife). Lefties and righties with large and small hands sat at dinner tables to try each blade, slicing through rare and well-done steaks—including moderately tough shell sirloin and tender strip steaks—served on ceramic plates.

Most knives were sharp out of the box (except for one that struggled from the start, making jagged, torn slices), and all but two showed only minimal loss of sharpness during testing. As for comfort, testers favored contoured wood handles, which were lightweight and easy to grip. We also preferred knives whose blades and handles were of nearly equal length, which made them easier to control. While testers gave a narrow edge to the Victorinox knives for their comfortable handles and slightly sharper blades, the Chicago Cutlery Walnut Tradition 4-Piece Steak Knife Set ($4.49 per knife) performed almost identically at a savings of nearly $24 per knife. –L.S.

UPDATE Jar Openers

A well-designed jar opener can eliminate the frustration of trying to pry open stubborn lids. We rounded up six tools (priced from $5.99 to $17.99) and compared them with our old standby, the Amco Swing-A-Way Jar Opener ($5.99). We tested the openers on jars of all shapes, sizes, and materials—from 2-ounce vanilla bottles with tiny plastic lids to 26-ounce jars of tomato sauce with large metal lids.

Basic versions resembling silicone potholders weren't much better at opening jars than our bare hands. Another style, The Original JarPop JarKey ($6.16), works like a bottle opener, slightly lifting the lip of the lid to break the jar's seal. (Testers loved the JarKey's easy-to-use design, but since it's only effective on metal lids less than ½ inch tall, you'd also need the company's Maxi JarKey for lids ½ to ¾ inch tall.)

The versatile Amco Swing-A-Way Jar Opener is still our top pick. It sports a clamp that grips any size jar, and its prongs can release metal lids or loosen plastic lids. –L.S.

NEW PRODUCT Grillbot

The Grillbot ($120.71) is a battery-operated robot with three rotating metal brush bristles designed for hands-free cleaning of charcoal or gas grill grates. You place the Grillbot on your grill grate; set its cleaning cycle for 10, 20, or 30 minutes; shut the grill lid; and, in theory, come back later to a perfectly clean grate. While its 10-minute cycle was enough to clean up after a few steaks or pork cutlets, the Grillbot failed miserably at tougher cleaning jobs: It barely made a dent in residue from burnt chicken or stuck-on glazes, even after two 30-minute cycles. Since the Grillbot weighs only 3.5 pounds, it depends on long rounds of lightweight brushing instead of pressure to attempt to remove grit. What's more, the tool must be used on a grill cooled to below 250 degrees (temperature sensors turn the robot off if it gets too hot). We'll stick with our favorite grill brush, the Grill Wizard 18-Inch China Grill Brush ($31.50), which relies on pressure to remove tough grime in just a few strokes. –L.S.

TESTING Insulated Shopping Totes

Insulated shopping totes are designed to keep refrigerated and frozen foods cold on the commute home from the supermarket. We purchased six (priced from $6.97 to $38.90), looking for a comfortable, easy-to-carry sack that could keep groceries at a food-safe temperature for at least an hour. The best bags insulated well, sealed tight, and were moderately sized, leaving little room for warm air to circulate around the groceries. We also found small or midsize bags more comfortable because they weren't as bulky or heavy to carry. Our favorite bag, the Rachael Ray ChillOut Thermal Tote ($17.99), is sized right and contains superior insulation that kept food cold for 2 hours in a 90-degree room. We also liked its shoulder straps, which made carrying its load easier. If you can plan ahead and chill the tote before you shop, the PackIt Freezable Grocery Bag ($27.26), which has gel packs sewn into its lining, offers exceptional 4-hour cold retention. Its only disadvantage: no shoulder straps. –K.S.

TESTING Cold Brew Coffee Makers

Cold brew coffee, made by steeping ground beans in cold or room-temperature water for several hours, produces a smoother, less acidic brew than does hot-water extraction and yields a concentrate that can be diluted with hot or cold water (or poured over ice) to make hot or iced coffee. We tested seven makers (priced from $24.99 to $75), following manufacturer directions and comparing them with our DIY cold brew method using a French press. We tasted the coffee cold and black. Tasters loved the "rich, chocolaty" brew made with our French press method, but the exorbitant cost per cup (we use a high concentration of ground coffee) and stirring and straining work make a case for the dedicated brewers. We eliminated smaller-capacity models and those that didn't allow the grinds and water to sufficiently interact, which yielded weak brews, and a model that yielded just 20 ounces of coffee—not concentrate—after 7 hours. That left makers from Filtron and Toddy, both of which yielded generous amounts of rich-tasting concentrate; however, the Toddy took top honors for its particularly smooth brew. –L.M.

For complete testing results, go to CooksIllustrated.com/aug15.

INDEX

July & August 2015

RECIPE VIDEOS
Want to see how to make any of the recipes in this issue? There's a video for that.

MORE VIDEOS
Recipes, reviews, and videos available free for 4 months at
CooksIllustrated.com/aug15
Science of Cooking: Secrets of Cooking Rice
Testing Asian Knife Sharpeners

Israeli Couscous Salad, 22

Grilled Whole Trout, 19

Ultimate Charcoal-Grilled Steaks, 9

Cherry Clafouti, 15

Modern Succotash, 20

Fried Brown Rice with Pork and Shrimp, 11

100 Percent Whole-Wheat Pancakes, 7

Roasted Tomatoes, 21

Peri Peri Grilled Chicken, 5

Italian Sausage with Grapes and Vinegar, 13

PHOTOGRAPHY: CARL TREMBLAY; STYLING: MARIE PIRAINO

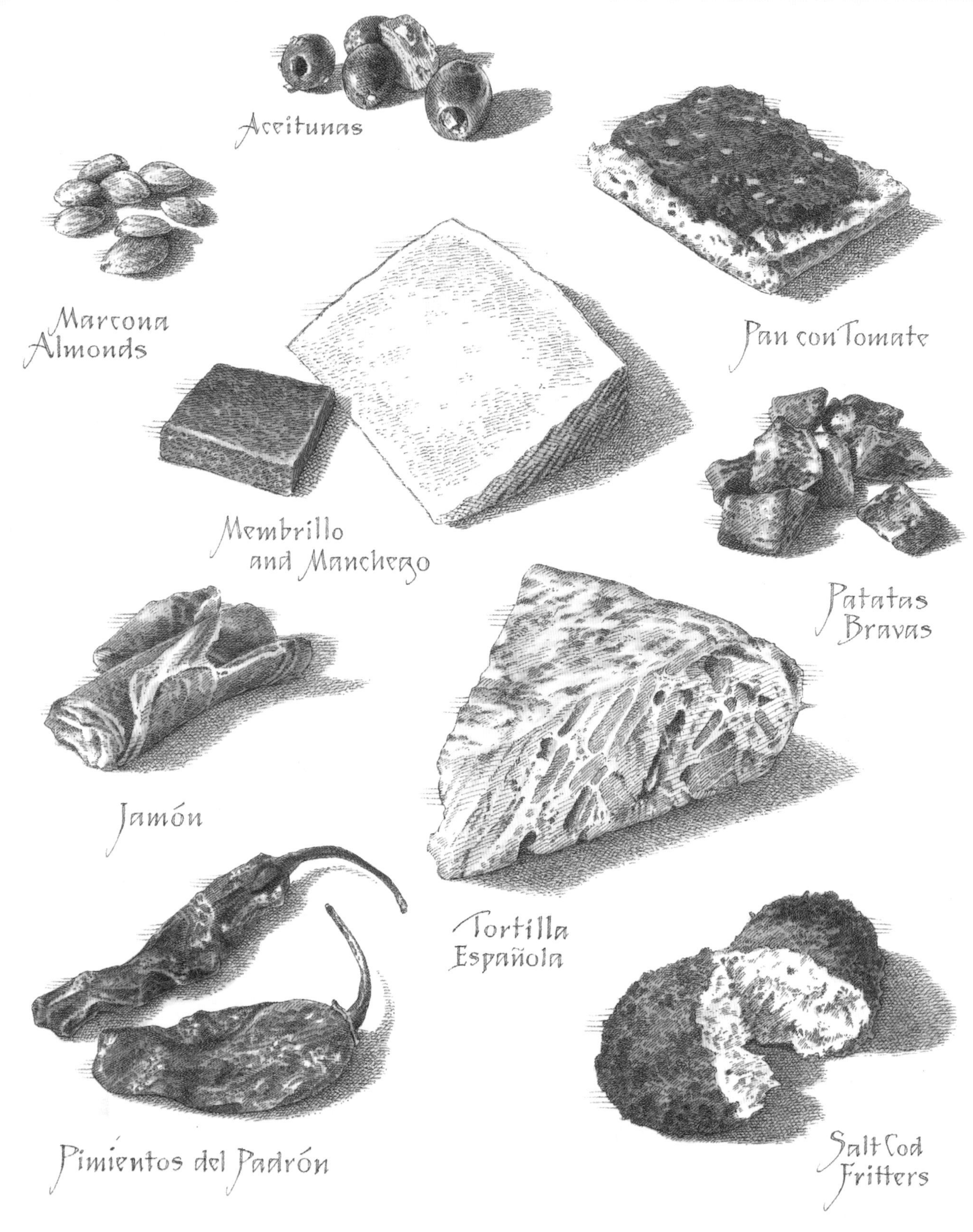

CLASSIC TAPAS

NUMBER 136

SEPTEMBER & OCTOBER 2015

COOK'S ILLUSTRATED

15-Minute Grilled Country Ribs

Superflaky Biscuits
More than 50 Layers

Spanish Chicken
Easy Braise, Bold Flavors

Carbon-Steel Skillets
Chefs' Secret Weapon

Chocolate-Caramel Layer Cake

Indoor Flank Steak
Even Better than Grilled

Freezer Tips and Tricks
Should You Freeze Flour?

Sausage Meatballs
Middle Eastern Bread Salad
Homemade Apple Butter
Best Black Bean Burgers

CooksIllustrated.com
$6.95 U.S. & CANADA

CONTENTS

September & October 2015

HEIRLOOM APPLES There are hundreds of centuries-old apple cultivars. KNOBBED RUSSETS, an old English breed, have rough-textured skin and rich sweetness. The exteriors of ROXBURY RUSSETS, supposedly the oldest species of American apple, are similarly sandpapery and give way to crisp, pleasantly tart flesh. Mustard-colored HUDSON'S GOLDEN GEMS share the potato-like skin of russet varieties but have softer flesh that tastes like pears. The French CALVILLE BLANC D'HIVER delivers big crunch and tartness, while its native cousin, the red-flushed ORLEANS REINETTE, is firm and sweet. BLACK OXFORDS from Maine are actually plum-colored, and beyond their thick skin their flavor is subtle. Conversely, Connecticut's deep red BLACK GILLIFLOWER is soft and floral. While WINTER BANANA apples don't taste like their namesake, they do hint at tropical fruits. German HOLSTEINS are bright with well-balanced sweet-tart flavor. COVER *(Cabbage)*: Robert Papp; BACK COVER *(Heirloom Apples)*: John Burgoyne

America's Test Kitchen is a very real 2,500-square-foot kitchen located just outside Boston. It is the home of *Cook's Illustrated* and *Cook's Country* magazines and the workday destination of more than three dozen test cooks, editors, and cookware specialists. Our mission is to test recipes until we understand how and why they work and arrive at the best version. We also test kitchen equipment and supermarket ingredients in search of products that offer the best value and performance. You can watch us work by tuning in to *America's Test Kitchen* (AmericasTestKitchen.com) and *Cook's Country from America's Test Kitchen* (CooksCountry.com) on public television.

PRINTED IN THE USA

THE ROCK

I recently visited my 19-year-old son, Charlie, in Utah where he was part of an Outward Bound–style adventure. The day I visited was rock-climbing day, replete with harnesses, carabiners, ropes, helmets, belay devices, and special climbing shoes. The group took more than an hour to set up the ropes as I sat around watching ripe-smelling twentysomethings crab their way up the cliff, legs akimbo. Then the inevitable happened—it was my turn.

When you are a tad over 60 and, while you are standing at the bottom of a cliff, someone shouts out "your turn," three things happen. First, you are transported back to third-grade physical education class—the one with the rope hanging from the gym ceiling—and it is now "your turn" to humiliate yourself in front of the jocks, the ones who, grinning, bulldoze you headfirst into the turf during football practice. Second, you make the mistake of looking upward, taking in the sheer height of the perfectly smooth outcropping, and imagining falling off the rock wall in slow motion, flailing your way to the ground. Finally, your digestive system seizes, drops, and leaves you with an intense desire to make a dash for the bushes. Of course with your son watching, there is no way out. Your choice is clear—death or humiliation.

The next step is education. Put on your harness. Strap in so the word "danger" does not appear on any buckles (when that word is obscured, the straps are properly threaded). Then you have to learn to tie a figure-eight follow-through knot that secures the rope to your harness. Put another way, you have seconds to learn how to tie a complicated knot—your life actually depends on it holding—and the person monitoring your progress is not old enough to remember sneakers without Velcro.

Then the signals. There is the climber, the belayer, and the backup belayer. (The last exists, in my mind, to step in if the glassy-eyed, slightly unhinged first belayer decides to separate from his right mind during the climb.) The climber says things such as "On rock!" to which the belayers say "Rock on!" And commands such as "Slack rope" and "Up rope" make sense. But I realized that the two most important commands, "Belay on!" and "Belay off!" sound remarkably similar. In fact, the previous climber called down "Belay on!" and the person on the ground thought he said, "Belay off!" This meant, of course, that instead of securing the climber firmly to the rope, the belayer took him off the rope, greatly increasing the chances of a chaotic, screaming descent and death. On that note, I headed upward.

Christopher Kimball

Ten minutes later, I was 35 feet above the ground on a sheer rock face. The footholds were ½ inch wide. My left leg was at a 75-degree angle to my torso, my left foot shoved into what I hoped was a deep crevice. My right arm was fully extended, sweeping the smooth rock face like a blind man touching the face of a stranger. I realized that I could not move. There was no down, no up, no sideways, just frozen inertia, like my childhood cat, Midnight, with her claws caught in the screen door, body hanging limply. Having been railroaded into this activity without much thought, I realized where I was—on a sheer, vertical rock face, tied to a rope held by a teenager for whom Beavis and Butthead are household gods. Then I remembered the only really useful command—"On rappel!"—which meant that I was quickly bounding off the rock face, gratefully heading back down to safety.

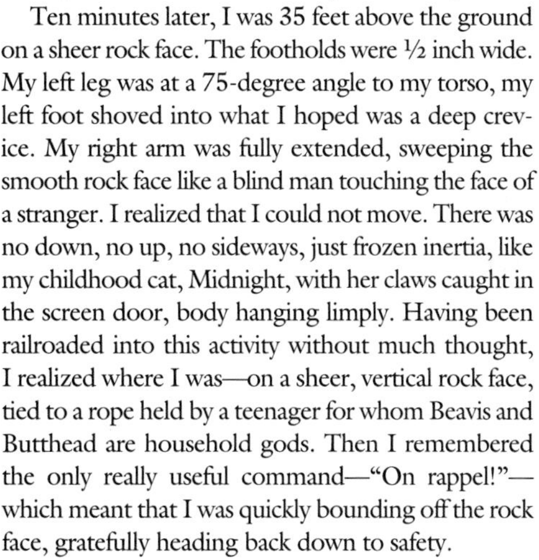

Things on the ground, however, were tense. Rock climbing, as it turned out, is a test of character. I learned later that some students are left for an hour or more, dangling from the rope, crying and begging to be returned to terra firma. Having given up in just a matter of minutes, I had despoiled the family name, embarrassed my son, and become an outsider.

Charlie cooked lunch on his portable stove—Minute Rice and dehydrated beans washed down with warm water. I think Dustin Hoffman ate better in the movie *Papillon*. After a brief rest and a bout of group motivational therapy, we headed back to the cliff face.

I grew angry. This was supposed to be a Bertie Wooster–type outing: a pleasant day in a Utah canyon, a slap on the back, a good feed, and a bit of mild adventure, all perfectly posed like snapshots in the family album. Instead, I had been sandbagged into rock climbing, dismissed it as a meaningless exercise, and then realized that I had broken the cultural code of the climber. I had given up.

So when the 6'7" guide—all muscle, shorts, and sinew—asked if anyone would like a second climb, I rushed over, put on climbing shoes, whipped together my figure-eight follow-through, clipped on the carabiner, and headed upward. It is not an exaggeration to say that I flew up that rock face like a giant spider chasing a juicy dinner. I lunged toward the top, spread-eagled to get a good grip, located those tiny footholds that I had missed that morning, and quickly found myself at the summit. I didn't even take in the view—I shouted "Rappel!" and pushed off the cliff like Sylvester Stallone in *Cliffhanger*.

Reveling in my success, I looked around for a note of celebration. Charlie was making googly eyes at the pigtailed German guide with bad breath, the two belayers were deep into a discussion of when *Star Wars* meets *The Lord of the Rings*, and most everyone else was in animated conversation about the last time they consumed copious amounts of alcohol.

That evening as Charlie was cooking yet another mess of rice and beans, each of the kids had to state what they had learned that day. I was tempted to shout out, "Go get a real job!" when I thought that maybe I actually had learned something. As one of my high school teachers, Bill Gillespie, said at commencement, "Some day you will come back to show us your trophies and your scars, and we'll be glad to see you." He meant that we struggle for ourselves, for our own dignity, not for the homecoming. It's just the rock face and you—everyone else is standing too far away to notice.

FOR INQUIRIES, ORDERS, OR MORE INFORMATION

CooksIllustrated.com
At CooksIllustrated.com, you can order books and subscriptions, sign up for our free e-newsletter, or renew your magazine subscription. Join the website and gain access to 22 years of *Cook's Illustrated* recipes, equipment tests, and ingredient tastings, as well as companion videos for every recipe in this issue.

COOKBOOKS
We sell more than 50 cookbooks by the editors of *Cook's Illustrated*, including *The Cook's Illustrated Cookbook* and *The Science of Good Cooking*. To order, visit our bookstore at CooksIllustrated.com/bookstore.

COOK'S *ILLUSTRATED* MAGAZINE
Cook's Illustrated magazine (ISSN 1068-2821), number 136, is published bimonthly by Boston Common Press Limited Partnership, 17 Station St., Brookline, MA 02445. Copyright 2015 Boston Common Press Limited Partnership. Periodicals postage paid at Boston, MA, and additional mailing offices, USPS #012487. Publications Mail Agreement No. 40020778. Return undeliverable Canadian addresses to P.O. Box 875, Station A, Windsor, ON N9A 6P2. POSTMASTER: Send address changes to *Cook's Illustrated*, P.O. Box 6018, Harlan, IA 51593-1518. For subscription and gift subscription orders, subscription inquiries, or change of address notices, visit AmericasTestKitchen.com/support, call 800-526-8442 in the U.S. or 515-248-7684 from outside the U.S., or write to us at *Cook's Illustrated*, P.O. 6018, Harlan, IA 51593-1518.

FOR LIST RENTAL INFORMATION Contact Specialists Marketing Services, Inc., 777 Terrace Ave., 4th Floor, Hasbrouck Heights, NJ 07604; phone: 201-865-5800.
EDITORIAL OFFICE 17 Station St., Brookline, MA 02445; 617-232-1000; fax: 617-232-1572. For subscription inquiries, visit AmericasTestKitchen.com/support or call 800-526-8442.

QUICK TIPS

COMPILED BY SHANNON FRIEDMANN HATCH

A Grate Idea for Almond Paste

Pat Wood of Broomfield, Colo., has found that stiff almond paste is difficult to incorporate into other ingredients, even if you crumble it. To break it up even more, she shreds it into fine pieces on a box grater.

Removing Eggshell Bits

Bits of broken eggshell can be hard to remove from a bowl of cracked eggs. Franklin English of Atlanta, Ga., suggests wetting two fingers. Because the water molecules naturally cling to the fingers and the shells, the water acts as a weak glue that makes it easy to pick out the pieces.

Pulling Up the Tab

The metal tab of a salt container lies flat against the top, which makes it hard to grab when it's time to refill the saltshaker. Miriam Hartman of Pasadena, Calif., suggests bending back the top of the tab with a pair of pliers to make the edge easier to grasp.

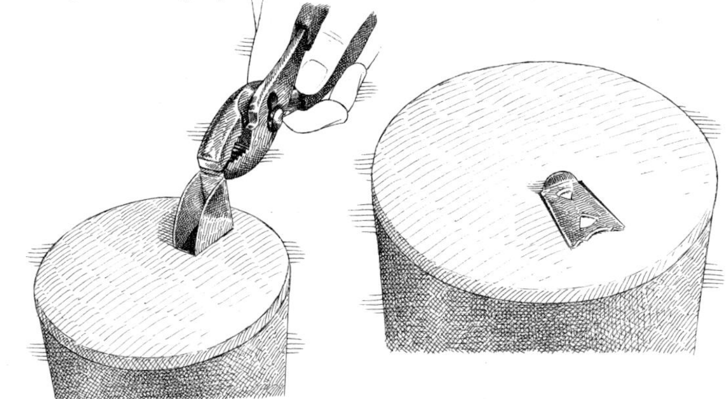

Getting Out the Last Drop

Lucy Shapiro of Gouldsboro, Maine, doesn't like to waste a drop of honey or syrup, so when the bottle is nearly empty, she sets it upside down inside a wide-mouthed funnel over a measuring cup to drain. The sticky substance can then be easily scraped out of the measuring cup with a rubber spatula.

Good Goodie "Bag"

When giving family and friends baked goods to take home, Cheryl Herbert of Plainfield, N.J., packs them in sturdy produce clamshell containers that she's saved.

Cool Container for Bacon Grease

Many cooks pour bacon grease into a lidded container, such as an old tin can, to let it cool before disposing of it or storing it, but the hot grease makes the metal container too hot to handle. Matt Donnelly of Los Angeles, Calif., instead uses an insulated disposable coffee cup with a lid to contain the grease when discarding it.

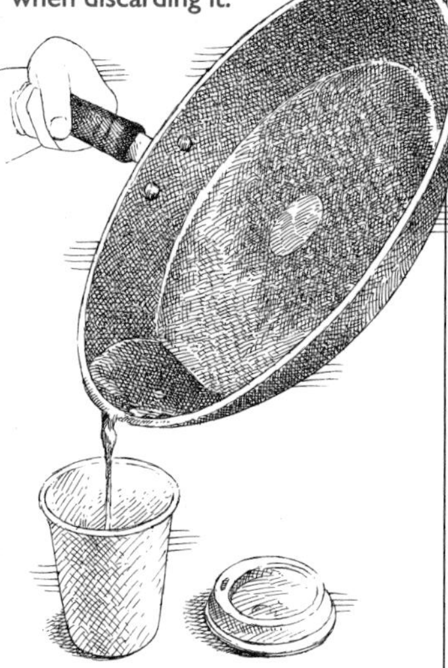

Keeping Dried Mushrooms Submerged

When rehydrating in a bowl of water, dried mushrooms tend to float on the surface. Chuck Nider of Columbus, Ohio, has a trick for keeping them submerged: He puts the mushrooms in a liquid measuring cup (a 2-cup measure works well), adds water, and nests a small bowl inside to press them into the liquid. The rim of the bowl rests on the rim of the measuring cup, preventing it from floating in the water, while its rounded base pushes the mushrooms into the liquid.

ILLUSTRATION: JOHN BURGOYNE

SEND US YOUR TIPS We will provide a complimentary one-year subscription for each tip we print. Send your tip, name, address, and daytime telephone number to Quick Tips, *Cook's Illustrated*, P.O. Box 470589, Brookline, MA 02447, or to QuickTips@AmericasTestKitchen.com.

A Key to Opening Tins Quickly

To pop the covers off metal tins with interlocking lids, such as those used for oatmeal, loose tea, and cocoa, Sharon Hladky of Midlothian, Va., keeps a paint key in her utensil drawer. Its flat edge easily slips under the container's top so that she can pry it off.

Recycling Lids for Mason Jars

Mary Zoll of Carlisle, Mass., covers her Mason jars with their two-part metal lids only when she's canning. If she's simply using the jars to store leftovers, she employs plastic lids from empty condiment jars like those from mayonnaise or peanut butter. She tests them for size and when she finds one that screws tightly onto a standard-mouth jar, she cleans it and keeps it handy.

Ice for Water Bottles

It can be difficult to cram ice cubes into water bottles, so Lisa Quentin of Randolph, N.J., adds a small amount of water to the bottle and stores it in the freezer. When she's ready to use the bottle, the ice is already built in.

Egg (Space) Saver

Wendy Fiero of Stuarts Draft, Va., often buys a new carton of eggs before she's completely finished with last week's dozen. So that she doesn't have to store two whole containers in her refrigerator, she cuts the older carton to hold just the remaining few eggs.

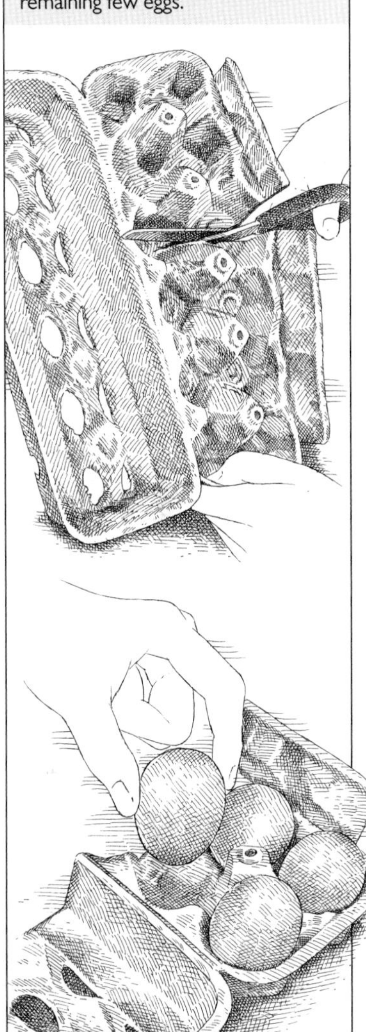

Clean Cupcake Carrier

Expanding on our recent tip about transporting a single cupcake in an upside-down deli container (which also allows you to pick up the cupcake without smearing the frosting), Marni Fylling of Hoboken, N.J., devised a way to transport a whole batch: She flips a plastic storage container upside down, places the cupcakes on the lid, and then snaps the container on top.

A New Way to Make Fudge

Rather than fashioning a parchment sling to prevent homemade fudge from sticking to a traditional baking pan, Amy Baranek of Randolph, Mass., uses a springform pan. After removing the sides, she slides an offset spatula under the prepared fudge to pop it onto a cutting board. (To create square pieces for serving, simply trim the rounded edges.)

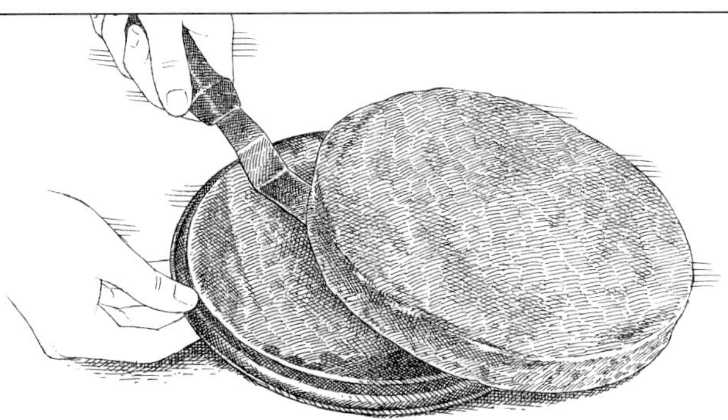

Great Pan-Seared Flank Steak

Flank steak has it all: rich, beefy flavor; lean meat; and a reasonable price tag. Its one downfall? It only seems to work on the grill.

BY ANDREA GEARY

In a perfect world, cooking a flank steak would be as simple as throwing it into a hot pan and searing it on each side. The outside would be crusty and brown by the time the inside was cooked to a rosy, even medium. But in the real world, flank steak can be too long to squeeze into a 12-inch skillet, so its ends reach up the sloped sides, making it awkward to cook. Plus, it's made up of long muscle fibers that contract when heated, causing the steak to buckle and therefore brown unevenly. The long muscle fibers also shrink unevenly as the meat cooks, so one end becomes thicker than the other. This means that the steak can turn out rare at the thick end and medium-well at the thin end. To top it off, the prolonged sear causes the meat just beneath the exterior to overcook and turn gray.

Moving outside to the grill solves most of these problems: There's no skillet to squeeze into (or smoke alarm to set off), and the more intense heat browns the steak better, even if it warps a bit. The uneven cooking and gray layer persist, but most cooks accept such imperfections as the price they pay for a quick grilled dinner.

To prevent the meat from buckling and therefore browning unevenly, we flip it frequently during searing. We slice the steaks before serving.

But I wanted a year-round way to cook this beefy, lean steak—and a tolerance of imperfection is not among my more notable qualities. I was determined to find a reliable indoor method for producing a well-browned flank steak that was cooked medium throughout. (We like loose-textured, wide-fibered steaks like flank cooked to medium because at this degree of doneness the fibers shrink a bit more, which translates to greater tenderness.)

Thinking Inside the Box

Hoping to limit smoke and spatter, I decided to try cooking the steak in the oven. To get any crust development, the meat was going to have to sit flat on a very hot, broad surface. But, alas, broiling the steak on a rimmed baking sheet was a failure. As it slowly heated up, moisture beaded on the wide, flat surface of the meat, inhibiting browning and leaving me with a gray steak that tasted steamed.

See Our Method
Video available free for 4 months at CooksIllustrated.com/oct15.

If I wanted that flavorful brown crust, I was going to have to use the direct heat of the stovetop. I started by dividing the steak into quarters. It was an unconventional move, but I had two reasons: First, doing so helped the steak fit neatly into the skillet. Second, it meant that I could remove the individual steaks from the skillet as they finished cooking, so they would all be cooked to a perfect medium.

I heated 2 tablespoons of oil in a skillet over medium-high heat until it was just smoking and added the steaks. Thinking that minimal interference would yield the best sear, I resolved to wait 3 minutes before moving them. The steaks buckled, though not as severely as the full steak had, and I hoped the warping would be reversed when I flipped them. Unfortunately, the damage was irreversible. The first sear had set a concave shape, so the steaks browned only around the edge of one side and only in the middle of the other.

I removed the two thinner steaks from the skillet after about 8 minutes when they reached 125 degrees. The thicker steaks took about 4 minutes longer. After resting, they were all cooked to medium, but there was a sizable band of gray, overcooked meat around the edges, and the browning—though better than my oven attempts—was still not up to par. As I wiped up the splatter on the stove, I knew there had to be a better way.

A Hybrid Approach

Cutting the steak into quarters gave me better control of the internal temperature of the meat and enabled me to fit it all in the pan, so I'd stick with that, but I had to reconsider the cooking method. Perhaps I had been hasty in eliminating the oven as a possibility.

One of the best methods for cooking thick steaks is the test kitchen's hybrid method that involves heating them gently in a 275-degree oven until they approach the perfect internal temperature and then transferring them to a hot skillet on the stovetop to brown. The oven step accomplishes three things: First, the precooked meat doesn't cool down a hot pan as drastically as a room-temperature steak would, so browning starts almost immediately. Second, some of the steak's surface moisture evaporates in the oven, so there's less to be converted to steam before browning can begin. Third, this accelerated browning means that the steak doesn't have to spend much time in the skillet, so the meat just below the crust doesn't overcook. There's also less time for splatter and smoke.

It's the best way to cook uniformly thick, hefty steaks like rib eyes or strip steaks, but would flank steak's irregular thinness be suited to this treatment? To find out, I divided my steak into quarters and seasoned them with salt. I also sprinkled on a teaspoon of sugar to assist in browning when the time came. I placed the meat on a wire rack set in a rimmed baking sheet and baked it in a 275-degree oven until the thickest steak reached 120 degrees, about 20 minutes. Then I seared the steaks in a hot skillet.

This time I was not as restrained about flipping the steaks. Reasoning that the buckling was caused not so much by the tightening of the fibers on each side of the steak as by the *unequal* tightening of those fibers, I flipped the steaks every minute to keep the surface tightening on each side pretty much

Fitting a Rectangle into a Circle

Squeezing a long flank steak into a 12-inch skillet usually means that the ends of the steak creep up the sloped sides of the pan, all but guaranteeing unevenly cooked meat. Cutting our flank steak into four pieces and warming it in the oven before searing (where it shrinks significantly) helps it fit neatly. Smaller pieces also have shorter muscle fibers, so the steaks don't buckle as much during searing.

TIGHT SQUEEZE
A 1½-pound flank steak is simply too big for a 12-inch skillet.

equal. It worked. This time the steaks were much flatter, which meant that more of the meat stayed in contact with the cooking surface. This, combined with the caramelizing effect of the sugar, yielded the best browning thus far.

But the doneness varied. The thicker ends were cooked to a perfect medium, but the thinner ends were closer to medium-well.

During my next test I was hypervigilant, repeatedly temping each steak and removing each from the oven as it reached 120 degrees. But such frequent temperature taking meant opening the oven several times, and every time it lost heat and had little time to recover before I opened it again. The thinnest steak was done in 20 minutes, but it took almost 50 minutes before the thickest steak reached the target temperature, which was a lot of fuss.

And yet these steaks won me over. They browned beautifully in the skillet, and I was happy with their juicy, rosy interiors and lack of overdone gray meat just below the surface. Was there a hassle-free way to get all the meat to the target temperature at once?

How Low Can You Go?

It occurred to me that high-heat methods like grilling or searing in a skillet had resulted in the biggest doneness differential between the thick and thin steaks. Could I close the gap by using a very low-temperature oven?

I reduced the oven temperature to 250 degrees and inserted a probe thermometer into one of the thicker steaks. When the thermometer registered 120 degrees (since I wasn't opening the oven, this took only about 30 minutes), I transferred all the steaks to a skillet to brown. Sure enough, these steaks were closer in terms of doneness, but the thinner steaks were still a bit overcooked.

Lowering the oven temperature even more did the trick. Steaks that were warmed for 35 minutes in a 225-degree oven registered between 120 and 130 degrees, so that after searing and resting they were a perfect rosy medium. (See "Getting Thick and Thin Ends More Evenly Cooked.")

Flank steaks this great deserved a bit of embellishment. I mixed up some flavorful compound butters and slathered them onto the warm steaks to melt over them as they rested. I sliced the steaks thinly across the grain for maximum tenderness and dotted them with just a bit more butter. Imperfection is no longer part of the flank steak bargain.

PAN-SEARED FLANK STEAK WITH MUSTARD-CHIVE BUTTER
SERVES 4 TO 6

Open the oven as infrequently as possible in step 1. If the meat is not yet up to temperature, wait at least 5 minutes before taking its temperature again. Slice the steak as thin as possible against the grain (for more information see "Making Flank Steak More Tender" on page 31). For our free recipes for Pan-Seared Flank Steak with Garlic-Anchovy Butter and Pan-Seared Flank Steak with Sriracha-Lime Butter, go to CooksIllustrated.com/oct15.

- 1 (1½- to 1¾-pound) flank steak, trimmed
- 2 teaspoons kosher salt
- 1 teaspoon sugar
- ½ teaspoon pepper
- 3 tablespoons unsalted butter, softened
- 3 tablespoons chopped fresh chives
- 2 teaspoons Dijon mustard
- ½ teaspoon grated lemon zest plus 1 teaspoon juice
- 2 tablespoons vegetable oil

1. Adjust oven rack to middle position and heat oven to 225 degrees. Pat steak dry with paper towels. Cut steak in half lengthwise. Cut each piece in half crosswise to create 4 steaks. Combine salt, sugar, and pepper in small bowl. Sprinkle half of salt mixture on 1 side of steaks and press gently to adhere. Flip steaks and repeat with remaining salt mixture. Place steaks on wire rack set in rimmed baking sheet; transfer sheet to oven. Cook until thermometer inserted through side into center of thickest steak registers 120 degrees, 30 to 40 minutes.

2. Meanwhile, combine butter, 1 tablespoon chives, mustard, and lemon zest and juice in small bowl.

3. Heat oil in 12-inch skillet over medium-high heat until just smoking. Sear steaks, flipping every 1 minute, until brown crust forms on both sides, 4 minutes total. (Do not move steaks between flips.) Return steaks to wire rack and let rest for 10 minutes.

4. Transfer steaks to cutting board with grain running from left to right. Spread 1½ teaspoons butter mixture on top of each steak. Slice steak as thin as possible against grain. Transfer sliced steak to warm platter, dot with remaining butter mixture, sprinkle with remaining 2 tablespoons chives, and serve.

SCIENCE Getting Thick and Thin Ends More Evenly Cooked

Our usual method for cooking steaks is to preheat them in a 275-degree oven and then transfer them to the stovetop to sear their outsides. But when we adapted this technique to flank steak, we ran into a problem: By the time the thick end of the steak reached the target temperature of 120 degrees, the thin end overcooked. The solution? Turn down the oven: At 225 degrees, both the thick and thin ends stay within an acceptable temperature range.

Here's why: The increase in the internal temperature of the steaks is not constant over the course of their time in the oven. Initially, the steaks heat up pretty rapidly, and then they slow as their internal temperature approaches that of the oven. But here's the interesting thing: The rate at which the temperature of the thin steaks and the thick steaks slows is different because their mass is different. The thin steaks heat more quickly, but their rate of increase starts to level off as it approaches the target temperature of 120 degrees. That gives the thicker steaks time to catch up. The lower the oven temperature, the more pronounced this leveling off effect is.

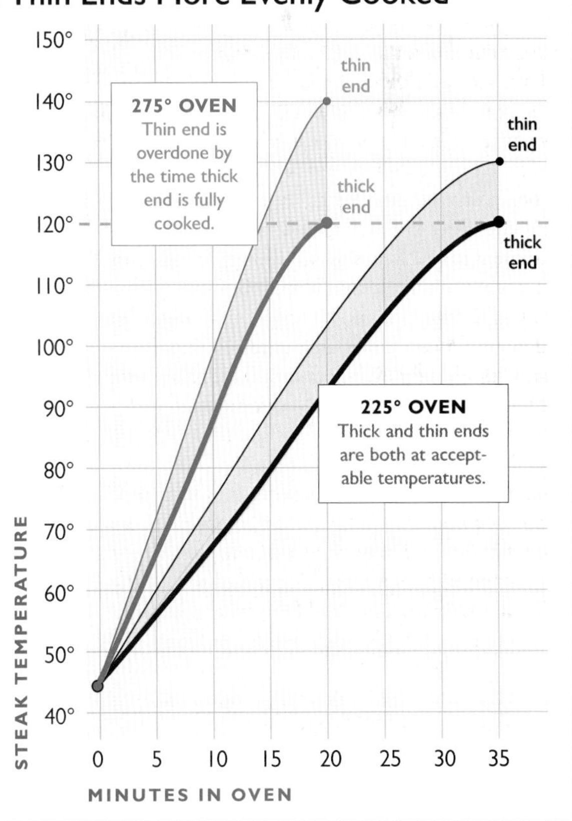

Ultimate Flaky Biscuits

For layered, ultraflaky biscuits, you've got to know when to fold them and when to hold them.

BY ANDREW JANJIGIAN

From the enormous soft and fluffy Southern cat head to the simple drop, I love biscuits of all kinds. But my current obsession is a specimen I've recently found in several restaurants. It's crisp and crunchy on the outside but tender and light as air inside, with flaky strata that peel apart like sheets of buttery paper in a way that rivals a croissant. No, this is not an everyday biscuit; it's an ethereal, once-in-a-while treat rich enough that there's no need to spread on any extra butter, just a slathering of jam, if that. But when I tried recipes billed as "rich and tender flaky biscuits," very few lived up to the promise, and those that did required a lengthy process of folding the dough and letting it rest that was as much work as making croissants. I set out to see what I could do to produce my ideal flaky biscuit with considerably less fuss.

Cutting biscuits into squares versus the usual rounds eliminates the need for rerolling scrap dough, which inevitably produces tough results.

A Flaky Foundation

Despite the failures, those early tests did help sort out a few things. First, I'd use only butter rather than a mixture of butter and shortening. Shortening lacks flavor, and I also found that it inhibited the formation of distinct layers. As in pie crusts, leaving distinct pieces of fat in the dough (what many recipes refer to as "pea-size" pieces) is key to producing flakiness. As the biscuits cook, the bits of fat melt into the dough, leaving small voids. Then, as the water in the dough turns to steam, it expands these gaps and creates layers. The problem with shortening is that it has a soft texture and tends to combine with the flour rather than stay distinct like butter. Most recipes I found called for 2 to 4 tablespoons of fat per cup of flour; I suspected that I could squeeze in more. I settled on 16 tablespoons butter to 3 cups flour—a little more than 5 tablespoons per cup.

As for the type of flour, unlike ultratender, fluffy Southern-style biscuits that demand a specialty low-protein flour (generally 7 to 8 percent) like White Lily, my early tests confirmed that flaky biscuits are better off made with all-purpose flour. This is because all-purpose flour has a little more protein (10 to 12 percent), and when combined with water, the protein in flour produces gluten. The more protein, the more gluten, which translates to a biscuit dough with more strength that can bake up with distinct, structured layers rather than cakey and fluffy. I tried bread flour (which is closer to 13 percent protein) but found that it created an overly strong gluten network that produced tough biscuits. The best results came from using King Arthur all-purpose flour, which is 12 percent protein.

See the Flakiness Happen
Video available free for 4 months at CooksIllustrated.com/oct15

I also determined that I'd use buttermilk rather than milk for its distinctive tang, a touch of sugar for complexity, a little baking soda to enhance browning and add some lift, and, finally, baking powder for additional lift. As for shaping, I settled on square biscuits. Round biscuits were pretty, but they left too much scrap dough and rerolling those scraps produced biscuits that were tough. Shaping the dough into a square slab and then cutting that into squared-off biscuits was fast and meant no rerolling—and no waste.

Cut the Fat

I moved on to the heart of the matter: mixing and shaping. Many biscuit recipes require that you spend a lot of effort getting the butter into small, even, pea-size pieces by cutting it into the dry ingredients using a dough cutter, a pair of knives, a food processor, or your hands. The problem with most of these approaches is that it's far too easy to over- or underdo it, both of which hamper flakiness. I found that the most consistent method was to grate the butter using the large holes of a box grater, a trick I picked up from our recipe for Blueberry Scones (July/August 2007).

Of course, the effort is moot if these shreds of butter soften during mixing and shaping. To avoid that, I froze the butter for 30 minutes before grating it. And to get around the awkwardness of grating the stubs, I saved the last tablespoon of each stick to melt and brush on the tops of the biscuits just before baking them, which would improve crisping and browning.

Between the Folds

The grated butter helped create some layering but not nearly what I was after. In a pie dough, leaving the butter in small pieces is sufficient to get the right flaky effect, but that's because pie dough contains far less liquid (and far more butter) and is rolled out thin, a pair of factors that inherently smears the butter into thin sheets among floury layers. But in a wet, minimally rolled-out slab of biscuit dough, the butter pieces just float randomly in the mixture like raisins in a muffin batter. And that's where folding comes in. This process starts with rolling out the dough into a large, thin rectangle and then folding it into thirds like a letter. You then press the dough together to seal the package tightly, turn it 90 degrees, and repeat. The special thing about folding dough is that the technique works by multiplication, not addition. Each fold doesn't simply give you one more layer; it creates an exponentially greater number of layers because it's a trifold every single time, not a single fold.

Folding my biscuit dough, at least in the early

stages, was a messy affair: It started out shaggy and crumbly—anything but a cohesive mass—and it seemed like I wasn't really doing anything useful. But slowly and surely, the dry bits and the wet bits came together; by the fourth fold, the process was pretty tidy. The interesting thing was, I found in subsequent tests that the messier—and less mixed—the dough was in the beginning, the better. Even in those first few messy "folds," the slivers of butter were getting pressed and stretched into thinner and thinner sheets among clumps of wet and dry dough. If I mixed the dough in the bowl to the point where it was uniform before I folded it (which is what most recipes call for) or if I added more liquid to help bring the dough together, I ended up with layers that were less defined.

Some recipes call for letting the dough rest for as long as 30 minutes after every set of folds. This is because with each set the gluten in the dough gets stronger, making the dough increasingly harder to roll out. But because my dough wasn't cohesive for the first few sets of folds, gluten didn't develop at the same pace, and I could make five folds without any resting.

When I cut this dough into squares, each biscuit looked like the side view of a book, with layers that pulled away from one another dramatically during baking—just the effect I'd hoped for. There was only one problem: Most of the biscuits were coming out of the oven lopsided. In fact, of the nine biscuits the recipe produced, only the one cut from the center of the dough came out square and level.

I realized that the edges of the dough slab were being compressed during the rolling and folding process. Trimming away ¼ inch from the perimeter of the dough before cutting the biscuits took care of that, but the biscuits were still a bit wonky. By the fifth fold, the layers of dough were taut like stretched rubber bands. Once the layers started to separate in the oven, this tension caused them to slip and slide in different directions, leaving the biscuits lopsided. A single 30-minute rest in the refrigerator—a far cry from the multiple rests other recipes required—gave them time to relax. With that, I had buttery, super-flaky biscuits that consistently rose up tall and true.

FLAKY BUTTERMILK BISCUITS

MAKES 9 BISCUITS

We prefer King Arthur all-purpose flour for this recipe, but other brands will work. Use sticks of butter. In hot or humid environments, chill the flour mixture, grater, and work bowls before use. The dough will start out very crumbly and dry in pockets but will be smooth by the end of the folding process; do not be tempted to add extra buttermilk. Flour the counter and the top of the dough as needed to prevent sticking, but be careful not to incorporate large pockets of flour into the dough when folding.

- **3 cups (15 ounces) King Arthur all-purpose flour**
- **2 tablespoons sugar**
- **4 teaspoons baking powder**
- **½ teaspoon baking soda**
- **1½ teaspoons salt**
- **16 tablespoons (2 sticks) unsalted butter, frozen for 30 minutes**
- **1¼ cups buttermilk, chilled**

1. Line rimmed baking sheet with parchment paper and set aside. Whisk flour, sugar, baking powder, baking soda, and salt together in large bowl. Coat sticks of butter in flour mixture, then grate 7 tablespoons from each stick on large holes of box grater directly into flour mixture. Toss gently to combine. Set aside remaining 2 tablespoons butter.

2. Add buttermilk to flour mixture and fold with spatula until just combined (dough will look dry). Transfer dough to liberally floured counter. Dust surface of dough with flour; using your floured hands, press dough into rough 7-inch square.

3. Roll dough into 12 by 9-inch rectangle with short side parallel to edge of counter. Starting at bottom of dough, fold into thirds like business letter, using bench scraper or metal spatula to release dough from counter. Press top of dough firmly to seal folds. Turn dough 90 degrees clockwise. Repeat rolling into 12 by 9-inch rectangle, folding into thirds, and turning clockwise 4 more times, for total of 5 sets of folds. After last set of folds, roll dough into 8½-inch square about 1 inch thick. Transfer dough to prepared sheet, cover with plastic wrap, and refrigerate for 30 minutes. Adjust oven rack to upper-middle position and heat oven to 400 degrees.

4. Transfer dough to lightly floured cutting board. Using sharp, floured chef's knife, trim ¼ inch of dough from each side of square and discard. Cut remaining dough into 9 squares, flouring knife after each cut. Arrange biscuits at least 1 inch apart on sheet. Melt reserved butter; brush tops of biscuits with melted butter.

5. Bake until tops are golden brown, 22 to 25 minutes, rotating sheet halfway through baking. Transfer biscuits to wire rack and let cool for 15 minutes before serving.

To Avoid Slumps, Relax and Trim

Folding the dough multiple times creates great layering—but it also compresses the edges and causes tension that makes the layers separate and slide in different directions in the oven. Our fixes: We let the dough relax for 30 minutes in the fridge after folding and then trim away the compressed edges before cutting the dough into individual biscuits.

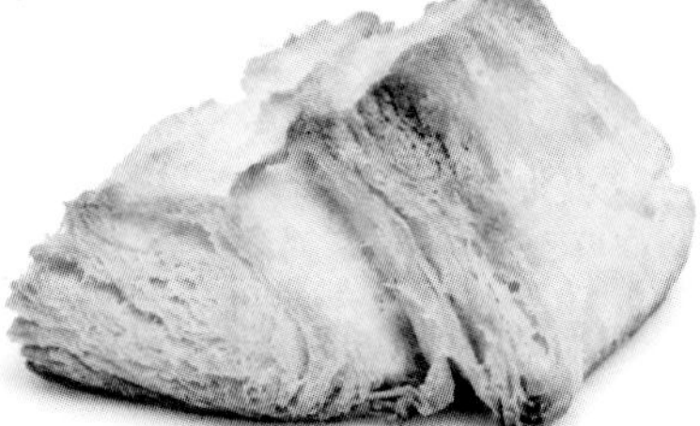

PREVENTABLE FLAW

Slumping is easily fixed by letting the dough rest.

STEP BY STEP | A SHAGGY DOUGH STORY

What's up with this scraggly looking dough? It allows the slivers of butter to be pressed and stretched into thinner and thinner sheets among the wet and dry clumps, ultimately creating more layers. Trust us: By the last fold, it will smooth out.

REALLY SHAGGY
The dough barely gets mixed before being transferred to the counter.

STILL SHAGGY
After the first fold, the dough remains very dry and crumbly.

GETTING LESS SHAGGY
By the third fold, the dough is starting to smooth out and look more like typical dough.

MOSTLY SMOOTH
After the fourth fold, the dough is only a little rough around the edges; the folds look distinct.

ALL SQUARED AWAY
After the fifth fold, the dough is rolled out, rests for 30 minutes, and is cut into squares for baking.

Spanish Braised Chicken

The rich flavor and lush consistency of this classic dish from Spain's Castilla–La Mancha region depend on a sherry-based sauce thickened with ground almonds and egg yolks.

⋺ BY ADAM RIED ⋹

At a Spanish restaurant not long ago, a chicken dish called *pollo en pepitoria* caught my attention. The meat, which had been braised until it was incredibly tender, arrived covered in a creamy, fragrant, subtly coarse sauce that featured three of the cuisine's star ingredients: sherry, saffron, and almonds. Scattered over the chicken were chopped egg whites and fresh parsley. The flavors and lush consistency were so appealing that I sopped up the extra sauce on the plate with pieces of crusty bread. I then hurried home to find recipes so that I could make the dish myself.

I quickly learned that the dish, which some sources note is a great specialty of the saffron-producing Castilla–La Mancha region of Spain, gets its creamy-but-not-quite-smooth consistency from a *picada.* This nut-based paste seasoned with garlic and herbs or spices is commonly used in Spanish cuisine to thicken soups, stews, and sauces. Interestingly, the picada for pollo en pepitoria is made even more rich by mashing hard-cooked egg yolks with the nuts. That explained the chopped egg white garnish.

Tomatoes and lemon juice balance the richness of the almonds and hard-cooked egg yolks in our sauce. We garnish the dish with chopped egg white.

But as stunning as this dish was in the restaurant, the versions I tried were not. Every one had richness in spades, but the creamy sauce usually came off as cloying and even a bit one-dimensional. With some work, though, I was sure I could produce a luxurious, complex-flavored sauce that was as rich and satisfying as it was balanced.

The Bright Side

Most Spanish cookbook authors note that the dish is traditionally made with a whole chicken (in those cases, it's called *gallina en pepitoria*), but plenty of modern recipes call for chicken parts—particularly thighs. The dark meat is especially nice for braising because it contains abundant connective tissue, which melts into gelatin as the chicken cooks, leaving the meat nicely tender. In fact, when we braise chicken thighs in the test kitchen, we maximize that texture by cooking them slowly and not just until they hit their target doneness temperature of 175 degrees, but well beyond that to 195 degrees; at that point, they're not just tender but downright silky. (For more information, see "Overcook Your Chicken Thighs—and Do It Slowly.")

The cooking method starts as does any classic braise: with browning the meat. I chose skin-on thighs, since the rendered fat from the skin would contribute big savory flavor to the dish. I would remove and discard the skin before serving since a long simmer makes chicken skin soggy.

From there, I softened a chopped onion with a couple of minced garlic cloves and salt in the rendered fat and saw to the sherry. We avoid "cooking sherry," which contains salt and preservatives that distract from the wine's nutty flavor. Sweet sherries, such as Pedro Ximénez, and cream sherries would also taste cloying in a savory braise. Instead, I reached for a dry, light-bodied variety called fino that's equally widely available. I poured a generous ⅔ cup into the pan, scraped up the flavorful browned bits known as fond, added chicken broth and brought the pot up to a simmer, and placed the parcooked thighs in the liquid. I simmered the thighs with the lid on for the better part of an hour, by which point the meat just barely clung to the bone.

Then came the picada, which is made like a pesto: Nuts—almonds are most traditional—get blitzed in the blender with more garlic, a pair of hard-cooked egg yolks, and a pinch of saffron (a little goes a long way) until the mixture is as smooth as possible. After stirring the thick paste into the pan, you simmer everything for another few minutes to meld the flavors and thicken it further.

Picada: A Nutty Thickener

Almonds processed with garlic, saffron, and hard-cooked egg yolks add body and flavor to the braise.

Unlike stews, sauces, and stir-fries that are thickened with starches or dairy, many Spanish stews and braises get their rich, hearty body from a pesto-like nut-based thickener called a *picada*. The basic formula, which many sources claim dates back to at least the 13th or 14th century, includes finely ground almonds or hazelnuts (*picar* means "to chop") and seasonings like garlic, herbs, and spices. But many versions also contain toasted or fried bread or even hard-cooked egg yolks, as in the recipe here. The ingredients are traditionally pounded to a thick paste with a mortar and pestle (we use a blender for speed) and stirred into the pot toward the end of cooking so that it can lend body, richness, and flavor to the cooking liquid.

COOKING ONLY

SHOPPING Sherry

What's What?

Sherry, a wine fortified with brandy, can be confusing to buy because it comes in a wide range of styles such as dry, sweet, cream, and "cooking." But for savory cooking purposes, stick with the dry kind. Sweet and cream sherries will taste overwhelmingly sweet when reduced in sauces, and cooking sherry, which has been treated with salt and preservatives to make it shelf-stable, can render a dish too salty.

Which Can I Use?

Dry sherries come in a variety of sub-classifications that represent degrees of aging and fortification—from drier, lighter-bodied, and less expensive fino to nuttier, heavier, and pricier oloroso. We've found that it's fine to cook with an inexpensive fino, such as Taylor Dry Sherry ($5.99 for 750 milliliters), but if you want a bottle that's as good to drink as it is to cook with, consider Lustau Palo Cortado Península Sherry ($19.99 for 750 milliliters). –A.R.

COOKING AND DRINKING

To brighten the rich almond-egg sauce, I finished it with a spritz of fresh lemon juice, which turned out to be a good move, albeit too subtle. I couldn't add much more lemon juice before the sauce would turn distinctly citrusy, but tomatoes also contain acid and were worth trying. Unlike in Italian sauces, where they're often the focal point, tomatoes are sometimes introduced in Spanish sauces to complement other flavors. Going forward, I experimented with chopped and grated fresh and canned whole tomatoes. I found that a small can of whole peeled tomatoes, drained and chopped fine, offered the necessary brightness along with nice savory sweetness. While I was making flavor tweaks, I also added a bay leaf and a dash of cinnamon—elements I'd seen in a handful of published recipes—when I sautéed the garlic, which made the sauce just a bit more fragrant.

The Grind

The sauce was just about there, but I had two quibbles with the almonds. Most recipes I found didn't call for toasting them, so I hadn't up until now, but not surprisingly this quick step noticeably deepened their flavor and, thus, the flavor of the sauce. The bigger issue was their texture; pepitoria is meant to have a rustic, slightly coarse consistency, but here the picada was too gritty to integrate well in the braising liquid. I tried simply buzzing the ingredients for longer in the blender, but even after 3 full minutes, they didn't break down sufficiently. I also tried replacing the nuts themselves with almond butter—an admittedly odd move that unfortunately did away with the sauce's pleasantly coarse texture.

I finally realized that the way to make a smoother picada was to treat it like soup and blend it with some of the braising liquid. The liquid not only saturated and smoothed out the dry nut mixture but also increased the volume of food in the blender jar, making it easier for the ingredients to engage the blade and process the picada more thoroughly. The resulting sauce was thick, creamy, and just shy of smooth—ideal for coating the moist chicken or swiping up with a piece of good crusty bread.

SPANISH BRAISED CHICKEN WITH SHERRY AND SAFFRON (POLLO EN PEPITORIA)

SERVES 4

Any dry sherry, such as fino or Manzanilla, will work in this dish. Serve with crusty bread.

- **8 (5- to 7-ounce) bone-in chicken thighs, trimmed**
- **Salt and pepper**
- **1 tablespoon extra-virgin olive oil**
- **1 onion, chopped fine**
- **3 garlic cloves, minced**
- **1 bay leaf**
- **¼ teaspoon ground cinnamon**
- **⅔ cup dry sherry**
- **1 cup chicken broth**
- **1 (14.5-ounce) can whole peeled tomatoes, drained and chopped fine**
- **2 hard-cooked large eggs, peeled and yolks and whites separated**
- **½ cup slivered blanched almonds, toasted**
- **Pinch saffron threads, crumbled**
- **2 tablespoons chopped fresh parsley**
- **1½ teaspoons lemon juice**

1. Adjust oven rack to middle position and heat oven to 300 degrees.

2. Pat thighs dry with paper towels and season both sides of each with 1 teaspoon salt and ½ teaspoon pepper. Heat oil in 12-inch skillet over high heat until just smoking. Add thighs and brown on both sides, 10 to 12 minutes. Transfer thighs to large plate and pour off all but 2 teaspoons fat from skillet.

3. Return skillet to medium heat, add onion and ¼ teaspoon salt, and cook, stirring frequently, until just softened, about 3 minutes. Add 2 teaspoons garlic, bay leaf, and cinnamon and cook until fragrant, about 1 minute. Add sherry and cook, scraping up any browned bits, until sherry starts to thicken, about 2 minutes. Stir in broth and tomatoes and bring to simmer. Return thighs to skillet, cover, transfer to oven, and cook until chicken registers 195 degrees, 45 to 50 minutes. Transfer thighs to serving platter, remove and discard skin, and cover loosely with aluminum foil to keep warm. While thighs cook, finely chop egg whites.

4. Discard bay leaf. Transfer ¾ cup chicken cooking liquid, egg yolks, almonds, saffron, and remaining garlic to blender jar. Process until smooth, about 2 minutes, scraping down jar as needed. Return almond mixture to skillet. Add 1 tablespoon parsley and lemon juice; bring to simmer over medium heat. Simmer, whisking frequently, until thickened, 3 to 5 minutes. Season with salt and pepper to taste.

5. Pour sauce over chicken, sprinkle with remaining 1 tablespoon parsley and egg whites, and serve.

SCIENCE

Overcook Your Chicken Thighs—and Do It Slowly

Unlike white meat, which dries out and toughens when overcooked, dark meat actually benefits from being cooked well beyond its doneness temperature (175 degrees). That's because dark meat contains twice as much collagen as white meat, and the longer the meat cooks, the more that collagen breaks down into gelatin, which coats the meat's protein fibers and makes it more moist and tender. (Dark meat also contains roughly twice as much fat, which coats the meat's proteins, and has a higher pH, which helps it retain moisture more effectively.) But it's also important to cook thighs low and slow so that they spend as much time as possible between 140 and 195 degrees—the temperature range in which collagen breaks down.

We proved the point by cooking two batches of chicken thighs to 195 degrees, one on the stovetop and one in a slower, gentler 300-degree oven. Whereas the stovetop-cooked thighs reached 195 degrees in about 25 minutes and were just moderately tender, the oven-cooked thighs lingered in that zone for nearly twice as long and were much more tender and pleasant to eat.

FORK-TENDER

For ultratender results, we slowly cook the chicken in the oven until it reaches 195 degrees.

Watch Every Step

Video available free for 4 months at CooksIllustrated.com/oct15

Sausage Meatballs and Spaghetti

A good meatball is tender enough to cut with a fork; sausage is inherently firm and springy. So is there any way to make a tender sausage meatball?

BY ANNIE PETITO

Like lots of Italian American families, mine always gathered on Sundays at my grandmother's for a big spaghetti dinner. She made her version especially hearty by serving the pasta with meatballs as well as links of sweet Italian sausage, which were my favorite part. Their rich, ultrasavory flavor and distinct seasonings—fennel, oregano, and red pepper flakes—made the dish particularly satisfying.

It'd be nice, I thought, to make meatballs with sausage, merging the links' savory flavor and the meatballs' tenderness into one package. The problem is that while meatballs are tender—a good one cleaves easily with the side of a fork—sausages are exactly the opposite: inherently dense and springy, which makes them awkward to cut and eat with spaghetti. This seemed like a problem worth solving.

Break It Up

Sausage is made by thoroughly blending and kneading meat, fat, and salt so that the meat's sticky proteins, called myosin, cross-link and bind together to create a strong network that gives the mixture its firm, springy texture. (To make links, the mixture is stuffed into a casing.)

To make tender sausage meatballs with store-bought Italian sausage, I'd need to break up that texture as much as possible. That's why I was surprised to see recipes that called for simply removing the sausage from the casing and rolling it into balls, which would inevitably cook up dense and springy. But what if I mixed up the sausage like a regular meatball, using a couple of egg yolks, grated Parmesan cheese, minced garlic, and a panade to break up its texture? The panade, a paste of bread and milk, would coat and lubricate the meat's protein molecules, preventing them from linking up tightly and thus keeping the mixture moist and tender.

An old Italian trick—briefly simmering the browned meatballs in the sauce—moistens the meat while lending the sauce savory depth.

I combined the ingredients with my hands, shaped the meatballs, and roasted them on a wire rack set in a rimmed baking sheet—our preferred setup for developing flavorful browning without making a greasy mess of the stovetop. Then I briefly simmered them in a simple tomato sauce. But rather than discreetly tenderizing the meatballs, the panade popped up in distinct pasty nuggets—a result that was not only unappetizing but also ineffective since much of the sausage was unable to reap its tenderizing benefits and thus cooked up with its characteristic firm, dense texture.

Plan B was to ditch the commercial sausage and simply make meatballs from ground pork seasoned with the herbs and spices typical of Italian sausage. The problem here was that seasoned ground pork didn't quite offer the rich juiciness that makes sausage so satisfying.

But why not combine the two? I mixed up another batch using equal parts sausage and ground pork and encouragingly found myself on the right track; though still firmer than I wanted, these meatballs were more tender than my sausage-only batch and had decent flavor and richness that I could surely improve down the line. For now, I needed to work on the distribution of the panade, which still appeared in doughy pockets.

Due Process

Most meatball recipes call for mashing bread into milk with a fork to make the panade and then gently incorporating the meat, eggs, and seasonings by hand to avoid overworking the meat and developing any of that sausage-like firmness.

But with dense sausage already in the mix, combining by hand simply wasn't effective enough to incorporate the panade. I needed a more powerful method. The paddle of a stand mixer would surely whip the meat mixture into a sticky paste, but what about a food processor? Its sharp blade would literally cut the panade into the meat—and I hoped I could use the staccato-like pulse button to avoid overmixing.

This turned out to be a good move; after a quick spin in the processor, the sausage-pork-panade mixture was relatively homogeneous and uniform. The problem was that even with my quick pulses, the meatballs cooked up a bit dense, indicating that the meat was still being worked too much. But I had an idea. I changed things up a bit and processed the nonmeat ingredients—the bread, milk, egg yolks, garlic, and Parmesan—so that they were thoroughly blended before the meat went in.

400 Meatballs to Perfection

When we started testing, our sausage meatballs were dense and springy. We made close to 400 meatballs before landing on just the right combination of ingredients and mixing methods that produced the savory, juicy, fork-tender meatballs we wanted.

FIRST WE TRIED
hand-mixing sausage with standard panade (bread-milk mixture)
BUT: meatballs dense, with mushy pockets of bread

THEN WE TRIED
subbing less-dense ground pork for sausage
GOOD: meatballs less dense
BUT: lacking sausage's rich juiciness

NEXT WE TRIED
combining sausage and ground pork
GOOD: richer meatballs
BUT: meat and panade not homogeneou

DISCOVERY

Don't Mix in Panade by Hand; Process It

To ensure that meatballs hold their shape, retain moisture, and stay tender during cooking, we typically combine the ground meat with a panade, a paste made of milk and bread. The starches and liquid form a gel that coats and lubricates the meat proteins, preventing them from linking together into a tough matrix.

The problem: It's hard to thoroughly incorporate a panade into the meat when blending by hand, so we use a food processor. Its sharp blade literally cuts the paste into the meat so that the mixture is homogeneous.

CLUMPY
By hand

HOMOGENEOUS
In a food processor

But even with this modification the meatballs weren't truly tender, and there could be only two possible explanations: The food processor was overworking the meat, or the panade and ground pork weren't doing enough to tenderize the sausage. So I made changes that addressed both. Instead of adding both the pork and the sausage to the processor at the same time, which made the bowl very full and the components hard to blend thoroughly without lots of mixing, I processed just the ground pork with the panade and seasonings, removed half the mixture before blending in the sausage, and then gently folded in the reserved portion of pork by hand until everything was just combined. I also briefly soaked the ground pork in a solution of salt and baking soda, which changes the meat's protein structure and raises its pH, both of which enable the pork to better retain moisture. (Because a lot of commercial sausage already includes water and other additives, I refrained from pretreating it.) Next I swapped the milk in the panade for heavy cream, which provided a little extra fat to coat the meats' sticky proteins and thus reduced their ability to stick together. Finally, to ramp up the now-muted sausage flavor, I added back some of those classic seasonings: coarsely ground fennel seeds, oregano, black pepper, and red pepper flakes.

All that was left was to fine-tune my tomato sauce. While the meatballs baked and the water boiled for the pasta, I sautéed minced garlic in a little olive oil and added both crushed tomatoes and tomato sauce for bright but smooth results. After a brief simmer, I tossed in fresh basil and added the meatballs, which soaked up the tangy sauce while lending it savory depth and richness.

I couldn't have been more pleased with my dish, which featured savory, well-seasoned, and tender sausage meatballs, or with my new-and-improved mixing method for making meatballs.

SAUSAGE MEATBALLS AND SPAGHETTI

SERVES 4 TO 6

The fennel seeds can be coarsely ground in a spice grinder or using the bottom of a heavy skillet. Use a light touch when rolling the meatballs to prevent them from being dense. To portion the meatballs, use 2 tablespoons or a #30 scoop, loosely filled, of the pork mixture. Our preferred brands of crushed tomatoes are Tuttorosso and Muir Glen.

Meatballs

- ½ teaspoon salt
- ¼ teaspoon baking soda
- 4 teaspoons water
- 12 ounces ground pork
- 2 slices hearty white sandwich bread, crusts removed, cut into ½-inch pieces
- ⅓ cup heavy cream
- ⅓ cup grated Parmesan cheese, plus extra for serving
- 2 large egg yolks
- 2 garlic cloves, minced
- 1 teaspoon fennel seeds, coarsely ground
- 1 teaspoon dried oregano
- 1 teaspoon pepper
- ½ teaspoon red pepper flakes
- 12 ounces sweet Italian sausage, casings removed and broken into 1-inch pieces

Tomato Sauce

- 2 tablespoons extra-virgin olive oil
- 1 garlic clove, minced
- 1 (28-ounce) can crushed tomatoes
- 1 (15-ounce) can tomato sauce
- Salt
- 1 tablespoon minced fresh basil

- 1 pound spaghetti

1. **FOR THE MEATBALLS:** Adjust oven rack to upper-middle position and heat oven to 500 degrees. Set wire rack in aluminum foil–lined rimmed baking sheet and spray with vegetable oil spray.

2. Dissolve salt and baking soda in water in large bowl. Add pork, fold gently to combine, and let stand for 10 minutes.

3. Pulse bread, cream, Parmesan, egg yolks, garlic, fennel seeds, oregano, pepper, and pepper flakes in food processor until smooth paste forms, about 10 pulses, scraping down sides of bowl as needed. Add pork mixture (do not wash out bowl) and pulse until mixture is well combined, about 5 pulses.

4. Transfer half of pork mixture to now-empty large bowl. Add sausage to processor and pulse until just combined, 4 to 5 pulses. Transfer sausage-pork mixture to bowl with pork mixture. Using your hands, gently fold together until mixture is just combined.

5. With your wet hands, lightly shape mixture into 1¾-inch round meatballs (about 1 ounce each); you should have about 24 meatballs. Arrange meatballs, evenly spaced, on prepared wire rack and bake until browned, about 15 minutes, rotating sheet halfway through baking.

6. **FOR THE TOMATO SAUCE:** While meatballs bake, heat oil in Dutch oven over medium heat until shimmering. Add garlic and cook, stirring frequently, until fragrant, about 30 seconds. Stir in crushed tomatoes, tomato sauce, and ¼ teaspoon salt and bring to boil. Reduce heat and simmer gently until slightly thickened, about 10 minutes. Stir in basil and season with salt to taste.

7. Add meatballs to sauce and gently simmer, turning them occasionally, for 10 minutes. Cover and keep warm over low heat.

8. Bring 4 quarts water to boil in large pot. Add pasta and 1 tablespoon salt and cook, stirring often, until al dente. Reserve ½ cup cooking water, then drain pasta and return it to pot.

9. Add ½ cup sauce and ¼ cup reserved cooking water to pasta and toss to combine, adjusting consistency with remaining reserved cooking water as needed. Transfer pasta to large serving platter and top with meatballs and remaining sauce. Serve, passing extra Parmesan separately.

Annie Makes the Meatballs
Video available free for 4 months at CooksIllustrated.com/oct15

SO WE TRIED ▶
mixing with food processor
GOOD: smooth, homogeneous
BUT: meatballs not truly tender and juicy

AFTER THAT WE TRIED ▶
mixing in portion of pork mixture by hand
GOOD: more tenderness
BUT: still not juicy

SO WE TRIED ▶
soaking pork in baking soda
GOOD: juicier meatballs
BUT: meat still a little sticky

FINALLY WE TRIED ▶
subbing heavy cream for milk
GOOD:
extra fat = less sticky meat

SUCCESS!
rich, savory, tender meatballs

Introducing Fattoush

This Middle Eastern bread salad is hard to beat—if you get the textures right. We set out to preserve the crunch.

BY LAN LAM

Middle Eastern cooks have a knack for making the most of leftovers. Take flatbreads, a mainstay of their tables. These thin breads stale quickly, so leftovers—and dishes designed to use them up—abound. Such recipes are called *fatteh*, derived from the Arabic word *fatta,* meaning "to crumble." Pita bread salad, or *fattoush,* is a prime example. The vibrant mix traditionally combines toasted, fried, or day-old bread with ripe tomatoes, cucumber, romaine lettuce, parsley, mint, scallions, and a potent green like watercress, all simply dressed with fresh lemon juice and extra-virgin olive oil.

Some cooks don't mind (or even prefer) if the pita softens in the vegetable juices and vinaigrette, but I like the bread to have some crunch. My goal: a refreshing, easy-to-make salad boasting plenty of textural contrast.

A simple lemon and garlic vinaigrette is all that is needed to dress a mix of tomatoes, cucumber, arugula, herbs, and pita chips.

Picking Produce

I jumped right into my salad-making adventure by selecting the vegetables and herbs. Farm-fresh tomatoes and a crisp English cucumber, which we have found to have fewer seeds than the American kind, were mandatory. A handful of chopped scallions was also a given. After sampling various combinations of lettuce, greens, and herbs, I eliminated the traditional parsley and romaine. The former was too grassy; the latter, too watery. Mint, cilantro, and peppery arugula, on the other hand, offered plenty of fresh, summery flavor and made the cut.

For the vinaigrette, I looked to a similar recipe, our Italian Bread Salad (July/August 2011), which is also based on bread, tomatoes, and cucumbers. Figuring that a similar dressing would be appropriate here, I whisked together 3 tablespoons of fresh lemon juice, ½ cup of extra-virgin olive oil, 1 small clove of minced garlic, and salt and pepper. (Sharply citrusy Middle Eastern sumac berries or *za'atar*, a spice mix that features sumac, dried herbs, and salt, are often included as well, but I decided to skip these since they can be hard to find.)

On to the pita. Untreated stale bread wasn't an option since it wasn't crisp enough to start. Could it be as convenient as tearing open a bag of store-bought pita chips? No. Though they were supercrunchy straight from the bag, commercially made chips are low in fat and so became mushy within minutes of mixing the salad. I would have to make my own.

Forging ahead and following the test kitchen's recipe for pita chips, I divided two rounds into wedges, lightly spritzed them with vegetable oil spray, and toasted them in a moderate oven. Once the brittle triangles cooled, I broke them into bite-size pieces and tossed them with my vegetables and vinaigrette. This try was a success in that it had the right combination and ratios of ingredients. However, the garlic flavor in the dressing was overwhelming even though I had used only a small clove. What's more, the pita failed to stay crunchy.

To tame the garlic, I used a tried-and-true test kitchen trick and let it soak in the lemon juice for 10 minutes. The citric acid chemically changed the harsh-tasting allicin in the raw garlic into more mellow flavor compounds.

Perfecting the Pita

As for the pita, one way to keep it crunchy would be to remove moisture from the vegetables. This meant seeding the tomatoes and cucumbers, salting them, and then letting their liquid drain away.

Seeking "Crunchewy" Pita

It took a few tries to figure out an easy way to produce pita chips that would maintain most of their crunch even when mixed with vinaigrette and juicy vegetables.

DAY-OLD PITA: LIMP FROM THE START
We dismissed day-old bread from the get-go for its lack of crunch.

STORE-BOUGHT CHIPS: MUSHY
Store-bought chips are low in fat and didn't stand up to moisture.

SPRITZED AND BAKED: SOGGY
A light misting of oil didn't adequately waterproof the pita.

DEEP-FRIED: TOO MUCH WORK
This option required 2 cups of oil and frying in multiple batches.

OVEN-FRIED: CRUNCHY
Our method produces chips that are truly water-repellent.

TECHNIQUE

NEATER, TASTIER TOMATOES

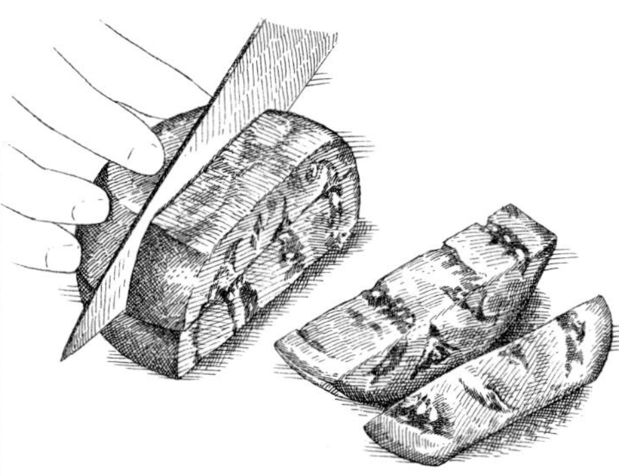

Hold tomato on counter with stem end facing to one side and cut into ¾-inch-thick slices. By orienting tomato this way, seeds and flavorful jelly will stay intact when you cut. Stack slices in pairs and cut into ¾-inch strips; then cut strips crosswise into ¾-inch pieces.

But aside from being time-consuming, the trouble with this approach was that as the salt pulled moisture out, it also caused the vegetables' cell walls to collapse slightly, softening their textures. What's more, the jelly that surrounds a tomato's seeds is its tastiest part—it contains three times more flavorful glutamates than the flesh. I was loath to toss it in the garbage.

Perhaps I needed an altogether different approach. Instead of removing moisture from the salad, what if I waterproofed the pita itself? Since oil repels water, my immediate thought was to deep-fry the pita, which would coat it in more oil than simply spritzing it. Sure enough, a batch of deep-fried pita chips retained its crunch even after being tossed with the vegetables and vinaigrette. What little liquid was absorbed flavored the chips and softened them enough to make them pleasantly chewy in spots and more fork-friendly. The drawbacks: The chips had to be fried in batches and in lots of oil—about 2 cups.

I was fairly certain that I could achieve this same effect in the oven if I could determine how much oil the pita absorbed during frying. To find out, I made a couple more batches, carefully measuring the amount of oil I began with and the amount that remained after frying. With a little math, I determined that two pita breads were soaking up about ¼ cup of oil. I set a rack in a rimmed baking sheet and arranged my pitas (first splitting them into two thin rounds and halving them) on the rack, brushing them with half the oil destined for the dressing. Then I baked the pitas in a 375-degree oven until crisp. Once they were cool, I broke the pitas into rough pieces and added the herbs, vegetables, garlic–lemon juice mixture, and remaining oil. It was a good start: The oil prevented most of the chips from absorbing so much moisture that they turned to mush while still allowing them to pick up flavor from the lemony dressing. But frustratingly, some of the chips were still soggy or oily.

I realized that I'd haphazardly arranged the pitas on the rack, with some smooth side up and others rough side up. The oil was sliding right off the smooth sides of the bread, whereas the craggy rough-side-up chips remained crisp because they had gripped the oil. I prepared another batch, this time making sure to arrange all my pita chips rough side up. I also reduced the oil to 3 tablespoons to eliminate any greasiness. These chips hit the mark: During baking, the oil spread and soaked all the way through the bread, giving the same effect as deep frying. When a colleague raved about the bright flavors and quipped that every last pita piece was "crunchewy," I knew I had a winner.

PITA BREAD SALAD WITH TOMATOES AND CUCUMBER (FATTOUSH)

SERVES 4

The success of this recipe depends on ripe, in-season tomatoes. A rasp-style grater makes quick work of turning the garlic into a paste. For our free recipe for Pita Bread Salad with Tomatoes and Cucumber (Fattoush) for Two, go to CooksIllustrated.com/oct15.

- **2 (8-inch) pita breads**
- **7 tablespoons extra-virgin olive oil**
- **Salt and pepper**
- **3 tablespoons lemon juice**
- **¼ teaspoon garlic, minced to paste**
- **1 pound tomatoes, cored and cut into ¾-inch pieces**
- **1 English cucumber, peeled and sliced ⅛ inch thick**
- **1 cup arugula, chopped coarse**
- **½ cup chopped fresh cilantro**
- **½ cup chopped fresh mint**
- **4 scallions, sliced thin**

1. Adjust oven rack to middle position and heat oven to 375 degrees. Using kitchen shears, cut around perimeter of each pita and separate into 2 thin rounds. Cut each round in half. Place pitas, smooth side down, on wire rack set in rimmed baking sheet. Brush 3 tablespoons oil over surface of pitas. (Pitas do not need to be uniformly coated. Oil will spread during baking.) Season with salt and pepper to taste. Bake until pitas are crisp and pale golden brown, 10 to 14 minutes. Set aside to cool. (Cooled pitas can be stored in zipper-lock bag for 24 hours.)

2. While pitas toast, whisk lemon juice, garlic, and ¼ teaspoon salt together in small bowl. Let stand for 10 minutes.

3. Place tomatoes, cucumber, arugula, cilantro, mint, and scallions in large bowl. Break pitas into ½-inch pieces and place in bowl with vegetables. Add lemon-garlic mixture and remaining ¼ cup oil and toss to coat. Season with salt and pepper to taste. Serve immediately.

TESTING

New-Generation Kitchen Trash Cans

Gone are the days when a kitchen trash can was nothing more than a simple plastic bin with a lid. These days, your choices include sleek models in fingerprint-proof stainless steel with motion sensors that can set you back close to $200.00. To find out what our money would buy, we purchased five tall kitchen trash cans, including both bargain bins and luxury models, priced from $17.99 to $180.00. To evaluate design, user-friendliness, and odor control, we started by stuffing the cans with identical assortments of garbage, docking points if the bags slipped down or were hard to fill or remove. We then loaded the cans with odoriferous ingredients, left them for a weekend, and sniffed around for smells on Monday. Our final consideration was the way the user opens the bin (step pedal, button, motion sensor, or manually); after using the cans daily for several weeks in home kitchens, a step pedal model won us over. Though it's an investment, the Simplehuman Rectangular Step Trash Can ($180.00) shows impressive attention to detail. Its lid opens fully and effortlessly for access to a roomy barrel and can be kept open with the flip of a switch; plus, it has a lightweight liner that can be removed for cleaning. If you don't want to spring for bells and whistles, our Best Buy, the Sterilite Lift-Top Wastebasket ($17.99), has to be opened by hand, but it's sturdy and easy to use. For complete testing results, go to CooksIllustrated.com/oct15. –Kate Shannon

SIMPLEHUMAN Rectangular Step Trash Can, 50 liter

PRICE: $180.00

COMMENTS: We appreciated the foot pedal on this luxe model as well as its sleek but spacious and sturdy frame that trapped odors. It boasts a fingerprint-proof stainless-steel exterior and a liner that can be lifted onto an interior rest for easy bag changes.

STERILITE Lift-Top Wastebasket

BEST BUY

PRICE: $17.99

COMMENTS: Although it lacks a hands-free opening mechanism, this model's lid opens completely and can be left open. It's also a snap to line the can and remove full bags, and it kept odors contained.

Watch It Become Fattoush

Video available free for 4 months at CooksIllustrated.com/oct15

Grilled Country-Style Ribs

Though not true ribs, this lesser-known cut pairs the rich flavor of ribs with the quick cooking of a chop.

BY LAN LAM

Country-style pork ribs are a favorite in the test kitchen—we've sliced them into small pieces for stir-fries and braised and shredded them for hearty ragus. But this cut is rarely prepared on its own, perhaps because the name causes confusion. Country-style ribs actually aren't anything like baby back ribs or St. Louis–style spareribs, which are sold as racks of bones joined by collagen-rich meat that takes hours to turn tender. Instead, they are more like well-marbled pork chops: They're a knife-and-fork cut, sold either boneless or with a portion of bone attached, containing both light, lean loin meat and a section from the dark, richly pork-flavored shoulder. And because they contain much less collagen, they cook quickly.

So why not treat them like pork chops and feature them front and center in a recipe? Grilling seemed like a great option. The trick, I knew, would be getting the white and dark meat to cook evenly. The pork chops we've grilled in the past contain only meat from the loin, so I'd need to come up with my own cooking method for country-style ribs that produced a flavorful, nicely browned exterior and juicy interior throughout.

We often brine or salt pork chops to help the meat stay juicy while it cooks. Since soaking chops in a saltwater brine would impede browning, it seemed more sensible to take a cue from barbecuing and apply a salt-heavy spice rub to my ribs, letting them sit to give the salt time to penetrate. I made a simple dry rub with chili powder, cayenne, a tablespoon of salt, and brown sugar, which would encourage browning while adding a complex sweetness. After coating the ribs with this spice mixture, I wrapped them tightly in plastic wrap and placed them in the fridge. A few stripped-down cooking tests showed that the ribs were nicely seasoned after just 1 hour but didn't suffer from sitting in the fridge for a full 24 hours if I wanted to apply the rub the day before.

Now it was time to move on to the key challenges. I decided to focus first on figuring out how much to cook the pork and then worry about the grill setup, so I began with a straightforward single-level fire, spreading 6 quarts of lit coals evenly over the grill. Though

See How They Cook
Video available free for 4 months at CooksIllustrated.com/oct15

Country-style ribs offer a lot more meat per bone than traditional pork ribs.

cooking the ribs to 175 degrees delivered perfect dark meat, the light meat was woefully dry. On the flip side, pulling the ribs off the grill when they reached 135 to 140 degrees produced juicy light meat but chewy, underdone dark meat. A compromise was in order. Tasters eventually voted in favor of ribs cooked to 150 degrees. The fat in the ribs moistened the light meat enough that the slight overcooking wasn't noticeable, while the dark meat still had a little tug to it but was nevertheless reasonably tender—and very flavorful.

All that was left was to fix the grill setup. On a single-level fire, the exterior of my ribs tended to dry out while I waited for the interior to come up to temperature. There were also hot and cool spots because of gaps between the coals, which meant that some ribs burned. When we want a combination of good char and a perfectly cooked interior, we often set up the grill with hotter and cooler sides, piling all the coals on one side; that was clearly the way to go here. I started the ribs over the more concentrated, even heat of the hotter side to produce excellent browning. I then finished them on the cooler side to slowly cook them through for juicy, tender results. On the cooler side, it was also easy to add sweetness and tang by basting the ribs with barbecue sauce and allowing it to slowly caramelize without burning.

Country-style pork ribs might be a misnomer, but there's no confusion that my recipe for sweet and tangy, meaty grilled pork was a winner.

SWEET AND TANGY GRILLED COUNTRY-STYLE PORK RIBS

SERVES 4 TO 6

For information on buying country-style pork ribs, see "Ribs That Aren't" on page 28. Be sure to trim the pork well to reduce flare-ups. This recipe requires refrigerating the spice-rubbed ribs for at least 1 hour or up to 24 hours before grilling. For our free recipe for Sweet and Tangy Barbecue Sauce, go to CooksIllustrated.com/oct15. Alternatively, use bottled sauce (our winning brand is Bull's-Eye Original Barbecue Sauce).

- **4 teaspoons packed brown sugar**
- **1 tablespoon kosher salt**
- **1 tablespoon chili powder**
- **⅛ teaspoon cayenne pepper**
- **4 pounds bone-in country-style pork ribs, trimmed**
- **½ cup barbecue sauce, plus extra for serving**

1. Combine sugar, salt, chili powder, and cayenne in bowl. Rub mixture all over ribs. Wrap tightly in plastic wrap and refrigerate for at least 1 hour or up to 24 hours.

2A. FOR A CHARCOAL GRILL: Open bottom vent halfway. Light large chimney starter filled with charcoal briquettes (6 quarts). When top coals are partially covered with ash, pour evenly over half of grill. Set cooking grate in place, cover, and open lid vent halfway. Heat grill until hot, about 5 minutes.

2B. FOR A GAS GRILL: Turn all burners to high, cover, and heat grill until hot, about 15 minutes. Leave primary burner on high and turn off other burners to maintain grill temperature around 350 degrees.

3. Clean and oil cooking grate. Place ribs on hotter side of grill. Cover and cook until well browned on both sides, 4 to 7 minutes total. Move ribs to cooler side of grill and brush with ¼ cup sauce. Cover and cook for 6 minutes. Flip ribs and brush with remaining ¼ cup sauce. Cover and continue to cook until pork registers 150 degrees, 5 to 10 minutes longer. Transfer ribs to serving platter, tent with aluminum foil, and let rest for 10 minutes. Serve, passing extra sauce separately.

A New Way to Sauté Summer Squash

A common kitchen tool gets around the core issue.

BY ANNIE PETITO

Everyone knows that summer squash has a lot going for it: It's inexpensive and abundant, its mild flesh pairs nicely with a variety of flavors, and it cooks quickly. But it's also 95 percent water and full of meddlesome seeds. That means that unless you do some finagling, you're inevitably in for soggy, steamy, seedy results. Excess moisture is commonly addressed by cutting or shredding the vegetable, salting it, and then waiting at least 30 minutes for the liquid to drain off—a nonstarter when I'm racing to churn out dinner. Some recipes skip salting to economize on time and call for simply sautéing the squash quickly over high heat. The goal is to tenderize the flesh before it completely breaks down and sheds liquid, but the technique doesn't work very well. Chunky pieces end up soft on the outside but firm in the middle. Slicing the squash thin is an option, but that still doesn't get rid of the seeds. I wanted nonwatery, seedless squash on the table in a flash.

What if I removed the core altogether? Using a spoon to scrape the seeds from a squash that I halved lengthwise left me with odd-looking half-moon shapes. A better plan would be to work around the core, cutting the flesh first into thick vertical planks and then into thin, bite-size pieces. This was doable, but as I cut, I thought about a few recipes I'd seen that called for trading the knife for a vegetable peeler and shaving the squash into ribbons.

I got out my peeler and trimmed the ends from a colorful mix of summer squash and zucchini. Using firm, steady pressure and stopping when I reached the seeds, I speedily produced a generous pile of strips. It was time to move to the stove.

After just 4 minutes, the squash is tender and translucent.

I placed a large nonstick pan over high heat and set out to cook the ribbons in a single batch. To prevent the strips from tangling in the pan, I tried coating them in plenty of extra-virgin olive oil before cooking, but this only made them greasy. Instead, I found that simply fluffing the squash with tongs as it hit the oil-coated skillet and tossing it occasionally during cooking adequately prevented clumping.

Normally, I want to develop as much browning as possible when cooking summer squash because of the rich flavor it adds. In this case, however, going overboard on browning detracted from the bright, colorful appearance of the graceful ribbons, so I dialed down the heat. In less than 5 minutes, I had crisp-tender, beautifully translucent squash that wasn't the least bit soggy or seedy.

Now I just needed to incorporate seasonings. A complex dressing would only overpower the delicate squash flavor, so I mixed together a straightforward vinaigrette. I started by squeezing a lemon and adding a clove of minced garlic. Next came extra-virgin olive oil and the zest from the lemon. When I tossed the dressing with the hot ribbons, they soaked it up and took on an attractive shimmer. With a final sprinkle of parsley, my work was done.

TECHNIQUE

MAKING SQUASH RIBBONS

Holding squash at slight angle, peel from the top downward. Rotate squash every few strokes, stopping when you reach the seedy core. A stack of four ribbons should be only ¼ inch thick.

SAUTÉED SUMMER SQUASH WITH PARSLEY AND GARLIC

SERVES 4

Be sure to start checking for doneness at the lower end of the cooking time. For our free recipe for Sautéed Summer Squash with Oregano and Pepper Flakes, go to CooksIllustrated.com/oct15.

- 1 small garlic clove, minced
- 1 teaspoon grated lemon zest plus 1 tablespoon juice
- 4 yellow squashes and/or zucchini (8 ounces each), trimmed
- 7 teaspoons extra-virgin olive oil
- Salt and pepper
- 1½ tablespoons chopped fresh parsley

1. Combine garlic and lemon juice in large bowl and set aside for at least 10 minutes. Using vegetable peeler, shave each squash lengthwise into ribbons. Peel off 3 ribbons from 1 side, then turn squash 90 degrees and peel off 3 more ribbons. Continue to turn and peel ribbons until you reach seeds. Discard core.

2. Whisk 2 tablespoons oil, ¼ teaspoon salt, ⅛ teaspoon pepper, and lemon zest into garlic mixture.

3. Heat remaining 1 teaspoon oil in 12-inch nonstick skillet over medium-high heat until just smoking. Add squash and cook, tossing occasionally with tongs, until squash has softened and is translucent, 3 to 4 minutes. Transfer squash to bowl with dressing, add 1 tablespoon parsley, and toss to coat. Season with salt and pepper to taste. Transfer to serving platter and sprinkle with remaining 1½ teapoons parsley. Serve immediately.

SAUTÉED SUMMER SQUASH WITH MINT AND PISTACHIOS

Substitute 1½ teaspoons cider vinegar for lemon zest and juice. Substitute ⅓ cup chopped fresh mint for parsley and sprinkle squash with 2 tablespoons pistachios, toasted and chopped, before serving.

Watch the Ribbons
Video available free for 4 months at CooksIllustrated.com/oct15

Guide to Freezing Ingredients

Too often, that extra half-can of tomato paste or handful of chopped onion gets thrown away. We tested dozens of ingredients to see which we could freeze for future use.

BY KEITH DRESSER AND LOUISE EMERICK

Freeze It Right

When freezing food, air is the enemy. Freezer burn, indicated by ice crystals and brownish-white discoloration, happens when frozen food is exposed to air and dehydrates and oxidizes. Here's how to ensure the best texture and flavor.

Keep Your Freezer Cold
The quicker foods freeze, and the fewer fluctuations in temperature once frozen, the better. Your freezer should register 0 degrees Fahrenheit or colder; use a thermometer to check.

Portion Liquids
Liquids can be frozen in ice cube trays and then transferred to a zipper-lock bag.

Minimize Headroom
In hard-sided containers, fill to ½ inch from the top and place plastic wrap on the food's surface before attaching the lid.

Double Wrap
For solid foods you're wrapping in zipper-lock bags, first wrap in plastic wrap and then put the food in the bag, pressing out as much air as possible before sealing.

PANTRY

These pantry ingredients can be frozen and thawed with virtually no noticeable change in quality.

Anchovies, Bacon

Prep: Coil up individually (to prevent sticking and to minimize surface area for freezer burn), freeze on plate, and transfer to zipper-lock bag.

Applesauce

Prep: Portion in ½- to 1-cup containers to freeze; transfer to zipper-lock bag.

Beans (Soaked and Canned)

Prep: Rinse soaked dried beans (we brine ours for better flavor and texture) and drain canned beans. Pat all beans dry with paper towels and transfer to zipper-lock bag. To save space, lay flat to freeze.

➢ Cooked homemade beans don't freeze as well as canned beans; the latter contain calcium chloride, which protects against ice crystal damage.

Bread

Prep: Wrap sliced loaves tightly in plastic wrap, wrap unsliced loaves in foil, and seal each in zipper-lock bag. Thaw individual slices at room temperature; no need to thaw slices before toasting. Place frozen loaves, still wrapped in foil, in 450-degree oven for 10 to 15 minutes; remove foil and return loaves to oven for 1 to 2 minutes to crisp crust.

SCIENCE **Never Refrigerate Bread**

Bread stales when starches crystallize and incorporate water into the crystalline structure, causing the loaf to harden. But the storage temperature dramatically affects how quickly this happens. We found that refrigerated bread staled in just a day and bread stored at room temperature staled in just two days—but frozen bread held up well for a month. Why? Staling, or retrogradation, occurs about six times faster at refrigerator temperatures (36 to 40 degrees) than at room temperature, but at below-freezing temps, it slows down significantly. Bottom line: Store bread at room temperature for no more than two days; otherwise, freeze it.

Broth

Prep: For smaller amounts, freeze in ice cube trays or muffin tin cups; transfer to zipper-lock bag. For larger portions, line 4-cup liquid measuring cup with zipper-lock bag and pour in broth. Seal bag, seal in second bag if desired, and lay flat to freeze.

Canned Tomato Paste

Prep: Open ends of can, push out paste, and freeze in zipper-lock bag. Cut off only as much as needed from frozen log.

Chipotle Chiles in Adobo Sauce

Prep: Freeze spoonfuls of chiles and sauce on parchment paper–lined baking sheet; transfer to zipper-lock bag.

Coconut Milk

Prep: Portion into ½- to 1-cup containers to freeze; transfer to zipper-lock bag. After thawing, process with immersion blender for 30 seconds to re-emulsify before use.

Cooked Grains

Prep: Spread cooked grains (we tested wheat berries and long-grain white and brown rice) on baking sheet to cool, transfer to zipper-lock bag, and lay flat to freeze. No need to thaw before use.

Tortillas

Prep: Separate corn or flour tortillas with waxed paper or parchment paper and place in zipper-lock bag. To thaw, defrost stacks of 3 to 4 tortillas in microwave at 50 percent power, 10 to 20 seconds per stack.

Used Frying Oil

Even strained, used frying oil contains microscopic particles of food that make it go rancid quickly at room temperature.
Prep: Freeze in airtight containers.

Wine

Prep: Freeze 1-tablespoon portions in ice cube tray; transfer to zipper-lock bag.

➢ Use only in cooking since freezing causes many of wine's organic compounds to precipitate out as solids (heat reintegrates them).

ILLUSTRATION: JOHN BURGOYNE

DAIRY AND EGGS

We found that freezing dairy products and eggs didn't affect flavor, only texture. Liquids seemed thinner and separated; yogurts and some cheeses were grainy. That's because freezing causes the water and proteins to separate; the water then forms ice crystals while the proteins clump. Blending liquids with an immersion blender will eliminate some but not all clumps, so it's best to use thawed dairy in baked goods where it's not a primary ingredient. (Freezing also separates water and protein in egg yolks. But we came up with a great fix: stirring a simple syrup into the yolks. The dissolved sugar interferes with ice crystal formation and also prevents clumping.)

Cream Cheese

Prep: Seal in zipper-lock bag.

➤ Don't use as spread or in recipes where grainy texture will be noticeable, such as in cheesecake. Fine for biscuits and pound cake.

Cultured Dairy (Buttermilk, Sour Cream, Yogurt)

Prep: Portion in ½- to 1-cup containers to freeze; transfer to zipper-lock bag.

➤ Not good for custards, puddings, and most uncooked applications. (Greek yogurt is the exception—since freezing thins its texture, it can be swapped for regular yogurt in uncooked recipes.)

➤ Thawed buttermilk mixes well in salad dressings that include emulsifying agents (e.g., mayonnaise).

Egg Whites

Prep: Freeze individually in ice cube trays; transfer to zipper-lock bag.

➤ Thawed whites will whip more quickly than fresh since freezing begins the process of unwinding their proteins that whipping continues.

Egg Yolks

Prep: Prepare syrup of 2 parts sugar to 1 part water; stir into yolks using ¾ teaspoon syrup per 4 yolks. Syrup will not impart noticeable sweetness; yolks are fine even for savory applications such as hollandaise sauce.

Hard and Semisoft Cheeses

Prep: Wrap cheese (cheddar, Brie, Pecorino Romano, mozzarella, and Parmesan all freeze well) tightly in foil; seal in zipper-lock bag.

➤ Cheddar turns crumbly after thawing; use only in melted applications.

Milk and Cream

Prep: Portion in ½- to 1-cup containers to freeze; transfer to zipper-lock bag.

➤ Avoid using in uncooked applications; custards and puddings; and coffee, cocoa, and other hot beverages. Fine for baked goods and mashed potatoes.

➤ Thawed heavy cream can be whipped, but use it immediately or it will start to weep.

Five to Always Freeze

There are a few ingredients that we always put directly in the freezer to preserve freshness and flavor and prevent spoilage.

Bay Leaves

Stored in the freezer for three months, bay leaves were far more flavorful than those stored at room temperature for the same amount of time.

Extra Butter

If kept in the fridge longer than a month, even unopened sticks of butter can pick up off-flavors. Freeze extra sticks sealed in a zipper-lock bag.

Extra Coffee Beans

Unless coffee beans are sealed in unopened, airtight containers, their flavor deteriorates noticeably after 10 days at room temperature. Before freezing, portion extra beans in one-day allotments to minimize exposure to air and moisture.

Nuts

The high fat content of nuts means that they can turn rancid surprisingly fast at room temperature. There's no need to thaw them before use.

Whole-Grain Flours, Oats, and Cornmeal

Freezing prevents fats in whole grains from oxidizing and producing off-flavors; transfer items to airtight containers first. Bring them to room temperature before baking with them.

PRODUCE

Freezing alters the texture of many types of produce, but their flavors can remain remarkably intact.

Bananas

Prep: Peel and then seal in zipper-lock bag.

➤ Best for quick breads (thaw first) and smoothies (keep frozen).

➤ Avoid pies, puddings, or any recipe where banana needs to hold its shape.

Citrus Zest

Prep: Freeze in packed ½-teaspoon mounds on baking sheet; transfer to zipper-lock bag.

➤ Avoid using as garnish since color fades.

Chopped Onions

Prep: Seal in zipper-lock bag.

➤ Freezing turns onions mushy. Use only in cooked applications (no need to thaw first).

SCIENCE

Cut Garlic and Onions Before Freezing

When cut, garlic and onions each release the same enzyme that reacts with their sulfur compounds to produce their characteristic pungent flavors. Because freezing reduces the activity of this enzyme, it needs to be able to do its job and produce the compounds before the garlic and onions go into the freezer, where the flavors will be preserved. There is one notable difference in how we freeze them: We coat garlic in oil to protect its pungent flavor compounds from oxidation. Onions contain an extra enzyme that does this job, so there's no need for the oil.

Fresh Herbs

Prep: Chop parsley, basil, tarragon, or cilantro; transfer by spoonful to ice cube trays, top with water, and freeze. Transfer to zipper-lock bag.

➤ Add frozen cubes directly to soups, sauces, and stews. Herb flavor won't be quite as strong as when fresh.

Garlic

Prep: Mince garlic, combine with ½ teaspoon vegetable oil per clove, and freeze in heaping teaspoons on baking sheet. Transfer to zipper-lock bag.

Ginger

Prep: Grate ginger (frozen whole ginger turns spongy), freeze in 1-teaspoon portions on baking sheet, and transfer to zipper-lock bag.

Keep a Record!

Storing leftovers in the freezer is great—until you forget about them. To keep track of what you have, affix a dry-erase board to the freezer and make notes when you add (or remove) items. Adding dates also reminds you to use up older items.

Really Good Black Bean Burgers

Earthy black beans should make a satisfying nonmeat burger. But most either fall apart when flipped or are so mushy that no one wants to eat them.

BY ERIKA BRUCE

When it comes to vegetarian recipes, veggie burgers have never been high on my list. Most rely on such a hodgepodge of ingredients, with multiple grains and vegetables that need to be individually prepared before they go into the burger, that they are a lot of work to put together. Black bean burgers seem more approachable. The earthy beans promise a hearty, satisfying meal, and because the beans themselves provide plenty of substance, ideally the process wouldn't be much more complicated than making an everyday beef burger—just mash up a couple of cans of beans, add a few complementary ingredients, shape into patties, and cook.

When I reviewed recipes, I found that there were a couple of approaches to handling the beans: They could be coarsely chopped, lightly mashed with a fork, or pureed until smooth. To bind the beans together, almost all recipes relied on eggs, and many also loaded up on starchy ingredients like bread crumbs or oats. Unfortunately, I wasn't impressed when I tried them. Lots of starch made it easy to shape chopped beans and eggs into patties, but these burgers turned into dry, tasteless hockey pucks once cooked. At the other end of the spectrum were the recipes that called for mashed or pureed beans. The cohesive, hummus-like texture held together nicely even with minimal binders, but it also produced a burger with a gluey, pasty consistency.

As for add-ins, recipes tended to follow the lead of veggie burgers by throwing in everything from porcini mushrooms and soy sauce to poblano peppers and cashew nuts. I was after burgers that featured earthy bean flavor at their heart with just enough seasoning and mix-ins to give them a little zest and intrigue. I also wanted patties that weren't wet or gluey but rather just cohesive enough to hold together when flipped in the pan, with a little textural contrast from chunks of beans and a nice crust.

A spicy chipotle mayonnaise enlivens the earthy-tasting burgers.

Look: It Really Works
Video available free for 4 months at CooksIllustrated.com/oct15

A Hill of Beans

After draining and rinsing a couple of cans of beans, I spread the beans on paper towels to rid them of moisture. My thinking was the drier they were, the less starchy binder they might require. And to avoid a smooth, mushy texture, the beans would have to retain some of their shape. But they still needed to be broken down enough to incorporate well, so I pulled out the food processor. A couple of pulses produced nicely chopped pieces that would offer a bit of texture.

To transform the chopped beans into a cohesive burger mix, I tried stirring in a beaten egg along with a handful of panko bread crumbs. (I used only a small amount so as to let the bean flavor come to the fore.) Like tiny sponges, the bread crumbs did an excellent job of absorbing the egg's moisture, but even a little bit made the burgers taste bready. What's more, one egg seemed insufficient since each and every burger broke apart into crumbles as I flipped it.

Many recipes call for some sort of precooked grains, such as rice or bulgur, to bind the beans, but in the interest of simplicity, I opted to avoid that path. Instead, I experimented with a different sort of starch that would complement the Latin American provenance of black beans: tortilla chips. Since I already had the food processor out, I quickly blitzed a few chips before pulsing in the beans. Then I added two beaten eggs to help hold the burgers together. Everything seemed great—that is, until I tried to pack the burgers into patties. The mixture was so wet and sticky that shaping them was nearly impossible.

Bound for Glory

Adding more ground chips would only mute the flavor of the beans, so I took a lunch break, hoping that an hour of hands-off time would allow the starches in the beans and the tortilla chips to absorb the liquid from the egg. Just as I had hoped, the mixture was much easier to handle after it sat in the fridge for an hour. These patties were easy to form, held their shape fairly well, and developed a crisp, golden brown crust when I fried them in a little bit of oil. Unfortunately, they still occasionally broke apart as I flipped them.

To glue the burgers together more effectively, I took the unorthodox step of adding a good sprinkling of flour. After all, we often use flour in combination with beaten egg to get a breading to cling to meat. Sure enough, since wheat contains sticky amylopectin starches, a mere 2 tablespoons all but guaranteed that the burger would stay together, without negatively affecting flavor.

Now the burgers just needed some personality. Avoiding additions that were high in moisture or that needed to be cooked down ahead of time (such as onions and peppers), I landed on minced garlic and scallions and chopped fresh cilantro. They were quick and easy and fit my Latin American theme. For even more complexity, I spiked the mixture with citrusy coriander and smoky cumin. Finally, a dash of hot sauce added zip.

These burgers were ready to be topped with the usual fixings—gooey melted cheese, thinly sliced onion, lettuce leaves, and tomato slices—or more deluxe toppings like a creamy avocado-feta spread, spicy chipotle mayonnaise, or a tangy roasted tomato-orange jam.

BLACK BEAN BURGERS
SERVES 6

The black bean mixture needs to be refrigerated for at least 1 hour or up to 24 hours prior to cooking. When forming the patties, it is important to pack them firmly together. Our favorite canned black beans are Bush's Best. Serve the burgers with your favorite toppings or with one of our spreads (recipes follow).

- 2 (15-ounce) cans black beans, rinsed
- 2 large eggs
- 2 tablespoons all-purpose flour
- 4 scallions, minced
- 3 tablespoons minced fresh cilantro
- 2 garlic cloves, minced
- 1 teaspoon ground cumin
- 1 teaspoon hot sauce (optional)
- ½ teaspoon ground coriander
- ¼ teaspoon salt
- ¼ teaspoon pepper
- 1 ounce tortilla chips, crushed coarse (½ cup)
- 8 teaspoons vegetable oil
- 6 hamburger buns

1. Line rimmed baking sheet with triple layer of paper towels and spread beans over towels. Let stand for 15 minutes.

2. Whisk eggs and flour together in large bowl until uniform paste forms. Stir in scallions; cilantro; garlic; cumin; hot sauce, if using; coriander; salt; and pepper until well combined.

3. Process tortilla chips in food processor until finely ground, about 30 seconds. Add black beans and pulse until beans are roughly broken down, about 5 pulses. Transfer black bean mixture to bowl with egg mixture and mix until well combined. Cover and refrigerate for at least 1 hour or up to 24 hours.

4. Adjust oven rack to middle position and heat oven to 200 degrees. Divide bean mixture into 6 equal portions. Firmly pack each portion into tight ball, then flatten to 3½-inch-diameter patty. (Patties can be wrapped individually in plastic wrap, placed in a zipper-lock bag, and frozen for up to 2 weeks. Thaw patties before cooking.)

5. Heat 2 teaspoons oil in 10-inch nonstick skillet over medium heat until shimmering. Carefully place 3 patties in skillet and cook until bottoms are well browned and crisp, about 5 minutes. Flip patties, add 2 teaspoons oil, and cook second side until well browned and crisp, 3 to 5 minutes. Transfer burgers to wire rack set in rimmed baking sheet and place in oven to keep warm. Repeat with remaining 3 patties and 4 teaspoons oil. Transfer burgers to buns and serve.

Bean Burgers Gone Bad

Mixing lots of starchy binders with whole or coarsely chopped beans makes a dry, crumbly burger without much flavor. Pureeing the beans allows you to use minimal binders but turns the patty mushy and gluey.

CRUMBLY AND TASTELESS
Lots of starchy binders mute the bean flavor and dry out the burger.

WET AND MUSHY
Pureed beans need fewer binders but lead to burgers with a hummus-like texture.

AVOCADO-FETA SPREAD
MAKES ABOUT 1¼ CUPS

- 1 ripe avocado, cut into ½-inch pieces
- 1 ounce feta cheese, crumbled (¼ cup)
- 1 tablespoon extra-virgin olive oil
- 1 teaspoon lime juice
- ⅛ teaspoon salt
- ⅛ teaspoon pepper

Using fork, mash all ingredients in medium bowl until mostly smooth.

CHIPOTLE MAYONNAISE
MAKES ABOUT ⅓ CUP

- 3 tablespoons mayonnaise
- 3 tablespoons sour cream
- 2 teaspoons minced canned chipotle chile in adobo sauce
- 1 garlic clove, minced
- ⅛ teaspoon salt

Combine all ingredients. Cover and refrigerate for at least 1 hour.

ROASTED TOMATO–ORANGE JAM
MAKES ABOUT 1 CUP

Line the baking sheet with foil for easy cleanup.

- 12 ounces cherry tomatoes, halved
- 1 shallot, sliced thin
- 1 tablespoon extra-virgin olive oil
- ¼ teaspoon salt
- ⅛ teaspoon ground cinnamon
- 2 tablespoons orange marmalade

Adjust oven rack to middle position and heat oven to 425 degrees. Toss tomatoes, shallot, oil, salt, and cinnamon together in bowl. Transfer to aluminum foil–lined rimmed baking sheet and roast until edges of tomatoes are well browned, 15 to 20 minutes. Let cool slightly; transfer tomato mixture to food processor. Add marmalade and process until smooth, about 10 seconds.

Keys to an Ideal Black Bean Burger

Here's what we did to create a burger full of earthy bean flavor that wasn't muted by too much starchy binder.

DRY BEANS
Removing excess moisture by draining on paper towels helps cut down on the need for absorbent binders.

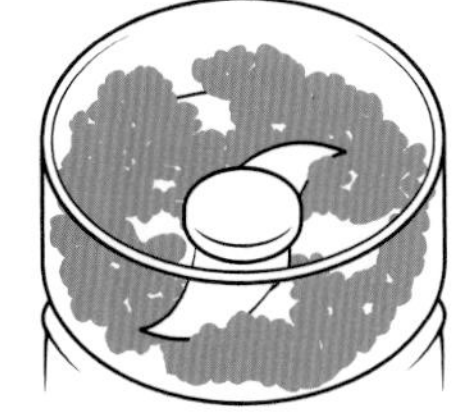

PULSE, DON'T PUREE
Pulsing the beans with tortilla chips (we processed them first) keeps the beans chunky for textural contrast.

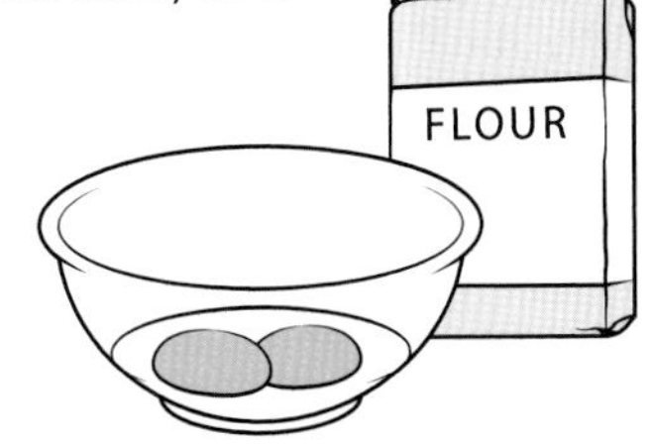

GIVE IT EXTRA CLING
In addition to eggs and starchy tortilla chips, we add flour, which contains sticky amylopectin, to hold the mix together.

LET IT REST
Letting the mixture sit gives the starches time to soak up the eggs so the burgers are easier to handle.

Chocolate-Caramel Cake

The cake and frosting we weren't worried about. But a caramel filling that was complex in flavor and spreadable, yet thick enough not to ooze out? That was another matter.

BY LAN LAM

I love making layer cakes. Tall, imposing ones that make a splash at parties and serve a crowd. The components should be pitch-perfect and strike that balance between kid birthday nostalgia and adult sophistication—a moist, tender crumb; distinct, spreadable filling that's just thick enough to glue the layers together; and frosting that's silky and full-bodied but not so sweet or rich that a forkful is overwhelming.

Chocolate cake is my favorite, and I've made plenty layered with buttercream, ganache, and mousse. But this time I wanted to home in on chocolate and caramel—a combination that has a kind of visceral appeal. A quick search turned up plenty of recipes with a wide range of profiles. Maybe all I had to do was bake off a few and find one I liked.

Wishful thinking. It wasn't that every recipe was a total failure; there were cakes with solid chocolate flavor, gooey caramels, and smooth frostings. And many of them had at least four layers so that the whole package looked rather majestic. But not one delivered the trifecta I had in mind: layers of dark, truly chocolaty cake separated by pleasantly bitter, soft but not runny caramel and generously (but judiciously) covered with glossy chocolate frosting that was a notch less dark and rich than the cake itself.

Think all layer cakes are fussy? This one isn't. The cake is a dump-and-stir, the caramel is simple, and the frosting takes minutes in a food processor.

Piece of Cake

Deep chocolate flavor was a must for the cake but so was getting the crumb just right. In addition to being moist and tender, it needed to be sturdy enough to hold up under the weight of the caramel and frosting. And given that this was a three-component dessert, I wanted to keep the cake-making process as simple as possible.

Those textural considerations would be affected by the mixing method, so I reviewed the two basic options. First—and most traditional for layer cakes—there was the creaming method. This involves beating softened butter with sugar in a stand mixer until it becomes light and fluffy, adding eggs one by one, and then gradually beating in the dry and liquid components alternately until just combined.

I was more keen on the second option, the dump-and-stir method, which involves simply whisking together the dry and wet ingredients in separate bowls and then whisking the wet into the dry until a smooth batter forms. This would be much faster and easier than hauling out my stand mixer, and stirring the liquid directly into flour that has not been coated with butter would create more gluten. This in turn would make for a sturdier but sufficiently tender cake that could be halved to make 4 layers (I'd cut each cake into 2 rounds) able to stand up to the filling and frosting.

I threw together a basic chocolate cake batter and divided it between two 9-inch round cake pans that I greased, floured, and lined with parchment paper (for more information about prepping cake pans, see "Do I Really Need to Use Parchment Paper?" on page 22). After baking for 25 minutes in a 325-degree oven, the cakes emerged nicely resilient, albeit tighter and drier than I wanted. The chocolate flavor was also a tad dull. Adding ½ cup of water moistened the crumb (more buttermilk would have increased the acidity in the cake and potentially compromised the leaveners), and swapping the melted butter for more neutral-tasting vegetable oil allowed the chocolate flavor to shine.

Lan Makes the Cake
Video available free for 4 months at CooksIllustrated.com/oct15

Buttering Up the Caramel

Making caramel sauce is a two-stage process. First, you heat sugar until it melts; some cooks also add a little water, which helps the sugar caramelize evenly without burning, and light corn syrup, which helps prevent crystallization. The degree to which you cook the sugar after melting determines the flavor of the caramel; the higher the final temperature, the more complex and bitter it will be. Next, cream, butter, and other flavorings (like salt and vanilla) are added, which creates a fluid caramel sauce. As the mixture cooks, the temperature increases, water evaporates, and the caramel sauce stiffens—eventually turning into hard candy.

Thus, the biggest key to making a faintly bitter and spreadable but not runny caramel was to zero in closely on its temperature at the two different stages. I boiled 1¼ cups of sugar with ¼ cup each of water and light corn syrup in a saucepan until the mixture turned amber, which took about 10 minutes. Then I lowered the heat and continued to caramelize the sugar mixture until it turned dark amber and its temperature registered between 375 and 380 degrees—a good indication that its flavor would be just a touch bitter but not burnt. Off the heat, I stirred in 1 cup of heavy cream, 6 tablespoons of butter, 1 teaspoon of vanilla, and a generous ¾ teaspoon of salt (salty caramel would be a great match for the sweeter frosting).

Now for the tricky part—figuring out just how much to reduce the liquidy caramel. I returned the heat to medium and simmered the mixture (stirring frequently to ensure even cooking) until it hit about 240 degrees; at that point, it looked a bit runny, but I hoped it would stiffen up a bit as it cooled. I poured it into a greased baking pan—spreading it out would help it cool faster—and waited until it was just warm to the touch.

Don't Be Afraid of Caramel

Caramel is simply sugar (sucrose) that's been heated until it melts, browns, and develops complex flavor. You can use it to make a fluid caramel sauce or chewy or hard candy by adding cream, butter, and other flavorings. The longer the mixture cooks, the more water will evaporate and the stiffer the caramel will become.

Though caramel gets a bad rap for being finicky to make, with the right recipe, it's easy to overcome its two main pitfalls: The sugar can melt unevenly and burn, or it can seize up and crystallize. The latter happens when some of the sucrose molecules are not hot enough to melt and break down into glucose and fructose and instead bond, creating a grainy texture. Here's what we do to make a caramel that works.

ESSENTIAL TECHNIQUES

Add Water

Water, which makes a "wet caramel," helps the sugar dissolve and spread across the pan so that it melts evenly and reduces the risk that some sugar burns before the rest caramelizes.

Add Corn Syrup, Not Acid

Adding acid or corn syrup to sugar as it caramelizes can prevent crystallization; both ingredients interfere with sucrose's ability to bond with itself.

Acids: A small amount of lemon juice, vinegar, or cream of tartar speeds the breakdown of sucrose into fructose and glucose. These molecules dilute the remaining sucrose molecules, decreasing their chances of bonding together before they, too, can break down.

Corn syrup: Corn syrup already contains glucose molecules (and water); thus, it dilutes the sucrose molecules faster. For this reason, we prefer it over acids.

Use a Heavy-Bottom Saucepan

Sugar is prone to burning in lightweight cookware, which does not transfer heat evenly. A heavy saucepan helps the sugar cook evenly.

Use Two Levels of Heat

Over high heat the sugar can heat unevenly or even burn, but over low heat it can crystallize. That's because there will be enough heat to evaporate the water, but not enough to melt the sugar, so the sucrose molecules can bond. We melt the sugar over medium-high heat and then reduce the heat to low to prevent it from burning.

"TIPS" TO AVOID

As long as you cook the sugar over a hot enough flame, it will melt, so skip these common caramel techniques.

Stirring

Stirring the sugar to help it melt isn't necessary. We simply swirl the pan occasionally as the syrup cooks to even out hot spots.

Washing/Covering

Brushing the walls of the pot with a wet pastry brush and covering the saucepan to create condensation are both meant to "rinse" away any sugar molecules that might be clinging to the sides, but they will melt eventually anyway.

TECHNIQUE
TAKING THE TEMPERATURE OF CARAMEL

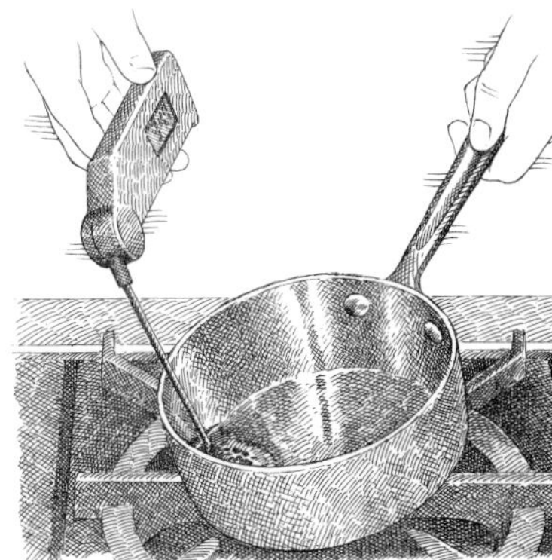

Before inserting an instant-read thermometer (which we prefer to a candy thermometer) into the caramel, swirl the caramel to even out any hot spots. Then tilt the pot so that the caramel pools 1 to 2 inches deep and move the thermometer back and forth in the caramel for about 5 seconds before taking a reading. If using a clip-on thermometer, swirl the caramel for at least 15 seconds and tilt the caramel toward the probe.

But it didn't stiffen up enough, so when I went to spread it on the prepared cakes, some of the caramel soaked into the cake while more of it gently oozed from between the layers. The obvious next test was to cook the caramel to a higher temperature—250 degrees—but that overdid it, producing a more viscous mixture that was too firm to spread.

I briefly changed course and made a dulce de leche–type caramel with sweetened condensed milk, since its thick, viscous consistency would be close to what I was after. But its duller, milkier flavor didn't offer the same complexity and depth as a traditional caramel.

What my filling needed, I realized, was something that is both solid and soft at room temperature—like butter. I made a couple more batches of caramel with increasing amounts of butter and found that adding 2 extra tablespoons produced a cooled caramel that was soft enough to spread but solid enough that it didn't soak into or leak out of the cake.

Icing on the Cake

Tasting the deep chocolate cake spread with the caramel filling confirmed that the frosting could stand to be a bit sweeter than the cake—and I had just the thing in mind. In the test kitchen archives is a chocolate frosting that has just the right rich body and glossy sheen; even better, it is a cinch to

The Five-Recipe Test: Not a Cakewalk

As with any new recipe, we started our chocolate-caramel cake testing by seeing what other recipes had to offer. The five we chose (from sources including *Martha Stewart Living* and *Bon Appétit*) ranged in technique and flavor—but all were flawed in some way. Beyond their glossy coats and tall statures were dry, dull cakes; caramel fillings that were too stiff or too runny; and frostings that were overly dense or achingly sweet.

make since it comes together in the food processor in just minutes.

I followed the recipe, processing softened butter with confectioners' sugar, cocoa powder, corn syrup (its moisture helps dissolve the confectioners' sugar and prevents that unpleasant graininess some frostings have), vanilla, and melted milk chocolate. It spread beautifully over the cake—thick and smooth. I even swirled some simple designs into the top coat for a more festive look. But my tasters and I agreed that the milk chocolate flavor was a few notches sweeter than it should be, so I swapped it for bittersweet.

The darker chocolate coat made the cake look and taste a bit more sophisticated, but the whole package still had a touch of whimsy and birthday party charm—exactly the type of cake I couldn't wait to make for my next dinner party. And for the salted caramel fans, I sprinkled on a bit of coarse sea salt, which gave it a delicate crunch and even a little sparkle.

CHOCOLATE-CARAMEL LAYER CAKE

SERVES 12

Baking spray that contains flour can be used to grease and flour the pans. Both natural and Dutch-processed cocoa will work in this recipe. When taking the temperature of the caramel in steps 3 and 4, remove the pot from the heat and tilt the pan to one side. Use your thermometer to stir the caramel back and forth to equalize hot and cool spots and make sure you are getting an accurate reading (see "Taking the Temperature of Caramel" on page 21). For ideas on finishing the cake, see "Frosting Cakes with Flair" on page 30.

Cake

- 1½ cups (7½ ounces) all-purpose flour
- ¾ cup (2¼ ounces) unsweetened cocoa powder
- 1½ cups (10½ ounces) granulated sugar
- 1¼ teaspoons baking soda
- ¾ teaspoon baking powder
- ¾ teaspoon salt
- ¾ cup buttermilk
- ½ cup water
- ¼ cup vegetable oil
- 2 large eggs
- 1 teaspoon vanilla extract

Caramel Filling

- 1¼ cups (8¾ ounces) granulated sugar
- ¼ cup light corn syrup
- ¼ cup water
- 1 cup heavy cream
- 8 tablespoons unsalted butter, cut into 8 pieces
- 1 teaspoon vanilla extract
- ¾ teaspoon salt

Frosting

- 16 tablespoons unsalted butter, softened
- ¾ cup (3 ounces) confectioners' sugar
- ½ cup (1½ ounces) unsweetened cocoa powder
- Pinch salt
- ½ cup light corn syrup
- ¾ teaspoon vanilla extract
- 6 ounces bittersweet chocolate, melted and cooled

- ¼–½ teaspoon coarse sea salt (optional)

1. **FOR THE CAKE:** Adjust oven rack to middle position and heat oven to 325 degrees. Grease two 9-inch round cake pans, line with parchment paper, grease parchment, and flour pans. Sift flour and cocoa into large bowl. Whisk in sugar, baking soda, baking powder, and salt. Whisk buttermilk, water, oil, eggs, and vanilla together in second bowl. Whisk buttermilk mixture into flour mixture until smooth batter forms. Divide batter evenly between prepared pans and smooth tops with rubber spatula.

2. Bake until toothpick inserted in center comes out clean, 22 to 28 minutes, switching and rotating pans halfway through baking. Let cakes cool in pans on wire rack for 15 minutes. Remove cakes from pans, discarding parchment, and let cool completely on rack, at least 2 hours.

3. **FOR THE CARAMEL FILLING:** Lightly grease 8-inch square baking pan. Combine sugar, corn syrup, and water in medium saucepan. Bring to boil over medium-high heat and cook, without stirring, until mixture is amber colored, 8 to 10 minutes. Reduce heat to low and continue to cook, swirling saucepan occasionally, until dark amber, 2 to 5 minutes longer. (Caramel will register between 375 and 380 degrees.)

4. Off heat, carefully stir in cream, butter, vanilla, and salt (mixture will bubble and steam). Return saucepan to medium heat and cook, stirring frequently, until smooth and caramel reaches 240 to 245 degrees, 3 to 5 minutes. Carefully transfer caramel to prepared pan and let cool until just warm to touch (100 to 105 degrees), 20 to 30 minutes.

5. **FOR THE FROSTING:** Process butter, sugar, cocoa, and salt in food processor until smooth, about 30 seconds, scraping down sides of bowl as needed. Add corn syrup and vanilla and process until just combined, 5 to 10 seconds. Scrape down sides of bowl, then add chocolate and pulse until smooth and creamy, 10 to 15 seconds. (Frosting can be made 3 hours in advance. For longer storage, cover and refrigerate frosting. Let stand at room temperature for 1 hour before using.)

6. Using long serrated knife, score 1 horizontal line around sides of each cake layer; then, following scored lines, cut each layer into 2 even layers.

7. Using rubber spatula or large spoon, transfer ⅓ of caramel to center of 1 cake layer and use small offset spatula to spread over surface, leaving ½-inch border around edge. Repeat with remaining caramel and 2 of remaining cake layers. (Three of your cake layers should be topped with caramel.)

8. Line edges of cake platter with 4 strips of parchment to keep platter clean. Place 1 caramel-covered cake layer on platter. Top with second caramel-covered layer. Repeat with third caramel-covered layer and top with final layer. Spread frosting evenly over sides and top of cake. Carefully remove parchment strips. Let cake stand for at least 1 hour. (Cake can be made 2 days in advance and refrigerated. Let stand at room temperature for at least 5 hours before serving.) Sprinkle with coarse sea salt, if using. Cut and serve.

Perfecting the Caramel Filling

Our caramel filling is soft enough to spread on the cake layers but not so fluid that it soaks into the cake or drips down the sides of a cut slice.

SOFT, BUT NOT RUNNY

Do I Really Need to Use Parchment Paper?

It may sound like overkill, but the most effective way to ensure that a cake releases cleanly from a baking pan is to grease the pan, line it with parchment paper, and then grease and flour the parchment and pan sides. The parchment guarantees that the cake pulls away from the pan bottom completely, and a coat of grease and flour on the parchment and up the pan sides helps the batter cling and rise and ensures that the parchment pulls away from the cake bottom without removing large crumbs.

GOT STUCK Just grease and flour

CLEAN RELEASE Grease, flour, and parchment

The Chef's Secret Weapon

What if one pan could do everything the best traditional stainless-steel, cast-iron, and nonstick pans can do—and, in some cases, even do it a little better?

BY LISA McMANUS

Even if you've never heard of a carbon-steel skillet, you've almost certainly eaten a meal made in one. Restaurant chefs use these pans for all kinds of tasks, from searing steak to sautéing onions to cooking eggs. French omelet and crêpe pans are made of carbon steel, as are the woks used in Chinese restaurants. Even Julia Child had a few carbon-steel pieces alongside her familiar rows of copper cookware. In European home kitchens, these pans are hugely popular. Somehow, though, despite their prevalence in restaurants, they've never really caught on with home cooks in the United States. Given their reputation for being as great at browning as they are at keeping delicate foods from sticking, we wondered if it was time that changed.

A well-seasoned carbon-steel skillet is so nonstick that fried eggs slip around in the pan.

We bought seven carbon-steel skillets, all as close as possible to our preferred size of 12 inches for a primary skillet, priced from $39.95 to $79.95. For fun we also threw in a $230 hand-forged version made in Oregon. Bearing in mind carbon steel's multipurpose promise, we decided on a range of recipes for our testing: frying eggs, turning out cheese omelets, pan-searing steaks, and baking the traditional French upside-down apple dessert known as tarte Tatin, which begins on the stove and moves to the oven. Along the way we'd evaluate the skillets' shape, weight, handle comfort, and maneuverability. Washing the pans after every test would let us judge how easy they were to clean and maintain. Our key question: Could this one type of pan actually make owning the other skillets we've always had in our arsenal—stainless-steel tri-ply, cast-iron, and nonstick—more of an option than a necessity?

In Season

The first thing we learned about carbon steel is that, like cast iron, it rusts when it's bare. It requires seasoning, a process that bonds oil to the pan to not only provide a layer of protection but also start the process of making the pan nonstick. While two of the skillets we ordered came preseasoned, the other six arrived sheathed in sticky beeswax or thick grease to block rust formation in transit. After scrubbing off this temporary coating (which was sometimes easier said than done), we followed each manufacturer's seasoning instructions. At first we wondered if the need for seasoning might end up being a deal breaker. But we found a favorite method that is relatively easy. (For more, see "Seasoning Carbon Steel" on page 24.)

When we got cooking, we were astonished at how nonstick even the initial seasoning made these pans. Our first test was to fry an egg in a teaspoon of butter. In nearly all of the pans, the egg slipped around like a puck on an air hockey table. Omelets slid out in perfect golden oblongs, and tarts popped out intact, with few exceptions. Each time we cooked, more patina built up. And as long as we cleaned it following manufacturers' instructions—no soap and a light coat of oil after drying, like cast iron—the nonstick surface kept gradually improving. Most of the time, we merely had to wipe out the pan with a paper towel—no washing at all—to find it clean as a whistle.

So our first discovery was a big one: Getting true nonstick performance from a carbon-steel skillet is remarkably quick. Another virtue of carbon-steel skillets came to light when we seared steaks. A smoking-hot traditional stainless-steel tri-ply skillet does a perfectly acceptable job at this task, and it's what most home cooks are likely to use, even though we're partial to cast iron and find that it does a superior job (cast iron's heat retention makes it incredibly good for high-heat tasks). The carbon-steel pans trumped both. The impressively deep, even browning these pans produced was easily on a par with cast iron, but because carbon-steel pans are lighter and thinner than cast-iron skillets of the same size, the carbon-steel pans were able to heat up in nearly half the time. Later, using our winning carbon-steel pan, we saw equally great browning when we tried an assortment of other recipes, including frying sliced potatoes, cooking burgers, and stir-frying Sichuan green beans. This is a skillet worth owning if only for pan frying and sautéing, besting our favorite traditional skillet and equaling the best cast-iron skillet in terms of results but with less weight to lug. Like both of these types of pans, it can also go under the broiler.

However, during these additional tests we did discover one downside. If you simmer an acidic tomato sauce in a carbon-steel skillet, as we did when we made a batch of skillet lasagna in our winning pan, the acid will strip off most of the pan's dark patina and the shiny silver interior of the skil-

Carbon Steel: A Very Versatile Material

The composition of carbon steel, an alloy made of about 1 percent carbon and 99 percent iron, makes it a particularly functional material for cookware. It contains slightly less carbon than cast-iron, which makes it less brittle; as a result, it can be made relatively thin and lightweight but still be plenty durable. It's heavy enough to retain heat well but thin enough to heat quickly. And unlike cast iron, which is so rough that it requires multiple rounds of seasoning to become truly nonstick, the smooth surface of carbon steel makes it easy to acquire a slick patina of polymerized oil during seasoning. For a detailed comparison of carbon steel and cast iron, go to CooksIllustrated.com/carbonsteel.

The Pan That Does It All

A good carbon-steel skillet can literally do it all: You can bake, broil, sear, and stir-fry in it; plus, you can cook delicate foods like fish and eggs in it with no fear of sticking. It's no wonder that these skillets are used by so many professional chefs in restaurant kitchens around the world. The only caveat? Cooking with acidic ingredients will take away some of the seasoning, but it can be easily restored.

SEARS LIKE CAST IRON
A carbon-steel skillet can brown food just as deeply and evenly as cast iron. It also has two advantages: It heats up more quickly, and its lighter weight makes it easier to handle.

PERFORMS LIKE STAINLESS TRI-PLY
Carbon steel heats virtually as evenly as stainless-steel tri-ply (aluminum sandwiched between stainless) but can brown more deeply; our winner costs one-third of the price of our favorite tri-ply skillet from All-Clad.

AS SLICK AS NONSTICK
Carbon steel is as slippery as brand-new nonstick, but it sears better, doesn't have a synthetic coating, has no oven-safe temperature limits, and lasts forever.

let will reappear. However, we didn't notice any off-flavors when we tasted the lasagna, and a few rounds of stovetop heating and wiping the skillet with oil, which took about 10 minutes, restored the slippery patina.

Finally, design. We found two basic styles: very thin, shell-like pans and a thicker variety. The thin pans scorched food and threw off recipe times (butter instantly browned and even blackened before we could crack an egg to fry), and they warped by the end of testing. We preferred the thicker skillets. Even if they were a bit harder to lift—some weighed up to twice as much as our favorite traditional skillet, though still a few pounds less than our favorite cast-iron pan—they regulated heat much better and did not warp.

Other design features—issues that have come up in every skillet testing we've done—mattered, too. Some pans felt unbalanced or had slightly cramped cooking surfaces. Others had too-high sides that impeded access to the food or too-low sides that let liquids (like the egg for omelets) splash out. And several of the pans had unusually long, steeply angled handles; these made shorter testers grab them at awkward angles, and they barely fit inside the oven when we baked tarte Tatin.

Lisa Explains It All
Video available free for 4 months at CooksIllustrated.com/oct15

Make Room on the Pot Rack

Despite these minor issues, though, our conclusion was clear: Carbon-steel skillets have earned a place in our kitchen. They possess some of the best attributes and lack several of the drawbacks from each type of standard skillet. They offer the versatility of a traditional pan, the heat retention of cast-iron at a lighter weight, and the slick release of a good nonstick skillet without the synthetic coating or the lack of durability. In fact, many of us would happily opt for just a carbon-steel pan in our own home arsenal. (Plus, perhaps, either a traditional or nonstick pan if we didn't want to fuss with reestablishing the seasoning after cooking acidic dishes.)

At the end of our testing, we had two top choices: First, the Matfer Bourgeat Black Steel Round Frying Pan, 11⅞", priced at an affordable $44.38. This is a simple, classic pan that cooks beautifully. It's sturdy, easy to maneuver, and quick both to acquire slick seasoning and to clean up, with a smooth, rivet-free interior that won't trap food particles—in other words, it's all you need. But if you want a pan that's a showpiece as well, we also loved the Blu Skillet Ironware 13" Fry Pan ($230.00). While our initial skepticism was well deserved given its price, we were surprised by what a great pan it was. It is beautifully crafted, sturdy, and well sized and shaped, and it performs perfectly, releasing food well from the get-go and only improving as we used it. However, its high price means it's not for everyone, and because the pans are made by hand one by one, wait times can be weeks long, depending on demand.

Seasoning Carbon Steel

Unless it comes preseasoned, a carbon-steel pan requires seasoning just as a cast-iron pan does. This process bonds oil to the surface, providing protection against rust and making the pan nonstick. The instructions that come with our winning pan, from Matfer Bourgeat, suggest an unusual method, but we found that it really works.

INITIAL SEASONING

First you'll need to remove the new pan's wax or grease coating (used to protect the metal from rusting in transit). Use very hot water, dish soap, and vigorous scrubbing with a bristle brush. Dry the pan and then put it on low heat to finish drying. Add ⅓ cup oil, ⅔ cup salt, and peels from two potatoes (these help to pull any remaining wax or grease from the pan surface). Cook over medium heat, occasionally moving the peels around the pan and up the sides to the rim, for 8 to 10 minutes. (The pan will turn brown.) Discard the contents, allow the pan to cool, and wipe with paper towels. You are ready to cook. (If you experience sticking, repeat once.) This method will work on any carbon-steel skillet.

MAINTENANCE

Avoid soap and abrasive scrubbing. Simply wipe or rinse the pan clean, dry it thoroughly on a warm burner, and rub it with a light coat of oil. If you accidentally scrub off some of the patina, wipe the pan with a thin coat of oil and place it over high heat for about 10 minutes until the pan darkens (it will smoke; turn on an exhaust fan).

Blotchy is OK.
As soon as you season and start cooking in a carbon-steel pan, it changes from shiny silver to brown and blotchy. The blotches are a sign that the pan is building up a slippery patina, which will help it become increasingly nonstick. The blotches and nonstick capability may initially wax and wane, but with use, the pan's cooking surface will gradually darken and become more uniform in color.

KEY
GOOD ★★★
FAIR ★★
POOR ★

TESTING: CARBON-STEEL SKILLETS

We tested eight carbon-steel skillets, all close to 12 inches in diameter, rating them on their cooking performance, sticking, and ease of use, including directions for seasoning. (Two pans were preseasoned; we seasoned the rest according to manufacturer instructions.) All pans were purchased online and appear in order of preference.

COOKING SURFACE
Official pan sizes are based on rim-to-rim measurements; we measured across the flat portion of the inside of each pan to assess the actual available cooking surface.

COOKING
We fried eggs, made omelets, pan-seared steaks, and baked tartes Tatin. Pans that performed well across the board earned higher ratings.

NONSTICK
Pans received high marks for consistently releasing food without sticking.

EASE OF USE
We considered design factors such as shape; weight; thickness; and handle angle, length, and comfort. We also rated pans higher if they were easier to clean.

HIGHLY RECOMMENDED

	CRITERIA	TESTERS' COMMENTS
MATFER BOURGEAT **Black Steel Round Frying Pan, 11⅞"** MODEL: 062005 PRICE: $44.38 WEIGHT: 4.7 lb COOKING SURFACE: 9 in	Cooking ★★★ Nonstick ★★★ Ease of Use ★★★	This affordable pan had it all: thick, solid construction; a smooth interior with no handle rivets to bump the spatula or trap food; an ergonomically angled handle; and sides flared just right for easy access but high enough to contain splashes. Steaks formed a deeply crisp crust, tarte Tatin caramelized beautifully and released neatly, and fried eggs just slipped around in the pan.
BLU SKILLET IRONWARE **13" Fry Pan** MODEL: SQ2281937 PRICE: $230.00 WEIGHT: 5.5 lb COOKING SURFACE: 10 in 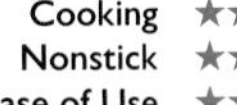	Cooking ★★★ Nonstick ★★★ Ease of Use ★★★	This costly, beautifully designed pan is a hand-forged piece of art, but it's also built to work hard. It arrived preseasoned, with the metal heat-treated to a lovely shade of slate blue, though it darkened with use. With its broad cooking surface, nicely flared sides, and perfect browning and release, it was a pleasure to use. Our only quibble (besides price): It's heavy. The large helper handle is a useful addition.

RECOMMENDED

	CRITERIA	TESTERS' COMMENTS
MAUVIEL M'steel **Round Fry Pan, Steel Handle 12.5"** MODEL: 3651.32 PRICE: $79.95 WEIGHT: 5.1 lb COOKING SURFACE: 10 in 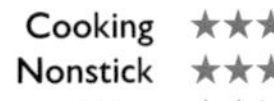	Cooking ★★★ Nonstick ★★★ Ease of Use ★★½	Very spacious and sturdy, with low sides and a reliably slick surface, this pan browned evenly but felt slightly heavier than ideal and lacked a helper handle to share the weight.
TURK **Heavy Steel Frying Pan 11"** MODEL: 66228 PRICE: $79.00 WEIGHT: 4.3 lb COOKING SURFACE: 8 in 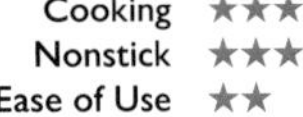	Cooking ★★★ Nonstick ★★★ Ease of Use ★★	Solidly built, handsome, and well-designed—with low flaring sides, a handle at an accessible angle, and a slippery surface that never stuck—this pan was maneuverable and easy to use. Its seasoning was nicely durable. Its only flaw: a too-small cooking surface that made the pan feel cramped for full-size recipes—it would be best for recipes serving two.
DE BUYER **Mineral B Frypan, 12.6"** MODEL: 5610.32 PRICE: $79.95 WEIGHT: 5.75 lb COOKING SURFACE: 9¼ in 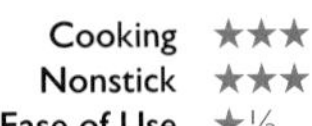	Cooking ★★★ Nonstick ★★★ Ease of Use ★½	This roomy, beautifully constructed pan browned foods well and with great release, eventually. The instructions for seasoning had us coat just the cooking surface with oil, leaving the sides to fend for themselves; they stuck and tore tarte Tatin. After more cooking, the sides caught up and the pan didn't stick. Its high-angled handle and heft made it more difficult to maneuver than other pans.
PADERNO **World Cuisine Heavy Duty Polished Carbon Steel Frying Pan, 12½"** MODEL: A4171432 PRICE: $42.34 WEIGHT: 6.2 lb COOKING SURFACE: 9½ in 	Cooking ★★½ Nonstick ★★½ Ease of Use ★½	With enough cooking space and the lower-angled handle we prefer, this pan had plenty of promise. But it provided a slightly less slippery release than the top pans, and its sides were a bit too shallow. Its weight made it hard for testers to maneuver.

RECOMMENDED WITH RESERVATIONS

	CRITERIA	TESTERS' COMMENTS
LODGE **12" Seasoned Steel Skillet** MODEL: CRS12 PRICE: $39.95 WEIGHT: 4.2 lb COOKING SURFACE: 9¼ in	Cooking ★★ Nonstick ★★ Ease of Use ★★	This comparatively light pan was very comfortable to lift and handle, and its factory preseasoning seemed like a plus because we could start cooking right away. But in contrast to the other pans in the lineup, its slick seasoning actually deteriorated as we cooked, and food began to stick. Slightly thinner, it also ran a little hot with a tendency toward hot spots; apples caramelized unevenly.

NOT RECOMMENDED

	CRITERIA	TESTERS' COMMENTS
VOLLRATH **12½" Carbon Steel Fry Pan** MODEL: 58930 PRICE: $45.01 WEIGHT: 3.3 lb COOKING SURFACE: 9¼ in 	Cooking ★★ Nonstick ★★ Ease of Use ★	This thin pan became superhot superfast—perfect for restaurants, where orders need to move fast, but not so great for home cooks. High, cupped sides made it hard to slide a spatula beneath foods, and an extra-long, steeply angled handle poked us as we stood before the stove. Hot spots made apples caramelize unevenly when we made tarte Tatin. The bottom warped by the end of testing.

Tapping into Maple Syrup's Secrets

Maple syrup continues to be produced on small farms in the same low-tech way that it has been for centuries. But that's not the whole story.

BY LAUREN SAVOIE

It's early March, and a team of editors and I are driving along a winding dirt road in Vermont on our way to visit a sugar shack tucked against a mountain covered with thousands of maples. At first glance, the passing forest scape is a canvas of barren trees and snowy fields, but a closer look brings into focus a web of silver taps and clear plastic tubing weaving among the trees—the sign that it's sugaring season.

We've timed our trip carefully because sugaring season is both short and temperamental. Not only is the majority of the world's maple syrup produced on relatively small-scale farms, like this one, throughout Canada and the northern United States over a period of just two months each year, but the sap production is entirely weather-dependent: Syrup makers must wait for freezing nights that are followed by warm days, a pattern that causes higher pressure within the tree to push sap out of the tree. Couple that with the fact that it takes 40 gallons of sap to produce just 1 gallon of maple syrup and it's not surprising that this product can fetch more than $1.50 per ounce.

Even when we sampled the syrups plain, we found only subtle flavor differences. We recommend buying the cheapest maple syrup you can find.

Anyone who's tasted real maple syrup on pancakes, in desserts, or even in savory glazes or dressings knows that there is no cheap substitute. We confirmed as much a few years ago when we compared a few maple syrups with pancake syrups; the latter, corn syrup–based products that are a fifth of maple syrup's price, tasted cloying and candy-like. This time, we decided to home in on pure maple syrup and gathered eight products, all Grade A Dark Amber since it's the most widely available grade, tasting them plain and baked into maple syrup pie.

From Sap to Syrup

Pure maple syrup is simply sap from sugar maple trees that has been boiled to concentrate its sugar. To harvest it, taps connected to plastic tubing are drilled into the trees; the sap flows through the tubing into large storage containers where it's held for no more than 24 hours (unprocessed sap is only about 2 to 3 percent sugar, so it spoils quickly). When it's time to boil, the sap is transferred to an evaporator pan set over a large fire and reduced until it reaches 66 percent sugar density. (If it's boiled much longer, the syrup will start to crystallize; any less and it will eventually spoil.)

After the sap has been boiled and filtered, it's graded according to color, which also helps categorize the strength of its flavor. David Lutz, a forest ecologist at Dartmouth College, explained that syrup color and flavor are primarily determined by changes in the chemical composition of the sap throughout the sugaring season. At the start of the season, the syrup is very light-colored because the sap is infused with stored sucrose from the winter and generally free from compounds that impart strong flavors or a dark color. (The earliest, clearest sap was historically graded "A, extra fancy" because it was the best representation of a neutral-tasting sugar substitute.) As the season progresses, the environment becomes more biologically active, the tree prepares to bloom, and hundreds of phenolic compounds—the same types of chemicals found in tea and wine—start flowing through the sap, darkening its color and deepening its flavor.

Although Vermont and some other states have their own grading systems, there are no universal grading standards in the syrup industry. But there are five main grades that range from Grade A Light Amber to Commercial—the latter a syrup so strong-tasting that it's reserved for industrial use. To assess color and assign a grade, some syrup producers use a spectrometer, a tool that measures the amount of light transmitted through the syrup, but more often grading is low-tech and subjective: Syrup makers simply compare their finished syrup to color charts or small vials of dyed glycerin. If the syrup falls between two hues, producers often choose the darker grade because syrup may darken with time due to oxidation. (Note: The U.S. Department of Agriculture and a handful of syrup-producing states will be issuing new grading

How Nature Colors Syrup

The color of maple syrup ranges dramatically over the course of the two-month sugaring season due to natural chemical changes in the sap. As the tree becomes more biologically active, phenolic compounds develop that infuse the sap, imparting color (and flavor). First-of-the-season sap is almost clear because it contains few of these compounds. As the season progresses and the tree prepares to bloom, more compounds deepen the color of the sap.

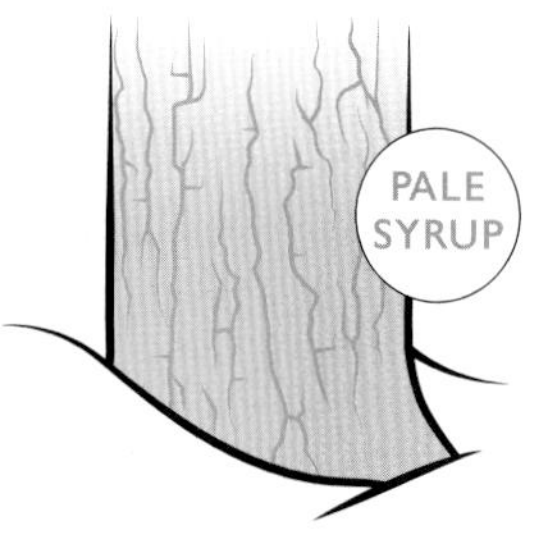

EARLY SEASON
Few phenolic compounds

LATE SEASON
Many phenolic compounds

conventions for maple syrup effective in 2017.)

Perhaps because grading is such an imprecise process, we noticed some color differences among the syrups in our testing, even though they were all labeled the same Grade A Dark Amber. Some were dark like molasses, while others were only faintly golden—but surprisingly these color differences did not correlate to the syrups' flavors. Most of the lighter-colored products tasted just as robust as darker ones. In fact, we were hard-pressed to find any distinct differences among the syrups other than color. Ultimately, we recommend them all.

Pooling Resources

Still, we were curious about the discrepancy between syrup color and flavor and turned to Michael Farrell, director of Cornell's Sugar Maple Research & Extension Field Station, Uihlein Forest, for an explanation. He noted that unless you're comparing the very lightest grade with the darkest one, the differences in flavor can be pretty subtle. More significantly, he added, the distinct flavors in maple syrup have been literally blended out of most supermarket brands. Because each maple tree averages only ¼ gallon of maple syrup over the entire season, it's impossible for most producers to acquire the land or resources necessary to yield enough volume for national distribution. Instead, most producers sell their syrup to large packagers, which pool hundreds of different products and bottle the blends under a brand name. Farrell and other experts told us that to get the color and flavor profile that falls within the Grade A Dark Amber spectrum, the most marketable grade of syrup, they blend different grades. "If their Dark Amber is looking a little too dark, they might mix in medium to lighten it up," Farrell said. The goal is "to try to make a consistent product."

Some packagers might even doctor the syrups with cheaper sweeteners to maximize their yield, but Farrell doesn't feel that it's a major issue in the industry. His bigger concern is pancake syrups masquerading as pure maple syrup, either from packaging that makes pancake syrup look like the real thing or from the inclusion of a small amount of pure maple syrup. "It changes people's opinions of real maple syrup," he said.

To us, there's a distinct advantage to blending: It means that all Grade A Dark Amber syrups sold in supermarkets are going to taste very similar, so our advice is to buy the cheapest all-maple product you can find.

PICK A SYRUP, ANY SYRUP

Twenty-one America's Test Kitchen staffers sampled eight nationally available supermarket brands of Grade A Dark Amber maple syrup in two blind tastings—plain and in maple syrup pie—and rated them on flavor, sweetness, and strength of maple flavor. We obtained information about processing methods from manufacturers and industry experts. Because we found all the syrups to be very similar and recommend them all, we don't have a favorite; instead, they appear in order of price per fluid ounce.

RECOMMENDED

UNCLE LUKE'S
Pure Maple Syrup, Grade A Dark Amber

PRICE: $20.69 for 32 fl oz ($0.65 per fl oz)
The least expensive product we tried, which looked particularly dark and "molasses-y," boasted "rich caramel flavor" that tasted "pleasantly toasty" in pie.

HIGHLAND SUGARWORKS
Pure Organic Maple Syrup, Grade A Dark Amber

PRICE: $23.87 for 32 fl oz ($0.75 per fl oz)
This "very light"-colored syrup was "buttery," "smooth," and "sweet." Some tasters picked up on "fruity" or even "coffee" flavors.

COOMBS FAMILY FARMS
Pure Maple Syrup, Grade A Dark Amber

PRICE: $24.54 for 32 fl oz ($0.77 per fl oz)
"Butter and vanilla" flavors stood out in this dark brown syrup, which some tasters likened to "maple sugar candy."

ANDERSON'S
Pure Maple Syrup, Grade A Dark Amber

PRICE: $26.19 for 32 fl oz ($0.82 per fl oz)
This syrup, which boasted the deepest "caramelized brown color," delivered "rich," "woody" smokiness and strong "caramel" notes that stood out particularly well in maple syrup pie.

MAPLE GROVE FARMS
Pure Maple Syrup, Grade A Dark Amber

PRICE: $6.99 for 8.5 fl oz ($0.82 per fl oz)
With "bold," "concentrated maple flavor," this syrup worked well in the pie's custard filling, where tasters deemed it "toasty," "caramelized," and "balanced."

MAPLE GOLD
Pure Maple Syrup, Grade A Dark Amber

PRICE: $16.50 for 12 fl oz ($1.38 per fl oz)
Tasters picked up on this dark-colored syrup's "toasty," "woodsy," "assertive vanilla" flavors and even noticed some "tanginess."

SPRING TREE
Pure Maple Syrup, Grade A Dark Amber

PRICE: $18.49 for 12.5 fl oz ($1.48 per fl oz)
This "balanced," "complex" syrup had flavor notes that ranged from "bright and tangy" to "woodsy," with a "sweet finish."

CAMP
Pure Maple Syrup, Grade A Dark Amber

PRICE: $19.95 for 12.7 fl oz ($1.57 per fl oz)
This "light-colored syrup" impressed tasters with its "good balance of maple depth and tang" and range of complex flavors—from "smoky" to a "hint of orange."

Single-Origin Syrups: Worth the Splurge?

While most maple syrup producers sell their products to large packagers who blend and sell them commercially, there are also some who sell their own unblended syrups directly from their farms (or through local specialty stores). Curious if these single-origin syrups would have more distinct, nuanced flavors—and if they would be worth mail-ordering—we tasted five (priced from $0.48 to $1.33 per ounce) alongside one of the supermarket brands. We liked them all, but none had distinct enough nuances to warrant the shipping charges—a result that maple syrup expert Michael Farrell said isn't surprising. "Most people," he noted, "aren't going to be able to tell the difference."

DID YOU KNOW?

All products reviewed by America's Test Kitchen, home of *Cook's Illustrated* and *Cook's Country* magazines, are independently chosen, researched, and reviewed by our editors. We buy products for testing at retail locations and do not accept unsolicited samples for testing. We do not accept or receive payment or consideration from product manufacturers or retailers. Manufacturers and retailers are not told in advance of publication which products we have recommended. We list suggested sources for recommended products as a convenience to our readers but do not endorse specific retailers.

INGREDIENT NOTES

BY KEITH DRESSER, ANDREA GEARY, LAN LAM & ANNIE PETITO

Tasting Fish Sauce

At first blush, fish sauce might seem like an odd concept. Like soy sauce, it's both a condiment and an ingredient, and it's full of glutamates that enhance flavor. But while soy sauce is made from comparatively mild-tasting fermented soybeans and grains, fish sauce gets its flavor from something far more potent: fermented anchovies. Manufacturing methods vary, but the basic process is the same: Fresh, whole anchovies are layered with sea salt and left to ferment for at least 12 months. Over time, the fish breaks down and the salty liquid that forms is collected and filtered before bottling. It's strong stuff with an intense aroma. But there's a reason this pungent sauce is a critical component of many Asian cuisines and is becoming increasingly common in American kitchens: Its savory, briny taste brings out depth in everything from dipping sauces and soups to stir-fries and marinades.

We gathered five products from grocery stores and Asian markets and sampled each over white rice, mixed into a Thai dipping sauce, and in our recipe for Vietnamese Caramel Chicken. Every sauce was intensely flavored, but the best balanced saltiness with a complex savory taste. Less successful sauces were either overwhelmingly salty or unpleasantly fishy. Protein content turned out to be key: An independent lab confirmed that our winner had nearly double or even triple the protein of other products. Though it also had more sodium, its abundance of protein prevented it from tasting overly salty. It was also the only product not to include sugar.

Our new favorite, Vietnamese import Red Boat 40° N Fish Sauce, is the most expensive sauce in the lineup, but we think its richly nuanced, balanced flavor is worth a few more pennies per ounce. For complete tasting results, go to CooksIllustrated.com/oct15. –Kate Shannon

RECOMMENDED

RED BOAT 40° N Fish Sauce
PRICE: $7.99 for 8.45 fl oz ($0.95 per fl oz)
INGREDIENTS: Anchovy, sea salt
PROTEIN: 20.58% by weight
SODIUM: 1,490 mg per 1-tbs serving
COMMENTS: With nearly double (or even triple) the protein of other brands, this fish sauce tasted "complex, not just fishy."

THAI KITCHEN Premium Fish Sauce
PRICE: $4.99 for 6.76 fl oz ($0.74 per fl oz)
INGREDIENTS: Anchovy extract, salt, sugar
PROTEIN: 11.44% by weight
SODIUM: 1,360 mg per 1-tbs serving
COMMENTS: Though this sauce was slightly milder than our winner, tasters thought that our runner-up provided a "good base flavor" that added depth to recipes.

Ribs That Aren't

We're not sure how country-style ribs, which we call for in our Sweet and Tangy Grilled Country-Style Pork Ribs recipe (page 14), got their name, since they are more like pork chops. Traditional spareribs or baby back ribs feature thin strips of meat separated by rib bones. The former is cut from the belly of the pig; the latter from the loin area near the backbone. Country-style ribs, however, come from the region where the loin meets up with the blade, or shoulder, of the animal. Therefore, they contain a mix of lean light meat from the loin, rich dark meat from the shoulder, and, if bone-in, part of the shoulder blade or rib bone. Even though their name is confusing, we are still big fans of country-style ribs: They are meaty, cook quickly, and boast rich pork flavor. –L.L.

NOT ALL COUNTRY-STYLE RIBS ARE ALIKE
Don't be alarmed if a single package of country-style ribs contains a motley assortment of pieces. It's common to find small and large bones, dark and light meat, and varied marbling.

Parmesan Rind Substitutes

We often borrow the classic Italian trick of adding a Parmesan rind to stews or soups to boost their savory depth. The rind is particularly good for seasoning because it's the part of the cheese where most of the bacteria and mold grow and, thus, the source of strong aroma and flavor compounds. Could the rinds from other aged cheeses do the same job? We experimented with adding a few different rinds to minestrone to find out. While an Asiago rind made the soup taste unappealingly gamey, tasters agreed that rinds from both Pecorino Romano and Gruyère added a savory flavor comparable to that of the Parmesan rind. If you don't have a rind, any one of these cheeses is also an acceptable substitute. This will result in some stringy melted cheese stuck to the bottom of the pot, but you can simply leave it behind when serving. –K.D.

Getting the Most out of Leeks

Since just the white and light green parts of a leek are tender—the tough dark green parts are suitable only for making stock—it pays to select specimens that have a higher proportion of the desirable light-colored base. How you prep them makes a difference, too: The traditional method is to simply chop off the leek at the point where light gives way to dark, but the usable pale, tender portion actually extends above this line in the interior of the vegetable. To preserve that part, we've adopted a new trimming method that results in a roughly 15 percent greater yield. –A.G.

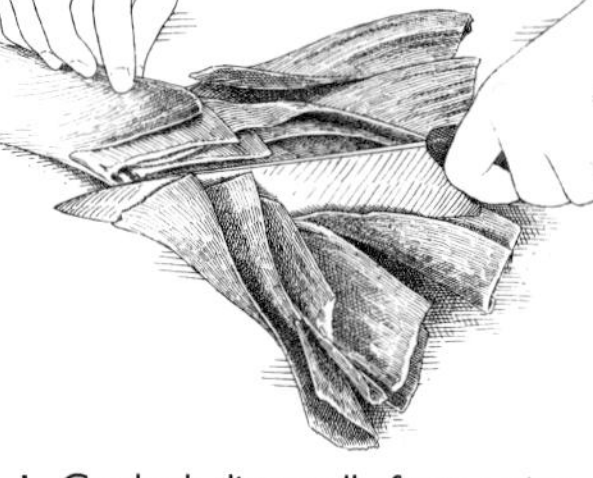

1. Cut leek diagonally from point where leaves start to darken to middle of dark green portion.

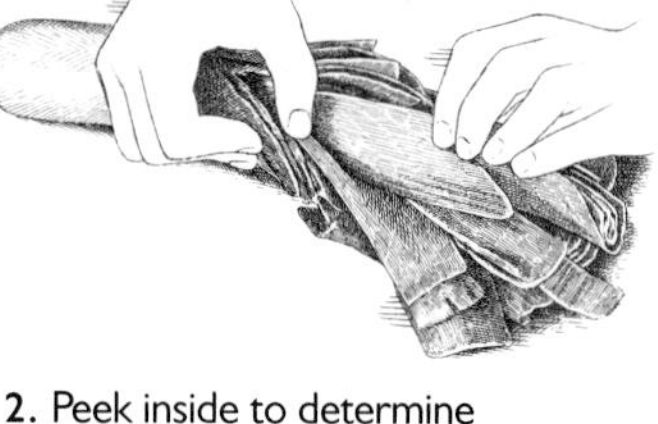

2. Peek inside to determine where light green turns dark. Cut diagonally again, preserving light portion.

3. Repeat twice to create pointed shape with pale leaves.

The Mayo Advantage for Grilled Cheese

Some cooks we know swear by spreading mayo on the bread for grilled cheese instead of butter. Since it saves the step of having to soften butter to make it spreadable, we decided to test this method ourselves. Both butter and mayonnaise produced sandwiches with crisp, well-browned exteriors. Unsurprisingly, the sandwiches made with butter tasted more buttery, while the mayonnaise versions had a slight but discernible tang. But both samples were deemed entirely acceptable.

A word of warning: Though we're fans of light mayonnaise (our favorite light mayo closely rivaled our favorite full-fat version in a side-by-side taste test), it won't work here. Because the low-fat product has only one-third of the fat of regular mayonnaise (water is the first ingredient listed), it makes a pale, soggy grilled cheese. –A.G.

Low-Fat versus Nonfat Buttermilk

Readers have asked us if low- and nonfat buttermilk are interchangeable in baking recipes. To find out, we made pancakes with both types and found that they produced comparable results in both appearance and texture. Our Flaky Buttermilk Biscuits (page 7) revealed a little more variation—those made with nonfat buttermilk were slightly denser and not as flaky—but both options produced acceptable biscuits. Buttermilk pie, though, was another matter: The filling made with nonfat buttermilk was grainy and slightly curdled. That's because low-fat buttermilk has an asset that nonfat buttermilk lacks: fat, which helps prevent eggs in a custard from curdling. Fat coats the proteins, making them less likely to clump. So you can use non- and low-fat buttermilk interchangeably in most recipes. However, if you're making a custard-style dessert (like pie or panna cotta), stick with the low-fat type. –A.P.

OK FOR BISCUITS AND PANCAKES
Nonfat buttermilk works just fine.

NOT OK FOR CUSTARD PIE
Filling made with nonfat buttermilk turns grainy and curdled.

Another Way to Thicken Soups

Many pureed soup recipes call for sliced white sandwich bread as a thickener. Since we don't always have sandwich bread on hand, we wondered if oats might work just as well. We made three of our soups that we thicken with bread—potato-leek, creamy tomato, and Italian garlic soup—subbing in ½ cup of oats for each slice of bread called for in the recipe. The oats worked well in the potato and garlic soups, but tasters found that they dulled the bright flavor of the tomato soup and created a slightly gelatinous consistency. We fixed both issues simply by reducing the amount of oats by half.

In sum: Whole oats can be used instead of bread to thicken soup. (Quick oats work fine, too.) Use ½ cup oats per slice of bread for most soups. For tomato-based soups, only use ¼ cup oats per slice. –A.J.

OATS INSTEAD OF BREAD
Substitute ½ cup oats per slice of bread, unless the soup is tomato based, in which case substitute only ¼ cup oats per slice.

DIY RECIPE Apple Butter

Although it's in the same family as applesauce, apple butter goes a step further, requiring cooking down apples to concentrate their flavor, drive off water, and caramelize their sugars. The result is a dark, complex-tasting spread that is ideal for serving with baked goods or cheese or as a sandwich spread. Most store-bought versions overwhelm the apple flavor with an abundance of cinnamon, nutmeg, and cloves. To keep the apple flavor up front in our homemade butter, we skip all the spices and instead add apple brandy, apple cider, and some lemon juice for brightness. Since firm texture wasn't an issue, we picked two types of apples for flavor complexity—Fuji for its sweet, honey-like notes and McIntosh for classic apple taste. Because softer McIntosh apples break down more quickly than Fuji apples, we cut them into larger pieces. Cooking them with their skins on extracts maximum flavor. –Christie Morrison

APPLE BUTTER

MAKES ABOUT 3 CUPS

A food mill is the easiest way to remove the skins and puree the apples.

- **2 pounds McIntosh apples, cored, quartered, and cut into 2-inch pieces**
- **2 pounds Fuji apples, cored, quartered, and cut into 1-inch pieces**
- **1 cup apple cider**
- **1 cup Calvados or applejack**
- **1 cup (7 ounces) granulated sugar**
- **½ cup (3½ ounces) packed light brown sugar**
- **3 tablespoons lemon juice**
- **¼ teaspoon salt**

1. Combine apples, cider, and Calvados in large Dutch oven and bring to boil over medium-high heat. Reduce heat to medium-low, cover, and simmer, stirring occasionally, until apples are very soft, about 30 minutes.

2. Working in batches, transfer apples to food mill and process. Discard skins and transfer puree to now-empty Dutch oven. Stir in granulated sugar, brown sugar, lemon juice, and salt. Simmer over low heat, stirring occasionally, until mixture is browned and thickened and rubber spatula or wooden spoon leaves distinct trail when dragged across bottom of pot, 1 to 1½ hours.

3. Transfer apple butter to jar with tight-fitting lid and let cool completely before covering and refrigerating. Apple butter can be refrigerated for up to 1 month.

Simmer apples, cider, and Calvados.

Process in food mill.

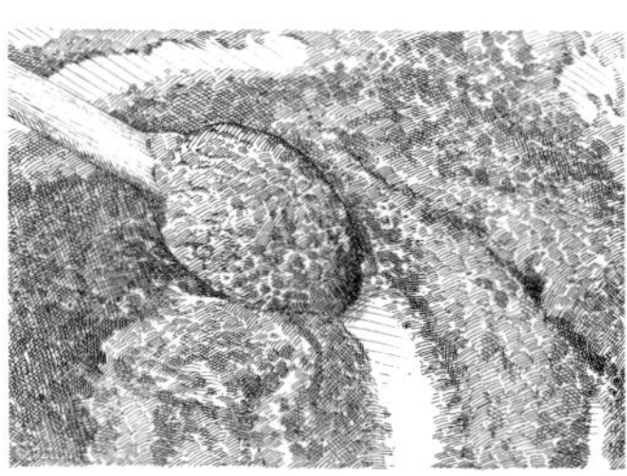

Simmer with sugars, lemon juice, and salt.

RECIPE UPDATE: Our New York Bagels recipe (May/June 2015) calls for 10 ounces of water to make the dough. While the recipe will work with this amount, some readers found that unless using the precise quantity of flour measured by weight, not volume, the dough could be somewhat sticky. To ensure the best results no matter how the flour is measured, we recommend using 9 ounces (1 cup plus 2 tablespoons) of water rather than 10 ounces.

KITCHEN NOTES

⋝ BY ANDREA GEARY, ANDREW JANJIGIAN, LAN LAM & DAN SOUZA ⋜

WHAT IS IT?

A perfectly poached egg is compact, saucer-shaped, and free of feathery whites. Could the tin Egg Poacher, a late-19th-century invention that we purchased on eBay for $25, help us achieve that goal? Its four circular molds contain the eggs as they sit on a perforated plate, which allows water to circulate during cooking and drain away afterward. When the eggs are done cooking, you remove the poacher from the water with the handle, which features a thumb-operated spring-loaded lever that lifts the molds away from the plate so the poached eggs can slide off. A cookery book of the era, *Miss Parloa's Kitchen Companion: A Guide for All Who Would Be Good Housekeepers* (1887), proclaimed the Egg Poacher "so convenient that one could hardly do without it . . ." Though we found that the tool did indeed produce four beautifully poached eggs, using it was a little harrowing. The only pan that could accommodate its low handle height was a shallow skillet, which we had to fill to the rim with water to cover the molds. When the water boiled, it shot through the center perforation like a geyser and threatened to bubble over. We'll pass on this gadget. –Shannon Friedmann Hatch

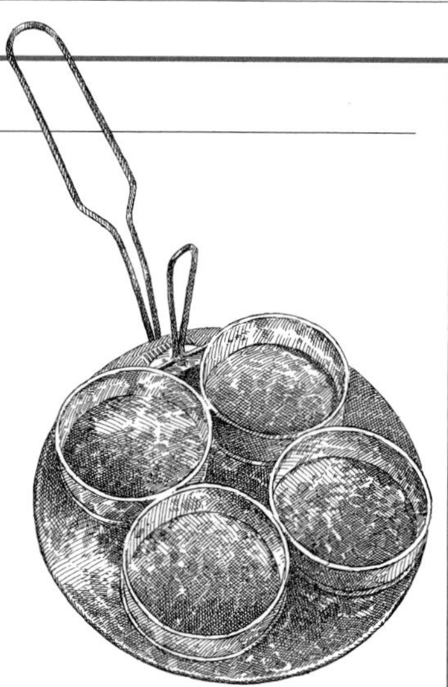

IMPERFECT POACHER
Though it poached eggs nicely, this gadget felt dangerous to use.

A Better Way to Keep Dough from Sticking

The usual way to keep pie, cookie, or biscuit dough (such as the dough for our Flaky Buttermilk Biscuits, page 7) from sticking is to first sprinkle the counter with a generous amount of flour before rolling out the dough. But dough can still stick and thus be vulnerable to tearing when you try to lift it from the counter. Here's an approach that allows you to bring flour directly to the area where the dough is sticking and to use just the amount of flour needed to release it. You will need a bench scraper for this method. –A.J.

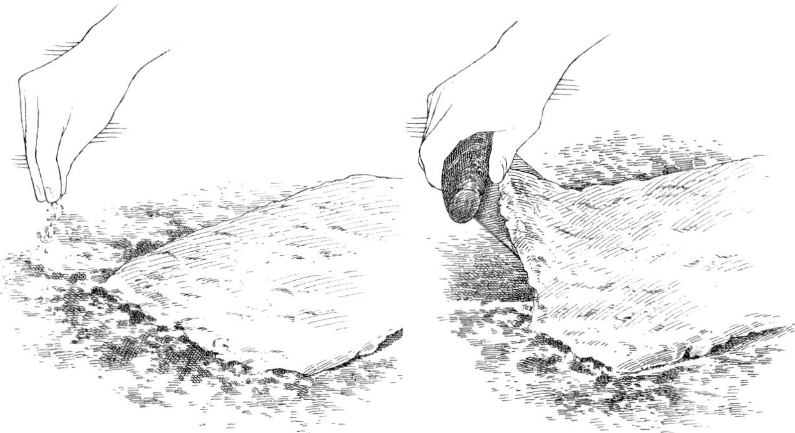

1. Place dough on lightly floured counter. If it sticks during rolling, sprinkle flour liberally around perimeter of dough.

2. Slide bench scraper under dough, dragging flour along with it. Repeat, sliding scraper and more flour under dough until it releases completely from counter.

Two Speedy Ways to Soften Butter

A stick of butter takes about an hour to soften at room temperature, so we came up with two methods for speeding the process.

For baking applications where butter is creamed, cut the stick into 1-tablespoon pieces (more exposed surface area helps the butter warm evenly) and stand them on a plate. The pieces will soften in about 20 minutes. For simply spreading butter on bread or making flavored butters (such as for Pan-Seared Flank Steak with Mustard-Chive Butter, page 5), microwave the pieces at 50 percent power in 10-second increments until the butter is still solid but yields completely to pressure. It's OK if the butter melts a little; simply stir it together until it's uniform. Just don't use the microwave method when baking since over-softened butter can compromise baked goods. –A.G.

Frosting Cakes with Flair

Giving cakes a polished look need not require pastry bags and years of practice. Here are three easy techniques for finishing layer cakes.

C-SHAPED SWIRL

Beginning on side of cake, use small spoon to make C-shaped swirl. Make second swirl next to first about ¾ inch away, orienting C in different direction. Make more swirls, oriented in different directions, over sides and top of cake until frosting is completely covered.

ZIGZAG

Gently run spatula (offset works best) over sides and top of cake to smooth frosting. Holding 12-inch-long serrated knife at both ends with blade facing down and centered over top of cake, gently move knife from side to side to create zigzag pattern.

SPIRAL

Set cake on turntable-style cake stand. Place tip of offset spatula or spoon at center of cake. Slowly rotate cake while dragging tip of spatula or spoon toward edge to create spiral. –L.L.

Brining Beans in Half the Water

In the test kitchen we soak dried beans in salt water overnight to soften their skins, which helps them cook more evenly and reduces the number of beans that rupture. Our formula uses a gallon of water and 3 tablespoons of salt to soak 1 pound of beans. But some readers have asked if a full gallon of brine is really necessary. We tested lesser amounts to see just how little liquid we could get away with using. We found that 2 quarts of water (and 1½ tablespoons of salt) will work perfectly well for a pound of beans, but it's a good idea to use a deep container (a bowl rather than a wide Dutch oven) to ensure that the beans remain submerged as they hydrate and swell. –A.G.

Don't Bother with a Dough Blade

Many food processors come with dough blades, which typically feature short, blunt arms that gently pull and tear dough to knead it. But because the short arms don't extend to the outside rim of the work bowl, they're limited in their ability to pick up flour when small amounts are processed. Thus our winning food processor, the Cuisinart Custom 14-Cup Food Processor, advises using its dough blade only for recipes that call for at least 3½ cups of flour. When we made batches of pizza dough with 4½ cups of flour using the metal blade and the dough blade, each did a comparable job of kneading the dough, but the metal blade did it 15 percent faster. In fact, we find that the efficiency of the metal blade makes it preferable for all dough. Given all this, we're not sure why manufacturers even bother including it as an accessory in the first place. We're sticking with the metal blade for all doughs. –A.J.

SUPERFLUOUS ACCESSORY

Why Burgers Need a Rest

Who hasn't eaten a burger on a bun so saturated with meat juices that it was practically falling apart? There's an easy way to mitigate that problem: Let your burgers rest briefly before placing them on buns. In raw meat, most of the juices are stored in individual structures called myofibrils. Cooking causes the proteins to contract and expel some of the liquid. If the meat is given a chance to rest off heat, the proteins relax, allowing some of the juices to be reabsorbed. We advocate a rest for most meat, but it's particularly important for burgers. Burgers are always cooked directly over high heat, which raises their temperature at the surface. This in turn causes the proteins to be squeezed harder, so more moisture is lost. Letting ground beef rest is also important because a significant amount of fat will drain away instead of collecting in the bun.

For perfect burgers (and buns), let the burgers rest for 5 minutes, tented with foil and preferably on a rack so moisture doesn't collect underneath, before transferring them to buns. –A.J.

SCIENCE Why Gas Grills Need to Preheat Longer

We call for preheating charcoal grills for 5 minutes but gas grills for a full 15 minutes. Why the difference? Both types of grills cook food through radiant heat and conductive heat. Radiant heat browns and cooks the portions of food between the bars of the cooking grate; the hot grate cooks food it touches through conductive heat. (Both types of grills also cook food through convection, the transfer of heat through air.) With a charcoal grill, because the hot coals produce an abundance of radiant heat, preheating the grill is simply serving to heat up the walls and cooking grate. But with a gas grill, preheating serves two functions. Gas flames do not produce much radiant heat, so manufacturers place metal bars, ceramic rods, or even lava rocks between the flames and the cooking grate. It takes about 15 minutes for these items to convert the heat of the flames into radiant heat that can both get the grate searing hot and cook food directly. So what happens when you skimp on the time? Our test—toasting bread for 1 minute on gas grills preheated for just 5 and 10 minutes—shows that the results suffer. –L.L.

PREHEATED 5 MINUTES

PREHEATED 10 MINUTES

PREHEATED 15 MINUTES

SCIENCE Making Flank Steak More Tender

We know that it's possible to make relatively tough cuts like flank steak more tender by thinly slicing them against the grain—that is, perpendicular to the orientation of the muscle fibers—rather than with the grain. But how much more tender? We decided to quantify just how much difference using the correct slicing method can make.

EXPERIMENT

We cooked a whole flank steak in a temperature-controlled water bath to 130 degrees, cut equally thick slices both with and against the grain, and used an ultrasensitive piece of equipment called a CT3 Texture Analyzer from Brookfield Engineering to test how much force was required to "bite" into the slices. We repeated the experiment three times and averaged the results. We also duplicated the tests with a more tender piece of strip loin.

RESULTS

Flank steak slices carved against the grain required 383 grams of force to "bite" 5 millimeters into the meat, while slices carved with the grain required a whopping 1,729 grams of force—more than four times as much—to travel the same distance. Strip loin slices carved against the grain required 329 grams of force; with the grain, 590 grams of force.

STEAK	CUT	FORCE NEEDED TO BITE
flank steak	against grain	383 grams
	with grain	1,729 grams
strip loin	against grain	329 grams
	with grain	590 grams

EXPLANATION

Flank steak contains wide muscle fibers and a relatively high proportion of connective tissue that make it chewy. Slicing it against the grain shortens those muscle fibers, making it easier to chew.

TAKEAWAY

Slicing against the grain dramatically narrowed the gap in tenderness between the strip and flank steaks. Flank steak sliced with the grain was 66 percent tougher than strip steak sliced with the grain, but that difference dropped to just 14 percent when both types of steak were sliced against the grain. So while all cuts benefit from slicing against the grain, it's especially important when slicing flank steak. In fact, slicing a flank steak properly can make it tender enough to rival premium steaks. –D.S.

SCIENCE OF COOKING: HOW TO SLICE STEAK

The way you slice steak can make all the difference. Here's why. Free for 4 months at CooksIllustrated.com/oct15

EQUIPMENT CORNER

BY HANNAH CROWLEY, LISA McMANUS & KATE SHANNON

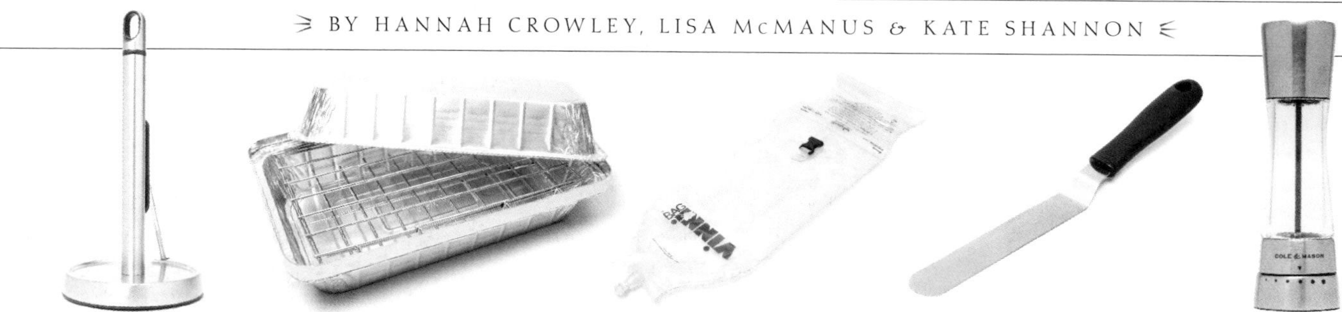

HIGHLY RECOMMENDED	RECOMMENDED WITH RESERVATIONS	HIGHLY RECOMMENDED	HIGHLY RECOMMENDED	RECOMMENDED
SIMPLEHUMAN **Tension Arm Paper Towel Holder** MODEL: KT1161 PRICE: $24.99	RIBALIZER **Rib Rack** MODEL: N/A PRICE: $29.95	VINNIBAG **Wine Travel Bag** MODEL: VB01 PRICE: $28.00	OXO **Good Grips Bent Icing Knife** MODEL: 73591V1 PRICE: $9.99	COLE & MASON **Derwent Gourmet Precision Pepper Mill** MODEL: H59401G PM PRICE: $40.00

TESTING Paper Towel Holders

A paper towel holder aids with tearing and protects the roll from wet spots and spills. Determined to find a sturdy holder that would make tearing quick, precise, and tidy, we purchased six models (priced from $13.00 to $24.99). All consisted of a center pole set on a metal base, sometimes with an arm to provide resistance for tearing. We tore off sheets in small and large increments and noted which models were easy—or not—to handle and move.

Whereas straight, stationary arms became useless once a few layers of towels had been pulled off, angled and hinged arms made one-handed tearing more precise, prevented sheets from drooping, and kept rolls looking tidy. Plus, they accommodated rolls of any size. Heavier models were more stable, and we liked tall, easy-to-grip center poles, as long as their tops didn't need to be removed each time a roll needed replacing. Meeting all those criteria was the Simplehuman Tension Arm Paper Towel Holder ($24.99), which was sturdy, secure, and easy to carry. –K.S.

TESTING Ribalizer

Most barbecued rib recipes require at least 4 hours of cooking and yield only a couple of racks. The Ribalizer ($29.95), which looks like a large toast rack set in a metal pan, promises as many as six racks in 2 hours when cooking ribs on a gas grill. Users prop up the rib racks between the bars and add liquid to the pan below. The ribs cook uncovered for 45 minutes and are then covered with a second pan (steam helps them cook faster) for another hour of cooking.

We cooked baby back and larger St. Louis–style ribs with the Ribalizer and found that it performed as promised; it was also a cinch to set up and use. But there's a considerable drawback: Since the ribs steam, they develop no deeply flavorful char and "bark"—arguably the best part of barbecued ribs. Ultimately, we think the Ribalizer is worth considering if you're a novice griller, want to shortcut the cooking process, or need to make a lot of ribs at once, but just know that their flavor won't be the same as true barbecue. –H.C.

TESTING Wine Travel Bags

You can tuck a bottle of wine between soft clothes in a suitcase and hope that it doesn't break, or you can shield it in a wine travel bag that's designed to protect bottles on the go. We tested four (priced from about $5.00 to $28.00) made of plastic or neoprene by dropping them from waist height, packing them in a suitcase and tossing them as an airplane baggage handler might, and rolling them down a flight of stairs. We even flew them back and forth across the country.

Two bags were useless: Their bottles frequently broke, and often the shards of glass slashed the bags' walls, allowing wine to spill everywhere. In the cushiony neoprene bag, bottles broke less often—but when they did, the wine wasn't contained because the neoprene is perforated. The VinniBag ($28.00), an inflatable bag made from thick, durable plastic (inspired by the dry bags that sailors use), was the best of the bunch; it protected the bottles during all but one extreme drop test and accommodated bottles of all shapes and sizes. We'll be packing one in our luggage from now on. –H.C.

TESTING Offset Spatulas

For frosting a cake, there's no better tool than an offset spatula. The long, narrow blade is ideal for scooping and spreading frosting, and it bends like a stairstep where it meets the handle for better leverage. We tested six (priced from $5.93 to $9.99) with blades that measured between 7 and 8 inches from handle to tip—long enough to frost layer cakes but short enough to maneuver inside baking pans—by slathering dozens of jelly rolls and layer cakes with heavy cream cheese frosting, glossy meringue, thick caramel, and smooth buttercream.

Every blade was strong enough to hold a big dollop of frosting, but we preferred those offset to a roughly 30-degree angle, which made it comfortable to frost the sides of a cake. Better blades also offered at least 6½ inches of flat usable surface area for covering the radius of a 9-inch layer cake and were thin enough to slide easily underneath cake layers. Our favorite, the OXO Good Grips Bent Icing Knife ($9.99), also offered an exceptionally comfortable rubber-coated handle that allowed us to frost cakes with ease. –K.S.

UPDATE Pepper Mills

The original version of our winning Cole & Mason Derwent Gourmet Precision Pepper Mill ($40.00) featured a row of painted-on dots that indicated the grind setting, but we found that these wore off over time. We notified the manufacturer, which has since changed to more durable etched-on dots. We purchased one of the improved models, and after more than 16 weeks of heavy test kitchen use, the dots are still intact. To determine whether a mill has the etched-on dots, check the batch number, which you can find printed on the swing tag, above the UPC, or on a product sticker. The number should be 140228 or higher. –L.M.

For complete testing results, go to CooksIllustrated.com/oct15.

INDEX

September & October 2015

RECIPE VIDEOS

Want to see how to make any of the recipes in this issue? There's a video for that.

MORE VIDEOS

Science of Cooking: How to Slice Steak

FOLLOW US ON SOCIAL MEDIA

facebook.com/CooksIllustrated
twitter.com/TestKitchen
pinterest.com/TestKitchen
google.com/+AmericasTestKitchen
instagram.com/TestKitchen
youtube.com/AmericasTestKitchen

Grilled Country-Style Pork Ribs, 14

Pita Bread Salad (Fattoush), 13

Sautéed Summer Squash, 15

Spanish Braised Chicken, 9

Pan-Seared Flank Steak with Mustard-Chive Butter, 5

Sausage Meatballs and Spaghetti, 11

Black Bean Burgers, 19

Flaky Buttermilk Biscuits, 7

Chocolate-Caramel Layer Cake, 22

PHOTOGRAPHY: CARL TREMBLAY; STYLING: MARIE PIRAINO

HEIRLOOM APPLES

NUMBER 137 NOVEMBER & DECEMBER 2015

COOK'S ILLUSTRATED

Everything Turkey
How to Buy, Prep, Cook, Carve, and Deal with Leftovers

Miso-Glazed Salmon
Better Flavor and Texture

Rustic Bread Stuffing
Light, Loose, and Crispy

Bringing Back Ground Beef Chili

Chicken Marsala
Not Supersweet

Taste Test: Cheap Extra-Virgin Olive Oils

New-Style Pecan Bars
Simpler and Nuttier

Modern Baked Alaska
Brussels Sprout Salads
Perfect Rack of Lamb

CooksIllustrated.com
$6.95 U.S./$7.95 CANADA

CONTENTS

November & December 2015

ON THE BACK COVER BY JOHN BURGOYNE

Classic American Cookies

The most iconic American cookie, CHOCOLATE CHIP, features a toffee-flavored base punctuated with semisweet chips or chunks. Chewy oats and plump raisins distinguish OATMEAL RAISIN cookies from other drop cookies. The SNICKERDOODLE is a variation of a sugar cookie leavened with cream of tartar and baking soda. PEANUT BUTTER cookies are distinctively marked with a crosshatch pattern. CHOCOLATE SANDWICH cookies are crisp on the outside with a creamy filling inside. Crackly MOLASSES cookies owe their chewy texture to their signature ingredient. Buttery JAM THUMBPRINTS are defined by a center indentation filled with preserves. HERMITS are usually shaped like thick-cut biscotti but can also be formed into round drop cookies or chewy bar cookies. Popular in New York City, BLACK AND WHITE cookies have a delicate crumb flavored with lemon extract and a contrasting glaze. To make GRAHAM CRACKERS, you roll out a dough, score it, and dock it with small holes to prevent any rising when baked.

CLASSIC AMERICAN COOKIES

America's Test Kitchen is a very real 2,500-square-foot kitchen located just outside Boston. It is the home of *Cook's Illustrated* and *Cook's Country* magazines and the workday destination of more than three dozen test cooks, editors, and cookware specialists. Our mission is to test recipes until we understand how and why they work and arrive at the best version. We also test kitchen equipment and supermarket ingredients in search of products that offer the best value and performance. You can watch us work by tuning in to *America's Test Kitchen* (AmericasTestKitchen.com) and *Cook's Country from America's Test Kitchen* (CooksCountry.com) on public television.

THANKS GIVING

The Nun Study investigated the process of aging and the onset of Alzheimer's disease in 700 nuns from the School Sisters of Notre Dame. What made this study unusual was that in 1930 these same nuns, who were then in their twenties, were asked to write a brief autobiography setting out their reasons for entering the convent. The 2001 results found that those nuns who had expressed positive emotions in their 1930 write-ups, including love, hope, and gratitude, were much more likely to be alive and well 60 years later. The increase in life expectancy was as much as seven years.

In the Old Testament, the Israelites complained about the lack of food and water in the desert, about the manna, and about the dangers they faced from the Egyptians during the Exodus. Moses warned that an even bigger danger would be a lack of gratitude once they had arrived in the Promised Land. "When you have eaten your fill and have built fine houses and live in them . . . do not say to yourself, 'My power and the might of my own hand have gained me this wealth.'"

The Carter family (the famous Depression-era singing group who sang "Keep On the Sunny Side") lived in an area of Virginia called Poor Valley where the ground was rocky and thin. (Next door was Rich Valley, which offered deep, loamy soil.) Even though some of their instruments were homemade—the harmonica was a comb with a piece of paper pulled tight across it—there was always music. The fiddler warmed up in the morning with "Pine Dreams," "Soap Suds," or "Johnny Put the Kettle On and We'll All Have Tea." For an impromptu Saturday night party, the furniture was carried out into the yard so folks would have a place to dance.

I live part-time in the Vermont equivalent of Poor Valley. Many of the town's 940 residents were born in their own homes. Sherman's Country Store is all penny candy, hot dogs, Pabst Blue Ribbon, and toilet paper. The firehouse is the center of the town's social life: Old Home Day carnival, chicken dinners, and barbecues. Some front porches are bric-a-brac dumping grounds, featuring threadbare sofas that drip their stuffing. We still have a 300-head working dairy farm. The "honey truck" is often seen going up and down Main Street on its way to spray liquid manure on a corn or hay field. We offer a weigh-in station for big game right next to the derelict gas pumps, which feature a sign reading, "Regular, $8.30/gal"—a local joke that keeps tourists from stopping.

Christopher Kimball

Right up the road is Rich Valley, a well-known Vermont hamlet with a golf course, a well-stocked country store populated by more New Yorkers than Vermonters, antique stores, a half-dozen postcard-perfect inns, a summer stock theater, a kitchen equipment outlet, and an outdoors farmers' market.

Just last weekend, someone asked me why I live in Poor Valley instead of the richer town to the north. Our town is a pretty town, a long strip of valley with a high ridge of rugged Vermont mountains on one side and low hills running down to New York State on the other, but it has its rough edges, like the double-wide trailer just north of town with the refrigerator in the front yard. It's a small town where folks volunteer at the drop of a hat, whether it's for the rescue squad, the firehouse, or to run the French fry booth at the annual carnival. Yet gossip is the town's currency. There is no shortage of feuds, slights, and jealousies. And our town is no stranger to tragedy—logging accidents and worse. Some residents have already erected their own tombstones in the cemetery by Main Street in public acceptance of the inevitable.

The reason to live in such a town is gratitude. A hard life is balanced by the joy of life. Tragedy is offset by community. Anger is suppressed with forgiveness. Stupidity is upended with laughter. In Rich Valley, many are proud of their success. In Poor Valley, folks are proud of their town.

Abraham Lincoln set aside a day in November to celebrate Thanksgiving. The Civil War—"the lamentable strife," in Lincoln's words—had devastated this country, and he urged all citizens to pursue a course of "humble penitence for our national perverseness and disobedience," looking to the Almighty Hand for the full "enjoyment of peace, harmony, tranquility and Union." He reminded us that our well-being is not entirely of our own making, that our happiness and success cannot be entirely ascribed to personal industry.

Starting with Lincoln, tales of Thanksgiving are, of course, stories of gratitude. A Mrs. Hulda Esther Thorpe remembered "one of the best Thanksgiving dinners we ever knew." A family of prairie settlers in the 1800s was sitting down to the Thanksgiving feast. A group of outlaws "came in silently and just shoved the folks back and ate up the dinner." After they were gone, the "women made a big cornbread and with what few things that were left, they had a feast." They were all deeply thankful that they were spared.

Sometimes, though, the best stories about gratitude are built around a character who is spectacularly ungrateful. A Vermont farmer had been married for thirty years and often compared his wife's cooking with his mother's, not in his wife's favor. One Thanksgiving his wife went all out to prepare the perfect feast, one that would be better than her mother-in-law's. The farmer sat down to the Thanksgiving table and ate with great relish. After he was done, his wife said, "Well, you seemed to like that meal well enough."

Her husband thought a bit, running the major items over in his mind. "'Twas good," he allowed at last. "The turkey was roasted just right and the dressing was well seasoned. The mashed potatoes were smooth and good. The other vegetables was done just the way I like them and even the pie and the pudding was good. But the gravy—that gravy . . . well, Mother's gravy always had lumps in it!"

Enjoy the day. Be grateful. Happy Thanksgiving!

FOR INQUIRIES, ORDERS, OR MORE INFORMATION

CooksIllustrated.com
At CooksIllustrated.com, you can order books and subscriptions, sign up for our free e-newsletter, or renew your magazine subscription. Join the website and gain access to 23 years of *Cook's Illustrated* recipes, equipment tests, and ingredient tastings, as well as companion videos for every recipe in this issue.

COOKBOOKS
We sell more than 50 cookbooks by the editors of *Cook's Illustrated*, including *The Cook's Illustrated Cookbook* and *The Science of Good Cooking*. To order, visit our bookstore at CooksIllustrated.com/bookstore.

***COOK'S ILLUSTRATED* MAGAZINE**
Cook's Illustrated magazine (ISSN 1068-2821), number 137, is published bimonthly by Boston Common Press Limited Partnership, 17 Station St., Brookline, MA 02445. Copyright 2015 Boston Common Press Limited Partnership. Periodicals postage paid at Boston, MA, and additional mailing offices, USPS #012487. Publications Mail Agreement No. 40020778. Return undeliverable Canadian addresses to P.O. Box 875, Station A, Windsor, ON N9A 6P2. POSTMASTER: Send address changes to *Cook's Illustrated*, P.O. Box 6018, Harlan, IA 51593-1518. For subscription and gift subscription orders, subscription inquiries, or change of address notices, visit AmericasTestKitchen.com/support, call 800-526-8442 in the U.S. or 515-248-7684 from outside the U.S., or write to us at *Cook's Illustrated*, P.O. 6018, Harlan, IA 51593-1518.

FOR LIST RENTAL INFORMATION Contact Specialists Marketing Services, Inc., 777 Terrace Ave., 4th Floor, Hasbrouck Heights, NJ 07604; phone: 201-865-5800.

EDITORIAL OFFICE 17 Station St., Brookline, MA 02445; 617-232-1000; fax: 617-232-1572. For subscription inquiries, visit AmericasTestKitchen.com/support or call 800-526-8442.

QUICK TIPS

COMPILED BY ANNIE PETITO

Smooth Cake Frosting

When frosting the sides of a cake, Antonia Chandler of Houston, Texas, finds that her bench scraper is the best tool for smoothing the sides. She spins the cake on a turntable-style stand, holding the edge of the scraper steady against the side of the cake so that it smooths any uneven patches.

Plastic Bag Space Saver

When he's short on storage space, Shawn Gagne of Los Angeles, Calif., uses pushpins to tack up cardboard boxes of zipper-lock bags on a wall in the pantry, where they're even more accessible.

Slow-Cooker Warming Tray

Janet McCarron of Seattle, Wash., likes to set up a station for making candy or decorating cookies during the holidays and has found that her slow cooker comes in handy as a warming tray. She places glass jars of chocolate in the vessel and pours in enough water to come partially up their sides, creating a warm bath, which keeps the chocolate warm and fluid for as long as she needs while assembling her treats.

Cabbage "Bowls"

When making cabbage-based recipes, like coleslaw, Bonnie Powers of Dublin, N.H., uses the discarded outer leaves as disposable bowls for collecting vegetable peels and scraps. When she's done prepping, she simply tosses the leaves into the garbage or compost.

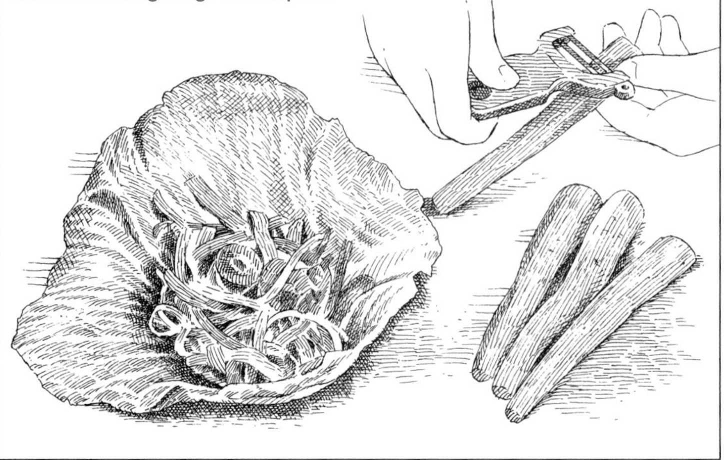

Keeping Tongs Closed

Helen Koenig of Bernardsville, N.J., stores tongs that don't have a lock in a 2-inch length of cardboard paper towel tube. One squeeze and the tongs slip right into their homemade "sleeve" for easy storage and removal.

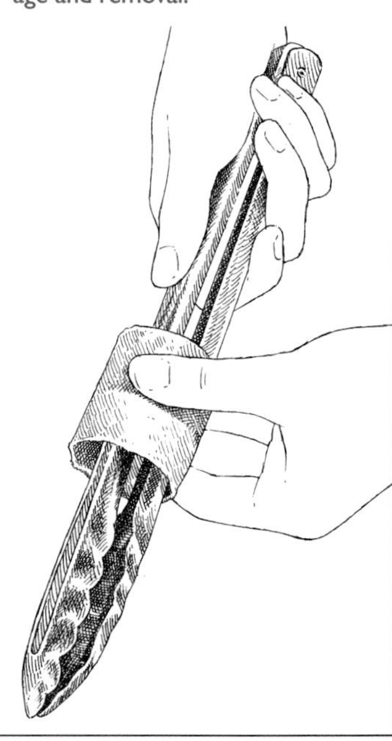

Breaking Up Ground Meat

Annie Guba-Boruch of Waterbury, Conn., reaches for her pastry blender whenever she needs to cut cold butter or shortening into flour. When attempting to break up a batch of ground meat during cooking, she came up with another use for the tool. The pastry blender's sharp, parallel blades easily and neatly chop meat for more even cooking.

SEND US YOUR TIPS We will provide a complimentary one-year subscription for each tip we print. Send your tip, name, address, and daytime telephone number to Quick Tips, *Cook's Illustrated*, P.O. Box 470589, Brookline, MA 02447, or to QuickTips@AmericasTestKitchen.com.

Making Plastic Wrap Stick

To help plastic wrap cling tightly to the rim of metal mixing bowls, Alex Barunas of Gilford, N.H., runs a bit of water around the sides of the bowl to give the plastic more purchase.

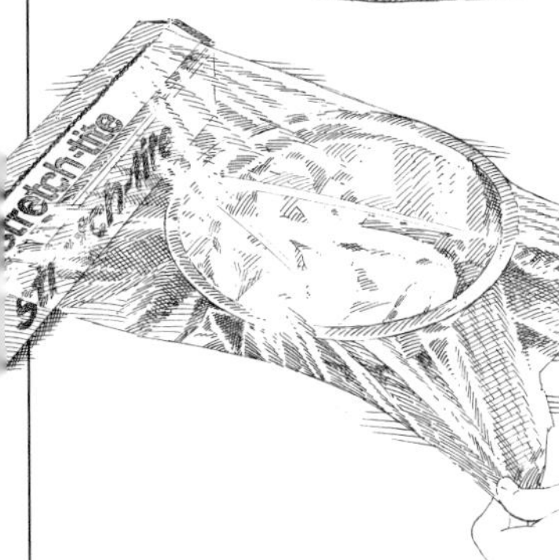

Makeshift Freezer Shelves

Rather than sift through her freezer to find hidden smaller items, Marsha Wianecki of Okemos, Mich., created shelves using plastic magazine holders. By arranging the holders on their sides with the openings facing forward, she's able to easily see and reach their contents.

Tea Bag in a Pinch

When her tea ball broke, Connie Basset of Omaha, Neb., devised this clever idea for steeping the loose leaves: She piles them in the center of a disposable paper coffee filter, bundles it up, and fastens the top with a clothespin. Once she's steeped her tea, she simply throws the "tea bag" away.

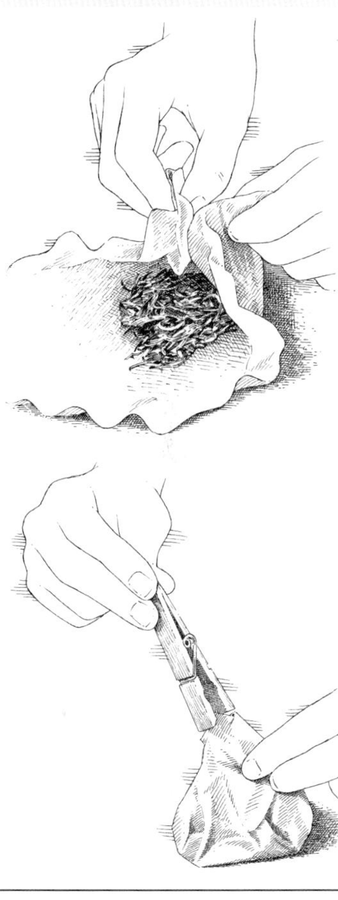

Aluminum Foil Covers

Robin Hamlin of Santa Barbara, Calif., saves the aluminum foil rounds that seal yogurt containers and reuses them to cover the cut side of fruits and veggies. The heavy-duty aluminum washes easily and stays put on the food without tearing.

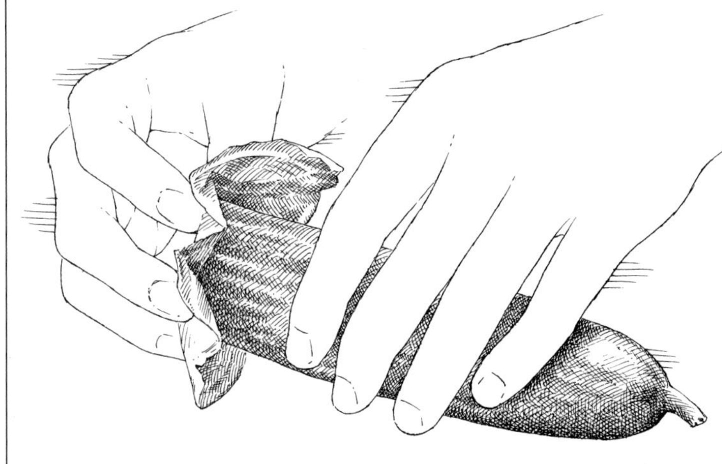

Hanger-Turned-Chip-Clip

Maryse Chevriere of San Francisco, Calif., recycles her unused skirt hangers by snapping off the pinchers to use as bag clips.

Protecting Stemware

To safely transport fragile wine glasses or champagne flutes, Mary Wilbor of Glastonbury, Conn., covers the stemware bowls with the stretchable plastic netting she saves from pieces of delicate fruit (such as tomatoes and Asian pears).

Saving Spent Lemons for Zest

Instead of tossing out her spent lemon halves after juicing, Susan Lacy of Miamisburg, Ohio, freezes them for zesting later. The halves can be easily stacked and stored in a zipper-lock bag, and the freezer firms them up for easy zesting.

Roasted Rack of Lamb

If you have the know-how, rack of lamb can be one of the simplest—and most elegant—holiday dishes you'll ever make.

⋙ BY LAN LAM ⋘

For many, hosting company at the holidays means pulling out all the stops to present a centerpiece-worthy entrée. Old standbys like turkey or prime rib are great choices—except that they are only for crowds. Plus, they eat up precious time and energy: From salting and trussing to roasting, resting, and carving, it can take hours or even days to get them from supermarket to table.

Enter rack of lamb. With elegantly curved rib bones attached to a long, lean loin, it is as grand as any beef roast or whole bird—but it cooks a whole lot faster and its small size makes it ideal for fewer guests. What's more, its tenderness and delicate but distinctive flavor make it approachable for those who have not tried lamb (and may surprise those who think they dislike it): Because the loin muscle of the animal gets little exercise, the meat doesn't get tough or develop much of a strong, gamy flavor. The fact that this particular cut is so lean also plays a role in its mild taste. (For more, see "The Funk Is in the Fat.")

Rack of lamb is a cinch to serve since the rib bones act as built-in carving guides. Just slice between them to produce handsome chops.

Rack 'em Up

A single rack of domestic lamb weighs about 2 pounds and contains seven or eight rib bones that arc from the loin. Traditionally, the racks are spiffed up via "frenching," a process that involves cutting away the sinew, fat, and small bits of meat that cover the bones. It can be tedious work, but happily, butchers often take care of this so it's easy to find a roast that is just about oven-ready. Given the small size of a single rack, I decided to cook two frenched racks, which would ably serve four to six guests.

Since lamb fat is the primary source of the musky flavor that some shy away from, I trimmed the fat cap to ¼ inch. Next, I scored crosshatch marks into the fat and sprinkled the racks all over with kosher salt. Cutting slits in the fat would allow the salt to quickly penetrate the meat as well as help the fat render.

With the meat ready to go, I got down to the business of cooking. There are a lot of recipes out there promising "simple but spectacular" results, with the usual recommendation being to roast the meat in a hot oven for about 30 minutes. Using this approach, the racks didn't brown very well; plus, they were pink only at the very center—the outer portion was a dry, dusty gray. If I was going to splurge on rack of lamb, I wanted dazzling results. That meant rosy, juicy, and tender meat surrounded by a rich mahogany exterior.

And yet, abandoning the so-called simple approach resulted in only minor advancements. Slow-roasting the racks in a more moderate oven meant that every bite was juicy, but this lamb wasn't full-flavored because there was zero browning on its exterior. In the test kitchen, we often turn to dual-temperature techniques to achieve both great browning and even cooking. The question was, how should I apply this approach to rack of lamb?

A sear-then-roast routine made sense. I fired up the stove and seared the racks in a skillet until they were good and brown, which took about 5 minutes per rack (and made a pretty good mess of my stovetop). I then placed the seared lamb on a wire rack set in a rimmed baking sheet and slipped it into a 250-degree oven to finish cooking.

The racks emerged gorgeously brown from the pan searing, but when I carved them into chops, frustration set in: Because the loin is relatively small, all that time in the skillet had overcooked most of the meat. I cleaned up and started over, this time placing a roasting pan in the oven and heating the oven to 500 degrees. My hope was that the racks would rapidly brown when they hit the preheated pan. Then I could dial down the oven and let the meat gently finish cooking. But this was another disappointment: The preheated pan wasn't hot enough to sufficiently brown the racks, and the initial high oven temperature overcooked the meat.

Slow Start

Searing followed by roasting was a no-go. How about the reverse? I placed the seasoned racks in a 250-degree oven and let them roast gently until they reached 120 degrees, or just shy of medium-rare. There were a couple of possible approaches for browning the exterior in the oven: Crank the heat as high as it would go or enlist the broiler. I tried both. The broiler browned the fat cap more quickly than the hot oven, so the rack overcooked less. But it still overcooked. Perhaps a skillet was the way to go after all.

I slow-roasted two more racks, this time pulling them from the oven when they were somewhat underdone. I then seared the fat caps one at a time in a hot skillet. To my surprise, each rack browned in less than 2 minutes. When I cut into the meat, I was again surprised, this time by how uniformly rare it was. The explanation was simple. I had assumed that the racks would require a substantial amount of time to brown and would therefore finish cooking in the skillet. But the browning happened so fast—there wasn't even time for the stovetop to get messy—that

Shopping for Lamb: For more information on what to look for and why, go to CooksIllustrated.com/lamb.

See Lamb's Virtues
Video available free for 4 months at CooksIllustrated.com/dec15

I clearly needed to let them roast all the way to their serving temperature, 125 degrees for medium-rare. Sure enough, using this method, I finally got the oohs and ahhs I sought: These racks had deeply browned exteriors and perfectly rosy interiors.

But why had they browned so quickly? The slow roasting time had warmed up the fat cap. This allowed it to immediately jump to the temperature necessary for stovetop browning to occur.

Spiced Salt

With a foolproof cooking method at hand, it was time to try salting the racks ahead of time to see if the treatment, which changes the meat's structure to help it hold on to more juices, was necessary. I salted two racks and let them sit for 1 hour. Then I asked tasters to compare their flavor and texture to racks that were seasoned and then immediately cooked. Tasters reported that the seasoned racks were just as juicy as the salted ones. That's because salt's ability to help meat retain juices is most apparent when meat is exposed to high temperatures, and my lamb was being cooked at only 250 degrees. That meant that it never got hot enough for much moisture to be squeezed out. It had one other thing going for it: Unlike steaks or many other roasts, rack of lamb is protected by a moisture-retaining fat cap on one side and bones on the other side. Given these factors, it was unnecessary to give the lamb a salt treatment.

What it did need was a little dressing up, so I went ahead and mixed some ground cumin with kosher salt. I used some of this cumin salt to season the racks; the rest I saved for garnishing the lamb. And while the roasts cooked, I mixed together a quick relish of roasted red peppers, fresh parsley, minced garlic, lemon juice, and extra-virgin olive oil. With the relish spooned alongside the cumin-scented chops, I knew I had a hit. I was so taken with the depth and texture that the cumin salt added that I whipped up an anise salt and paired it with a mint-almond relish. With these ultrasimple recipes at hand, lamb will surely be at the center of my holiday table more often.

ROASTED RACK OF LAMB WITH ROASTED RED PEPPER RELISH

SERVES 4 TO 6

We prefer the milder taste and bigger size of domestic lamb, but you may substitute lamb imported from New Zealand or Australia. Since imported racks are generally smaller, in step 1 season each rack with ½ teaspoon of the salt mixture and reduce the cooking time to 50 to 70 minutes.

Lamb

- 2 (1¾- to 2-pound) racks of lamb, fat trimmed to ⅛ to ¼ inch and rib bones frenched
- Kosher salt
- 1 teaspoon ground cumin
- 1 teaspoon vegetable oil

Relish

- ½ cup jarred roasted red peppers, rinsed, patted dry, and chopped fine
- ½ cup minced fresh parsley
- ¼ cup extra-virgin olive oil
- ¼ teaspoon lemon juice
- ⅛ teaspoon garlic, minced to paste
- Kosher salt and pepper

1. FOR THE LAMB: Adjust oven rack to middle position and heat oven to 250 degrees. Using sharp knife, cut slits in fat cap, spaced ½ inch apart, in crosshatch pattern (cut down to, but not into, meat). Combine 2 tablespoons salt and cumin in bowl. Rub ¾ teaspoon salt mixture over entire surface of each rack and into slits. Reserve remaining salt mixture. Place racks, bone side down, on wire rack set in rimmed baking sheet. Roast until meat registers 125 degrees for medium-rare or 130 degrees for medium, 1 hour 5 minutes to 1 hour 25 minutes.

2. FOR THE RELISH: While lamb roasts, combine red peppers, parsley, olive oil, lemon juice, and garlic in bowl. Season with salt and pepper to taste. Let stand at room temperature for at least 1 hour before serving.

3. Heat vegetable oil in 12-inch skillet over high heat until just smoking. Place 1 rack, bone side up, in skillet and cook until well browned, 1 to 2 minutes. Transfer to carving board. Pour off all but 1 teaspoon fat from skillet and repeat browning with second rack. Tent racks with aluminum foil and let rest for 20 minutes. Cut between ribs to separate chops and sprinkle cut side of chops with ½ teaspoon salt mixture. Serve, passing relish and remaining salt mixture separately.

The Funk Is in the Fat

Unique branched-chain fatty acids are responsible for many of lamb's musky flavors. To find out just how important these fatty acids are, we combined ground lean lamb meat and fat to create two blends: 90 percent lean meat/10 percent fat and 80 percent lean meat/20 percent fat. When we made burgers from the blends as well as from 100 percent lean meat and rated the intensity of the lamb flavor, tasters unanimously found the meat/fat blends to have more characteristic lamb flavor than the 100 percent lean patties. When it comes to lamb, the old adage that fat equals flavor can't be overstated: Trimming some fat will result in a milder taste. –Dan Souza

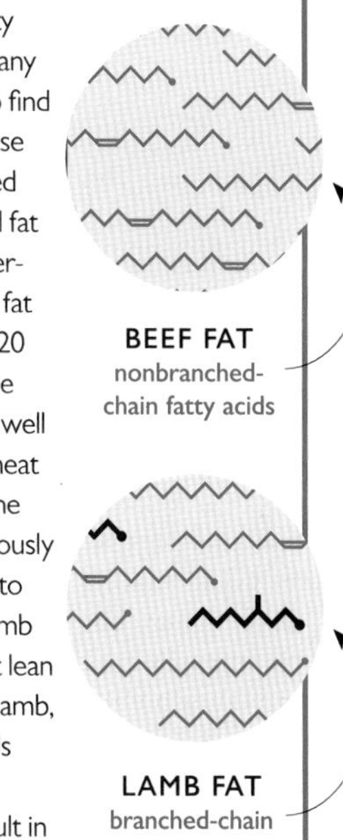

ROASTED RACK OF LAMB WITH SWEET MINT-ALMOND RELISH

Substitute ground anise for cumin in salt mixture. Omit red pepper relish. While lamb roasts, combine ½ cup minced fresh mint; ¼ cup sliced almonds, toasted and chopped fine; ¼ cup extra-virgin olive oil; 2 tablespoons red currant jelly; 4 teaspoons red wine vinegar; and 2 teaspoons Dijon mustard in bowl. Season with salt and pepper to taste. Let stand at room temperature for at least 1 hour before serving.

Easy as 1-2-3

Putting an impressive roast on the table doesn't have to be stressful or take all day. Our rack of lamb is ready in less than 2 hours.

1. SEASON There's no need to salt ahead of time. Because of the insulating bones and thin layer of fat, rack of lamb sprinkled with salt right before roasting is just as juicy as meat salted an hour in advance.

2. SLOW-ROAST For juicy meat that's a rosy medium-rare from center to edge, we simply roast the racks in a 250-degree oven until they reach 125 degrees, 1 hour 5 minutes to 1 hour 25 minutes.

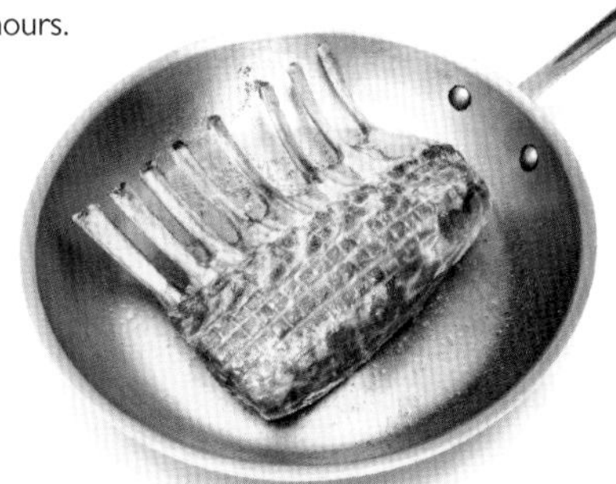

3. SEAR The fat cap warms up in the oven, so when it hits a hot skillet, it quickly reaches the temperature necessary for browning. Because the rack browns in just 2 minutes, none of the meat overcooks during this step.

Great Chicken Marsala

Chicken cutlets napped with a silky mushroom-Marsala sauce are a restaurant standard. So why doesn't anyone cook them at home?

BY ANDREW JANJIGIAN

Everyone knows chicken Marsala, a menu staple at virtually every Italian American restaurant in the United States. But despite its wide-ranging appeal, the dish is rarely made at home. That's too bad, because it's relatively simple to prepare and—when done right—truly satisfying: thinly pounded chicken cutlets, dusted lightly with flour, pan-seared until golden brown but still tender and juicy, and napped with a sumptuous sauce of Marsala wine and thinly sliced mushrooms. What's not to like?

Well, as it turned out, quite a bit. When I prepared a handful of recipes, not one dish could hold a candle to the best restaurant versions. For starters, the thin cutlets tended to dry out by the time they browned. What's more, their flour coating turned gummy as soon as I spooned the sauce on top. Then there was the sauce itself, which ranged from thin and watery to syrupy and sweet. Clearly there was lots of room for improvement.

Most homemade versions of chicken Marsala feature dry cutlets cloaked in an overly sweet sauce. A few simple tricks fix both issues.

Crafting Cutlets

My first step was to streamline the preparation of the cutlets themselves. I knew of two approaches: Either use a meat pounder to flatten a whole breast, or cut the breast in half horizontally into two thinner pieces. The problem with the former method is that all that pounding virtually guarantees tearing the meat. On the other hand, it's difficult to evenly halve a breast horizontally since the meat becomes thinner as you approach the tapered end.

Eventually, I came up with a better way: First, halve the breast crosswise. Then, split the thick side horizontally, leaving three similarly sized pieces that require only a minimum of pounding to become cutlets (see "A New Way to Cut Cutlets"). To season the cutlets and help them stay moist, I tossed them with salt and set them aside for 15 minutes.

Starch Relief

Normally in this dish the cutlets are dredged in flour before they're seared. The flour serves a few purposes. First, it absorbs any surface moisture (a plus since moisture inhibits browning), and then it browns. It also gives the Marsala-mushroom sauce something to grab on to, so the cutlets become nicely coated. The problem was that the flour didn't cook through in the short time that the cutlets were in the pan, causing that gummy mess once the sauce (for now, a placeholder recipe) was introduced.

I wondered if cornstarch would fare better, but it behaved similarly. I even tried using precooked starch in the form of ground saltines. The resulting cutlets were less sticky, but the coating had a gritty texture instead of a smooth one. I also tried cooking the cutlets bare, but that was a dead end: Without a flour coating, the sauce slid right off the chicken; plus, since the flour offers the chicken some protection from the heat, it was tricky to get the cutlets fully browned before they overcooked.

Maybe I needed to reconsider the approach of arranging the seared cutlets on a platter and spooning the sauce on top. Did the sauce and cutlets need to spend more time together?

Back at the stove, I returned the browned cutlets to the skillet after preparing the sauce and let it bubble gently for a few minutes. Problem solved: During simmering, any excess flour sloughed off into the sauce where it gelatinized, leaving the coating thin, silky, and not the least bit gummy. And because the salting step was effective at maintaining moisture, this additional gentle cooking didn't harm the meat.

Marsala and Mushrooms

With perfectly cooked cutlets at hand, I turned my attention to the sauce. White button mushrooms, sliced thin and sautéed, are typically used. They are fine but subtle, and I wanted more complexity. Switching to earthier cremini mushrooms and adding garlic, shallot, and tomato paste was a good start. I had seen recipes that also included pancetta, and indeed, I liked the meatiness it contributed.

As for the Marsala, this Sicilian fortified wine is produced in both sweet and dry styles. Obviously, sweet Marsala tastes sweeter than dry, but I also found that the dry type offered more depth of flavor. In addition, I came to prefer the complexity of moderately priced ($10 to $12) Marsala, rather than the supercheap bottles.

Most recipes rely on a combination of chicken broth and Marsala; I liked a 1:1 ratio. I reduced both before adding them to the mushroom mixture, starting with the Marsala and then adding the broth. As we have found in previous recipes, reducing the wine and broth together prevented sufficient alcohol evaporation, producing a boozy taste. However, last-minute additions of ¼ cup of raw Marsala, lemon juice, and chopped oregano brightened the sauce without making it taste of alcohol. Finally, adding dried porcini mushrooms to the reduction rounded out the flavor.

Reducing the wine and broth helped intensify the sauce but did little to add body. (The flour from the cutlets contributed some viscosity but not nearly enough.) A few tablespoons of butter, whisked in at the very end, helped a bit more. Then, thinking about the way a restaurant chef might give the sauce some heft, reduced veal stock (demi-glace) crossed my mind. This spoonable, gelatinous ingredient can provide a luxurious consistency. I wasn't about to buy (or make) demi-glace for this recipe, but I knew of a good stand-in: gelatin. Four teaspoons added to the reducing wine gave the sauce velvety body.

After a sprinkle of parsley, everything was in its place in my new and improved classic.

Unassuming Superhero: Flour

Don't be tempted to skip flouring the chicken cutlets before pan-searing them. It is a quick step that's key to the success of the final dish.

ABSORBS MOISTURE
Flour soaks up any wetness on the raw chicken but remains dry enough to brown.

BROWNS EXTERIOR
When the cutlets are seared, it's the flour that browns and develops flavor, not the meat.

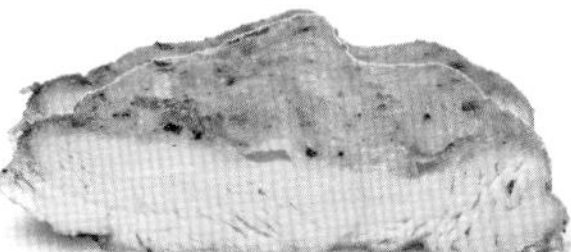

PROTECTS INTERIOR
Flour browns faster than meat, so the coated chicken can come off the heat before it overcooks.

THICKENS SAUCE
As the cutlets simmer in the sauce, some flour sloughs off and gives the sauce body.

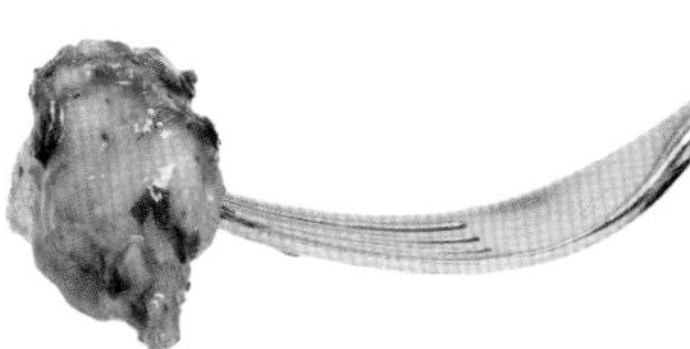

GRABS SAUCE
The flour coating on the cutlets helps the sauce cling to the meat.

BETTER CHICKEN MARSALA

SERVES 4 TO 6

It is worth spending a little extra for a moderately priced dry Marsala ($10 to $12 per bottle). Serve the chicken with potatoes, white rice, or buttered pasta. For our free recipe for Better Chicken Marsala for Two, go to CooksIllustrated.com/dec15.

- 2¼ cups dry Marsala
- 4 teaspoons unflavored gelatin
- 1 ounce dried porcini mushrooms, rinsed
- 4 (6- to 8-ounce) boneless, skinless chicken breasts, trimmed
- Kosher salt and pepper
- 2 cups chicken broth
- ¾ cup all-purpose flour
- ¼ cup plus 1 teaspoon vegetable oil
- 3 ounces pancetta, cut into ½-inch pieces
- 1 pound cremini mushrooms, trimmed and sliced thin
- 1 shallot, minced
- 1 tablespoon tomato paste
- 1 garlic clove, minced
- 2 teaspoons lemon juice
- 1 teaspoon minced fresh oregano
- 3 tablespoons unsalted butter, cut into 6 pieces
- 2 teaspoons minced fresh parsley

1. Bring 2 cups Marsala, gelatin, and porcini mushrooms to boil in medium saucepan over high heat. Reduce heat to medium-high and vigorously simmer until reduced by half, 6 to 8 minutes.

2. Meanwhile, cut each chicken breast in half crosswise, then cut thick half in half again horizontally, creating 3 cutlets of about same thickness. Place cutlets between sheets of plastic wrap and pound gently to even ½-inch thickness. Place cutlets in bowl and toss with 2 teaspoons salt and ½ teaspoon pepper. Set aside for 15 minutes.

3. Strain Marsala reduction through fine-mesh strainer, pressing on solids to extract as much liquid as possible; discard solids. Return Marsala reduction to saucepan, add broth, and return to boil over high heat. Lower heat to medium-high and simmer until reduced to 1½ cups, 10 to 12 minutes. Set aside.

4. Spread flour in shallow dish. Working with 1 cutlet at a time, dredge cutlets in flour, shaking gently to remove excess. Place on wire rack set in rimmed baking sheet. Heat 2 tablespoons oil in 12-inch skillet over medium-high heat until smoking. Place 6 cutlets in skillet and lower heat to medium. Cook until golden brown on 1 side, 2 to 3 minutes. Flip and cook until golden brown on second side, 2 to 3 minutes. Return cutlets to wire rack. Repeat with 2 tablespoons oil and remaining 6 cutlets.

5. Return now-empty skillet to medium-low heat and add pancetta. Cook, stirring occasionally, scraping pan bottom to loosen browned bits, until pancetta is brown and crisp, about 4 minutes. Add cremini mushrooms and increase heat to medium-high. Cook, stirring occasionally and scraping pan bottom, until liquid released by mushrooms evaporates and mushrooms begin to brown, about 8 minutes. Using slotted spoon, transfer cremini mushrooms and pancetta to bowl. Add remaining 1 teaspoon oil and shallot to pan and cook until softened, 1 minute. Add tomato paste and garlic and cook until fragrant, 30 seconds. Add reduced Marsala mixture, remaining ¼ cup Marsala, lemon juice, and oregano and bring to simmer.

6. Add cutlets to sauce and simmer for 3 minutes, flipping halfway through simmering. Transfer cutlets to platter. Off heat, whisk in butter. Stir in parsley and cremini mushroom mixture. Season with salt and pepper to taste. Spoon sauce over chicken and serve.

A New Way to Cut Cutlets

Because a chicken breast is unevenly shaped and has a thick and a thin end, it can be tricky to turn into uniform cutlets. Our novel method makes the process foolproof: Cut each breast in half crosswise (1); then cut the thicker piece in half horizontally (2). Place the pieces between two sheets of plastic wrap and gently pound them ½ inch thick.

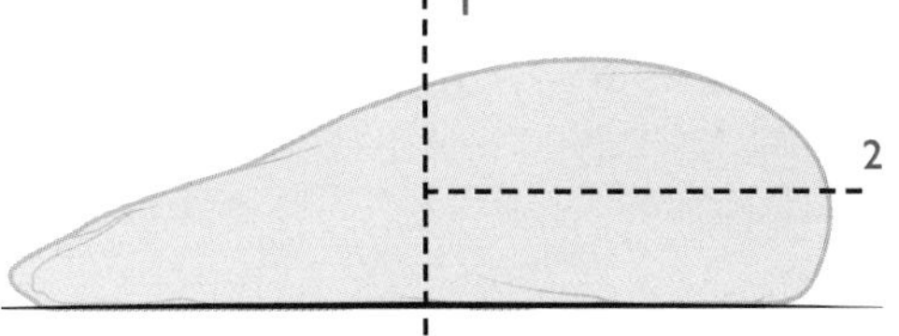

TESTING Spatula-Spoons

We use a wooden spoon to scoop food and scrape up flavorful browned bits when making stews and pan sauces, and we use a flexible spatula to fold ingredients and swipe bowls clean. A spatula-spoon (or "spoonula") promises to serve both functions in one handy item. We purchased eight models ($7.51 to $14.95) and stirred jam, scraped up fond in chili, tossed a stir-fry, and folded scrambled eggs. For scraping up fond, firm and blunt top edges were most effective. We also preferred thin, straight sides that could glide along skillets. The best tools could also transfer generous amounts of food into storage containers. Ultimately, the Starpack Premium Silicone Spoonula ($8.49) and the Rubbermaid High-Heat Spoon Scraper ($9.13) combined all our desired qualities. We still consider our favorite wooden spoon and silicone spatula to be essential, but we'll reach for either of these spoonulas when making a recipe that requires both a wooden spoon and a spatula. For complete testing results, go to CooksIllustrated.com/dec15. –Kate Shannon

HIGHLY RECOMMENDED

STARPACK
Premium Silicone Spoonula
MODEL: N/A
PRICE: $8.49
COMMENTS:
This tool felt especially comfortable, and its spacious and sturdy head presses flush to cookware.

RUBBERMAID
High-Heat Spoon Scraper
MODEL: FG196600
PRICE: $9.13
COMMENTS:
Our co-winner boasts the largest head capacity in the lineup, and its edges felt extra-precise.

Andrew Makes It for You
Video available free for 4 months at CooksIllustrated.com/dec15

Best Ground Beef Chili

Ground beef chili offers more convenience than chili made with chunks of meat. But before you can make a truly great version, you need to understand the nature of ground beef.

BY ANDREW JANJIGIAN

I'm not from Texas, so I've never had any trouble thinking that chili by definition could only mean a bowl made with hand-cut chunks of beef. If anything, I'm always more drawn to ground beef versions, since they skip the tedious step of breaking down a whole roast. That said, I've rarely encountered a ground beef chili that can hold its own against the chunky kind. It often suffers from dry, grainy, somewhat tough meat. I set myself the challenge of changing that.

I wanted a big batch of thick, spicy, ultrabeefy chili—the kind I'd pile into a bowl with tortilla chips or rice and enjoy with a beer. In order to create that, I would first have to sort out how to give the ground meat the same juicy, tender texture found in chili made with chunks of beef.

Tortilla chips (or rice) are a must with this thick, rich chili that's deeply spiced with an easy-to-make ancho chile powder.

Ground Plan

As a first step toward improving dry meat, I opted to use 2 pounds of 85 percent lean (15 percent fat) ground beef. The fat in the mix would lubricate the meat fibers, creating a sense of moistness. As for how to cook it, most chili recipes—whether using ground beef or chunks—call for browning the meat in oil to build a flavor base. Since ground beef sheds a fair amount of liquid as it cooks, and liquid precludes browning, I cooked it in three batches so that any moisture could evaporate quickly.

The next big question was how long to simmer the meat in the liquid ingredients for the most tender results. Recipes vary widely: Some suggest an hour, others call for 2 hours, and more than a few say "the longer the better." But would the fact that the meat was ground make its proteins and collagen break down more quickly than stew meat, which requires roughly 2½ hours of simmering? All this confusion could, I figured, be cleared up by one simple test.

But first I needed a basic chili recipe to work from. After setting the browned meat aside, I sautéed a few spoonfuls of store-bought chili powder (a stand-in for the homemade blend I planned to mix up later), diced onions, and minced garlic in the residual fat. Once the aromatics were softened, I returned the beef to the pot along with a can of pinto beans and a small can of whole tomatoes that I pureed in the food processor. (I used judicious amounts of each since I wanted the beef to be the star of the show.) Finally, I stirred in 2 cups of water. I brought the mixture to a boil, put the lid on the pot, and transferred it to a 275-degree oven where the ambient heat would cook it gently. After about an hour, the result was only mediocre: The flavors were no longer raw-tasting, but they were somewhat blah. Plus, the beef still had the dry, tough texture I was trying to avoid.

Watch: Ground Beef Triumphs
Video available free for 4 months at CooksIllustrated.com/dec15

Trying for Tenderness

Sixty minutes of simmering clearly wasn't long enough to tenderize the meat. I put the chili back into the oven, pulling it out and sampling it every 15 minutes or so. The Goldilocks moment, when the meat was fairly tender, came at the 90-minute mark.

This suggested that just because meat is ground doesn't mean it doesn't take time to tenderize: The pieces might be smaller than meat chunks, but the muscle fibers are made of the same proteins and collagen that require similar exposure to heat to break down. Heat penetrates the fibers more quickly when they are in small pieces, which is why chunks of chuck roast might take 2 to 2½ hours to tenderize, while ground beef requires only 90 minutes.

I had made progress, but the ground beef still wasn't living up to its full potential: I wanted it to be even more tender, and it wasn't perfectly moist like beef chunks are after proper browning and simmering. That's because fine pieces of ground meat give off far more moisture during the browning step than larger meat chunks do. The muscle fibers tighten up when heated, squeezing out some of the liquid they contain. And the smaller the piece, the more liquid will be lost to the surrounding environment.

There are a few tricks to help keep ground beef tender and juicy. One of them I was already doing: using meat with a relatively high fat content. Another is to add salt and let the meat sit for about 20 minutes. In addition to seasoning the meat, salt alters the structure of the meat proteins to better allow it to retain moisture. Finally, you can raise the pH of

When It Comes to Cook Time, Chuck Is Chuck

You might think that just because ground beef is made up of tiny pieces of meat, it doesn't need much time to cook. But ground chuck is exactly that—cut-up pieces of chuck roast—and as such contains the same proteins and collagen that require adequate exposure to moist heat to properly break down. Many chili recipes cook the ground meat for 45 minutes or even less. For optimally tender results, we simmer ours for 1½ to 2 hours—almost as long as we do stew meat.

=

CUBED VS. GROUND
Both benefit from longer cooking.

the meat with a little baking soda to help the proteins attract more water and hold on to it (see "Better Browning Through Chemistry").

Indeed, incorporating baking soda—¾ teaspoon plus 2 tablespoons of water to help it dissolve—not only kept the meat juicy and made it even more tender, but it also produced an unforeseen benefit: Since the beef now barely shed any moisture during cooking (not even the small amount of water that I added to dissolve the baking soda) and a higher pH significantly speeds up the Maillard reaction, the meat browned much more quickly. This meant that I could cook it in a single batch rather than in three—a major timesaver.

Fat and Flavor

With that, I shifted my focus to giving the chili memorably spicy flavor. Store-bought chili powder is convenient, but it's not that much trouble to make a homemade blend that tastes significantly better. I started with six dried whole ancho chiles, toasted to bring out their raisin-like sweetness and fruity heat. But it was hard to grind the small quantity of chiles in a food processor, since the pieces just bounced around the workbowl. One trick we've used in the past is to add cornmeal to the mix to bulk it up. The cornmeal also serves to slightly thicken and add corn flavor to the chili. I used the same approach, but substituted a few tortilla chips for the cornmeal, since I always have them on hand to serve with chili.

Keep That Orange Slick

Because the main flavor compounds in most spices are fat soluble, skimming the bright orange fat from the finished chili will rob it of flavor. For deep, richly spiced complexity, don't remove the fat—stir it back in.

For another layer of heat and smokiness, I stirred in minced chipotles in adobo. And to boost the chile notes without adding more heat, I threw in some sweet paprika. Of course, chili powder isn't made from just chiles. I also added a generous amount of ground cumin, plus garlic powder, ground coriander, dried oregano, black pepper, and dried thyme.

Finally, about that fat. After the chili came out of the oven, it was covered in a layer of bright orange grease. When I reflexively skimmed it off, my tasters complained that the chili tasted a little flat and lean. The Day-Glo color should have been a giveaway that the fat was loaded with oil-soluble compounds from my spice blend. Discarding it robbed the chili of flavor. So for my next batch, instead of removing the fat, I just stirred it back in. Now the chili boasted deeply spiced complexity.

To cut some of its richness, I added 2 teaspoons of sugar and a couple of tablespoons of cider vinegar. I served the chili with lime wedges, fresh cilantro, chopped onion, and plenty of tortilla chips and/or steamed white rice. This chili was full-flavored and rich but certainly not so rich that my guests didn't come back for seconds.

SCIENCE Better Browning Through Chemistry

Browning ground beef is a challenge since it expels juices more rapidly than chunks of meat do, and most of that moisture needs to evaporate before browning can occur. To limit the amount of liquid, the usual solution is to brown in batches. We stick with one batch but toss the meat with baking soda before cooking, which helps lock in moisture. To quantify baking soda's impact, we ran a simple experiment.

UNTREATED
Meat is flooded with liquid and fails to brown.

EXPERIMENT We cooked three batches of ground beef treated with baking soda and compared them with three otherwise identical untreated batches. We calculated the pre- and postcooking moisture level of each batch and compared degrees of browning.

RESULTS On average, the untreated meat lost about 10 percent more moisture during cooking than the treated meat. That may not sound like much, but it makes a significant difference in how well ground meat browns: The treated batches were deeply browned, whereas the untreated batches didn't brown at all. (If we kept cooking the untreated meat, it would have eventually browned but would have been overdone.)

TREATED WITH BAKING SODA
Meat barely sheds moisture and browns nicely.

EXPLANATION Raising the pH of meat increases its water-holding capacity, meaning that the proteins attract more water and are better able to hold on to it—not just during browning but throughout cooking. Besides keeping the meat from losing water that would make it steam versus brown, a higher pH also speeds up the Maillard reaction, making the treated meat brown even better and more quickly.

BEST GROUND BEEF CHILI
SERVES 8 TO 10

Diced avocado, sour cream, and shredded Monterey Jack or cheddar cheese are also good options for garnishing. This chili is intensely flavored and should be served with tortilla chips and/or plenty of steamed white rice.

- **2 pounds 85 percent lean ground beef**
- **2 tablespoons plus 2 cups water**
- **Salt and pepper**
- **¾ teaspoon baking soda**
- **6 dried ancho chiles, stemmed, seeded, and torn into 1-inch pieces**
- **1 ounce tortilla chips, crushed (¼ cup)**
- **2 tablespoons ground cumin**
- **1 tablespoon paprika**
- **1 tablespoon garlic powder**
- **1 tablespoon ground coriander**
- **2 teaspoons dried oregano**
- **½ teaspoon dried thyme**
- **1 (14.5-ounce) can whole peeled tomatoes**
- **1 tablespoon vegetable oil**
- **1 onion, chopped fine**
- **3 garlic cloves, minced**
- **1–2 teaspoons minced canned chipotle chile in adobo sauce**
- **1 (15-ounce) can pinto beans**
- **2 teaspoons sugar**
- **2 tablespoons cider vinegar**
- **Lime wedges**
- **Coarsely chopped cilantro**
- **Chopped red onion**

1. Adjust oven rack to lower-middle position and heat oven to 275 degrees. Toss beef with 2 tablespoons water, 1½ teaspoons salt, and baking soda in bowl until thoroughly combined. Set aside for 20 minutes.

2. Meanwhile, place anchos in Dutch oven set over medium-high heat; toast, stirring frequently, until fragrant, 4 to 6 minutes, reducing heat if anchos begin to smoke. Transfer to food processor and let cool.

3. Add tortilla chips, cumin, paprika, garlic powder, coriander, oregano, thyme, and 2 teaspoons pepper to food processor with anchos and process until finely ground, about 2 minutes. Transfer mixture to bowl. Process tomatoes and their juice in now-empty workbowl until smooth, about 30 seconds.

4. Heat oil in now-empty pot over medium-high heat until shimmering. Add onion and cook, stirring occasionally, until softened, 4 to 6 minutes. Add garlic and cook until fragrant, about 1 minute. Add beef and cook, stirring with wooden spoon to break meat up into ¼-inch pieces, until beef is browned and fond begins to form on pot bottom, 12 to 14 minutes. Add ancho mixture and chipotle; cook, stirring frequently, until fragrant, 1 to 2 minutes.

5. Add remaining 2 cups water, beans and their liquid, sugar, and tomato puree. Bring to boil, scraping bottom of pot to loosen any browned bits. Cover, transfer to oven, and cook until meat is tender and chili is slightly thickened, 1½ to 2 hours, stirring occasionally to prevent sticking.

6. Remove chili from oven and let stand, uncovered, for 10 minutes. Stir in any fat that has risen to top of chili, then add vinegar and season with salt to taste. Serve, passing lime wedges, cilantro, and chopped onion separately. (Chili can be made up to 3 days in advance.)

Rustic Bread Stuffing

We've updated our turkey methods but never reworked stuffing. The time had come.

BY ANDREA GEARY

Back when cooking methods were primitive and every turkey was free-range, smart cooks filled the cavity of the bird with scraps of bread to capture the flavorful juices that would otherwise be lost during roasting. With a moist, dense texture, this stuffing no doubt provided a welcome counterpoint to meat that was probably a bit dry and tough.

Today's cooks have all the tools to produce a juicy turkey, yet we still tend to serve a soft, steamy stuffing—even when it's baked in a dish alongside the bird instead of inside its cavity. I thought that a moist and tender turkey might be better served by a stuffing that boasted a looser, lighter texture similar to that of a bread salad. With chew and crunch, my new stuffing would restore balance to the Thanksgiving spread.

A typical stuffing recipe goes like this: Combine cubes of toasted white sandwich bread with buttery sautéed aromatics, a handful of fresh chopped herbs, and maybe some browned sausage, nuts, or dried fruit. Douse the lot with broth and mix in some beaten eggs to promote that cohesive, pudding-like texture. Finally, transfer the mixture to a baking dish, and bake it in a moderate oven.

Since I wanted a bread salad–esque result, I decided to cut up a loaf of rustic bread instead of the usual sandwich bread. It also made sense to try eliminating the eggs and decreasing the broth. Otherwise, my first attempt was fairly canonical: onions, celery, butter, sage, and chicken broth. But using less liquid (I cut it by half) didn't mean that the stuffing was half as moist; it meant that half of the cubes were soggy and the rest were rock hard.

Perhaps the rustic bread was too coarse? I decided to try a baguette, but not an expensive one: The chewy, light-yet-uniform crumb of a supermarket baguette seemed like it would work well. I would need two to fill a 13 by 9-inch baking dish.

To maintain the rustic effect, I tore the loaves into bite-size pieces. After arranging the pieces on a baking sheet and drizzling them with olive oil, I toasted them briefly in a 450-degree oven until the jagged edges were browned and crisped but the interiors were still soft. Then I drizzled 2 cups of broth onto the chunks while they were still on the baking sheet, which ensured that each piece was moistened—but not drowned. Next came the sautéed celery, onions, and sage; I transferred the mixture to a baking dish and returned it to the oven for about 30 minutes.

I was almost there. This batch had a pleasantly varied texture—soft in some spots, crisp in others, and even a bit chewy. The very bottom and end pieces of baguette became tough, though, so for the next batch I trimmed them off before ripping up the loaf. I also added a handful of dried cranberries before baking to play up the Thanksgiving angle and stirred in some chopped parsley. A sprinkle of toasted walnuts contributed a bit more savory richness.

This new approach to stuffing was so successful that it seemed a shame to confine it to Thanksgiving, so I created a year-round variation with Italian flavors and another with Middle Eastern ones.

Look: New-Style Stuffing
Video available free for 4 months at CooksIllustrated.com/dec15

No eggs, less broth, and baguettes torn into bite-size pieces give the stuffing a rustic, coarse texture.

RUSTIC BREAD STUFFING WITH CRANBERRIES AND WALNUTS

SERVES 6 TO 8

Baguettes from the bakery section of the supermarket, which have a slightly soft crust, work well in this recipe. The weight should be listed on the wrapper. To make the stuffing ahead, wrap it with plastic wrap immediately after transferring it to the baking dish, and refrigerate it for up to 24 hours. Add 5 minutes to the baking time. For our free recipe for Rustic Bread Stuffing with Dates and Almonds, go to CooksIllustrated.com/dec15.

- **3 tablespoons unsalted butter**
- **2 baguettes (10 ounces each), bottom crust and ends trimmed and discarded**
- **3 tablespoons extra-virgin olive oil**
- **2 cups chicken broth**
- **3 celery ribs, cut into ½-inch pieces**
- **1 teaspoon salt**
- **¼ teaspoon pepper**
- **2 large onions, cut into ½-inch pieces**
- **½ cup dried cranberries**
- **3 tablespoons chopped fresh sage**
- **3 tablespoons chopped fresh parsley**
- **¼ cup walnuts, toasted and chopped coarse**

1. Adjust oven rack to upper-middle position and heat oven to 450 degrees. Grease 13 by 9-inch baking dish with 1 tablespoon butter and set aside. Tear baguettes into bite-size pieces (you should have about 12 cups) and spread into even layer on rimmed baking sheet. Drizzle with oil and toss with spatula until oil is well distributed. Toast in oven for 5 minutes. Stir bread, then continue to toast until edges are lightly browned and crisped, about 5 minutes longer. Transfer sheet to wire rack. Drizzle broth over bread and stir to combine.

2. Melt remaining 2 tablespoons butter in 10-inch skillet over medium heat. Add celery, salt, and pepper. Cook, stirring frequently, until celery begins to soften, 3 to 5 minutes. Add onions and cook until vegetables are soft but not browned, about 8 minutes. Add cranberries and sage and cook until fragrant, about 1 minute.

3. Add vegetable mixture to bread and toss with spatula until well combined. Transfer stuffing mixture to prepared dish and spread into even layer. Bake for 20 minutes. Stir with spatula, turning crisp edges into middle, and spread into even layer. Continue to bake until top is crisp and brown, about 10 minutes longer. Stir in parsley, sprinkle with walnuts, and serve.

RUSTIC BREAD STUFFING WITH FENNEL AND PINE NUTS

Substitute extra-virgin olive oil for butter (6 tablespoons in total). Substitute 1 fennel bulb, stalks discarded, bulb halved, cored, and cut into ½-inch pieces, for celery and increase pepper to ½ teaspoon. Omit cranberries. Substitute 1½ tablespoons chopped fresh rosemary, 1 minced garlic clove, and ½ teaspoon ground fennel for sage. Substitute toasted pine nuts for walnuts.

Warm Brussels Sprout Salads

Salads made with these hearty leaves can be a lot to chew on. We fixed that.

⋟ BY LAN LAM ⋞

Though most often sautéed or roasted, raw Brussels sprouts make a great salad green. My method has always been to slice the raw sprouts thin, dress them, and let them sit—steps that help tenderize the tough leaves and brighten their pungent flavor. Sprouts also take well to punchy dressings and bold additions like rich nuts and cheeses, tangy dried fruit, and even smoky, salty bacon.

A drawback to these slaw-like salads is that thin-slicing the sprouts is tedious—and they can literally be a lot to chew on. I had one idea that sounded faster: pulling the leaves from the stem whole instead of slicing them. But it only took a few minutes of plucking for me to realize that pulling apart the tightly packed leaves was actually more time-consuming than slicing. Scratch that.

In the end, I was able to streamline the shredding process with an assembly line approach: Rather than trimming, halving, and slicing the sprouts one by one, I worked through all the trimming before moving onto the halving, and so forth.

Even shredded, the sprouts were very dense to eat; I decided to incorporate a second leafy vegetable. A handful of bitter but more tender radicchio, shredded into fine strips, was just the thing to break up the salad's slaw-like density and add complexity.

Softening raw Brussels sprouts with a regular dressing takes about 30 minutes, but what if I dressed them with a warm vinaigrette? Surely the heat would wilt them faster, and a warm dressing would be a nice change.

Like regular vinaigrettes, warm ones are mixtures of fat and acid (usually in a 3:1 ratio). The difference is that the fat in warm vinaigrettes is heated, which meant that I had options other than oil. This seemed like a perfect opportunity to use my favorite Brussels sprouts pairing: bacon.

While I crisped a few chopped slices in a skillet, I used the microwave to lightly pickle some thinly sliced shallots in a mixture of red wine vinegar, whole-grain mustard, sugar, and salt. Then I whisked the shallot mixture into the bacon. Instead of dressing the greens in a bowl, I added them to the skillet, where they were warmed not just by the dressing but also by the pan's residual heat.

Now for those aforementioned bold additions—toasted almonds and shaved Parmesan for the bacon version and dried cranberries, toasted hazelnuts, and Manchego for another variation with brown butter. These salads were as complex as they were elegant and will play a starring role on my holiday table.

Shreds of tender radicchio lighten the salad's texture.

BRUSSELS SPROUT SALAD WITH WARM BACON VINAIGRETTE

SERVES 6

A food processor's slicing blade can be used to slice the Brussels sprouts, but the salad will be less tender. For tips on slicing them with a knife, see page 31. For our free recipe for Brussels Sprout Salad with Warm Mustard Vinaigrette, go to CooksIllustrated.com/dec15.

- ¼ cup red wine vinegar
- 1 tablespoon whole-grain mustard
- 1 teaspoon sugar
- Salt and pepper
- 1 shallot, halved through root end and sliced thin crosswise
- 4 slices bacon, cut into ½-inch pieces
- 1½ pounds Brussels sprouts, trimmed, halved, and sliced thin
- 1½ cups finely shredded radicchio, long strands cut into bite-size lengths
- 2 ounces Parmesan, shaved into thin strips using vegetable peeler
- ¼ cup sliced almonds, toasted

1. Whisk vinegar, mustard, sugar, and ¼ teaspoon salt together in bowl. Add shallot, cover tightly with plastic wrap, and microwave until steaming, 30 to 60 seconds. Stir briefly to submerge shallot. Cover and let cool to room temperature, about 15 minutes.

2. Cook bacon in 12-inch skillet over medium heat, stirring frequently, until crisp and well rendered, 6 to 8 minutes. Off heat, whisk in shallot mixture. Add Brussels sprouts and radicchio and toss with tongs until dressing is evenly distributed and sprouts darken slightly, 1 to 2 minutes. Transfer to serving bowl. Add Parmesan and almonds and toss to combine. Season with salt and pepper to taste, and serve immediately.

BRUSSELS SPROUT SALAD WITH WARM BROWN BUTTER VINAIGRETTE

SERVES 6

A food processor's slicing blade can be used to slice the Brussels sprouts, but the salad will be less tender.

- ¼ cup lemon juice
- 1 tablespoon whole-grain mustard
- 1 teaspoon sugar
- Salt and pepper
- 1 shallot, halved through root end and sliced thin crosswise
- ¼ cup dried cranberries
- 5 tablespoons unsalted butter
- ⅓ cup hazelnuts, toasted, skinned, and chopped
- 1½ pounds Brussels sprouts, trimmed, halved, and sliced thin
- 1½ cups baby arugula, chopped
- 4 ounces Manchego cheese, shaved into thin strips using vegetable peeler

1. Whisk lemon juice, mustard, sugar, and ¼ teaspoon salt together in bowl. Add shallot and cranberries, cover tightly with plastic wrap, and microwave until steaming, 30 to 60 seconds. Stir briefly to submerge shallot and cranberries. Let cool to room temperature, about 15 minutes.

2. Melt butter in 12-inch skillet over medium heat. Add hazelnuts and cook, stirring frequently, until butter is dark golden brown, 3 to 5 minutes. Off heat, whisk in shallot mixture. Add Brussels sprouts and arugula and toss with tongs until dressing is evenly distributed and sprouts darken slightly, 1 to 2 minutes. Transfer to serving bowl. Add Manchego and toss to combine. Season with salt and pepper to taste, and serve immediately.

Look: It's Easy
Video available free for 4 months at CooksIllustrated.com/dec15

Sweet Potato Soup

The secrets to creamy sweet potato soup with deep, earthy-sweet flavor? Use those peels, and turn off the heat.

BY LAN LAM

In Asia and Africa, sweet potatoes are regarded as one of those foods that need no adornment. In fact, street vendors sell whole sweet potatoes—steamed, baked, grilled, or roasted—to passersby who enjoy their earthy, sweet complexity out of hand, skin and all. Americans also eat sweet potatoes cooked every which way, but we tend to pile them high with a slew of extras—like marshmallows, orange juice, brown sugar, curry powder, cinnamon, or nutmeg—that overpower their taste.

Some cooks riff on butternut squash soup and turn sweet potatoes into a creamy puree. But, like other types of sweet potato dishes, the soups I tried were so loaded with extras that it was hard to identify the main ingredient. I wanted to strip away the nonessentials to make a silky, luxurious soup in which the sweet potatoes really stood out. I planned on garnishing the soup with a flavorful topping, just as one might dress up a baked potato. With complementary ingredients on the soup instead of inside it, the sweet potato flavor would be front and center.

A drizzle of maple sour cream and a sprinkle of fresh chives highlight the pure, simple flavor of the soup.

Soup Starter

Following the classic protocol for a pureed vegetable soup, I began by cooking *mirepoix* (diced onion, carrot, and celery) in melted butter. To the softened aromatics, I added 2 pounds of peeled and sliced sweet potatoes along with 4¼ cups of vegetable broth. I let the mixture simmer until the potatoes were tender and then pureed the mixture in batches in the blender, adding another couple of cups of broth to the puree to create a lightly thickened consistency. The result was nice and smooth, but the savory-sweet flavor I was looking for was missing. Comments from colleagues like "generically vegetal" and "watery and lacking in richness" echoed my opinion. Evidently, the classic approach wasn't going to work.

I started over, this time with a focus on eliminating ingredients to allow the sweet potatoes to come to the fore. After a few tries, I landed on sautéing just one sliced shallot and a few sprigs of fresh thyme in butter and then adding the potatoes along with water and salt. I let the pot simmer until the spuds were tender and then thinned the mixture with more water (for a total of about 6 cups) during blending. It was an austere list, but the fewer ingredients I used, the better (and the more like sweet potatoes) the soup tasted.

I seemed to be on the right track, but the deep earthiness I wanted wasn't there. As I peeled my way through another couple of pounds of sweet potatoes, it struck me that perhaps the skins themselves were the missing link. I made a few more batches, cooking different amounts of potato skins in each and blending them into the soup. Using too many skins gave the soup a dark, murky appearance and a muddy flavor to match. But adding just a quarter of the peels to the pot yielded a lightly speckled soup with a mildly earthy taste. (For more information, see "Putting Peels to Work.")

See It Become Soup
Video available free for 4 months at CooksIllustrated.com/dec15

Culinary Chemistry

Could I make the soup better still? Before I thinned the puree with water to create a more soup-like consistency, it had a marvelously deep potatoey flavor. I wondered if there was a way I could avoid adding any liquid beyond the 4¼ cups of water I was using for cooking the potatoes and still get a silky, sippable consistency. It wasn't a far-fetched idea.

I had been looking over a recipe in our archives, Roasted Sweet Potatoes (November/December 2008). Here we do a neat trick: We start the spuds in a cold oven. As the oven comes to temperature, the potatoes slowly heat up. During that time, some of the potato starches are converted into sugars by a family of amylase enzymes. The result is sweeter sweet potatoes with a silkier texture than those that simply go into a hot oven. I hoped I could use a similar approach to reduce the amount of starch in my soup so I wouldn't need to thin down its consistency (and its flavor) with extra water.

I tried to mimic the cold-oven approach by starting the potatoes in 4¼ cups of cold salted water and slowly bringing them up to a simmer. Disappointingly, the soup turned out just as starchy as ever. After a consultation with our science editor, I understood why. It turns out that the amylase action only takes place under certain conditions: First, the temperature must be between 140 and 170 degrees. Second, salt cannot be present. (Our roasted sweet potatoes call for salt, but because the salt doesn't penetrate as quickly during roasting as in simmering, the conversion still takes place.) Third and finally, the pH of the cooking liquid must be between 4 and 7. Satisfying two of the three requirements was easy. I was already cooking the sweet potatoes in water (pH 7), and I would wait to add salt to the water until after the starch conversion period. As for the temperature, I would have to experiment with ways to get the potatoes to the right heat level and hold them there.

Eventually I settled on gently cooking the shallot and thyme in butter and then adding the water and bringing it to a simmer (about 195 degrees). Next, I removed the pot from the heat and added the potatoes and peels. I kept the pot off the heat and let the water (which registered 150 degrees, right in the sweet spot for the enzymatic reaction) spur the amylase into action. After 20 minutes, the temperature of the water had dropped to 135 degrees, and the slices were bright orange and pliable. I returned the pot to the heat, added salt, and brought the mixture to a boil to finish cooking the potatoes, which took about 10 minutes. As soon as I fished out the thyme and whizzed the mixture in a blender, I knew that the amylase had done its work. The soup's satiny consistency was just right—no extra water was necessary—plus, it tasted cleaner and more vibrant than ever (see "Thinning Sweet Potatoes with Less Liquid").

For the next go-round, I seasoned the final cooking water not just with salt and pepper but also with touches of brown sugar and cider vinegar. The former underscored the sweet taste of the potatoes; the latter balanced it out. And before assembling my colleagues to sample the soup, I put together an assortment of potential toppings.

Using classic baked potato toppings as inspiration, I mixed up some sweet potato–friendly ideas, including buttery rye croutons, candied bacon bits, and maple sour cream. When served with one of these garnishes plus a sprinkle of fresh chives, pure sweet potato flavor was apparent in every spoonful.

SWEET POTATO SOUP

SERVES 4 TO 6 AS A MAIN DISH OR 8 AS A STARTER

To highlight the earthiness of the sweet potatoes, we incorporate a quarter of the skins into the soup. In addition to the chives, serve the soup with one of our suggested garnishes (recipes follow). The garnish can be prepared during step 1 while the sweet potatoes stand in the water. For our free recipe for Sautéed Mushroom Topping, go to CooksIllustrated.com/dec15.

- 4 tablespoons unsalted butter
- 1 shallot, sliced thin
- 4 sprigs fresh thyme
- 4¼ cups water
- 2 pounds sweet potatoes, peeled, halved lengthwise, and sliced ¼ inch thick, ¼ of peels reserved
- 1 tablespoon packed brown sugar
- ½ teaspoon cider vinegar
- Salt and pepper
- Minced fresh chives

1. Melt butter in large saucepan over medium-low heat. Add shallot and thyme and cook until shallot is softened but not browned, about 5 minutes. Add water, increase heat to high, and bring to simmer. Remove pot from heat, add sweet potatoes and reserved peels, and let stand uncovered for 20 minutes.

2. Add sugar, vinegar, 1½ teaspoons salt, and ¼ teaspoon pepper. Bring to simmer over high heat. Reduce heat to medium-low, cover, and cook until potatoes are very soft, about 10 minutes.

3. Discard thyme sprigs. Working in batches, process soup in blender until smooth, 45 to 60 seconds. Return soup to clean pot. Bring to simmer over medium heat, adjusting consistency if desired. Season with salt and pepper to taste. Serve, topping each portion with sprinkle of chives.

BUTTERY RYE CROUTONS

MAKES 1½ CUPS

The croutons can be made ahead and stored in an airtight container for 1 week.

- 3 tablespoons unsalted butter
- 1 tablespoon olive oil
- 2 slices light rye bread, cut into ½-inch cubes (about 1½ cups)
- Salt

Heat butter and oil in 10-inch skillet over medium heat. When foaming subsides, add bread cubes and cook, stirring frequently, until golden brown, about 10 minutes. Transfer croutons to paper towel–lined plate and season with salt to taste.

CANDIED BACON BITS

MAKES ABOUT ¼ CUP

Break up any large chunks before serving.

- 4 slices bacon, cut into ½-inch pieces
- 2 teaspoons dark brown sugar
- ½ teaspoon cider vinegar

Cook bacon in 10-inch nonstick skillet over medium heat until crisp and well rendered, 6 to 8 minutes. Using slotted spoon, remove bacon from skillet and discard fat. Return bacon to skillet and add brown sugar and vinegar. Cook over low heat, stirring constantly, until bacon is evenly coated. Transfer to plate in single layer. Let bacon cool completely.

MAPLE SOUR CREAM

MAKES ⅓ CUP

Maple balances the sweet potatoes' earthiness.

- ⅓ cup sour cream
- 1 tablespoon maple syrup

Combine ingredients in bowl.

DISCOVERY

Putting Peels to Work

Instead of discarding the potato peels, we blend some of them into our soup to take advantage of an earthy-tasting compound they contain. The compound, called methoxypyrazine, is potent—it's detectable in water in levels as low as one part per trillion—so we use only one-quarter of the peels in order to avoid overwhelming the soup.

SCIENCE

Thinning Sweet Potatoes with Less Liquid

Soaking sweet potatoes in hot water before cooking is the trick.

Creating a soup with prominent sweet potato flavor meant using a minimal amount of water. The only catch? Sweet potatoes require more water than less starchy vegetables like squash or carrots to be thinned to a soupy consistency after boiling. That's because their large starch molecules form a loose mesh that traps added water, preventing the texture from turning runny. Eventually, if enough water is added, the mesh can't hold any more liquid, and the texture loosens and thins.

But we discovered a trick: By adding the sweet potatoes to simmering water and then letting them sit off heat for 20 minutes before boiling them, the large starch molecules are converted into much smaller sugar molecules that are unable to create a mesh. This meant that we only needed to puree the sweet potatoes with the 4¼ cups of cooking liquid to get just the right consistency, with no additional liquid needed. But that's not the only benefit: The conversion of starch to sugar also makes the potatoes taste even better.

USUAL WAY: BOIL THEN PUREE

OUR WAY: SOAK BEFORE BOILING

Reinventing Pecan Bars

By banishing the custard filling in favor of a topping that emphasizes the pecan's nutty richness, we made this bar cookie simpler, too.

BY ANNIE PETITO

Most pecan bars take their cue from pecan pie, with a single layer of nuts dominated by a thick, gooey, ultrasweet filling sitting atop a pat-in-the-pan crust. I'm not opposed to that style, but it's mainly about the filling and only a little about the nuts. As a lover of nuts (pecans especially), I've always thought it would be great to have a bar that emphasized the star ingredient.

The closest I've come are recipes that ditch the rich, egg-based custard in favor of a toffee-like topping. These call for heating sugar and butter together until thickened, stirring in the nuts, and spreading the mixture over a parbaked crust before popping it into the oven. But when I tried a few such approaches, I found that the resulting bars still had a one-note sweetness that distracted from the pecans—and there were never enough pecans in the first place. My ideal was a pecan bar featuring a buttery crust piled high with nuts held in place not by a filling, per se, but by a not-too-sweet glaze whose only jobs were to enhance the flavor of the pecans and glue them to the crust. For that kind of a bar, I was on my own.

Making these pecan bars couldn't be easier. The crust requires no parbaking, and both it and the topping are simply stirred together in bowls.

Going Nuts

I started with a placeholder crust, a food processor–blended mixture of flour, sugar, salt, and cold butter that I borrowed from our archives and scaled up to fit a 13 by 9-inch pan (you can never have too many cookies on hand during the holidays). I patted the sandy dough into the pan and parbaked it for 20 minutes at 350 degrees until the crust was light brown—standard procedure to prevent a wet filling from seeping in and making it soggy.

Since I wanted a topping that was all about the nuts, I wondered what would happen if I simply tossed the pecans with corn syrup, which is one-third less sweet than granulated sugar, before spreading them over the crust. I tried this, stirring ½ cup into a relatively modest 2 cups of chopped pecans, which I toasted first to enhance their rich flavor (see "Pretoasting Nuts Before Baking"). But it was a bust, as the corn syrup's flat taste did nothing to bring out the flavor of the nuts, and now the bar wasn't sweet enough overall. Next, I experimented with maple syrup, thinking its caramel-like flavors might complement the pecans, heating it with some butter to cut some of the sweetness and bring extra nuttiness to the glaze. Its flavors matched nicely with the pecans, but the syrup dried out and crystallized in the oven, making the topping crusty with an unappealing matte finish. Honey didn't work either. Though it produced a moist, glossy, slightly chewy topping that my tasters liked for its texture, its prominent flavor was a distraction from the pecans. Ultimately, I landed on a combination of corn syrup and brown sugar, the latter's molasses-like notes a good match for the pecans. I heated ½ cup of corn syrup and ¾ cup of brown sugar with 7 tablespoons of butter on the stove until the mixture was bubbly and syrupy; I then took the glaze off the heat and stirred in vanilla extract to add complexity, followed by the pecans. This glaze had a lot going for it: It was glossy and stayed slightly moist and chewy in the oven. But its sweetness still dominated the pecans. I wondered if I could fix that simply by increasing the amount of nuts, which had been my goal anyway.

I upped the nuts from 2 cups to 3 cups and left them in halves, which gave them a more impressive presence. This worked so well to offset the glaze's sweetness that I added another cup. The nuts were now the main event of the topping, enhanced but not overpowered by the glaze. There was another bonus: With this many pecans, the nuts did not sit neatly in a single layer on the crust but were more haphazardly layered on top of one another, allowing for a variety of textures—some nuts were chewy, sitting directly in a slick of glaze, while those sitting on the very top were crisp.

Cool Before Cutting

To ensure that the bars slice into neat squares, make sure to let them cool completely so the topping and crust have time to firm up.

Crust Control

With the topping settled, I turned my attention back to the crust. I'd been using the food processor to cut the cold butter into the flour, but it occurred to me that there was an even easier crust I could use. In our French Apple Tart (November/December 2014), we make an easy press-in crust using melted butter instead of chilled, stirring it right into the dry ingredients. Buttery and sturdy, this shortbread-like crust was ideal for the pecan topping and a snap to make.

I had an additional thought: Now that the topping was barely wet at all, did I even need to parbake the crust? I tried skipping this step, spreading the hot topping over the unbaked crust and baking it for 20 minutes. When I turned the bars out of the pan, I found that the bottom of the crust was still pale and slightly pliable. Baking the bars on the bottom rack and for a little longer produced a crust that was evenly golden, but it also created a new problem: Since the bars were closer to the heat source, more moisture was evaporating from the topping, which was getting crunchy and brittle in parts, especially at the edges.

Watch Annie Make the Bars
Video available free for 4 months at CooksIllustrated.com/dec15

SCIENCE Pretoasting Nuts Before Baking

For deep nutty flavor, don't rely on baking to brown nuts. Toast beforehand.

We're always surprised when recipes for baked goods that call for nuts don't specify toasting them first. Like browning meat or caramelizing sugar, the simple act of toasting nuts makes them taste remarkably more complex. Toasting not only produces Maillard browning reactions that create hundreds of new flavor compounds but also brings the nuts' oils to the surface, where they oxidize and produce rich, roasted aromas. But baking nuts as part of a bar cookie or quick bread isn't enough to produce these results. Nuts need to reach at least 300 degrees and be held there for several minutes for significant browning to occur. Nuts folded into batter or cookie dough won't rise above the temperature of the crumb's interior, which is done at about 200 degrees. Nuts used as a topping can reach higher temperatures, but only after any surrounding moisture has burned off, which doesn't give them enough time to brown before the item is taken out of the oven.

To prove the point, we baked two batches of our Ultranutty Pecan Bars, one made according to the recipe with toasted nuts and the other made with untoasted nuts. Though the caramelized glaze helped to darken both nuts, the pretoasted ones were noticeably more brown and tasted more complex.

TECHNIQUE | HOW TO TOAST NUTS

Nuts (especially irregularly shaped ones) toast more evenly in the oven, but the stovetop is more convenient for amounts less than 1 cup. To avoid overbrowning, transfer toasted nuts to a plate to cool.

IN THE OVEN
Spread nuts in single layer on rimmed baking sheet and toast in preheated 350-degree oven until fragrant and slightly darkened, 8 to 12 minutes, shaking sheet halfway through to prevent burning (for smaller nuts like pine nuts, check them earlier).

ON THE STOVETOP
Place nuts in single layer in dry skillet set over medium heat and toast, stirring frequently, until fragrant and slightly darkened, 3 to 5 minutes.

Up until now I had been boiling the glaze on the stove before adding the nuts. If I didn't do that, I thought, maybe enough moisture would stay in the glaze to keep the topping more pliable. Plus, it would make the recipe even quicker. It was worth trying.

For my next test, I combined the brown sugar, corn syrup, vanilla, and salt in a bowl. I melted the butter separately and then stirred it, piping hot, into the mixture so the sugar would melt, continuing to stir until the mixture was homogeneous and glossy. But it was so thick that after I stirred in the nuts, there was no question of spreading it evenly across the crust. All I could do was push it to the edges as best I could, leaving patches of crust bare. I was sure this was a dead end, but as I watched the bars cook, I could see the thick brown sugar mixture begin to melt. After 25 minutes, the topping was bubbling across the crust, and all the empty spots were completely coated.

Once the bars were cooled, I turned them out of the pan. They were golden brown on the bottom, with a glossy, even sheen on top. I trimmed the edges to neaten them up and cut them into squares. The bars were chewy and moist, not overly sweet, and loaded with pecans. For a final touch, I sprinkled the bars with flake sea salt as they came out of the oven.

Topping Clumps? Not to Worry

To streamline our Ultranutty Pecan Bars recipe, we skipped the step of heating the topping on the stovetop. Instead, we stirred the ingredients together off heat and spread the thick mixture as best we could over the crust. Don't worry if there are bare patches: The topping melts during baking, distributing itself evenly over the crust.

ULTRANUTTY PECAN BARS

MAKES 24 BARS

It is important to use pecan halves, not pieces. The edges of the bars will be slightly firmer than the center. If desired, trim ¼ inch from the edges before cutting into bars. Toast the pecans on a rimmed baking sheet in a 350-degree oven until fragrant, 8 to 12 minutes, shaking the sheet halfway through.

Crust

- 1¾ cups (8¾ ounces) all-purpose flour
- 6 tablespoons (2⅔ ounces) sugar
- ½ teaspoon salt
- 8 tablespoons unsalted butter, melted

Topping

- ¾ cup packed (5¼ ounces) light brown sugar
- ½ cup light corn syrup
- 7 tablespoons unsalted butter, melted and hot
- 1 teaspoon vanilla extract
- ½ teaspoon salt
- 4 cups (1 pound) pecan halves, toasted
- ½ teaspoon flake sea salt (optional)

1. FOR THE CRUST: Adjust oven rack to lowest position and heat oven to 350 degrees. Make foil sling for 13 by 9-inch baking pan by folding 2 long sheets of aluminum foil; first sheet should be 13 inches wide and second sheet should be 9 inches wide. Lay sheets of foil in pan perpendicular to each other, with extra foil hanging over edges of pan. Push foil into corners and up sides of pan, smoothing foil flush to pan. Lightly spray foil with vegetable oil spray.

2. Whisk flour, sugar, and salt together in medium bowl. Add melted butter and stir with wooden spoon until dough begins to form. Using your hands, continue to combine until no dry flour remains and small portion of dough holds together when squeezed in palm of your hand. Evenly scatter tablespoon-size pieces of dough over surface of pan. Using your fingertips and palm of your hand, press and smooth dough into even thickness in bottom of pan.

3. FOR THE TOPPING: Whisk sugar, corn syrup, melted butter, vanilla, and salt together in medium bowl until smooth (mixture will look separated at first but will become homogeneous), about 20 seconds. Fold pecans into sugar mixture until nuts are evenly coated.

4. Pour topping over crust. Using spatula, spread topping over crust, pushing to edges and into corners (there will be bare patches). Bake until topping is evenly distributed and rapidly bubbling across entire surface, 23 to 25 minutes.

5. Transfer pan to wire rack and lightly sprinkle with flake sea salt, if using. Let bars cool completely in pan on rack, about 1½ hours. Using foil overhang, lift bars out of pan and transfer to cutting board. Cut into 24 bars. (Bars can be stored at room temperature for up to 5 days.)

Our Guide to Turkey

Turkey can look and taste great, or it can be a dry, pale disaster. Even if this is your first turkey, our guide will help you buy, prepare, and roast the perfect bird. BY ELIZABETH BOMZE

SHOPPING

Around the holidays, turkeys come fresh and frozen, large and small, and often stamped with confusing package labels. Here's what to look for—and what to avoid.

Fresh Isn't Always Best

Unless you're buying a turkey fresh from a local farm, a frozen turkey is a better bet. Why? Frozen turkeys are frozen quickly and completely, which prevents large ice crystals from forming and damaging the meat. Turkeys labeled "fresh" may be chilled to as low as 26 degrees, a temperature at which tiny ice crystals can still form in the meat. If these crystals melt (which can happen if the temperature fluctuates during transport or thawing), they can merge with neighboring crystals, refreeze, and puncture the meat, allowing juices to escape during cooking and the meat to cook up dry and tough.

Don't Buy Big

The bigger the bird, the harder it is to get the white and dark meat to cook evenly. Plus, some ovens can't accommodate large turkeys. We recommend birds that weigh between 12 and 14 pounds. If you're feeding a crowd, consider supplementing the whole bird with turkey parts.

Buyer Beware

The terms below aren't always plainly stamped on package labels, so be sure to check the fine print for notations about water retention or added ingredients.

Water-Chilled

Most poultry is water-chilled—that is, dunked in a cold chlorinated bath, which causes it to retain water, diluting flavor and inflating cost. We've found that these birds can taste "bland" and "spongy" compared with air-chilled poultry. (Air-chilling is typically noted on labels.) The only water-chilled poultry we do buy is kosher, since the process saves you the trouble of brining.

Pre- or Self-Basted

Pre- or self-basted (also called "enhanced") turkeys are water-chilled birds injected with a solution (look for turkey broth, oil, sugar, or sodium phosphate on the label) to enhance flavor and moisture. We've found them somewhat wet with a mild, almost bland flavor.

Our Favorite Turkeys

We prefer air-chilled poultry, which is hung from a conveyor belt and circulated around a cold room, because the process produces birds with better flavor and texture than water-chilled birds. However, air-chilled turkeys can be hard to find, so we have two alternatives.

Timesaver: Kosher

Per Jewish dietary law, kosher turkey carcasses are covered in kosher salt and then rinsed multiple times in cold water, which seasons the meat and helps it retain moisture. As a result, kosher turkeys do not need to be brined or salted.

➢ **Our favorite:** Empire Kosher Turkey ($2.49 per lb)

Splurge: Heritage

Because heritage turkeys are conceived naturally and allowed to live longer than conventional birds, they have longer legs and wings, more fat and dark meat, and richer flavor. The downside: They can cost 10 times more than conventional turkeys.

➢ **Our favorite:** Mary's Free-Range Heritage Turkey ($166.72 for 7- to 14-lb bird, plus shipping)

EXCLUSIVE ONLINE RECIPE

Roasted Brined Turkey

PLUS our test kitchen experts can help you:

- Shop smarter for ingredients and equipment.
- Make the most of your time with handy scheduling tips.
- Ensure success with step-by-step cooking videos.

Available free through December 31, 2015, at **CooksIllustrated.com/thanksgiving.**

MUST-HAVE TURKEY TOOLS

Instant-Read Thermometer:

➢ **Our favorite:** ThermoWorks Splash-Proof Super-Fast Thermapen ($96.00)

We love this thermometer's accuracy, how rapidly it registers temperatures, and its large, easy-to-read display.

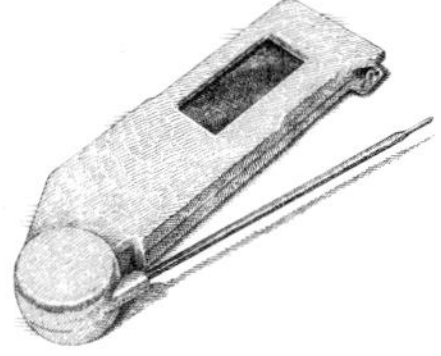

Roasting Rack:

➢ **Our favorite:** All-Clad Non-Stick Roasting Rack ($24.95)

This durable rack has conveniently located handles and is large enough to hold a 14-pound turkey.

Roasting Pan:

➢ **Our favorite:** Calphalon Contemporary Stainless Roasting Pan with Rack ($99.99)

The sturdy construction of this pan and its roomy, secure handles earned it our top rating. It comes with a decent U-shaped rack.

Don't Bother:

➢ **Covered Oval Roasting Pans**

Problems: narrow, crowded, small handles

➢ **Disposable Aluminum Roasting Pans**

Problems: flimsy construction, no handles

➢ **Bulb Baster**

Problems: basting prevents skin from drying and crisping (see "Six Roasting Rules")

BEFORE YOU COOK

Defrost Early

Whole turkeys take several days to thaw. Plan on one day for every 4 pounds—and if your bird isn't kosher or prebasted, factor in at least 6 hours to brine or at least 24 hours to salt.

➢ **Emergency Quick-Thaw:** Place turkey in its wrapper in bucket filled with cold water and thaw for 30 minutes per pound. Change water every half-hour to prevent bacteria growth.

Save (Most of) the Giblets

Turkey cavities often contain the neck, heart, and gizzard—flavor powerhouses that should be used for gravy. Brown and sweat them to extract their flavor; then discard. Just don't use the liver (large, shiny, dark red); its strong flavor ruins gravy.

Brine or Salt for Better Flavor and Texture

Brining and salting both season and enhance juiciness in lean meat like turkey. Which method you use depends on how much time and space you have and how much you care about having really crisp skin.

Brining

Pros: faster (6 to 12 hours)
Cons: requires a lot of fridge space; adds extra moisture that can prevent skin from crisping

➢ **Brining Bags:** Ziploc Big Bags XL ($5.79 for four 2 by 1.7-foot foodsafe bags)

Salting

Pros: requires less fridge space; helps skin dry out and crisp
Cons: slower (24 to 48 hours)

SCIENCE If You Salt, Don't Rush It

To quantify just how far salt moves through turkey muscle fibers, we applied 1 teaspoon of kosher salt per pound evenly to four turkey breasts, wrapped them in plastic wrap, and refrigerated them for 1, 12, 24, and 48 hours, respectively. Then we cut slivers from each breast and tested them (alongside an untreated control breast) with a sodium ion meter.

The data confirmed that longer salting times led to more evenly seasoned meat—and that shorter salting times are actually detrimental. Whereas the exterior of turkey salted for just 1 hour was inedibly salty and its interior bland, the bird salted for 24 hours was more evenly seasoned, and better still after 48 hours.

THE BOTTOM LINE: If you're salting, it is essential to do it for at least 24 hours to ensure that the meat is evenly seasoned. Shorter salting times will merely leave the outer layers overly salty and are not worth the trouble.

CORE TECHNIQUE | TAKING TURKEY'S TEMPERATURE

The most reliable way to gauge the doneness of turkey is to take its temperature with an instant-read thermometer.

Breast: Insert the thermometer from the neck end, holding it parallel to the bird. (Avoid hitting the bone, which can give an inaccurate reading.) It should register 160 degrees.

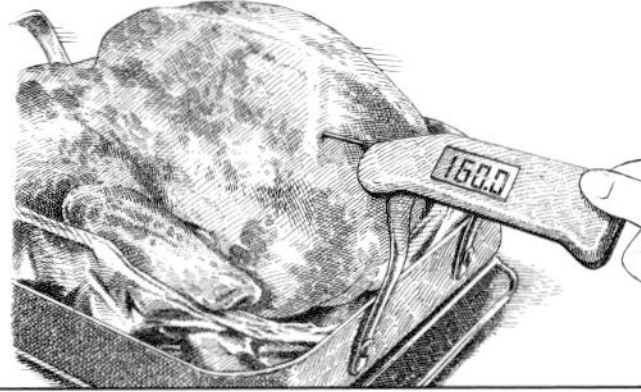

Thigh: Insert the thermometer at an angle into the area between the drumstick and breast away from the bone. It should register 175 degrees.

Pink Turkey Is OK

Pink-tinted turkey isn't necessarily undercooked. Often, the color is simply an indication that the pH of the meat is relatively high, which stabilizes the meat's pink pigment so that it doesn't break down when exposed to heat. (We've observed that pork with a high pH can also remain pink when fully cooked.) As long as the meat registers the prescribed temperature, it's safe to eat.

Reheating Leftover Turkey

Our gentle method helps ensure moist meat and crisp skin.

1. Wrap all leftovers in aluminum foil, stacking any slices, and place on wire rack set in rimmed baking sheet. Heat in 275-degree oven until meat registers 130 degrees.
2. Place any skin-on pieces skin side down in lightly oiled skillet over medium-high heat, heating until skin recrisps.

1. WARM GENTLY
Heat all leftovers in 275-degree oven.

2. RECRISP SKIN
Recrisp any skin-on pieces in oiled skillet.

SIX ROASTING RULES

1. Don't stuff

Stuffing cooked in the turkey cavity tastes great, but by the time the stuffing reaches a safe temperature (165 degrees), the meat is overcooked.

2. Roast on a rack

Roasting a turkey on a V-rack allows air to circulate around the bird, which helps the meat cook evenly and the skin dry out and crisp.

3. Flip during cooking

Start the bird breast side down to shield the white meat from the heat; then turn it breast side up halfway through cooking to crisp the skin. Use clean paper towels to grab the turkey at the top and bottom ends, tip it so the juices in the cavity run into the pan, and flip it breast side up.

4. Don't baste

Basting does nothing to moisten dry breast meat. The liquid just runs off the turkey, and it actually prevents the skin from drying and crisping.

5. Don't rely on pop-up thermometers

If your turkey comes with a pre-inserted thermometer, ignore it (but don't remove it). These devices can pop up above or below a food-safe temperature.

6. Let rest before carving

Resting the turkey for about 30 minutes allows its muscle fibers to reabsorb juices; skip this step and that liquid will run all over your carving board, leaving the meat dry. No need to tent the turkey with aluminum foil; as long as it's intact, it will cool slowly.

Miso-Marinated Salmon

Turns out, miso is one of the best ways to flavor salmon—inside and out.

⋟ BY ANNIE PETITO ⋞

The Japanese technique of marinating fish in miso started as a way to preserve a fresh catch without refrigeration during its long journey inland. In the last few years, however, after its introduction by chef Nobu Matsuhisa at his namesake restaurant, it has become a popular restaurant preparation in this country. The technique itself is quite simple. Miso is combined with sugar, sake, and mirin (sweet Japanese rice wine) to make a marinade that is typically applied to oily fish like salmon or black cod and left to sit for about three days; during that time, the marinade seasons the fish and draws moisture out of its flesh so that it becomes quite firm and dense. The fish is then scraped clean and broiled, producing meaty-textured, well-seasoned fillets with a lacquered savory-sweet glaze.

Those flavors pair particularly well with a rich fish like salmon, and the marinade takes minutes to make. But to me, three days is just too long to wait for such a simple dish—and frankly, I don't prefer the salmon to be quite so dense. I wondered if I could tweak the traditional technique to produce miso-marinated salmon just to my liking: moist, well-seasoned fillets that were slightly firmer than usual and evenly burnished on the surface.

I started by applying a riff on the Nobu marinade to the salmon and was happy with its flavor balance and consistency: A loose paste made from ½ cup of white miso, ⅓ cup of sugar, and 3 tablespoons each of sake and mirin, it clung nicely to the fillets. The question was how long to let the fish marinate. To find out, I made several more batches of the marinade, coated four skin-on salmon fillets with each, and let the fish sit for 30 minutes, 1 hour, 6 hours, and 24 hours—the longest I was willing to wait. After wiping off the excess paste, I placed the fillets on a foil-covered wire rack set in a baking sheet and broiled them 6 inches from the element. To confirm that there was a benefit to marinating, not just glazing, the fish, I also coated another four unmarinated fillets with the marinade mixture just before cooking.

The results were convincing: The flavor of the glazed fillets was merely skin-deep, while the batch that had been marinated for 24 hours delivered deep, complex seasoning throughout. There was a textural bonus to marinating, too: The salmon had firmed up just a bit at the surface, which made for a nice contrast to its silky interior. There was some flexibility with the marinating time; I could achieve largely the same effect when I marinated the fish for anywhere from 6 to 24 hours.

The only remaining problem was that the glaze was overbrowning before the interior was cooked. Reducing the sugar to ¼ cup helped (and nobody missed the extra sweetness), but the real fix was lowering the oven rack. By moving the rack 8 inches from the element, the fillets cooked up tender and silky just as the glaze took on an attractively deep bronze color—and if the edges started to burn, I simply pulled up the foil underneath to act as a shield. It was just the result I wanted in a fraction of the time.

See It Happen
Video available free for 4 months at CooksIllustrated.com/dec15

MISO-MARINATED SALMON
SERVES 4

Note that the fish needs to marinate for at least 6 or up to 24 hours before cooking. Use center-cut salmon fillets of similar thickness (see page 29). See page 31 for tips on removing pinbones. Yellow, red, or brown miso paste can be used instead of white. For our free recipe for Miso-Marinated Salmon for Two, go to CooksIllustrated.com/dec15.

- ½ cup white miso paste
- ¼ cup sugar
- 3 tablespoons sake
- 3 tablespoons mirin
- 4 (6- to 8-ounce) skin-on salmon fillets
- Lemon wedges

1. Whisk miso, sugar, sake, and mirin together in medium bowl until sugar and miso are dissolved (mixture will be thick). Dip each fillet into miso mixture to evenly coat all flesh sides. Place fish skin side down in baking dish and pour any remaining miso mixture over fillets. Cover with plastic wrap and refrigerate for at least 6 hours or up to 24 hours.

2. Adjust oven rack 8 inches from broiler element and heat broiler. Place wire rack in rimmed baking sheet and cover with aluminum foil. Using your fingers, scrape miso mixture from fillets (do not rinse) and place fish skin side down on foil, leaving 1 inch between fillets.

3. Broil salmon until deeply browned and centers of fillets register 125 degrees, 8 to 12 minutes, rotating sheet halfway through cooking and shielding edges of fillets with foil if necessary. Transfer to platter and serve with lemon wedges.

Broiling the fish 8 inches from the element ensures even browning.

Why Marinate with Miso?

A miso marinade works much like a typical curing technique. The miso (a paste made by fermenting soybeans and sometimes other grains with salt and a grain- or bean-based starter called *koji*), sugar, and alcohol all work to season and pull moisture out of the flesh, resulting in a firmer, denser texture. Miso also adds flavor benefits: sweetness, acidity, and water-soluble compounds such as glutamic acid that, over time, penetrate the proteins and lend them deeply complex flavor.

MANY SHADES OF MISO
We prefer the sweet, fruity flavor of white miso for this recipe, though earthier yellow, red, or brown types can also be used.

Pasta e Ceci

Pasta and chickpeas is a homey Italian standard. Our tweaks added depth but not fuss.

⋟ BY ANDREW JANJIGIAN ⋞

Pasta e ceci—pasta and chickpeas—have been paired up in Italian cuisine for centuries. The combination is cheap, simple, and pantry-ready, and the dish itself—a sibling of *pasta e fagioli*—is hearty, flavorful, and fast to make. It's one of those one-pot meals that home cooks turn to over and over again.

Just about every Italian household has a version, which explains why published recipes range dramatically—from brothy soups to hearty stews and even lightly sauced pastas. Simple aromatics like onion, celery, carrot, and garlic are common but not compulsory, as are additions like pancetta, tomato, rosemary, and parsley. In fact, the only constants are the namesake ingredients—and even those can vary. It's common to see both dried and canned chickpeas, as well as fresh and dried pasta of various shapes. Using up broken strands of spaghetti or linguine befits the dish's frugal nature, but short pastas match particularly well with the chickpeas.

Preparing a handful of recipes helped me develop my own ideal: a loose stew that's thick with creamy beans and stubby pasta but is also savory enough to balance the starchy components. And it had to be on the table in well under an hour.

A quick version meant I'd be using canned chickpeas, but it wasn't a sacrifice. We've found that many canned chickpeas are uniform and well seasoned. I started by sautéing a soffritto—minced onion, carrot, celery, and garlic—in olive oil. I then stirred in a couple of cups of water (cleaner-tasting than either chicken or vegetable broth) and two 15-ounce cans of chickpeas along with their liquid (we've found that the starchy, seasoned liquid adds body and flavor). I also added 8 ounces of ditalini, a popular choice for their chickpea-like size. The mixture simmered for about 10 minutes, by which point the pasta was tender and had released some starch that thickened the stew.

I liked that the pasta and chickpeas were chunky and distinct (some recipes puree some or all of the chickpeas), but I did want to soften up the beans a bit more. So rather than adding them along with the pasta, I gave them a 10-minute head start. The extra simmering time changed their texture from snappy to creamy, and because they broke down a bit, they added even more body to the cooking liquid.

This dish takes just 30 minutes from pantry to table.

With the consistency of the stew just right, I circled back to its flavor—which, despite the soffritto, was lackluster. My instinct was to add some diced pancetta, which I'd seen in a few recipes. It lent the stew meaty depth, but it also added chewy bits that marred the overall creamy texture. The solution was to grind the pork to a paste in the food processor and then incorporate it into the soffritto. While I had the appliance out, I saved myself some knife work and blitzed the vegetables, too.

Tomatoes and a minced anchovy, both packed with umami-enhancing glutamates, were good additions as well. I also opted for a small can of whole tomatoes, chopped coarsely. The final tweaks—minced rosemary and a dash of red pepper flakes added to the soffritto, plus last-minute additions of parsley and lemon juice—provided bite and brightness.

I topped my bowl with grated Parmesan and a drizzle of oil and tucked into a savory, rib-sticking stew that I'd thrown together in about 30 minutes.

Cook Those Chickpeas

We simmer our chickpeas for 10 extra minutes to give them a creamy texture. Unlike most canned beans, chickpeas are not processed with skin-strengthening calcium chloride, which means they are capable of softening with further cooking.

PASTA E CECI (PASTA WITH CHICKPEAS)

SERVES 4 TO 6

Another short pasta, such as orzo, can be substituted for the ditalini, but make sure to substitute by weight and not by volume.

- 2 ounces pancetta, cut into ½-inch pieces
- 1 small carrot, peeled and cut into ½-inch pieces
- 1 small celery rib, cut into ½-inch pieces
- 4 garlic cloves, peeled
- 1 onion, halved and cut into 1-inch pieces
- 1 (14-ounce) can whole peeled tomatoes, drained
- ¼ cup extra-virgin olive oil, plus extra for serving
- 1 anchovy fillet, rinsed, patted dry, and minced
- ¼ teaspoon red pepper flakes
- 2 teaspoons minced fresh rosemary
- 2 (15-ounce) cans chickpeas (do not drain)
- 2 cups water
- Salt and pepper
- 8 ounces (1½ cups) ditalini
- 1 tablespoon lemon juice
- 1 tablespoon minced fresh parsley
- 1 ounce Parmesan cheese, grated (½ cup)

1. Process pancetta in food processor until ground to paste, about 30 seconds, scraping down sides of bowl as needed. Add carrot, celery, and garlic and pulse until finely chopped, 8 to 10 pulses. Add onion and pulse until onion is cut into ⅛- to ¼-inch pieces, 8 to 10 pulses. Transfer pancetta mixture to large Dutch oven. Pulse tomatoes in now-empty food processor until coarsely chopped, 8 to 10 pulses. Set aside.

2. Add oil to pancetta mixture in Dutch oven and cook over medium heat, stirring frequently, until fond begins to form on bottom of pot, about 5 minutes. Add anchovy, pepper flakes, and rosemary and cook until fragrant, about 1 minute. Stir in tomatoes, chickpeas and their liquid, water, and 1 teaspoon salt and bring to boil, scraping up any browned bits. Reduce heat to medium-low and simmer for 10 minutes. Add pasta and cook, stirring frequently, until tender, 10 to 12 minutes. Stir in lemon juice and parsley and season with salt and pepper to taste. Serve, passing Parmesan and extra oil separately.

Look: It's Supereasy
Video available free for 4 months at CooksIllustrated.com/dec15

Bringing Back Baked Alaska

The classic cake, ice cream, and meringue combo is a science experiment you can eat. Our modern, less-sweet version is one you'll actually enjoy.

BY ANDREA GEARY

Baked Alaska is the unicorn of the dessert world; everyone has heard of it, but few have seen one in real life. Maybe that's because its three components—a circle of cake topped with a dome of ice cream and covered in meringue—make it sound too fussy to cobble together at home. Or maybe Baked Alaska seems intimidating since it appears to defy the laws of thermodynamics: Baking this dessert in a very hot oven browns and crisps the billowy meringue exterior while leaving the ice cream core frozen and firm. Some restaurants further heighten the drama by lowering the lights, dousing the creation with liqueur, and setting it ablaze at the table.

Nevertheless, the dessert is still basically a dressed-up ice cream cake, and it's no more difficult to make than any other version. My own reasons for not throwing one together more often have always been that Baked Alaska is very sweet, and the traditional bombe shape—while visually impressive when whole—is difficult to slice and serve neatly. Even if you do manage to cut neat slices, the meringue and ice cream invariably part company when you move the slices from the platter to dessert plates. My goal was to reengineer Baked Alaska so it would be as enjoyable to eat as it is impressive to behold.

A trio of chocolate chiffon cake, coffee ice cream, and lightly sweetened meringue makes a memorable—and great-tasting—dessert.

Bombes That Bombed

My first move was to pick a style of meringue: French, Italian, or Swiss. With the French kind, the egg whites don't fully cook, and the result is relatively coarse and foamy. I prefer the other styles because the sugar completely dissolves. The results are creamier, denser, and more stable.

Ultimately, I chose the Swiss version, which is a bit easier to make. The basic method is to gently whisk egg whites and sugar in a bowl over simmering water (I cook it until the mixture reaches 160 degrees for food safety) and then whip it in a stand mixer until stiff peaks form.

Andrea Shows You How
Video available free for 4 months at CooksIllustrated.com/dec15

As for the cake, Baked Alaska can be made with anything from a lean and airy genoise to a rich and tender pound cake to a brownie. I thought that the brownie sounded like a nice flavor and visual contrast to the meringue. Sticking with the traditional bombe shape for now, I baked a basic brownie in an 8-inch round pan and packed softened vanilla ice cream into a plastic wrap–lined bowl with the same diameter. To form the ice cream cake, I pressed the cooled brownie round onto the ice cream and popped the whole thing in the freezer. Once it was firm, I unmolded the cake and covered the surface with a thick layer of meringue (which was tricky, because it tended to slip down the surface of the ice cream). Finally, I baked the Alaska in a 500-degree oven for just a few minutes until the exterior was brown and crisp.

Why It Doesn't Melt

How is it that ice cream wrapped in cake and covered in a layer of meringue can remain frozen solid for a good 5 minutes in a 500-degree oven? Meringue (and, to a lesser extent, cake) is full of tiny air bubbles that provide terrific insulation, since they conduct heat poorly. Heat causes molecules to vibrate and bump into one another, transferring energy. Since air bubbles contain fewer molecules, heat transfer is slow.

I was right—everyone liked the chocolate flavor and visual contrast of the brownie, but in combination with the ice cream and that thick coat of meringue, the whole package was much too sweet. Plus, the ice cream turned icy when I refroze it before baking. Decreasing the amount of meringue reduced some of that sweetness, but doing so came at a cost. When I baked off another Alaska covered with about half as much meringue, the ice cream core turned to soft-serve.

Foam Sweet Foam

Lesson learned: That voluminous meringue coat isn't there just for aesthetics. Its primary function is insulation. The meringue protects the ice cream at the center from melting in the heat of the oven.

Here's how it works: When egg whites are beaten, they form a foam—a liquid (egg whites are primarily water) that traps millions of tiny air bubbles and holds them together in a solid shape. Foams make great insulators because the air bubbles contain relatively few molecules and thus conduct heat energy poorly. The more meringue I used, the better the insulation would be.

If I couldn't reduce the amount of meringue, maybe I could at least make it less sweet by replacing ¼ of the sugar with corn syrup, which is less sweet. But recalibrating the meringue only marginally reduced the dessert's overall sweetness. To really make a difference, I would need to reduce the amount of meringue, too, which would bring me back to my compromised insulation problem. Or so I thought.

Splendid Insulation

Up until that point, I'd been relying almost exclusively on the meringue for insulation. But cakes are also foams with the ability to insulate, so maybe I could make better use of that component. I'd actually seen a couple of Baked Alaska recipes in which the ice cream was completely encased in cake and had dismissed them as overkill. Now I recognized this as a potentially genius move that would allow me to cut way back on the meringue while keeping the ice cream well insulated.

But in order to do so, I had to make some changes—starting with the type of cake. The brownie was not only too sweet but also too inflexible to encase the ice cream, so I switched to a chiffon cake. Because this cake is made with whipped egg whites, it's not only spongier and more flexible than a brownie but also contains much more air, making it a better insulator. (Its plain flavor wasn't an incentive, but I'd revisit that later.)

Using the more-resilient chiffon cake also allowed me to change the way I assembled my Baked Alaska. Rather than line a bowl with cake pieces and soft ice cream, which always resulted in icy ice cream and messy slicing, I abandoned the bombe shape and instead turned the ice cream into a cylinder and wrapped cake around it.

First, I cut the cardboard off two pint containers of ice cream, pressed them together to form a cylinder, and stashed it in the freezer. To make a wide, flat cake that could be wrapped around the cylinder, I baked the chiffon batter in a rimmed baking sheet, cutting the cake into pieces that I used to encase the ice cream. I halved the cylinder lengthwise, placed the halves cut side down on another piece of cake, and placed my creation on a wire rack set in a rimmed baking sheet (to separate it from the sheet's surface, which would get hot in the oven). I spread the cake with just two inches of meringue, appreciating how much better it clung to the surface of the cake than it had to the ice cream, and baked it.

The final results were even more encouraging: Not only were there no drips of melted ice cream, but the slices I cut were tidy and intact and the cross-section view was striking: a half circle of ice cream surrounded by cake and just enough meringue.

A Grown-Up Ice Cream Cake

All I had left to revisit was the flavor. Since the chocolate brownie had been a good match for the meringue, I made the chiffon cake chocolate by substituting cocoa for some of the cake flour.

To make the flavors even more complex, I tried a series of tart sorbets in place of the plain old vanilla ice cream; they had good flavor but were too lean. Instead, I used a premium coffee ice cream that was rich, creamy, and had just the right hint of bitterness—a great match for the other components.

My version of Baked Alaska wasn't just an edible science project about insulation; it was a showpiece dessert that tasted every bit as good as it looked.

TESTING Perfecting the Three Components

Conventional recipes for Baked Alaska often look impressive but tend to be achingly sweet and hard to slice neatly. We reengineered all three components, including wrapping the entire ice cream core in cake, which allowed us to use less meringue, for a dessert that looks and tastes great.

CAKE

All cakes insulated the ice cream from heat to varying degrees; genoise and chiffon cakes were the most effective because they contain more insulating air bubbles that keep the ice cream colder. Both chiffon and genoise were also resilient enough to be wrapped around the ice cream, but we chose chiffon for its slightly richer flavor and more tender texture.

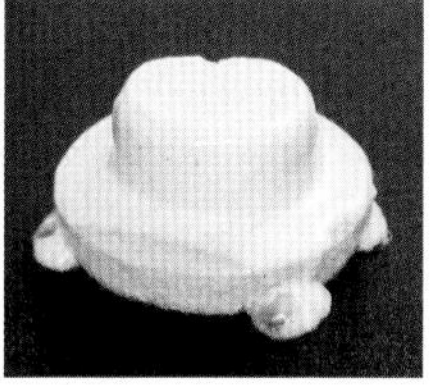

POUND CAKE
Too dense to be effective

BROWNIE
Also not a great insulator

GENOISE
Airy but too lean

CHIFFON ★
Airy, moderately rich, resilient

MERINGUE

We wanted a creamy meringue that was easy to make. After experimenting with the three classic types, we chose a Swiss meringue and made it less cloying by replacing some of the sugar with corn syrup.

FRENCH
Easy to make, but grainy and not food-safe

ITALIAN
Creamy and smooth, but requires fussy hot syrup

SWISS ★
Creamy, smooth, and food-safe when cooked to 160 degrees

ICE CREAM

Our goal was a complex-tasting, not-too-sweet frozen core.

VANILLA ICE CREAM
Rich and creamy but too sweet

RASPBERRY SORBET
Bright-tasting but too lean

COFFEE ICE CREAM ★
Creamy with a hint of bitterness

Thermal Connection

Accounts vary, but many sources attribute the invention of Baked Alaska to Count von Rumford, an 18th-century physicist and pioneer of thermodynamics who is also credited with the invention of the double boiler, the modern kitchen range, and—most fittingly—thermal underwear. A popular version of the story is that Rumford's original name for the dessert, *omelette surprise*, changed decades later when chef Charles Ranhofer of Delmonico's in New York City dubbed it Baked Alaska in celebration of the United States' acquisition of the territory in 1867.

Bonus Baked Alaska

Our Baked Alaska recipe leaves just enough leftover cake and ice cream to make an additional for-two version. For our free recipe for Bonus Baked Alaska, go to CooksIllustrated.com/dec15.

BAKED ALASKA
SERVES 8

Coffee ice cream provides the best contrast with sweet meringue in this recipe, but other flavors may be substituted, if desired. A high-quality ice cream such as Häagen-Dazs works best because it is slower to melt. To ensure the proper texture when serving, it is necessary to remove the cake from the freezer before making the meringue. This recipe leaves just enough leftover cake and ice cream to make an additional for-two version. For our free recipe for Bonus Baked Alaska, go to CooksIllustrated.com/dec15.

2 (1-pint) containers coffee ice cream

Cake

- 1 cup (4 ounces) cake flour
- ⅓ cup (1 ounce) unsweetened cocoa powder
- ⅔ cup (4⅔ ounces) sugar
- 1½ teaspoons baking powder
- ¼ teaspoon salt
- ½ cup vegetable oil
- 6 tablespoons water
- 4 large eggs, separated

Meringue

- ¾ cup (5¼ ounces) sugar
- ⅓ cup light corn syrup
- 3 large egg whites
- 2 tablespoons water
- Pinch salt
- 1 teaspoon vanilla extract

1. Lay 12-inch square sheet of plastic wrap on counter and remove lids from ice cream. Use scissors to cut cardboard tubs from top to bottom. Peel away cardboard and discard. Place ice cream blocks on their sides in center of plastic with wider ends facing each other. Grasp each side of plastic and firmly press blocks together to form barrel shape. Wrap plastic tightly around ice cream and roll briefly on counter to form uniform cylinder. Place cylinder, standing on end, in freezer until completely solid, at least 1 hour.

2. FOR THE CAKE: Adjust oven rack to middle position and heat oven to 350 degrees. Lightly grease 18 by 13-inch rimmed baking sheet, line with parchment paper, and lightly grease parchment. Whisk flour, cocoa, ⅓ cup sugar, baking powder, and salt together in large bowl. Whisk oil, water, and egg yolks into flour mixture until smooth batter forms.

3. Using stand mixer fitted with whisk attachment, whip egg whites on medium-low speed until foamy, about 1 minute. Increase speed to medium-high and whip whites to soft, billowy mounds, about 1 minute. Gradually add remaining ⅓ cup sugar and whip until glossy, soft peaks form, 1 to 2 minutes. Transfer one-third of egg whites to batter; whisk gently until mixture is lightened. Using rubber spatula, gently fold remaining egg whites into batter.

4. Pour batter into prepared sheet; spread evenly. Bake until cake springs back when pressed lightly in center, 10 to 13 minutes. Transfer cake to wire rack and let cool for 5 minutes. Run knife around edge of sheet, then invert cake onto wire rack. Carefully remove parchment, then reinvert cake onto second wire rack. Let cool completely, at least 15 minutes.

5. Transfer cake to cutting board with long side of rectangle parallel to edge of counter. Using serrated knife, trim ¼ inch off left side of cake and discard. Using ruler, measure 4½ inches from cut edge and make mark with knife. Using mark as guide, cut 4½-inch rectangle from cake. Trim piece to create 4½ by 11-inch rectangle and set aside. (Depending on pan size and how much cake has shrunk during baking, it may not be necessary to trim piece to measure 11 inches.) Measure 4 inches from new cut edge and make mark. Using mark as guide, cut 4-inch rectangle from cake. Trim piece to create 4 by 10-inch rectangle, wrap rectangle in plastic, and set aside. Cut 3½-inch round from remaining cake and set aside (biscuit cutter works well). Save scraps for Bonus Baked Alaska.

6. Unwrap ice cream. Trim cylinder to 4½ inches in length and return remainder to freezer for Bonus Baked Alaska. Place ice cream cylinder on 4½ by 11-inch cake rectangle and wrap cake around ice cream. (Cake may crack slightly.) Place cake circle on one end of cylinder. Wrap entire cylinder tightly in plastic. Place cylinder, standing on cake-covered end, in freezer until cake is firm, at least 30 minutes.

7. Unwrap cylinder and place on cutting board, standing on cake-covered end, and cut in half lengthwise. Unwrap reserved 4 by 10-inch cake rectangle and place halves on top, ice cream side down, with open ends meeting in middle. Wrap tightly with plastic and press ends gently to close gap between halves. Return to freezer for at least 2 hours and up to 2 weeks.

8. FOR THE MERINGUE: Adjust oven rack to upper-middle position and heat oven to 500 degrees. Spray wire rack set in rimmed baking sheet with vegetable oil spray. Unwrap cake and place on rack. Combine sugar, corn syrup, egg whites, water, and salt in bowl of stand mixer; place bowl over saucepan filled with 1 inch simmering water, making sure that water does not touch bottom of bowl. Whisking gently but constantly, heat until sugar is dissolved and mixture registers 160 degrees, 5 to 8 minutes.

9. Place bowl in stand mixer fitted with whisk attachment. Beat mixture on medium speed until bowl is only slightly warm to touch, about 5 minutes. Increase speed to high and beat until mixture begins to lose its gloss and forms stiff peaks, about 5 minutes. Add vanilla and beat until combined.

10. Using offset spatula, spread meringue over top and sides of cake, avoiding getting meringue on rack. Use back of spoon to create peaks all over meringue.

11. Bake until browned and crisp, about 5 minutes. Run offset spatula or thin knife under dessert to loosen from rack, then use two spatulas to transfer to serving platter. To slice, dip sharp knife in very hot water and wipe dry after each cut. Serve immediately.

STEP BY STEP | ENGINEERING

A NEW BAKED ALASKA

1. Cut ice cream tubs from top to bottom and peel away cardboard. Place blocks on plastic wrap on their sides with wider ends facing each other.

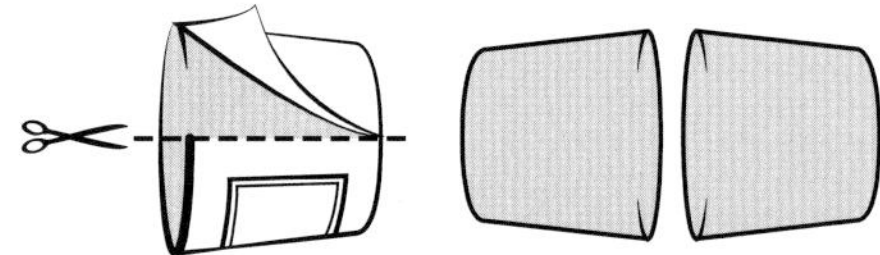

2. Wrap plastic tightly around ice cream and roll on counter to form even cylinder. Place in freezer, standing on end, for 1 hour.

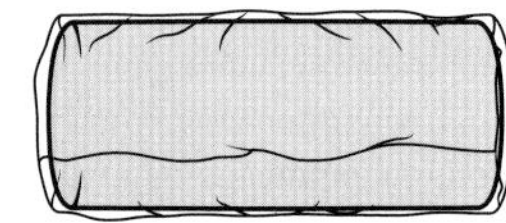

3. Trim ¼ inch off left side of cake. Cut 4½ by 11-inch rectangle (A), 4 by 10-inch rectangle (B), and 3½-inch round (C). Save scraps (D) for Bonus Baked Alaska.

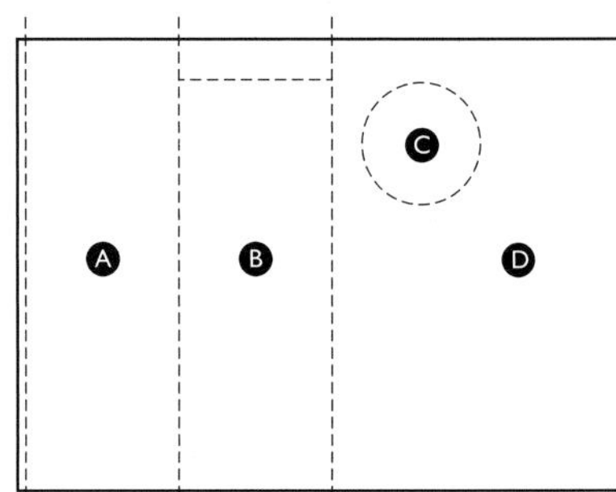

4. Unwrap ice cream and trim cylinder to 4½ inches in length. Return remainder to freezer.

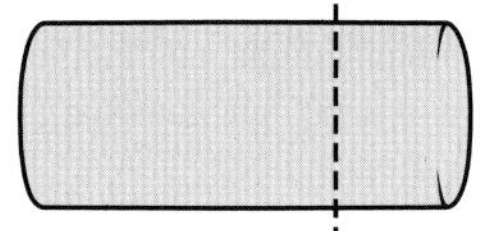

5. Place ice cream on 4½ by 11-inch rectangle and wrap cake around ice cream. Place cake circle on one end of cylinder. Wrap in plastic. Freeze, standing on cake-covered end, for 30 minutes.

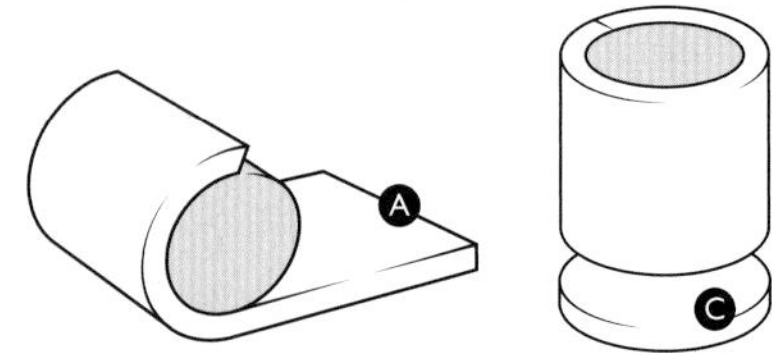

6. Unwrap cylinder, stand on cake-covered end, and cut in half lengthwise. Place halves on 4 by 10-inch rectangle, ice cream side down, with open ends meeting in middle.

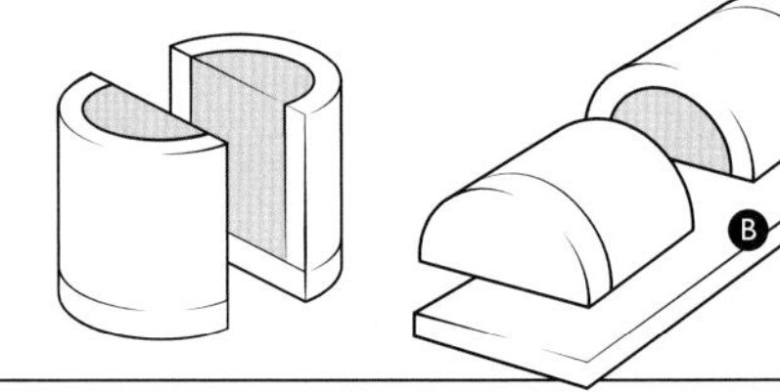

Like an Extra-Virgin?

Often dull or even rancid-tasting, supermarket olive oils never seem to live up to their extra-virgin designation. Have new industry standards improved the options?

⋟ BY LISA McMANUS ⋞

Olive oil, which is simply juice pressed from olives, tastes great when it's fresh. The highest grade, called extra-virgin, is lively, bright, and full-bodied at its best, with flavors that range from peppery to buttery depending on the variety of olives used and how ripe they are when harvested. (In general, an earlier harvest yields greener, more peppery oil; a later harvest results in a mellower, more golden oil.) But like any other fresh fruit, olives are highly perishable, and their pristine, complex flavor degrades quickly, which makes producing—and handling—a top-notch oil time-sensitive, labor-intensive, and expensive. But the results couldn't be more worth it. We use extra-virgin olive oil as a condiment on grilled meat, fish, vegetables, and pastas; a source of richness and body in soups and sauces; and a star player in vinaigrette.

Unfortunately, the supermarket extra-virgin olive oils we tasted seven years ago were wan facsimiles of the good stuff. Most were either as bland as vegetable oil or, worse, funky, overpowering, and stale. We learned that Americans were literally getting the bottom of the barrel, and a number of more recent articles and books have pointed out a big reason why: With no meaningful U.S. standards for olive oil, lower-quality oils found a ready market here. In fact, one widely reported 2010 University of California, Davis Olive Center study revealed that a whopping 69 percent of tested supermarket olive oils sold as "extra-virgin" actually weren't according to the standards set by the International Olive Council (IOC), the industry's worldwide governing body. They were in fact lesser grades being passed off at premium prices.

Since then, the U.S. olive oil industry has taken steps to be more stringent. California, where olive oil production has grown tenfold over the past decade, passed its own standards in 2008 and tightened them last year. And in 2010, after the UC Davis Olive Center study and at the urging of domestic producers, the U.S. Department of Agriculture (USDA) adopted chemical and sensory standards for olive oil grades similar to those established by the IOC. Among the chemical standards: An oil must not exceed certain levels of free fatty acids and peroxides, which would indicate olive deterioration, poor processing, and oxidation. To meet sensory criteria, an oil must taste not just flawless—or have what experts call "zero defects"—but also possess good fruity flavor.

The Globe-Trotting Path of Many Supermarket Olive Oils

Many brands of oils labeled "extra-virgin" in supermarkets contain blends of oils sourced from multiple countries, which can indicate that the oils were collected from a price-driven bulk market that prioritizes cheap, not high-quality, oil. Traveling far distances before bottling also increases the risk that spoiled oil may wind up in the final product. The oil that went into one of our lower-ranked brands, Olivari, traveled from Italy, Greece, Spain, Turkey, Tunisia, and/or Morocco before being bottled in Rome, New York. Our winning oil from California Olive Ranch, on the other hand, uses oil from olives harvested within 150 miles of its Northern California pressing and bottling facility.

To see if these new standards have led to better-quality oils in supermarkets, we decided to take a fresh look. We sampled 10 top-selling nationally available supermarket extra-virgin olive oils in a series of blind tastings: plain, with bread, over tomatoes and mozzarella, and in a vinaigrette served over salad greens. We also sent each of the oils to an independent laboratory for chemical evaluation and to 10 trained olive oil tasters to get a second opinion on their flavor quality.

Flavor Savers

Every stage of the process affects the quality of the oil. Producers must start with good fruit—that is, ripe olives that have been harvested carefully and aren't bruised or fermented—and get it to the mill as quickly as possible, before spoilage sets in. Extra-virgin olive oil (sometimes abbreviated EVOO) must also be pressed—or, in modern terms, spun out by a centrifuge to separate the water from the oil—with clean equipment that won't add impurities and without using high heat or chemicals. While heat and chemicals extract more oil from the olives, it's at the cost of preserving important aromatics and antioxidants that help keep the oil fresh-tasting. That said, producing high-quality oil is only half the challenge. Because olive oil begins to degrade as soon as it's exposed to air, heat, and light, producers must transport and store it carefully to preserve its freshness.

Any of these factors might account for the fact that, while all the oils in our tasting did just pass the lab tests we commissioned (a limited spectrum of some of the same freshness and quality tests required by the IOC and USDA), only one passed all the tests with solid scores. The rest showed spotty results that weren't indicative of a truly fresh, high-quality oil. As for our sensory evaluations, these were even more discouraging. Both panels agreed that only two out of the 10 oils had good fruity flavor without off-notes. Our in-house panel found these remaining oils merely lackluster, but the experts were harsher

How Oil Gets Robbed of Its Extra-Virginity

In the multibillion dollar olive oil industry, there can be many detours on the way to true extra-virgin status.

BAD FRUIT
Bruised or fermented olives can lead to off-notes in oil.

IMPROPER PROCESSING
Use of high heat and chemicals extracts more oil but damages flavor.

ADULTERATION
To mask defects, some makers cut oil with tasteless, odorless refined olive oil.

SHODDY STORAGE
Heat, air, and light all make an oil degrade faster.

OLD AGE
Even under ideal conditions, all olive oils will oxidize and become rancid over time.

in their criticism. Oils that we deemed simply flat or dull they decried as borderline rancid or "fusty," an industry term for a fermented taste.

When we spoke about these results with Alexandra Kicenik Devarenne, an independent California-based olive oil consultant and educator, judge in international olive oil competitions, and author of *Olive Oil: A Field Guide* (2014), she confirmed what we suspected: "If this had been an official panel tasting, the problems in these oils would make them a lower grade. They would be virgin, as opposed to extra-virgin."

But how could so many subpar oils labeled "extra-virgin" still appear in supermarkets, given the standards the USDA has put in place? The answer is simple: The standards aren't enforced. In fact, they're not enforced anywhere in the olive oil industry. A 2013 U.S. International Trade Commission report noted that even in Europe, the IOC standards are "widely unenforced," allowing "a wide range of oil qualities to be marketed as extra-virgin." (In the United States, a different reason might eventually force more compliance: Manufacturers of two of the oils in our lineup, Bertolli and Filippo Berio, are the targets of class-action suits for misleading labeling. Both have denied the claims.)

Standard bottling practices and "best by" dates also might be part of the problem. Devarenne explained that the oils in our lineup may have had the necessary flavor profile to qualify as extra-virgin when they were first pressed, but the fact that oils are commonly stored in stainless-steel tanks for multiple years and given a "best by" date from the time of bottling rather than harvest may have meant that they weren't especially fresh by the time we tasted them.

For Devarenne, the issue with most of the oils we tasted is not that they don't have a place in the kitchen—she thinks most would be acceptable as cooking oils rather than condiment oils, and we agree. Instead, it's what she calls "the 'truth in labeling' thing." "If, overnight, all of the olive oil in the supermarket magically relabeled itself to accurately reflect what was inside the bottle, we would have a vigorous trade in virgin grade olive oil in this country," she said. Instead, mislabeling cheapens the consumer's impression of what a real extra-virgin oil should be.

Grade Inflation

For an oil to qualify as true extra-virgin, it must meet certain chemical standards (including minimal levels of free fatty acids, which indicate fermentation), be free of off-notes, and contain some positive fruity flavors. The problem is, the USDA doesn't enforce these criteria. According to olive oil consultant Alexandra Kicenik Devarenne, many oils labeled "extra-virgin" in supermarkets fall short enough of these benchmarks that they would more accurately be described as "virgin," a lesser category of olive oil you almost never see in stores. Without enforcement of the stricter extra-virgin standards, there's no incentive for bottlers to change their labels (or their pricing).

Consider the Source

So what about those better-quality oils in our lineup? Our runner-up was from Lucini, a supermarket brand of extra-virgin we've liked in the past. Our top-ranking sample was from California Olive Ranch, the winner of our 2009 tasting of California extra-virgin olive oil. The latter stood out for its "fragrant," "complex," and "fruity" flavors. Not surprisingly, it also was the oil that bested the others in our chemical tests. So what does California Olive Ranch do differently that makes their product better than the others? Mostly, it boils down to the company's control over every stage of the production process, which preserves the freshness of the oil as much as possible.

It starts with the source. Six of the 10 brands we tasted are sourced from multiple regions—and from one to as many as 11 different countries—which increases the likelihood that the oils were collected from a price-driven global bulk market that prioritizes cheap, not high-quality, oil. Conversely, California Olive Ranch, the lone domestic oil in our tasting, is made from olives that are grown within 150 miles of the pressing and bottling facility. The company knows exactly what types of olives go into its oils and is willing to share the information, whereas the bottlers of some lower-ranking brands wouldn't reveal the varieties used in their products, making us wonder if they even tracked such information (one brand admitted that it didn't).

Second, the company uses a relatively new growing and harvesting process called super-high-density planting, in which the trees are planted together much more tightly than they would be in traditional groves. As a result, the olives can be harvested by machines more efficiently than they would be if they were picked by hand or shaken into nets on the ground. (Speed is of the essence, since olives begin to change flavor from the moment they are separated from the tree and must be pressed as quickly as possible to ensure they retain the desired flavor profile.) Then, by bottling very close to the source, the company cuts out the risk that the oil oxidizes and spoils during transport to another facility. And unlike some producers that sell their oil in clear glass or even plastic bottles, which expose the oil to more damaging light, California Olive Ranch uses dark-green glass bottles that help shield the oil. The upshot of all these factors: fresher and cheaper olive oil.

We hope we'll be seeing more choices like California Olive Ranch Extra Virgin Olive Oil on supermarket shelves. While it costs more than mediocre oils from industrial bottlers like last-placed Bertolli ($0.59 per ounce compared to $0.36), it's far less expensive than our high-end extra-virgin favorite from Columela, which costs $1.12 per ounce. (We even found these oils comparable when we tasted them side by side.) In fact, its price is so reasonable that we can use it as a condiment, but we won't feel bad about also using it in cooking.

SHOPPING

Indications of a Fresher Oil

These three things can help you assess the quality of an extra-virgin olive oil before you buy it.

HARVEST DATE
Since a "best by" date might be 24 to 32 months after the oil was bottled and 1 to 2 years after it was pressed, a harvest date is a more precise indication of freshness. Look for the most recent date, and note that in Europe and the United States, olives are harvested in the fall and winter, so most bottles will list the previous year.

DARK GLASS
Avoid clear glass; dark glass shields the oil from damaging light. Avoid clear plastic, too; it's not a good barrier to light or air.

OIL ORIGIN
Bottlers often print where their oil has been sourced from on the label; look for oil that has been sourced from a single country.

TASTING SUPERMARKET EXTRA-VIRGIN OLIVE OIL

We tasted 10 top-selling extra-virgin olive oils plain, with bread, over tomatoes and mozzarella, and in vinaigrette, rating the oils on their fruity, fresh, bitter, and peppery flavors and overall appeal. Information about source, olive varieties, and bottling location were obtained from manufacturers. We also had the oils tested at an independent laboratory for quality and freshness. (An independent group of trained olive oil tasters conducted a separate double-blind tasting of the oils, but we didn't factor their assessment into our rankings.) Results were averaged and products appear below in order of preference.

RECOMMENDED

CALIFORNIA OLIVE RANCH Everyday Extra Virgin Olive Oil

PRICE: $9.99 for 500 ml ($0.59 per oz)
OLIVE VARIETIES: Arbequina, Arbosana, Koroneiki
SOURCE: Northern California
BOTTLED IN: Artois, California
COMMENTS: "Fruity," "fragrant," and "fresh" with a "complex finish," this top-ranked oil is a supermarket standout. In fact, its flavor rivaled that of our favorite high-end extra-virgin oil. Not surprisingly, its lab scores for freshness and quality were also better than the other brands across the board.

"Rivals the flavor of our favorite high-end EVOO."

RECOMMENDED

LUCINI Premium Select Extra Virgin Olive Oil

PRICE: $20.99 for 500 ml ($1.24 per oz)
OLIVE VARIETIES: Frantoio, Moraiolo, Leccino, Maurino, and Pendolino
SOURCE: Tuscany and Central Italy
BOTTLED IN: Tuscany
COMMENTS: Drizzled over tomatoes and mozzarella and as a dip for bread, this pricey Italian oil—our former supermarket favorite—tasted "incredibly rich," "bright," and "buttery" with a pleasantly "peppery aftertaste," though those flavors became somewhat muted in vinaigrette. There, it was deemed "subtle."

RECOMMENDED WITH RESERVATIONS

COLAVITA Extra Virgin Olive Oil, Premium Italian

PRICE: $18.99 for 34 oz ($0.56 per oz)
OLIVE VARIETY: Coratina (other varieties included to lesser extent, to temper bitterness)
SOURCE: Italy
BOTTLED IN: Pomezia, Italy
COMMENTS: With a "fresh, light, green taste" and a "mildly peppery finish," this oil earned acceptable but not stellar scores. Several tasters deemed it "mild—just OK," especially in vinaigrette, where it was a little too "neutral."

GOYA Extra Virgin Olive Oil

PRICE: $5.99 for 17 oz ($0.35 per oz)
OLIVE VARIETIES: Hojiblanca, Lechin, Picual, Arbequina, Picudo, Cacereña, and Manzanilla
SOURCE: Andalucia, Spain
BOTTLED IN: Andalucia
COMMENTS: Notes for this Spanish oil ranged from "balanced, but mild" and "middle-of-the-road" to just plain "boring." In vinaigrette, it made a "mellow and balanced dressing, but has no real distinct EVOO flavor."

RECOMMENDED WITH RESERVATIONS CONTINUED

BOTTICELLI Extra Virgin Olive Oil

PRICE: $8.99 for 25.3 oz ($0.36 per oz)
OLIVE VARIETIES: Arbequina, Arbosana, Koroneiki
SOURCE: Italy, Spain, Greece, Tunisia
BOTTLED IN: Italy
COMMENTS: On its own, this blended oil tasted "mild" and "not that fresh" with a "bitter aftertaste"; in vinaigrette, it came across as "fine" but "heavy" and without "much character to it." As one taster summed it up, "it could be any old regular oil off the shelf."

FILIPPO BERIO Extra Virgin Olive Oil

PRICE: $5.99 for 16.9 oz ($0.35 per oz)
OLIVE VARIETIES: Proprietary information
SOURCE: Italy, Spain, Greece, and Tunisia
BOTTLED IN: Massarosa (Lucca), Italy
COMMENTS: While a few tasters appreciated this oil's "slight peppery aftertaste" and even found it "smooth" in vinaigrette, many others detected "medicinal," "vinegary" notes and a "greasy consistency"—possible signs that the olives weren't processed quickly enough after picking or that the oil was on the verge of going rancid.

OLIVARI Extra-Virgin Olive Oil

PRICE: $6.99 for 17 oz ($0.41 per oz)
OLIVE VARIETIES: Special blend; proprietary information
SOURCE: Italy, Greece, Spain, Turkey, Tunisia, and Morocco
BOTTLED IN: New York
COMMENTS: Disappointingly, this oil's "bright [and] fruity" aroma gave way to a "flat," "thin" flavor that "dissipates quickly." Over tomatoes and mozzarella, it tasted more "punchy" but still "a little stale," even though the "best by" date was more than a year away.

STAR Extra Virgin Olive Oil

PRICE: $9.99 for 500 ml ($0.59 per oz)
OLIVE VARIETIES: Company does not track, saying, "There are many varieties grown in the countries we source from."
SOURCE: Spain, Italy, Greece, and Tunisia
BOTTLED IN: Spain and Tunisia
COMMENTS: This "acceptable but not distinctive" oil "smelled brighter, grassier, and more peppery than it tasted." In vinaigrette, it was "lost in other flavors" and offered little more than a "greasy mouthfeel."

POMPEIAN Extra Virgin Olive Oil

PRICE: $12.99 for 32 oz ($0.41 per oz)
OLIVE VARIETIES: Arbosana, Koroneiki, Coratina, Arbequina, Picual, Frantoio, Picholine, and Hojiblanca
SOURCE: May include Italy, Greece, Spain, Argentina, Tunisia, Turkey, Morocco, Chile, United States, Uruguay, Portugal
BOTTLED IN: Maryland
COMMENTS: This oil was "neutral" and "timid" at best; one taster even said, "Nothing. I've got nothing here." But the more alarming comments were about its off-flavors—"metallic," "soapy," and "acidic" among them.

BERTOLLI Extra Virgin Olive Oil

PRICE: $8.99 for 25 oz ($0.36 per oz)
OLIVE VARIETIES: Proprietary blend
SOURCE: Italy, Spain, Portugal, Greece, Morocco, Tunisia, Chile, Argentina, and Australia
BOTTLED IN: Italy and Spain
COMMENTS: Straight out of the bottle, this oil's "dull" flavor and "quick finish" left tasters underwhelmed—and unlike many other samples, its flavor didn't improve much when it met up with other ingredients. It tasted "greasy and flat" with tomatoes and mozzarella, and tasters found it boring in vinaigrette. "Nothing special. Could be vegetable oil in here."

Finding a Good Oven Thermometer

An oven thermometer is the only reliable way to know what's happening inside your oven—unless you have a model that's inaccurate, hard to read, or falls off the racks.

BY KATE SHANNON

For reliable, consistent results with recipes, a good oven thermometer is critical. When we used a high-tech digital thermometer to take the temperature of five different home ovens preheated to 350 degrees, some missed the mark by as much as 50 degrees. Here's one big reason why: An oven's internal thermometer only gauges the temperature of the location where it's installed, which is necessarily in an out-of-the-way spot in the back, front, or side of the oven box. But these areas can be subject to hot spots or drafts that make their temperatures differ from the center of the oven. Only a good freestanding oven thermometer can tell you what's really going on right in the middle of the oven, where most food cooks.

For several years, we've relied on our winning dial-face oven thermometer from Cooper-Atkins, but we've also noticed new models on the market and wondered if anything better had come along. We scooped up nine dial-face models priced from $4.63 to $20.94 to pit against it. (We avoided bulb models since we've found that their tinted alcohol can get stuck and give inaccurate readings.) Most of our lineup had the option to hang from the racks or sit upright. Either way, we wanted a thermometer that was easy to position and remove for a periodic reading. In addition to ease of use, we rated the legibility of the faces and, most importantly, the models' accuracy. Finally, to assess quality control, we purchased four copies of each thermometer and ran the entire set through testing.

TOO COLD: 425°　TOO HOT: 475°　JUST RIGHT: 450°

Do 25 Degrees Really Matter?

A number of the products in our lineup have a logo on their packaging and/or the thermometer itself showing that they have been tested by the independent certification organization NSF International and meet standard requirements. The problem is, those standards allow a thermometer to be off by as much as 25 degrees—just the variance we found in some of our brands. To see the impact of such a discrepancy, we baked popovers in ovens that we set to 25 degrees above and below the desired initial temperature of 450 degrees. The popovers in the too-cold oven didn't rise properly, while those in the too-hot oven were misshapen and overly dark.

Temperature Trackers

An unreliable oven thermometer is worse than none at all, so we started by evaluating each brand's accuracy at 250, 350, and 450 degrees, using the same oven for all of our tests. We clipped a lab-grade thermocouple to the center of the middle oven rack and arranged all four copies of a model closely around the probe. We then compared their readings to the thermacouple's.

All dial-face thermometers work by the same internal mechanism. A bimetallic strip (that is, two pieces of different metals pressed together) is wound into a tight coil and connected to a tiny dial. The two metals expand and contract at different rates when heated or cooled, moving the dial on the face. As simple a mechanism as this is, quality controls clearly vary from factory to factory. With three products, one out of the four copies faltered, registering temperatures 10 to 25 degrees off the real oven temperature.

Lisa Explains It All
Video available free for 4 months at CooksIllustrated.com/dec15

Easy Reading

Most of the models in our lineup had thin, flat bases designed to sit atop the oven racks. Models with bases less than 2¼ inches wide were difficult to position and prone to tipping over. We found similar fault with two models with clamp-like bases designed to clip onto the grates. The space between the open jaws of the clamp was too narrow to slide over the racks in all five of the different oven styles we tested. At best, they slid on crooked and were difficult to read. At worst, they fell off completely and landed on the oven floor. After one such tumble, the silicone backing on one model melted and warped. The glass face of another top-heavy model cracked when it hit the oven floor.

Finally, we focused our attention on how easy it was to read each model with the oven door open and closed. Our testers favored models that had minimal markings beyond 50- and 25-degree indications, since having more tick marks made them harder to read, and the extra marks were unnecessary anyway. We also knocked off points on models with metal casings that obscured the numbers or cast long shadows on them, forcing us to crouch or squint to read the temperature.

In the end, nearly half our lineup failed to meet our basic criteria for legibility and stability. Add to that the three models that faltered in our accuracy tests, and we were left with just four oven thermometers that met our expectations. Of these, the CDN Pro Accurate Oven Thermometer ($8.70) earned the top marks. It has large temperature markings and a simple, streamlined face—plus, a wide base that fits securely on all types of oven racks without fiddling or fussing. It's our new winner, and one that we'll be keeping within easy reach to check our own ovens.

Put Your Thermometer Where the Food Is

Many cooks let their oven thermometer live in the oven in an out-of-the-way place where they can check it every time they cook. This is actually unnecessary (with typical home use, an oven's accuracy should remain relatively consistent over time). A better approach: Periodically check your oven's basic accuracy. Place your thermometer in the middle of the center rack, where most food cooks. As a benchmark, set the oven to 350 degrees. After the oven indicates that it has preheated, check the thermometer's reading. (But don't wait too long—ovens cycle off and on to maintain a stable temperature.) Remove the thermometer and adjust the temperature setting accordingly the next time you cook. Repeat the process every three to six months.

KEY

GOOD ★★★
FAIR ★★
POOR ★

TESTING OVEN THERMOMETERS

We tested 10 dial-face thermometers, priced from $4.63 to $20.94, all with a temperature range of at least 150 to 500 degrees Fahrenheit. Prices shown were paid online. Models appear in order of preference.

ACCURACY

We weighed this criterion most heavily in our rankings. We tested four units of each model in ovens set to 250, 350, and 450 degrees Fahrenheit, using a lab-grade thermocouple to assess their accuracy. Models lost points if one unit was off by more than 10 degrees.

EASE OF USE

We rated each model on how easy it was to position and remove and on its stability on the rack. Thermometers lost points if they tipped over, fell off the rack, or were difficult to install.

LEGIBILITY

We evaluated how easy it was to see the thermometers' temperature readings with the oven door open and closed. Models with sharp color contrast and clear temperature indications fared best.

RECOMMENDED

CDN
Pro Accurate Oven Thermometer

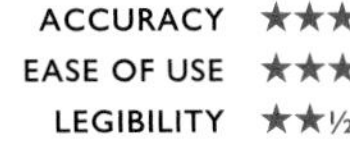

ACCURACY ★★★
EASE OF USE ★★★
LEGIBILITY ★★½

MODEL: DOT2
PRICE: $8.70
TEMPERATURE RANGE: 150–550 F
COMMENTS: All copies of this model aced our accuracy tests. It sports a wide, sturdy base and clear temperature markings with large numbers and boldly visible dashes at 50- and 25-degree increments. Its silver face is more prone to glare and light reflection than models with white backgrounds, but it's still fairly easy to read.

TAYLOR
TruTemp Thermometer

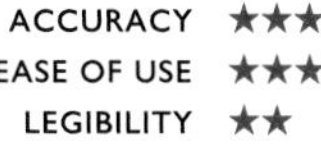

ACCURACY ★★★
EASE OF USE ★★★
LEGIBILITY ★★

MODEL: 3506
PRICE: $6.10
TEMPERATURE RANGE: 100–600 F
COMMENTS: As with our winner, all units of this model gave consistently accurate readings. Testers appreciated the large display and the color indications (cooler temperatures are shaded in blue and hotter in red), but we found its tiny dashes denoting temperature increments of less than 25 and 50 degrees distracting.

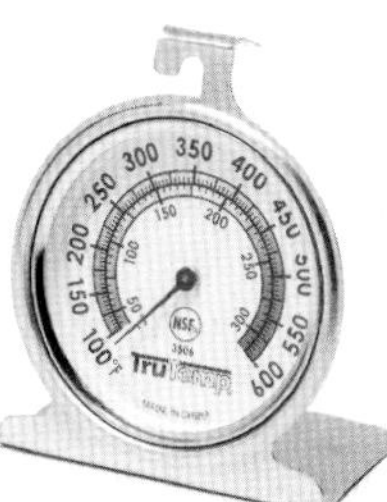

RECOMMENDED WITH RESERVATIONS

POLDER
Commercial Oven Thermometer
MODEL: THM-550N **PRICE:** $7.19
TEMPERATURE RANGE: 50–500 F

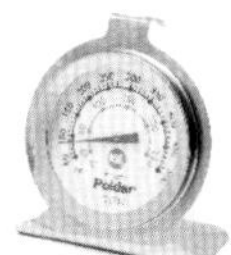

ACCURACY ★★★
EASE OF USE ★★★
LEGIBILITY ★½

This thermometer was small but mighty, providing readings that matched the oven's ambient temperature in test after test. When we looked at it straight on, the numbered markings were clear as day. But its metal casing obscured some numbers entirely and cast shadows on others, posing serious problems for tall cooks and frustrating even our more petite testers.

COOPER-ATKINS
Dial Oven Thermometer
MODEL: 24HP-01-1 **PRICE:** $4.63
TEMPERATURE RANGE: 100–600 F

ACCURACY ★★★
EASE OF USE ★★★
LEGIBILITY ★½

Our old winner continued to impress us with consistently accurate temperature readings and a wide, sturdy base. But the metal casing hid some numbers from view, drawing criticism especially from taller testers. The food safety instructions printed on the bottom of the face were distracting.

NOT RECOMMENDED

WILLIAMS-SONOMA
Oven Thermometer
MODEL: 21-4024691 **PRICE:** $19.95
TEMPERATURE RANGE: 150–600 F

ACCURACY ★★★
EASE OF USE 0
LEGIBILITY ★★

We found no faults with the accuracy of this thermometer, and we liked how its numbers are located close to the center of the face, where they never became obscured by shadows. But its clamp-like clip was incompatible with every oven grate we tried. Frustrated testers struggled to clip it on facing forward and often watched with dismay as it fell forward or swiveled sideways.

NORPRO Oven Thermometer
MODEL: 5973 **PRICE:** $7.97
TEMPERATURE RANGE: 150–600 F

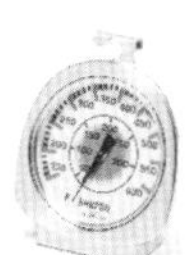

ACCURACY ★★★
EASE OF USE ★
LEGIBILITY 0

The accuracy of this model wasn't enough to offset its flaws: Its slim base, just 1¾ inches across, is just barely bigger than the gaps between most oven grates and required painstaking placement so it didn't tip into the grates. The positioning of numbers between temperature increments (instead of directly over them) made it impossible to read at a glance.

TAYLOR
Connoisseur Oven Thermometer
MODEL: 503 **PRICE:** $13.22
TEMPERATURE RANGE: 150–600 F

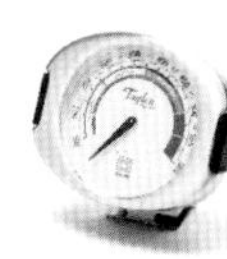

ACCURACY ★★★
EASE OF USE 0
LEGIBILITY ½

Though this thermometer gave consistently accurate readings, it had a clamp-like clip (in place of a traditional flat base) that was difficult to slide onto the grates in all five different styles of oven we tested it in. It routinely clipped on crooked or fell over, making its otherwise bright, easy-to-read face illegible. The silicone backing on one unit melted and warped when it fell onto the oven floor.

TAYLOR
Oven Thermometer
MODEL: 5932 **PRICE:** $6.90
TEMPERATURE RANGE: 100–600 F

ACCURACY ★
EASE OF USE ★★★
LEGIBILITY ★★★

One unit of this model was off by 25-degree variations in two accuracy tests. It's too bad, because the temperature markings are easy to read, and its wide base easily supports its extra-large face.

MAVERICK
Oven Thermometer
MODEL: OT-01 **PRICE:** $12.00
TEMPERATURE RANGE: 100–600 F

ACCURACY ★
EASE OF USE ★★★
LEGIBILITY ★

One copy of this thermometer gave readings 10 to 25 degrees below the actual oven temperature in all three temperature tests. The model is also quite small, with tiny numbers that are often obscured by its metal casing or hidden in shadows, but it did sit securely on the oven rack.

MAVERICK
Large Dial Oven Thermometer
MODEL: OT-02 **PRICE:** $20.94
TEMPERATURE RANGE: 100–600 F

ACCURACY ★
EASE OF USE ★
LEGIBILITY ★★★

Like its sibling, this thermometer faltered in accuracy. One unit was off by 25 degrees in two temperature tests. The base also couldn't support the weight of its oversized face, and it toppled over enough times to crack one unit's glass front. With these flaws, we didn't care that it was easy to read.

INGREDIENT NOTES

BY ANDREA GEARY, LAN LAM & ANNIE PETITO

Tasting Multigrain Gluten-Free Sandwich Bread

In a recent tasting of white gluten-free loaves, we were hard-pressed to find any we could recommend. Would branching out beyond white bread provide better options? We bought nine brands of multigrain and whole-grain gluten-free sandwich bread, sampling them plain and toasted with butter, and were pleasantly surprised by two of the options.

Our top-ranked bread had plenty of salt, while the two lowest-ranked breads contained the least. Our favorite was also one of two breads with the highest level of fat, helping to create a crumb that was fluffy and moist. It was also the only bread to add baking soda, while the runner-up added baking powder. In addition to boosting lift, both leaveners produce flavorful browning through the Maillard reaction for a better-tasting loaf.

But here's the catch: To be labeled "multigrain" (whether gluten-free or traditional), breads only have to contain more than one type of grain—and that can be in the form of refined flours lacking the fibrous bran and nutrient-rich germ. Our favorite "multigrain" gluten-free bread, Glutino Gluten Free Multigrain Bread, actually contains no fiber or protein at all, a clear sign that it contains no whole grains. Meanwhile, our second-place bread, Three Bakers 7 Ancient Grains Whole Grain Bread, Gluten-Free, contains 4 grams of protein and 10 grams of fiber in a 100-gram serving.

For a loaf with texture and flavor that resembles traditional bread, choose Glutino Gluten Free Multigrain Bread. In fact, it might be the best choice for anyone looking for a "white" gluten-free sandwich bread (we preferred it to the white gluten-free loaves we tasted). For bread with whole-grain fiber, Three Bakers 7 Ancient Grains Whole Grain Bread, Gluten-Free is a flavorful option. For complete testing results, go to CooksIllustrated.com/dec15.
–Lisa McManus

RECOMMENDED

GLUTINO
Gluten Free Multigrain Bread
PRICE: $5.49 for a 14.1-ounce loaf ($0.39 per oz)
COMMENTS: With the most salt of all the breads we tasted, one of the highest fat contents, and good browning on the crust, this loaf had a flavor advantage. It also had the best texture. "It has chew and some structure" with an interior that was "fluffy and light, almost like challah." Overall, as one happy taster wrote, "Miles better than the others."

THREE BAKERS
7 Ancient Grains Whole Grain Bread, Gluten-Free
PRICE: $5.99 for a 17-ounce loaf ($0.35 per oz)
COMMENTS: With "a yeasty, rich flavor," a "crust that is very chewy," and "seeds and grains (that) add interest," this bread, with its "very open crumb," was appealing to many tasters. Toasted, it had "nice crunch and chew" but became "gummy in the middle."

Comparing Kale

Three types of kale are commonly available in supermarkets— black (also known as dinosaur, cavolo nero, Lacinato, or Tuscan), curly (also known as Scottish or green), and red (also known as Russian Red or Winter Red). To examine their differences, we sampled the greens braised and in a salad that called for soaking the raw leaves in a warm water bath to tenderize them. While they all had pleasant flavor, we preferred the tenderness of black and curly kale. Red kale was too tough to enjoy, even when braised. –A.P.

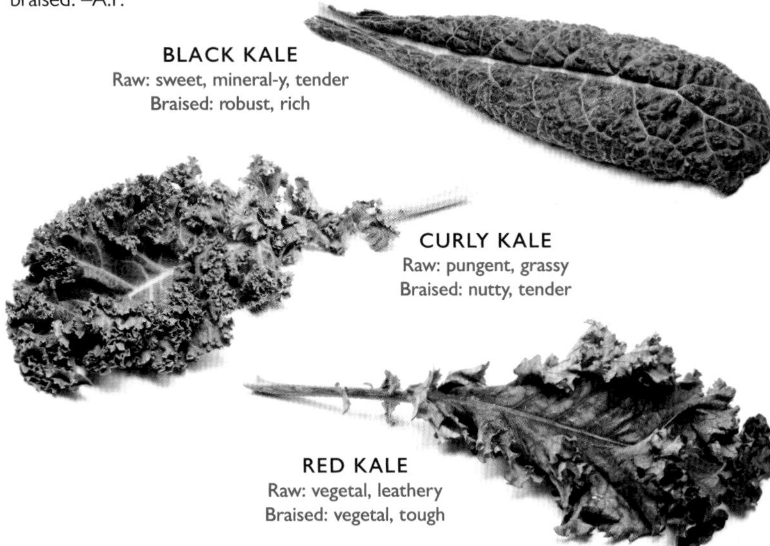

BLACK KALE
Raw: sweet, mineral-y, tender
Braised: robust, rich

CURLY KALE
Raw: pungent, grassy
Braised: nutty, tender

RED KALE
Raw: vegetal, leathery
Braised: vegetal, tough

Cracking the Cocoa Nib

Cocoa nibs are the fermented, roasted, and cracked pieces of cacao beans that manufacturers process to make chocolate. They are dry and crunchy and have the bitterness of unsweetened chocolate or coffee, tempered by a slightly fruity acidity. Cocoa nibs don't melt when heated, but their cocoa butter comes to the surface. While they can be sprinkled on oatmeal or yogurt or cooked into a chili, they are usually incorporated in baked goods. In tests, we found that they are best suited to applications like banana bread where there aren't a lot of other competing flavors (or textures), although we did like them a lot in a granola made with dried cherries and almonds. Use ½ to ⅔ cup of cocoa nibs per 9-cup batch of granola, loaf of quick bread, or dozen muffins. –L.L.

Chestnuts: Buying and Shelling

Chestnuts are available jarred and canned, but we've found that processing causes them to lose their rich, nutty flavor and take on a molasses-y sweetness. For that reason, we recommend using fresh chestnuts when they are available in the fall or early winter. Look for nuts with glossy shells, a sign of freshness and proper storage. Also choose nuts that do not rattle when shaken, as this indicates that they have dried out.

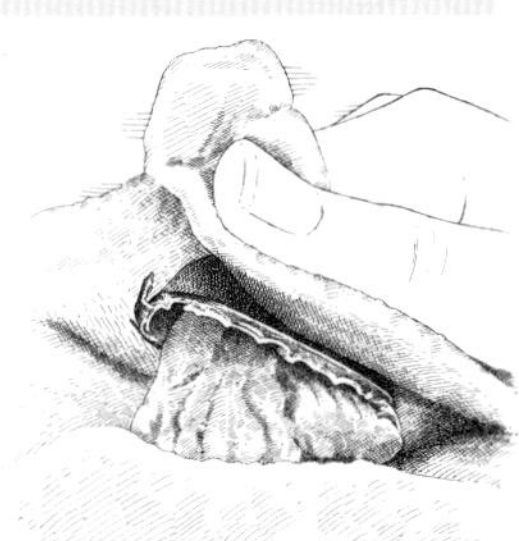

EASY SQUEEZE
Extract nutmeats by squeezing blanched nuts.

To shell 1 pound of chestnuts: Cut whole nuts in half crosswise, then blanch for 8 minutes in 8 cups boiling water. Turn off heat; leave nuts in water. One at a time, hold nut with a folded towel and squeeze shell to extract nut. Using paring knife, trim any bits of husk. One pound of chestnuts will yield roughly 10 ounces of nutmeats. –L.L.

Cut Your Own Salmon Fillets

When making Miso-Marinated Salmon (page 18) or any salmon recipe that calls for fillets, it's important to use fillets of similar thickness so that they cook at the same rate. We find that the best way to ensure uniformity is to buy a large center-cut fillet (1½ to 2 pounds if serving 4) and cut it into 4 equal pieces. –A.P.

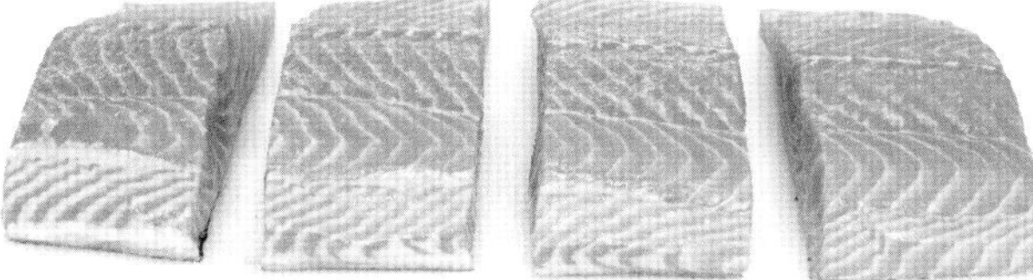

FOR EVEN COOKING, CUT PORTIONS AT HOME

The Nicest Rice for Pudding

Rice pudding is usually made with long-grain rice, but we wondered if it could be improved by swapping in Arborio or sushi rice. Since these short-grain rices have a high proportion of amylopectin—the starch that makes risotto creamy and sushi rice cling—could they make a more luxurious, creamier rice pudding?

To find out, we compared stovetop rice pudding (served cold) made with long-grain rice, Arborio rice, and sushi rice. Some tasters objected to the softness and lack of "bite" in the sushi rice grains, while Arborio was panned for contributing a slight grittiness. Turns out this is due to a genetic "defect" in their cores called chalk that never softens completely. It's what gives risotto a desirable al dente texture, but we found it unwelcome in pudding.

For pudding with a creamy texture boasting rice with a pleasant, mild chew, long-grain rice is still the best choice. That's because it contains a good amount of a starch called amylose that retrogrades, or rearranges into crystalline structures, when the rice turns cold, giving it the chew sushi rice lacks without making it too firm. –A.G.

Flavoring Whipped Cream

A small amount of extract or ground spices can be whisked into whipped cream to dress it up, but we wanted a way to infuse the flavor of ingredients like citrus zest, herbs, or tea leaves so that their texture wouldn't be distracting.

Heating the cream with the flavoring will extract the most flavor, but the strained cream won't whip to the proper volume unless it's chilled long enough for most of its fat to resolidify. Refrigerating overnight is an option, but we found a faster approach. To make 2 cups of whipped cream:

1. Heat ¼ cup heavy cream to 125° over medium heat.
2. Off heat, add flavoring.
3. Steep for 10 minutes, then strain.
4. Refrigerate for 30 minutes.
5. Whip ¾ cup heavy cream until starting to thicken. Add infused cream and sugar to taste; whip to soft peaks.

INGREDIENT	AMOUNT	PAIRINGS
TEA LEAVES	2 tablespoons	Earl Grey–Berries, Jasmine-Chocolate
CITRUS ZEST	½ teaspoon	Lemon or Lime-Berries, Orange-Chocolate, Lemon-Almond
MINCED HERBS	2 tablespoons	Rosemary-Lemon, Basil-Peach, Mint-Chocolate

DIY RECIPE Marshmallows

Homemade marshmallows are easy to make. Simply heat up a sugar mixture and beat it with unflavored gelatin until the mixture transforms from a translucent liquid into a white, fluffy goo. Spread this into a pan (we line it with greased foil for easy removal), let it set up, and cut it into cubes. The gelatin is key for structure. Without it, you'd end up with something like marshmallow crème. Serve with our Hot Chocolate Mix (November/December 2014), or cut them into mini marshmallows to use in our 15-Minute Rocky Road Fudge (January/February 2007). –Louise Emerick

MARSHMALLOWS

MAKES 117 MARSHMALLOWS

You will need a candy thermometer or another thermometer such as an instant-read probe model that registers high temperatures for this recipe.

- **⅔ cup (2⅔ ounces) confectioners' sugar**
- **⅓ cup cornstarch**
- **1 cup cold water**
- **2½ tablespoons unflavored gelatin**
- **⅔ cup light corn syrup**
- **2 cups (14 ounces) granulated sugar**
- **¼ teaspoon salt**
- **2 teaspoons vanilla extract**

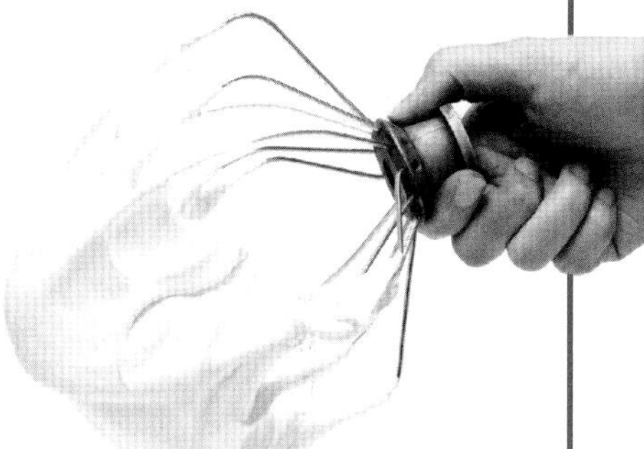

JUST RIGHT

When the mixture is thick enough to coat the whisk, it will set up firm.

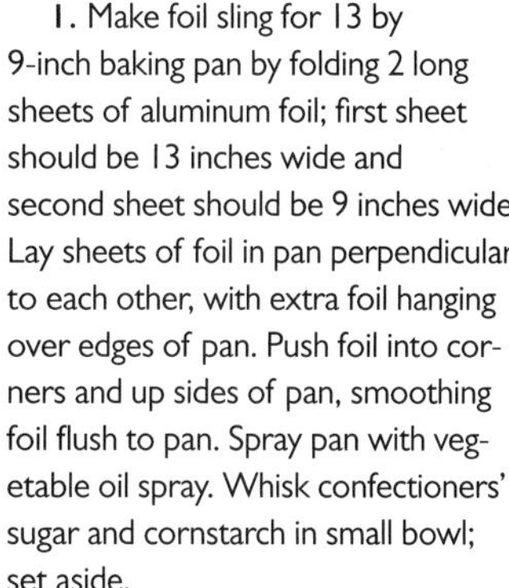

1. Make foil sling for 13 by 9-inch baking pan by folding 2 long sheets of aluminum foil; first sheet should be 13 inches wide and second sheet should be 9 inches wide. Lay sheets of foil in pan perpendicular to each other, with extra foil hanging over edges of pan. Push foil into corners and up sides of pan, smoothing foil flush to pan. Spray pan with vegetable oil spray. Whisk confectioners' sugar and cornstarch in small bowl; set aside.

2. Pour ½ cup water into bowl of stand mixer fitted with whisk. Sprinkle gelatin over water. Let stand until gelatin becomes very firm, about 15 minutes.

3. Meanwhile, combine remaining ½ cup water and corn syrup in medium saucepan. Pour granulated sugar and salt into center of saucepan (do not let sugar hit saucepan sides). Bring to boil over medium-high heat and cook, gently swirling saucepan, until sugar has dissolved completely and mixture registers 240 degrees, 6 to 8 minutes.

4. Turn mixer speed to low and carefully pour hot syrup into gelatin mixture, avoiding whisk and bowl. Gradually increase speed to high and whip until mixture is very thick and stiff and coats whisk, 10 to 12 minutes, scraping down bowl as needed. Add vanilla and mix until incorporated, about 15 seconds.

5. Working quickly, scrape mixture evenly into prepared pan using greased rubber spatula and smooth top. Sift 2 tablespoons confectioners' sugar mixture over pan. Cover and let sit overnight at room temperature until firm.

6. Lightly dust cutting board with 2 tablespoons confectioners' sugar mixture and lightly coat chef's knife with oil spray. Turn marshmallow slab out onto cutting board and peel off foil. Sift 2 tablespoons confectioners' sugar mixture over slab. Cut into 1-inch-wide strips, then cut crosswise into 1-inch squares. Working with 3 or 4 marshmallows at a time, toss marshmallows in bowl with remaining confectioners' sugar mixture, then toss in fine-mesh strainer to remove excess powder. Marshmallows can be stored in zipper-lock bag or airtight container for up to 2 weeks.

KITCHEN NOTES

⋟ BY ANDREA GEARY, ANDREW JANJIGIAN, LAN LAM & ANNIE PETITO ⋞

WHAT IS IT?

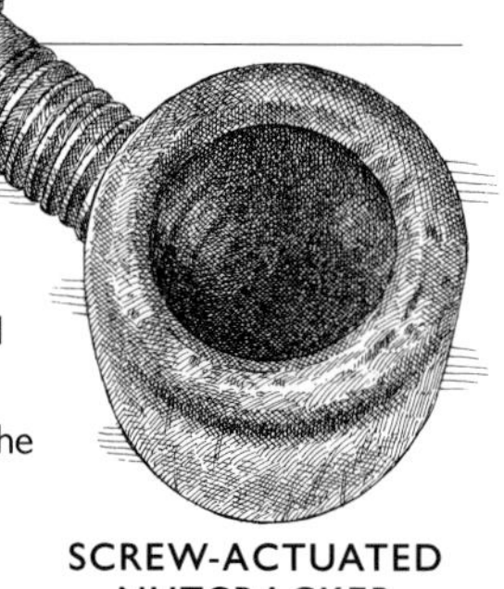

It might look like an old-fashioned toy, but this gadget is a screw-actuated nutcracker. The screw nutcracker first appeared in the 17th century, although this particular version is a more contemporary model crafted in the early 1950s. To use it, a nut is placed in the cup and pressure is applied to the shell by turning the screw. When the shell breaks, the screw is backed out to allow access to the nutmeat. When we gave it a try, we found that it worked exceedingly well. Moderate pressure applied to the screw easily cracked any nut—from walnuts, almonds, and pecans to hazelnuts and Brazil nuts. –Steve Dunn

SCREW-ACTUATED NUTCRACKER
Though rudimentary in appearance, this tool made easy work of cracking a variety of nutshells.

Ensuring Weight and Temperature Accuracy

Small inaccuracies in measuring temperature and weight can lead to problems like overcooked roasts and cookies that spread too much, so it's important to routinely test scales and thermometers to make sure that they are accurate. Here's how to do it. –A.G.

SCALE

If your scale measures in both grams and ounces, testing in grams will provide a more accurate assessment. One nickel should weigh 5 grams. If you are testing in ounces, 4 quarters and 1 nickel should weigh 1 ounce. If your scale is off and cannot be calibrated (check the manufacturer's instructions), write the discrepancy on a piece of masking tape and affix it to the scale so you can take it into account when you weigh.

THERMOMETER

A thermometer can be tested in boiling water, which should register 212 degrees at sea level, or in a glass of ice filled with just enough water to reach the top of the ice, which should register 32 degrees. For the most definitive results, test both ways. As with your scale, either calibrate according to the manufacturer's instructions or make a note of any discrepancy.

COOKING LESSON The Solution to Searing Meat

When cooking meat, including recipes like our Roasted Rack of Lamb with Roasted Red Pepper Relish (page 5), we've found that the best way to achieve a rosy pink interior and nicely browned exterior is to roast the meat in a low oven until nearly done and then sear it on a very hot stove. The low oven's gentle heat ensures a smaller temperature gradient between the center and exterior of the meat, so the meat cooks through evenly from edge to edge; the stove's intense heat then rapidly browns just the surface so there's no time for the meat beneath it to overcook.

Browning meat via this oven-to-stove method may be a bit more work than simply turning up the oven temperature or blasting the meat under the broiler, but here's why it's better than either of those methods. –L.L.

CONVECTION: INEFFICIENT
Transfers heat poorly so browning falls short.

Why Not a Hot Oven?

Air is an inefficient conductor of heat, so even if the oven is cranked to 500 degrees, the surface of the meat won't brown quickly enough before the interior overcooks.

RADIANT: OVERKILL
Browns well but heats the oven's air, causing overcooking.

Why Not the Broiler?

Broilers produce radiant heat waves that brown the top of food rapidly. But they also heat up the air inside the oven, so the other sides of the meat will absorb that heat at the same time and overcook the interior.

CONDUCTION: DIRECT
Quickly browns only what's in contact with the pan for perfect results.

Why the Stove?

Searing meat in a very hot skillet conducts heat directly to only the side of the meat in contact with the pan. The other sides of the meat aren't exposed to additional heat, so they don't continue cooking. The result: a great crust without a band of overcooked meat beneath it.

HOMEMADE PIE SHIELD

Sometimes the edges of a pie get too brown before the rest of the pie is finished cooking. The standard advice for dealing with the situation is to crimp strips of foil around the affected areas, but it's easier said than done because the pie plate is perilously hot. And the strips of foil have a tendency to fall off as the pie is returned to the oven. We've devised a much easier method. We cut a circle out of a square piece of foil and then place that square on top of the pie. –A.G.

1. For 9-inch pie, fold 12-inch square piece of foil in half and then in half again to make 6-inch square.

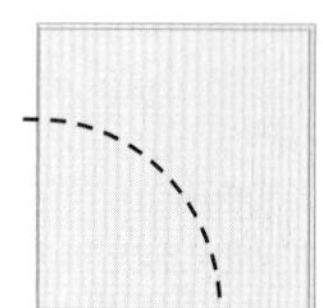

2. Working with folded corner as reference point, make two marks, one on each folded side, 4 inches from corner. Draw curved line connecting marks to form quarter circle. Tear foil along line.

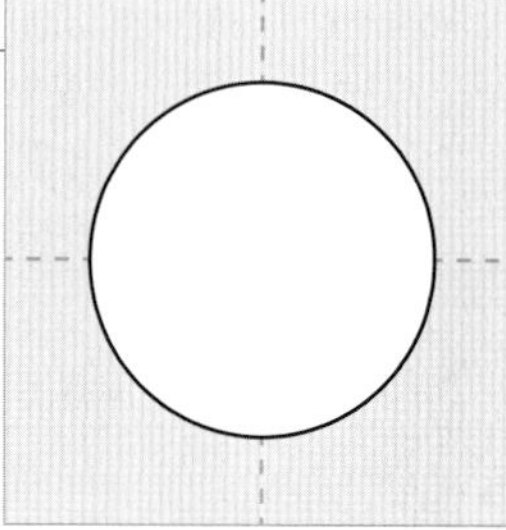

3. Unfold foil. Place shield over pie and crimp lightly to hold it in place before returning pie to oven.

TECHNIQUE | REMOVING PINBONES FROM SALMON

When a fish is filleted, the flesh is removed from the backbone and ribs, but the relatively soft, thin, needle-like pinbones, also known as intermuscular bones, are not attached to the main skeleton and thus must be removed in a second step. While most fish are sold with the pinbones removed, they are difficult to see and are sometimes missed by the fishmonger. When preparing recipes like our Miso-Marinated Salmon (page 18), it's always a good idea to check for bones before cooking. –A.P.

1. Drape fillet over inverted mixing bowl to help any pinbones protrude. Then, working from head end to tail end, locate pinbones by running your fingers along length of fillet.

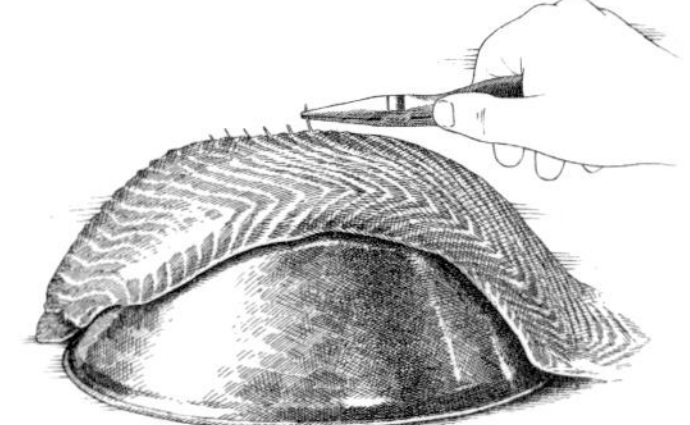

2. Use tweezers to grasp tip of bone. To avoid tearing flesh, pull slowly but firmly at slight angle in direction bone is naturally pointing rather than straight up. Repeat until all pinbones are removed.

Use a Bowl for Simpler Seasoning

When seasoning meat before cooking, we normally lay the pieces on a baking sheet, sprinkle the salt over them in an even layer on one side, and then flip them over and repeat on the second side. This is fine for larger cuts like whole chicken breasts or steaks, but it is tedious when working with smaller pieces, like cutlets or meat for stir-fry. In this case—as we found when developing our Better Chicken Marsala recipe (page 7)—it is far easier, more efficient, and just as effective to place the meat in a bowl, add the salt, and then toss thoroughly to distribute the salt evenly over the meat. –A.J.

TECHNIQUE | SPEEDIER BRUSSELS SPROUTS PREP

We prefer to thinly slice 1½ pounds of sprouts for Brussels Sprout Salads (page 11) by hand rather than use a food processor, since its blades tend to cut the leaves unevenly. We've found it most efficient to complete one task at a time on all the sprouts and use an assembly line setup on the cutting board. In fact, employing this approach made some cooks more than 30 percent faster at the task. –L.L.

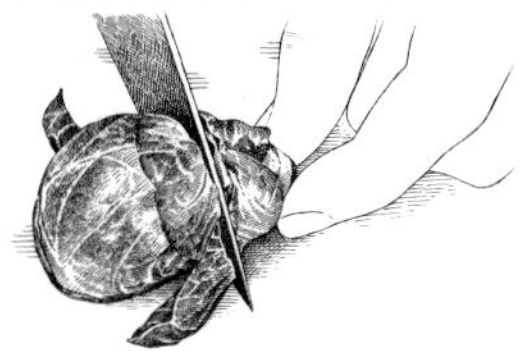

1. TRIM GENEROUSLY
Trim base from sprouts, cutting high enough so that each sprout is roughly as tall as it is wide. This will allow tough outer leaves to fall away; pull off and discard any that remain.

2. HALVE
Pile trimmed sprouts at one end of board. Cut each in half, pushing halved sprouts to opposite end of board.

3. SLICE
Divide cutting board into three regions: keep halved sprouts at one end near nondominant hand, reserve center for slicing, and pile shredded sprouts on remaining third of board.

SCIENCE When to Treat Chicken: Before or After Freezing?

Brining or salting chicken before cooking not only seasons the meat but also subtly changes its protein structure, which enables it to retain more moisture as it cooks. We know that many of our readers buy poultry in bulk and freeze it for later use, so we wondered: Is there any advantage to treating chicken prior to freezing and, if so, which method is preferable?

EXPERIMENT

We soaked three boneless, skinless chicken breasts in brine for 45 minutes, sprinkled three others with salt and let them rest for 1 hour, and left nine breasts untreated before freezing all of the samples for one week. After thawing the samples, we brined three and salted three of the previously untreated ones. We then cooked the chicken breasts using a *sous vide* machine and measured their moisture loss by comparing their cooked weight to their original weight prior to treating and freezing.

RESULTS

We found that salting the chicken before freezing worked best, resulting in chicken that was well seasoned and that lost only 11 percent of its weight when cooked (the samples that were brined before freezing lost 15 percent). Chicken that was salted or brined after thawing did not fare as well, losing 16 and 20 percent of its weight, respectively. The frozen chicken that was never treated lost 22 percent of its original weight.

METHOD	TIME FRAME	MOISTURE LOST
salting	before freezing	11%
	after freezing	16%
brining	before freezing	15%
	after freezing	20%
no salt or brine	n/a	22%

EXPLANATION

Treating the chicken before freezing works better than after because it gives the salt additional time to do its job—while the meat is freezing and then again while it is thawing. Salting the chicken before freezing works better than brining since salting creates a more concentrated brine at the surface of the meat, allowing more salt to travel into the meat. A higher concentration of salt within the meat allows it to hold onto more moisture (up to a point, at least; concentrations above a certain amount can actually have a negative effect).

TAKEAWAY

Salting chicken breasts before freezing is the best choice for well-seasoned meat that will retain the maximum amount of moisture. And happily, salting a bulk batch of chicken breasts before freezing is also more convenient than salting each smaller batch after thawing. To do it, sprinkle both sides of the chicken breasts with kosher salt (1½ teaspoons per pound) and refrigerate for one hour so that the salt can do its job. Pat dry, wrap, and freeze. –A.G.

SCIENCE OF COOKING: The Secrets of Seasoning Meat
Should you sprinkle your pork chop and turkey breast with the same amount of salt? Not if you want them to taste right. Free for 4 months at CooksIllustrated.com/dec15.

EQUIPMENT CORNER

BY HANNAH CROWLEY, LISA McMANUS, LAUREN SAVOIE & KATE SHANNON

HIGHLY RECOMMENDED

CILIO
Champagne Bottle Sealer
Model: C300888
Price: $7.50

HIGHLY RECOMMENDED

PREPWORKS
Collapsible Party Carrier
Model: BCC-4
Price: $23.81

RECOMMENDED

NINJA
Nutri Ninja Pro
Model: BL450
Price: $89.00

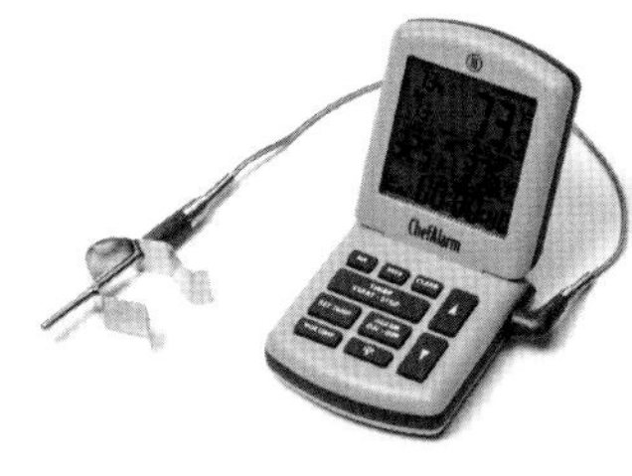

RECOMMENDED

THERMOWORKS
Pro-Series High Temp Air Probe and Stainless Steel Grate Clip
Model: TX-1003X-AP
Price: $17.00

RECOMMENDED

CUISINART
MultiClad Pro Stainless 3½-Quart Sauté Pan with Helper and Cover
Model: MCP33-24HN
Price: $78.13

TESTING Champagne Savers

Champagne savers promise to keep champagne and sparkling wine fresh for anywhere from three days to a few months (a week would be plenty to us). We tested six ($4.44 to $35.00), pouring a glass and a half from six bottles of sparkling wine, sealing them with the savers, and storing them in the refrigerator. We tasted them daily against a freshly opened bottle, one we sealed with just plastic wrap and an elastic band, and a bottle we left entirely open. One model did such a poor job that the wine saved with it tasted almost as flat as the open bottle after a day. Three other sealers (and the plastic wrap) kept wines reasonably drinkable for two days. But the standout model, the Cilio Champagne Bottle Sealer ($7.50), featured an easy-to-use, airtight seal that kept the contents just as lively as a newly opened bottle for two days and perfectly acceptable for a third. Even better, in a separate test where we didn't open the bottle daily, the wine stayed fresh for a week. –H.C.

TESTING Pie Carriers

Traveling with a delicate pie can feel like tempting fate, but a good pie carrier can make the task easier and more secure. We tested five models ($11.88 to $25.99)—a pair of basic pie-shaped plastic containers and three handled carriers—by loading the carriers with a variety of shallow double-crust pies and taller cream-topped pies, walking with them around the block, and driving with them down 3 miles of bumpy roads.

The simple plastic containers were too shallow to fit anything taller than a 2-inch-high apple pie without crushing the top crust. These pies also slid around recklessly on the carriers' wide, slippery bases, damaging the crusts' delicate edges. Handled carriers were more secure and easily transportable with one hand. The best model, the Prepworks Collapsible Party Carrier ($23.81), sported a large, nonskid base that kept pies of all diameters perfectly stable and a tall dome that accommodated a lofty meringue topping. –L.S.

TESTING Personal Blenders

A full-size blender is a must for large-batch cooking, but "personal blenders" offer smaller footprints, lower price tags, and lids that allow them to transition from pitchers to travel cups when making smoothies and shakes. To see if any are worth owning in addition to a full-size blender, we evaluated nine models ($16.99 to $89.00) with pitchers sized 24 ounces and smaller, using them to blend smoothies with hard frozen berries and fibrous kale, thick milkshakes, and Green Goddess dressing.

Skinny pitchers were generally harder to fill and struggled to incorporate ingredients more than gently tapered U-shaped models did; the only downside of the wider shape is that they don't fit in most standard cup holders. Longer blades (the best were at least 1⅛ inches) sporting at least four sharply angled prongs were better able to grab and process ingredients. Travel lids were a necessity, and we preferred spouts that were wide enough for thick liquids to flow through and snapped shut with a tight seal.

Our favorite, the Ninja Nutri Ninja Pro ($89.00), encompassed all these traits with results as smooth as those from our full-size Best Buy blender, The Hemisphere Control from Breville ($199.99). It was also the quickest at blending, which compensated for the fact that users must continuously hold down the pitcher to engage the motor, and it excelled in our 100-smoothie and 100-milkshake abuse tests. While not a necessity, it might be worth shelling out for if you're a smoothie enthusiast. –K.S.

UPDATE ChefAlarm Digital Thermometer

While evaluating oven thermometers (page 26), we discovered that the ThermoWorks ChefAlarm ($59.00), our favorite digital probe thermometer for meat, deep frying, and candy making, offers an alternative to the dial-face models we tested. The company sells a separate ambient temperature probe ($17.00), which connects to the thermometer and tracks the temperature of the oven. The probe clipped easily to the grate and was accurate to within a single degree. We also like that the remote thermometer, with its large digital display and intuitive user interfaces, allows you to easily check the oven temperature without opening the door. If you already own a ChefAlarm, it's an excellent alternative to our winning dial-face model from CDN, the Pro Accurate ($8.70). –K.S.

UPDATE Cuisinart Sauté Pan

Our 2012 Best Buy sauté pan from Cuisinart was recently redesigned; the new model features squared-off handles made of stainless steel that resist heating up on the stovetop. When we compared the updated and the older pans, we found the new handle design easier to grip without slipping. Other than that, the pans were still similar: Both models browned equally well (though the new pan retains the old model's too-narrow cooking surface) and felt nicely balanced for easy lifting and pouring. We recommend the updated model, the Cuisinart MultiClad Pro Stainless 3½-Quart Sauté Pan with Helper and Cover ($78.13), as our new Best Buy. –L.M.

For complete testing results, go to CooksIllustrated.com/dec15.

INDEX

November & December 2015

FOLLOW US ON SOCIAL MEDIA
facebook.com/CooksIllustrated
twitter.com/TestKitchen
pinterest.com/TestKitchen
google.com/+AmericasTestKitchen
instagram.com/TestKitchen
youtube.com/AmericasTestKitchen

Better Chicken Marsala, 7

Baked Alaska, 22

Roasted Rack of Lamb with Red Pepper Relish, 5

Brussels Sprout Salad, 11

Sweet Potato Soup, 13

Rustic Bread Stuffing, 10

Ultranutty Pecan Bars, 15

Best Ground Beef Chili, 9

Pasta e Ceci (Pasta with Chickpeas), 19

Miso-Marinated Salmon, 18

PHOTOGRAPHY: CARL TREMBLAY; STYLING: MARIE PIRAINO

CLASSIC AMERICAN COOKIES